Allied Railways of the British Sectors of the Western Front

NARROW GAUGE in the SOMME SECTOR
Before, during and after the First World War

Allied Railways of the British Sectors of the Western Front

NARROW GAUGE in the SOMME SECTOR
Before, during and after the First World War

Martin & Joan Farebrother

PEN & SWORD
TRANSPORT
AN IMPRINT OF PEN & SWORD BOOKS LTD.
YORKSHIRE - PHILADELPHIA

First published in Great Britain in 2018 by
Pen and Sword Transport
An imprint of
Pen & Sword Books Ltd
Yorkshire - Philadelphia

Copyright © Martin and Joan Farebrother, 2018

ISBN 978 1 473 88763 3

The right of Martin and Joan Farebrother to be identified as Authors of this work has been asserted by them in accordance with the Copyright, Designs and Patents Act 1988.

A CIP catalogue record for this book is available from the British Library.

All rights reserved. No part of this book may be reproduced or transmitted in any form or by any means, electronic or mechanical including photocopying, recording or by any information storage and retrieval system, without permission from the Publisher in writing.

Typeset in Palatino by Aura Technology and Software Services, India.
Printed and bound in India by Replika Press Pvt. Ltd.

Pen & Sword Books Ltd incorporates the Imprints of Pen & Sword Books Archaeology, Atlas, Aviation, Battleground, Discovery, Family History, History, Maritime, Military, Naval, Politics, Railways, Select, Transport, True Crime, Fiction, Frontline Books, Leo Cooper, Praetorian Press, Seaforth Publishing, Wharncliffe and White Owl.

For a complete list of Pen & Sword titles please contact

PEN & SWORD BOOKS LIMITED
47 Church Street, Barnsley, South Yorkshire, S70 2AS, England
E-mail: enquiries@pen-and-sword.co.uk
Website: www.pen-and-sword.co.uk

Or
PEN AND SWORD BOOKS
1950 Lawrence Rd, Havertown, PA 19083, USA
E-mail: Uspen-and-sword@casematepublishers.com
Website: www.penandswordbooks.com

Contents

List of Figures	vi
List of Tables	vii
Acknowledgements	ix
Abbreviations	x
Introduction	xii

Chapter One	Introducing the Somme sector and its railways	1
Chapter Two	The metre gauge railways of the Somme *département* 1888 to 1914	11
Chapter Three	The metre gauge railways of the Oise and Aisne *départements* 1895 to 1914	35
Chapter Four	Railways and light railways (60cm gauge) during the First World War (1914-1918)	56
Chapter Five	Light and metre gauge railways of the Somme battlefields 1915 - 16 March 1917	71
Chapter Six	Light and metre gauge railways of the Somme sector 17 March 1917 to 20 March 1918	96
Chapter Seven	Light and metre gauge railways of the Somme sector 21 March to 7 August 1918	129
Chapter Eight	Light and metre gauge railways of the Somme sector 8 August to 11 November 1918	151
Chapter Nine	Light railways of the Somme sector 12 Nov 1918 to 1974	175
Chapter Ten	The metre gauge railways of the Somme *département* 12 November 1918 to 1955	192
Chapter Eleven	The metre gauge railways of the Oise and Aisne *départements* 12 November 1918 to 1955	206
Chapter Twelve	Things to see and do now	222

Bibliography	249
Index	251

List of Figures

Introduction
0.1 Sectors and Armies on the northern part of the Western Front 1914 - 1918

Chapter one
1.1 Railways in the Somme Sector in Spring 1914

Chapter two
2.1 The Doullens-Albert line, with stations and other stops, up to 1914
2.2 The Albert-Ham line, with stations and other stops, up to 1914
2.3 The Albert-Montdidier line, with stations and other stops, up to 1914
2.4 Fricourt junction station
2.5 Ham station before 1914

Chapter three
3.1 The Noyon-Montdidier line, the Noyon-Ham line, & the Offoy-Ercheu-Bussy loop line, up to 1914
3.2 Boulogne-la-Grasse as opened in 1913
3.3 Noyon station 1896
3.4 Roye-sur-Matz station MG opening 1913

Chapter five
5.1 Allied railways in the Somme Sector 1 July 1916
5.2 Allied railways west of the Ancre March 1917
5.3 Allied railways Railways Ancre Valley and east of the Ancre and North of the Albert - Bapaume Road March 1917
5.4 The Aveluy Area February 1917
5.5 Allied Railways south of the Albert to Bapaume road & north of the Somme March 1917
5.6 Allied Railways south of the Somme river and North of the Amiens - Chaulnes railway March 1917

Chapter six
6.1 Main Allied railways Somme Sector after the German retreat to the Hindenburg Line, March 1917 - 20 March 1918. Light railways (60cm gauge) not shown.
6.2 Allied railways in the 1916 Somme battlefield area, north of the Somme, 20 March 1918
6.3 Allied railways in the 1916 Somme battlefield area, south of the Somme, 20 March 1918
6.4 Allied railways in the 'new' areas, Bapaume to Péronne, March 1917 to 20 March 1918
6.5 Allied railways in the 'new' areas, Péronne to Ham, March 1917 to 20 March 1918
6.6 Allied railways in the Fifth Army South area, Ham to Barisis, December 1917 to 20 March 1918

Chapter seven
7.1 The great retreat, Somme sector, 21 March 1918 to 5 April 1918
7.2 Railways in the Somme Sector north of the Somme, April 1918 - 7 August 1918

Chapter eight
8.1 Allied Railways in the final advance in the Somme Sector, 8 August 1918 to 11 November 1918. Light railways (60cm gauge) not shown
8.2 British Army Light Railways, Somme Sector, 29 September 1918 - 15 November 1918

Chapter Nine
9.1 MRL Light Railways, Somme Sector, to end of 1922
9.2 Passenger services, MRL Light Railways, Somme Sector, 1921 to 1927
9.3 *Sucrerie Centrale de Santerre*, Dompierre, Light Railways, 1930s

Chapter Ten
10.1 Ham station about 1930

Chapter Eleven
11.1 Noyon station from 1932

Chapter Twelve
12.1 Walk 1 Railways & cemeteries behind the line at Beaumont Hamel
12.2 Walk 2 Albert
12.3 Walk 3 Péronne-Flamicourt
12.4 Walk 4 Bellicourt to Nauroy
12.5 Walk 5 St-Quentin

List of Tables

Chapter one
1.1 Standard gauge lines of *Intérêt Général* in the Somme sector
1.2 Standard gauge lines of *Intérêt Local* in the Somme sector

Chapter two
2.1 Doullens - Albert, stations and other stops, up to 1914
2.2 Albert - Ham, stations and other stops, up to 1914
2.3 Albert - Montdidier, stations and other stops, up to 1914
2.4 Offoy - Ercheu & Ercheu - Bussy, stations and other stops, up to 1914
2.5 Major bridges on the eastern Somme metre gauge lines up to 1914
2.6 Principal industrial branch lines and sidings up to 1914
2.7 Technical details of SE Somme locomotives up to 1914
2.8 Probable main allocations of some SE locomotives before 1914
2.9 Doullens - Albert Summary Timetable May 1914
2.10 Albert - Péronne - Ham (SE) Summary Timetable May 1914
2.11 Albert - Montdidier (SE) Summary Timetable May 1914
2.12 Offoy - Ercheu & Ercheu - Bussy (SE) Summary Timetable May 1914

Chapter three
3.1 Noyon - Ham & Noyon - Montdidier, Stations and other stops, up to 1914
3.2 Major bridges on the Noyon to Ham and Noyon to Montdidier metre gauge lines up to 1914
3.3 Noyon to Ham & Noyon to Montdidier, Principal industrial branch lines and sidings up to 1914
3.4 Technical details of Lambert NGL and RH locomotives up to 1914
3.5 Noyon to Guiscard and Ham (NGL) Summary Timetable May 1913
3.6 Noyon to Lassigny and Montdidier (NGL) Summary Timetable May 1914
3.7 St-Quentin - Le Catelet - Caudry, stations and other stops up to 1914
3.8 Caudry to St-Quentin (CFC) Summary Timetable May 1914

Chapter four
4.1 Somme Sector 1916-1918 Allocation of Groups of Railway Construction Companies/Engineers (RCC/RCE) to British Armies
4.2 Technical details of British and French Army Light Railway Steam Locomotives 1914-1918
4.3 Technical details of British Army Light Railway Petrol Tractors 1916-1918
4.4 Technical details of British Army Light Railway Wagons 1916-1918
4.5 British Army Light Railway route miles and tonnage 1917 and 1918, Western Front (Belgium and France)

Chapter six
6.1 Summary Timetables for Somme Sector metre gauge lines July 1917

Chapter eight
8.1 Somme Sector Light railway units, and those doing light railway work, transferred to standard gauge work October and November 1918

Chapter nine
9.1 Light Railway units still working in the Somme Sector after the Armistice
9.2 Motive power, 1st Aus LROC February and March 1919
9.3 Goods carried by category, 1st Aus LROC February and March 1919
9.4 Passenger services on the MRL Somme Oise and southern Pas-de-Calais lines as at 1 August, 1923

Chapter ten
10.1 Technical details of SE Somme locomotives from 1919
10.2 Technical details of SE Somme railcars from 1925
10.3 Doullens - Albert (SE) Summary Timetable October 1938

10.4 Albert - Péronne - Ham (SE) Summary Timetable October 1938
10.5 Albert - Montdidier - Rollot (SE) Summary Timetable October 1938
10.6 Offoy - Ercheu & Ercheu - Bussy (SE) Summary Timetable October 1936

Chapter eleven
11.1 Noyon to Guiscard and Golancourt (VFIL) Plessis to Ham (MRL) Timetable June 1921
11.2 Noyon to Guiscard and Ham (VFIL) Summary Timetable January 1922
11.3 Noyon to Lassigny and Montdidier (VFIL) Summary Timetable January 1922
11.4 Technical details of Noyonnais (VFIL) locomotives from 1919
11.5 Noyon to Ham and Noyon to Rollot (VFIL) Summary Timetable October 1936

Chapter twelve
12.1 Present location of some relevant narrow gauge rolling stock

Acknowledgements

We wish to thank the following, without whose help this book could not have been produced:

Jonathan Clay, for the illustration on the jacket; the National Archives at Kew; the Somme archives at Amiens; the Oise archives at Beauvais; the Imperial War Museum (IWM) Photograph Archive for their assistance and for permission to reproduce photographs from the archive, and the Australian War Memorial (AWM), Canberra, for similar assistance; the IWM map archive at Duxford, for help with finding other information on the First World War; the Royal Engineers Museum and Library, Brompton Barracks, Gillingham, Kent for help, and access to War Diaries of the Royal Engineers Railway Companies; the French Railways Society (formerly The SNCF Society) Librarian Roger Ongley, and Curator of Timetables Patrick Bennett; Gordon Wiseman (French Railways Society), for some timetable information; Sue Jenkins, for access to the private war diary of her grandfather, Leonard Atkins, who served with the 1st LROC in the First World War; David Blondin, APPEVA (CFCD, Le P'tit Train de la Haute Somme) for help, and for permission to use photographs from the APPEVA collection; Jean-Louis Rochaix, Bernard Rozé, René Brugier, and R K Blencowe, for help, and for permission to use photographs from their collections; Trevor Edmonds, for information on First Anzac Light Railways; Kim Winter and Ian Hughes, War Office Locomotive Trust; William Shelford, Archivist, Leighton Buzzard Narrow Gauge Railway; Tony Nicholson, Lynton and Barnstaple Railway Trust; Philip Pacey, West Lancashire Light Railway; Adrian Gray, Honorary Archivist, Ffestiniog Railway Company; Simon Lomax and Gareth Roberts, Moseley Railway Trust; Gerry Cork, Amberley Museum and Heritage centre. Finally, John Scott-Morgan, for help with the production, and for the use of photographs from his collection; Carol Trow, for the editing; and Pen & Sword Books Limited, for the use of photographs from their archives, and for the production.

Images and permissions:
We have attempted to contact all possible copyright holders. If any have been missed, the copyright holder should contact the publisher. We have done our best to make this book as accurate as possible. We are responsible for any errors and would be pleased to hear about them.

Abbreviations

Railways and Railway Companies, past and present, including heritage organisations

AMHC	Amberley Museum and Heritage Centre
AMTP	*Association du Musée des Transports de Pithiviers*
APPEVA	*Association Picarde pour la Préservation et l'Entretien des Véhicules Anciens*
CDA	*Société des Chemins de Fer Départementaux de l'Aisne*
CdN	*Compagnie du Nord*
CEN	*Compagnie des Chemins de Fer Économiques du Nord*
CFBS	*Chemin de Fer de la Baie de Somme*
CFC	*Société des Chemins de Fer du Cambrésis*
CFCD	*Chemin de Fer Cappy Dompierre (P'tit train de la Haute Somme)*
FR	Ffestiniog Railway
GC	*Chemin de Fer de Guise au Catelet*
HB	*Compagnie du Chemin de Fer de Hermes à Beaumont*
L&BR	Lynton and Barnstaple Railway, North Devon
LBNGRS	Leighton Buzzard Narrow Gauge Railway Society Ltd.
MRT	Moseley Railway Trust
MTVS	*Musée de Tramways à Vapeurs et des chemins de fer Secondaires français (Valmondois)*
NE	*Compagnie des Chemins de Fer Secondaires du Nord-Est*
NF	*Compagnie des Chemins de Fer d'intérêt local du Nord de la France*
NGL	Noyon, Guiscard, Lassigny (a Lambert Company, later part of VFIL)
RTA	*Régie départemantale des Transport de l'Aisne*
SE	*Société Générale des Chemins de Fer Économiques*
SNCF	*Société Nationale des Chemins de Fer Français*
SNCV	*Société Nationale des Chemins de Fer Vicinaux (Belge)*
StQG	*Société du Chemin de fer de St. Quentin à Guise*
TPT	*Tramway de Pithiviers à Toury*
VBStQ	*Compagnie du Chemin de fer de Velu-Berlincourt à St. Quentin*
VFIL (or CGL)	*Compagnie Générale des Voie Ferrées d'Intérêt Local*
WHHR	Welsh Highland Heritage Railway
WHR	Welsh Highland Railway
WLLR	West Lancashire Light Railway
WOLT	War Office Locomotive Trust

British and Dominion Armies, First World War

ADGT	Assistant Director General of Transportation (with Roman numerals for each army).
ADLR	Assistant Director of Light Railways (with Roman numerals for each army)
ALR	Anzac Light Railways
APB	Australian Pioneer Battalion
Aus. or (Aus)	
LROC	Australian Light Railway Operating Company
BGROC	Broad Gauge Railway Operating Company
BTLC	British Transport Liquidation Commission
Bttn	Battalion
CCS	Casualty Clearing Station
CORCC	Canadian Overseas Railway Construction Company
CRCE	Chief Railway Construction Engineer (GHQ)
CRT	Canadian Railway Troops
DGT	Director General of Transportation
DRL	Director of Light Railways
FWC	Foreways Company
GHQ	General Headquarters
LRCE	Light Railway Construction Engineer
LRFC	Light Railway Forward Company
LROC	Light Railway Operating Company
NCO	Non-Commissioned Officer
POW	Prisoner of War

Abbreviations

RARE	Royal Anglesey special reserve Company, RE
RC	Railway Company (RE)
RCC, or RCE (with Roman numerals)	Group of Railway Construction Companies, or Railway Construction Engineers (RE)
RE	Royal Engineers
RMRE	Royal Monmouth special reserve Company, RE
ROD	Railway Operating Division (RE)
RTO	Railway Transport Officer
TC CE	Tramways Company, Canadian Engineers
TCC	Train Crews Company (light railways, RE)
WD	War Department

Other abbreviations (some used mainly or wholly in tables, maps, and diagrams)

ACNF	*Ateliers de Construction du Nord de la France (de Blanc Misseron)*
AWM	Australian War Memorial, Canberra, Australia
BV	*Bâtiment des Voyageurs* (passenger building)
CGIT	*Compagnie Générale Industrielle de Tranports*
CWGC	Commonwealth War Graves Commission
HM	*Halle aux Marchandises* (goods building)
IWM	Imperial War Museum, London
LGV	*Ligne de Grande vitesse* (high speed railway line)
LR	Light railway (60cm gauge)
MG	Metre gauge
MRL	*Ministère des Régions Libérées* (Ministry for the Liberated Regions)
MTP	*Ministère des Travaux Publics* (Ministry of Public Works)
PN	*passage à niveau* (level crossing)
SACM	*Société Alsacienne de Construction Mécanique*
SG	Standard gauge

Introduction

In our previous book, *Narrow Gauge in the Arras Sector - before, during and after the First World War* (Pen & Sword Transport, 2015), we described the history of railways of less than standard gauge in the Arras sector of the Western Front. These were put into the context of the existing and new standard gauge lines. In addition, the narrow gauge history of that area was followed from the beginnings, through the First World War, and then on into their subsequent use, up to final closure of the last lines in 1958. In this book we have addressed this subject for the Somme sector of the Western Front.

Many in France regard the term 'narrow gauge' as not including the metre gauge but only gauges less than this. This was also the view of the British Army in the First World War, to whom the metre gauge was coupled with the standard gauge as 'Broad Gauge Railways'. 'Light Railways' were, with very few exceptions, of 60 cm gauge. However, we have concentrated here on all railways of less than standard gauge in the Somme sector. There is also some information on standard gauge railways to set the scene for this.

Those who have read our previous book will realise that there are parts of this book which are the same, starting with the immediately following outline history of the First World War. We have done this so that this book can stand alone, and new readers are not disadvantaged. All the photographs except one (8.1, Chapter Eight) are new, and all the figures with the exception of Figure 0.1, which has been modified to correct some inaccuracies, and for the dates to fit better with the key events in the Somme sector.

Throughout this book the term 'British Army' means the British and British Empire (now Commonwealth) Army units which were under the command of the British Expeditionary Force (BEF) General Headquarters (GHQ). This included important Armies from the Dominions of Canada, Australia, New Zealand, and South Africa, and from India.

The British sectors and approximate Army positions from 1914 are shown in Figure 0.1. From October 1914, the Belgian Army held the front line from north of Ypres (now Ieper), in Belgium, to the sea. After the formation of the British First and Second Armies at the end of December 1914, the British Army held the front line from Ypres south to around La Bassée in France, in the east of the *département* of Pas-de-Calais north of Lens. The French held it from La Bassée south. The British Second Army were responsible for the line in Belgium from Ypres south, and in France in the Nord *département*, down as far as the Armentières area. The British First Army extended south in the Pas-de-Calais *département* as far as just north of Lens, until the Battle of Loos in September 1915. From March 1916, the British Army took over the responsibility for the front from Ypres down to the river Somme. The British First Army now took over the front almost to the Scarpe valley just north of Arras; and the British Third Army from there south to Hébuterne, at the north end of the 1916 Somme battlefield but still in the Pas-de-Calais *département*. From there south was the British Fourth Army, and later also the Fifth, to the beginning of the French Sixth Army almost on the Somme river. The Fifth Army held some of the front line around Bapaume, in the south of the Pas-de-Calais *département* in 1917, until this was taken over again by the Third Army from 1 June, 1917.

The British front line from March 1916 until Summer 1918 falls easily into three sectors, which are from north to south:

The Ypres sector, held by the Second Army, from Ypres in Belgium to north of Armentières in the Nord *département* in France. This corresponds with the ancient territory of Flanders (*Flandres* in French, *Vlaanderen* in Flemish) in Belgium and the northern part of the Nord *département* in France.

The Arras sector, held by the First Army (and from April 1918 also partly by the Fifth Army) south from Armentières to Arras, and by the Third Army in Arras and south to the area of the Somme *département* border; this corresponds roughly with the eastern part of the Pas-de-Calais *département* (the Pas-de-Calais *département* being the historical *Comté*, or County, of Artois), and parts of the adjacent southern part of the Nord *département*.

The Somme sector, held at times by part of the Third Army, by the Fourth Army, and later also the Fifth Army until April 1918. This corresponds in 1916 with the part of the Somme *département* to just north of the Somme river, but later extended south of the river. There was

Introduction

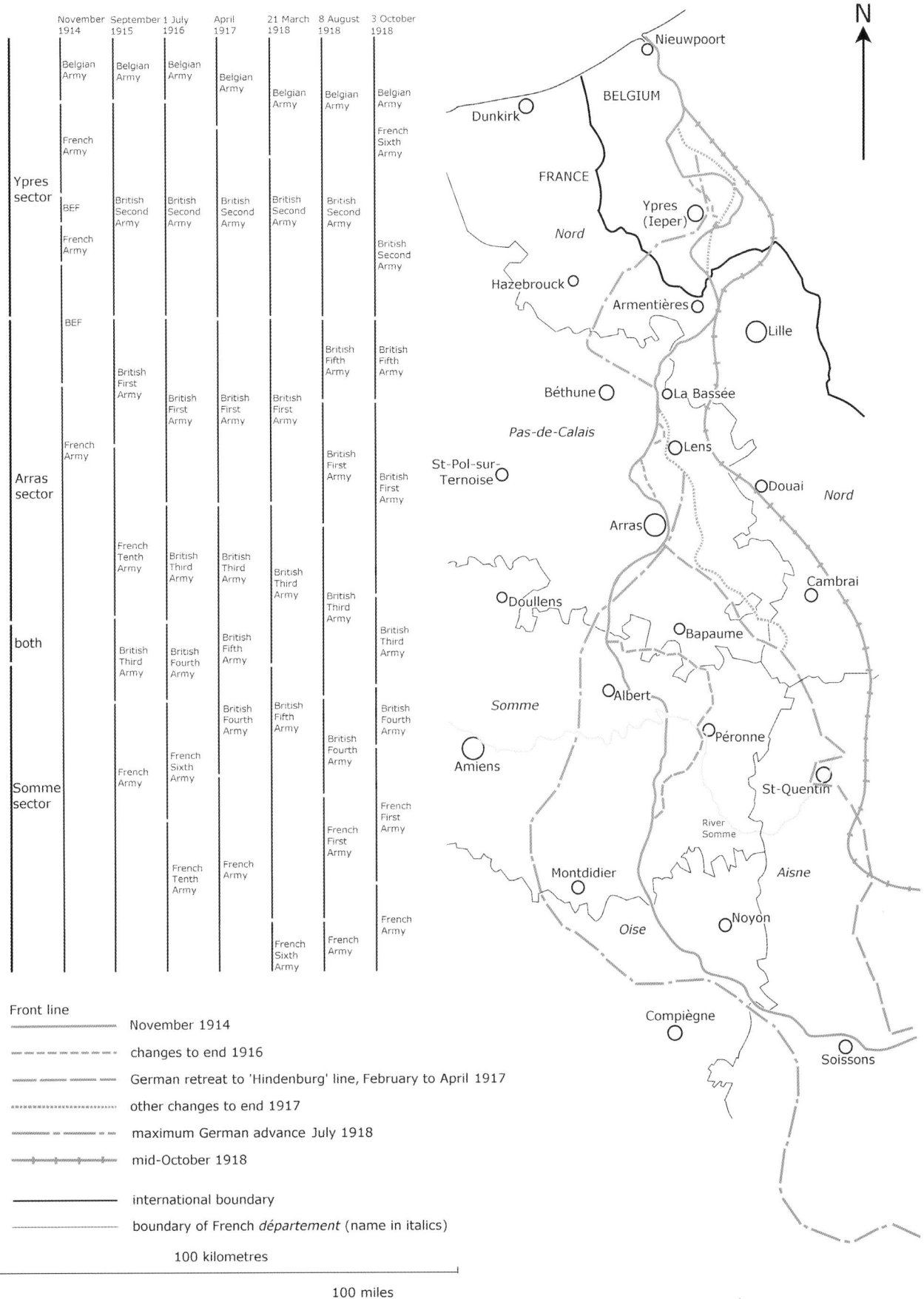

Figure 0.1

also considerable French involvement. For the (first) Battle of the Somme, which began on 1 July 1916, the French Sixth Army held the line and took part in the battle from Maricourt south. The maximum extent of the British Army commitment to the south was between January and 21 March 1918, when the Fifth Army was responsible for the front line down to Barisis, east of Noyon.

The Somme sector is therefore in the ancient region of Picardie (Picardy in English), comprising the *départements* of Somme, Oise and Aisne. There is a grey area at the north end of the 'Somme sector' and the south end of the 'Arras sector' as we have defined them. This overlap is identified in Figure 0.1. In the Summer of 1916 the Third Army extended south to Hébuterne, in the south of the Pas-de-Calais *département*. This was at the north end of the 1916 Somme battlefield, and is properly considered with the Somme sector. However, the area east of there, around Bapaume, formed the starting points for the Fifth Army Bullecourt attacks in 1917. These are very much part of the story of the Arras sector. The Battle of Cambrai in Autumn 1917 (Third Army) also mainly concerns the Arras sector, but some railway units at the north end of the Somme sector became involved. Some material about the Battle of Cambrai is therefore included in this book (see Chapter Six).

It was during the Battle of the Somme in the summer of 1916 that grave deficiencies in the supply lines became most apparent. As part of general mobilisation at the beginning of the war, the French government had placed all railways in the country under military control, although the railways generally continued to be run by the regular personnel. In 1916, Sir Eric Geddes, an experienced railway manager who had previously worked in London with Lloyd-George when the latter was Secretary of State for War, was appointed Director General for Transportation, France, and given the rank of Lt Colonel in the Engineering and Railway Staff Corps. He was given responsibility for standard gauge and 'light' railways, roads, and canals, but not 'mechanical transport' (presumably motor road vehicles).

This recognised the importance of transport, and especially railway transport, in the effort to win the war. In 1915, it was agreed that the British Army could operate on French standard gauge lines, and in December 1916 there was a further agreement for the British Army to import wagons and engines for these lines. The British Army Railway Operating Division (ROD) operated extensively on the standard and metre gauge railways in Belgium and the north of France from 1915. The agreement also led to the building and operating in Belgium, Nord-Pas-de-Calais and Somme of military standard gauge railways exclusive to the British Army, which we have called 'British Army lines'. An increase in the rate of railway building and upgrading followed, culminating in an enormous effort in 1917 and 1918.

The railway infrastructure before the First World War was key to the developments during the war. After the war, these railways played a major part in the recovery and reconstruction. However, the war had a major effect on the later development of railways in these parts of France. If the war had not occurred, railways, particularly secondary lines (those of *Intérêt Local*), might have been more extensive, and might have been in a much better position to compete against road transport. The war, and financial problems afterwards, impaired infrastructure investment, including in particular electrification.

It was the French (and in the Ypres Sector the Belgians) who had been fighting on their own territory and had to live with the major consequences. The British and Dominion Armies, and the American Army, and others, came and 'did the business'. They then contributed to clearing up, for a very few years, and mainly their own material, and went home.

In the Somme Sector before the First World War there was an extensive network of metre gauge lines. The 60cm gauge lines were short and industrial. During the war, the metre gauge lines played a significant part, but the major military developments, first French and then British, were standard and 60 cm gauge lines. After the war both the narrow gauges continued, but as in the Arras sector, the 60cm gauge survived the longest, serving the sugar beet industry.

In Chapter One, we provide an introduction to some of the relevant history, geography, and industrial and railway development of this area. Chapters Two and Three cover the history of the metre gauge railways of this area before the First World War. Chapter Four deals with the general history of railways, and particularly British and Dominion Armies' light railways, during the First World War.

Chapters Five to Eight address the detailed First World War narrow gauge history of this sector. In our previous book, *Narrow Gauge in the Arras Sector*, we described the railways area by area. In the Somme sector, there were distinct chronological phases, fought over a considerable depth of territory west to east. The chapters divide the story into these chronological phases. The demarcation points are, firstly, the end of the retreat of the German Army to the Hindenburg Line in March 1917; secondly, the start of the German offensive and advance in the Somme sector on 21 March, 1918; and thirdly, the start of the Allied offensive in the Somme sector, and of the final advance east, on 8 August, 1918. The titles of Chapters Five to Eight describe the period covered in each, and a background history of the war and of battles in the Somme sector for that period is given at the beginning of each chapter.

After this we describe the post-war history of these railways, and finally, in Chapter Twelve, summarise what can be seen now, including some walks.

We have made all the translations from French. We have followed the British convention for the configuration of wheels on locomotives. The French convention is only to count the wheels on one side of the locomotive and not to use hyphens, so that a locomotive that is to the British a 2-6-0 is to the French a 130.

French local government

In 1790, during the French revolution, the country was re-organised into administrative units called *départements* (departments), roughly equivalent to counties in the UK. The old counties and regions were swept aside. Each *département* has a *Préfet* (Prefect) who is appointed from Paris to run the services of the State and is accountable to central government. Each *département* also has an elected assembly, the *Conseil Général*, with a President, to run local services. The *Préfet* and the *Conseil Général* run the *département* from the main administrative town or city, the *préfecture*. Outside the largest conurbations, *départements* are divided into *sous-préfectures*: these in turn are each composed of a number of *cantons*, which are themselves composed of *communes*. In the countryside each village is a *commune*, with its own *Maire* (Mayor). The reintroduction of *régions* in 1982, between the central government and the *départements*, is irrelevant to this book.

Times and timetables

In summary timetables all times have been given in the 24-hour clock. All these tables are abstracted from the originals. All of the original timetables are in the 24-hour clock, except for some in the nineteenth and early twentieth centuries which are in the 12-hour clock, with the trains marked *matin* (morning) or *soir* (evening) over the departure from the station of origin. In the text we have given times related to timetables in the 24-hour clock, and other times in the 12-hour clock with am or pm. In France, the timetables were published by the *Librairie Chaix*, of Paris, often referred to simply as the *Chaix*.

Units of measurement

Length and distance

1 metre = 100 centimetres (cm) = 1,000 millimetres (mm) = 3.28ft = 3ft 3⅜ inches

1 kilometre (km) = 1,000 metres = 0.62 miles = approx. ⅝ mile

1 mile = 1.609 kilometres

Weight

1 kilogram (kg) = 1,000 grams (gm) = 2.2046 pounds (lb)

1 tonne (metric ton) = 1,000 kilograms = 2,204.6 pounds

1 ton (Imperial ton) = 2,240 pounds

In this book most units are metric, except where the originals are in Imperial units, as in most British Army documents from the First World War. Some important distances and heights are given in both.

Chapter One

Introducing the Somme sector and its railways

The Somme sector as we have defined it includes all the major battlefields of Picardie (Picardy in the English spelling) in the First World War from 1915 to 1918. The ancient region of Picardie was reformed after the French revolution into the modern *départements* of Somme (*Préfecture*, or administrative centre, Amiens), Oise (*Préfecture* Beauvais) and Aisne (*Préfecture* Laon). Some of the battlefields, especially those of the 1916 (First) Battle of the Somme, included a strip along the south of the Pas-de-Calais *département* (*Préfecture* Arras).

Geography

Outside the main towns, the countryside is mainly one of chalk plateaux, many with rich alluvial soils over the chalk, rising between mostly gentle river valleys. Some of the valley sides inland are steeper, and the hills rise to more than 150m (500ft). The majority of the land is farmed, but there are woods and forests, especially in the south-east. The chief crops are grains, oil plants (rape and flax), potatoes, beans, peas, and fruit; and of course, sugar beet (see below).

The coastline on the English Channel is short, squeezed between the Authie estuary in the north (boundary with the Pas-de-Calais *département*) and the Bresle river in the south, which reaches the sea at Eu-Le-Tréport, (boundary of the Seine-Maritime *département*, Normandy). The largest river is the Somme, which gives its name to the *département*, and to the main First World War battles of this sector. The port of St-Valéry-sur-Somme lies on its extensive estuary. This port played some part towards the end of the First World War but is better known as the final departure point of William the Conqueror for England in 1066.

In the north-west of the region, the rivers run from south-east to north-west. Furthest north is the Authie, which is for most of its course the boundary between *départements* of Pas-de-Calais and Somme, and therefore historically the division between Artois and Picardie. The Somme flows into Amiens from the east, then turns north-west to the sea.. Further east, between St-Quentin and Péronne, it loops down to the south around Ham. The Somme is notable for its broad flood plain, with lakes and swampy areas, making it difficult to cross. The second largest river of the Region, the Oise, flows south-west just over the plateau east of St-Quentin, then past Noyon to Compiègne to join the Seine just west of Paris. The Aisne, which gives its name to the eastern *département* of Picardie, flows west from the Argonne Forest past Soissons to join the Oise at Compiègne, and is therefore south of our area.

There is an extensive network of canals. The Somme is navigable in its lower reaches, and further up is accompanied by a lateral canal, through Péronne and Ham. East of Ham it meets the St-Quentin Canal. This runs northeast from Noyon on the Oise, crosses from the Oise to the Somme north from Tergnier, and then runs north through St-Quentin all the way to Cambrai and into the northern industrial area. The *Souterrain* (tunnel) *de Riqueval* which takes the St-Quentin canal north into the valley of the Escaut past Marcoing and Cambrai was important in the closing stages of the First World War in 1918.

From Tergnier the *Canal de la Sambre à l'Oise* (the Sambre Canal) follows the Oise valley northeast. The *Canal du Nord* runs north from the lateral canal of the Oise at Pont l'Évêque (Noyon). It has a common section with the Somme canal between Ham and Péronne, then follows the Tortille valley north and on into the industrial area west of Cambrai, to meet the La Sensée canal at Arleux (Nord *département*). Construction did not begin until 1908 and the canal was incomplete at the start of the First World War, during which the works were extensively damaged. Works did not recommence until 1960 and the canal was opened in 1965. There are tunnels at Ruyaulcourt and Panneterie (east of Roye and north of Noyon).

This is not a major industrial region. Industries include cement (from the chalk), sugar beet processing, and a large glass factory at St-Gobain.

Sugar beet

Sugar beet is widely grown in northern France and in 2013 France was still the second largest producer of beet sugar in the world (after Russia). Picardie is the largest producer of beet sugar in France, with a production of more than one third of the French total.

To produce sugar, the sugar beet is washed and then shredded, and the sugar extracted with hot water. The raw juice is purified and condensed down and the sugar is then crystallised from the concentrated syrup. After extraction, the beet strips are pressed to remove water and remaining sugar, and the waste (*pulpe*, pulp) can be used as animal feed. Frequently the whole process is carried out in one factory (*sucrerie*). In some areas, the initial extraction was carried out in a *râperie*, and the juice was then transferred to a central factory for final sugar production. Sugar beet can also be used to produce alcohol, in which case the factory is often called a *distillerie*. Sugar refineries used to use railways and particularly narrow gauge lines extensively.

History

The area which forms the background to this book has for centuries been much fought over. Examples to start with, close to English hearts, were Edward III's and Henry V's successes at Crécy and Agincourt. The relevance to this book lies not in the battles but in their routes, which were through our area. Edward III crossed to France in 1346, landing at St.Vaast on the Cherbourg Peninsula. He took Caen and Lisieux before crossing the Seine and reaching the Somme. He tried to cross at Picquigny and Pont-Remy but was forced to turn towards the sea. At Mons-en-Vimeux his scouts picked up a French peasant who was willing to do a deal – freedom and gold in return for information about a river crossing. He led them to Blanchetaque, a crossing clearly named after the white tracks made by horses and wagons. The army crossed after waiting for the tide to ebb and rested for four days in the Forest of Crécy. They chose a site for battle near the village of Crécy-en-Ponthieu and the battle took place late on 26 August. It was a great victory with the English slaughtering 10,000 Frenchmen. However, a mere 69 years later, the French suffered a repeat performance.

Henry V invaded France in 1415, landing at Harfleur, where he lost 3,000 men (20 per cent of his force), and valuable time, besieging and finally capturing the port. Against his counsellors' advice he opted to march to Calais, 144 miles away. He failed to emulate his predecessor Edward, who quickly crossed the Somme, and he was forced to track upstream tailed by the French on the other bank. He skirted Abbeville and Amiens and he, also, is now entering our area. The French were closing in from south and east but a solution was at hand. Where the Somme loops to the North, he was able to outdistance the French by cutting the corner. He was able to cross the river at Voyennes and Berthancourt by improvising bridges with planks torn from nearby houses. While the English rested, the French occupied Péronne. Henry, however, was able to keep ahead of them through Forceville, Acheux and Lucheux before skirting Doullens and heading north. At some point heralds came to his camp from the French leaders seeking to 'inform you that ere you come to Calais they will meet you and fight you'. He finally faced the French at Agincourt, beat them soundly and became heir to the French throne, as the king's son-in-law.

Turning now from English invaders to other struggles that the French had to face. France had for centuries been aware of its vulnerability in the north. In the thirteenth century, steps were taken to absorb the territory of warring magnates into France. In the fourteenth century, the problem to the north was Burgundy, which had grown from a duchy, given by the French king to a younger brother in 1356, to a major European power. It stretched across the area which we know as Belgium and Holland into a large part of what is now northern France. Not only was Burgundy now encroaching on France, but it was becoming powerful and aggressive. It was in these areas that towns that feature in this book are sited. They have therefore for many centuries been frontier towns. Louis XIV in the seventeenth century employed that master of military architecture, Vauban, to build for him a chain of fortresses in the north-east for this very reason. Finally, moving on to the nineteenth century, a new enemy arrived, Germany, newly on the scene as a military power and anxious to prove it. After the Franco-Prussian War of 1870-71, the German state acquired Alsace and parts of Lorraine. When Germany invaded France in 1914, it was yet again through this area and the towns we have highlighted below were once again 'frontier towns'. The histories of a selection of such towns will make the point.

St-Quentin

St. Quentin began life as a Roman fortified town, Augusta Viromanduorum, built to guard a ford over the Somme. Towns in this region, due to their position found themselves on the frontline many times through the centuries. Thus, in 1465, the last Duke of Burgundy, Charles the Bold, joined a revolt of French nobles against the Crown. Charles was one of seven Dukes and his main purpose was to recover the towns which his father had ceded to France. One of these was St. Quentin, which he took before joining the revolt. In 1471, in a surprise attack, Louis XI retook the town. Charles was killed by the Swiss at Nancy in 1476 leaving an only daughter, Mary, as his heir. This valuable heiress eventually married Maximillian Hapsburg, Holy Roman Emperor from 1508, and had a son Phillip who, by marriage, became King of Spain. Thus, Spain became the main power that France had to contend with in this area. In 1557, St. Quentin was under siege by the Spaniards. When it fell it was looted and virtually destroyed. The population fled and it was deserted for two years. The Spaniards then won a battle against the French nearby and their king, Phillip II, as homage to St Lawrence, whose name-day it was, vowed to build a great palace. This was the Escorial near Madrid, which took the form of a grid-iron representing St Lawrence's martyrdom. The French retook it in 1559, and strengthened its fortifications,

1.1 The west end of the basilica at St-Quentin, taken from up the hill along the path of the former metre gauge railway from St-Quentin to Caudry, May 2016. *(Authors)*

1.2 Remains of the Hindenburg Line in the western suburbs of St-Quentin, May 2016 (see Walk 5 in Chapter Twelve). *(Authors)*

demolishing two districts to do so. By the middle of the seventeenth century, although it escaped siege, the town was surrounded by the fighting in Picardy. By the end of the seventeenth century the military successes of Louis XVI had pushed the French border further North and St. Quentin was no longer on the front line. However, come the Napoleonic Wars, in 1814, the town was occupied by the Russians, who left without causing much damage. In January 1870 during the Franco-Prussian War the citizens managed to repel the Prussians, and they congratulated themselves by erecting a statue, which still stands. They were, however a little premature since a second attack was soon successful. For their bravery during this war, the town was awarded the Legion d'Honneur. At the outset of war in 1914, St. Quentin was taken by the Germans. The occupation was harsh and in 1916 the population was expelled and the town was fortified as part of the Hindenburg Line. By the end of the war, 80 per cent of the town was damaged including the Basilica.

Noyon

Another town that can serve as an example of being on this frontier is Noyon. This city was also founded by the Romans and clearly, they saw it in this light too. They fortified it strongly and remains of these fortifications can still be seen. These fortifications have been cited as one reason why Bishop Medardus, in 531, moved the see here from Vermand. Another possible reason has been suggested that he thought the wine was better! Be that as it may, in 859, the Vikings attacked, occupied the town and killed the bishop. In the following centuries, Noyon suffered a similar fate to St. Quentin in the power struggle between France and Burgundy. It was taken and ravaged in 1552 by Charles V but 'sold' back to France seven years later. However, France, in the second half of the sixteenth century, had a civil war on its hands as the king Henry IV, a Protestant was challenged by the Catholic League. Noyon appeared centre-stage when, in 1591, Henry captured it from the League after a two week siege. Its importance lay in its position on the route from Spanish controlled Flanders to Paris and the Spanish were set on invading France in pursuit of their Catholic European Empire. In both world wars, Noyon was occupied by the Germans and suffered great damage. Although the cathedral was hit, it survived. However, the Germans cut down the organ pipes and used them for shell cases.

Péronne

This town could be said to be our third frontier town. French historians consider it to have suffered more damage over the centuries than any other French town. The ramparts were built in the ninth century. The only part remaining is the imposing Porte de Bretagne. It was besieged and occupied by the Normans in the eleventh century. The town figured prominently in the long-drawn-out contest between France and Burgundy. Its fortress was used to house notable prisoners. The most notable of these was Louis XI. His struggle with Charles the Bold raged for many years over our area. In 1468, with Charles as a newly empowered ruler, the two were embroiled in a rebellion in Liège. The rebels had hoped for help from France to free themselves from Burgundy. Louis agreed to meet Charles at Péronne. Historians have wondered what made Louis put himself at the mercy of Charles. The only answer seems to be that he relished the contest and believed he could outsmart him. His nickname was, after all, 'The Spider King'. Louis arrived at Péronne with a small company of fifty lords and attendants to be met by Charles with two hundred 'knights and squires in glittering array'. Although he was offered the finest lodgings available, he insisted on moving into the castle, which although in a bad state of repair, was secure. After several days of tricky negotiations, things deteriorated with news of assaults against Burgundian prelates in Liège. Charles flew into a rage, blaming Louis for the attacks, and that he had only come to Péronne to distract Charles from the plots in Liège. Louis found the city gates closed against him. One particularly alarming thought was that in 927 a Count of Vermandois had imprisoned his ancestor, Charles the Simple, in this castle until he died. Several sleepless nights followed, until thanks to the calming influence of Phillipe de Commynes, Charles agreed to consider a more peaceful way forward. A treaty was to be signed and Louis would accompany him to Liège. De Commynes served Charles for ten years until one night in 1472 he secretly left for Louis' camp to become his close adviser. The struggle in Péronne continued and in 1536, Spanish Burgundy besieged the town. This siege became famous for the courage of a woman, Catherine de Poix, who rallied the citizens and is reported to have thrown Spaniards off the battlements. The Spaniards finally took the town and razed it to the ground. In the nineteenth century, during the Franco-Prussian War it was occupied and flattened again. Péronne suffered badly in 1917 and was then fire bombed in May 1940 by the Germans. For this the town received two Croix de Guerre and a Légion d'Honneur.

The damage suffered in the First World War by these medieval towns represented a new departure in warfare. This was the deliberate targeting of medieval landmarks along the Western Front. It began in the city of Rheims where the Germans, having been forced from the city centre, fired deliberately on the cathedral. From then on, the cathedrals of Northern France, notably St. Quentin and Noyon, became war targets. It was recognised that destruction of such glorious medieval landmarks was a potent psychological weapon. They were symbols of past glory, independence and prosperity. The buildings represented the community's historic identity.

Albert

This is yet another Roman foundation, this one from 54BC. It was later called Ancre, after its river. The name was changed after it was given to Charles d'Albert, Duc de Luynes by Louis XIII in 1617. Its main claim to fame, nowadays, comes from events in the First World War. In 1915 and 1916, it was very near the front line, on the British side, hence it was often bombarded. The Basilica, a popular pilgrimage site, had been rebuilt between 1885 and 1895. Surmounting the tower was a gold Virgin and Child by a local artist, Albert Roze. On 15 January 1915, the tower was struck and the statue slumped to one side. The statue now became a potent symbol to the troops of both sides. The British came to believe that whoever caused the statue to fall would lose the war. The Germans believed the opposite. They took Albert in March 1918 and following bombardment by the British the Basilica was destroyed. The statue was never found. The rebuilt Basilica is an exact copy of the nineteenth century one by the son of the original architect.

1.3 The basilica of Notre-Dame de Brebières at Albert before 1914. *(Authors' collection)*.

1.4 The basilica of Notre-Dame de Brebières at Albert in 1917. After the bombardment in 1916, the golden statue of the Virgin is leaning in a precarious position. *(Authors' collection)*

Ham

Our next town is Ham, a pleasant town on the Canal de la Somme. Its main claim to fame is its fortress. The date of its foundation is not clear, but it is mentioned in a charter of 1052. By the thirteenth century, it had acquired its characteristic shape, a polygon with numerous cylindrical towers. It was besieged by Phillip of Spain in 1557, on the same campaign that saw him attack St. Quentin. It was remodelled for Louis XIV by Vauban and by the nineteenth century it had become a prison for holding political opponents. The most famous prisoner was Louis Napoleon, the nephew of the Emperor. He had, in 1839, from exile in England, attempted an 'invasion' of France to coincide with the arrival of his uncle's body in Paris. With 56 bemused soldiers, who had been told this was a 'pleasure cruise', he landed at Wimereux near Boulogne. He marched into Boulogne, fully expecting that the population would welcome him and the soldiers rush to his cause. There was no support and he was soon captured and sent to Paris for trial. He was sentenced to life imprisonment in the fortress of Ham. The fortress was dark and dank from the mists generated by the nearby Somme canal. Louis Napoleon spent just over five years as a prisoner in Ham. He had books and a suite of rooms. He was allowed to take a mistress and he chose Eleanora Vergeot, who worked in the prison as an ironer. With her he had two sons. When he escaped he was 38 years old and it had been a formative experience. He escaped dressed as a workman, with staining to hide his white face, and a plank over his shoulder. His beloved dog Ham went with him.

1.5 The town hall at Doullens in April 2015. Posters of Field-Marshal Sir Douglas (later Earl) Haig and Marshal Foch advertise an exhibition of the meeting the Army Commanders held there on 26 March 1918. *(Authors)*

Doullens

This town began life as a Roman settlement, Dulcinum. In 1225, France, worried about the defence of its northern borders, took control of the area from the ruling Counts of Vermandois. In 1475, Louis XI burned it to the ground for supporting Burgundy. In 1523, it was given the name Doullens-le-Hardi in acknowledgement of its fierce defence against the Anglo-Burgundian armies. In 1593, the Spaniards besieged, then captured the town, massacring all the inhabitants. It was returned to France in 1598 by the Peace of Vervins. Vauban built another of his citadels here which failed to impress Victor Hugo on a visit in 1837 who remarked 'I don't like citadels'. On 26 March 1918 Doullens town hall was the site of the meeting of Allied Army Commanders at which Marshal Foch became supreme allied commander.

Amiens

We turn now to the largest and most spectacular place in the area covered by this book, Amiens. It was founded by a Gallic tribe who named it Samerobriva, simply Somme Bridge. The modern name comes from the Romans who named it Ambianum, after the local tribe, the Ambiani. In the following centuries it was much fought over but became French in 1185. It suffered the same fate as the 'frontier towns' described above, taken by the Burgundians in 1435 but bought back in 1463 by Louis XI. It was captured by the Spaniards in 1597. They gained entry to the hungry city disguised as peasants selling, oddly enough, walnuts and apples! The French king, Henry IV, retook the city after a siege. Later peaceful times allowed the city to become rich from manufacturing velour cloth which they dyed with woad which had long been an Amiénois skill. The cathedral, which is the largest in France, was built between 1220 and 1288. The cathedral survived both world wars which was fortunate, since Amiens was seen as a crucial prize by both sides due to its importance as a railway centre. Railways arrived in 1846 with the Gare du Nord serving the Paris line. As other lines were developed, the city began to turn away from the Somme to such an extent that City Hall moved its entrance from the riverside to face the station. In 1914, it was the Advanced Base for the British Expeditionary Force but was taken by the Germans in August. Its importance as a railway centre led its recapture to become a high priority and it was taken by the French in September 1914. It remained in Allied hands, never far behind the front line, throughout the war. As a result, the local people had a difficult time and showed their feelings with strikes. There were 25 in 1918!

In the Second World War, it fell to the Germans in May 1940. In 1944, after the Normandy landings, 200 RAF bombers flew in to destroy those railways that had made Amiens a target for a hundred years. They were aiming especially for the important junction south-east of the city, Longueau. In this attack of 12 and 13 June, much damage was inflicted on the city.

Development of railways in the Somme sector

The main networks of standard and metre gauge lines in the Somme sector, as they were in spring 1914, are shown in Figure 1.1. This includes all the major battlefield areas of the First World War in this sector, but not some of the supply lines further west. It also extends south to the village of Barisis, in the forest of St-Gobain due east of Noyon. This was the southernmost part of the front that the British Army held in the War, but they only held it from January to March 1918.

The definitions of lines of *Intérêt Général* and those of *Intérêt Local* were codified in the *Loi Migneret* of 1865. Lines of *Intérêt Général* were those of sufficient length, importance, or strategic worth to be at least partially a

Introducing the Somme sector and its railways

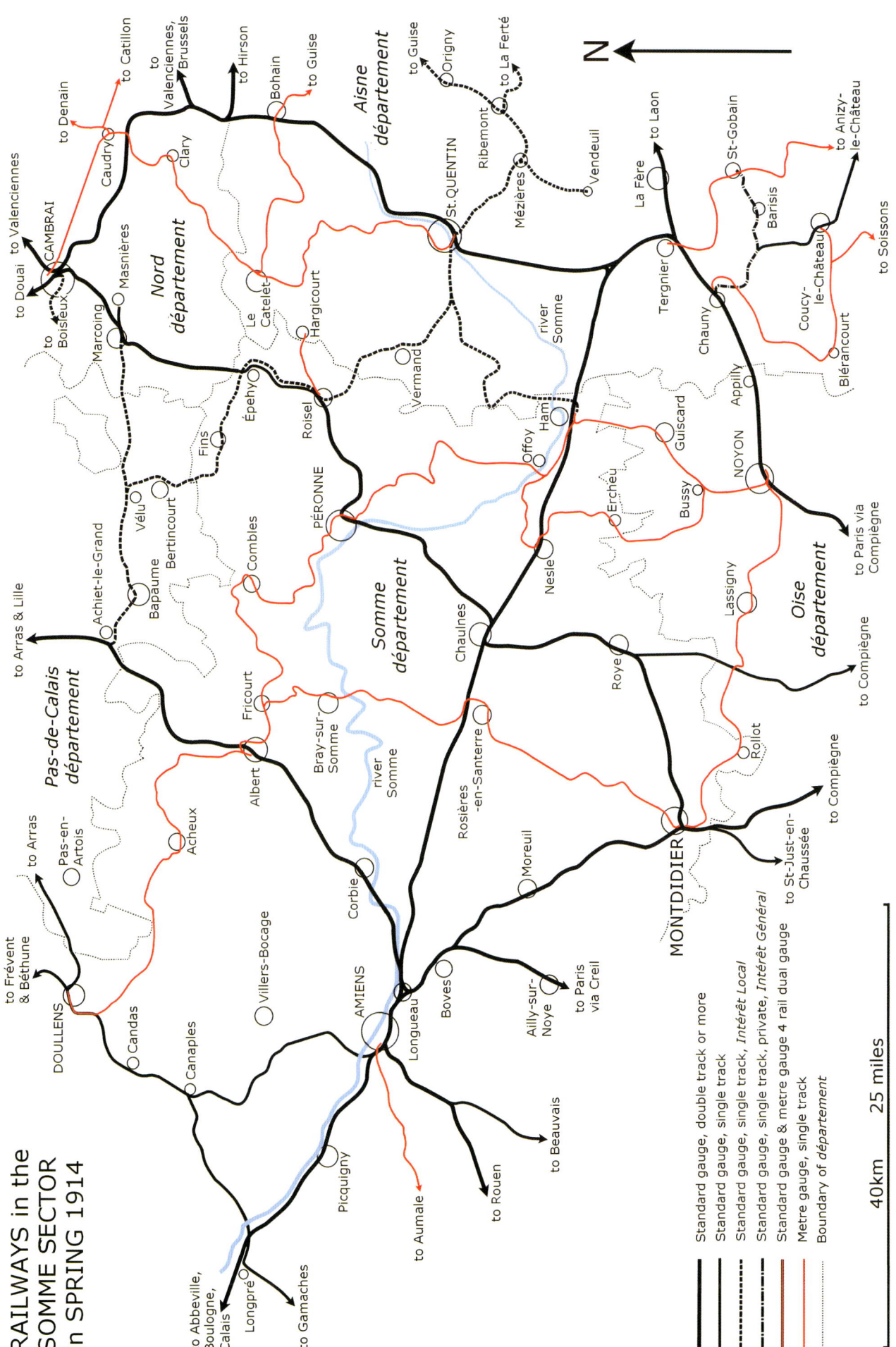

Figure 1.1

charge on the State and were administered by the Ministry of Public Works in Paris. Those of *Intérêt Local* were administered by the *département* concerned and were (and are still) a responsibility of the *Préfet* (Prefect). The Chief Engineer of *Ponts et Chaussées* (bridges and highways) for the *département* reported to the Préfet and was also responsible for railways. Local Engineers were based in the chief towns. Unless otherwise qualified, the terms 'Chief Engineer', 'Local Engineer' or 'Engineer' in this book refer to these departmental employees, not to employees of the operating companies. Although the right to build and operate the railways was conceded to companies, the State and the *départements* kept very firm control over them. They had to give permission for all changes to the *Cahier des Charges*, which was the original very detailed agreement about building and operating each line. It is for this reason that so much of the paperwork survives in the departmental archives, even when most of the individual companies' archives have disappeared.

The Freyciney Plan in 1879-1880 further encouraged the development of lines of *Intérêt Local*. Within this category, tramways were also defined. These were lines built at least 70 per cent in roads, or on the verges of roads. For a full discussion of all these decisions and their effects we recommend Chapter 1 of *Minor Railways of France* (W J K Davies, Plateway Press, 2000).

A businessman or a company would usually be the originator of plans for railways of *Intérêt Local*, frequently with local encouragement. If found suitable after public and other enquiries, the proposed line would be declared of *utilité publique* ('in the public interest'), and the concession to build and operate the line would be granted to the businessman or company for a fixed number of years. A *Compagnie* or *Société Anonyme* (limited company) would be formed at or before this stage. At the end of its life, local agreement was sufficient to close a line, but the formal decree of *déclassement* (declassification) had to come from the office of the President of France, and would be published in the official journal of the Republic.

The *Compagnie du Nord*, formed in 1845, was eventually responsible for almost all lines of *Intérêt Général* in the area covered by this book. These are listed in Table 1.1. Many of these lines are now closed. In general, standard gauge lines were of *Intérêt Général*, and those of metre gauge and narrower gauges were of *Intérêt Local*, but there were exceptions both ways. In the area of interest of this book, there were a number of standard gauge lines of *Intérêt Local*. The only standard gauge line of *Intérêt Général* which was in private ownership, was that from Chauny to St-Gobain (Aisne *département*).

Table 1.1 Standard gauge lines of Intérêt Général in the Somme sector

Line	via	type	département (in Somme sector)	opened	closed pass.	decl. goods	notes
Paris–Lille	Amiens, Arras	DT	Oise, Somme	1847			
Paris–Brussels	Noyon, St-Quentin	DT	Oise, Aisne				
Amiens–Boulogne	Abbeville, Noyelles	DT	Somme	1848			
Chauny–St-Gobain (1)		ST	Aisne	1860	1950	1993(2)	SNCF 1983
Amiens–Tergnier	Rosières, Ham	DT	Somme, Aisne	1867			
Amiens–Rouen	Saleux, Abancourt	DT	Somme, Oise	1867			
Amiens–Beauvais	Saleux (junction)	ST	Somme, Oise	1872	1939, 1945	1979	
Longpré–Longroy–Gamaches			Somme	1872	1938	1993	
St.Just-en-Chaussée–Chaulnes	Montdider, Roye	DT, ST	Oise, Somme	1873	1970	1975, 1996	
Chaulnes–Cambrai	Péronne, Roisel	DT, ST	Somme	1873	1970		
Doullens–Frévent		ST	Somme	1876 (3)	1938, 1944		
Doullens–Arras		ST	Somme	1876	1936, 1941		
Doullens–Longpré	Canaples	ST	Somme	1874	1938, 1941	1971 & 2005	
Canaples–Amiens		ST	Somme	1877	1945		
Compiègne–Roye		ST	Oise, Somme	1881	1939, 1942		
Compiègne–Amiens	Montdidier	DT	Oise, Somme	1883			
Tergnier–Laon		DT	Aisne				
Chauny–Anizy-Pinon (4)		ST	Aisne	1882			

DT double track
ST single track – where both stated, predominant stated first
(1) Private IG line, owned and from 1869 operated by CSG - all other lines *Compagnie du Nord*
(2) Remains open Chauny-Usines–Chauny (1995)
(3) Classed as *Intérêt Local* until 1880
(4) Part line shared with Chauny–St-Gobain
CSG *Compagnie des manufactures de glaces et produits chimiques de St.Gobain, Chauny et Cirey*
SNCF *Société Nationale des Chemins de Fer Français*

Standard gauge lines of Intérêt Local

Table 1.2 Standard gauge lines of Intérêt Local in the Somme sector

Line	via	type	département(s)	length Km	opened	closed pass.	goods	decl.	notes
Achiet–Marcoing (AB)	Bapaume	ST	Pas-de-Calais Nord	33	1871–1878	1966	1969 (1)	1973	VFIL 1930 RPdeC 1961
Vélu–St-Quentin (VBStQ)		ST	Pas-de-Calais Somme, Aisne	52 (2)	1879–1880	1955			VFIL 1930
Vélu–Bertincourt–Fins–Sorel			Somme	13	1880	1955	1955		VFIL 1930
Fins–Sorel–Vermand			Somme, Aisne	27	1879	1955	1955/69		VFIL 1930 RTA 1956
Vermand–St-Quentin			Aisne	12 (2)	1880	1955	1972/92		VFIL 1930 RTA 1956 SNCF 1981
St-Quentin–Ham (CDA)		ST	Aisne, Somme	27 (2)	1910–12	1955	1981/90		NE 1922
St-Quentin–Villers-Aubigny			Aisne	15 (2)	1910	1955			RTA 1951-52
Villers-Aubigny–Ham			Aisne, Somme	6	1912	1955			SNCF 1981
St-Quentin–Guise via Mézières, Ribemont		ST	Aisne	40	1874–75				CDA 1919
St-Quentin–Origny-Ste-Benoîte (3)			Aisne	23	1874	1968			NE 1922 RTA 1952 SNCF 1981
Origny-Ste-Benoîte–Guise			Aisne	17	1874–75	1965	1966		CDA 1920 NE 1922 RTA 1952
Appilly–Coucy-le-Château (French Army)		ST	Oise, Aisne	19	1917	1928	1928		CDA 1919
Appilly–Blérancourt			Oise, Aisne	6	1917	1928			NE 1922
Blérancourt–Coucy-le-Château (4)			Aisne	13	1917	1928 (5)	1963		CDA 1919 NE 1922 RTA 1952

ST   single track
AB   Compagnie du Chemin de fer d'Achiet à Bapaume
CDA   Société des Chemins de fer Départementaux de l'Aisne
NE   Compagnie des Secondaires du Nord-Est
RPdeC   Régie départementale des transports du Pas-de-Calais
RTA   Régie départementale des Transports de l'Aisne
StQG   Société du Chemin de fer de St. Quentin à Guise
VBStQ   Compagnie du Chemin de fer de Vélu-Bertincourt à St. Quentin
VFIL   Compagnie Générale des Voie Ferrées d'Intérêt Local (also often abbreviated as CGL)
(1)   In use until recently from Achiet to Bapaume as a private industrial line
(2)   5km at St-Quentin end common to Vélu – St-Quentin and St-Quentin – Ham
(3)   Now also the *Chemin de Fer Touristique du Vermandois* (CFTV)
(4)   Dual standard/metre gauge 1920s to 1948
(5)   Metre gauge service continued to 1948

Standard gauge lines of *Intérêt Local* in the Somme sector are shown in Table 1.2. The first two lines were built by companies associated with Émile Level, who had many other railway interests. These two lines were part of a larger network in the south-eastern part of the Pas-de-Calais *département*, which is fully described in Chapter One of *Narrow Gauge in the Arras Sector* (Pen & Sword, 2015), but the other lines are not relevant to the Somme Sector. The west-east line from Achiet to Marcoing is in the 'grey area' which is common at different times to both the Arras Sector and the Somme Sector. It forms a natural northern boundary to the Somme Sector railways. Since these lines were built by companies associated with Level, it is no surprise that in 1930 the management of these lines was taken over by the *Compagnie Générale des Voie Ferrées d'Intérêt Local* (VFIL), who by that time had taken over many other lines in the 'Level empire', mostly metre gauge, in the Nord, Pas-de-Calais, Oise and Aisne *départements*. VFIL is often known as CGL in French publications.

The lines in Table 1.2 were important during the First World War. All of these were single track, but some were made double track during this conflict. The only one which remains open is part of the St-Quentin-Guise line from St-Quentin to Origny-Ste-Benoîte. This functions under SNCF for goods, and at weekends in the season as the Heritage Railway *Chemin de Fer Touristique du Vermandois* (CFTV).

Metre Gauge lines

In this book we have only examined in detail the metre gauge lines in or closely involved with the battlefields of the First World War. Information on other metre gauge lines in the Somme, Oise and Aisne *départements* can be found in books in the bibliography. In the Somme *département* we have not included the western network (*Réseau des Bains de Mer*). These only played a small part in spring 1918. In the Oise *département* we have not covered the lines Crévecoeur-le-Grand–St. Just-en-Chaussée–Estrée-St-Denis, Formerie–Milly-sur-Thérain, La Bosse–Méru, and Hermes–Persan-Beaumont. In the Aisne *département* we have only covered lines in the west of the *département* and north of Soissons.

Chapters Two and Three deal with the metre gauge lines of the Somme sector up to 1914. The metre gauge lines in the First World War are described in Chapters Five to Eight, with the light railways. In Chapters Ten and Eleven the story of the metre gauge railways is followed from the end of the War to closure.

Chapter Two

The metre gauge railways of the Somme département *1888 to 1914*

The subjects of Chapter Two are the eastern Somme network of metre gauge lines. The first three of the lines listed below centred on Albert, the nexus of the system. The fourth was a branch from the Albert line. Hence, we have called them the Albert group of lines. The whole network ran to 329 km (204 miles). These lines, were:

Doullens–Albert
Albert–Fricourt–Péronne–Ham
Albert–Fricourt–Montdidier
Offoy–Ercheu–Bussy (as a loop line leaving the Albert–Ham line and continuing to Bussy in the Oise *dèpartement*)

Note that the first in the list is headed by Doullens not Albert. This is in line with the listings in the *Chaix*.

We must also mention very briefly the line west from Amiens to Aumale, and on to Envermeu in the Seine-Inférieure (now Seine-Maritime) *département*. This played a minor part in the First World War. The short line from Roisel to Hargicourt is described in Chapter Three; although mainly in the Somme *département*, it ended in the Aisne *département*, close to the St-Quentin–Caudry line at Bellicourt.

The Somme *département* decided in 1882 to entrust the building of a network of metre gauge railways to one company, the *Société Générale des Chemins de Fer Economiques* (SE). They had a good working relationship with the *Compagnie du Nord* and this enabled them to resolve any problems with connections and the sharing of stations. The network was declared *d'utilité publique* in 1885.

Building and Opening

The lines opened in sections. The first to open was the Doullens to Albert line, from Doullens to Beauval, on 15 November 1888. It was extended to Beauquesne on 14 February 1889 and reached Albert on 3 August 1891. Albert to Péronne was completed 1 April 1889 and the line reached Ham on 24 October 1889. The Albert–Montdidier line was opened from Montdidier to Rosières 28 June 1889, and it was joined to the Albert to Ham line at Fricourt 26 October 1889. You will note that we listed the final section of the Albert network as Offoy to Ercheu and Bussy, and that the line was only in the Somme *département* as far as Ercheu, before entering Oise. The section of track from Offoy to Ercheu was completed 14 July 1890. The link from Ercheu to Bussy was completed 5 June 1897, built by the *Noyon Guiscard Lassigny* Company (NGL) (part of the Lambert Group), who operated the line from Noyon to Guiscard, which it joined at Bussy. However, although in the Oise *département*, it was run by SE from the time of opening, and it is therefore included in this chapter.

Description of the lines

The heights and distances along the lines are shown with the stations and other stops in Tables 2.1 to 2.4.

Doullens to Albert

This line, 44.4km (27½ miles) long, served a number of large agricultural communities and for 4km from Doullens it shared the Amiens to Frévent standard gauge line to Gèzaincourt. Climbing through valleys, it crossed the high ground between the Authie and Ancre valleys. The high ground reached 143m (469ft) at Beauquesne station, and after descending a little, the line climbed again to the highest point on the line, at 155m (508ft), between Acheux and Mailly-Maillet.

Table 2.1 Doullens–Albert, stations and other stops, up to 1914

Name	Type	Distance km		Altitude m (ft)
		From Chaix	from Profile	
Doullens	CdN shared	0		64 (210)
Connection with SG Amiens to Béthune, Abbeville to Arras				
Gézaincourt	CdN halt	4		79
end of dual gauge with SG				
Beauval	station type 2	8	7.36	86
Beauquesne	station type 2	13	12.66	143 (469)
Raincheval-Arquèves	station type 2	15	14.96	108
Vauchelles	halt	19	18.81	102
Louvencourt	station type 2	21	21.61	106
Acheux-Varennes	station type 1	26	25.99	133
Bertrancourt	halt	30		149 (489)
Mailly-Maillet	station type 2	33	32.44	146
Auchonvillers	*arrêt*	34		139
Mesnil-Martinsart	station type 2	38	38.24	108
Martinsart	*arrêt*	40		86
Aveluy	*arrêt*	42		84
Albert	CdN shared	44	44.12	68 (223)
Connection with SG line Amiens–Arras. Origin of MG lines to Ham & Montdidier				

Narrow Gauge in the Somme Sector

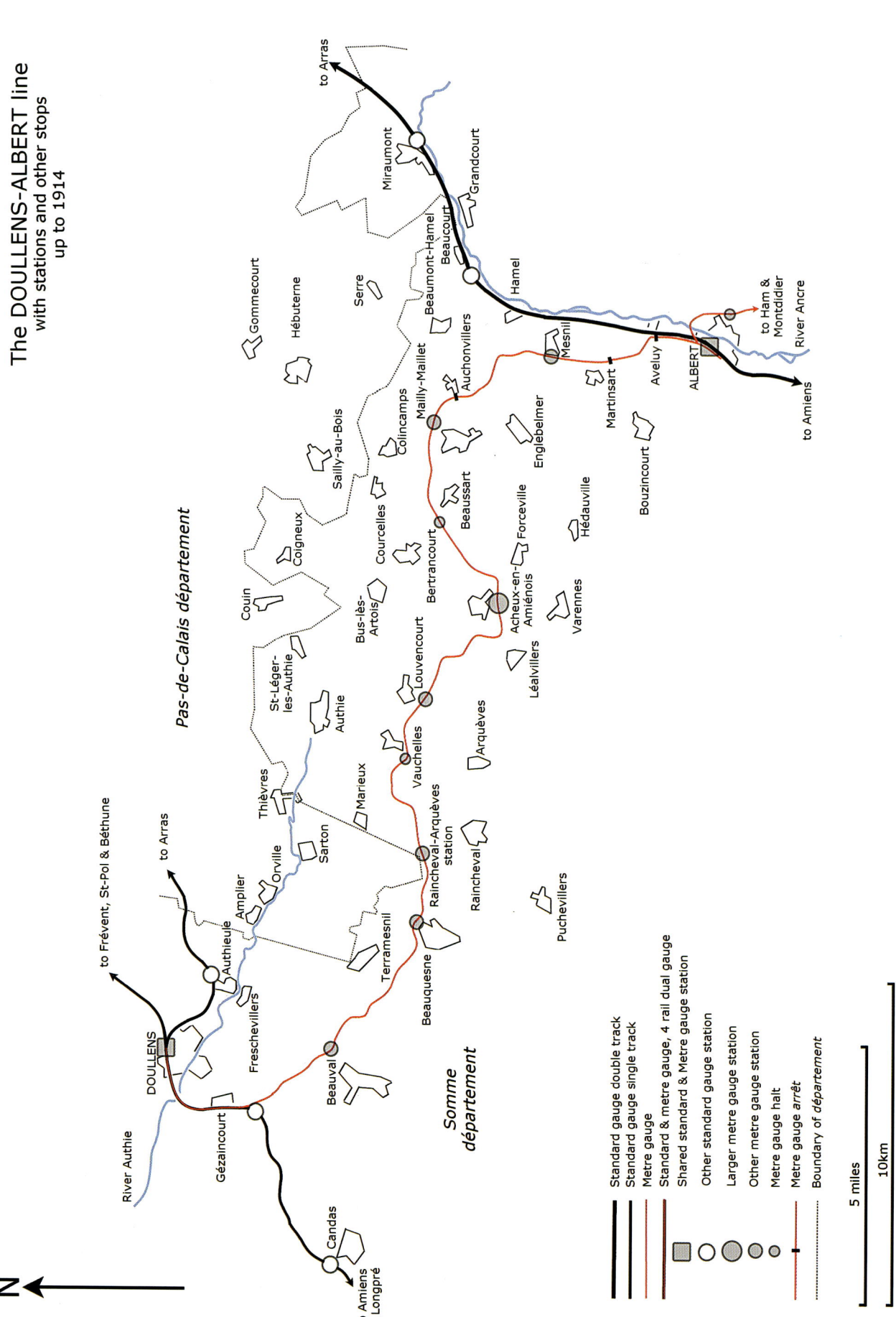

Figure 2.1

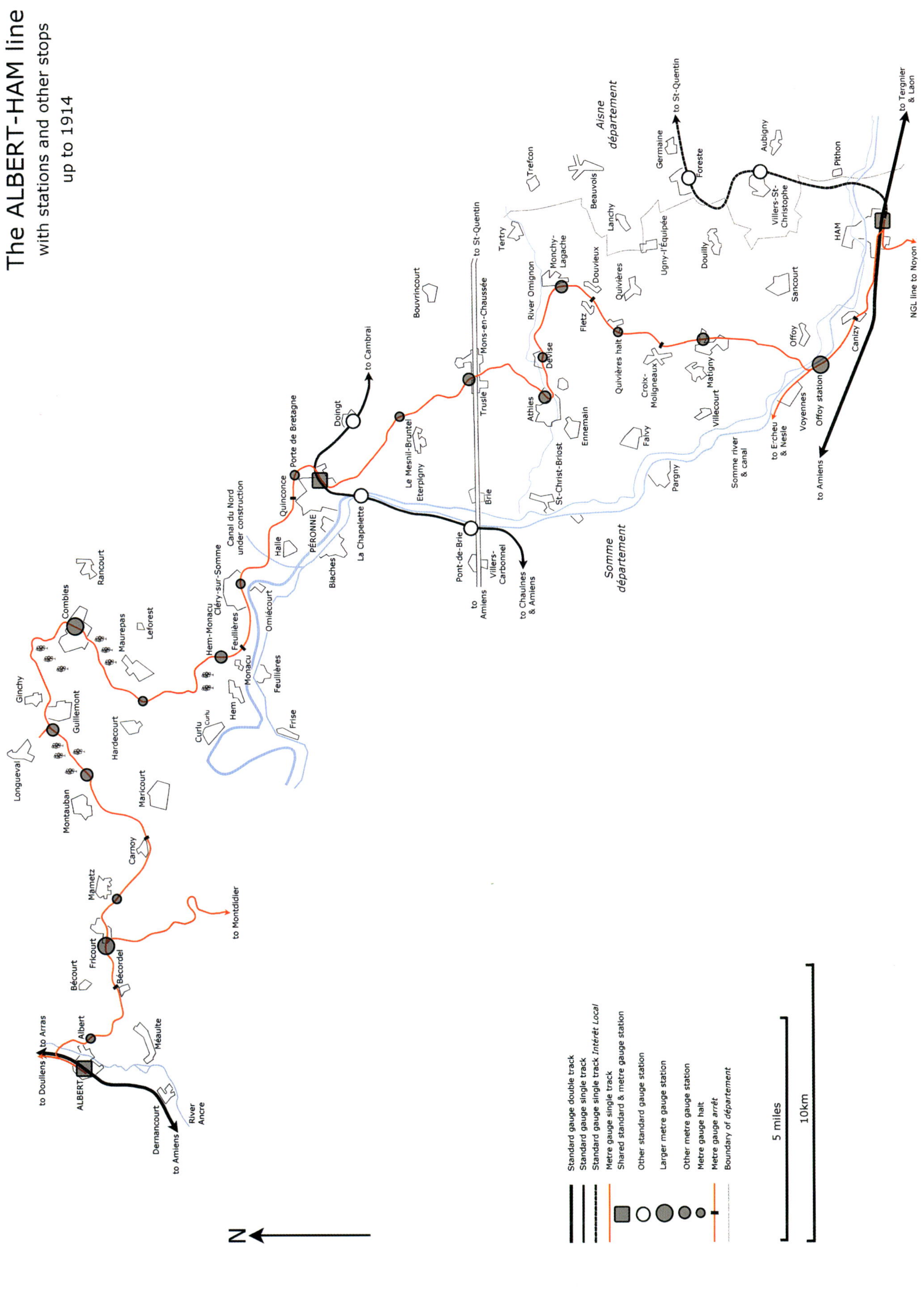
The ALBERT-HAM line
with stations and other stops
up to 1914
Standard gauge double track
Standard gauge single track
Standard gauge single track Intérêt Local
Metre gauge single track
Shared standard & metre gauge station
Other standard gauge station
Larger metre gauge station
Other metre gauge station
Metre gauge halt
Metre gauge arrêt
Boundary of département
5 miles
10km
N
to Doullens
to Arras
ALBERT
Albert
Dernancourt
to Amiens
River Ancre
Méaulte
Bécourt
Bécordel
Fricourt
to Montdidier
Mametz
Carnoy
Montauban
Maricourt
Longueval
Guillemont
Ginchy
Hardecourt
Combles
Rancourt
Maurepas
Leforest
Curlu
Hem
Monacu
Hem-Monacu
Feuillères
Cléry-sur-Somme
Omiécourt
Frise
Canal du Nord
under construction
Halle
Quinconce
Porte de Bretagne
PÉRONNE
Biaches
La Chapelette
Doingt
to Cambrai
Le Mesnil-Bruntel
Eterpigny
Bouvrincourt
to St-Quentin
Mons-en-Chaussée
Trusle
Brie
Pont-de-Brie
Villers-Carbonnel
to Amiens
to Chaulnes & Amiens
Athies
Devise
River Omignon
Tertry
Monchy-Lagache
Douvieux
Fletz
St-Christ-Briost
Ennemain
Falvy
Pargny
Somme département
Quivières halt
Quivières
Croix-Moligneaux
Matigny
Villecourt
Voyennes
Somme river & canal
Trefcon
Beauvois
Lanchy
Ugny-l'Équipée
Aisne département
Germaine
Foreste
Aubigny
Villers-St-Christophe
Douilly
Sancourt
Pithon
HAM
Offoy
Offoy station
Canizy
to Eccheu & Nesle
to Amiens
NGL line to Noyon
to Tergnier & Laon
to St-Quentin

Figure 2.2

Table 2.2 Albert–Ham, stations and other stops, up to 1914

Name	Type	Distance km		Altitude m (ft)
		From Chaix	From profile	
Albert	CdN shared	0	0	68 (223)
SG line Amiens–Arras. Origin of line to Doullens				
Albert	halt	3		
Bécordel-Bécourt	arrêt	6		
Fricourt	station type 1	8	7.95	64
junction with line Albert–Montdidier				
Mametz	halt	10	11.40	75
Carnoy	arrêt	12		
Montauban	station type 2	16	17.53	144 (472)
Guillemont-Longueval	station type 2	18	20.43	139
Combles	station type 1	23	24.88	101
Maurepas	halt	28		68
Hem-Monacu	station	32		51
Feuillières	arrêt	33		50
Cléry	halt	36	35.65	47
Le Quinconce	arrêt	41		
Pt-de-Bretagne	halt	41		
Péronne-Flamicourt	CdN shared	44	44.06	50 (164)
Connection with SG lines to Montdidier, Paris, Cambrai				
Mesnil-Bruntel	halt	5	4.82	52
Mons-en-Chaussée	station type 2	8	8.49	84
Athies (Somme)	station type 2	12	12.85	55
Devise	halt	13		54
Monchy-Lagache	station type 2	16	16.30	67
Fletz-Douvieux	arrêt	18		87 (285)
Quivières	halt	19	19.84	85
Croix-Moligneaux	arrêt	21		51
Matigny	station type 2	23	23.72	74
Offoy	station type 1	28	28.12	63
origin of line to Ercheu (and Bussy)				
Canisy	arrêt	30		67
Ham	CdN shared	34	34.22	64 (210)
connection with SG lines to Amiens & Tergnier, and MG line to Noyon				
Total Albert to Ham		78	78.28	

CdN *Compagnie du Nord*

Albert to Ham

At 75.9km (47 miles) this was the longest of the lines of the Somme network. Leaving the line to Doullens north of Albert station, it crossed the standard gauge main line from Amiens to Arras on a bridge. The line was shared with that to Montdidier for 8km (5 miles) to Fricourt, then it climbed the plateau before reaching the valley of the Somme river near Cléry. The maximum height was 144m (472ft) near Montauban station. At Péronne it crossed the river Cologne. This river divided two stations in Péronne, the halt at Péronne Porte de Bretagne and Péronne-Flamicourt, the latter being the main station in Péronne. This was also the site for a major depot and workshop. It was the place to change trains if you wanted the standard gauge main line to Montdidier, Cambrai and Paris. It then wandered south to Ham, crossing the Somme river and canal just north of Offoy, junction of the branch to Ercheu and Bussy. This was a lower section, reaching only 87m (285ft). At Ham, there was a network of sugar factory branches, and it met the *Compagnie du Nord* line from Amiens to Tergnier, the standard gauge *Société des Chemins de Fer Départementaux de l'Aisne* (CDA) line to St-Quentin and later, from 1912, the NGL metre gauge line to Guiscard, Bussy and Noyon.

Albert to Montdidier

Because Albert was regarded as the centre point of the network the first section of this line is in fact the first 8km (5 miles) of the Albert to Ham line. They parted company at Fricourt and this line then ran for 52km (32 miles) to Montdidier. Crossing the hill between Fricourt and the Somme Valley at Bray, it reached 103m (338ft). South of Bray, it crossed the Somme river and at Froissy, the Somme canal. Climbing onto the Santerre plateau,

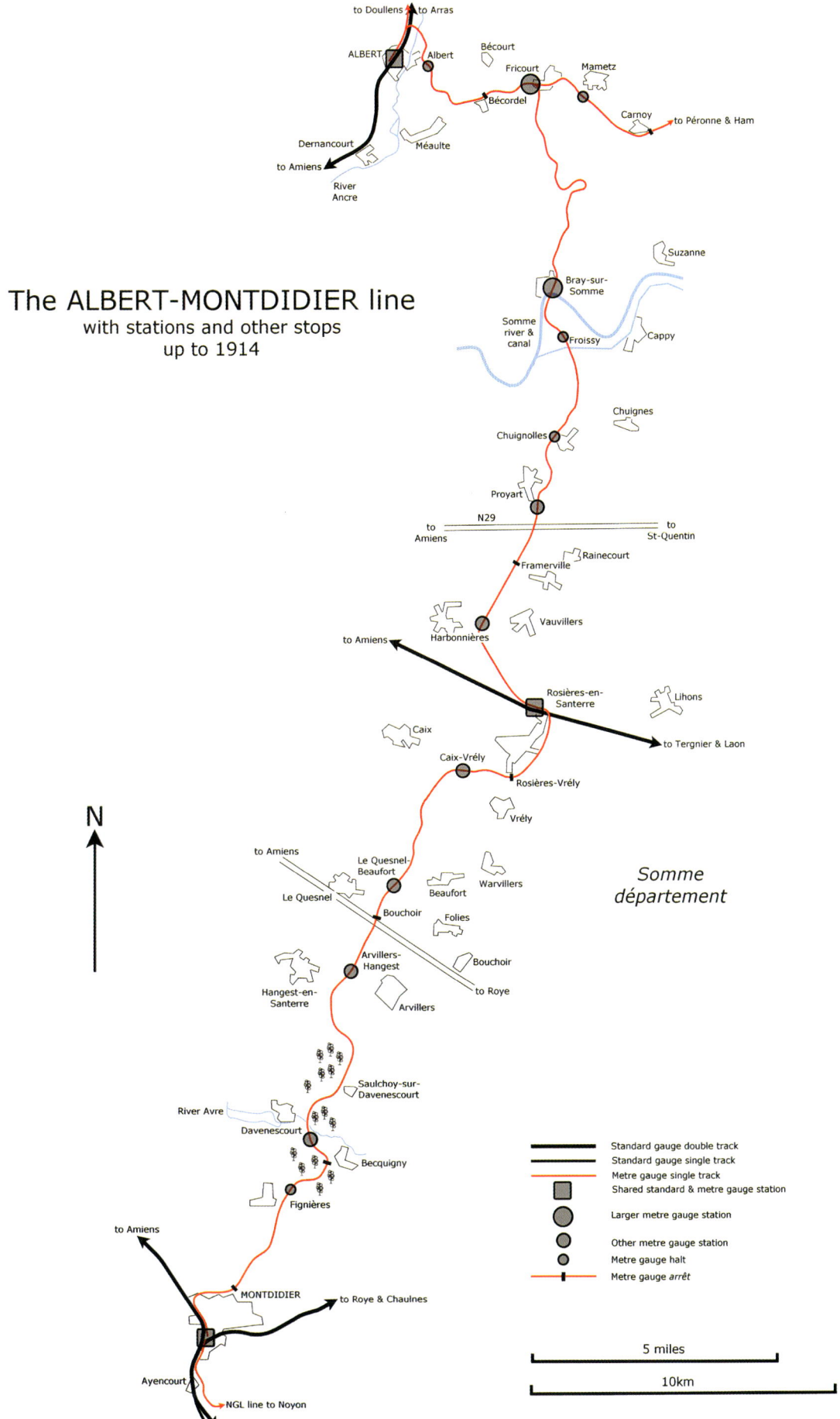

Figure 2.3

Table 2.3 Albert–Montdidier, stations and other stops, up to 1914

Name	Type	Distance km		Altitude m (ft)
		From Chaix	from Profile	
Albert	CdN shared	0	0	68 (223)
SG line Amiens–Arras. Origin of MG line to Doullens				
Albert	halt	3		
Bécordel-Bécourt	arrêt	6		
Fricourt	station type 1	8	7.95	64
junction with line Albert–Ham				
(highest point)				103 (338)
Bray(-sur-Somme)	station type 1	16	16.80	41
Froissy	halt	18		42
Chuignolles	halt	22		78
Proyart	station type 2	24	24.99	84
Framerville	arrêt	26		89
Harbonnières	station type 2	28	28.40	89
Rosières(-en-Santerre)	CdN shared	32	31.97	90
SG Line Amiens to Tergnier				
Rosières-Vrély	arrêt	34		86
Caix-Vrély	station	36	36.21	69
Le Quesnel-Beaufort	station	41	40.96	94
Bouchoir	arrêt	42		98
Arvillers-Hangest (Hangest-en-Santerre)				
	station type 2	44	43.86	103 (338)
Davenescourt	station type 2	50	49.36	60
Becquigny	arrêt	51		69
Fignières	halt	54	53.96	102 (335)
Montdidier	arrêt	58		76
Montdidier	CdN shared	60	60.27	60 (197)
MG line to Rollot (Somme) and Noyon (Oise)			(52.32 from Fricourt)	
SG lines to Amiens and Compiègne				

CdN *Compagnie du Nord*

at Rosières it crossed on the level the *Compagnie du Nord* standard gauge line from Amiens to Tergnier. The line reached another high of 103m (338ft) near Hangest, before descending through wooded valleys to cross the Avre at Davenescourt. Climbing once more to about 102m (335ft) at Fignières, the line descended to enter Montdidier from the north, joining the standard gauge line from Amiens to Compiègne. There was a depot and workshop, and junctions with the line from St-Just-en-Chaussée to Cambrai. The metre gauge line from Noyon also terminated here from 1913 (see Chapter Three).

Offoy to Ercheu and Ercheu to Bussy

The route of this line is shown with those of the lines based on Noyon in figure 3.1 (Chapter Three). The line was 33km (20 miles) long. It left the line from Albert to Ham at Offoy. At Nesle, it crossed the standard gauge line from Amiens to Tergnier. At the station at Ercheu, it met the line from Bussy, conceded by the Oise *département* but operated by SE as an extension of the Somme network. At Bussy, it met the line run by NGL from Noyon to Guiscard from 1895, and on to Ham from 1912. The length of the line in the Oise *département* was 11.6km (7 miles).

Engineering

All lines ran mostly in their own path, with only short sections along the edges of roads. In accordance with general SE practice, the rails were of Vignole type of 15 or 20kg/m, mostly the latter. Junctions with standard gauge lines, and common (dual gauge) lines were protected with standard *Compagnie du Nord* mechanical signals. More important level crossings would have a crossing keeper and cottage, with some sort of control when a train crossed the road.

Doullens to Albert

This line had a common line (4 rail dual gauge) from Doullens to Gézaincourt, a distance of 4km.

Albert to Ham

This line crossed the standard gauge line from Montdidier via Chaulnes to Cambrai at Péronne. The original plan was for a crossing on the level just at the north east end of Péronne-Flamicourt station, where the standard gauge line crossed the road from Flamicourt to Doingt. This may have been the initial arrangement, but by 1914, there was a bridge over the standard gauge line 600m north east of the station

The metre gauge railways of the Somme département 1888 to 1914

Table 2.4 Offoy–Ercheu & Ercheu–Bussy Stations and other stops, up to 1914

Name	Type	Distance km		Altitude m (ft)
		From Chaix	from profile	
Offoy		20		63 (207)
Junction with SE Albert–Ham line, 72km from Albert, 6km from Ham				
Voyennes	halt	18		57
Rouy-le-Petit	station	15		57
Mesnil-St-Nicaise	station type 2	12		77
Nesle	CdN shared	10		79
Connection with SG CdN line Amiens–Tergnier				
Languevoisin	*arrêt*	7		
Breuil	*arrêt*	5		
Moyencourt	station type 2	3		63
Ercheu	station type 1	0		73 (236)
Ercheu	station type 1	0	0	73 (236)
Ognolles	station type 2*	1	1.61	76
Beaulieu	*arrêt*	6	5.07	
Beaulieu-Ecuvilly	station type 2*	7	6.07	76
Catigny	station type 2*	9	8.43	56
Sermaize	halt	11	10.04	54
Haudival	*arrêt*	12	11.43	49
Bussy	station type 2*	13	12.88	47 (154)
Junction with Noyon–Ham line, 7km from Noyon, 18km from Ham				

* Lambert type stations
CdN *Compagnie du Nord*
SE *Société Générale des Chemins de Fer Économiques*

2.1 The SE type 2 station at Montauban, on the line from Albert to Ham. Nearest the camera is the crossing over the GC 64 (now the D 64) road from Montauban to Guillemont, with a cottage for the crossing keeper, and a wooden barrier which can be slid across on the right side of the track, for traffic control. (Authors' collection)

(see Image 6.1, Chapter Six, and walk 3 in Chapter Twelve). At Ham, there was a crossing on the level to lead to the metre gauge station south of the main lines (see Figure 2.5).

Offoy to Ercheu

This line crossed the main line from Amiens to Tergnier and on to Laon at the station at Nesle, which it shared with the *Compagnie du Nord,* on the level at the east end of the station.

Ercheu to Bussy

We know more about the engineering of the track for this line, as we do also for some of the other Oise lines (see Chapter Three). Like most of Oise lines, it had maximum radius of curvature of 150m and maximum gradient 2 per cent. The gauge of 1.00m on the straight and on curves of radius more than 500m, was increased to 1.01m on curves of radius 300 to 490m, and to 1.015m on curves of radius 150 to 290m. Sleepers were all of oak laid at 0.88m centres, 13 per 11m rail on the straight and 14 on curves.

Bridges

The more important bridges on the Somme metre gauge lines up to 1914 are shown in Table 2.5. All the details are not available for all the bridges. All the bridges carried a single metre gauge track, and all the bridges of *tablier métallique* (metal platform) type had brick abutments.

Construction of the Canal du Nord from Noyon to the Somme canal south of Péronne had started before the First World War. Before August 1914 it had reached the stage at which bridges for the lines from Offoy to Ercheu (at Rouy-le-Petit) and from Bussy to Ercheu (between Haudival and Béhancourt) were required, even though the canal was probably still dry. They would have been similar to the bridges over the Somme canal on the other lines.

Stations and other stops

Lists of the stations and other stops for the lines in this chapter up to 1914 are given in tables 2.1 to 2.4. Sometimes the larger stations are called *gares*, but

2.2 The bridge of the line from Albert to Montdidier over the River Somme at Bray. A train coming from Montdidier is entering from the south. Postcard postmarked at Bray station in 1901. *(Authors' collection)*

Table 2.5 Major bridges on the eastern Somme metre gauge lines up to 1914

Section at	distance (km)	over/ under	what	span (m)	type	notes
Albert to Fricourt	(from Albert Station)					
Albert	0.75	over	Amiens to Arras railway	8	TM oblique	fence on top, lattice girder under
Albert	c.1.05	over	canalised Ancre river	12		
Fricourt to Ham	(from Albert station)					
Péronne	c.43	over	Cologne river	5		
Péronne	c.43.5	over	Montdidier to Cambrai railway		TM oblique	
Offoy	71.64	over	Somme river	12	TM	lattice girder sides
Offoy	71.77	over	Somme canal	25	TM	lattice girder sides
Fricourt to Montdidier	(from Albert station)					
Bray	c.17.2	over	Somme river		TM	lattice girder sides
Froissy	c.18.9	over	Somme canal		Brick	with elliptical arch combined with road bridge

TM *Tablier Métallique*

commonly before 1914, most of the stations are still called *stations* in French. Distances are given from the *Chaix* timetables, and where available, the more accurate distances from the original profiles for the lines. Heights are from satellite images for the known locations of the stations and other stops, which mostly accord well with the surveys for the original line profiles.

Buildings

The stations on the lines built by the *Société Générale des Chemins de Fer Economiques* (SE) had a common pattern, similar to those of other SE lines, including the *Réseau des Bains de Mer* (*Baie de Somme*), and the line from Amiens to Aumale. The other line in this chapter, from Bussy to Ercheu, was built for the Noyons Guiscard Lassigny company (NGL), although operated by SE. NGL was part of the group of Alfred Lambert, and the line had 'Lambert' type stations. These are identified in Table 2.4 and are fully described with the other NGL lines in Chapter Three.

The stations all had a main building, with the roof ridge at right angles to the track. This was flanked by an annexe on one side and a goods hall on the other. There were two types of station building, larger and smaller, which we have designated type 1 and type 2 respectively. Except in the few cases where the type of station is not known, it is shown in tables 2.1 to 2.4.

Type 1 stations were placed at locations considered important (Acheux-Varennes, Combles, and Bray), and in two cases at junctions (Fricourt and Offoy).

The other was at Ercheu, the end of the SE line from Offoy. The main building was double width, with two doors on the track side, and two windows above. The annexe had a single door on the track side, and a small window above, also often an end door. The goods hall had two doors on the track side, and a larger door on the forecourt side.

Type 2 stations were smaller, the main building being single width, with a single door and a single window on the first floor at the building ends. The annexe had a single door on the track and forecourt sides, and a small 'attic' end window. The goods hall was smaller with single doors on each side. Halt buildings were similar to the main building of type 2 stations, without the annexe or the goods hall. At *arrêts* there might be a wooden or brick shelter.

Most of the stations and halts were finished in brick, but a few had partial rendering. Type 1 stations had the station name on the end of the annexe as well as on the track end of the main building, while type 2 stations and halts only had the name on the track end of the main building. All stations and halts had 'Chemin de Fer' on the road (forecourt) end of the main building.

Track layouts

A station might have one or two loop lines, so that there were two or three tracks and one or two platforms. There was also sometimes a fourth line at the back of the passenger building around the station forecourt. An example of a larger station is Fricourt, junction of the line from Albert to Ham with that to Montdidier (Figure 2.4). Fricourt had four tracks and

2.3 The SE type 1 station at Fricourt, junction of the metre gauge lines from Albert to Ham and to Montdidier. Undated, but before the First World War. This station was on the front line on 1 July 1916. *(Authors' collection)*

2.4 The SE type 2 station at Beauval, now a private house, in April 2015, from the road (forecourt) side. *(Authors)*

2.5 The SE halt building at Froissy, now a private house, May 2016. *(Authors)*

three platforms, and some services terminated here (see operations and timetables). At a station the line nearest the passenger building would also serve the goods platform, so that passengers would have to cross this line to join the train at a further line.

At halts, there might sometimes be a loop line. An *arrêt* (literally, a 'stop') would just have a through line, but there might be a rudimentary platform, and a shelter.

The stations shared with the Compagnie du Nord standard gauge tracks were the ends of lines (Doullens, Albert, Ham, Montdidier), or places where the lines crossed along the way (Péronne, Rosières-en-Santerre, Nesle).

Albert

Albert was a large station on the through double main line from Amiens to Arras and on from there to Lille. The metre gauge lines to Doullens, Ham and Montdidier had an island platform with two tracks immediately west of the standard gauge platforms. At the north end of the station SE had a depot and workshops, and a goods area with transhipment facilities. The rolling gantry crane probably spanned standard and metre gauge lines, as elsewhere.

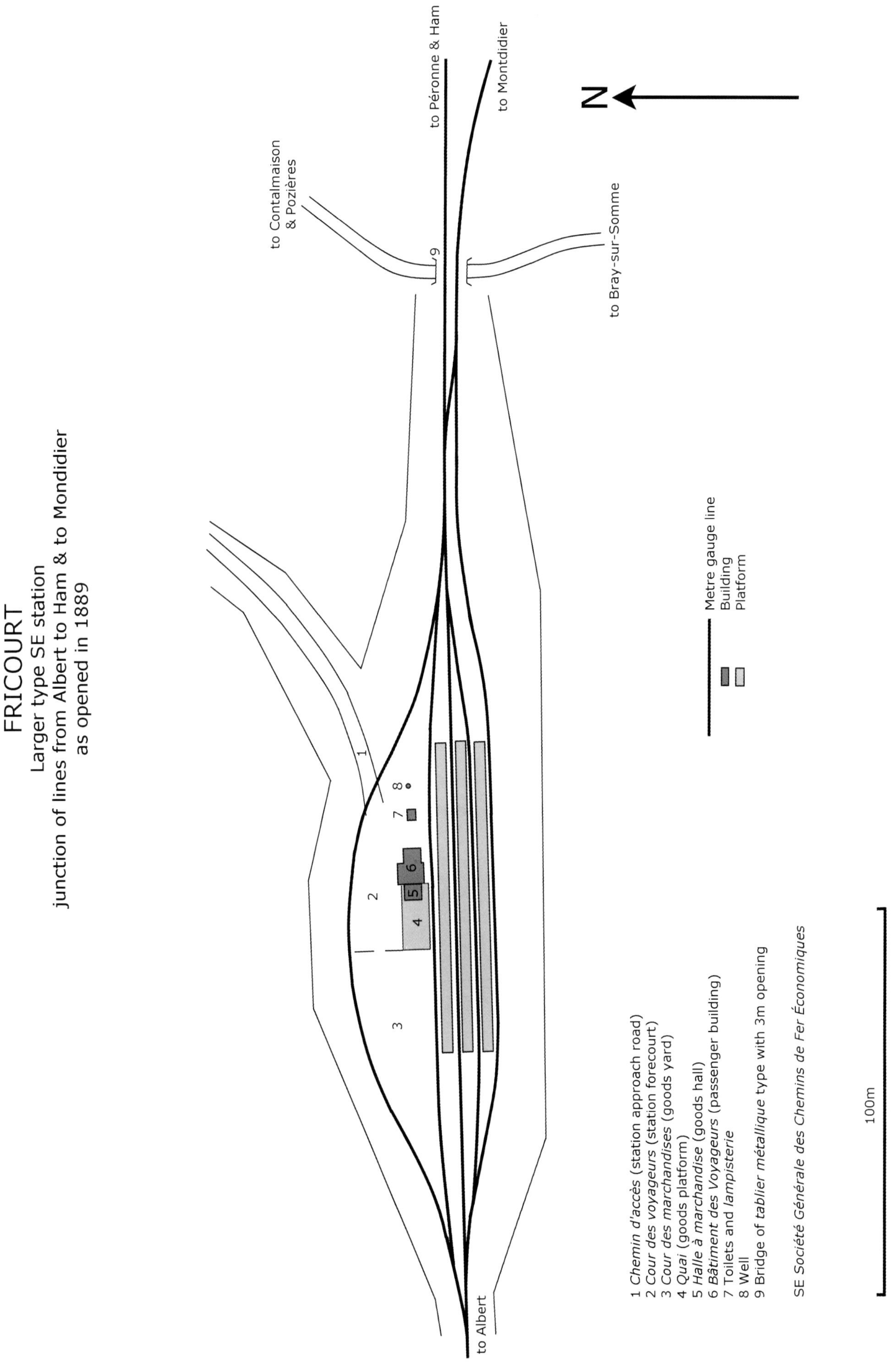

The metre gauge railways of the Somme département 1888 to 1914

FRICOURT
Larger type SE station
junction of lines from Albert to Ham & to Mondidier
as opened in 1889

to Péronne & Ham
to Montdidier
to Contalmaison & Pozières
to Bray-sur-Somme
to Albert

N

— Metre gauge line
▪ Building
▫ Platform

1 *Chemin d'accès* (station approach road)
2 *Cour des voyageurs* (station forecourt)
3 *Cour des marchandises* (goods yard)
4 *Quai* (goods platform)
5 *Halle à marchandise* (goods hall)
6 *Bâtiment des Voyageurs* (passenger building)
7 Toilets and *lampisterie*
8 Well
9 Bridge of *tablier métallique* type with 3m opening

SE *Société Générale des Chemins de Fer Économiques*

100m

Figure 2.4

21

2.6 Albert station, looking east, with the Basilica of Notre-Dame in the town centre in the background. The metre gauge lines are nearest the camera, with the standard gauge line from Amiens to Arras behind, in front of the main station buildings. Metre gauge carriages are parked on the line nearest the camera, with the gantry crane left and the depot off picture to the left. Postcard postmarked 1910. *(Authors' collection)*

2.7 The gantry crane 'marooned' in the now disused yard at Albert station. October 2016. *(Authors)*

Ham

The station track plan as in early 1914, after the arrival of the line from Noyon in 1912, is shown in Figure 2.5. This shows the metre gauge facilities, including transhipments *en fosse* (metre gauge line below) and *en estacade* (metre gauge line above).

Montdidier

At Montdidier from 1889, the metre gauge line from Albert joined the east side of the double track standard gauge line from Amiens to Compiègne north of the station and had a platform on the same side of the standard gauge lines. This station was north of the standard gauge line branching off to Roye, and eventually Cambrai.

From 1913, the extension from Lassigny of the line from Noyon, of the Noyon-Guiscard-Lassigny Company (NGL) came in from the south, also on the east side of the standard gauge lines. We do not have full details, but we think that this had a separate station, south of the line branching off to Roye. There was almost certainly a connection on the level between the two metre gauge lines, across the standard gauge lines to Roye, before 1914. Later, after the First World War, when SE ran trains through from Albert to Rollot, there was a bridge over the line to Roye.

The metre gauge railways of the Somme département 1888 to 1914

HAM
Compagnie du Nord station
shared with the MG lines to Albert & to Noyon
& the SG *Intérêt Local* line to St-Quentin
in early 1914

Lines (from top) -
SG to Eppeville sugar factory
MG (SE) to Péronne & Albert
SG (CdN) lines from & to Amiens
MG (NGL) to Guiscard & Noyon

Lines (from top, all SG) -
Private branch line
CdN lines to and from Tergnier
CDA *Intérêt Local* line
to St-Quentin
(turns north over Tergnier
lines on bridge)

to Ham centre

to Guiscard & Noyon

― Standard gauge line
― Metre gauge line
― Dual standard and metre gauge
▪ Building
▫ Platform

MG   Metre gauge
SG   Standard gauge
CdN *Compagnie du Nord*
SE   *Société Générale des Chemins de Fer Économiques*
NGL Noyon-Guiscard-Lassigny
CDA *Société des Chemins de fer Départementaux de l'Aisne* (Ham-St-Quentin SG line)

1 *Bâtiment des Voyageurs* (Main station building)
2 *Cour des Voyageurs* (Forecourt)
3 *Buvette*
4 *Cour des Marchandises* (Goods yard) (CdN & SE)
5 Coal platform
6 Coal store
7 Water tower
8 *Halle à marchandises* (goods hall)
9 Loading gauge
10 Rolling gantry crane
11 *Quai à bestiaux* (cattle loading platform)
12 Covered goods platform
13 *Transhipments en fosse* (right) and *en estacade* (left)
14 *Remise de machines* (Locomotive shed)(SE)
15 *Remise de voiture* (carriage shed)(SE)
16 Turntable
17 *Remise de machine* (Locomotive shed)(NGL)
18 Platform (NGL and CDA)
19 *Cour des Marchandises* (Goods yard) (NGL & CDA)
20 *Halle à marchandises* (goods hall) & platform (NGL)
21 *Remise de machines* (Locomotive shed)(CDA)

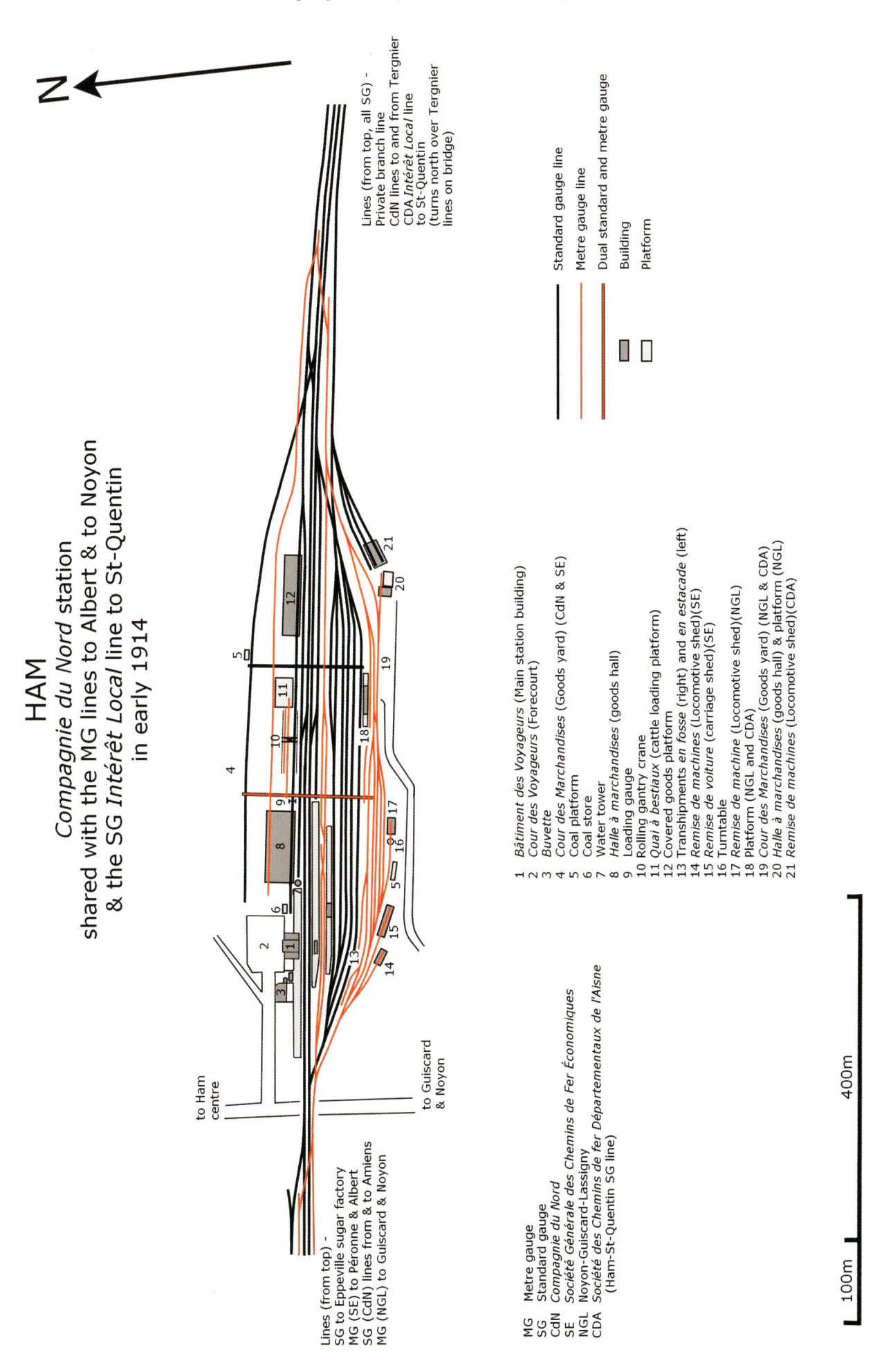

Figure 2.5

Narrow Gauge in the Somme Sector

2.8 Montdidier station, on the main line from Amiens to Compiègne. At the single metre gauge platform, a train hauled by SACM 0-6-2T No. 3.564, with a *fourgon* (baggage van) and one carriage, is waiting to leave for Albert. 1908 or before. *(Authors' collection)*

Rosières-en-Santerre

At Rosières-en-Santerre the metre gauge track came in from the north-west, from Albert via Fricourt and the platform with two lines was on the north side of the standard gauge lines further away from the station building. The line crossed the road on a level crossing with the standard gauge line to the east of the station and then turned south to cross the standard gauge lines on the level.

Nesle

The facilities for the metre gauge lines at Nesle were very similar to those at Ham.

Depots

The SE depot and workshops for the eastern Somme network were at Albert and at Péronne-Flamicourt. There were also facilities for stabling two locomotives and train sets at Acheux, for the service between Doullens and Albert, and at Ercheu, for the services to Offoy and to Bussy. The timetable pattern before 1914 suggests that one locomotive would also need to be based at Offoy. It does not suggest the need for facilities at Bussy, junction with the line from Noyon to Guiscard and Ham, but at some time a shed for one locomotive was provided at Bussy, it is said by the SE Company. Other locomotives were stationed at Doullens, Fricourt, Ham, Montdidier, Nesle, and Rosières.

Industrial links

The more important industrial links are shown in Table 2.6. This shows the importance of the sugar beet industry in this area.

2.9 The locomotive shed at Bussy station, junction of the line from Ercheu operated by SE with the line from Noyon to Guiscard and Ham operated by NGL. The shed is said to have been for a locomotive of SE, operating the line to Ercheu. May 2016. *(Authors)*

The metre gauge railways of the Somme département 1888 to 1914

Table 2.6 Principal industrial branch lines and sidings up to 1914

Location	Distance (km)	Nature of business	Proprietor	Date built (most probably)	Notes
Doullens to Albert	(from Doullens)				
Doullens	0		Delmotte		Works by line to Frévent, north east of station
Beauval	7.36	Bâche (tarpaulin) factory	Saint-Frères		Factory by line at station
Beauval	7.36	Phosphate extraction		before 1907	60cm gauge line with transhipment at Beauval to MG
Albert station	0		M Norman et Compagnie	1897	Dual gauge lines into factory at south west end of station
Albert to Ham	(from Albert)				
Guillemont	20.4	Guillemont sugar factory		before 1914	branch from station 0.60km to factory and further 1km to Longueval
Cléry-sur-Somme	34.9	not known		before 1914	branch from 700m west of halt c. 2km long to Bouchavesnes
Cléry-sur-Somme	36.7	Canal du Nord works		1910	60cm gauge line crossing metre gauge line
Le Quinconce-St-Denis	41	St-Denis sugar factory (sucrerie)		before 1914	Branch 700m long from Quinconce arrêt
Between Mons-en-Chaussée and Athies					
Croix-Molingeaux	c.54	Quarries		before 1914	2 sidings to quarries, 700m and 500m
	66	Factory (prob sugar factory)		before 1914	Branch 900m long, junction 700m south of arrêt
Athies	57.2	not known		before 1914	triangular junction 400m south west of station Branch 5km long to St-Christ
Monchy-Lagache	60.6	Factory		before 1914	150m branch 300m south of station
Eppeville (Ham)	c. 77.5	Sugar factory (sucrerie)		before 1914	Addition of metre gauge to existing standard gauge siding
Albert to Montdidier	(from Albert)				
Froissy	c. 18	Sugar factory (sucrerie)		c. 1889–90	Branch to south side of Froissy lock, for sugar factory
Offoy to Ercheu	(from Ercheu)				
Mesnil-St-Nicaise	12	Sugar factory (sucrerie)	Mme Vve Horrie	1899–1900	Branch to sugar factory
Mesnil-St-Nicaise	12	Sugar factory (sucrerie)	M Théry (Athies)	1907	Second branch to sugar factory
Nesle	10	Distillerie	M Savary	1895	Second branch in 4 rail dual gauge, adjacent to Nesle station
Moyencourt	3	Sucrerie			branch about 500m long, 250m south of station
Ercheu	0	Râperie		before 1914	Short branch, adjacent to Ercheu station
Ercheu to Bussy	(from Ercheu)				
Beaulieu-Ecuvilly	6.1	Sugar factory			

25

2.10 A locomotive and train in the *Rue du Bas* at Beauval, on the 60cm gauge line from Beauval metre gauge station to the unknown site for phosphate extraction. Postcard written and postmarked 3 November 1907. *(Authors' collection)*

2.11 The SE type 2 station at Beauval, before the First World War. A Passenger train heading towards Albert is standing in the station. Behind the wall is the *bâche* (tarpaulin) factory of Saint-Frères. *(Authors' collection)*

Rolling stock

The rolling stock in use on these lines corresponded with the classic types of the SE Company. Vehicles had one central buffer, couplings below and no continuous braking.

Steam locomotives

The steam locomotives of the *Société Générale des Chemins de Fer Economiques* (SE) were distributed between the depots at Abbeville (Baie de Somme network), Amiens (Amiens to Aumale and Invermeu line), Albert, Acheux, Péronne and Montdidier. There must also have been a depot at Ercheu for the locomotives used on the NGL line from Ercheu to Bussy. Some details of steam locomotives used on the line up to 1914 are shown in table 2.7.

There is insufficient information to show a complete allocation of locomotives on the SE Somme networks before 1914. There is no evidence of the use of the three Blanc-Misseron-Tubize locomotives on any of the eastern Somme lines.

Two of the later *Nord de la Chapelle* locomotives, 3.571 and 3.572, were intended for the Ercheu to Bussy line but had not arrived when the line opened on 5 June 1897. Locomotives 3.601 and 3.602 were initially used instead, but only for a short period. Later, with increased traffic, five locomotives were transferred from other networks. We have shown the probable main

The metre gauge railways of the Somme département 1888 to 1914

Table 2.7 Technical details of SE Somme locomotives up to 1914

Manufacturer	NC	SACM	SACM	NC	NC	NC	BMT	BMT
Year(s) of manufacture	1886-89	1889-90	1890-93	1897	1897		?1900	1900
Wheel configuration	0-6-2T	0-6-2T	0-6-2T	0-6-2T	0-6-2T	0-6-2T	2-6-0T	2-6-0T
Company No(s)	3.519-533	3.534-540	3.561-570	3.601-602	3.571-572*	3.510 & 512** 3.623 & 639#	3.651-652	3.661##
Year(s) put in service	1887-89	1889-					pr 1908	'later'
Number put in service	15	7	10	2	2	4	2	1
Weight empty (tonnes)	19.18	19.18						
Weight loaded (tonnes)	25.03	25.03						
Diam. of driving wheels(m)	0.91	0,91						
Boiler capacity (m^3)	2.53	2.92						
Boiler pressure (Kg/cm^2)	9 - 10	10						
Heating surface (m^2)	55.11	61.28						
Diam. of pistons (m)	0.35	0.35						
Piston travel (m)	0.46	0.46						
Max speed (kph)	28							

BMT – Blanc-Misseron-Tubize
NC – Ateliers de la Compagnie du Nord à La Chapelle
SACM – Société Alsacienne de Construction Mécanique, Belfort

*   for the Ercheu – Bussy line in the Oise département
** transferred from the Allier network
\#   transferred from another network
\#\# transferred from the Flanders network

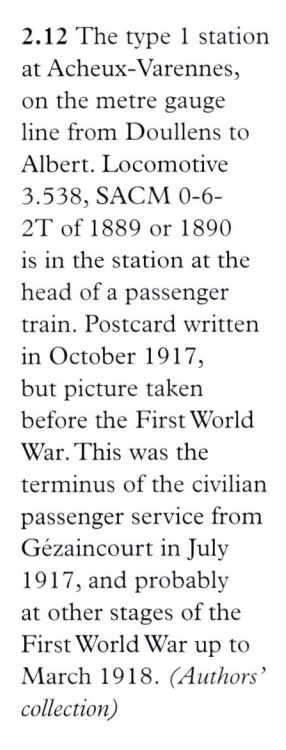

2.12 The type 1 station at Acheux-Varennes, on the metre gauge line from Doullens to Albert. Locomotive 3.538, SACM 0-6-2T of 1889 or 1890 is in the station at the head of a passenger train. Postcard written in October 1917, but picture taken before the First World War. This was the terminus of the civilian passenger service from Gézaincourt in July 1917, and probably at other stages of the First World War up to March 1918. *(Authors' collection)*

allocations of some of these locomotives, with some of their names, in Table 2.8.

The timetables before 1914 (see Operations below) required two locomotives and train sets based at Acheux, Albert, Péronne, and Ercheu, and one each at Montdidier and Offoy. This adds up to ten locomotives. In practice, there would need to have been one or two spare at each location to allow for servicing and breakdowns. The information in Table 2.8 indicates at least 17 locomotives allocated to these lines before 1914.

Passenger carriages

These were of the classical SE type, that is bogie carriages with a body finished with wooden planking, and one

Table 2.8 Probable main allocations of some SE locomotives before 1914

Number	Name	year in service	Manufacturer	line(s) mainly used on
3.524	Beauval	1889	Nord Chapelle	Albert–Péronne
3.525	Péronne	1889	Nord Chapelle	Albert–Péronne
3.529	Carnoy	1889	Nord Chapelle	Rosières–Montdidier
3.530	Combles	1889	Nord Chapelle	Rosières–Montdidier
3.531	Nesle	1889	Nord Chapelle	Albert–Péronne
3.532	Ham	1889	Nord Chapelle	Albert–Péronne
3.533	Rosières	1889	Nord Chapelle	Albert–Péronne
3.534	Crécy	1889	SACM	Albert–Ham & Montdidier
3.535	Moliens-Vidame	1889	SACM	Albert–Ham & Montdidier
3.536	Hornoy	1889	SACM	Albert–Ham & Montdidier
3.537	Acheux	1890	SACM	Doullens–Albert
3.538	Bray	1890	SACM	Doullens–Albert
3.540	Dompierre	1890	SACM	Doullens–Albert
3.564	Forest L'Abbaye	1891	SACM	Albert–Montdidier
3.566	La Picardie	1892	SACM	Albert–Montdidier
3.571	Bussy	1897	Nord Chapelle	Ercheu–Bussy
3.572	Beaulieu	1897	Nord Chapelle	Ercheu–Bussy

Nord Chapelle – Ateliers de la Compagnie du Nord à La Chapelle
SACM – Société Alsacienne de Construction Mécanique, Belfort

2.13 The type 2 station at Mailly-Maillet, on the line from Doullens to Albert. Postcard postmarked 1908. The passenger train, going towards Doullens, is headed by SACM 0-6-2T locomotive 3.537 of 1889 or 1890, and is composed of two bogie carriages and a *fourgon*. (Authors' collection)

entered them from their end platforms. Prior to 1914, they were constructed by Desouche & David, or Decauville. Each carriage had various combinations of classes. There were first and second, first and third or second and third. At one extreme some carriages had seats for all the classes, at the other, some were only third class.

Wagons

On the Albert network there were 16 fourgons, 890 goods wagons and four moving cranes of 4 tonnes. There were four types of goods wagons on the network:

Type K Covered 129 (of which three were equipped as rescue wagons)

Type U *Tombereaux* (open wagons) 560 (of which 32 had bogies)

Type H flat *wagons à ridelles* 165 (of which 5 had bogies, and of which some were specially modified for oil, phosphates, or molasses)

Type T *couplable* flat wagons with mobile traverse 36

The metre gauge railways of the Somme département 1888 to 1914

Table 2.9 Doullens–Albert (SE)
Summary Timetable May 1914

	(1)		(2)		
Doullens		07.58	12.40	15.50	20.33
Connection with CdN SG lines to Arras, St-Pol-sur-Ternoise, Amiens and Longpré					
Gézaincourt		08.05	12.49	15.59	20.42
Connection with CdN SG lines to Amiens and Longpré					
Beauval		08.18	13.02	16.12	20.54
Beauquesnes		08.35	13.18	16.30	21.09
Louvencourt	(06.08)	09.01	13.41	17.02	21.34
Acheux-Varennes	06.21	09.17	13.57	17.17	<u>21.46</u>
Mailly-Maillet	06.40	09.36	14.17	17.32	
Albert	07.10	10.11	14.49	18.02	
Connection with CdN SG line Amiens–Arras. Origin of MG SE lines to Ham, Montidier and Rollot					
			(2)		(1)
Albert		09.05	12.30	16.00	19.22
Connection with CdN SG line Amiens–Arras. Origin of MG SE lines to Ham, Montidier and Rollot					
Mailly-Maillet		09.35	13.01	16.32	20.02
Acheux-Varennes	05.15	09.52	13.23	16.49	<u>20.22</u>
Louvencourt	05.29	10.07	13.40	17.02	(20.34)
Beauquesnes	05.52	10.30	14.01	17.25	
Beauval	06.11	10.47	14.22	17.43	
Gézaincourt	06.22	11.02	14.33	18.00	
Connection with CdN SG lines to Amiens and Longpré					
Doullens	06.30	11.10	14.41	18.08	
Connection with CdN SG lines to Arras, St-Pol-sur-Ternoise, Amiens and Longpré					

Underlined – terminates, other than at end of line
SG   standard gauge   MG   metre gauge
CdN   *Compagnie du Nord*
SE   *Société Générale des Chemins de Fer Économiques*
(1) Between Louvencourt and Acheux-Varennes and *vice versa* only runs for the Fairs of St. Matthew (24 Feburary), St. Éloi (25 June) and St. Simon (28 October)
(2) As a trial and only until further notice

Operations

The general pattern from the opening of these lines up to 1914 was for two, or in most cases three, passenger trains per day in each direction, plus an additional service over part of the route. Journey times varied a little, perhaps because some of these were mixed passenger and goods trains and required time to drop off or pick up wagons.

Doullens to Albert

The timetable for May 1914 (Table 2.9) shows that there were three trains over the full length of the line each way daily. There were also trains running part of the way. There was one from Acheux to Doullens and a similar one from Acheux to Albert, both in the early morning, and returning in the evening. The latter was extended between Acheux and Louvencourt on three named feast days.

There were probably only two trains each way the whole length of the line when it opened fully in 1891. In 1909, the Town Council of Albert petitioned SE to provide an additional train in the middle of the day, at least between Albert and Acheux. SE responded that receipts did not justify putting on another train in the middle of the day, and this view was supported by the Local Engineer. Nevertheless, by 1914 the third train in the middle of the day ran the whole length of the line, but was still marked as a 'trial until further notice'. These services required facilities for two locomotives and train sets based at Acheux. The journey times between Doullens and Albert varied between 2 hours 8 minutes and 2 hours 15 minutes.

Albert to Ham

The timetable for May 1914 (Table 2.10) shows that there were also three tains a day each way between Péronne and Albert, and the same between Péronne and Ham, which appears to have been run as a separate service. It was possible twice a day to travel through from Albert to Ham or vice versa, but it required a change of train at Péronne. The waiting time at Péronne was 24 minutes, or later 2 hours 46 minutes, in the Ham direction, and 1 hour 24 minutes, or later 41 minutes in the Albert direction. Table 2.10 also shows

Table 2.10 Albert–Péronne–Ham (SE)
Summary Timetable May 1914
Main stops only, not including halts and *arrêts*

		(1)	(1)			(2)	(1)		(2)
Albert		05.45	09.00	09.00	12.10		16.20	19.25	
Connection with CdN SG line Amiens–Arras. Origin of MG SE line to Doullens
Fricourt		06.04	09.20	09.21	12.32	13.55	16.44	19.50	19.55
junction with MG SE line Albert–Bray–Montdidier
Montauban			09.45		13.00			20.17	
Guillemont			09.53		13.09			20.28	
Combles			10.09		13.25			20.45	
Hem-Monacu			10.31		13.47			21.09	
Péronne(-Flamicourt) a			10.58		14.16			<u>21.40</u>	
Connection with CdN SG lines to Montdidier, Paris, Cambrai & Douai
	d	05.20			11.22	17.02			
Mons-en-Chaussée		05.38			11.40	17.22			
Athies (Somme)		05.47			11.49	17.32			
Monchy-Lagache		06.00			12.02	17.48			
Matigny		06.20			12.22	18.09			
Offoy		06.33			12.36	18.31			
junction with SE MG line to Ercheu
Ham		06.48			12.51	18.48			
connection with CdN SG lines to Amiens, Tergnier and Laon, and NGL MG line to Noyon
Ham					08.40		14.00		19.35
connection with CdN SG lines to Amiens, Tergnier and Laon, and NGL MG line to Noyon
Offoy					09.03		14.20		20.02
junction with SE MG line to Ercheu
Matigny					09.23		14.39		20.15
Monchy-Lagache					09.45		15.00		20.34
Athies (Somme)					10.00		15.16		20.47
Mons-en-Chaussée					10.12		15.27		21.06
Péronne(-Flamicourt) a					10.31		15.44		<u>21.15</u>
Connection with CdN SG lines to Montdidier, Paris, Cambrai & Douai
	d		05.20		11.55		16.25		
Hem-Monacu			05.48		12.29		16.51		
Combles			06.11		12.55		17.11		
Guillemont			06.24		13.12		17.24		
Montauban		(3)	06.33	(4)	(4)	13.22	(3)	17.30	(4)
Fricourt		<u>06.51</u>	06.55	10.00	13.50	13.50	<u>17.45</u>	17.50	19.52
junction with MG SE line Albert–Bray–Montdidier
Albert			07.13	10.19	14.02	14.08		18.07	20.11
Connection with CdN SG line Amiens–Arras. Origin of MG SE line to Doullens

a arrive   d depart

underlined – terminates, not at end of line
SG standard gauge CdN Compagnie du Nord
MG metre gauge SE Société Générale des Chemins de Fer Economiques
      NGL Noyon Guiscard Lassigny Company
(1) to Bray and Montdidier
(2) to Bray
(3) from Bray
(4) from Montdidier and Bray

the services between Fricourt and Albert on the Albert to Montdidier line.

The service between Péronne and Albert required one locomotive and train set based at Péronne, and one at Albert. The service between Péronne and Ham required one locomotive and train set based at Péronne. Journey times between Péronne and Albert were from 1 hour 42 minutes to 2 hours 15 minutes, the longer times probably being for mixed trains. Times between Péronne and Ham were from 1 hour 28 minutes to 1 hour 53 minutes.

Albert to Montdidier

The timetable for May 1914 (Table 2.11) shows that there were three trains each way per day over the full length of the line. There were also two 'shuttles' between Fricourt and Bray, which connected at Fricourt with trains on the line between Albert and Péronne. Actual journey times were between 2 hours 33 minutes and 3 hours 15 minutes. One train per day in each direction took over 3 hours, and for one of these an extra 19 minutes is allowed at Froissy for the train to manoeuvre at the canal, where the sugar factory

The metre gauge railways of the Somme département 1888 to 1914

Table 2.11 Albert–Montdidier (SE)
Summary Timetable May 1914
Main stops only, not including halts (except for Froissy) and *arrêts*

				(1)	(1)			(1)	
Albert			05.45	09.00	09.00	12.10		16.20	19.25
connection with CdN SG line Amiens–Arras. Origin of SE MG line to Doullens
Fricourt			06.04	09.20	09.21	12.32	13.55	16.44	19.50	19.55
junction with MG SE line Albert–Péronne–Ham
Bray			06.28	09.43			14.16	17.10		20.15
Froissy (halt)			06.33	09.48				17.16		
Proyart			06.52	10.04				17.34		
Harbonnières			07.11	10.15				17.50		
Rosières	a		07.19	10.24				18.00		
connection with CdN SG line to Amiens, Tergnier and Laon
	d		07.58	12.39				18.45		
Caix-Vrély			08.07	12.48				19.02		
Le Quesnel - Beauf.			08.17	12.59				19.15		
Arvillers - Hangest			08.25	13.07				19.26		
Davenescourt			08.38	13.26				19.44		
Montdidier			08.59	13.50				20.08		
connection with CdN SG lines Amiens to Compiègne and St-Just-en-Chaussée to Cambrai
Origin of NGL MG line to Noyon

						(2)	(3)
Montdidier			06.03	10.22			16.30	16.44
connection with CdN SG lines Amiens to Compiègne and St-Just-en-Chaussée to Cambrai
Origin of NGL MG line to Noyon
Davenescourt			06.31	10.53			17.02	17.12
Arvillers - Hangest			06.51	11.13			17.21	17.31
Le Quesnel - Beauf.			06.59	11.24			17.32	17.40
Caix-Vrély			07.09	11.37			17.46	17.51
Rosières	a		07.20	11.50			18.02	
connection with CdN SG line to Amiens, Tergnier and Laon
	d		08.21	12.45			18.46	
Harbonnières			08.34	12.55			18.55	
Proyart			08.51	13.06			19.08	
Froissy (halt)			09.27	(4)	13.19		19.21	
Bray		06.31	09.39	(4)	13.27	17.25	19.29	
		(5)			(5)	(5)		
Fricourt		06.51	06.55	10.00	13.50	13.50	17.45	17.50	19.52
junction with SE MG line Albert–Péronne–Ham
Albert			07.13	10.19	14.02	14.08		18.07	20.11
connection with CdN SG line Amiens–Arras. Origin of SE MG line to Doullens

a   arrive   d   depart
underlined – terminates, not at end of line
SG   standard gauge   CdN   *Compagnie du Nord*
MG   metre gauge   SE   *Société Générale des Chemins de Fer Economiques*
                          NGL   Noyon Guiscard Lassigny Company

(1) to Péronne and Ham
(2) except Saturdays
(3) Saturdays only (note times same as (2) from arrival at Rosières to Albert)
(4) If the train does not have to manœuvre at the canal leaves Froissy at 09.08 and arrives at Bray at 09.14
(5) from Péronne and Ham

branch was. These must have been the mixed passenger and goods trains.

In fact, journey times were longer, up 4 hours 50 minutes, if there were long layovers at Rosières-en-Santerre, the range being 39 minutes to 2 hours 15 minutes. These must have been to allow connections on the Amiens to Tergnier and Laon line. Table 2.11 also shows the services at Fricourt and Albert on the Albert to Péronne and Ham line. These services would have required one locomotive and train set at Albert and one at Montdidier to operate the main services, and one at Bray to operate the shuttle to Fricourt.

Offoy to Ercheu and Ercheu to Bussy

The timetable for May 1914 (Table 2.12) shows these two lines, although they were both run by SE, listed

31

2.14 The SE type 1 station at Bray-sur-Somme, with a train consisting of a locomotive and at least two passenger carriages coming from Montdidier. Undated but probably before the First World War. *(Authors' collection)*

2.15 Part of the track side of the former SE type 1 station at Bray-sur-Somme. This has been much extended as a *Centre de Secours* (Fire and Rescue service station), but the name is still prominent, in beautifully preserved bas-relief. April 2016. *(Authors)*

separately. There were three trains each way on both these lines. Within a few months of opening in 1897, the line from Ercheu to Bussy had an extra train on Saturdays and the first Tuesdays each month, market days at Noyon. It is worth noting the layovers at Nesle, which ranged from 1 hour 5 minutes to 2 hours 25 minutes. The latter was extended to 2 hours 55 minutes on Fridays. This must have been to connect with the CdN standard gauge trains between Amiens and Laon. At Ercheu, passengers had to change trains if they wanted to go on to Bussy. As we have noted above, both these lines were operated by one company, although owned by different ones. However, clearly they were very much separate organisations. As an example of this, note the arrival at Ercheu from Bussy at 16.48 but the departure for Offoy timed for 16.45!

With the layovers at Nesle, the journey between Ercheu and Offoy took anything up to 3 hours 35 minutes, or 4 hours 5 minutes on a Friday for the last train towards Offoy. The actual travelling times were between 1 hour 7 minutes and 1 hour 40 minutes, probably the longer times being for mixed trains. Between Ercheu and Bussy journey times were between 33 and 39 minutes. The service required two locomotives and train sets based at Ercheu, one for the service to Bussy. The other would have provided the service to Offoy, with another locomotive and train set based at Offoy.

Fares

In 1914 fares were about 11 cents per km for first class, 8 cents for second and 6 cents for third. This made the fares from Albert to Péronne (44km) 4.85 francs first class, 3.75 second class, and 2.65 third class.

The metre gauge railways of the Somme département 1888 to 1914

2.16 The type 2 station at Harbonnières, on the line from Albert to Montdidier. No date, but from the dress of the ladies almost certainly before the First World War. A passenger train in the station is hauled by locomotive No. 3.566, one of ten 0-6-2 SACM tank locomotives manufactured between 1890 and 1893. *(Authors' collection)*

11. – HARBONNIERES. – La Gare.

Table 2.12 Offoy–Ercheu & Ercheu–Bussy (SE)
Summary Timetable May 1914
Main stops only, not including halts and *arrêts*
Note - in the original Ercheu–Offoy and Ercheu–Bussy are separate tables

			(1)	(2)
Offoy		06.35	11.00	16.25	16.25
connection with MG SE Ham–Péronne–Albert line				
Rouy-le-Petit		06.54	11.25	16.45	16.45
Mesnil-St-Nicaise		07.02	11.39	16.59	16.59
Nesle	a	07.08	11.45	17.05	17.05
connection with SG CdN Amiens to Tergnier and Laon line				
	d	08.21	12.50	19.30	20.00
Moyencourt		08.46	13.13	19.54	20.24
Ercheu		08.52	13.20	20.00	20.30

			(3)	
Ercheu	06.01	11.13	14.08	17.51
Ognolles	06.07	11.19	14.13	17.57
Beaulieu-Ecuvilly	06.19	11.31	14.24	18.09
Catigny	06.26	11.37	14.30	18.16
Bussy	06.40	11.50	14.42	18.29
connection with MG NGL line Noyon to Ham				

			(3)	
Bussy	09.10	13.22	16.15	19.50
connection with MG NGL line Noyon to Ham				
Catigny	09.23	13.34	16.26	20.04
Beaulieu-Ecuvilly	09.29	13.40	16.32	20.11
Ognolles	09.40	13.50	16.43	20.23
Ercheu	09.45	13.55	16.48	20.28

Ercheu		06.35	11.25	16.45	
Moyencourt		06.48	11.37	16.54	
Nesle	a	07.10	11.55	17.20	
connection with SG CdN Amiens to Tergnier and Laon line				
	d	08.20	13.24	19.21	
Mesnil-St-Nicaise		08.27	13.33	19.31	
Rouy-le-Petit		08.37	13.46	19.42	
Offoy		08.58	14.10	19.58	
connection with MG SE Ham–Péronne–Albert line				

a	arrive		d	depart
SG	standard gauge		CdN	*Compagnie du Nord*
MG	metre gauge		SE	*Société Générale des Chemins de Fer Economiques*
			NGL	Noyon Guiscard Lassigny Company

(1) Except Friday
(2) Friday only (note times same Offoy - Nesle)
(3) Saturday, and the first Tuesday of each month, only (market day in Noyon)

2.17 The crossing cottage at Rosières-Vrély, on the line from Albert to Montdidier, now a private house. April 2016. (*Authors*)

Chapter Three

The metre gauge railways of the Oise and Aisne départements *1895 to 1914*

The lines covered in this chapter do not fit easily into a *départemental* classification. They do however form three groups. The first is the Noyonnais network of two lines, that ran mainly in the Oise *département* but also extended into the Somme. These lines are Noyon–Guiscard–Ham, and Noyon–Montdidier. The second is the Cambrésis system north from St-Quentin in Aisne to Caudry in the Nord *département*, and the related line from Le Catelet to Guise via Bohain. This line ran entirely in the Aisne *département*, and only merits brief mention in this book. We include in this group also the short isolated line from Roisel in Somme to Hargicourt in Aisne. It is included because of its near relationship with the St-Quentin–Caudry line. In addition, we offer a short section on the tramways of St-Quentin. The final group lies in the southwest of the Aisne *département* where we have covered Chauny–Coucy-le-Château–Montécouvé–Soissons, and Tergnier–Anizy-Pinon. This group need to appear on some maps of our area, but are peripheral to the main story, and are only mentioned very briefly.

Noyonnais network (Noyon to Ham, Noyon to Montdidier)

These lines are shown in Figure 3.1. The lines of *intérêt local* from Noyon to Guiscard and Ham, and from Noyon to Lassigny and Montdidier (along with the separate line from Milly-sur-Thérain to Formerie) were conceded in 1890 to Alfred Lambert, and declared *d'utilité publique* in 1891. Shortly after the *Société anonyme des Chemins de fer de Milly à Formerie et de Noyon à Guiscard et Lassigny* (MF & NGL) was formed. In 1893 this company was also conceded the line from Bussy to Ercheu, to link the Guiscard branch to the network at Ercheu. This branch was operated by the *Société Générale des Chemins de Fer Economiques* (SE), and has therefore been included in Chapter Two. The extensions of the network into the Somme *département*, from Guiscard to Ham and from Lassigny to Montdidier, were much delayed by long discussions.

Building and Opening

The lines from Noyon to Guiscard and Noyon to Lassigny were opened together on 6 April 1895. The delayed extensions were finally built jointly by the Oise and Somme *départements*, and operation was entirely allocated to NGL in an agreement signed in 1912. Guiscard to Ham finally opened on 1 September 1912, and Lassigny to Rollot and Montdidier on 24 August 1913.

Description of the lines

The line to Ham was 25km long, and that to Montdider 44km long. Distances and heights along the lines are shown in Table 3.1. Distances are given from the *Chaix* timetables, and where available the more accurate distances from the original profiles for the lines, only available for the parts of the lines within the Oise *département*. Heights are from satellite images for the known locations of the stations and other stops, which mostly accord well with the surveys for the original line profiles.

Noyon

The lines began on the south side of the *Compagnie du Nord* station at Noyon (see Figure 3.3). In Noyon there was an embankment with bridges over the Petite Verse and then the Grande Verse rivers, before the line curved north to a bridge over the standard gauge line to Paris, and then to the bifurcation of the lines to Ham and to Montdidier at 1.21km.

Noyon to Ham

The line then followed the valley of the River Verse to Bussy, where there was the junction with the line operated by SE to Ercheu (& Offoy), and on to Guiscard. After Guiscard, the line entered the Somme *département* between Golancourt and Muille-Villette and proceeded to Ham. Between Guiscard and Ham it crossed the watershed between the Verse and the Somme, reaching a maximum height of 93m (305ft) at Plessis station. At Ham it met the SE metre gauge line to Albert, the CdN standard gauge line from Amiens to Tergnier and Laon, and the *Société des Chemins de Fer Départementaux de l'Aisne* (CDA) standard gauge *intérêt local* line to St-Quentin.

Noyon to Montdidier

This line ran for 44km. From the junction in Noyon, the line followed the *Compagnie du Nord* standard gauge line to Pont-l'Evêque and then travelled along the valley of the Divette. After Lassigny the line

35

Narrow Gauge in the Somme Sector

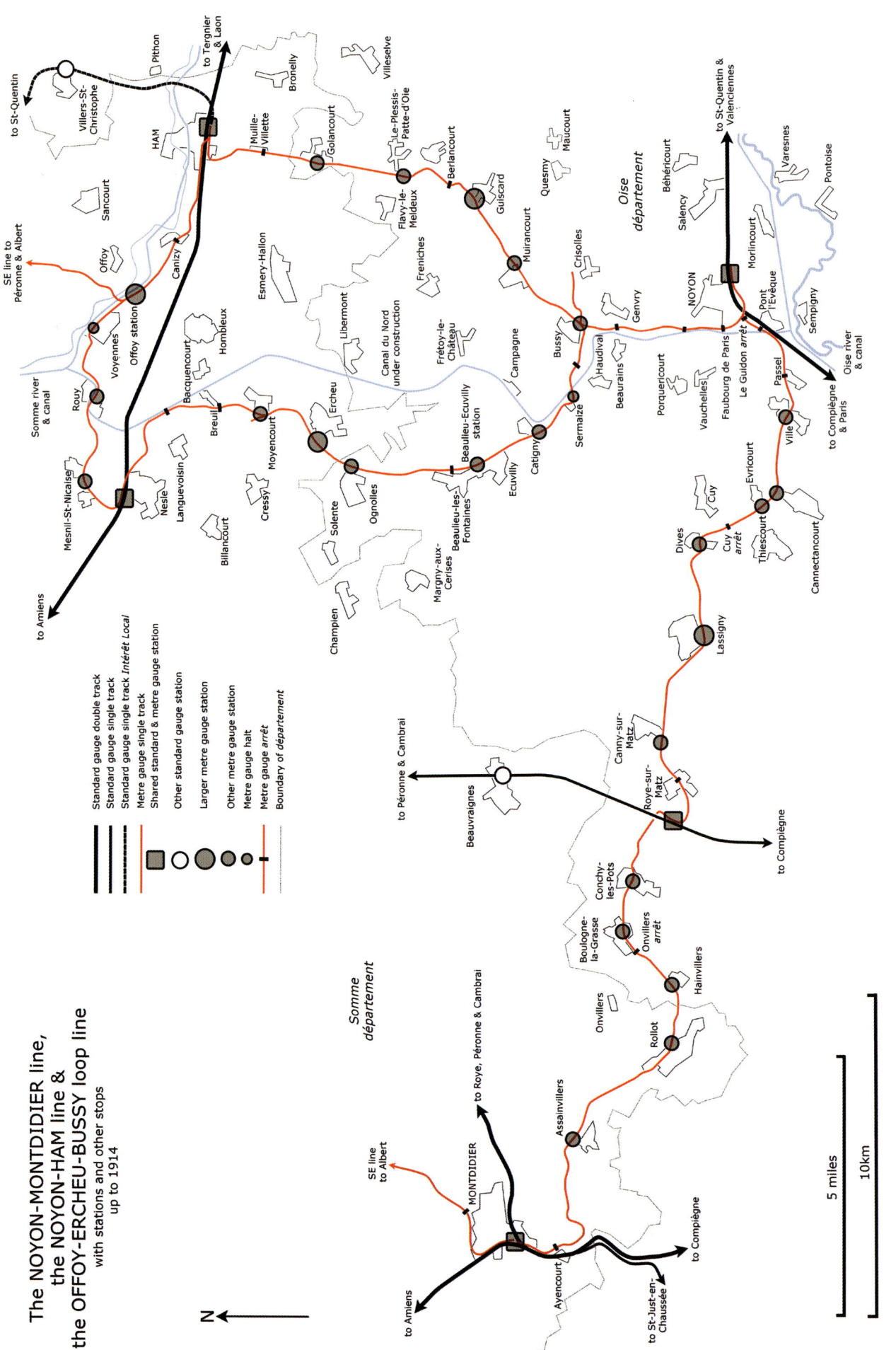

Figure 3.1

The metre gauge railways of the Oise and Aisne départements 1895 to 1914

Table 3.1 Noyon–Ham & Noyon–Montdidier, stations and other stops, up to 1914

Name	Type	Distance km From Chaix	from Profile	Altitude m (ft)
Noyon	CdN shared	0		45 (148)
SG line Paris Compiègne Noyon Brussels				
junction to Lassigny & Montdidier		(1)	1.21	
Route de Montdidier* (Faubourg de Paris)	arrêt	3	(2.10)	
Vauchelles	arrêt	4	3.84	
Beaurains	arrêt	6	5.83	
Bussy	station type 2	8	7.33	47
Junction with SE MG line to Ercheu, Offoy				
Muirancourt	station type 2	11	10.68	49
Guiscard	station type 1	14	13.52	55
Berlancourt	arrêt	16	14.49	58
Plessis-Flavel-Berlancourt	station type 2	17	16.47	93 (305)
Golancourt	station type 2	20	19.45	66
(boundary Oise - Somme *départements*)			20.22	
Muille-Villette	arrêt	22		64
Ham	CdN shared	25		64 (210)
CdN SG line Amiens, Rosières, Chaulnes, Ham, Tergnier, Laon				
CDA SG line to St Quentin				
SE MG line to Albert				
Noyon	CdN shared	0	0	45 (148)
SG line Paris Compiègne Noyon Brussels				
junction to Guiscard & Ham		(1)	1.21	
Le Guidon*	arrêt	2		
Pont l'Evéque	arrêt	3	2.52	
Passel	arrêt	5	4.24	41
Ville	station type 2	6	5.68	43
Cannectancourt	station type 2	9	8.29	51
Thiescourt	station type 2	9	8.94	51
Cuy*	arrêt	11		55
Dives	station type 2	12	11.68	55
Lassigny	station type 1	16	15.11	72
Canny-sur-Matz	station type 2	20	18.87	75
Roye-sur-Matz	arrêt	22	20.54	71
Roye-sur-Matz	CdN shared	23	22.10	71
Connection with SG line Compiègne–Roye (Somme)				
Conchy-les-Pots.	station type 2	26	25.07	85
Boulogne-la-Gr.	station type 2	28	26.84	112
Onvillers	arrêt	29	27.84	97
Hainvillers	station type 2	31	29.39	113
(boundary Oise - Somme *départements*)			29.96	
Rollot	station type 2	33		115 (377)
Assainvillers	station type 2	37		90
Ayencourt-les-M.	arrêt	42		64
Montdidier	CdN shared	44		60 (197)
SE MG line to Albert (Somme)				
SG CdN lines Amiens to Compiègne, and St-Just-en-Chaussée to Cambrai				

arrêt   for picking up and setting down passengers without luggage only
* not open at opening of line in 1895   SG standard gauge   MG metre gauge
CdN   *Compagnie du Nord*   SE *Société Générale des Chemins de Fer Économiques*
CDA   *Société des Chemins de Fer Départementaux de l'Aisne*

crossed, at Roye-sur-Matz, the *Compagnie du Nord* line from Compiègne to Roye. It entered the Somme *département* before Rollot. Rollot was the highest point on the line, at 115m (377ft), as the line crossed the watershed between the Oise basin and the Somme basin.

Engineering

Canal du Nord
Work on the Canal du Nord began before the First World War, but in this section, it was still dry at the beginning of hostilities in 1914. The line to Ham may have been diverted to keep it on the east side of the canal. The line to Montdidier must have crossed the new canal works near the *arrêt* at Pont-l'Evêque. We do not have any details of this bridge, but it was probably of lattice girder type, and may have been shared with the bridge for the standard gauge lines from Paris.

Path and trackbed
Most of the route was away from roads, in its own path. There were short sections by roads, especially between Guiscard and Ham, but there were no 'tramway' sections in roads.

Gradients and curvatures
These lines like most of the other Oise lines had minimum radius of curvature 150m and maximum gradient of 2 per cent.

Rails
Like most of the other Oise lines, these lines had 20kg/m Vignole rails, 11m long. As originally laid, sleepers were of pine cresosoted or injected with copper sulphate for the straight sections. For curves more than 300m radius alternate sleepers were of oak, and all were oak for curves of 150 to 300m radius. Of minimum length 1.70m., they were laid at most 0.88m from centre to centre, 13 per rail on straight sections and 14 on curves.

Bridges
Major bridges on these lines are shown in Table 3.2. See also the section on the construction of the Canal du Nord, above.

Stations and other stops
A list of the stations and other stops up to 1914 has been given in Table 3.1.

Buildings
The *Société anonyme des Chemins de fer de Milly à Formerie et de Noyon à Guiscard et Lassigny* (MF & NGL) was one of the companies associated with Alfred Lambert, and the stations on these lines are similar to those of other lines associated with this entrepreneur, for instance the line from Aire to Berck in the Pas-de-Calais département. This was also the case for the line from Ercheu to Bussy, built by NGL but operated by SE as part of the eastern Somme network (see Chapter Two).

The buildings were of brick, with the long axis and the roof ridge parallel with the platforms and the track. For the original lines from Noyon to Guiscard and to Lassigny, there were two types.

Larger stations, which we have called type 1, were at the original ends of the lines at Guiscard and Lassigny. The central two storey building had a ground floor office, a *salle de baggages* (baggage hall), and two exits onto the platforms. There was one exit to the station forecourt. On the first floor were three rooms and a kitchen, with two chimneys. At one end of the main building was a single story waiting room opening from the baggage hall, and a *consigne* with access to the baggage hall and the platform. At the other end of the main building there was a goods hall 57m long with a 53m long platform, and a livestock platform with ramp. There was good loft space over the main

Table 3.2 Major bridges on the Noyon to Ham and Noyon to Montdidier metre gauge lines up to 1914

Section at	distance (km)	over/ under	what	span (m)	type	notes
Noyon (common)	0.60	over	river La Petite Verse	3.50	TM	
	0.90	over	river La Grande Verse	4.00	TM	
	1.15	over	SG railway Paris-Noyon	8.00	TM oblique	
Noyon to Montdidier						
Pont l'Evêque		over	Canal du Nord (works)		lattice girder	?shared with SG ?when
Roye-sur-Matz		under	SG railway Compiègne-Roye	4.20	TM oblique	4.20m opening, 4.30m vert clearance

SG standard gauge
TM *Tablier Métallique*

The metre gauge railways of the Oise and Aisne départements 1895 to 1914

3.1 A Corpet-Louvet 0-6-2T waits to depart from Lassigny for Noyon with a passenger train in 1908 or before. At this time, Lassigny was the end of the line from Noyon. Note that the train is standing on the second line away from the passenger building, leaving the first line for access to the goods hall. The locomotive, a Corpet-Louvet 0-6-2T, is one of those manufactured between 1890 and 1893, and has an open cabin. Postcard postmarked 1908. *(Authors' collection)*

3.2 The track side of the 'Lambert' type 1 station at Lassigny, now a departmental road repair depot. November 2015. *(Authors)*

building and the waiting room, and a cellar under the main building. At the end of the loft space there was a full size rectangular window.

Smaller stations, which we have called type 2, were expected to have fewer passengers, and were smaller. There was no extension for the waiting room, and there was only one exit to the platforms. Upstairs there was only one room plus the kitchen. Reflecting this there was only one chimney. From the end view the buildings appear slimmer. There is a round window for the attic, over the end away from the goods hall, and a rectangular attic window at the goods hall end, but smaller than that for the type 1 stations. The goods hall was the only extension, 21m long with a 24m long platform, and usually a livestock platform. This type of building was used for all other stations on the lines, and for the later extensions to Ham, and to Montdidier.

All stations had a toilet block with two WCs, one each for ladies and for gentlemen, and an external *pissoir*. All stations also had a *lampisterie* (lamp store). For type 2 stations, the lampisterie and the toilet blocks were smaller.

At an *arrêt* there would often be a shelter (*abri*) with internal seating. A typical *abri* was 7.5m long and 2.5m wide inside, and open at the front, on the track side.

3.3 The 'Lambert' type 2 station at Conchy-les-Pots with the church of St-Nicaise behind on the left. No date, but this station was built for the extension of the line from Lassigny to Montdidier, opened in 1913. *(Authors' collection)*

Track layouts

Stations on these lines and their extensions had one loop line, so that there were two tracks through the station. The track nearest the station building served the goods platform, but a crossover line allowed wagons to be parked alongside the goods yard without obstructing access to the goods platform. However, it seems that, as on other systems, passengers usually had to cross the 'goods line' to join or leave a train.

A typical type 2 station track plan on the Lassigny line extension, at Boulogne-la-Grasse, is shown in Figure 3.2.

Transhipment facilities were provided at the end of the line joint stations with the Compagnie du Nord network, Noyon, Ham, and Montdidier.

Ham

Prior to the First World War, all termini of the secondary network were south of the CdN lines and buildings. The track plan for Ham station as in about 1910 is shown in Figure 2.5 in Chapter Two.

Noyon

The track plan for Noyon station as in 1896, the year after the opening of the lines to Guiscard and to Lassigny, is shown in Figure 3.3. This shows the metre gauge facilities.

Roye-sur-Matz

At Roye-sur-Matz main station, 1.5km (1 mile) west of the village, the line shared a station the standard gauge single track line from Compiègne to Roye. The track plan for the station, as at the time of opening of the extension from Lassigny to Montdidier in 1913, is shown in Figure 3.4. North of the station the metre gauge line towards Montdidier passed under the standard gauge line.

Depots

The Depot for the Noyonnais network was at the eastern end of Noyon station (see Figure 3.3). This had a shed for two locomotives and three carriages, a workshop, a lamp store and an office for the chief of the depot.

Sheds for one locomotive were provided at each of the initial termini (Guiscard and Lassigny). There was also a shed for one locomotive at Bussy (see picture 2.10, Chapter Two). The timetable pattern for the line to Ercheu (see Chapter Two) does not suggest the need for facilities at Bussy, but it is said that this shed was for a locomotive of SE, for the service between Bussy and Ercheu.

Industrial links

We have not made a complete list of the many metre gauge industrial branches and sidings. Some of these were simply a very short private single line into some premises adjacent to the track. The more important industrial links are shown in Table 3.3. We have not included the standard gauge industrial links at Noyon station.

The metre gauge railways of the Oise and Aisne départements 1895 to 1914

BOULOGNE-LA-GRASSE
Smaller type NGL station
line from Noyon to Montdidier
as opened in 1913

to Lassigny & Noyon

GC27 (now D27) to Roye-sur-Matz

GC27 (now D27) to Rollot

to Rollot & Montdidier

— Metre gauge line
▪ Station building
▫ Platform
▪ Other building

1 *Cour des marchandises* (goods yard)
2 *Cour des voyageurs* (station forecourt)
3 *Halle à marchandise* (goods hall)
4 *Bâtiment des Voyageurs* (passenger building)
5 Toilets and *lampisterie*
6 *Avenue d'accès* (station approach road)

NGL Noyon-Guiscard-Lassigny (Lambert group)

100m

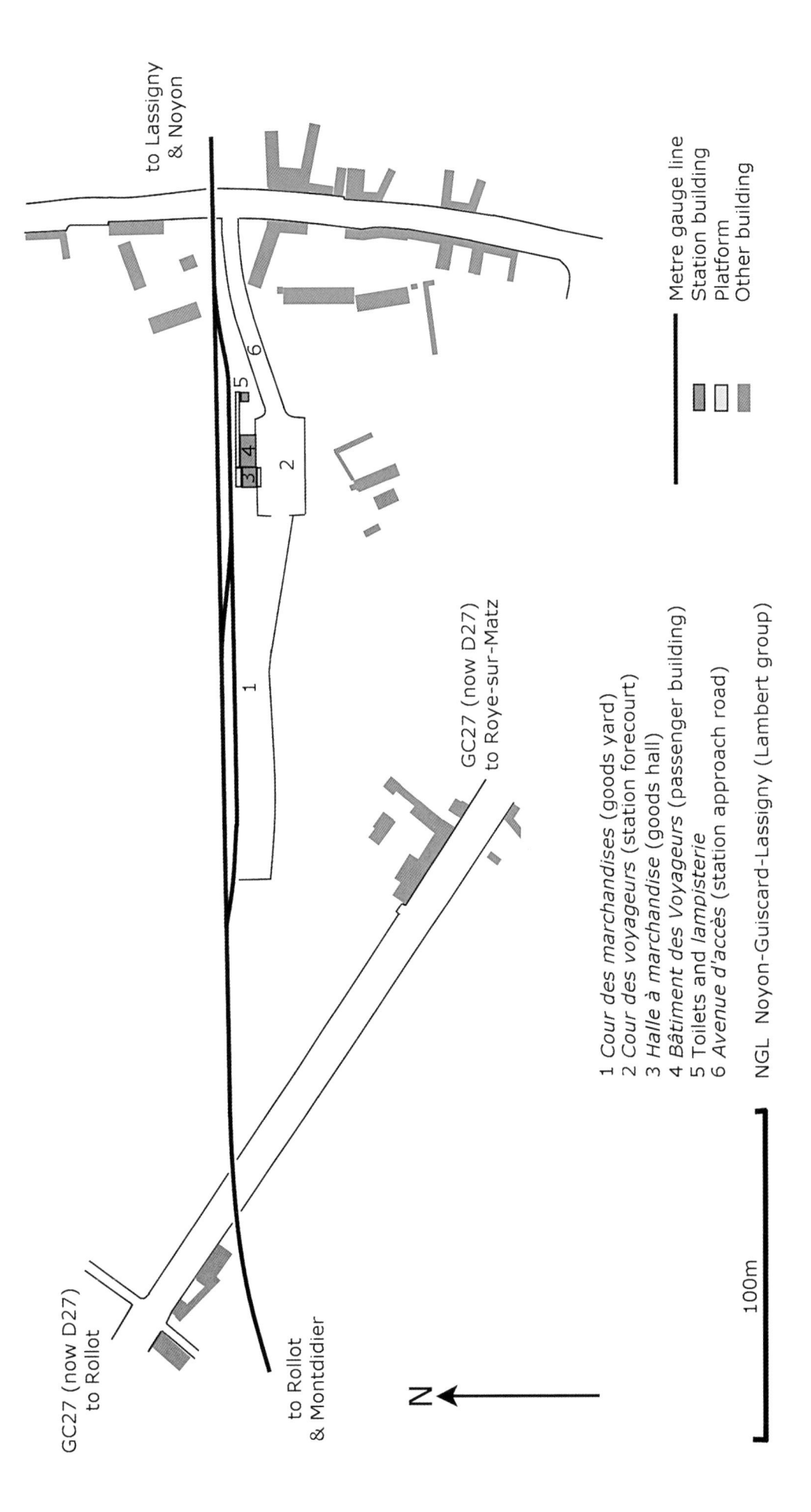

N

Figure 3.2

Narrow Gauge in the Somme Sector

NOYON
Compagnie du Nord station
shared with the MG lines to Ham & to Montdidier
1896

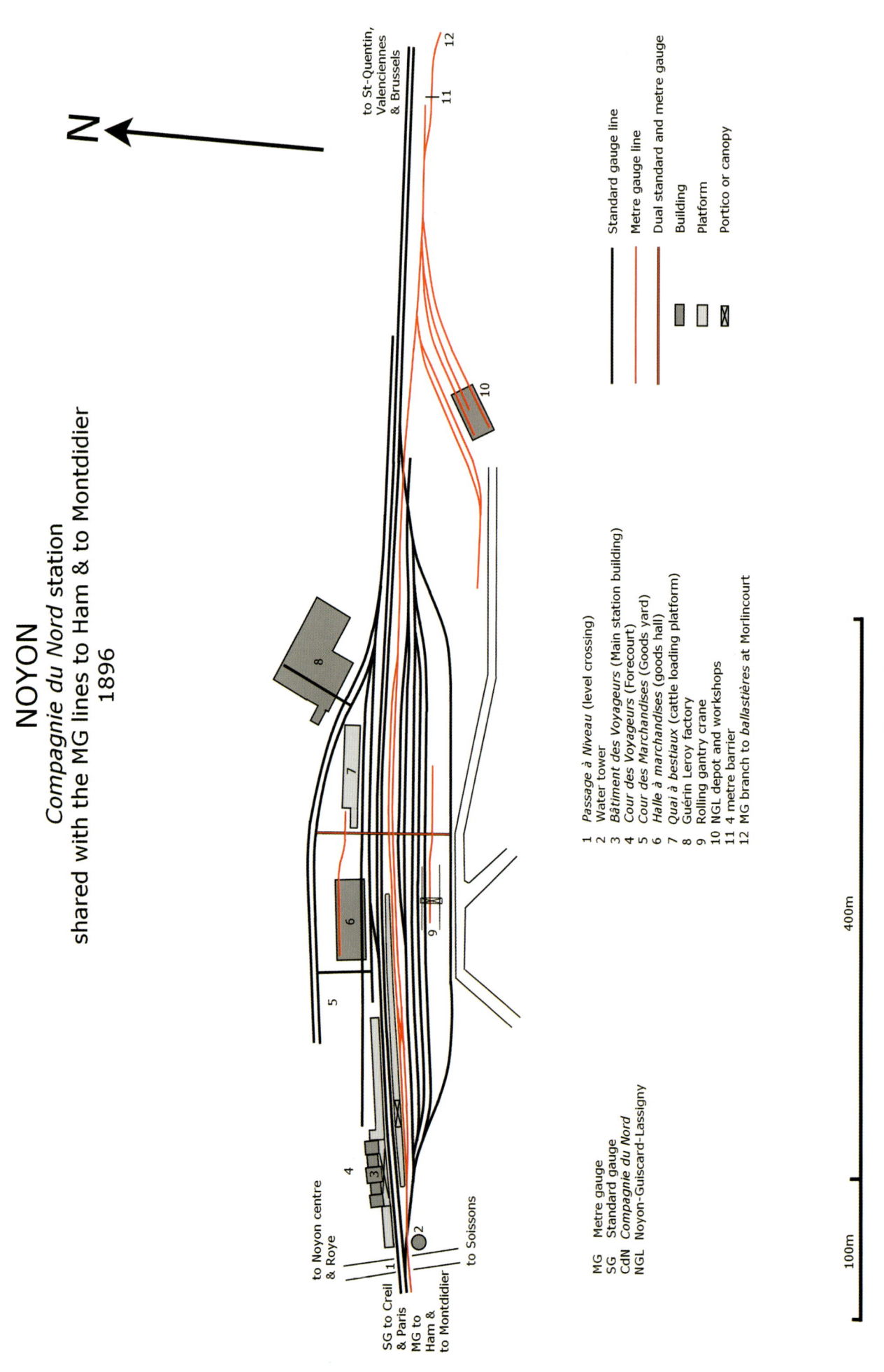

to St-Quentin, Valenciennes & Brussels

to Noyon centre & Roye
SG to Creil & Paris
MG to Ham & to Montdidier
to Soissons

1 *Passage à Niveau* (level crossing)
2 Water tower
3 *Bâtiment des Voyageurs* (Main station building)
4 *Cour des Voyageurs* (Forecourt)
5 *Cour des Marchandises* (Goods yard)
6 *Halle à marchandises* (goods hall)
7 *Quai à bestiaux* (cattle loading platform)
8 Guérin Leroy factory
9 Rolling gantry crane
10 NGL depot and workshops
11 4 metre barrier
12 MG branch to *ballastières* at Morlincourt

MG Metre gauge
SG Standard gauge
CdN Compagnie du Nord
NGL Noyon-Guiscard-Lassigny

— Standard gauge line
— Metre gauge line
— Dual standard and metre gauge
▪ Building
▫ Platform
▨ Portico or canopy

Figure 3.3

ROYE-sur-MATZ
Compagnie du Nord station
shared with the MG line from Lassigny to Montdidier
opened in 1913

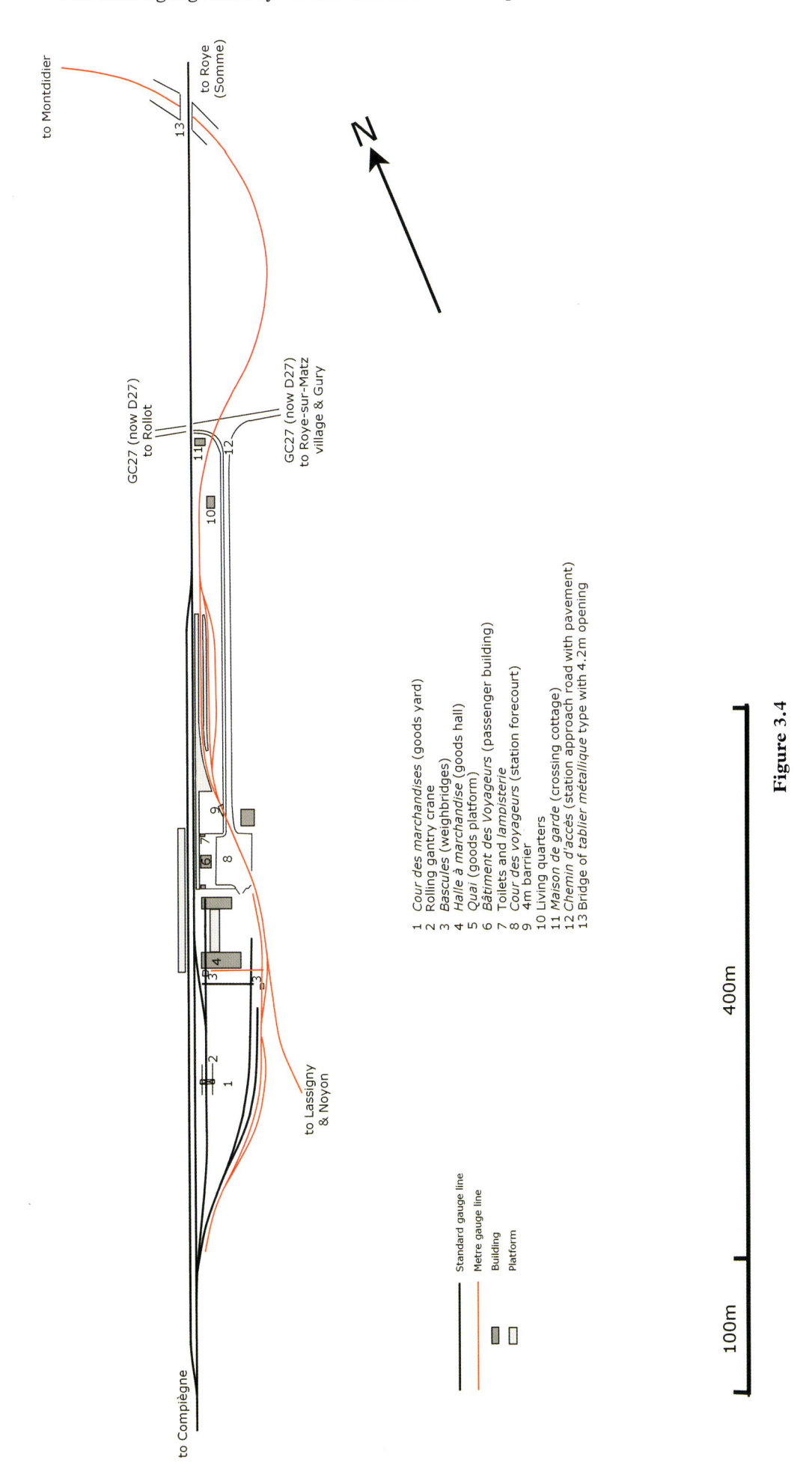

1 *Cour des marchandises* (goods yard)
2 Rolling gantry crane
3 *Bascules* (weighbridges)
4 *Halle à marchandise* (goods hall)
5 *Quai* (goods platform)
6 *Bâtiment des Voyageurs* (passenger building)
7 Toilets and *lampisterie*
8 *Cour des voyageurs* (station forecourt)
9 4m barrier
10 Living quarters
11 *Maison de garde* (crossing cottage)
12 *Chemin d'accés* (station approach road with pavement)
13 Bridge of *tablier métallique* type with 4.2m opening

Figure 3.4

Table 3.3 Noyon to Ham & Noyon to Montdidier
Principal industrial branch lines and sidings up to 1914

Location	Distance (km)	Length (km)	Nature of business	Proprietor (most probably)	Date built	Notes
Noyon						
Le Jonquoy (Morlincourt)	0	1.6	*Ballastière*		1897	By the Oise canal
Noyon to Ham	(from Noyon)					
Bussy station	7.2	2.5	Sugar Factory, Crisolles		before 1914	
Noyon to Montdidier	(from Noyon)					
Pont l'Evêque	1.2		*Briqueterie*	Albert Lefévre	1904	Loop line and branch at *arrêt*
Passel	3.1		Travaux Publics	M. Frot, Meaux	1913	Siding at Passel *arrêt*
Conchy-les-Pots	24.5		*Briqueterie*	Baraque	before 1914	Loop line and siding 500m east of station

Table 3.4 Technical details of Lambert NGL and RH locomotives up to 1914

Manufacturer	Hunslet	all Corpet-Louvet							
Year(s) of manufacture	1878	1890	1891	1893	1893	1879	1901 & 1905	1912	1912
Wheel configuration	0-4-0T	0-6-2T	0-6-2T	0-6-2T	0-6-2T	0-6-0T	0-6-0T	0-6-2T	0-6-2T
Manufacturer's No(s)									
Company No(s)		2 & 4	34	8	7			10	11 & 12
Name		La Vosgienne							
Year(s) put in service	1895	1894*	1894**	1893	1895#	c. 1899	1901 & 1905	1912	1913
Number put in service	1	2	1	1	1	1	2	1	2
Lines	RH	NGL## RH	NGL	NGL	NGL	RH	RH	NGL for Ham extension	NGL for Montdidier extension
Weight empty (tonnes)		16	16	16	14-16		17	17	17
Weight loaded (tonnes)		21.00	21.00	21.00					21.095
Diam. of driving wheels (m)		1.00	1.00	1.00				1.00	1.00
Boiler capacity (m³)		2.018	2.018	2.018				2.018	2.018
Boiler pressure (Kg/cm²)		10	10	10				12.5	12.5
Heating surface (m²)		46.50	46.50	46.50				46.52	46.52
Diam. of valves (mm)								55	55
Diam. of pistons (m)		0.30	0.30	0.30				0.30	0.30
Piston travel (m)		0.45	0.45	0.45				0.45	0.45

NGL Noyon–Guiscard–Lassigny lines (later extended to Ham and Montdidier)
RH   Roissel–Hargicourt line
*   transferred from Estrées–Froissy line (Oise *département*)
**   transferred from Aire–Rimeux–Berck line (Pas-de-Calais *département*), to Milly–Formerie line (Oise *département*) 1895
\#   transferred from Milly–Formerie line (Oise *département*)
\#\#   No. 2 NGL 1894, RH 1899 for second opening, later NGL again
     No. 4 RH 1894 for first opening

Rolling stock

The rolling stock had a single central buffer and coupling equipment of relatively low quality. There were many interchanges of stock between the Milly–Formerie and the Noyon lines, also with other Lambert lines, causing a confused situation.

Steam locomotives

Some details of steam locomotives used on the line up to 1914 are shown in table 3.4. During construction, Corpet 0-6-0T locomotives were used. In the 1890s, twelve Corpet-Louvet 0-6-2T locomotives of 14-16 tonnes were allocated for operations to the Lambert lines in the Oise *département*, and the Roisel to Hargicourt line in the Somme and Aisne *départements*. They were numbered sequentially over all the Lambert lines. In addition to other Lambert lines in the Oise département (Estrées–Froissy and Milly–Formerie), this included also the Aire–Rimeux–Berck line in the Pas-de-Calais *département*, and the Flanders network in the Nord *département*. At first, locomotives were moved from place to place as the need arose. Before the opening of the extensions to Ham and to Montdidier, there were certainly three locomotives based at Noyon, numbers 2, 7 and 8.

For the extensions to Ham and to Montidier three additional Corpet-Louvet 0-6-2T locomotives were ordered, but only one, number 10, had been delivered when the Ham extension opened in September 1912. The other two, numbers 11 and 12, had arrived for the opening of the extension to Montdidier in August 1913.

The Corpet-Louvet locomotives of the 1890s had open cabins, but the locomotives delivered in 1912 and 1913 had enclosed cabins. Apart from that there was little difference, except for a slight increase in empty weight and in boiler pressure.

Passenger carriages & wagons
While waiting for delivery of their own carriages, the Lambert organisation used for several months some 2-axle rolling stock known as 'Rosario'. These were made by *Forges de St-Denis* and intended for a French *société* who had the concession for the Rosario railway in Argentina. It seems that in the end they never took delivery.

The lot consisted of five passenger carriages, two first class, one mixed first and second class, and two second class. There were also two *fourgons*, ten covered wagons, and six open wagons. From 1895, the greater part of the goods stock went to the Roisel–Hargicourt line. With the arrival of the line's own carriages, the passenger carriages went first to Milly–Formerie, then to the Roisel to Hargicourt line in 1901.

The definitive rolling stock for Noyon–Guiscard–Lasigny (and Milly–Formerie) came from the *Ateliers du Nord de la France* at Blanc-Misseron.

Passenger carriages
As definitive stock soon after the opening in 1895, the Noyon network received two 2-axle carriages, one mixed first and third class and two third class, also three bogie carriages, all mixed first, second and third class with integral baggage area (*fourgon*).

The bogie carriages had end platforms and were numbered 51 to 53 (in sequence with other lines in the Lambert group). The single first class compartment had six places, the single second class compartment six places, and two and a half third class compartments had twenty places, with four more places on *banquettes* in the baggage area. A postal compartment opened to the outside. The 2-axle (4 wheel) carriages also had end platforms. Number 71 had six first and twenty third class places, and number 81 had eight second and twenty-four third class places. There were also three covered wagons to serve as *fourgons*. All the passenger stock had vacuum brakes.

By 1912, six additional carriages and three *fourgons* were delivered, in anticipation of the opening of the extensions to Ham and Montdidier. Two of the extra carriages had 2 bogies, and four were 2-axle (4 wheel) carriages. Some of these vehicles were labelled G.H.L.M. (Guiscard–Ham et Lassigny–Montdidier).

Wagons
For opening in 1895, the Noyon network received 13 covered wagons, 41 open wagons, 22 flat wagons, and 4 flat wagons with pivoting traverse. In 1910, they had 15 covered wagons, 38 open wagons, and 12 flat wagons. While waiting for the extensions of the lines, some wagons were loaned to the Estrées–Froissy Company.

Operations
The basic pattern up to the First World War was of three trains each way per day, augmented for market days in Noyon, Saturdays and the first Tuesday each month.

The timetable for the service between Noyon and Ham from May 1913 is shown in Table 3.5. There were three trains each way daily, with an extra train on market days in Noyon. During part of the year, from 5 October to 10 December, one train in the middle of the day becomes a mixed passenger and goods train, except on market days in Noyon. This suggests an increased demand for goods traffic in the autumn, almost certainly related to the sugar beet season. The extra time allowance is greatest for the middle of the day train to Ham, suggesting that wagons of sugar beet are being collected for the Ham (Eppeville) *sucrerie*. The journey time was 57 to 60 minutes for passenger trains, and 1 hour 8 minutes to 1 hour 25 minutes for mixed trains.

The timetable for the service between Noyon, Lassigny and Montdidier from May 1914 is shown in Table 3.6. This is a complex timetable. Following the opening of the line between Lassigny and Montdidier on 24 August 1913 the timings between Noyon and Lassigny hardly changed. The usual journey time between Noyon and Lassigny was 38 or 39 minutes. We have not been able to identify the mixed passenger and goods trains, as we have for the service to Ham in 1913. However, in May 1913, before the extension to Montdidier opened, the mixed trains were the equivalents of the 09.13 and 13.18 from Noyon, and the 11.24 from Lassigny, all allowed more time in the autumn (sugar beet) season.

Table 3.5 Noyon to Guiscard and Ham (NGL)
Summary Timetable May 1913
Main stops only, not including halts and *arrêts*

		(1)	(2)	(3)		
	MV	TL	MV	TL	TL	
Noyon	08.40	12.55	13.07	15.54	19.27	
Connection with CdN SG line Compiègne–St-Quentin (Paris–Brussels)						
Origin of MG NGL line to Lassigny and Montdidier						
Bussy	09.05	13.13	13.34	16.13	18.45	
junction with MG SE line to Ercheu, and Ercheu to Offoy						
Muirancourt	09.14	13.21	13.48	16.21	19.53	
Guiscard	09.28	13.29	14.02	16.29	20.01	
Plessis-Flavy-Berlancourt	09.38	13.38	14.13	16.38	20.10	
Golancourt	09.46	13.45	14.23	16.45	20.17	
Ham	09.55	13.54	14.32	16.54	20.25	
Connection with CdN SG lines Amiens, Tergnier and Laon. Origin of MG SE line to Albert						

			(3)		
	TL	MV	TL	TL	
Ham	06.10	11.10	14.08	17.56	
Connection with CdN SG lines to Amiens, Tergnier and Laon, Origin of MG SE line to Albert					
Golancourt	06.19	11.20	14.17	18.06	
Plessis-Flavy-Berlancourt	06.27	11.28	14.25	18.14	
Guiscard	06.35	11.41	14.33	18.22	
Muirancourt	06.42	11.48	14.40	18.29	
Bussy	08.52	12.02	14.49	18.39	
junction with MG SE line to Ercheu, and Ercheu to Offoy					
Noyon	07.08	12.18	15.05	18.55	
Connection with CdN SG line Compiègne–St-Quentin (Paris–Brussels)					
Origin of MG NGL line to Lassigny and Montdidier					

MV	Mixed passenger and goods trains	TL	Passenger trains
SG	standard gauge	CdN	*Compagnie du Nord*
MG	metre gauge	SE	*Société Générale des Chemins de Fer Economiques*
		NGL	Noyon Guiscard Lassigny Company

(1) Daily 11 December to 4 October, then only Saturdays and the first Thursday in the month (market days in Noyon) until 10 December
(2) Daily 5 October to 10 December, except Saturdays and the first Thursday in the month (market days in Noyon)
(3) Only on Saturdays and the first Thursday in the month (market days in Noyon), trial only

The section from Lassigny to Montdidier was being run essentially as a separate service, with poor connections except for one train per day in each direction, the 05.54 from Montdidier and the 19.22 from Noyon. For these, the timetable suggests that the same train was running through. With the opening of the line through to Montdidier, the opportunity was used to provide an extra servce from Lassigny to Roye-sur-Matz on a Saturday, to change for Compiègne for the market day there. The best journey times were 1 hour 7 minutes, but waiting time at Roye-sur-Matz, for connections, could be up to 54 minutes, making the longest journey time 1 hour 58 minutes. There was no provision for mixed trains or for autumn delays on the Lassigny to Montdidier section.

There were set rules for delays to allow connections at Ham, Noyon, Roye-sur-Matz and Montdidier, if the standard gauge trains were delayed. Depending on the importance of the connection, which included if it was the last of the day, the delay allowed could be from nothing to 35 minutes but was usually in the range 5-20 minutes.

The basic service between Noyon and Ham could be provided by one locomotive and train set, and the timetable suggests that it was based at Ham. One additional locomotive and set would be required for at least one of the autumn mixed services, and there were probably extra goods-only services during the sugar beet season. The service between Noyon and Lassigny could also be provided by one locomotive and train set, based at Lassigny. The service between Lassigny and Montdidier could be provided likewise by one locomotive and set based at Montdidier, but one extra would be required, based at Lassigny, on Saturdays. The whole pattern suggests one locomotive based at each of Ham and Montdidier, with two at Lassigny, and the remaining two probably at Noyon, for goods services and back up.

The metre gauge railways of the Oise and Aisne départements 1895 to 1914

Table 3.6 Noyon to Lassigny and Montdidier (NGL)
Summary Timetable May 1914
Main stops only, not including halts and *arrêts*

		(1)	(2)	(3)	(4)	(3)	(4)	(5)	(6)		
Noyon				09.13	09.13	12.48	13.02	15.59	15.59	19.22	
Connection with CdN SG line Compiègne to St-Quentin (Paris to Brussels).
Origin of MG NGL line to Guiscard and Ham
Ville				09.28	09.29	13.02	13.18	16.13	16.15	19.36	
Cannectancourt				09.35	09.36	13.09	13.25	16.20	16.22	19.43	
Thiescourt				09.38	09.42	13.12	13.31	16.23	16.28	19.46	
Dives				09.45	09.52	13.19	13.41	16.30	16.38	19.53	
Lassigny	a			09.52	09.59	13.26	13.48	16.37	16.45	20.00	
	d	06.25	08.20			12.18					20.01
Canny-sur-Matz		06.34	08.29			12.28					20.10
Roye-sur-Matz	a	06.41	08.36			12.31					20.17
	d		08.40			12.45					20.21
Connection with CdN SG line Compiègne to Roye
Conchy-les-Pots			08.47			12.51					20.28
Boulogne-la-Grasse			08.52			13.02					20.33
Hainvillers			08.59			13.10					20.40
Rollot			09.04			13.20					20.45
Assainvillers			09.14			13.31					20.55
Montdidier			09.27			13.44					21.08
Connection with CdN SG lines Amiens to Compiègne and St-Just-en-Chaussée to Cambrai
Origin of SE MG line to Albert

		(7)	(1)	(2)	(8)	(4)	(3)	(8)	
Montdidier				05.54			10.15		18.45
Connection with CdN SG lines Amiens to Compiègne and St-Just-en-Chaussée to Cambrai
Origin of SE MG line to Albert
Assainvillers				06.09			10.31		19.00
Rollot				06.19			10.46		19.10
Hainvillers				06.24			10.52		19.15
Boulogne-la-Grasse				06.31			11.03		19.22
Conchy-les-Pots				06.36			11.12		19.27
Roye-sur-Matz	a			06.42			11.18		19.33
	d		07.00	07.21			11.30		20.27
Connection with CdN SG line Compiègne to Roye
Canny-sur-Matz			07.08	07.29			11.39		20.35
Lassigny	a		07.16	07.37			11.47		20.43
	d	06.35			07.42	11.24	11.30	14.22	18.12
Dives		06.43			07.50	11.32	11.38	14.30	18.20
Thiescourt		06.50			07.57	11.43	11.46	13.37	18.27
Cannectancourt		06.53			08.00	11.46	11.49	14.40	18.30
Ville		07.00			08.07	11.55	11.57	14.47	18.37
Noyon		07.13			08.20	12.10	12.12	15.00	18.50
Connection with CdN SG line Compiègne to St-Quentin (Paris to Brussels).
Origin of MG NGL line to Guiscard and Ham

a	arrive	d	depart
SG	standard gauge	CdN	*Compagnie du Nord*
MG	metre gauge	SE	*Société Générale des Chemins de Fer Économiques*
		NGL	Noyon Guiscard Lassigny Company

(1) Saturdays only, market day in Compiègne
(2) Not between Lassigny and Roye-sur-Matz on Saturdays, market day in Compiègne
(3) Daily 11 December to 4 October
(4) Daily 5 October to 10 December
(5) 11 December to 4 October, only on Saturdays and the first Thursday each month, market days in Noyon
(6) 5 October to 10 December, only on Saturdays and the first Thursday each month, market days in Noyon
(7) Except Saturdays and the first Thursday each month, market days in Noyon
(8) Saturdays and the first Thursday each month, market days in Noyon

Following the outbreak of War on 3 August 1914, nearly all the motive power staff departed for army service. From 20 August, the service was reduced to one train each way daily from Monday to Saturday Noyon to Ham and Noyon to Lassigny. There was no mention of any service between Lassigny and Montidier, and there was no service on Sundays to allow time to attend to the locomotives, and to allow the remaining crews to rest. The service provided was:

Noyon	12.05	Noyon	14.30
Lassigny	12.50	Ham	15.40
Lassigny	13.05	Ham	16.20
Noyon	13.50	Noyon	17.30

This service could be provided by one locomotive, train set and crew.

Fares
In 1914, fares were about 10 cents per km for first class, 8 cents for second and 6 cents for third. This made the fares from Noyon to Montdidier (44km) 4.55 francs first class, 3.80 second class, and 2.75 third class.

St-Quentin–Le Catelet–Caudry (SQLeCC)
In 1878, Pierre Chevalier, Alfred Lambert & Louis Rey were asked to set up a tramway network in the rich agricultural area bounded by Cambrai, Caudry, St-Quentin and Denain. In 1880 the *Société des Chemins de Fer du Cambrésis* (CFC) was set up and obtained a declaration of *utilité publique* for the first line from Cambrai to Catillon, under the tramway regulations.

Building and Opening
The whole system was extensive, and the first section from Cambrai was opened in 1881. A second route from Denain to Le Catelet via Caudry could not be built on the verges of roads and was conceded under the *intérêt local* regulations in 1882, with the extension to St-Quentin conceded in 1885. The relevant line for this book was this line from St-Quentin via Le Catelet to Caudry. The line was built from Denain to Le Catelet via Caudry between 1887 and 1891. The link between Le Catelet and St-Quentin was opened firstly to the St-Quentin-Cambrésis station on 14 April 1892. The line finally reached St-Quentin-Nord on 28 March 1904.

Description of the line
The line was 57km long. Distances and heights along the line are shown in table 3.7. It branched off the Cambrai to Catillon line at the station/depot of Caudry, which was situated at the entrance to the village. It crossed the CdN Busigny to Cambrai line,

Table 3.7 St-Quentin–Le Catelet–Caudry, stations and other stops, up to 1914

Name	Type	Distance km	Altitude m (ft)
Caudry-Cambrésis	station (depot)	0	
Caudry-Nord	station	4	
Connection with CdN Cambrai–Le Cateau–Maubeuge–Charleroi			
Ligny	halt	6	
Clary	station	9	
Hurtevent	station	14	
Walincourt	station	14	
Malincourt	station	17	
Villers-Outréaux	station	19	
(boundary Nord and Aisne *départements*)			
Aubenchal-aux-Bois	station	21	
Le Catelet-Gouy	station	25	
Origin of MG Le Catelet–Bohain–Guise			
Bony	station	27	
Bellicourt	station	30	137 (449)
Nauroy	station	32	144 (472)
Estrées	halt	34	138
Joncourt	station	35	135
Levergies	station	40	
Le Tronquoy	station	45	
Lesdins	station	46	
Omissy	station	47	
Moulin-Brûlé	station	50	
St-Quentin-Cambrésis	station	50	106 (348)
(St-Quentin) St-Jean	halt	52	82
(St-Quentin) Monplaisir	*arrêt*	53	
(St-Quentin) La Tombelle	*arrêt*	54	
(St-Quentin) Rocourt	shared station	55	90
Connection with SG IL lines to Vélu & Ham			
St-Quentin-Nord	CdN shared station	57	75 (246)
Connection with SG CdN Paris–Brussels & SG IL line St-Quentin–Guise & SG IL lines to Vélu & Ham			

SG Standard gauge   MG Metre gauge
CdN *Compagnie du Nord*

on a bridge, and there was a connection with this line here, at Caudry-Nord station. The line then went south and crossed the departmental border between Villers-Outréaux (Nord) and Aubenchal-aux-Bois (Aisne) to reach Le Catelet-Gouy, which was the end of the line from Guise and Bohain. The line crossed the Escaut, which was here not very far from its source. It followed a sinuous course with some industrial links to the station at St-Quentin-Cambrésis. This station faced the Faubourg du Moulin-Brûlé. From here a tram route linked it with the town centre. From 1904 to 1914 the line went on round to the west of the town, joining at Rocourt the *intérêt local* standard gauge lines from Vélu and Ham, which it joined to cross the Somme and the Somme canal to reach St-Quentin-Nord, on the Paris to Brussels main line, and also the origin of the *intérêt local* standard gauge line to Guise.

3.4 The station at Rocourt, on the western edge of St-Quentin, before the First World War. The picture is taken from the level crossing over what is now the D930 Rue de Paris, with the standard gauge line to Ham and to Vélu on the left, and the metre gauge line to Caudry on the right. A standard gauge train headed towards St-Quentin Nord is standing in the station. Postcard written in German in July 1916 and posted at a German Army Field Post Office. *(Authors' collection)*

Engineering

The line from Caudry to Catillon was classified as a tramway, but the the line of concern here, from Caudry to St-Quentin, was built in its own path, mostly away from roads.

Rails

The track was constructed of Vignole rails at 20kg/m.

Dual gauge, and rail crossings on the level

The track was dual gauge at St-Quentin from Rocourt to St-Quentin-Nord, with the standard gauge *intérêt local* lines from Vélu and from Ham (see Chapter One).

Gradients and curvatures

The maximum gradient was 3 per cent with a maximum curvature of 100m radius.

Bridges

Before the First World War, there was a bridge to the south of Caudry-Cambrésis. It was just before Caudry-Nord where the line crossed the Busigny-Cambrai line. There was also a bridge over the Escaut river, near its source to the south of Le Catelet-Gouy and it shared with the Standard Gauge *intérêt local* lines from Vélu and Ham a bridge over the Somme and the Somme canal at St-Quentin (see walk 5, Chapter Twelve).

Stations and other stops

CFC did not build any common stations with CdN, except at St-Quentin-Nord. In other locations, they had their own stations. The one in Cambrai (not on this line) was extremely large and imposing.

Buildings

The stations followed a common pattern of linked one storey and two storey buildings. Naturally they differed in size and the arrangement of windows and doors. The larger stations, for instance that at Caudry, had imposing two storey accomodation, presumably for the station master, and an attached single storey building for passengers set alonside the track. The two storey building also had a small round feature under the eaves. The larger building was set at 90 degrees to the track with no doorway onto the platform. The smaller stations merely had fewer windows to both sections. The station name was on the side of the two storey building and the end of the one storey building.

Saint-Jean (St-Quentin) had a single storey building with its name on the track side. It had two doors and a window on the track side. It was sometimes called a *gare* although it was classified as a halt.

Track layouts

There was a transhipment facility at each point of contact with the Standard Gauge CdN lines, at Caudry and St-Quentin.

Depots

The depot and workshops for repair of rolling stock was at Caudry. There were sheds for locomotives at termini and at stations where trains had to turn round.

Narrow Gauge in the Somme Sector

3.5 A mixed train at Le Catelet-Gouy, on the line from St-Quentin to Caudry, hauled by Corpet-Louvet 0-6-0T of series 5-10 (1888-92) with an open cabin. This also shows the typical station building for this network. The locomotive has two buffers, therefore the photograph was taken before the First World War. *(Collection Bernard Rozé)*.

3.6 Bellicourt station from the road side, April 2016. *(Authors)*

Industrial links

The line had significant goods tonnage. This was fed by the sugar beet industry and the mining industries of lime (*chaux*) and coal. For coal, metre gauge wagons were loaded at Denain onto Standard Gauge truck transporters belonging to the mines of Anzin. They were then taken to the *fosse* Renard to be loaded with coal.

There were branches to various industrial and agricultural businesses. There was a line to a factory at Mont-St-Martin, at Bellicourt for a brick works and a *sucrerie* and one at Lesdins for a *râperie*. The branch about 2km (1¼ miles) long, which left the main line 1km east of Bellicourt station (in the direction of St-Quentin), was of particular importance in the closing stages of the First World War (see Chapter Eight, and walk 4 in Chapter Twelve).

Rolling stock

Until 1914, the line had rolling stock fitted with two buffers and central couplings. This was unusual for a metre gauge line in France. During the First World War, these were replaced by a central buffer with couplings below, but the continuous vacuum braking system was kept. Our description of the rolling stock below relates to the whole *Cambrésis* network.

Steam locomotives

The tramway from Cambrai to Catillon was set up with four 0-6-0T 12 tonne locomotives ordered from Fives-Lille. However, CFC, being part owned by Alfred Lambert, was mostly faithful to the firm of Lucien Corpet, later Corpet-Louvet and took delivery of twelve 0-6-0Ts as follows:

2 of 10 tonnes in 1880 and 1881 (No. 1 'L'Escaut' and No.2 'La Selle'). (Note the duplicated numbers with the Fives-Lille locomotives above)

6 of 15 tonnes delivered between 1888 and 1892 (No.5 'Clary', No.6 'Le Catelet', No.7 'Denain', No.8 'Quiévy', No. 9 'St.Quentin' and No.10 'Levergies')

2 of 15.8 tonnes delivered in 1895 (No.11 'Anzin' and No.12 'Douchy')

2 of 16.5 tonnes delivered 1899 (No.13 'Caudry' and No.14, taken from an order for Saône-et-Loire)

Shortly before the First World War, increases in traffic necessitated more powerful locomotives:

2x 0-8-0T from Jung (Germany) delivered in 1907 and 1911 (No.15 'Denain-Anzin' and No.16 'Valenciennes')

2x 2-6-0T from Piguet in 1912 (No.30 and No. 31)

2x 2-6-0T from Corpet-Louvet, 1 delivered in 1913 (No.33) and one retained in the factory until 1921 because of the First World War (No.32).

Passenger carriages

For the opening of the Cambrai–Catillon line carriages were ordered from the workshop of Chevalier. They were shareholders in CFC. Initially there were 15 x 2 axle carriages and 1 bogie carriage.

With expansion of the network there was a maximum of 48 carriages by 1911. Of those with 2 axles, some had compartments with side doors, and some had a central and an end platform. Those with bogies were of wood covered in sheet metal, with open end platforms, or, for a series of carriages for mixed 3rd class and baggage (*fourgon*), a closed intermediate platform.

Wagons

There were 52 goods wagons in 1881. This increased to 276 in 1888 and 309 by 1927. They included baggage vans, covered wagons, flat wagons, open wagons and some specialised types such as open coal wagons, tipper trucks and tank wagons.

Operations

At the beginning, CFC offered three passenger classes. In 1912, first class was stopped. Presumably this better reflected the demands of the service.

A summary timetable for May 1914 is shown in Table 3.8. There were two trains daily over the whole length of the line from Caudry to St-Quentin-Nord. There was, in addition one train from Caudry to St-Quentin-Cambrésis, two Le Catelet to St-Quentin-Nord, and one from Caudry to Le Catelet. The latter was marked 3rd class and ran from Caudry at 5.50am on weekdays only, clearly a workers' train. It was due to arrive at Le Catelet at 8.17am but the connection with the train to St-Quentin-Nord which departed 8.34am was not guaranteed.

There were two trains from St-Quentin-Nord to Caudry, two from St-Quentin-Cambrésis to Caudry, one at midday from St-Quentin-Nord to St-Quentin-Cambresis and one in the early evening from St-Quentin-Nord to Le Catelet. This shows that trains were based at St-Quentin-Cambrésis and Le Catelet as well as at Caudry.

The journey times from Caudry to St-Quentin-Nord were 3 hours 7 minutes and 3 hours 47 minutes. Layovers at Le Catelet were 15 minutes and 57 minutes and at St-Quentin-Cambrésis 13 minutes and 19 minutes. St-Quentin-Nord to Caudry took 3 hours 43 minutes and 5 hours 17 minutes. Layovers at St-Quentin-Cambrésis were 13 minutes and 2 hours

Narrow Gauge in the Somme Sector

Table 3.8 Caudry to St-Quentin (CFC)
Summary Timetable May 1914
Not all stations and other stops shown

			(1)				
Caudry-Cambrésis			05.50		09.42	13.00	16.14	20.08
Origin of CFC MG lines to Cambrai, Denain and Catillon								
Caudry-Nord	a		06.05		09.50	13.08	16.23	20.16
	d		06.35		09.57	13.10	16.35	20.32
Connection with CdN SG line St-Quentin to Cambrai								
Ligny			06.53		10.07	13.19	16.47	20.41
Walincourt			07.27		10.27	13.38	17.11	21.02
Villers-Outréaux			08.04		10.43	13.52	17.30	21.17
Aubenchal-aux-Bois			08.09		10.47	13.56	17.35	21.21
Le Catelet-Gouy	a		<u>08.17</u>		10.55	14.04	17.43	<u>21.29</u>
	d		06.40	08.34	11.10	15.01	18.25	
Origin of NF MG line to Bohain and Guise								
Bellicourt			06.54	08.48	11.24	15.14	18.41	
Nauroy			07.00	08.54	11.30	15.21	18.48	
Joncourt			07.09	09.01	11.38	15.29	18.57	
Lesdins			07.34	09.28	12.03	15.54	19.24	
St-Quentin (Cambrésis)	a		07.46	09.40	12.15	16.06	<u>19.37</u>	
	d		07.51	09.47	12.28	16.25		
Connection with No 1 tram route of St-Quentin, to and from St-Quentin Nord								
St Jean (halt)			07.55	09.51	12.32	16.30		
Rocourt			08.06	10.02	12.43	16.41		
Connection with CDA SG line to Ham, VBStQ SG line to Vélu								
St-Quentin (Nord)			08.12	10.08	12.49	16.47		
Connection with CdN SG line to Noyon and Bohain (Paris to Brussels)								
Origin of CDA SG line to Ham, VBStQ SG line to Vélu, SG IL line to Guise								
St-Quentin (Nord)				08.40	10.30	13.20		18.33
Connection with CdN SG line to Noyon and Bohain (Paris to Brussels)								
Origin of CDA SG line to Ham, VBStQ SG line to Vélu, SG IL line to Guise								
Rocourt				08.47	10.37	13.27		18.40
Connection with CDA SG line to Ham, VBStQ SG line to Vélu								
St Jean (halt)				08.57	10.48	13.38		18.49
St-Quentin (Cambrésis)	a			09.02	10.54	<u>13.44</u>		18.54
	d		06.30	09.15	12.55		17.00	19.39
Connection with No 1 tram route of St-Quentin, to and from St-Quentin Nord								
Lesdins			06.41	09.29	13.06		17.13	19.51
Joncourt			07.09	09.56	13.32		17.41	20.17
Nauroy			07.17	10.04	13.39		17.50	20.15
Bellicourt			07.23	10.10	13.45		17.57	20.31
Le Catelet-Gouy	a		07.35	10.22	13.57		18.09	<u>20.43</u>
	d		07.48	10.58	14.15		18.28	
Origin of NF MG line to Bohain and Guise								
Aubenchal-aux-Bois			07.56	11.06	14.23		18.36	
Villers-Outréaux			08.02	11.11	14.28		18.42	
Walincourt			08.21	11.27	14.44		19.00	
Ligny			08.40	11.46	15.05		19.12	
Caudry-Nord	a		08.49	11.55	15.14		19.30	
	d		09.05	12.15	15.39		19.38	
Connection with CdN SG line St-Quentin to Cambrai								
Caudry-Cambrésis			09.13	12.23	15.47		19.46	
Origin of CFC MG lines to Cambrai, Denain and Catillon								

(1) Weekdays only, 3rd class only   a arrive   d depart   underlined – terminates, not at the end of the line
IL   *Intérêt Local*   SG   standard gauge   MG   metre gauge
CdN   *Compagnie du Nord*
CDA   *Société des Chemins de Fer Départementaux de l'Aisne*
CFC   *Société des Chemins de Fer du Cambrésis*
NF   *Compagnie des Chemins de Fer d'intérêt local du Nord de la France*
VBStQ   *Compagnie du Chemin de fer de Vélu-Berlincourt à St.Quentin*

1 minute and at Le Catelet 26 minutes and 18 minutes. Passengers for the latter at St-Quentin-Cambrésis would have been well advised to take the No 1 tram from St-Quentin Nord to the Cimetière du Nord, which was just by St-Quentin-Cambrésis station.

Fares
In 1914, the fare for the whole length of line was 4 francs 21 centimes for second class, 3 francs 25 centimes for third class. At 7.4 cents per km second class, and 5.7 third class, this was slightly cheaper than the the Somme and Oise lines. There was no first class.

Tramways of St Quentin
The electric tramways of St-Quentin were standard gauge and opened in 1908. There were three lines:

1 Gare Nord (*Compagnie du Nord*) to Cimetière du Nord (adjacent to St-Quentin-Cambrésis metre gauge station)
2 Gare Nord (*Compagnie du Nord*) to Faubourg de l'Isle
3 Gare Nord (*Compagnie du Nord*) to Rocourt and Rémicourt

Depending on the times of the trams on line 1, it may have been quicker to join or leave trains on the line between St-Quentin and Caudry at St-Quentin-Cambrésis, and travel between St-Quentin-Cambrésis and the Gare Nord by tram. In any event, the tram would take you through the centre rather than round the edge of the town.

Guise to Bohain and Le Catelet (GBC)
This line connected with the line from St-Quentin to Caudry at Le Catelet. It only needs very brief mention, because part of the formation was used for a British Army light railway in 1918 (see Chapter Eight). The line crossed the main line from St-Quentin to Brussels at Bohain, and went on to Guise. It was 40km long and opened in 1900.

Roisel - Hargicourt
Plans were afoot to develop industry in the area between the Somme and the Aisne rivers. This area was rich in phosphate seams. It was also hoped to link the line of *Intérêt Local* from St-Quentin to Vélu (where it linked with Achiet–Marcoing line) with the Cambrésis MG line from St. Quentin to Caudry, on the Cambrésis network, at Bellicourt. The same gauge and the same concessionnaire were chosen, with Alfred Lambert receiving the concession in 1892. The 1892 plans for the link to Bellicourt shows it going round the north side of the village to join the St-Quentin to Caudry line at Bellicourt station, with a junction facing towards St-Quentin. This would have made the whole line 11.7km long, with at *arrêt* for a factory at Villeret at 8km. In the end this link was only achieved during the First World War with standard and 60cm gauge lines (see Chapter Eight).

Building and Opening
The line from Roisel to Hargicourt opened at the end of May 1894. Having not yet received the declaration *d'utilité publique*, it served only a private industrial function. Failing regularisation of its status, operations were suspended from August 1895 by decree of the *Préfet*. Lambert ceded the rights to a group of entrepreneurs and engineers, Michon, Grosselin and Morment. These obtained a new concession in 1899, with the approval of the *Compagnie du Nord*, followed by a declaration *d'utilité publique* in 1900. Nothing then prevented putting the track in usable state and the reopening, with passenger services, on 2 July 1901. Two months later the *Compagnie des Chemins de fer d'intérêt local du Nord de la France* (NF) officially took over the branch, with the technical support of the St-Quentin - Vélu company.

Description of the line
The line was 7.4km long. It started at Roisel (Somme *département*) with a station shared with the standard gauge line of *intérêt local* from Vélu to St-Quentin, and the Compagnie du Nord line from St-Just-en-Chaussée to Cambrai via Péronne. This was 77m (253ft) above sea level. Leaving the *intérêt local* line 1km north of Roisel station, the line went east to serve the industrial area, with mining operations for phosphates and lime, which had motivated its construction. Templeux-le-Guérard station was at 4.3km (2¾ miles), at 95m altitude. The line then entered the Aisne *département* in its last kilometre to reach the terminus at Hargicourt-Villeret, at 7.4km (4½ miles), and altitude 111m (364ft).

Stations
The two brick station builings at Templeux and Hargicourt were quite small. The main building had two storeys, but the only window upstairs was on the end away from the goods hall. The small goods hall was attached.

Depots
The passenger services began and ended at Hargicourt, and there was a shed for at least one locomotive there.

Industrial links
The branches for exploitation of phosphates and lime went to a number of quarries and factories. At Templeux-le-Guérard a branch north for 200m had a

3.7 The station at Templeux-le-Guérard, on the line from Roisel to Hargicourt. looking towards the village, with two wagons, before the First World War. *(Authors' collection)*

triangular junction just east of the station. There was no indication of this in 1901, and the branch was built some time between then and 1914. There was large group of quarries 1km west of Hargicourt station, and another group 1km east of the station, to which the line may have extended before 1914.

Rolling stock
Given the nature and history of the line not surprising that there was heterogeneous rolling stock.

Steam locomotives
The steam locomotives for the Roisel to Hargicourt line before 1914 are shown with those of the Noyon network in Table 3.4. For the start of services in 1894, Lambert moved 0-6-2T Corpet No. 4 (1890) from the Oise network and then, in 1895, purchased one 0-4-0T Hunslet (1879) from the Lecomte enterprise at Dunkirk.

In 1899, for the reopening, the new concessionnaire received another Corpet, No. 2, from the Oise network, then a 0-6-0T Corpet called 'La Vosgienne' purchased from the enterprise Giron & Roncol. However, the operations required more powerful locomotives, so they acquired two 17 tonne 0-6-0T Corpets, one in 1901 and the other in 1905.

Passenger carriages & wagons
The 'Rosario' rolling stock has already been descibed (see the Noyon lines in this chapter). The lot consisted of five passenger carriages, two first class, one mixed first and second class, and two second class. There were also two *fourgons*, ten covered wagons, and six open wagons. From 1895, the greater part of the goods stock went to the Roisel–Hargicourt line. In 1900, they were refurbished and fitted with continuous braking by the *ateliers Nord* at Tergnier.

The passenger carriages were transferred to the Roisel–Hargicourt line in 1901 for the beginning of passenger services. Four of these, two mixed first and second class and two all second class, were refurbished at the *Nord* workshops at Longueau (Amiens) before entry into service.

Operations
The mainstay of the line remained essentially the goods traffic, with only modest passenger activity. For passengers, there were four or five *navettes* (shuttles) per day each way, with accommodation in first and second class only. The journey time was 24 to 42 minutes. The pattern could be provided by one train set, starting from and finishing at Hargicourt, where there was a locomotive shed. The timetable for May 1914 shows five trains each way per

day, of which one is marked as a trial which did not run on Sundays, Mondays, feast days or the day after feast days.

Tergnier to Anizy-Pinon

This metre gauge electric tramway appears on some maps in the south of the area covered, but only needs very brief mention. From Tergnier the line crossed the forest to St-Gobain and then Anizy-le-Château. It was 31km (19 miles) long and opened in 1910.

Chauny to Coucy-le-Château, and the Soissons network links

These metre gauge lines also appear on some maps in the south of the area covered and are also peripheral to the story of the Somme sector, needing only brief mention. The line from Chauny to Coucy-le-Château was 30.5km long and opened in 1909. The link south to the line from Soissons to Vic-sur-Aisne at Montécouvé opened in 1910.

3.8 A tram on the line to St-Gobain and Anizy in the Boulevard Henri-Martin at Tergnier. Postcard written in 1912. *(Authors' collection)*

Chapter Four

Railways and light railways (60cm gauge) during the First World War (1914-1918)

It was inevitable that the railways of the north of France would play a vital role in supply and communication for the Allied armies As part of general mobilisation at the beginning of the war, the French Government had placed all railways in the country under military control. The British front lines from autumn 1914 to 1918 have already been described in the introduction. Figure 0.1 also shows the distribution of British, French and Belgian armies at various stages of the War. The British armies which were involved in the Somme sector were the Third, Fourth and Fifth. A brief statement of the changes to the British approach to railway transport from 1916 has also been given in the introduction.

There is a general map of railways in the Somme sector up to 1914 in Chapter One (figure 1.1), and there are railway overview maps near the beginning of Chapters Five to Eight. In 1915, there were some standard gauge lines behind the front line in this area, and the French Army were responsible for most of that front line. The main line north from Amiens to Arras was cut by the front line just north of Albert, and that from Amiens to Tergnier in the area of Chaulnes. From March 1916, with the build up to the 'big push' (the Battle of the Somme), the British Third and Fourth Armies were in the front line south to Maricourt, and the French Sixth Army south of that.

Line of railway command

The Battle of the Somme was the major stimulus for the appointment of Sir Eric Geddes and a Special Commission in August 1916, to consider the whole question of transportation for the British Armies in France. The Commander-in-Chief, Field-Marshal Sir Douglas Haig, wanted light railways used extensively along the whole British front, to help relieve the deterioration of the roads, and the need for manual labour by the troops. In October 1916, Geddes, who had been General Manager of the North Eastern Railway in Britain, was appointed Director-General of Transportation (DGT), with a rank of Lieutenant-Colonel and a headquarters near Montreuil. Later, in March 1918, the title of the Directorate of Transportation was changed to Directorate of Railway Traffic.

Railway Companies

Many RE and Dominion Railway Companies took part in work in the Somme sector during the First World War. Railway companies often moved with the Army to which they were attached, so that with the movement of the British Armies many units were in the Somme sector for only part of the war.

Before the beginning of the First World War there were only two regular RE Railway Companies, the 8th and the 10th, based at Longmoor Camp in Hampshire. There were also three special reserve Railway Companies, the 2nd and 3rd Royal Monmouth (2nd and 3rd RC RMRE) and the 3rd Royal Anglesey (3rd RC RARE) Railway Companies.

Later in the war, there were many more construction and operating Companies. The Companies of the Royal Engineers were numbered consecutively regardless of their speciality. Therefore reference, for instance, to the 296th Railway Company does not mean that there were more than 296 railway companies, but that there were more than 296 Companies of which the 296th happened to be a railway company. The exceptions were the light railway (LR) companies, which were numbered separately (see below). Canadian, Australian, New Zealand and South African railway troops were also available. The Canadians were organised into battalions, each consisting of four companies, which were often deployed on differing tasks, although usually in the same area. The skilled workers of the Engineers were supported by much larger numbers of less skilled workers. These included British and Indian Labour Companies, the Belgian, Chinese and Egyptian Labour Forces, and German prisoners of war (POWs).

Typically, a Railway company (RC) (RE) would be responsible for constructing and maintaining railways in a designated area. They were also responsible for operating their lines during construction, but later in the war, operations were handed over to the Railway Operating Division (ROD) when construction was complete. The work of the railway companies was mainly on standard gauge railways, but there was some work on metre gauge lines, which were included together by the British army as 'Broad Gauge' railways. A few Railway Companies were more specialist, for instance the 287th and 297th, which were bridging companies. In 1915 and 1916 there was some work on light railways (mostly 60cm gauge), but from later 1916, with the establishment of a Directorate of Light Railways, this was mostly undertaken by Light Railway (LR) companies.

The exception to this were the Battalions of Canadian Railway Troops (CRT), many of whom undertook broad gauge and light railway work, changing from one to the other at different times. The thirteen Battalions of CRT were formed between December 1916 and March 1918. One was formed in Halifax, Nova Scotia, seven in England (one at Bordon and six at Purfleet), and five 'in the field' in France. Some had previously been Pioneer or Labour Battalions, and one, 2nd CRT, an Infantry Battalion. In addition, in December 1916, the Canadian Overseas Railway Construction Corps were divided into the 1st and 2nd Canadian Overseas Railway Construction Companies (CORCC).

From 26 May 1918, Canadian Railway Troops were brought together as the Corps of Canadian Railway troops. These were placed under HQ CRT for administration, reinforcements, promotions, and other personnel matters. However, they remained under local orders within each army for day to day work. Units affected were the 13 Battalions of Canadian Railway Troops (CRT), the 1st and 2nd Tramway Companies, Canadian Engineers (TC CE), the 13th (Can) LROC, the 58th (Can) BGROC, 69 Wagon Erecting Co, 85 Engine Crew Co., and the 1st and 2nd Canadian Overseas Railway Construction Companies.

In all there were, by the end of the war, 32 RE Railway Companies on the Western Front, of which 12 served in the Somme sector. In addition, there were the 13 Battalions of CRT, a total of 52 Companies. There were also occasional railway units which were not officially part of the RE; in the Somme sector an example was the 17th Battalion Northumberland Fusiliers.

Groups of Railway Construction Companies, or Engineers

By April 1915, there were three Headquarters for groups of railway companies. Then and later, these variously called themselves at different times groups of 'Railway Construction Companies' or 'Railway Construction Engineers' using the abbreviation RCC or RCE, with roman numerals for their numbers. We have used the abbreviation most commonly used by each unit, and the roman numerals, throughout this book. In the end there were five such groups, RCC I-IV and RCE V. However, they did not relate consistently to the five British armies.

The three groups in existence by the end of April 1915, were RCC I, RCC III, and RCC IV. All were formed at the large British Army railway depot at Audruicq, near Calais. Although we know from other records that RCC I was formed by April 1915, there are no unit records until October 1917, and from then, and probably before, the group HQ served the First Army and was probably based at Barlin. The first RCC III served in the Second Army (Ypres) area, and in June 1916 was renamed RCC II. This group continued to work in the Second Army area for the rest of the War. Neither RCC I nor RCC II form part of the story of this book.

The three groups in the Somme sector were RCC III, RCC IV and RCE V. The groups were responsible for construction, repair and maintenance work on standard

Table 4.1 Somme Sector 1916-1918
Allocation of Groups of Railway Construction Companies/Engineers (RCC/RCE) to British Armies

	HQ based at (main locations)	*Army*	*from*	*to*
3rd Group RCC (RCC III)				
formed Audruicq 8 February 1915				
renamed RCC II 1 June 1916 (see text)				
(re)formed 20 February 1917	Doullens, Beaumetz-lès-Loges	Third	20 February 1917	5 January 1918
4th Group RCC (RCC IV)				
formed 15 April 1915				
	possibly Buire-sur-Ancre	Fourth	1916	16 July 1917
	Doingt (near Péronne)	Fifth	18 January 1918	March 1918
	St-Léger-les-Domart, Doingt, Aulnoye, Louvroil			
		Fourth	April 1918	July 1919
		Third	31 October 1918	July 1919
5th Group RCE (RCE V)				
formed 20 October 1916	Léalvillers, Grévillers,	Fifth	20 October 1916	31 July 1917
	Bernaville	Third south	1 August 1917	5 Jan 1918
	Grévillers, Bernaville, Acheux, Boisleux-St-Marc			
		Third	5 January 1918	30 October 1918
	Somain	First (east)	31 October 1918	March 1919

and metre gauge railways undertaken by railway companies working in their army area. In 1915 and early 1916, they had some part in the development of policy for light railways and trench tramways. After the establishment of the Directorate of Light Railways in late 1916, they maintained liaison with the Assistant Director of Light Railways (ADLR) for the army area in which they worked. Because the movement of these groups, and their relationship with the different armies, is complex, it is summarised for the groups involved in the Somme sector in Table 4.1.

The Railway Operating Division (ROD)

The Railway Operating Division (ROD) were an amorphous group of maintenance and operating railway staff. Officially part of the British Army, they were in fact under rather looser discipline, it being accepted that the main task was to operate railway services. In November 1915, they took over operating the line between Hazebrouck and Poperinghe, in the Ypres Sector. By January 1917, they had taken over all standard gauge and metre gauge locomotive operating on British lines and some on French lines, except advanced lines still under construction. They also operated some light railways, pending the formation of the Light Railway Operating Companies (LROCs).

French Railway Engineers

The French had an equivalent organisation of railway engineers. From 1889, the 5th Génie of French Military Engineers was entirely devoted to railway work. Before the First World War there were three Battalions each of four Companies. During the war this increased to 85 Companies, with 450 officers and 21,500 men, and up to 100,000 men as supporting labour, who included Chinese, Indochinese, and Malagasy personnel.

Metre gauge railways

The role of the metre gauge railways during the war has been estimated to be small. Col. Henniker in *Transportation on the Western Front* (1937) (pages 65 to 70) considered their important use confined to a few months in Spring 1918. Certainly in 1916, the decision was taken to develop 60cm gauge (light) railways, and to develop metre gauge railways only in relation to existing lines, and to link them. However, in the Somme sector, the metre gauge railways made a considerable contribution to the support of the French and British Armies in 1915 and 1916 (see Chapter Five). Later with the fuller development of new standard gauge lines and light railways, some utilising the paths of former metre gauge lines, they played less part. However, some did operate throughout the war.

Metre gauge locomotives

In September 1915, the War Department ordered ten 18 ton 0-6-0T metre gauge locomotives of *bicabine* (*Vicinaux Belge*) type, known in British railway parlance as 'tram engines'. In March 1916, a further forty were ordered. A further twenty similar locomotives of 26.5 tons were supplied by the American Locomotive Company (Alco) and were used with the Belgian Army north of Ypres. The metre gauge lines in the Somme sector were all properly engineered railways rather than tramways. No *bicabine* type locomotives had been used on these lines before the war, and we have seen no evidence of their use during it.

Light (60cm gauge) railways.

This gauge was made popular by the French Decauville Company in the nineteenth century. They developed a system of prefabricated light track with steel sleepers. It was widely used in France for shorter industrial

4.1 Lengths of prefabricated 60cm gauge 'Decauville' track stacked by a canal, somewhere on the Western Front. *(Pen & Sword Archive)*

lines, and for some public passenger and goods lines. Because of this origin, 60cm gauge lines and track are often known as 'Decauville' lines and track, even if not manufactured by them, or not prefabricated. Although sometimes loosely equated with the Imperial gauge of 2 ft (610mm), 60cm (600mm) is in fact 1ft 11⅝in. This is close to another gauge of some British lines, including the Ffestiniog and Welsh Highland railways, which are 1ft 11½in (597mm) gauge.

The French and the German armies quickly realised the potential usefulness of light railways for military purposes, and both adopted the 60cm gauge well before the First World War. The British army also recognised this, although rather later, and developed a system based on the 2ft 6in gauge. However it became clear that the use of a different gauge from the other armies would be unwise, and the 2ft 6in equipment was sent to the Suez Canal Zone. The term light railways usually refers to the 60cm gauge, but very occasionally smaller gauges (50cm or 40cm) were used for short 'trench tramways'. We have included a general summary to provide background. Light railways of 60cm gauge were also built and operated by the British Army in the First World War in Egypt, around Salonika (Northern Greece), and to a limited extent in Italy.

War Department Light Railways (WDLR)

By February 1916, there were increasing problems with roads breaking up and road transport getting bogged down in mud. Feeder lines of 60cm gauge between standard gauge railheads and the front were agreed. In March 1916, it was also agreed to use heavier rails, 20lb/yd (about 10kg/m), to allow mechanical traction. Some track, locomotives, and other rolling stock were ordered. Also, in March 1916, the British Third and Fourth Armies took over from the French some existing 60cm gauge lines in the Somme and Arras sectors. The (First) Battle of the Somme, which began on 1 July 1916, increased the pressure on transport and the difficulties on the roads, especially when the autumn rains came. By October 1916, the British were operating 130km of light railways, 49km taken over from the French. Motive power was mainly mules and men, and there were only about 20 locomotives and petrol tractors and 200 wagons. French and German light railways were much more advanced.

When Sir Eric Geddes arrived as Director-General of Transportation (DGT) in October 1916, he appointed a Director of Light Railways (DLR). It was estimated that 200,000 tons of goods per week needed moving from standard gauge railheads, and during intensive fighting this could reach 2,000 tons per mile of front per day. An Assistant Director of Light Railways (ADLR) was appointed in each army area, supported by a Light Railway Construction Engineer, and a Superintendent of Light Railways for operations. Later (in 1917) there were 2 ADLRs for the Third Army, ADLR III North and III South. It was the south of the Third Army area that was in the Somme sector. In early 1918, when the Fifth Army took over the long section of front line south to Barisis, this army also split the organisation between an ADLR V North and V South.

The DGT decided to establish a complete system of light railways behind the whole length of the front. The first order was for 1,000 miles of track, 700 steam locomotives, 100 petrol tractors and 2,800 wagons, and 25,000 men to construct and operate these. The track estimate was based on 10km per km of front for the 62km (39 miles) where intensive fighting was expected, and half that for the remaining 83km

4.2 German troops being transported towards the front line by light railway, in 1914. *(Authors' collection)*

(52 miles) of front, plus 25 per cent for contingencies and 200 miles (320km) in reserve. Later with greater line lengths behind the front, this was increased. 'Feeder' lines extended forward, linking the standard gauge railheads with the front. These would be in loops, linked by lateral lines at the medium and heavy artillery positions, so that if one line was cut by shell fire there would always be another route. Standard gauge railheads were at least 7 miles (11km), and often 10 miles (16km) or more, behind the front. At the other end, the light railways would extend to the beginning of the trench tramway systems (see below), about 3,000yd (2.5-3km) from the front line. Geddes remained in France as DGT until May 1917.

Construction of light railways was mostly undertaken by specialist railway troops supported by Labour Companies. However, many Operating Companies were called upon to construct part or all of the lines they were to operate, and most were expected to carry out maintenance and repairs. By the end of 1916, 95 miles (153km) were being operated, carrying 7,500 tons per week. Construction was slowed in early 1917 by very bad weather, with continuous frost for five weeks from the beginning of February. Track materials were not delivered from the UK in sufficient quantities until March 1917. From April to October 1917, about 110 miles (177km) of line were constructed each month. After the German advances of spring 1918, the average from early August to November 1918 was 61 miles constructed, and 163 miles reconstructed, per month. The reconstruction was mainly of former British lines recaptured, or of German lines captured. During this period in 1918, an average of 4,330 skilled and 4,610 unskilled men were employed on light railway construction. All of these figures relate to the whole British force in France and Belgium, not just to the Somme sector.

By September 1917, it had been agreed that there should be a north-south 'main' line, called a lateral route, behind the whole length of the British front line, and linking all the armies. This would allow transfer of goods and men without using the standard gauge lines and without transhipment. The first 'main line' was planned approximately 6,000yd (5.5km) behind the front line and was complete by March 1918. By this time, it had been decided to construct another about 12,000yd (11km) behind the front line, with further lines running back from this. This would allow light railways to bring goods from dumps and railheads further back, and to evacuate stock in the case of a German advance.

Light Railway Companies

For operations, Light Railway Operating Companies (LROCs) were recruited in England, and in the Dominions, or by taking men with the right background from other units in France. Recruitment began in England in January 1917, with the formation of the 1st LROC at Longmoor on 20 January. Eight further British LROCs (numbered 2-4, 6, and 9-12) were formed at Longmoor or the nearby Bordon Camp from 4 February to 17 May 1917. The 5th (New Zealand) LROC was formed at Codford Camp on 4 February 1917. We are not sure where the 7th and 8th (South African) LROCs were formed but both were in France by early summer 1917. The 13th (Canadian) LROC was formed at Aldershot on 9 June 1917.

Numbering of the Companies was often confusing, especially for the three Australian LROCs. These were originally variously named and numbered, but by the time they reached France, they were numbered in sequence with the RE LROCs as the 15th, 16th and 17th (Aus) LROCs respectively. The 15th was formed from professional railwaymen in Victoria, Australia in November 1916 and originally called the 'Victorian Railway Unit', probably later called the 1st Australian LROC before arriving in Europe. They arrived in France on 29 May 1917, moving to Belgium (Ypres sector) on 3 June. The 16th was formed in Australia on 21 March 1917, and originally called the 2nd Australian LROC. They arrived at Bordon Camp in England on 21 July 1917 and were renamed the 16th (Aus) LROC on 28 July. The 16th were in France from 6 September 1917, moving on to Belgium (Ypres Sector) on 26 September. The 17th were formed in France, at Fricourt Brigade Camp on 11 June 1917. They were formed from the 1st (Anzac) LROC which was disbanded at Fricourt on that date. The 1st (Anzac) were probably formed in France in December 1916, as the operating company for Anzac Light Railways. The 17th were initially known as the 17th (Anzac) LROC, but by early 1918 were the 17th (Aus). From 5 March 1918 the 15th, 16th and 17th became the 1st, 2nd and 3rd Australian LROC (Aus LROC) respectively. On 7 September 1918, the 3rd officially became the 3rd Aus. Light Railway Forward Company (Aus LRFC).

Companies with higher numbers (such as the 17th (Aus) LROC), were generally formed in France by 'combing out' suitable personnel from other support units and from the infantry. The 29th to 31st and the 33rd were formed at Boulogne in February and March 1917. The formation of the 31st is described by T.R. Heritage in *The Light Track from Arras* (2nd Ed 1999). The 32nd was formed 'in the field'. The 34th was raised from men of the XV Corps on 28 February 1917, in the Fourth Army area, as the XV Corps LR Troops, and renamed 34th LROC on 25 May 1917. The 35th were probably the first proper Light Railway Company, having been formed as the XIV Corps LR Company at Trones Wood on the Somme battlefield on

7 December 1916, and renamed the 35th LROC on 10 May 1917. Finally, the 54th LROC was formed 'in the field', almost certainly in the Somme sector, in May 1917.

In addition to the 13th (Can) LROC, the Canadians had two 'Tramway Companies'. The Canadian LROC was formed from the No1 Section Canadian Corps Tramway Company on 14 November 1917, at Lens Junction (Arras Sector). No2 Section became the Canadian LR Construction Company. In early 1918, they became the 1st and 2nd Tramway Companies, Canadian Engineers (TC CE) respectively. They mostly supported the Canadian Corps in the First Army, but 1st TC CE spent a short time in the Somme Sector in August 1918 (see Chapter Eight). They were not Tramway Companies in the sense of Trench Tramways, and did operate more forward sections of LRs, with petrol tractors but not steam locomotives as motive power. This served to a large extent as a model for the LR Forward Companies formed later in 1918 (see Chapter Eight).

The LROCs were supported by five LR Train Crew companies (TCCs), numbered the 18th to the 22nd. At least three were formed in England, the 19th and 20th at Bordon Camp in February and March 1917 respectively, and the 22nd at Longmoor Camp in May 1917. In some cases, these were closely associated with particular LROCs. By summer 1917, the 19th TCC had been split up, with men supporting the 4th, 6th and 9th LROC, But in later 1918, the 19th was reformed as an LROC, operating independently until early 1919. The 18th TCC also became a 'proper' LROC.

There were two companies of miscellaneous trades, the 23rd and 24th, three Workshop companies, the 25th to 27th, and one tractor repair company, the 28th. These were based mostly at the Central LR Workshops, initially at La Lacque and later at Beaurainville.

A typical LROC consisted of between 220 and 260 men, most commonly about 250. Of these about eighty-five would be train crews, forty telephone and control post operators, thirty on station yard and traffic duties, fifty to sixty on shed duties (repairs and maintenance), and the rest in support roles.

In addition, there were four United States Regiments for the construction and operation of light railways, the 12th, 14th, 21st, and 22nd US Engineers. Of these the 14th worked with the British Army at Boisleux and Pozières until May 1918, and the 12th in the Somme valley until July 1918, after which they joined the main force of US infantry further south.

Telephones and other signals services were provided by Army Signals. More detail of rolling stock is given in the next section, but in general steam locomotives were used further away from the front line, and petrol or petrol electric locomotives were used nearer the front where the greater visibility of steam locomotives, from the smoke and steam during the day or visible fire at night, would be a hazard.

The LR Companies which were not formed in France and Belgium usually arrived in France through the port of Le Havre, before deployment to an army and sector in France or Belgium. Near Le Havre and Rouen there were major RE railway works and facilities, and an Australian Base Depot. After the War most were demobilised through Le Havre.

Trench Tramways

From October 1915, the British Army on the Western Front sanctioned short narrow gauge lines known as trench tramways. These were mostly of 60cm gauge but occasionally 40cm and 50cm gauge. These lines were laid to bring goods into the trench areas using trolleys, usually manually propelled. There were no locomotives, and the rails were very light, 9lb/yd (4.5kg/m), or sometimes made of wood. These tramways were also sometimes called 'push car lines', especially by the Canadians. Supplies were brought to standard gauge railheads as close to the front as practicable, and the goods moved from there to the trenches or trench tramway ends by horse and cart or motor lorry. British trench tramways were initially built and operated on an *ad hoc* basis by individual army units.

At the beginning of major light railway development in 1916, it was decided that although the light railways should extend to the end of the trench tramway systems, they should not be joined. The very light rails made them unsuitable for the light railway rolling stock. However, this policy led to the need to have transhipment points, some under enemy observation. Ammunition for heavy guns was delivered by light railway to group stations from which it was distributed by hand trolley along numerous spurs. Other goods were delivered to bulk delivery points, with tramways beyond.

By autumn 1917, ten Army Tramway Companies (RE) had been formed on a divisional basis. The main work was laying tramlines from light railway group stations to heavy batteries as they moved forward and salvaging the tramlines from battery positions as they were vacated. In later 1917, some tramways were allowed a light railway connection, but only four wheel wagons were allowed to travel through from one to the other. A large number of 1 ton, four wheel box wagons were provided to the tramways, and some low power petrol tractors, mainly the 10hp tractors built by McEwen and Pratt. Selected tramways also received the heavier rails, allowing use by bogie wagons, and some were effectively absorbed into the light railway systems. Towards the end of 1917, some men from the Tramway Companies were sent to the Light Railway

Workshops at La Lacque, near Isbergues, for training on petrol tractors.

After the difficulties experienced with this model of trench tramways during the Third Battle of Ypres in 1917, it was decided in early 1918 to reform the Tramway Companies. The new companies were initially known as Forward Transportation Companies, but by February or March 1918 they had been named Foreways Companies (FWC). A depot was set up at Savy-Berlette, later renamed the Forward LR Training School.

Track

French track of Decauville type was supplied in lengths already riveted to steel sleepers. British track of light railway weight was supplied loose, mostly in lengths of 5m, but with some of 2.5m and 7.5m. This could be clipped onto steel sleepers before being laid but could also be spiked down onto wooden sleepers. Because of the tolerance of the gauge to sharp curves, heavy earthworks were usually avoided. On average, it took 2,000 man days, 75 per cent unskilled, to construct and ballast 1 mile (1.6km) of track. Maintenance could require up to twenty men per mile in forward areas vulnerable to damage.

Ballast for the track was provided from various sources. Some was obtained from the rubble of ruined buildings. In the Somme sector, much ballast was chalk, obtained from chalk pits along the lines. One disadvantage of this was the visibility of white chalk from the air, and this sometimes had to be camouflaged.

Rolling Stock

In 1916 and early 1917, some mules were used. The British also used some French locomotives, taken over with the early French lines in the Arras sector in 1916, and later some captured German locomotives. These were mostly 0-8-0T locomotives of *Feldbahn* type.

Steam and petrol locomotives were ordered by the British Army in small numbers in early 1916 and in increasingly large numbers after that. Petrol mechanical (PM) and petrol electric (PE) locomotives were known by the British Army as tractors, and we have used this term for them. We have given technical details of the principal types of steam locomotive used in Table 4.2, and of petrol tractors in Table 4.3. In these tables we have used Imperial units, except where otherwise indicated, because these are the units in which most of these locomotives were designed and built. The numbers given are those put into service in France. More were produced. Some of these went to other fronts, and some had not been delivered when the war ended. We have included in Table 4.2 details of the Péchot-Bourdon locomotive, and the 8 tonne 0-6-0

4.3 A pile of preconstructed lengths of light rail on metal sleepers is carried slung across two 2 axle (4 wheel) wagons, near High Wood, October 1916. The motive power is a Simplex 20hp tractor, which looks quite new, and at this early stage is marked ROD (Railway Operating Division). *(IWM Q4381)*

Railways and light railways (60cm gauge) during the First World War (1914-1918)

4.4 An Orenstein and Koppel 0-8-0T of German Army *feldbahn* type on display at the CFCD museum at Froissy, May 2016. *(Authors)*

Table 4.2 Technical details of British and French Army Light Railway Steam Locomotives 1914-1918

Manufacturer		Hunslet	Baldwin	Alco-Cooke	Hudson	Barclays	Péchot	Decauville
Country		UK	USA	USA	UK	UK	France	France
Dates(s) of	from	08.1916	10.1916	02.1917	06.1916	early 1917		1914
manufacture	to	09.1917	04.1917	05.1917	08.1917			1918
Wheel configuration		4-6-0T	4-6-0T	2-6-2T	0-6-0WT	0-6-0WT	0-4-4-0T	0-6-0T
Number put in service in France		75	495	100	32	25		390
Length inc. buffers (ft-ins)		19-10¾	19-6⅛	22-1½	15-5¼	14-8⅜	19-8	15-6⅛
Height (ft-ins)		8-11½	9-3¼	8-10½	8-6	8-4⅝	8-5½	5-3¾
Width (ft-ins)		6-3½	6-11	6-9	5-8	5-3	6-8	8-6¼
Weight empty (tons)		10.90	11.04	13.39	5.76	5.13	12.59 (12.79 tonnes)	8.2
Weight loaded (tons)		14.05	14.50	17.19	6.85	6.38		10.4
Wheelbase (ft-ins)		13-0	12-2	16-6	4-2	4-4	12-7 (2.3 m)	4-7⅛
Driving wheelbase (ft-ins)		5-6	5-10	5-6	4-2	4-4	(2 of 2-11½) (0.9m)	4-7⅛
Diam. of driving wheels (ft-ins)		2-0	1-11½	2-3	1-11	1-10	2-1½ (0.65 m)	1-11⅝
Boiler pressure (lb per sq inch)		160	178	175	180	160	12 Kg/cm^2	178
Heating surface (sq ft)		205	254.5	262	126	131	26.99 m^2	188.8
Water capacity (gallons)		375	396	395	110	110	1514 L	264
Coal capacity (cwt)		15	15.7	15	3.5	3.5	400 Kg	10
Diam. of cylinders (inches)		9½	9	9	6½	6¾	6⅞ (175 mm)	8½
Piston travel (inches)		12	12	14	12	10¾	9½ (240 mm)	11
Centre of gravity (ft-ins) Above track level - loaded		2-10½	3-0	2-10	2-7½	2-9½		

T	side tanks WT well tanks
Hunslet	Hunslet Engine Company Ltd, Leeds, England Baldwin Baldwin Locomotive Company, Philadelphia, USA
Alco-Cooke	American Locomotive Company, USA (constructed at Cooke Locomotive works)
Hudson	R Hudson Ltd, Leeds, England (construction subcontracted to Hudswell Clarke)
Barclay	Andrew Barclay Company Ltd, Kilmarnock, Scotland
Péchot	Péchot-Bourdon, plus 280 manufactured for the French Army by Baldwin, USA
Decauville	Decauville, including 70 manufactured for the French Army by Kerr Stuart, Stoke-on-Trent, England (the 'Joffre' class)

4.5 Hudswell-Clarke (Hudson) 0-6-0WT (well tank) locomotive, WD No. 102, near Fricourt in November 1916. *(Collection John Scott-Morgan)*

4.6 Hunslet 4-6-0T WD No. 302 with a train of bogie wagons at an unknown location on the Western Front. There are troops of a Scottish Regiment behind, possibly waiting to board the train. *(Collection R. Blencowe)*

Decauville locomotive, the main locomotives used by French Army light railways.

The light locomotives, with well tanks located between the wheel frames and with a low centre of gravity, were used mainly for yard work. Of the heavier locomotives, those from Hunslet were ordered first, but when it became apparent that they could not meet the demand, a larger order was placed with Baldwin in the USA. Steam locomotives on light railways required watering points every 5 to 8 miles (8 to 13km) and coaling every 20 to 30 miles (32 to 48km). The 4-6-0 locomotives were liable to derail when running tender first, but less when the quality of the track improved later in the war. However, the 2-6-2 Alco-Cooke (Alco) locomotives were still found best when running tender first. Later in the war, Baldwin also produced 2-6-2 locomotives, but only for the American Army.

The Péchot-Bourdon was the main locomotive used by French Army light railways. A double ended 0-4-4-0 side tank locomotive of Fairlie type, it was developed by Captain Péchot of the French artillery, and they had sixty-two by 1914. During the war, 280 were built for the French Army by the Baldwin Locomotive Company in the USA. The French also used 8 tonne 0-6-0 tank locomotives of

4.7 Baldwin 4-6-0T WD No. 883 at an unknown location on the Western Front. *(Collection R. Blencowe)*

4.8 Alco TPT/AMTP No. 3-22, works No. 57131, WD No. 1240, is preserved in static display at AMPT at Pithiviers. September 2015. *(Authors)*

Decauville type. Between 1914 and 1918, 320 of these were delivered to the French Army by Decauville. A further 70 were supplied to the French by Kerr Stuart of Stoke-on-Trent, England (the 'Joffre' class).

Petrol tractors (see Table 4.3) were needed for the forward area lines, for their greater flexibility on track which might be of poorer quality, and their ability to avoid enemy observation. Of these, both the Simplex type and the petrol electrics were excellent, but the latter had longer wheelbases, and they were said to be slow. There were only minor differences between the Dick Kerr and the British Westinghouse types. The former had fixed side openings ('windows') on the cab, and louvres on the sides of the engine compartment, which the latter did not have. On both, the cab entrance was at the back.

The McEwan and Pratt 10hp tractors were intended mainly for trench tramways, and very forward spurs. In practice, they were found to be under-powered. In the end they were mainly used in yards, and in forestry areas. The Crewe tractor was designed around a Model T Ford engine and chassis, with interchangeable road and railway wheels. It did not perform adequately on light railways.

4.9 A Péchot-Bourdon 0-4-4-0T locomotive at a French Army supply dump. *(Authors' collection)*

4.10 'Joffre', Kerr Stuart Joffre Class 0-6-0T works number 2405 of 1915, owned and restored by the West Lancashire Light Railway, at Froissy, 7 May 2016. *(Authors)*

The 20hp Simplex tractors (see picture 4.3) were all open to the elements. The 40hp Simplex tractors were supplied in three types. The 'open' type had some protection at the front and back and on top. Eighty-four were supplied to France but some were subsequently converted. Twenty were built as 'armoured', and a few more, perhaps seven, were converted from the 'open' type. When the side doors were closed these were said to be unbearably hot inside. The compromise was the 'protected' type, with side doors but more opening

Railways and light railways (60cm gauge) during the First World War (1914-1918)

4.11 Motor Rail Simplex 40hp PM tractor of 'Protected' type, WD number 3090 at Apedale Valley Light Railway on 13 May 2016, during the 'Tracks to the Trenches' event. This locomotive is owned by the Moseley Railway Trust. *(Authors)*

Table 4.3 Technical details of British Army Light Railway Petrol Tractors 1916-1918

Manufacturer			Simplex PM	Simplex PM (1)	Dick Kerr PE (BW PE)	McEwan & Pratt	Crewe Tractor (Ford)
Horse power			20	40	45	10	20
Dates (s) of	from		2.1916	5.1917	2.1917	6.1917	1916
manufacture	to		11.1918	late 1918		6.1918	1917
Wheel configuration			4 wh (2 axle)	4 wh (2 axle)	0-4-0	0-4-0	4 wh (2 axle)
Number put in service			749	292 (2)	DK 100 BW 100	42	132
Length over buffers (ft-ins)			8-11	11-1½	15-1	9-0¼	11-0
Height (ft-ins)			4-4¾ (or 4-6)	7-8	8-8	8-3¾	5-0⅛
Width (ft-ins)			4-10	6-6	5-6	3-6	4-10½
Weight empty (tons)			1.68	5.73	7.50	0.95	
Weight loaded (tons)			1.93 (3)	6.00 (3)	8.00	1.89	1.07
Wheelbase (ft-ins)			3-6½	4-0	5-6	3-0	4-5
Diam. of wheels (ft-ins)			1-5¾	1-6	2-8	1-6	
Engine			Dorman 2JO	Dorman 4JO	Dorman 4JO	Baguley	Ford model T
Cylinders Number			2	4	4	2	4
Diameter			4 5/16 (ins)	120 (mm)	120 (mm)	4 (ins)	3¾ (ins)
Stroke			5½ (ins)	140 (mm)	140 (mm)	5 (ins)	4 (ins)
Cooling			Water	Water	Water	Water	Water
Petrol capacity (gallons)				26	40	24	

(1) details are for the 'open' type (see text)
(2) all types (see text)
(3) includes 12 stone driver

Simplex	Motor Rail & Tramcar Company, Simplex Works, Bedford, England
Dick Kerr	Dick, Kerr and Company, Preston.
BW	Those made by British Westinghouse were very similar (see text)
McEwan & Pratt	McEwan, Pratt & Company (taken over in 1913 by Baguley Cars), London and Baguley Works, Burton-on-Trent, England
Crewe Tractor	London & North-Western Railway Works, Crewe

around the top than the 'armoured' type. One hundred and eighty-eight were supplied to France, and some more produced by conversion.

Wagons were supplied by British manufacturers in a variety of types, listed in table 4.4. The open bogie wagons with sides were able to carry heavy loads of shells, one of their main uses. Special wagons were used to carry some types of artillery. The light P class wagons with slatted sides were for rations and could be moved on trench tramways, either by hand or by light tractor. As a rough guide, it was reckoned that bogie wagons would carry thirty men, or ten tons of ammunition, eight tons of ballast, or five or six

Table 4.4 Technical details of British Army Light Railway Wagons 1916-1918

Class	Type	Wheels	Length Over buffers (ft-in)	Centre of wheels or bogies (1) (ft-in)	Tare (tons)	Maximum load (tons)	Cubic capacity (cu ft)
A	6ft open box, fixed sides and ends	4, 2 axle	8-11½	3-0	0.834	3.666	60
A	6ft open box, loose sides and ends	4, 2 axle	8-8	3-0	0.864	3.636	60
A	6ft open box, folding sides and ends	4, 2 axle	8-8	3-0	0.900	3.600	43
B	8ft open box, loose sides and ends	4, 2 axle	10-8	3-0	0.975	3.525	80
C	12ft open bogie, fixed sides and ends	8, 2 bogie	16-5½	8-0	1.975	7.025	122
C	12ft open bogie, loose sides and ends	8, 2 bogie	16-5½	8-0	1.960	7.040	122
D	17ft open bogie, falling side doors	8, 2 bogie	20-6½	13-9	2.250	9.750	175
E	17ft well bogie, centre falling doors	8, 2 bogie	20-6½	13-9	2.600	9.400	225 (2)
F	17ft well bogie, detachable stanchions	8, 2 bogie	20-6½	13-9	2.100	9.900	323 (3)
H	17ft bogie tank	8, 2 bogie	20-6½	13-9	3.938	8.700	1500 (4)
K	double sided tipper wagon	4, 2 axle	5-6	1-10			18
L	American side dump car 6ft in inside	4, 2 axle		2-10			40
N	hopper wagon, 6ft 9in inside	4, 2 axle		3-6			
P	light wagon, slat sides and ends (push use only?)	4, 2 axle	6-6 (inside)	2-6	0.425		36, 50 if piled
R	ration wagon, push and tractor use	4, 2 axle				1 (notional)	
	bogie workshop wagon (5)	8, 2 bogie	20-6½	13-9			
	covered goods, ambulance fittings	8, 2 bogie	23-3½	16-6	4.500	7.500	605

(1) The internal wheelbase of all bogies was 3ft 0in
(2) 167 cu ft if not using well
(3) assumed, 265 cu ft if not using well
(4) gallons
(5) 3 falling side doors, or double swing doors, or workshop office wagon with windows

4.12 Restored WD D class bogie wagon L.R.2574 at Froissy, 7 May 2016. Behind is a Decauville 0-6-0T of 1916, owned by CFCD. This was the model on which the 'Joffre' class was based. *(Authors)*

Railways and light railways (60cm gauge) during the First World War (1914-1918)

4.13 Restored WD water tank wagon L.R.7092 at Tacot des Lacs, November 2015. *(Authors)*

tons of most other materials. Box wagons with four wheels would carry ten men, four tons of ammunition, three tons of ballast, or two tons of most other materials.

In spring 1918 it was estimated that 19 per cent of steam locomotives and 25 per cent of petrol tractors were in maintenance or under repair at any one time. However only 4 per cent of wagons were unavailable for these reasons.

Depots and Workshops

The central light railway depot and workshops were a resource for all the British armies. The initial depot and workshops were at La Lacque, near the standard gauge line between Isbergues and Aire-sur-la-Lys, and repair and maintenance work began there in March 1917.

Following the German Army attack on the plain of the Lys beginning on 9 April 1918, the depot and workshops were moved to Beaurainville, between Montreuil and Hesdin, on the standard gauge line from Étaples to Arras. The new facilities were repairing rolling stock by July 1918. The workshops at Beaurainville are fully described in *Narrow Gauge in the Arras Sector* (2015).

In addition to the fixed central light railway depot and workshops, one and later two standard gauge trains were fitted out as repair shops for light railway stock. Also, a 60cm gauge repair train was provided for each army. Each train consisted of a generating car, two machinery cars, a tools car, a stores car, and an office car.

Operations

The development of light railways under the British army on the whole Western Front is outlined in Table

Table 4.5 British Army Light Railway route miles and tonnage 1917 and 1918, Western Front (Belgium and France)

Month	miles operated	tonnage carried per week
1917		
January	100	10,000
June	360	95,000
September	600	208,000
December	700	160,000
1918		
March	920	250,000
May	350	100,000
August	500	160,000
November	650	50,000

4.5. This shows the rapid build up during 1917, with maximum support for the battles of that autumn. After a lull in the winter, the maximum mileage and usage was reached just before the German attacks and advances of March, 1918, (on the Somme), and April, 1918, (the Lys pocket). As the ground was regained, lines were built, rebuilt or repaired, but by the autumn the advances to the east were leaving the light railways behind.

Apart from ballast and other railway materials, half of the goods carried on light railways was delivered by them to the final destination. This included all heavy artillery ammunition, which was generally given first priority, and a little field artillery ammunition and RE stores, which were second and third priority. Of the other half, roughly one quarter was for the field artillery, not delivered directly, and one quarter was for the most forward trench areas, including water and rations.

With very few exceptions the light railways were single track. Traffic control was initially based on the methods used on the French lines taken over in March 1916, using verbal or written permission to proceed. Gradually, the British light railways established greater local and central control. For local control, manned control posts with or without signals were established at passing loops and junctions, often in dugouts if far forward. These were linked by telephone, and trains could only proceed with permission to use the next section, which might be given verbally or, at some busy places, by semaphore or colour light signals rigged up locally. Each LROC was responsible for operating 20 to 30 miles of track, which they did by telephone from a district control post, with a board showing the position of all trains. Very close to the front line, train control was the responsibility of a named Officer or NCO.

Central control was exercised from a control post for each army area. These were able to receive requests from each Army Corps through their Light Railway Officers, and reallocate motive power and wagons as needed. However, most train ordering and scheduling was done within each district control. Initially, there was no traffic between armies on the light railways. With the completion of a north-south lateral line in early 1918, GHQ was able to coordinate activity. One notable use of the light railways to transfer men from north to south is described by Col. Henniker in *Transportation on the Western Front* (1937). Following the German advance towards Amiens on the Somme front, from 21 March 1918, General Byng moved the British Third Army Headquarters to Bernaville, west of Doullens, on 25 March. The Deputy Director General of Transportation (Construction) also opened a headquarters there, with orders to acquire all possible railway construction troops to construct a second defensive line. The 60cm lines and the Lens-Frévent metre gauge line were used to bring men over the north-south lateral line from the Second and First Army areas, using a more direct route than the standard gauge lines and easing the burden on them. Another use of the north-south lateral line in 1918 is described later, in *A Journey* (Chapter Six).

Following the German advance on the Somme front beginning 21 March 1918, the north-south line was lost from near Bapaume to the south. After the further German attack north and south of the Lys river and canal, which began on 9 April 1918, it was also lost for a considerable distance on the plain of the Lys.

There were some well recognised causes of delay and disruption on the light railways. The obvious one was damage from shell-fire or aerial bombardment. Mostly this could be quickly repaired, but much manpower was needed to ensure this. Track was also damaged at times by lorries or tanks not using authorised crossing points, and by men using the track as a footpath. Delays in loading wagons at standard gauge railheads, and in unloading at the destination, were more tightly controlled as experience increased. Between November 1917 and August 1918, the productivity of motive power units trebled and that of other rolling stock doubled by reducing these delays.

Reorganisation from June 1918

From the end of June 1918, transportation came under the control of the Quartermaster General (QMG) of the British Army on the Western Front. One consequence was that construction of all railways, and ports, came under a Director of Construction. Probably the QMG was regaining 'territory' lost to Sir Eric Geddes as DGT in 1916. One might ask why it was thought worth bothering with such a reorganisation at that time, but in spring 1918 it was widely expected that the war would continue into 1919 or 1920.

Light Railway Forward Companies (LRFCs) would be formed, for construction, maintenance and operation in the forward areas, still under the Directorate of Light Railways. Forward Companies were seen as operating from the point of hand over from steam traction, at about 3½ miles (5.6km) behind the front line, to the limit of mechanical traction at about 1 mile (1.6km) from the front. Steam traction further back would continue to be the responsibility of LROCs. In this respect, the LRFCs resembled the existing Canadian Tramway Companies (TC CEs). There were to be complex regulations for inter-running, if this became necessary. Operations would be entirely with petrol tractors, mainly 20hp Simplexes, which would be fitted with a small cab. Wagons would be of 4 wheel (2 axle) type only.

Ten LRFCs were designated, the 231st, 232nd, and 234th to 240th (RE), and the 3rd Aus. LRFC, the latter formed from the 3rd Aus. LROC. In practice these were not formed until October 1918, when the events of that autumn overtook them anyway. Some functioned as tractor based LROCs after the Armistice, and some were used to support standard gauge railway units.

Light Railways in the Somme Sector

The detailed history of light railways in the Somme Sector during the First World War is given in Chapters Five to Eight, and that of 60cm gauge railways in the area after the war in Chapter Nine.

Chapter Five

Light and metre gauge railways of the Somme battlefields 1915 - 16 March 1917

Although the German Army reached Amiens briefly in 1914, the front line in the Somme Sector from later 1914 to early 1916 settled across the chalk uplands of Picardy. By 1916, both sides were dug into well defended positions.

The story of the British armies in the Somme Sector is that of the Third, Fourth and Fifth Armies. The British Third Army was formed in France on 13 July 1915 and took over from the French the front line south to Maricourt, on the high ground north of the River Somme and east of Albert. The Fourth Army was formed in France on 5 February 1916 and took over from the Third Army from Serre south. From Maricourt south was held by the French Sixth Army.

This chapter divides the history of railways, and particularly light railways, during this period into three parts: the first concerns the preparations for the Battle of the Somme; the second the Battle itself, from 1 July to 18 November 1916; and the third the period from then until the end of the German withdrawal to the Hindenburg Line, completed by 16 March 1917.

Preparations for the First Battle of the Somme

The later part of 1915 and the first part of 1916 was a period of preparation for the First Battle of the Somme, which began on 1 July 1916. This only involved the Third Army to a limited extent, based in the north around the villages of Gommecourt and Hébuterne. The Fourth Army from Serre to Maricourt was the main British unit at the beginning of the battle. The French Sixth Army held from Maricourt south, to near Chaulnes, on the main Amiens to Tergnier railway. In March 1916 the Headquarters of the BEF moved from St-Omer to Montreuil to be more centrally positioned behind the lengthening British front.

Railways

The British and French armies worked on the Standard Gauge railways, to improve the supply lines to the front. The French also undertook extensive light railway works, but the British did very little to develop the few French light railways and tramways already existing in the part of the front they took over from 1915.

The Somme battle front was chosen because it was the meeting place of the British and the French parts of the front line. It was hoped that an offensive here might take pressure off the French at the desperate battle at Verdun. It was not a good choice in supply terms. Railways to the Somme front came from around Amiens. Some of the lines into Amiens from the west and south were single track, impairing the service from the existing French Army main supply yards (*gares régulatrices*, regulating stations) at Creil and Le Bourget.

The Allied railways into the Somme Sector before the First Battle of the Somme are shown in Figure 5.1. There were two main standard gauge lines from Amiens. The first was the double track main line which before the war had run from Amiens to Arras and on to Lille, in use to just north of Albert. It supplied both the British and the French parts of the front but was only open to Aveluy. The second was the double track main line from Amiens to Tergnier, open as far as Rosières-en-Santerre, which supplied the French part of the front line.

Standard Gauge works

Most of the extra works on the existing lines were undertaken by the French. From the south, the French doubled the line from Creil to Amiens via Beauvais. In 1915, they doubled the line north from Amiens to St-Pol via Doullens and Frévent and in spring 1916, a chord was provided at Amiens near St-Roch station so that traffic could run through from Rouen towards Doullens. In spring 1916 the line from Longpré to Canaples was doubled.

The French also rebuilt the yards at Longueau, immediately east of Amiens, so that the supply streams for the British Army (Albert line) and the French Army (Albert and Rosières lines) could be separated. From January 1916, new larger stations and yards were installed along the line to Chaulnes, at Les Buttes, L'Equipée and Wiencourt.

The French are also said to have provided the major supply yard (*gare régulatrice*) for the British armies in this sector, at Romescamps (Abancourt) on the main double track line from Rouen to Amiens. Rouen and Le Havre were major supply ports for

Figure 5.1

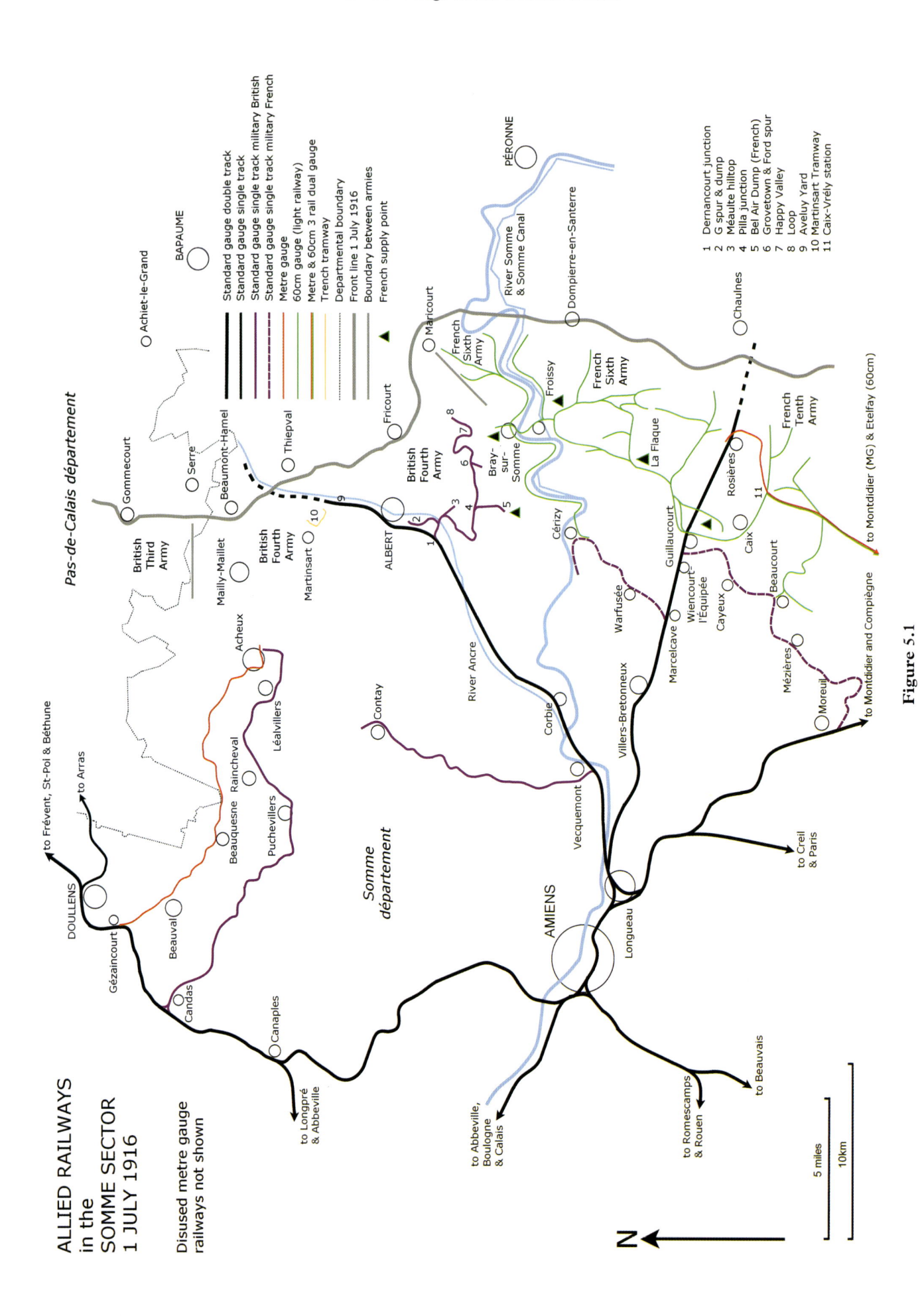

Light and metre gauge railways of the Somme battlefields 1915 - 16 March 1917

British troops on the southern part of the British part of the front from 1916 to 1918. The other major ports for British supplies, Calais and Boulogne, fed supplies down the main line south along the coast to Abbeville, the site of the other *gare régulatrice* for the British Somme front.

However, some works were done by British units, for instance extensions to the Yard at Vignacourt, on the Amiens to Doullens line. Here, two new sidings were built by the 3rd RC RMRE in April and May 1916. British units also built a large new railway yard at Aveluy, just north of Albert. Both the French and the British built additional military standard gauge lines in preparation for the battle.

British Military Lines
Candas to Acheux
In late 1915, it was proposed to convert the metre gauge line from Gézaincourt to Acheux to standard gauge, but in December the decision was taken to build a separate line. This single track line was built in early 1916, and was taken over by the ROD for operation on 1 April 1916. Further work was complete by June. Starting from Candas on the existing *Compagnie du Nord* line from Amiens to Doullens, it ran east through moderately hilly country to Acheux. The line was 17¼ miles (27km) long. There were many passing loops and sidings, and three major yards, used as supply rail heads. The first was at Candas, adjacent to the Amiens to Doullens line, which could serve as an exchange yard between French and British motive power. The second was at Puchevillers, a little over half way to Acheux. The third was at Acheux, where the line turned north to the yard adjacent to the existing metre gauge station. The line was already heavily used for supply trains before the start of the First Battle of the Somme.

Vecquemont to Contay
This was a British Army single track line 10 miles (16km) long, which began at a junction with the Amiens to Albert line just west of Vecquemont. It ran north and then somewhat northeast along the valley of the small River Hallue, to the village of Contay. The track was complete by the middle of March 1916. There were yards at Vecquemont near the junction with the main line, and at a large ammunition dump at Contay. Contay was in the back areas of the British front line, about 4 miles (6.5km) west of Albert.

Dernancourt to Loop (the Plateau Line)
Leaving the main Amiens to Arras line at Dernancourt junction (height 54m, 175ft), this is said to have been started in November 1915 as a series of gun spurs. It was extended on to the plateau to the east, for limited loads only, with quite severe gradients (maximum 3 per cent) and curves. By the beginning of the First Battle of the Somme on 1 July 1916, British units had built the line to the re-entrant valley called 'Loop', at 100m (330ft), where it crossed the metre gauge line from Fricourt to Montdidier. Many yards were built along the line, particularly in the valley around Méaulte, and a branch south from Pilla junction to a French rail head at Bel Air.

French Military Lines
Moreuil to L'équipée
Between 15 February and 23 June 1916, the French built a standard gauge single track link from Moreuil, on the Montdidier to Amiens line, to Wiencourt L'Equipée on the Amiens to Rosières main line, connecting these lines without going through Amiens.

Les Buttes to Gailly
This single track line was built between Les Buttes, on the Amiens to Chaulnes main line, north east to Cérizy (now Cerisy) and Gailly, on the Somme canal. This was opened on 24 June.

Metre gauge lines
Doullens - Albert
This line, behind the British part of the front, was entirely in Allied hands, but the eastern part between Acheux and Albert was exposed to enemy shelling. It was in use from Gézaincourt to Acheux in 1915 and 1916 before the Battle of the Somme. At the Doullens end the service terminated at Gézaincourt. The dual gauge section may have been removed when the line was doubled. Plans before the First Battle of the Somme included providing one train of ammunition per day at Gézaincourt for transhipment to the metre gauge and placing ambulance trains at Gézaincourt.

Albert to Péronne and Ham
This line was cut by the front line near Fricourt. It was not used on the British side of the front at this stage of the War. The German Army probably did use it. In general, the German Army used more military metre gauge lines than the allies. On plans before the beginning of the battle, there was a metre gauge German line down the valley past Mametz Wood, which had a junction with the Albert to Péronne line at Trones Wood.

Fricourt to Montdidier
The line from Montdidier north to Caix-Vrély and Rosières was used by the French for military traffic. An extra rail was laid into the metre gauge track to

73

make this section dual gauge with a 60cm light railway. At the southern end, a branch was built to the main light railway materials depot established at Etelfay, just north east of Montdidier, and headquarters of the French light railways for the Somme sector. North of Rosières, the line was disused.

Light Railways (60cm gauge)
At this stage of the war, the French army (and the German army) were way ahead of the British in developing light railways to supply the front line. This can be seen in Figure 5.1.

French Light Railways
During 1915, the French ordered 1,500km of 60cm gauge track for the Somme front. Deliveries began in April 1916, but only the first 500km had been delivered by the start of the 1916 Battle. Some metre gauge track from the line north of Rosières was also used.

Light Railway (60cm) lines were laid from the end of February 1916 to supply the French Sixth and Tenth Armies on the Somme front. Nine lines supplied the Sixth Army, who took part in the First Battle of the Somme with the British. These ran from just west of Chaulnes towards the north. Five lines supplied the Tenth Army, who held the front from Chaulnes south, not part of the 1916 offensive. For the Sixth Army, transhipment points were at Villers-Bretonneux, Marcelcave and Wiencourt-L'Equipée on the Amiens to Rosières line. For the Tenth Army, south of the Amiens to Rosières main line, transhipment points were probably at Guillaucourt, and where the light railways met the new Moreuil to Wiencourt line at Beaucourt. In May, General Foch insisted that the network must be finished for the start of the battle, originally set for 25 June. The whole was completed by that date.

British Light Railways
Although there were undoubtedly British Army trench tramways, man or mule hauled, in the British area of the Somme front before July 1916, we have very little evidence about these. Only one is shown on Figure 5.1. We have no evidence for proper light railways in this period. Although Hudson 0-6-0T Well Tank locomotives were supplied in limited numbers from June 1916, and Simplex 20 petrol tractors from February 1916 (ex works), few would have been available before the battle.

In November and early December 1915, a detachment of the the 3rd RC RMRE were based at Aveluy, building the 'Martinsart Tramway' for the 51st Division. They regarded this a particularly difficult piece of work, because of severe gradients, and the need to 'box the route in' for mule haulage. This tramway ran from Martinsart, near the metre gauge Doullens to Albert railway, for about 1 mile through Aveluy Wood towards the Aveluy to Beaucourt road. There were also trench tramways from Loop station toward the front line in the Fricourt area.

The First Battle of the Somme 1 July to 18 November 1916
This Battle is one of the best-known events of the war in the UK, ranking with Vimy Ridge (Arras) and Passchendaele (Ypres), both in 1917.

At the north end, Gommecourt and Serre were attacked by the British Third Army from the first day, with heavy losses, in what was really just a diversion. The British Fourth Army, under General Rawlinson, attacking from Beaumont-Hamel in the north west to Maricourt in the south east, had the eventual objective to reach Bapaume. On 1 July 1916, they were cut down by concentrated machine fire from posts which should have been inactivated by the week long preliminary bombardment. In the heaviest ever one day British loss in warfare, there were 57,450 casualties, of whom more than 20,000 were dead. In the south from Fricourt to Maricourt there was some breakthrough which was not properly exploited. The French Sixth Army under General Fayolle, whose objective was to take Péronne, also made immediate gains on a twelve mile (16km) front south from Maricourt to near Chaulnes.

The British army used the first tanks in warfare at the opening of the Battle of Flers-Courcellette on 15 September. During the autumn, the battle deteriorated into one of attrition in very wet and cold weather. The logistical supply nightmare that accompanied this, with roads sinking into mud, was a major stimulus for the British development of railways from later in 1916. From 1 November, the British Reserve Army became the Fifth Army (General Gough) and was put into the line between the Third and Fourth Armies for the final phases of the Battle.

Little progress was made between 1 July and 18 November anywhere north of Beaumont Hamel. There was some advance along the road from Albert to Bapaume, past Martinpuich and as far as Le Sars, two thirds of the way to Bapaume. The British advance was at most six miles on a ten-mile front, the French six miles north of the River Somme and four miles south of it on a twelve mile front. They advanced south of the river three quarters of the way to Péronne. In all the British and French gained 125 square miles for 420,000 British and 165,000 French casualties, but the German army also lost 650,000 men. It should be noted that the main French effort at the time was at Verdun (February to December 1916).

74

5.1 British troops pushing lorries through the mud. The light railway or trench tramway has been used for stacking shells. Location unknown but this was typical of the Somme front in autumn 1916. *(Pen & Sword Archive)*

Railways during the 1916 Battle of the Somme

The topography of the Somme battlefield is of river valleys (the Somme, the Ancre, and the willow stream through Fricourt) interspersed with plateaux. The highest of these, along the Albert to Bapaume road, reached more than 150m (490ft). This meant that in the early part of the battle British and French troops were attacking uphill. It also meant that in general, railways had to climb onto the plateaux from the existing lines in the valleys.

The period of the battle was one of intense railway development, particularly on the British front. Initially this was more standard gauge, but later the planning for light railways began to bear fruit. Following the appointment of Sir Eric Geddes as Director-General of Transportation (DGT) in October 1916 (see Chapter Four) his plans were swiftly implemented. Light railways (60cm gauge) began to be developed in greater numbers. More steam locomotives and petrol tractors also gradually began to arrive. There was a major conference on light railways at XIII Corps HQ (Fifth Army) on 7 November, but we have found no record of the discussions. General Gough (Fifth Army) had already written to the Quartermaster General in October, stating that sparing the roads by using the railways more had become a matter of extreme urgency.

Some use was made of existing metre gauge lines. For the rest of this section (during the First Battle of the Somme) and for the next section (after the Battle) railways are described in areas.

West of the Ancre Valley

This area, the main supply area for the north of the Somme Battle front, centred on the small town of Acheux-en-Amiénois, not far behind the front line at Auchonvillers. This area also stretches south to the Somme and the main Amiens to Arras railway at Vecquemont. Beaumont Hamel and the valley there were captured on 13 November, and Beaucourt in the Ancre valley, on the main railway line to Arras, on 15 November. Railways in this area during the First Battle of the Somme and up to 16 March 1917 are shown in more detail in Figure 5.2.

Standard gauge railways

Traffic on the existing lines became intense during the battle. On the line from Candas to Acheux, the heavy traffic in ammunition trains, troop reinforcements, and other supplies was supplemented by frequent ambulance trains. The line was being maintained by only half a Company, the 3rd RC RMRE. The other half was maintaining the Vecquemont to Contay line to the south. They said that they could scarcely cope. Later, when the autumn rains required more drainage to be dug, they were helped by POW labour, but in September there were two serious derailments of ambulance trains on curves in the middle part of the line. RCE V reported in October that the line was in 'deplorable' condition.

At the end of October improvements to the line were agreed, including doubling much of the line in loops more than 3km long. The 1st Bttn CRT arrived to undertake much of this work from the beginning of November. The developments were made more necessary by the increased traffic arising from the extensions of the line to the east (see next sections).

Narrow Gauge in the Somme Sector

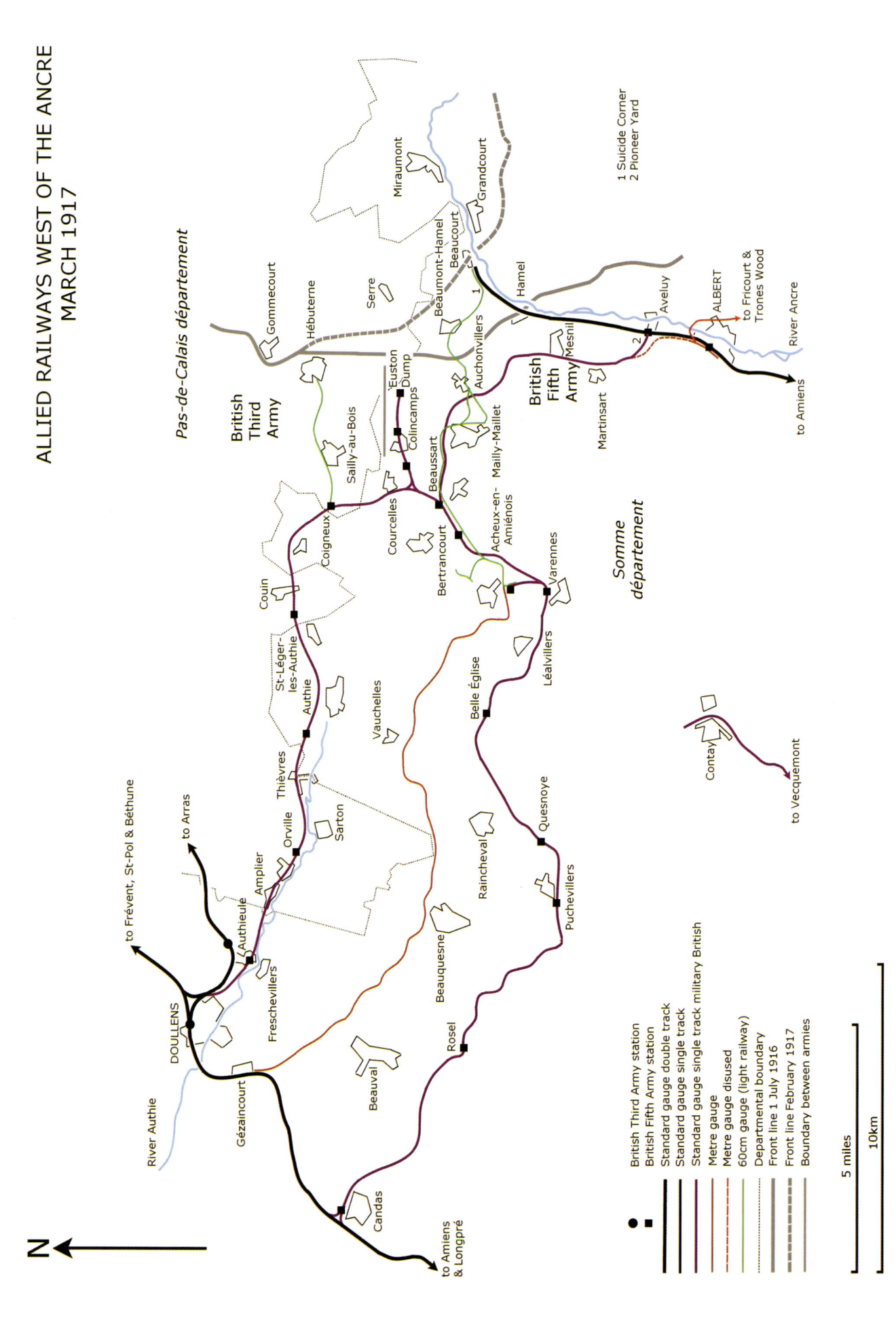

Figure 5.2

Varennes to Euston Dump (Colincamps)
The line from Candas was extended to Euston Dump just east of Colincamps. Work began in August 1916 and was complete by the end of September (119th and 277th RC RE). The line left the existing Acheux line at a junction near the station at Varennes, just south of Acheux, and ended not far behind the front line at Serre. Five miles (8km) long, the line was continually under heavy gun fire. Maintenance was initially taken over by 3rd RC RMRE, already overstretched on the Candas to Acheux section. In November, the supply rail head at Varennes was enlarged to hold supplies for two divisions.

Standard gauge petrol tractors were used on the line from Varennes to Euston Dump. Only one tractor was allocated, and from 5 to 9 November, breakdowns and accidents caused problems with the ammunition supply.

Beaussart to Aveluy
The existing metre gauge line from Doullens to Albert was at this time disused between Acheux and Albert. At Beaussart, north east of Acheux, the standard gauge station on the new line to Euston Dump was adjacent to the metre gauge halt. Between 10 and 30 October 1916, 277th RC RE, assisted by the 17th Bttn Northumberland Fusiliers, converted the metre gauge to standard gauge and left the metre gauge material lying by the track. In the valley just north of Aveluy, the standard gauge line left the metre gauge formation to join the main Amiens to Arras railway at Aveluy yard. Another yard, Pioneer or Pioneer Road yard, was built in the valley (figure 5.4). The metre gauge line from Aveluy into Albert remained disused.

The CRCE ordered RCE V to relay the metre gauge line in parallel with the standard gauge line now occupying the formation. RCE V, who had already stated why this was inadvisable, objected and the parallel line was never laid. The line was maintained and at least in November was operated by 277th RC.

Vecquemont to Contay
This line was now being maintained by half of 3rd RC RMRE, who were finding it difficult to cope. Throughout July 1916, heavy use by ammunition and supply trains, and ambulance trains, required long hours of work and continuous movement of working parties. In August, two new loops were constructed in 3 days for ambulance trains.

Metre gauge railways
Doullens to Albert
The conversion of the section of line from Beaussart to Aveluy into standard gauge in October 1916 caused a problem for metre gauge operations on the Albert to Péronne line, which was now in use to Fricourt and beyond. Because shelling made the use of the Albert station metre gauge workshops unsafe, locomotives and other rolling stock needing work had been transferred to the workshops at Beauval, on the Gézaincourt to Acheux line. This was no longer possible.

We know that the section from Gézaincourt to Acheux was in use, at least for military purposes. Among other things, it was used to take casualties from Acheux to Casualty Clearing Stations (CCS) at Beauval, a station on the line. Burials of soldiers in the Beauval Communal Cemetery extension (CWGC) are mostly from this period.

Light Railways
In October and November 1916 some preliminary work was undertaken in the Acheux area for a line or lines towards the front line. However, RCE V thought the project inadvisable, and work was discontinued. Further work was done after the 1916 Somme Battle (see below).

East of the Ancre and north of the Albert to Bapaume Road
This was the area of some of the heaviest fighting during the First Battle of the Somme in 1916. On the first day, La Boisselle, on the main Albert to Bapaume road, was captured, but only a small triangle of territory north of the road had been taken in the first two weeks, around Ovillers. By the middle of September, Pozières, on the main road, had been taken after a long struggle. Thiepval and Courcelette were not captured until later in September. By the end of the battle, British forces had also taken St Pierre Divion, on the east side of the Ancre. The furthest extension along the main road was to the chalk mound called the Butte de Warlencourt, situated just on the Bapaume side of Le Sars. Railways in this area during the First Battle of the Somme and up to 16 March 1917 are shown in more detail in Figure 5.3.

Standard Gauge Railways
Aveluy and Pioneer (Road) Yards
During the 1916 Somme battle, the yards at Aveluy, at the north end of the useable section of the main line from Amiens, were maintained and extended. There were standard gauge steam locomotives and petrol tractors at Aveluy, the latter probably to operate the line to Mouquet Farm (see below). In September 1916, with the construction of the light railway to Pozières, Aveluy yard also became a transhipment yard for the light railway. Detail of these yards is shown in Figure 5.4.

Narrow Gauge in the Somme Sector

ALLIED RAILWAYS
ANCRE VALLEY AND EAST OF THE ANCRE
AND NORTH OF THE ALBERT-BAPAUME ROAD
MARCH 1917

1. Martinsart tramway 1915
2. Lancashire dump
3. Ancre valley line, Parsley dump
4. Thiepval wood
5. Thiepval Château
6. Danube post
7. Mouquet Farm
8. Rifle dump
9. Pozières windmill
10. Centre Way dump
11. K dump
12. Tulloch's corner
13. Nab (Blighty) Valley
14. Donnet(t) Post
15. Crucifix Corner
16. Aveluy yard
17. Pioneer yard
18. Usna Valley
19. Usna Hill
20. Mash Valley
21. Tara Hill
22. Sausage Valley

Legend:
- Supply dump
- Standard gauge double track
- Standard gauge double track, disused
- Standard gauge single track military British
- Metre gauge
- Metre gauge disused
- 60cm gauge (light railway)
- Trench tramway
- Departmental boundary
- Front line 1 July 1916
- Front line February 1917

5 miles

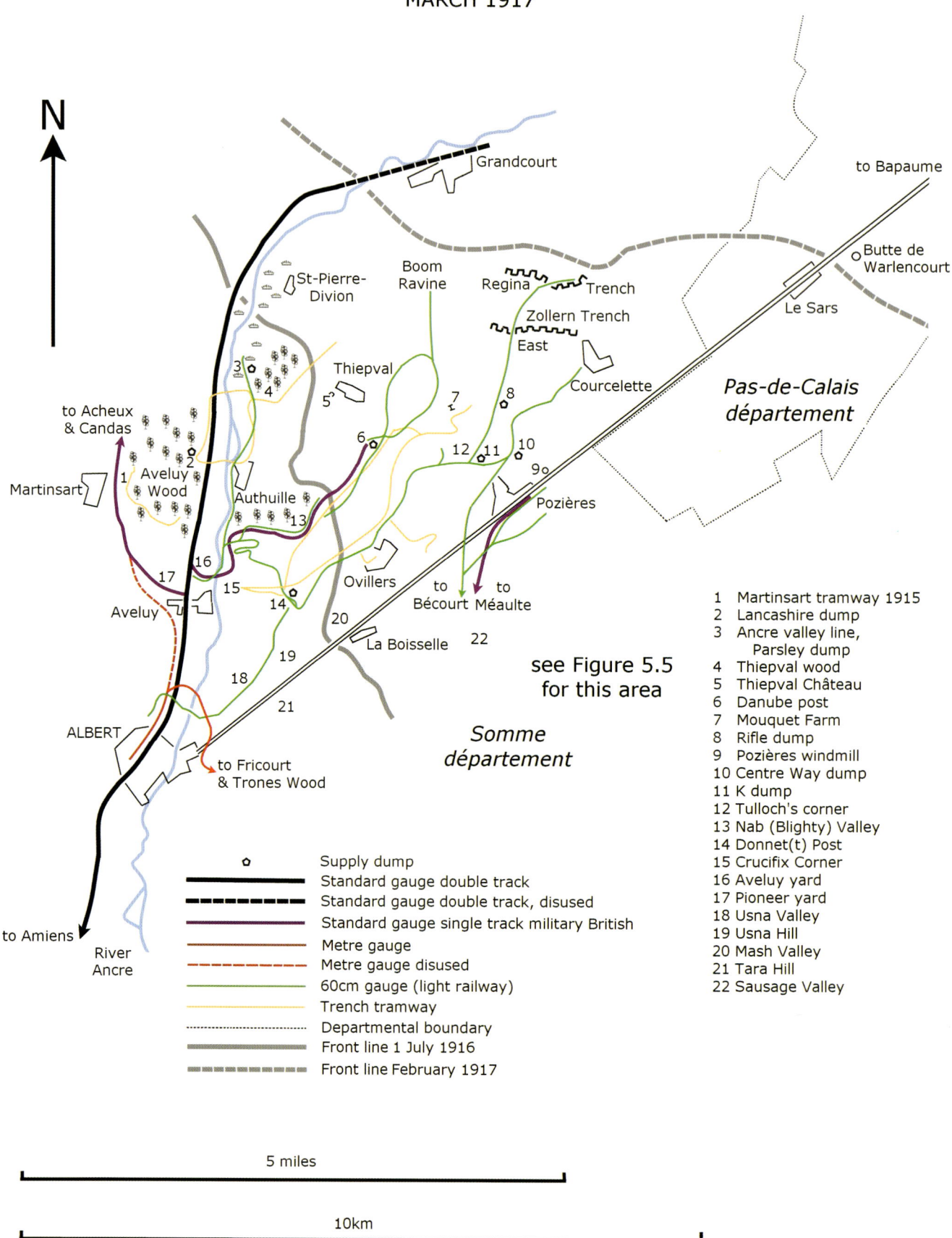

10km

Figure 5.3

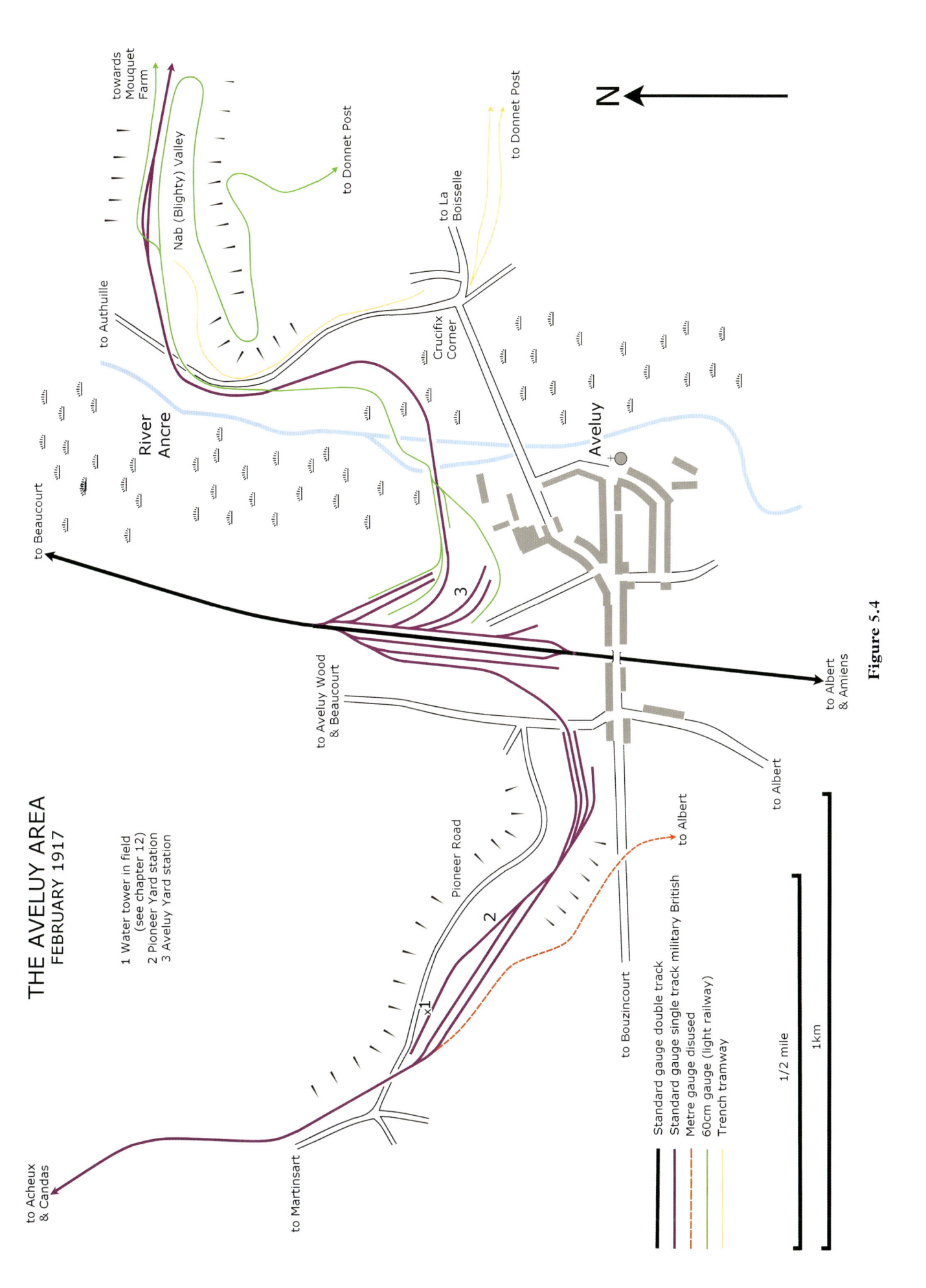

Light and metre gauge railways of the Somme battlefields 1915 - 16 March 1917

**THE AVELUY AREA
FEBRUARY 1917**

1 Water tower in field (see chapter 12)
2 Pioneer Yard station
3 Aveluy Yard station

Standard gauge double track
Standard gauge single track military British
Metre gauge disused
60cm gauge (light railway)
Trench tramway

Figure 5.4

Aveluy - Mouquet Farm (Nab Valley line)
In October, there had been plans to build a light railway from Aveluy Yard to Mouquet or Moquet Farm (*Ferme du Mouquet*), just over one mile east of Thiepval village. Mouquet Farm had been an objective for the first day of the battle, but was not finally taken until the third week of August. On 29 October, after a meeting with the DGT (Geddes), RCE V instructed that this should be a standard gauge line, to be completed by 20 November. The construction was mainly by 277th RC RE, with the 17th Bttn Northumberland Fusiliers, and with help for bridging from Canadian railway troops.

The single track line began with a junction facing towards Arras, within the Aveluy Yard. Curving east, it crossed the Ancre on a timber bridge (completed 6 November) and then up the east side of the river. After half a mile, it turned up Nab Valley, also known as Blighty Valley. The line was practically complete by 19 November. We do not think that the the line actually reached Mouquet Farm; later maps (February 1917) show it ending in a yard one mile short.

Light Railways (60cm gauge)
Tramways
A map during the 1916 Somme battle shows some tramways (see figure 5.3). These were mule-hauled. Of interest is the circular tramway from Lancashire Dump, in Aveluy Wood on the main road from Albert to Arras, up the Ancre Valley. This had two routes across the Ancre to the south west corner of Thiepval Wood. Here they met and then followed the edge of the Wood to the 1 July front line. The site of Lancashire Dump is now Aveluy Wood CWGC cemetery.

The other early major tramways began at Crucifix Corner, just east of Aveluy, also on the British side of the 1 July front line. Climbing east onto the plateau at Donnet (or Donnett's) Post, a supply dump and encampment, one tramway split into two lines, both going on north east, and linked further up, called the 'Inner Circle'. Most of the other tramways further east were replaced later by light railways. During August, the 1st and 2nd Australian Pioneer Battalions (APB) extended tramways around Pozières, including to K Dump north of the village.

Aveluy to Pozières and Courcelette
At the beginning of September 1916, part of the 119th RC RE moved into dugouts at Aveluy to start building a light railway to Pozières. Work on the formation and a bridge over the Ancre river was underway by 11 September. On 26 September, the railway was broken in two places by tanks passing over. Despite this, and shelling throughout the month, the line was finished during October.

From transhipment facilites in Aveluy standard gauge yard, the line crossed the Ancre and followed close to the Mouquet Farm standard gauge line into the

5.2 A Hunslet 4-6-0T hauls a train of bogie well wagons towards Aveluy, across the bridge over the Ancre, on 7 November 1916. The line is that from Aveluy via Blighty Valley to Donnet Post and Ovillers, on the high ground behind. Behind men are working on another bridge, for the standard gauge line from Aveluy Yard to Blighty (Nab) Valley. (*IWM Q6187*)

5.3 A Howitzer is hauled along the path of a light railway at Pozières in November 1916. *(Pen & Sword Archive)*

first part of Nab Valley. It then doubled back up a steep gradient along the south side of the valley to curve back again onto the plateau near Donnet Post. Turning past two supply dumps north of Ovillers, it then reached K Dump north of Pozières. Just east of the Dump was the junction with the line from Sausage Valley (see South of the Albert to Bapaume Road, below).

At the end of October, instructions were issued to rebuild the line from Ovillers Post (one of the supply dumps) to Pozières, using 'heavy rail' and standard gauge sleepers, for heavier trains. Unable to get metre gauge rails from the regauged Beaussart to Aveluy line in time, the existing 20lb/yd (10kg/m) rails were relaid on standard gauge sleepers. The whole line from Aveluy was complete by 5 November, with three new sidings at Pozières. The work was done mainly by the 17th Bttn Northumberland Fusiliers.

South of the Albert to Bapaume Road

This was the area of greatest advance on the first day of the 1916 Battle of the Somme, and in the first three weeks. The front line ran west to east from Fricourt to the boundary with the Fernch Army at Maricourt. By late July, the British troops had moved north past Mametz Wood to Contalmaison, Bazentin and Longeuval. Thereafter, progress was slower. By the end of the battle, the front line was just beyond Le Sars (on the Albert to Bapaume road), Gueudecourt and Lesbœufs. Railways in this area up to 16 March 1917 are shown in Figure 5.5.

Standard Gauge Railways

There were major standard gauge railway developments in this area during the 1916 Somme battle.

Dernancourt to Plateau and Trones Wood
The line from Dernancourt junction was extended during July 1916 from Loop to Plateau, on the more level high ground to the east (360ft (110m)), where a large station was built. Then, the line was extended from Plateau station to Trones Wood, with a station at Maricourt, mainly for French use. This was doubled in October by French troops, using British material. The line from Dernancourt junction was operated and maintained by the French from 1 August 1916.

The French constructed another single line up the hill between Ancre junction and Pilla junction, with easier gradients. This had to be sited to the west of the existing line, but, since this became the up line, trains had to cross over at the bottom. The old, steeper line became the down line, with a strict speed limit.

Méaulte junction to Longueval
This British line was commenced by 277th RC RE in mid-July 1916 and built as far as Willow Avenue Station at Mametz by the end of August. By the end of October, the railway had been extended to Bazentin and Longueval.

Starting from Méaulte junction, immediately to east of the bridge over the Ancre on the line from Dernancourt, the single track line followed the valley of the Willow Stream to meet the metre gauge line from

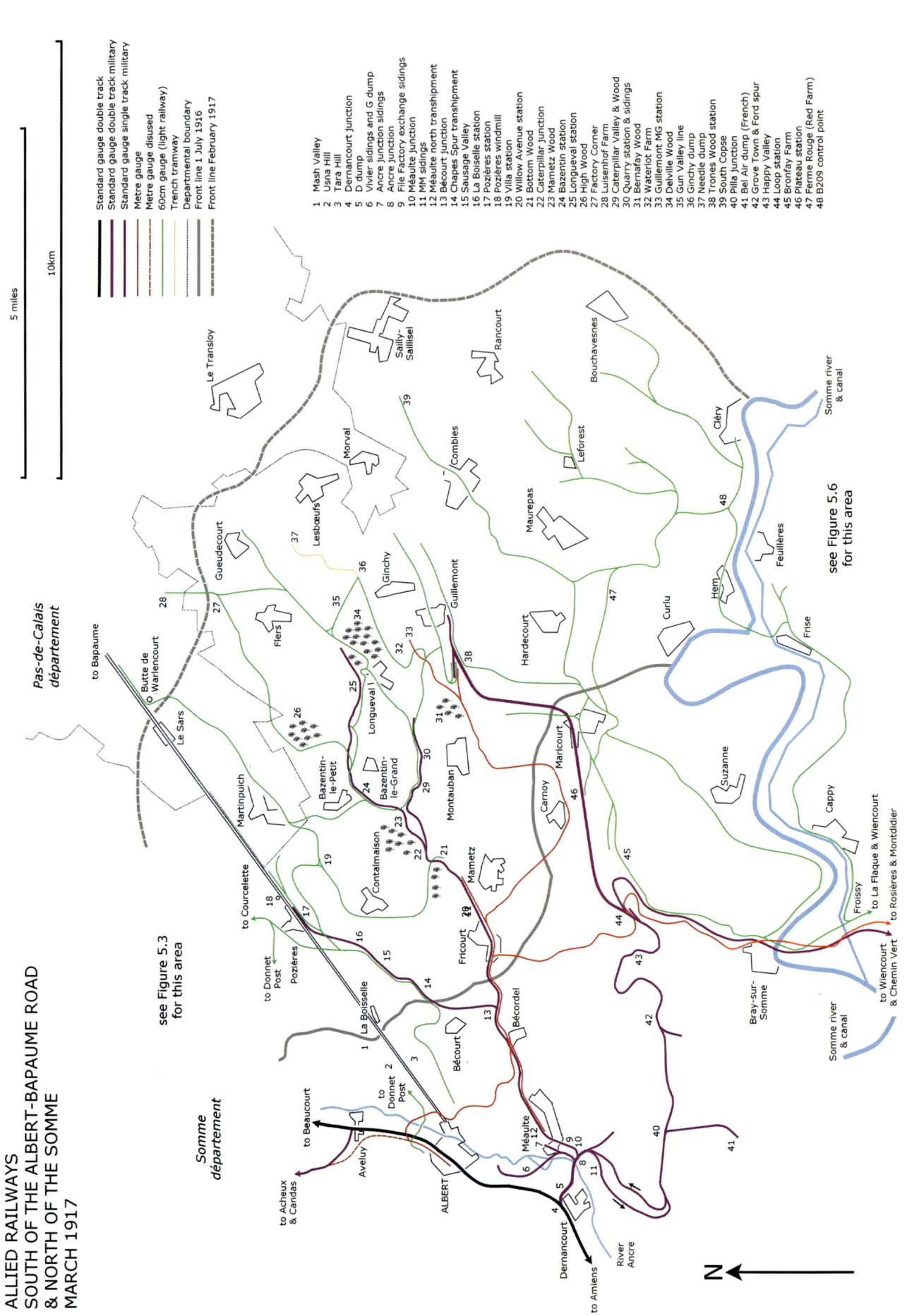

Figure 5.5

Albert to Péronne at the metre gauge halt at Bécourdel-Bécourt (Bécourdel Crossing). The line paralleled the metre gauge line through Fricourt station, and then continued to follow the valley past Mametz Wood. The line curved east around the north of the remains of Bazentin-le-Grand village to reach Longueval. By the end of October there were yards at Méaulte north, Willow Avenue station (Mametz), Bazentin station, and Longueval station. There were also sidings by Bottom Wood and Mametz Wood. Between Méaulte junction and Méaulte north yard were the extensive File Factory Exchange Sidings, indicating French operation up to there. Given the intense fighting for Mametz Wood and Bazentin in mid-July, it is difficult to imagine these valleys full of railways only a few months later.

Caterpiller Wood branch
From a junction in the valley by Mametz Wood, this branch followed the narrow and winding Caterpiller Valley to Quarry sidings, north of Montauban.

Chapes Spur branch
Another branch originated at Bécourt junction and went north to Chapes Spur where there was a light railway transhipment to the Sausage Valley line. Later, after the battle, the standard gauge line was extended along Sausage Valley to Pozières.

Metre gauge railways
Albert to Péronne and Montdidier
Early during the battle, British units restored the line from Albert as far as Fricourt, using French material and rolling stock. The French had started to restore the line north from Bray, and British units worked south from Fricourt, allowing Bray to Fricourt to open from 14 July. A metre gauge spur was built back along the new standard gauge line from Bécourt-Bécourdel halt to a transhipment station at Méaulte North yard. There was also a short metre gauge spur from Fricourt station to the new Willow Avenue station north of Mametz. The line was later reopened on to Montauban and Trones Wood. British units took over maintenance and operation from Albert to Trones Wood, probably from the end of October, using French rolling stock already on the line.

Light Railways
It was during the autumn of 1916 that very wet weather led to mud becoming a major problem. The 5th APB based at Montauban arrived on 22 October and were working on communication trenches towards Flers, and then road repairs. They described their transport lines as 'a sea of mud' and the route from them to the main road 'fearful'. In November, the 5th APB also undertook light railway work.

5.4 Hudswell-Clarke (Hudson) 0-6-0WT (well tank) locomotive WD No. 107 derailed at a crossing of the Albert to Fricourt road, September 1916. *(IWM Q4343)*

83

Albert–Avoca Valley–Sausage Valley–Pozières
There is evidence of trench tramways in the Avoca Valley, west of Bécourt, in August 1916. From 20 August both the 2nd and the 4th APBs, under the direction of the Chief Engineer of the Anzac Corps, were working on a proper 'Decauville' railway in the Avoca Valley, probably extending a line already coming into this area from the Albert. Work continued into September, and the line was eventually extended up Sausage Valley to Pozières, to join the line from Aveluy.

Trones Wood
At the Trones Wood standard gauge yard, the British proposed to build light railway transhipments on both sides, because there were gun emplacemnts towards Guillemont and Ginchy on both sides. This caused some concern to the French operating the yard. It was finally agreed that there could be a light railway link across the standard gauge line, but only for occasional use, for instance to transfer rolling stock.

Bernafay, Longueval, Flers (east)
From 6 November 1916, 4th APB moved to Mametz (Wood) Camp and Longueval. They were constructing 'tramways', probably from Mametz Wood to Quarry Sidings, in parallel with the Caterpiller Valley standard gauge branch. On 15 November the 2nd APB commenced constructing a 'tramline' on from Quarry Sidings, at the end of the standard gauge branch, to Bernafay Wood, Trones Wood, Longueval and Flers. This is probably the line that went to the east side of Flers, and eventually on to Gueudecourt (see developments after the 1916 Battle).

Longueval, Flers (west)
Meanwhile one company of 2nd APB were working on a line from Longueval to the west of Flers.

5.5 A light railway north of Mametz Wood, October 1916. Soldiers are manhandling a 2 axle (4 wheel) trolley between the light railway and the end of a trench tramway, seen to the left. *(IWM Q4446)*

5.6 Two Simplex 20hp tractors and a train of wagons are covered with soldiers, said to be Gordon Highlanders and Durham Light Infantry. Near High Wood, October 1916. *(IWM Q4387)*

By 22 November, just after the end of the battle, this line had reached the road from Flers to Eaucourt l'Abbaye.

The French Area, south east of the line from Maricourt to Morval

In the first two weeks of the First Battle of the Somme, the French Sixth Army made some progress to the east. Between Maricourt and the north bank of the Somme, they took Curlu and Hem, and by mid-September they had captured Cléry-sur Somme. This was well on the way to Péronne. However, between then and the end of the battle in November, they failed to get much nearer. They did however make a lot of progress north east, capturing Combles, Rancourt and Morval (see Figure 5.5).

South of the Somme and north of the main road from Amiens to St Quentin, the French Army also made considerable ground. They reached Biache, which was near Péronne. South of the road they made less progress, not quite reaching Chaulnes on the main railway from Amiens. Railways in this area are shown in Figure 5.6.

Standard gauge railways
Wiencourt–L'Equipée to Bray

The Moreuil to Wiencourt line was extended from Wiencourt (on the main Amiens to Rosières line) to Bray. Work commenced was complete on 20 August, with 18km (11 miles) of main line and 13km (8 miles) of other lines. There were four major stations, at La Flaque, Mérignolles, Froissy and Bray.

La Flaque station was quickly targeted by German artillery on 18 August. Wiencourt was then attacked on 25 August. A new station was built at Chemin Vert, west of Guillaucourt, and the line was doubled from there to Froissy. Doubling finished on 1 Jan 1917. Altogether, with the lines laid earlier in 1916, the French Engineers had laid 230km (143 miles) of lines in 6 months. The 5° Génie ran 6,768 trains to transport troops, including 1,701 in August and 1,478 in September

Because of the problems with the Plateau line, the French decided to extend this line from Bray to Loop, meeting the Plateau line there. This was built roughly parallel with the metre gauge line. The rails were linked through in October, but the French did not open

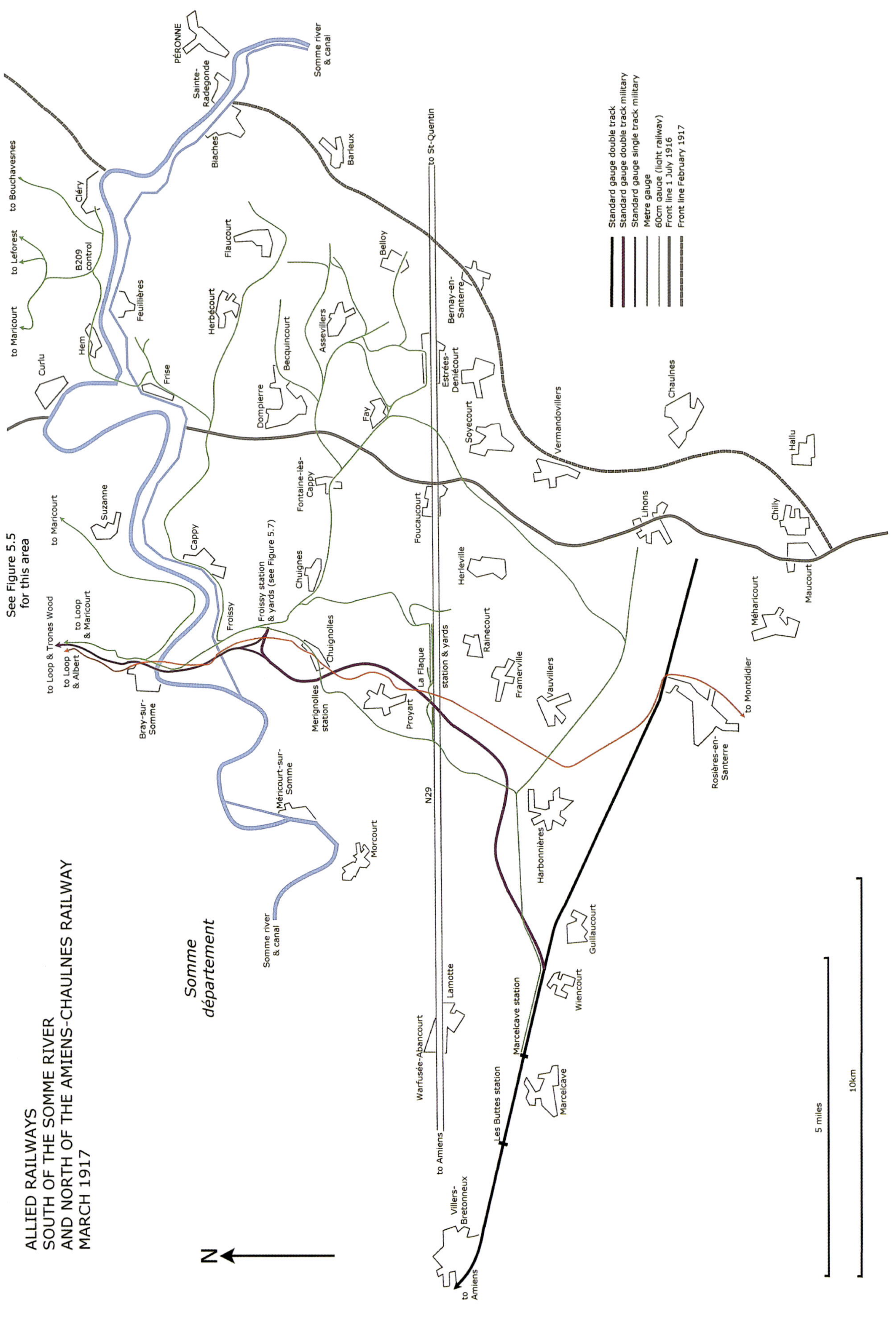
ALLIED RAILWAYS
SOUTH OF THE SOMME RIVER
AND NORTH OF THE AMIENS-CHAULNES RAILWAY
MARCH 1917
N
Somme département
Standard gauge double track
Standard gauge double track military
Standard gauge single track military
Metre gauge
60cm gauge (light railway)
Front line 1 July 1916
Front line February 1917
5 miles
10km
See Figure 5.5 for this area
PÉRONNE
Sainte-Radegonde
Somme river & canal
Biaches
Barleux
to St-Quentin
to Bouchavesnes
Cléry
to Leforest
B209 control
Flaucourt
Belloy
Bernay-en-Santerre
to Maricourt
Feuillières
Herbécourt
Becquincourt
Assevillers
Curlu
Hem
Frise
Dompierre
Estrées-Deniécourt
Chaulnes
Fay
Soyecourt
Vermandovillers
Hallu
Fontaine-lès-Cappy
Foucaucourt
Lihons
Chilly
Suzanne
to Maricourt
Cappy
Chuignes
Herleville
Maucourt
Froissy station & yards (see Figure 5.7)
Froissy
Rainecourt
Méharicourt
to Loop & Trones Wood
to Loop & Maricourt
to Loop & Albert
Chuignolles
La Flaque station & yards
Framerville
Vauvillers
to Montdidier
Bray-sur-Somme
Merignolles station
Proyart
Rosières-en-Santerre
Méricourt-sur-Somme
N29
Harbonnières
Morcourt
Guillaucourt
Wiencourt
Lamotte
Marcelcave station
Warfusée-Abancourt
Les Buttes station
Marcelcave
to Amiens
Villers-Bretonneux
to Amiens

Figure 5.6

Light and metre gauge railways of the Somme battlefields 1915 - 16 March 1917

5.7 A French Army light railway train at Froissy in late 1916. Shells are being transported on model 1888 Péchot flat wagons, hauled by a Decauville locomotive. *(Collection APPEVA)*

the line to traffic until ballasting and other work was finished, on 2 December.

Light Railways

It is almost certain that the French engineers extended the light railway system into the captured areas during the 1916 Somme Battle. More extensions were made after the battle before the British took over this area. Because it is not certain which extensions were made during which period, we have included all of them in the section concerned with the period after the battle (see Figures 5.5 and 5.6). With the building of the standard gauge line from Wiencourt to Bray, the Froissy yard included standard gauge faciliies and a transhipment area.

After the First Battle of the Somme

From 12 December 1916, the British army took over from the French responsibility for some of the front line north of the Somme. In February 1917 the British Army took over another section, down to the Amiens to Roye main road just west of Roye. The front line did not change much between the end of the 1916 Battle and the German retreat to the Hindenburg Line, completed by 16 March 1917.

Railways

This was a period of very active railway construction. The weather was very wet in the latter half of December 1916. This was followed by six weeks of intense frost lasting until February. This interfered considerably with railway construction and operations.

West of the Ancre

Railways in this area after the Battle of the Somme up to 16 March 1917 are shown with those during the 1916 battle in Figure 5.2.

Standard Gauge railways

On 17 January 1917, RCEV met the DGT (Geddes) at GHQ (Montreuil) to agree new standard gauge works in the Fifth Army area.

Vecquemont to Contay

From mid November 1916, a new branch line was built by 3rd RC RMRE to a quarry at Vecquemont for ballast. The quarry output was particularly needed in February 1917 for the construction of the extension of the Bécourt line to Pozières, but in general this line was less needed.

Candas to Acheux
During December 1916 the yard at Acheux was reorganised for a new ammunition yard and stone spur. Supply sidings were also built at Varennes, at the junction of the line to Colincamps (Euston Dump). In January 1917 a new yard was completed at Rosel. Doubling of the whole line, agreed in January, did not happen.

Acheux–Colincamps–Euston Dump–Serre
In late November the ROD took over from 119th RC RE the handling of ammunition trains to Euston Dump. In mid January the doubling of the line from Varennes junction to Euston Dump was agreed, with a rail head at Bertrancourt. The doubling was probably not achieved.

Authie Valley line (Doullens to Courcelles via Coigneux)
RCE V had been pressing the Fifth Army for this line since November 1916, and preliminary surveys were made in December. Construction of the line from Doullens to Coigneux (25 miles including rail heads) was approved in mid January 1917, but approval for construction from Courcelles to Coigneux (8.5 miles including rail heads), to meet it from the other end, was held up until the end of January, after the DGT (Geddes) had inspected the proposed lines.

Work began in early February but was held up by lack of grading teams. On 4 March, the Chief Railway Construction Engineer said that work on the line should stop, but again the DGT intervened, and on the next day, work proceeded. The whole line was connected up on 17 March, permitting traffic.

Metre gauge railways
Beaussart to Aveluy
This was the line converted to standard gauge in October 1916. The length of the converted section was about 7 miles (11km). After the 1916 Somme battle, the arguments about relaying the metre gauge line continued. Initial proposals had been to lay a third rail into the standard gauge, not for regular traffic, but to allow transfer of stock to Beauval for repair. Later, it was agreed to relay the metre gauge in parallel with the standard gauge. This meant clearing a new formation most of the way. In early December 1916, RCE V advised the CRCE that they did not have sufficient labour to do this, but were instructed to proceed when men were available. On 17 January 1917, at a meeting with the DGT at GHQ, it was agreed that relaying should not go ahead.

From the end of Janaury 1917, the situation was further complicated by the conversion of the section of metre gauge line from Acheux yard to Beaussart to light railway (60cm gauge). This was completed during February and was the first stage of the construction by 2nd Bttn CRT of a light railway network in this area.

Light Railways
Before the end of the 1916 Somme battle, there were no major light railways west of the Ancre. RCE V was asked to look into transportation requirements in the Fifth Army area in relation to standard gauge and 60cm railways, and they reported on 10 December 1916, but a copy is unavailable. In February, there was a meeting about policy for V Corps trench tramways, but we have no details of tramways in this area.

The 2nd Bttn CRT arrived at Varennes on 20 January 1917 to start construction of light railways in the Fifth Army area, under the ADLR V. The 6th LROC were also based at Acheux from 7 March to 9 April 1917, operating these lines.

Rolling stock and Track Material
Rolling stock began arriving at Acheux for these lines on 4 February, when the first steam locomotive, a 15 ton Baldwin, was unloaded. By March, there were seven steam locomotives. The last arrived on 9 March and was unloaded by the 6th LROC. Three petrol tractors arrived in February, with 22 bogie well wagons and 45 four wheel (two axle) wagons. There were also 78 tipper wagons for construction. Three more petrol tractors arrived in March.

Construction in February was held up by a severe shortage of track material. The situation improved and by the end of February, stock at Acheux yard included 40,000 wooden sleepers (also suitable for metre gauge track), 17,000 steel sleepers, and 33km of 20lb/yd rails.

Courcelles to Hébuterne
A light railway was laid between Courcelles and Hébuterne, possibly with standard gauge material. Work began at the end of November, with the 277th RC RE helped by the 17th Bttn Northumberland Fusiliers, and was completed by 22 December.

Acheux Yard
On arrival in Acheux, 2nd Bttn CRT surveyed the yard and made changes to support the light railway developments. Some new track was laid, and metre gauge track was regauged. In February, the frost was at times so hard that explosives had to be used to move earth. A coal bunker, eventually holding 400 tons, was constructed for light railway locomotives. Rolling stock repairs were undertaken, but there was a shortage of parts.

Acheux to Beaussart
Beginning at the end of January 1917, 2nd Bttn CRT converted the metre gauge line between Acheux Yard

and Beaussart to 60cm gauge. 200ft of sidings were built. The first train ran on 12 February.

Acheux Wood to Bertrancourt Dump
In February, a spur was constructed from Acheux Wood to Bertrancourt Dump, on the road from Acheux to Bertrancourt. The line was ready for light traffic on 4 March and ammunition trains were run from the Dump from 6 March. However, on 13 March, it was still priority to make the line ready for steam operation.

Beaussart to Beaumont-Hamel, Beaucourt and Grandcourt
Although other plans for lines from Beaussart did not come to fruition, the line from Acheux to Beaussart was extended to Mailly-Maillet, Auchonvillers, and Beaumont-Hamel. The plan was eventually to extend the line to Beaucourt, in the Ancre valley, and on to Miraumont, both on the standard gauge line from Albert.

On 21 February, work began to extend the line to Auchonvillers. Four steam locomotives were employed on construction trains from the Acheux Yard, with one petrol tractor in the yard and on the Bertrancourt Dump spur. Two petrol tractors were sent to Beaussart to operate to Auchonvillers. Orders were to be able to move ammunition to Beaumont-Hamel by 8 March. The original plan was to lay heavy rail (40lb/yd, 20kg/m) but there was lack of bolts and fishplates. It was agreed to use 20lb/yd rail. Track was laid from Beaussart to Auchonvillers all day and night to 5am on 5 March. A trial trip was made on the line to Beaumont-Hamel later on 5 March, and bad spots were remodelled on 6 March. By that date, the line was open at least for tractor traffic to Beaumont-Hamel.

From 6 March, ammunition was moved from Bertrancourt Dump to Beaumont-Hamel, often at night because of shell fire. In the first three days, 99 tons were moved. From 11 March, operating the line for goods traffic including ammunition was handed over to 'ADLR operating staff'; this was the 6th LROC, who had arrived at Acheux on 7 March.

Beyond Beaumont-Hamel, the line was to follow the valley south east to the Ancre valley, to the place known as 'Suicide Corner'. There had been a German line here. It was then to turn along the Ancre valley to Miraumont in parallel with the standard gauge line. For construction past Beaumont-Hamel, much broken machinery, old rails and other debris had to be removed, and holes and craters filled in. The artillery wanted 128 tons of ammunition daily for an attack on 18 March, but were told that the line was still being constructed. During this period 2nd CRT took over ammunition delivery on the new line from 6th LROC. Only 50 tons were promised, but in the event, 90 tons were delivered to Beaumont-Hamel on 15 March. Trains for the wounded were run from Mailly-Maillet or Beaumont-Hamel to Acheux on 14 to 16 March, so presumably the attack had been brought forward. Details are few, but since the German Army had mostly retreated to the Hindenburg Line by 17 March, they were leaving anyway.

The Army required the line to Beaucourt to be ready for tractor traffic by 20 March. It was delayed by failure of the ROD to supply track, presumably because the

5.8 The village of Beaumont-Hamel, with the end of the German field railway (*feldbahn*) from Beaucourt-Hamel main line station. A German soldier is standing on the left. The picture must have been taken before the First Battle of the Somme, which commenced 1 July 1916. (*Authors' collection*)

Albert to Arras main line was being reconstructed. The line never reached Miraumont.

The Ancre Valley, east of the Ancre and north of the Albert to Bapaume Road

Railways in this area after the Battle of the Somme up to 16 March 1917 are shown with those during the 1916 Battle in Figure 5.3.

Standard Gauge Railways
Albert to Arras
After the 1916 Somme battle, the main line from Albert to Arras was reconstructed towards Beaucourt by the end of March 1917. Although owned by the *Nord* railway, the line, because it was in the battle zone, was being operated by the French 5° Génie. Reconstruction was supposed to be undertaken by French Engineers assisted by British units. On 26 February, RCE V were instructed to ignore the French, who were being slow, and get on with it. Instead officers of RCE V met the French to coordinate matters. A series of high level meetings led to 5th CRT being instructed on 6 March by the DGT and Brig. Gen. Stewart, CO of CRT, to hand it all over to the French. In practice, they continued to assist the French until they left the area on 13 March.

Aveluy to Mouquet Farm
From 24 December, the line was operated by ROD, using petrol tractors based at Aveluy yard, which moved 600 to 1,000 tons of goods per day on the line. In February, it was decided that the bridge over the Ancre at Aveluy need not be strengthened to take steam locomotives.

Light Railways
Much of the work on light railways in this period in this area was undertaken by D Company of 2nd Bttn CRT, which arrived at Donnet Post and Aveluy on 24 January 1917 and left on 2 March, replaced by 4th Bttn CRT.

Aveluy Yard
On moving into Aveluy yard at the end of January 1917, D Company of 2nd CRT constructed new 60cm lines, locomotive sheds, stables, and dugouts there. During February light railway material began to arrive at the yard in larger quantities.

Aveluy to Ovillers and Pozières
During December 1916, battery spurs and ammuniton spurs were added to the Aveluy to Pozières line. At the end of January, 2nd CRT took over maintenance of this line (6 miles).

Ovillers to Rifle Dump and Zollern and Regina Trenches
This was sometimes called the Ovillers to Mouquet Farm line, because Rifle Dump was only ¾ mile east of Mouquet Farm. Construction from Ovillers to Rifle Dump was begun on 26 January 1917. Work was pushed ahead from 11 February, with ballasting all night on 14 February, because the line was required to Rifle Dump by 17 February, when there was to be some local offensive operation. The 2nd CRT reported on 16 February that the line would be ready next day at 11am to handle light loads, and to evacuate wounded, using petrol tractors.

Work started on 19 February on an extension to Zollern and Regina trenches, 2½ miles north east, and was taken over by A and B Companies of 4th Bttn CRT from 2 March.

Courcelette extension (Centre Way line)
This left the Ovillers to Rifle Dump line near Tulloch's Corner and joined the Sausage Valley line coming from the south at Centre Way Dump. Work had started towards Courcelette from Centre Way Dump on 31 January 1917, but was stopped on 3 February. On 23 February 2nd CRT were again instructed to build this line. By 25 February, considerable progress had been made, with fog screening the work from the enemy.

Nab Valley to Nicholl's Loop and towards Grandcourt
This line began at Danube Post, the railhead at the end of the standard gauge line to Mouquet Farm and connected to the pre-existing tramway at Nicholl's loop. Construction was begun on 26 January 1917. By 9 February, the line was ready for petrol tractor traffic. A line on from the left fork of the loop towards Grandcourt had been surveyed on 23 January. Work was taken over by 4th Bttn CRT from 2 March, and by 14 March they were at Boom Ravine chalk pit and had almost reached Grandcourt.

Ancre Valley Line
This line left the Aveluy to Pozières line at a junction at the entrance to Nab Valley. It would have been 5 miles (8km) long when completed. The route of the line followed the east bank of the Ancre, past Authuille to St. Pierre-Divion. Work commenced on 5 February, but was held up on 15 February because of the failure of the 63rd Division to provide labour, and again a few days later for lack of fish plates. Then on 24 February, 2nd CRT were ordered to cease all work on this line. The three miles of track laid had reached Parsley Dump by Thiepval Wood, and more had been graded. It would have been finished by 5 March. But now the track was to be taken up and the material used for the Courcelette extension and for the Nicholl's Loop extension toward Grandcourt.

South of the Albert to Bapaume Road
On 12 December 1916, the British Fourth Army took over the area south to the Somme from the French

Sixth Army. They took over responsibility for the railways during the following weeks. Railways in this area up to 16 March 1917 are shown in Figure 5.5. Note that in some cases by 16 March, light railways extended beyond the February 1917 front line. By the middle of March there had been some further advances, before the full extent of the German withdrawal became clear.

Standard Gauge Railways
Méaulte junction - Pozières
In January 1917, the extension to Pozières of the standard gauge line from Bécourt junction to Chapes Spur was discussed. The extension was built, probably in February.

Dernancourt junction - Trones Wood
This line was handed back by the French to maintenance by 3rd RC RMRE on 18 December 1916. In January 1917, Trones Wood yard was damaged by shell fire, and from 26 January to 17 February, a very severe frost held up works and damaged machinery.

Metre gauge railways
British units continued to operate the line from Albert to Montauban and Trones Wood, using French rolling stock. On later maps (January 1918), there is a metre gauge link from the line through Trones Wood to the standard gauge and light railway yard at the south end of the wood, but it is not known when this was built. The line from Bray to Fricourt was also operated, probably by the British.

Light Railways
Sausage Valley line
It was probably in January 1917 that this line was extended up Sausage Valley to Pozières, to join the lines from Aveluy. These were already being built and maintained by 2nd Bttn CRT, who took over maintenance of the Sausage Valley line from 17 February. They salvaged two flat cars and eight tipper cars on the line, and repaired damage. However, the Company operating the line promised two petrol tractors, but these did not appear, so 2nd CRT had to push ballast in salvaged tipper wagons by hand. Sheds and Nissen Huts were erected at Chapes (or Cheape's) Spur, north of Bécourt. The 4th Bttn CRT took over in March, and continued to maintain the line.

Bottom Wood to Contalmaison and Villa station
This line started from a transhipment at the yard at Bottom Wood. This was on the standard gauge line up the valley towards Bazentin and Longueval. There was probably a German line along part of the route before the 1916 Battle. The line followed the branch valley west past woods, including 'railway copse', one of the clues to a German line found here during the battle. The line then went north, passing Contalmaison village, where there was a link to the nearby Sausage Valley line. Finally, a route north east took it to Villa station, and a junction with the line from Pozières.

At the Bottom Wood end of the line, there was probably no light railway connection between this line and the Quarry to Bazentin line through Caterpiller Valley. For five days towards the end of February, 1st Anzac Light Railways provided a limber at Caterpiller Valley to take coal to Bottom Wood, presumably for steam locomotives on this line.

Pozières to Villa Station
This line began from a junction with the Sausage Valley line just south west of Pozières (Pozières junction). It was built as far as Villa Station by 1st Bttn CRT in January 1917, despite repeated shelling on the exposed site where it met, at Martinpuich junction, the line from 1st Anzac Light Railways HQ at Quarry Sidings.

Trones Wood
Trones Wood (*Bois des Troncs* in French), back in British maintenance and operation from December 1916, was a major railway centre. This was situated at the south end of the wood, across the road, and not where the Albert to Péronne metre gauge line went through the middle of the wood. It was here, on 7 or 11 December 1916, that the unit we believe to be the first 'proper' Light Railway Operating Company (LROC) in France was formed. This was the XIV Corps LR Company, renamed the 35th LROC on 10 May 1917. The 1st Anzac LROC, later (June 1917) to become the 17th Australian LROC, was also formed in December 1916, at Pozières.

The construction and operation of light railways to the north, north west and north east of Trones Wood during this period were associated with First Anzac Light Railways (1st ALR), formed to support the Anzac Corps. They were supported by some of the Australian Pioneer Battalions, initially mainly the 4th, but later the 1st, 2nd and 5th, and by some other Australian Engineers Companies. The 1st Anzac LROC was their operating company. The most important of these lines are described below. All are shown on Figure 5.5.

Quarry Sidings
The 1st ALR, and probably the 1st Anzac LROC, were based at or near Quarry Sidings. This was at the end of the branch standard gauge line up Caterpiller Valley from Mametz Wood, and there was a light railway transhipment. During February 1917, locomotives and petrol tractors began arriving.

During January 1917, the 4th APB built hospital and heavy ammunition sidings at or near Quarry Sidings.

5.9 Hunslet 4-6-0T WD No. 309 takes on water at Trones Wood, December 1916. Note the icicles, and that the locomotive is still labelled ROD (Railway Operating Division). Men appear to be filling cans with water from a leak in the hose. *(IWM Q1692)*

They continued to maintain this area in February, and widened a cutting, probably to take the steam locomotives which were arriving.

Longueval to Bazentin and High Wood
These lines started at the Bazentin rail head and transhipment, on the standard gauge line to Longueval. One branch followed quite close to the standard gauge to Longueval; this was probably the line known as the the 'Longueval long line'. The other branch went north to the area of High Wood. The 1st APB were working on these lines in January 1917. Work included the construction of Siege Sidings, on the Longueval line, and on 22 January the line was connected to the standard gauge yard at Longueval. The lines were complete by early February 1917. 4th APB took over maintenance, and the line was improved to allow steam locomotive operation.

Quarry to Bazentin and Martinpuich
This light railway, constructed, maintained and operated by 1st ALR, followed the standard gauge line west through Caterpiller Valley to just below Mametz Wood. Here there was a crossing on the level of the standard gauge line up the valley, and a water point for locomotives. From there it followed the standard gauge line north to Bazentin yard and transhipment. From there a path north through Bazentin Wood took it to Martinpuich junction, on the line from Pozières.

At least the section north from the end of Caterpiller Valley was probably constructed in early February by 4th APB, reaching Bazentin after the construction of the line from there to Longueval.

Martinpuich to Le Sars
In February, the 2nd APB moved to Martinpuich and from 10 February extended this line as a 'light tramway' past Martinpuich to Le Sars and the Butte de Warlencourt. The Butte is a chalk mound, about 50ft high, which by the end of the 1916 battle had been stripped bare. By 21 February, the line had been finished to the sunken road just south of the Butte.

There had been a German standard gauge line along the main road from Bapaume to Le Sars, with a terminal station west of the Butte between it and Le Sars village. By 9 March, 2nd APB had extended the light railway through the German station area to the main Albert to Bapaume Road, and some way along the road towards Bapaume.

High Wood to Le Sars
From the station and triangular junction just on the north side of High Wood, the line was extended to Le Sars, joining the railway from Martinpuich just short of the Butte de Warlencourt. The work was commenced in the middle of March 1917.

High Wood to Factory Corner and Luisenhof Farm
Factory Corner was named for a destroyed sugar factory at this road junction. This line reached Factory Corner by the end of February, when work commenced to

extend it to Luisenhof Farm, about 1 mile further. By the middle of March, salvaged rails were being moved from Siege Sidings on the Longueval long line up to Factory Corner for this work.

Quarry to Longueval, Flers and Gueudecourt
The line from Quarry sidings, north of Montauban, to Longueval was also known as the 'Longueval short line'. The line started from the transhipment at Quarry sidings, at the end of the Caterpiller Wood branch of the Méaulte to Longueval standard gauge line. At Longueval, it met the 'Longueval long line' from the Bazentin rail head. At Longueval there was a yard and probably transhipment at the Longueval standard gauge rail head. The line was extended past Flers to Gueudecourt. From north east of Longueval there was a link, called the Gun Valley line, to the Trones Wood to Ginchy line, which it met at Ginchy Dump just north of Ginchy.

The 4th APB were working on the Quarry to Longueval section in December 1916. Work on the rest of the line to Gueudecourt continued in January, and the line was connected with Longueval standard gauge yard. The main line was open by the end of January, and the Gun Valley link line in February. Also, in February 1917, bridges were strengthened between Quarry Sidings and Longueval to carry steam locomotives.

Trones Wood to Waterlot Farm and Ginchy Dump
Work started on the section from Trones Wood yard (north side) to Waterlot Farm at the end of November 1916, by the 5th APB. Waterlot Farm is on the road from Guillemont to Longueval, near the former sugar factory. There had been a metre gauge branch to the factory and on into Longueval, from the station at Guillemont, before the war. On this line, there were junctions with a line going on through Guillemont, eventually to Combles, and, at Waterlot junction, with a line to Quarry Sidings. In January 1917, 4th APB took over and the line was completed to Ginchy Dump, north of Ginchy village.

In February the line from Trones Wood to Waterlot Farm was improved, probably for the introduction of steam locomotives. This included the bends west of Waterlot junction, one known as Horseshoe bend.

Ginchy Dump to Gueudecourt
From 25 February 1917, the above line was built on towards Geuedecourt, by the 5th APB from Ginchy Dump. This was always a mule hauled line, and mule tracks were made alongside to facilitate this. By 5 March, the line was complete to past Needle Dump, between Flers and Lesbœufs, and was 750yds from the front line trenches. Much of the work had to be undertaken at night because of shell fire. The line opened for mule hauled traffic to Needle Dump on 11 March.

Lines from Plateau station
On 10 December 1916, 1st Bttn CRT moved to Plateau station for light railway work on the lines in the former French area. There appears to have been no operating company at Plateau at that time, and 1st CRT lent officers and a considerable number of men to help the ADLR IV operate the 'Decauville' lines. 1st CRT also built material sidings on the north side of Plateau standard gauge station, and on 23 December completed an inventory of permanent way material on the lines taken over from the French.

During January and February, Plateau station continued to be attacked by long range guns. On 3rd February the 1st LROC arrived at Plateau. This Company, formed at Longmoor Camp in Hampshire on 20 January 1917, from men who were mostly railway workers, was the first complete LROC to be sent to the Western Front from the UK. A detachment was sent to Bray-sur-Somme. The Company seemed to spend most of their time at Plateau and Loop stations unloading railway wagons, probably standard gauge. On 13 February, they moved on to Froissy.

Probably, 1st CRT continued to operate the light railway lines until the XVth Corps Light Railway Company was formed, almost certainly at Plateau, on 28th February. Formed from men already serving XV Corps, the Company operated the light railways of XV Corps taken over from the French in December 1916. They were officially named the 34th LROC on 25 May 1917.

Plateau - Bray-sur-Somme
On 29 January, 1st CRT were instructed to abandon the maintenance of the line from Bray-sur-Somme to Bronfay Farm, just south west of Plateau, and they withdrew the maintenance party. Probably this light railway was not considered necessary after the French opened the standard gauge line from Bray to Loop on 2 December 1916.

Plateau to Combles
This was a French built main line light railway through the former French area. It took an easterly course from Plateau station and transhipment past Maricourt and south of Hardecourt to west of Maurepas. Here, at the site of Maurepas *halte*, it met the disused metre gauge line from Albert to Péronne and took its path north east into Combles. When it was inspected for the takeover by RCE V on 22 December 1916, the French officer handing over reported average traffic of 350 tons daily. Improvements to the line were made in February, probably for the introduction of steam locomotives.

93

Combles to Haie Wood and South Copse
Before 22 December 1916, the main line from Combles went on north east to Haie Wood. On 22 December, 1st CRT commenced extending the line to South Copse, south west of Sailly-Saillisel. There was a lot of shelling, but despite this, the extension was ready for light tractor traffic on 12 January 1917.

The 1st CRT continued to work on the line. On 17 March, their CO walked the line from Combles to South Copse and found a party of 200 men working under instructions from the Chief Railway Engineer of XIVth Corps; this was still in the XVth Corps area. There is no record, but it is likely there were words about responsibilities and communications. Later this line became the important link through to Étricourt (see next chapter).

Maricourt to Le Forest (Maurepas) and Cléry via Ferme Rouge
This was another French built line, which also went east from Maricourt, to the south of the line to Combles. It turned south when it met the disused metre gauge line from Albert to Péronne and took its path to a junction north of Hem, from where it reached Maurepas, on the edge of the village of Le Forest (now Leforest). From the junction another line followed the metre gauge path to Cléry-sur-Somme. East of Hem, the Cléry line met the line from Froissy coming across the Somme river and marshes from Frise. At Cléry, there was a branch up to Bouchavesnes. On 13 January, improvement work started on the line, specifically on 'widening curves between Maricourt, Ferme Rouge and Maurepas to allow operation of the Hunslet type engine'.

Le Forest extensions to Rancourt
The British made two extensions to the line from Le Forest, both towards the Rancourt area, and both starting from a junction just east of Le Forest. Surveys were made in late December 1916 and early January 1917, and work began. The whole area was under very heavy enemy shell fire and destruction of the formation or the track was frequent. On 24 January, the German Army directed fire on one portion of track for three hours, destroying twenty lengths of track and most of the underlying formation. The reporting officer said that it was obvious that the fire was being directed by an enemy aeroplane which remained almost directly above during the firing.

Maricourt Bois to Trones Wood
A line north from the former French area at Maricourt Bois (wood) to the Trones Wood yard was built by 1st CRT in February 1917. It was ready for all traffic by 2 March.

South of the Somme
This area was taken over by the British Army from the French in February 1917. The front line for which the British were responsible now extended to the Amiens to Roye main road, with the front line just west of Roye. At the end of the 1916 Somme battle, the front line immediately south of the Somme was just east of Biaches. Railways in the 1916 Somme battlefield area, from the Amiens to Chaulnes railway north to the Somme River, up to 16 March 1917, are shown in Figure 5.6.

Light Railways
During or after the 1916 battle, the French extended their lines east and north. Most of these lines, shown on Figure 5.6, need no further explanation. However, two were of importance to our story.

Froissy to Cappy, Frise and Hem
The line from the junction at Froissy along the Somme canal to Cappy was extended to Frise and for a short distance beyond along the south side of the Somme. The line was also later extended north across the river to Hem, and this then joined other lines north of the river between Hem and Cléry, probably on the line of the Albert to Péronne metre gauge railway. In this way, it provided an important through route from Wiencourt-L'Equipée (on the main standard gauge line to Rosières) towards Bouchavesnes, north of the river. During this period petrol tractors replaced steam locomotives at Frise. Up to 1,500 tonnes of ammunition was hauled along this route daily.

On 15 February 1917, 1st Bttn CRT moved headquarters from Plateau to Froissy, which was also an important yard and light railway transhipment. Having reviewed the situation, they reported that some of the 60cm railways (still being called 'Decauville lines') were in bad condition and required much attention to be fit for operation. However, the main line was operated.

On 13 February, 1st LROC moved to Froissy, where the lines were still being operated by the French. 1st LROC spent some days dealing with coal and other stores, and 'learning the road' towards Frise (sometimes Freeze in British documents), and back through Proyart towards Wiencourt. They were scheduled to take over operation of these lines from the French on 20 February. However, one of their number contracted measles, and they were quarantined until 27 February. On 7 March, they were joined by part of the 18th TCC. Control posts were taken over including some north of the Somme in the Hem and Cléry area, about 2 miles behind the front line, and still under shell fire. During this period, 1st LROC only had one petrol tractor operating from Frise to north of the river, but by the middle of March this was busy with traffic day and night.

Cappy to Herbécourt and Flaucourt
There was probably a French branch line east from Cappy towards Herbécourt. On 25 February, 1st Bttn CRT commenced an extension from Herbécourt and Flaucourt to two termini east of Flaucourt. The line was ready for 'push car' traffic by 3 March, and shortly afterwards for petrol tractors.

The retreat to the Hindenburg Line
From late February, there were reports of abandoned German front line positions. By 17 March, the German Army had definitely gone from their former front line, and, as was discovered, had retreated to the Hindenburg Line further east.

Chapter Six

Light and metre gauge railways of the Somme sector 17 March 1917 to 20 March 1918

From late February or early March 1917, the German army retreated from the Somme battlefields to the Hindenburg line, which ran south east from Quéant to just west of Le Catelet and then south to St Quentin and Soissons. The proper German title for this heavily fortified prepared position was the *Siegfried Stellung* (Siegfried position), and the withdrawal was named Operation Alberich, after the dishonest dwarf in the Niebelung legends. The withdrawal achieved a considerable shortening of the German front line, During the retreat, the German army laid waste to the land and destroyed the infrastructure as far as possible.

It is probable that the German army's withdrawal to the Hindenburg Line was complete, or almost so, by 17 March 1917. At this point, the Allied Armies were faced with a vast area of vacated territory, up to 40km (24 miles) deep, from just south of Arras in the north to Soissons, on the River Aisne, in the south. The Allied Armies proceeded to advance and occupy this territory. They found a wasteland. Villages and towns had been systematically destroyed, crops burnt, fruit trees cut down and wells poisoned. Most railway, road, river and canal bridges had been blown, and railways destroyed or rendered unusable, and there were many delayed action mines and other traps. The Allied Armies established a new front line facing the Hindenburg Line, and proceeded to restore roads, railways and waterways.

In April and May 1917, the Battle of Arras resulted in important advances north and south of Arras, but only as far south as Bullecourt, attacked by the Australians. South of the railway from Achiet to Marcoing there was no major offensive until the Battle of Cambrai, from 20 November to 3 December 1917. After that, the responsibility of the British army was extended to the south, and preparations were made for the expected German offensive. This began on 21 March 1918.

The British responsibility had been extended south to the Amiens to Roye road, just northwest of Roye, in February 1917. In April 1917, the limit moved north, to the new front line immediately west of St Quentin. In June, it was moved again to a line to the east of Brie. After the Battle of Cambrai, in December, the Fifth Army returned from the Ypres area, and was given responsibility as far south as the small town of Barisis, east of Noyon. These areas, and their main railways to March 1918, are shown in Figure 6.1.

Before the Battle of Cambrai - 17 March to 19 November 1917
Standard Gauge railways
Albert to Achiet-le-Grand and Arras
The German retreat enabled the reopening of the pre-war main line from Amiens to Arras via Albert. After some disagreement as to whether the British or the French were to undertake the reconstruction, in the end RCE V did it. It was open for traffic all the way in April 1917.

Candas–Acheux–Colincamps–Achiet-le-Petit (Irles junction)
It was agreed to extend this line as soon as possible to a junction with the Amiens to Arras main line between Miraumont and Achiet-le-Grand, just east of Achiet-le-Petit, also known as Irles junction. In March 1917, RCE V were instructed to concentrate all Fifth Army labour on this. The line was completed through to Achiet-le-Grand in early April and the ROD took over operation from Colincamps on 15 April.

Beaussart to Aveluy
The line from Beaussart to Aveluy was converted back to metre gauge during 1917 and early 1918 (see the metre gauge section). However, the standard gauge Pioneer yard at Aveluy was kept, connected to the Amiens to Arras main line.

Achiet-le-Grand to Bapaume and Marcoing
This line of *Intérêt Local* had been present before the First World War. Now it would form an important route east towards Marcoing. It also led to the junction at Vélu, for the line towards St. Quentin.

In their retreat the Germans had virtually destroyed this line. The infrastructure was damaged, all the bridges had been destroyed, and the track had been removed. The 2nd Bttn CRT began work on 22 March. Bapaume was reached on 3 April. From 10 April, 2nd CRT pushed on east and by 30 April the 3½ miles of wrecked line to Vélu via Frémicourt had been relaid.

On 1 May, 2nd CRT were instructed by RCE V to survey alternative schemes for the extension towards Marcoing. The pre-war line had been through Hermies,

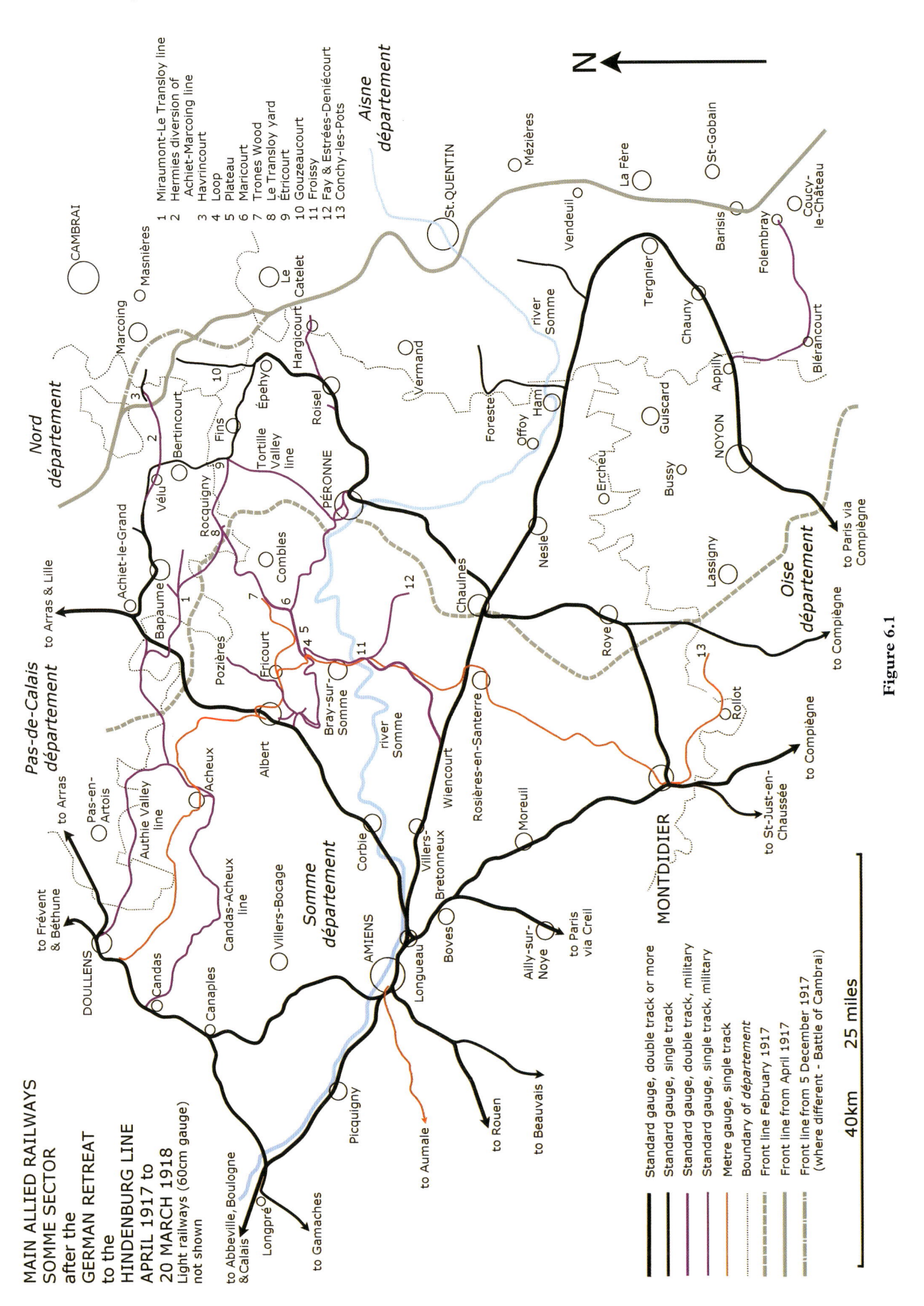

Light and metre gauge railways of the Somme sector 17 March 1917 to 20 March 1918

1 Miramont-Le Transloy line
2 Hermies diversion of Achiet-Marcoing line
3 Havrincourt
4 Loop
5 Plateau
6 Maricourt
7 Trones Wood
8 Le Transloy yard
9 Étricourt
10 Gouzeaucourt
11 Froissy
12 Fay & Estrées-Deniécourt
13 Conchy-les-Pots

Figure 6.1

then across the dry bed of the Canal du Nord on a high level bridge, now destroyed, to reach Havrincourt. The adopted solution was to divert the line along the north side of the canal itself, sheltering it from shell fire, but this was not fully implemented until December.

Vélu to Ytres and Étricourt
This was the first part of the *Intérêt Local* single track line which before the war had finished at St. Quentin. This section was constructed from the north end at Vélu by 2nd CRT working under RCE V, and from the south end at Étricourt by troops working under RCC IV. Construction began on 1 May, and the tracks were joined up on 18 May.

Ancre junction to Longueval
The line from Méaulte to Bécourt junction and Pozières was retained. However, the entire system beyond Bécourt junction, to Longueval and Quarry Sidings, was dismantled, and the track material dispatched for new lines.

Ancre junction to Plateau, Maricourt and Trones Wood
During October 1917, the branch line from Pilla junction to the French rail head at Bel Air was dismantled.

Trones Wood to Rocquigny, Ytres and Épehy
The Plateau line was extended from Trones Wood to Étricourt, where it met the line from Vélu to Épehy. At the end of July 1917, some of 3rd RC RMRE moved to Rocquigny to take over parts of the lines between Trones Wood and Étricourt, and beyond, from 295th RC RE. The Épehy railhead was not in use because it was under direct German observation. From September, the 11th United States Engineers were also working on parts of these lines.

Maricourt to Péronne
This new line, 10½ miles long, left the Ancre junction to Trones Wood line at Maricourt. It followed a route across country to Ferme Rouge (Red Farm), and just east of this, south of Maurepas, it met the disused metre gauge line from Albert and followed the route of it to Péronne.

On 22 March 1917, 1st Bttn CRT started work on the line, working from several places, and tracklaying began on 26 March. The battalion (about 1,200 men) was assisted by a labour force of 39 officers and more than 1,500 men. We quote these figures not because they were exceptional, but to illustrate the effort put into some of these urgent railway construction projects. The first supply train was run into Péronne on 15 April.

Chaulnes to Péronne, Roisel and Épehy
This line was reconstructed in single track from Chaulnes by the British army, starting on 25 March 1917. The line reached the bridge over the Canal du Nord at La Chapelette, just short of Péronne, by 14 April, when the line from Maricourt also reached the river bridge. Work on the bridges started on 20 April and the lines were connected on 22 April.

As soon as the line from Maricourt reached Péronne on 14 April, work started laying track towards Roisel and then on to Épehy. Péronne to Roisel was handed over to ROD to operate on 14 May. By 28 May, the 19 miles (31km) from Chaulnes to Roisel had been doubled. From Roisel to Épehy there was more enemy shelling, but by 16 May it was possible to lay track into

6.1 The former metre gauge bridge over the standard gauge line to Roisel, north east of Péronne station. The bridge has been reconstructed to take the standard gauge line from Maricourt. One line was present under the bridge in April 1917, but now on 16 May 1917 this has been doubled. *(IWM Q47004)*

Épehy during dull and hazy weather. The 1st Bttn CRT left for the Ypres sector on 18 June.

Amiens to Chaulnes, Ham and Tergnier
The main line from Amiens to Tergnier was repaired and reopened by French engineers to Chaulnes, Nesle and Ham. The double track reached Flavy-le-Martel on 27 April. The line was extended in single track to Tergnier by June 1917.

Wiencourt to Froissy, Bray and Loop
This line, built by the French in 1916, was in the British area from February 1917.

Other French lines
The other military lines built by the French in preparation for the 1916 Battle of the Somme, from Moreuil to L'Equipée, from Les Buttes to Gailly, and the branch from Froissy to Bois-Touffu (Fay), had been dismantled by French engineers by January 1918.

Metre gauge lines
Doullens–Albert
Beaussart to Aveluy and Albert, and Acheux to Beaussart - In 1916, the section from Beaussart to Aveluy had been converted to standard gauge by the British Army. In April 1917, the CRCE was instructed that this line should be taken up. It had been suggested that the metre gauge should be relaid alongside the standard gauge first, and then the standard gauge removed using metre gauge rolling stock. This was rejected, probably because it would have required another complete parallel formation. Pioneer Yard at Aveluy was to be kept as standard gauge.

A prime mover for the reinstatement of the metre gauge was the *Société Générale des Chemins de Fer Économiques* (SE), who wanted to restart the commercial exploitation of the whole line.

In June, 260th RC RE were instructed to undertake the conversion work. From June to October, there were problems with materials. Some of it had been used for 60cm gauge lines. The French stated that they were not going to supply any material for the reinstatement. However, the available metre gauge rails needed screws rather than spikes to fix them to the sleepers, and special bolts, and not enough were available. In addition, the French thought that the priority was to complete and open the line, whilst the British priority was to salvage standard gauge track material.

The 1st CORCC took over responsibility for the line but could not get enough ballast. On 6 November, they were moved to Frémicourt for urgent work, and despite requests from the British Army CRCE, there was still no definite date for metre gauge reopening. It is clear that in reality this was not a very high priority for British army railway troops at that time.

Gézaincourt to Acheux - Meanwhile, the section of the Doullens to Albert line from Gézaincourt to Acheux continued to operate, and still had some military use. It was also now safe for a limited civilian service to operate. The service was provided by the owners SE, who ran two trains per day, with the rolling stock based at Acheux Yard. The times for July 1917 are shown in Table 6.1. These trains were slower than most of the 1914 services, by 20 to 30 minutes. There were some possible connections with the very limited standard gauge service at Gézaincourt.

Albert to Fricourt and Trones Wood, and to Montdidier
British Army maps of early 1918 show that these lines were still present. It is probable that they were still in military use, and that the line from Albert to Trones Wood was operated by the British using French rolling stock.

During 1917, SE ran a civilian service once a day each way between Bray-sur-Somme and Montdidier, based at Bray. The times for July 1917 are shown in Table 6.1. This train was slower than most of the 1914 services, by 20 to 40 minutes. In the morning, it lay over at Rosières from 8.00am to 8.50am to connect with the single civilian train of the day from Ham to Amiens on the standard gauge line, stopping at Rosières at 8.41am. In the evening passengers could change from the single daily train at 6.34pm from Amiens to Ham but would have to wait until 8.05pm for the Bray train.

Noyon to Montdidier
From the outbreak of war, the service was much reduced due to lack of manpower (see Chapter Three). The service ceased altogether with the advance of the German army to the Marne, and in autumn 1914 the static front line was just west of Lassigny, cutting off the Noyon end of the line.

From March 1917, it was safe to reopen a civilian service from Montdidier as far as Conchy-les-Pots. From July 1917, the service, provided by the *Compagnie du Chemin de Fer de Hermes à Beaumont* (HB), ran once daily, as shown in Table 6.1. There were limited standard gauge connections at Montdidier. We do not have any details of French military use of the line. In August, HB, with the support of the Oise *département*, wanted to extend the service to Lassigny. If temporary buildings were provided at the damaged station at Lassigny, a train could be based there. However, the line required some repair along the former trench lines, for which the *Compagnie* did not have the personnel. An inspection of the line from Canny-sur-Matz to Lassigny by train on 5 September, by the Company Engineer, found a very deformed track, with the locomotive driver having to proceed very carefully at walking pace. On 8 September, the Military Commission of the *Réseaux du Nord* informed the *Préfet* of Oise that the line could not be

Narrow Gauge in the Somme Sector

Table 6.1 Summary Timetables for Somme Sector metre gauge lines July 1917

Acheux–Gézaincourt *(Doullens–Albert) (SE)*			*Bray-sur-Somme–Montdidier* *(Albert–Montdidier) (SE)*		*Montdidier–Conchy-les-Pots* *(Noyon–Montdidier) (HB)*	
Acheux-Varennes	05.33	13.00	Bray-sur-Somme	07.00	Montdidier	11.00
Louvencourt	05.52	13.19	Froissy (halt)	07.06	Ayencourt	11.03
Beauquesnes	06.32	13.54	Proyart	07.30	Assainvillers	11.15
Beauval	07.00	14.11	Harbonnières	07.52	Rollot	11.30
Gézaincourt	07.11	14.22	Rosières a	08.00	Hainvillers	11.36
			d	08.50	Boulogne-la-Grasse	11.45
			Caix-Vrély	09.01	Conchy-les-Pots	11.50
			Le Quesnel-Beaufort	09.12		
			Arvillers-Hangest	09.35		
			Davesnescourt	09.55		
			Montdidier	10.27		
Gézaincourt	09.15	17.51	Montdidier	18.25	Conchy-les-Pots	12.00
Beauval	09.34	18.10	Davesnescourt	19.00	Boulogne-la-Grasse	12.08
Beauquesnes	09.56	18.32	Arvillers-Hangest	19.28	Hainvillers	12.15
Louvencourt	10.31	19.15	Le Quesnel-Beaufort	19.36	Rollot	12.25
Acheux-Varennes	10.48	19.32	Caix-Vrély	19.50	Assainvillers	12.35
			Rosières a	20.00	Ayencourt	12.45
			d	20.05	Montdidier	12.48
			Harbonnières	20.20		
			Proyart	20.34		
			Froissy (halt)	20.55		
			Bray-sur-Somme	21.00		

a   arrive   d   depart
SE   *Société Générale des Chemins de Fer Économiques*
HB   *Compagnie du Chemin de Fer de Hermes à Beaumont*

6.2 The *Compagnie du Nord* halt at Gézaincourt, showing the metre gauge platform of the line from Doullens to Albert. Postcard written August 1911. It was from here that the civilian passenger service to Acheux-Varennes started in July 1917, and probably at other stages of the First World War up to March 1918. *(Authors' collection)*

6.3 The remains of the SE type 1 station at Fricourt after the 1916 Somme battle. The end of a passenger carriage can be seen on the right. *(Authors' collection)*

6.4 The destroyed station at Lassigny, on the metre gauge line from Noyon to Montdidier. Postcard written April 1918. *(Authors' collection)*

extended to Lassigny because the necessary work had not been done. And there, we think, the matter rested.

By stopping at Conchy, the service did not reach the next station of Roye-sur-Matz, which was also on the standard gauge line from Compiègne to Roye (Somme). However, there was a single daily civilian service from Roye-sur-Matz in each direction.

Light Railways (60cm gauge lines)

As for the standard gauge railways, there was much new building of light railways in the territory from which the German army had retreated to the Hindenburg Line. On the 1916 Somme battlefield, there was some work, completing that started before the German withdrawal, but also some demolition of lines thought to be no longer needed.

In the new territory to the east there was a great deal of new building of light railways, up to the Hindenburg line. These will be described from north to south. Before the retreat to the Hindenburg Line in February 1917, the German army had a long light railway from the Bourlon area, probably on the standard gauge line towards Boisleux. They also had lines going south from Ytres and Fins (Somme), with yards and transhipments at Ytres and probably at Fins. It is likely that some use was made of these lines or alignments.

From July 1917, many railway units, or parts of units, moved north to the Ypres sector to support the Fourth Army (moved to Ypres 5 July 1917) and the Fifth Army (moved 31 July 1917). Many of these returned in early 1918 (Fifth Army) or from April 1918 (Fourth Army). Some other companies and battalions moved between the Somme sector and Third Army North (Arras sector).

Rolling stock
Locomotives and wagons were still in short supply in spring and into the summer of 1917. In June, 6th Bttn CRT noted that tractors were particularly scarce. From 6 August, 6th CRT sent two of their four companies to the Arras sector until the end of September, and then from 14 October two were sent to the Ypres Sector. However as early as 20 July, all their petrol tractors were sent north, leaving them to depend on steam locomotives for their construction and operation of the BW system.

Weather
The weather in the area was generally very bad in spring 1917, causing problems for light railway construction and operation. In early April, there were heavy falls of snow, followed by periods of exceptionally heavy rain from April until August.

Light railway accidents
There had been accidents since the introduction of light railways, but with their increased use during 1917 they became more frequent. Collisions between standard gauge and light railway trains on crossings were a particular problem. If near the front line, both trains might be operating without lights.

The 1916 Somme battlefield

Light railways in the area of the 1916 Somme battlefield, north of the Somme, as at 20 March 1918, are shown in Figure 6.2.

Acheux area, including Acheux to Miraumont
These lines, built between January and March 1917, were complete for tractor operation to Beaucourt by 19 March. On 20 March, ADLRV advised 2nd CRT that in view of the military situation construction should cease. The light railways should be used to move salvaged ammunition to standard gauge rail heads and then taken up. The track material would be moved forward nearer the new front line. Since January, 25¼ miles of light railway had been laid.

Demolition began on 21 March. By 28 March, almost all the track between Acheux and Auchonvillers had gone. It must have been heartbreaking to undo all that work so soon. On 25 March, 2nd CRT took over operations from 6th LROC, and the same day at Acheux oversaw the loading onto standard gauge wagons of seven locomotives, thirty-five wagons, one petrol tractor, and five miles of 20lb/yd rails with all the fittings. In the same period, another company of the battalion moved ammunition and rails to a dump at Suicide Corner, near the standard gauge line.

The demolition ended with taking up the light railway in Acheux Yard itself on 7 April, the same day that salvaging of the Auchonvillers to Beaucourt section was complete at the Suicide Corner dump. The HQ of 2nd CRT moved to east of Bapaume, with large parts of the unit. Throughout April and into May 1917 2nd CRT shipped railway material east on the standard gauge line from Acheux, assisted by 29th LROC, based at Acheux from mid-March to mid-May. On 12 May, the final stores were transferred east, and the last of 2nd CRT left Acheux.

North of the standard gauge line from Colincamps to Achiet-le-Petit, the X7 line was built from Achiet-le-Grand to Bucquoy and Gommecourt by October 1917. It then turned north to join the C12 line towards Arras. There were branches south to sidings north of Puisieux, and to the standard gauge line west of Puisieux.

East of the Ancre, Pozières and Longueval to Bapaume

Aveluy to around Pozières
The 4th Bttn CRT remained at Donnet Post, west of Pozières, until the end of April 1917, maintaining lines

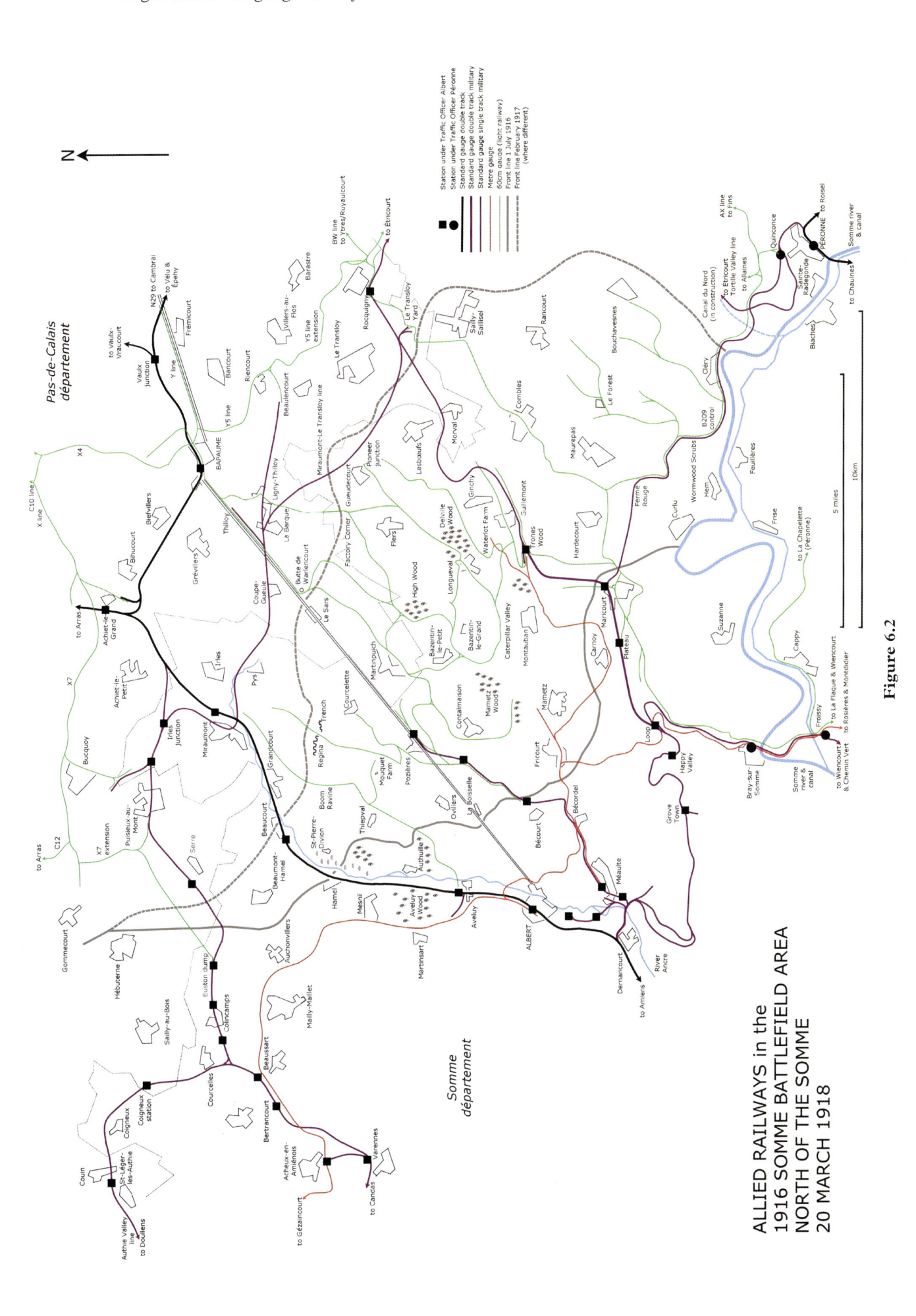

Light and metre gauge railways of the Somme sector 17 March 1917 to 20 March 1918

Figure 6.2 ALLIED RAILWAYS in the 1916 SOMME BATTLEFIELD AREA NORTH OF THE SOMME 20 MARCH 1918

in the area. The 29th LROC were at Pozières from 16 May to 2 June, operating the area before they were sent to the Ypres sector. They were replaced at Pozières by 19th TCC, who took over their huts, possibly at Donnet Post. Their time at Pozières is described in *The Light Track from Arras* (1931, and Plateway Press, 1999). When they arrived, they found no rolling stock, but did eventually find a Péchot (No. 202) in a shed. A few Hudson locomotives were sent later, and they made some wagons from wheels found in shell holes. The lines then still ran to Aveluy, Ovillers, Mouquet Farm, Contalmaison and Bapaume. They were mainly salvaging and stayed for about two months.

The 14th US Engineers were assigned to the Third Army from August 1917. They were based at Boisleux, and further south at Pozières, where they arrived on 18 August, probably replacing 19th TCC. At Pozières, they operated lines to Aveluy and Albert, to Grandcourt, to the Longueval and Ginchy area, and to Bapaume, and salvaged material. They were still at Pozières (and Boisleux) on 21 March 1918.

Pozières to Bapaume
After the German withdrawal Anzac Light Railways (ALR), working with some of the APBs, rapidly extended the line along the Albert to Bapaume road into Bapaume. The 1st APB worked on this in later March, partly by using the existing German standard gauge line along the road, transferring one set of rails to 'close the gauge'.

During March and April 1917, ALR moved to north and east of Bapaume to support the Australian forces for the British and Australian attacks on Bullecourt, which began on 11 April. The line from Pozières to Bapaume continued to be operated by the companies based at Pozières.

Pozières to High Wood, Factory Corner and Thilloy
During April 1917, 1st APB extended the line from Luisenhof Farm to Thilloy, and north of Thilloy the line was joined to the line from Pozières to Bapaume on the Albert to Bapaume road.

Longueval to Ginchy, Gueudecourt and Beaulencourt
5th APB moved back from Bapaume to near Flers, and from 20 to 24 March 1917, extended the light railway from Pioneer junction (Gueudecourt) nearly two miles to Beaulencourt, including restoring 900 yards of German track. From 25 March, they operated the line with mule traction, bringing up supplies from Ginchy Dump to Beaulencourt, despite snow and then heavy rain. In the first week in April, 683 tons of material were handled, and 812 tons in the second week. Traffic between Ginchy and Pioneer Junction

6.5 Men of the 2nd Australian Division taking up bombs to the forward area by light railway; in the background is the Butte de Warlencourt. March 1917. *(IWM Q1861)*

ceased after 13 April, by which time Ginchy Dump had been almost cleared.

From 7 April 5th APB left half a company at Ginchy. They continued to run the line from Pioneer junction to Beaulencourt, and the line from Ginchy until 13 April. After that the parallel railway from Longueval to Pioneeer junction (the Flers line) continued to be used, but presumably locomotives were still scarce, because material would be pushed by hand from Flers and Longueval Dumps to Pioneer Junction, and then taken on by mule to Beaulencourt. The line from Pioneer Junction to Beaulencourt is not shown on later light railway maps and was probably only used for a short time.

Plateau to Rocquigny and Péronne
Plateau Station
The XVth Corps Light Railway Company continued to operate the light railways from Plateau station until 25 May. They were officially named 34th LROC at that date.

Plateau to Maricourt, Cléry and Péronne
The French line, which was taken over in December 1916, extended almost to Cléry, which had been close to the front line until the German withdrawal. There was also a branch up towards Bouchavesnes from just west of Cléry village. The triangular junction near Hem with the line from Froissy and Frise, across the Somme was the site of the B209 control manned by 1st LROC based at Froissy. It is probable that they also operated the line towards Bouchavesnes. We have a first-hand account of activities at the B209 control from the personal diaries of Sgt. Leonard Atkins of 1st LROC, who was based at B209 from 12 March to 8 May when the control closed. On 12 March Atkins writes, 'Left Frise at 2.00pm, arrived B209 at 3.00pm. … I am now about 2 miles from the trenches. This is a cosy little dugout, all boarded-in and no rats or mice. Shells whizzing over us all the time.'

In early March there was much shell fire but not much traffic. By 16 March the one tractor allocated was running day and night. With the German withdrawal, the shell fire ceased, but there were frequent German bombers (Taubes) overhead. On 22 March they were very busy with troop movements passing 'up the line', and on 26 March there were 30 trains. The junction had become a yard, where trains were shunted and sorted out. Probably XVth Corps LRC were running trains from Plateau, joining those from Froissy. Now steam engines were running well beyond B209.

It is not certain when the light railway was extended to Quinconce, following the path of the disused metre gauge line from Albert to Péronne. The standard gauge railway from Maricourt to Péronne also followed this route. Much of the traffic from Froissy and Frise was to bring up ballast for this line. By 4 April, the light railway yard at B209 required a yardmaster, a shunter and a signalman on duty 24 hours a day. The first standard gauge supply train from Maricourt into Péronne ran on 15 April. Thereafter the light railway traffic decreased.

The B209 control was closed with the line across the Somme valley from Frise on 8 May. Possibly the light railway from Maricourt was also closed for a time; it is not shown on the Third Army railway map on 1 January 1918, but it was available for use during the retreat in March 1918.

Plateau and Maricourt to Combles, Rocquigny and Ytres
The 1st CRT continued to work on this mostly French line, to reach the road between Le Transloy and Sailly-Saillisel in April 1917. The 6th Bttn CRT built the link line from Ytres as far as an ammunition dump at Bus by June 1917, and in September this met the line coming from Maricourt at Rocquigny. This formed an important through route. The line from Ytres to Rocquigny was considered part of the BW system.

South of the Somme river and west of Péronne
The lines in this area from up to 20 March 1918 are shown in Figure 6.3. The lines from Froissy continued to be operated by the 1st LROC until July. Following the closure of the line across the Somme, Frise station closed on 15 May, but the line along the Somme canal to Cappy remained open. By the end of March 1917, this line had been extended by 1st Bttn CRT from Flaucourt to La Chapelette, on the standard gauge line just south of Péronne. The line was used by ammunition trains and other trains from 3 April. However, it was not extended across the Somme canal and river. Cappy was a very busy station, second only to Froissy yard. On 12 May, 30 trains were recorded in 12 hours.

With the extension of the British army front down to the road from Amiens to Roye in February 1917, it became responsible for the light railways built by the French south of the Amiens to St Quentin road. Although the British responsibility moved back to the north of that road after April 1917, British operating companies continued to run these light railways at least until June 1917.

The British army also undertook some other construction in these areas. Between 21 and 31 March 1917, 1st Bttn CRT constructed a light railway from Le Quesnoy to Fresnoy-lès-Roye, a short extension of the existing French line east from Mézières and Fresnoy-en-Chaussée and converted a section of 'push car line' at Lihons for steam operation. By June, spurs from La Flaque to Framerville, and from the Vauvillers–Fay line to Foucaucourt, had also been constructed.

Figure 6.3

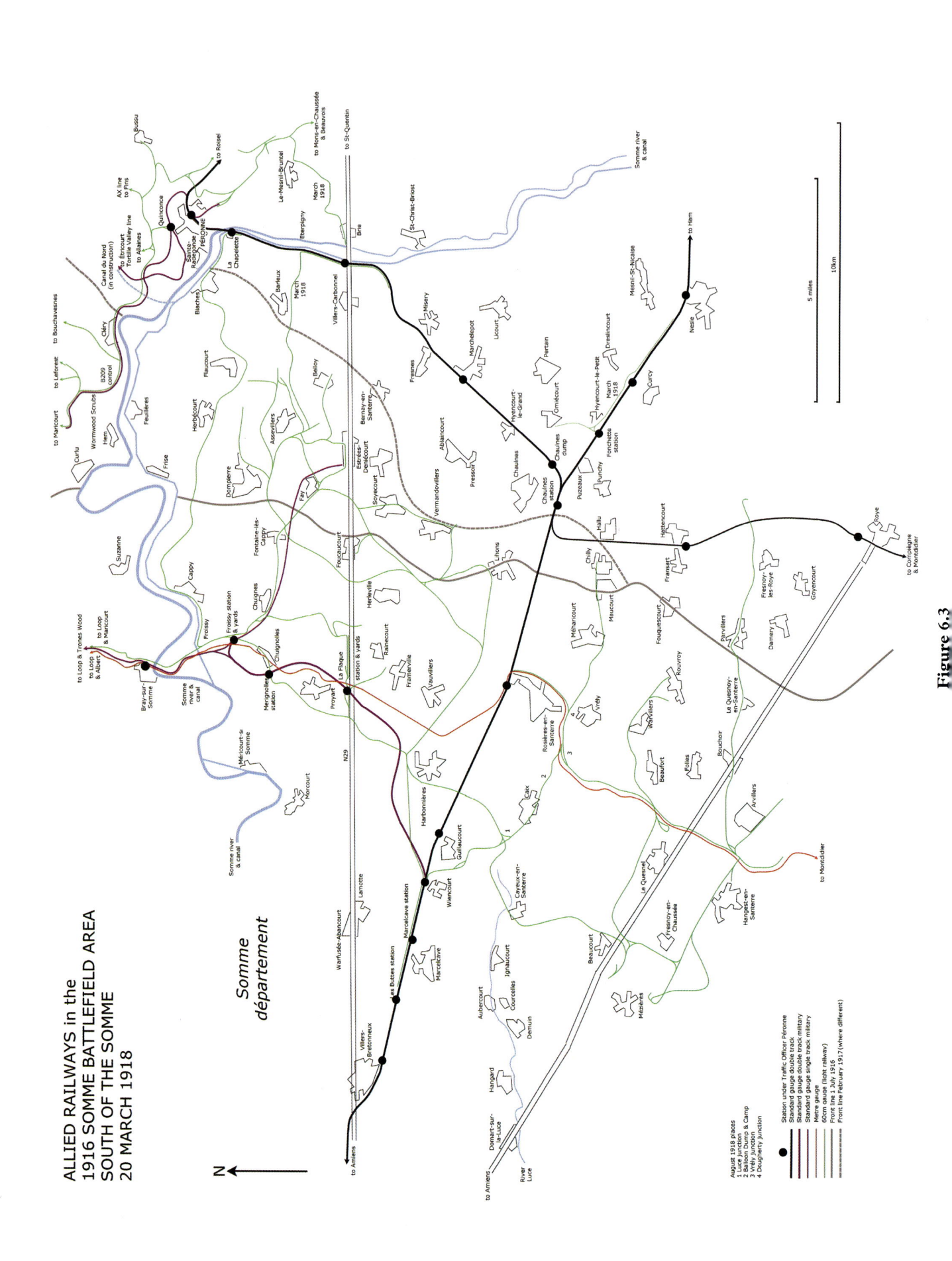

In addition to 1st LROC operating at Froissy, 10th LROC operated from Estrées-en-Santerre from 7 to 30 April. On 25 April, 9th LROC moved to Beaucourt-en-Santerre, just north of the Amiens to Roye main road, and took over the French lines south of the Amiens to Chaulnes main line, with a link across east of Guillaucourt to the lines north of that.

It is not certain for how long 9th LROC stayed, but on 28 May, 34th LROC moved to a camp close to Caix. From there they operated lines south and north of the Amiens to Chaulnes main line, mainly collecting salvage. On 6 July, they moved to Froissy, when the lines south of the Amiens to Chaulnes line were handed back to the French. At Froissy, 34th LROC was employed by the Third Army, the Fourth and Fifth moving to the Ypres sector during July 1917. They stayed at Froissy until 7 March 1918, working all the Third Army south back area lines, mainly handling salvage.

The new territory facing the Hindenburg Line
South of the Achiet to Marcoing line and north of the Péronne to Roisel line

Railways in this area are shown in Figure 6.4.

The Y lines
These lines were north and south of the standard gauge railway from Achiet-le-Grand to Bapaume and on towards Marcoing. In this book we are mainly concerned with light railways south of that line.

The main Y (or Y0) line went east from Bapaume parallel to the standard gauge line. East of Vélu it followed the Hermies diversion of the standard gauge line, but along the south side of the dry bed of the Canal du Nord, to Havrincourt. At Bapaume it connected south west to the line to Pozières and Aveluy, and north with the X4 line to Mory, which was also the light railway route to Achiet-le-Grand and then west along the X7 line towards Hébuterne. North from the main Y line the Y1, Y2, Y8, Y3, Y4 and Y7 lines (in that order, west to east) went north into the Arras sector. From just east of Bapaume the Y5 line went south to Riencourt-lès-Bapaume, and from Vélu the Y6 line also went south, to meet the BW system from Ytres at Bertincourt. Further east the BW lines from the south connected directly with the main Y line.

Anzac Light Railways (ALR), supported by some of the APBs, were mainly concerned with construction and operation north of the main Y line. In early May 1917, B Company of 1st APB were constructing light railways at Lebucquière, and the junction of the Y3 line with the Y main line near there was called Anzac Junction.

However, it was mainly Canadian units who constructed the Y system. The 2nd Bttn CRT moved their headquarters to near Frémicourt in the middle of April. On 25 May 1917 they took over all the light railways in the Fifth Army area from 4th Bttn CRT. Starting from then, they constructed, or in some cases completed the construction of, light railways around and to the east of Bapaume, including Achiet-le-Grand light railway yard. West of Mory the X line was later connected with the C10 line from Boyelles, another connection with Arras.

By the end of June 1917, the Y line extended through Vélu to the bend in the Canal du Nord north of the Ruyaulcourt canal tunnel, meeting a line north from Ytres. The line from Mory south to Bapaume, the X4 line, was constructed later in 1917. The X and X4 lines formed the main light railway route from Achiet to Bapaume, much separated from the more direct standard gauge line.

The operating company was 2nd LROC based at Bapaume until 15 July 1917, when they were moved to the Ypres Sector in support of the Fifth Army. They were relieved by the 4th LROC, always a Third Army company. In August, and possibly after that, they were supported by a detachment of the 19th TCC. By November, the 9th and 12th Bttns CRT were constructing and maintaining light railways in this area.

The BW, AX and CY systems
These systems of light railways were built between the Y lines in the north and Péronne in the south. They were bounded by the German front line, mainly the Hindenburg Line, in the east, and in the west by the British military standard gauge line from Péronne to Etricourt (the Tortille Valley line) and the standard gauge line south from Vélu to Ytres. For the overall layout of this area during this period please see Figure 6.4.

The main systems were built between May and November 1917. The 6th Bttn CRT, formed at Purfleet in Essex on 31 March 1917, arrived in France on 3 April. On 11 May, the Battalion HQ moved to Lechelle, just south west of Ytres, and remained there until 23 March 1918. This battalion was unusual in numbering the constituent Companies 1 to 4 throughout, rather than the more usual lettering A to D. Two Companies (1 and 3) were with Third Army North, in the Arras Sector, in August and September 1917, and then two Companies (1 and 4) went to the Ypres Sector in Belgium from October 1917 until December (No 4 Company) or early January 1918 (No 1 Company). However, 6th CRT were responsible for the core construction of these systems.

The BW lines were the most northerly, just south of the Y lines. The AX lines were in general south and

Narrow Gauge in the Somme Sector

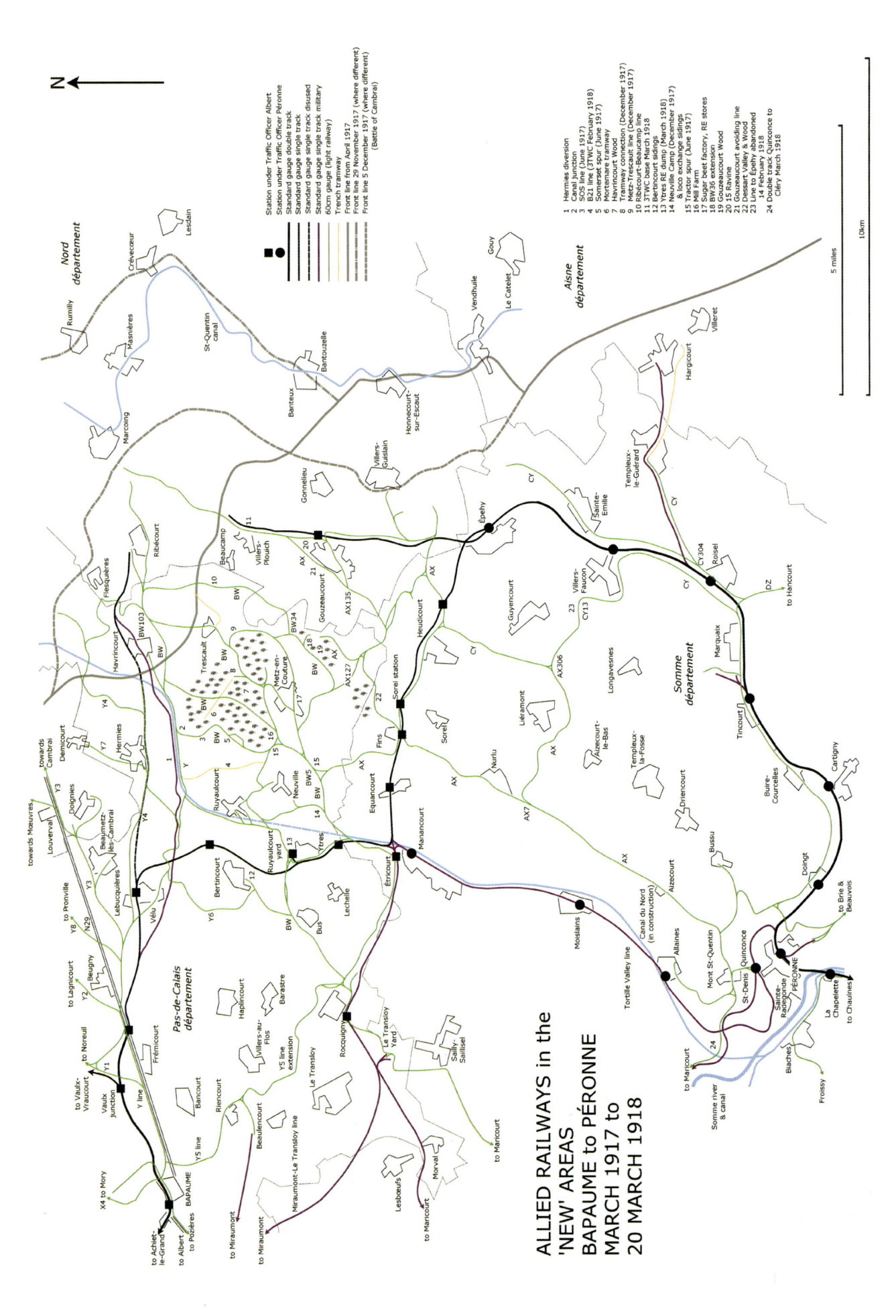

Figure 6.4

east of the BW lines, but eventually included a long line south from Fins to Quinconce (Péronne). The CY lines were all south of the standard gauge line from Étricourt to Épehy, and further to the east.

From 15 May 1917, 6th CRT took over responsibility for all Fourth Army light railways. The meeting point with Fifth Army light railways was near Bertincourt, where a branch north from the BW line met the Y6 line south from Vélu. From 23 May, 6th CRT started to receive locomotives and other rolling stock.

BW lines - Some confusion may be caused by the naming of the standard gauge stations in this area. Ytres station was in fact about 1 mile south of the centre of Ytres village. In view of this, the British army called the rail head and transhipment just north of Ytres 'Ruyaulcourt', even though Ruyaulcourt village was further away than Ytres. The 6th CRT constructed yards at Ytres station with light railway sidings and transhipments, and built light railways east, and then from these north and south, as shown on Figure 6.4.

The first lines were built east to the sugar factory (referred to as 'the beet root factory' in some documents) at Metz-en-Couture, and to Mill Farm near Havrincourt Wood. During May, shortages of track material were blamed on the operators at Ytres standard gauge yard, where wagons were waiting to be unloaded for 40 hours or more, overlooked by the troops responsible. So 6th CRT decided to use the rail head at Fins instead and take material from there by road until the light railway to Fins had been connected. The day after this decision, eight wagons of sleepers and ten wagons of track material were unloaded at Fins, followed by much more. Shortages of track material continued into June. Old German lines in the area were inspected, but no track material had been left.

By the end of May 1917, the lines had been extended south and east from the Metz sugar factory to Gouzeaucourt Wood, north up the west side of Havrincourt Wood, and west from Mill Farm back to the standard gauge line north of Ytres village (Ruyaulcourt station). Here standard gauge spurs were built at some time both east and west of the main line from Vélu to Étricourt, and almost certainly there was another transhipment. Almost 10½ miles of track had been laid in three weeks.

Construction continued in June. On 5 June, an urgent request came through from the Army for the extension of the line up the west side of Havrincourt Wood to the south bank of the dry bed of the Canal du Nord. This was completed three days later. Here it would later meet the Y line, extended along the south side of the canal in December 1917. By the end of the month, the line from Metz had been extended to Trescault, and a line south from Ruyaulcourt completed to link the main west to east lines. The BW link from Ytres village (Ruyaulcourt station) to Rocquigny, was fully open for traffic to Plateau on 18 July, There was a yard and rail head at Rocquigny station on the standard gauge line from Plateau to Étricourt.

By the end of June, the main construction of the system was complete, and 90 per cent of the Battalion were occupied maintaining and upgrading the lines. In that month, 13 miles of track had been constructed, and 34 miles of track were being maintained. The operating company based at Ytres from 20 May were the 9th LROC, who probably remained in this area until at least February 1918.

Towards the end of June, the lines were inspected by a party including General Stewart, CO of Canadian Railway Troops, and then on 29 June by Field Marshall HRH Duke of Connaught and his staff. There were further visitors on 2 July, the fiftieth anniversary of the Confederation of Canada.

AX lines - In early April 1917, 1st Bttn CRT began construction of the line north from Quinconce (Péronne) to Nurlu and Fins, open by the end of the month. By the end of May, the line had been extended north east from Fins to a junction with another AX line. This line extended from the BW Gouzeaucourt Wood line, and by the end of May had reached the edge of Gouzeaucourt Village, at the AX135 control point. The line also went south east to meet the line from Heudicourt rail head to the path of the standard gauge line north of Épehy, which was not in operation at that time. From 1 to 14 May, 10th LROC were the operating company based at Nurlu, and they moved to Fins to operate from 15 May, remaining to 6 July.

In June, a line was built east, from the Fins–Quinconce line just south of Nurlu, to the CY line near Liéramont. On 15 June, 6th Bttn CRT took over the AX lines. They were not impressed with state of the line from Quinconce to Fins, which they thought would 'practically have to be rebuilt'. Heavy rains on 20 June caused part of the line between Nurlu and Aizecourt to subside. Nevertheless, they put the lines in shape and by 30 June could use them and the CY lines to carry out troop movements for divisional relief.

The 6th CRT continued repair and maintenance in July and built a line parallel with the standard gauge line from Fins to Heudicourt. Also, by 30 July, a line was built into Villers-Guislain along an old German formation. Progress was slow because proximity to the front line necessitated night work.

CY lines - The 6th Bttn CRT worked on the CY lines from June 1917, with 3rd RC RARE, who arrived at Tincourt on 18 June. They took part in the Battle of Cambrai and by the time they left at the end of January 1918 they had constructed 40 miles of light railway.

The CY system based around Roisel was authorised in early June. Construction of the line from Heudicourt (or Heudecourt) began at the junction with the AX line east of there on 13 June. By the end of June, nearly 6 miles of track had been laid, to the AX junction near Liéramont and on to west of Villers-Faucon. A company of 6th CRT moved there on 4 July to work on a line from there to Épehy, but this was abandoned 2 days later on the orders of Fourth Army ADLR.

A line from Hamel, between Tincourt and Marquaix, to Roisel and on to join the Heudicourt line at Villers-Faucon was completed in June. In July, a line was built from Roisel which followed close to the standard gauge line almost to Épehy. A line from Tincourt to Quinconce (Péronne) was prospected in July but was concluded to be a very bad route. It may have been on an old German formation. It was not built until early 1918. which meant that all the CY links before the Battle of Cambrai were to the north and then the west.

South of the Péronne to Roisel standard gauge line - DZ lines

These are shown on Figure 6.5 (page 121). The DZ lines extended south from Roisel. With the departure of the Fifth and then the Fourth Army to the Ypres area, this area was run by Third Army South. There were no links west, and since there was no line from Tincourt to Quinconce until early 1918, the light railway connections in 1917 were all through Roisel and then east and north to Heudicourt, or to the Quinconce to Fins line.

The lines were constructed by 6th Bttn CRT, beginning in early August 1917. By 27 August, they had laid and ballasted nearly five miles of track. Track had been laid from Roisel to Montigny Farm and on to the main road from Amiens to St. Quentin just west of Vermand, the boundary of British responsibility until January 1918. There was also a spur from a junction south west of Herville towards Bernes.

The 12th US Engineers arrived in the area on 18 August 1917 and established their base at the sugar factory at Montigny Farm, taking over the DZ lines on 28 August. By the end of October, they were operating 41 miles of light railway, and maintaining another 25 miles. This included AX, CY and DZ lines with Chief Dispatchers at Fins, Tincourt, and Montigny Farm respectively. They worked within the British Third Army organisation, and the rolling stock was provided by the British Army, although it did include locomotives of American manufacture.

During the summer of 1917, the 1st LROC were also operating from the base at Montigny Farm, until about the middle of September. They may have been replaced by another operating company, explaining why the 12th US Engineers were maintaining more track than they operated.

The 6th CRT were also still constructing. In September, a branch was extended to Hancourt, and branches were built to Hesbecourt and to Jeancourt with a short branch to Le Verguier by early October, with spurs and sidings added until early November.

BW, AX, and CY lines, August to November 1917

Meantime, work continued on these systems north of the Péronne to Épehy standard gauge line (see Figure 6.4). The yards at Quinconce (Péronne) were considerably extended in September 1917. In September and early October, the BW link from Ruyaulcourt to the Ytres to Metz line, and the AX link south from that to Fins, were constructed, completed on 10 October. It was also in October and November that the AX line south of Gouzeaucourt was extended through the village, and on along the standard gauge route to Villers-Plouich. All this led to the link up with the other line at AX135 and the construction of the Gouzeaucourt avoiding line as part of the preparations for the Battle of Cambrai. Also, in September 1917, a branch of the CY line from Roisel was built near the route of the metre gauge line to Hargicourt.

The Battle of Cambrai 20 November to 4 December 1917

On 20 November 1917, the IIIrd and IVth Corps of the British Third Army attacked from Boursies, on the Bapaume to Cambrai road, in the north, to Gonnelieu, in the south. The Cambrai Offensive was led by nearly 500 tanks. There was no preliminary bombardment, and infantry followed immediately behind the tanks at walking pace. It is regarded as the first major tank battle.

The attack opened a gap six miles wide in the German front line, breaching part of the Hindenburg Line and some support lines behind. The breach was opened up into a salient, penetrating as far as Bourlon Wood in the north and beyond Marcoing and part of the St-Quentin canal further south. Why the breakthrough was not properly exploited is beyond the scope of this book. On 30 November, the German Second Army counterattacked, and by 4 December, the British had withdrawn from part of the area gained, losing Marcoing. Havrincourt, Flesqières and Ribécourt were held, but in the south the villages of Gonnelieu and Villers-Guislain were lost.

There were important light railway developments in the Somme Sector associated with the battle. Please refer to Figure 6.4 (page 108), which shows the principal locations described, and the front lines before, during and after the Battle.

Standard gauge railways

Much of the standard gauge preparation was to ensure facilities for delivery and unloading of the tanks as close as possible to the battlefield. Ramps already existed at Plateau station, and new ramps were built at Ruyaulcourt, Sorel, and Heudicourt, and also at Méaulte, in case trains could not get up to Plateau.

Light railways

On 1 November 1917, 6th Bttn CRT received orders from the ADLR III South to construct ammunition, stone and ration spurs, and to undertake main line works, on the BW and AZ light railway systems in the forward area, on the front between Havrincourt and Gouzeaucourt. The 3rd RC RARE also constructed new spurs on the AX lines in the Fins area. By 10 November, this had been completed. Further orders were now received to prepare for the construction of lines from Villers-Plouich to Marcoing, an extension of the AX line north past Gouzeaucourt, and from Trescault to Marcoing via Ribécourt, an extension of the BW system. Both these lines extended into enemy territory. Work was begun building Forward Supply Dumps to hold material for this construction.

The 6th Bttn CRT undertook work for these dumps at Fins and Heudicourt standard gauge stations, and on the western edge of Gouzeaucourt. They also worked at Villers-Plouich, and they revised track on the AX line. By 17 November, four miles of light railway material had been delivered to Villers-Plouich and five miles to Trescault. During the preparations, crossings were kept open for 380 tanks, on their way to the assembly areas. The 3rd RC RARE also undertook preparatory work, in the Fins area.

On 17 November, the 6th Bttn CRT were told that the Villers-Plouich to Marcoing line, and 3rd RC RARE that the Trescault–Ribécourt–Marcoing line, were to be completed within 48 hours of the attack on 20 November.

Because of better records, we know more about the preparations of 6th Bttn CRT than we do for 3rd RC RARE. By 18 November, the necessary materials had been assembled just south of Villers-Plouich village, in the area of the old station on the standard gauge line. The material included 22 'cars' (wagons) each with 125 16ft steel rails for the main line (2686 in all), each with a complete set of fish plates, bolts, and spikes. More than 8,500 'ties' (sleepers) were loaded from another 25 wagons. Eight-foot track sections (600 sets) for loops and sidings were pre-assembled and loaded separately, with four right hand and four left hand 'switches' (points). There was also bridging material. Ten petrol tractors were available to haul the material. One tractor, one wagon and tools for emergency repairs were placed at the AX135 control point, at the junction of the new Gouzeaucourt cut-off line just south west of the village, and two more tractors with wagons were placed further back at AX127 for emergency repair gangs.

Two companies, Nos 2 and 3 (500 men) of 6th Bttn CRT were allocated to this work, with five attached labour companies (more than 1,600 men), and 15 signals men. The companies were reformed into gangs with specific tasks, and on 19 November they rested.

The intention was to construct the line close behind the advancing infantry, with sidings provided at least every mile. From midnight on 19 November, an officer was stationed at AX135, and from then until the line could be opened for traffic, only construction and ambulance trains were allowed. On 20 November, the opening day of the offensive, the two railway and five labour companies were moved up from Fins on the railway, and formed up into working parties at AX135 at 6.00am. They moved up to Villers-Plouich at 8.30am and commenced work at 9.15am, about 600yds from the German front line. By 4.30pm, 1.5 miles track had been laid and finished, including 2 bridges, one of 40ft span, and one siding (AX509). At 8pm the first ammunition train travelled on the track from Villers-Plouich to the first siding. The operating company was the 12th US Engineers.

Work restarted at 9am on 21 November and continued to 6am on 22 November. By the evening of 21 November, 1.75 miles of track had been finished, passing around two large craters, to the second siding. Ammunition was carried all day to the first and second sidings. The new line was connected with the captured German line just south west of Marcoing at 6am on 22 November, 3.5 miles from Villers-Plouich. The first ammunition train reached this junction at 3pm, but the German track, although in good condition, was found to be too lightly constructed for the heavy British-US trains.

The Canadian troops were allowed to rest until noon, and then they worked back down the line, finishing off. No 3 Company moved into billets at Marcoing, where the houses were practically intact except for window glass, and No 2 Company and the attached labour returned to their original accommodation. However, No 3 Company were heavily shelled during the night at Marcoing, and on 23 November pulled back to make camp about two miles down the line towards Villers-Plouich, with a captured German field kitchen.

Further north, 3rd RC RARE started work at the BW54 control point, near Trescault as soon as the attack started on 20 November, and three days later they had extended the line by three miles. Traffic was being run on the line almost as soon as it was built. However, they did not link up with the captured German light railway near Ribécourt until 30 November. This was the same line as the one to which 6th Bttn CRT had linked on 22 November, about 2½ miles further west.

It was also on 30 November that the German counterattack started, forcing 3rd RC RARE to withdraw. Because of the German advance, No 3 Company of 6th CRT had to evacuate their camp, leaving almost all their tools and equipment. They evacuated by train south along the AX line, but north west of Gouzeaucourt they came under fire from the village, temporarily occupied by the German army. They were forced to leave their train and retreat west in small groups, first to Fins, which was being heavily shelled, and then to 6th Bttn CRT HQ at Lechelle.

The 12th US Engineers also had to make a hasty retreat, fortunately without casualties. The Canadians (6th CRT) recorded one killed, three missing and four wounded, all of No 3 Company. The German army did not hold Gouzeaucourt, but the front line at the end of the battle on 4 December was much closer to the AX lines south of Villers-Plouich than it had been before. The Battle of Cambrai showed that the key role of light railways in maintaining supplies to the front line during an attack had been recognised.

After the battle of Cambrai 5 December 1917 to 20 March 1918

On 14 December, the Supreme War Council decided that the British should take over 24 miles (38km) of French front covering the sector from just north of St Quentin southwards to Barisis, a small town in the St Gobain forest, due east of Noyon. The area was taken over by the end of January by the Fifth Army under General Gough, returning from the Ypres sector. At the same time the Fifth Army took over from the Third Army the existing British front line from Gouzeaucourt almost to St Quentin, another 12 miles (20km).

A major German offensive was generally expected. This was thought at first to be scheduled for 1 March 1918. The main priorities were strengthening the front line and improving communications. This was less of a concern north of St Quentin, which had been held by Third Army for a long time. Fifth Army were thinly spread on a long front, of which two thirds was newly taken over from the French Army, and General Gough expressed his concern to GHQ about being able to do enough work in the time available to hold the front successfully.

Weather

The winter of 1917-1918 was again very cold. Towards the end of the hard frost there were periods of thaw when the ground turned to soft mud, then froze again. In the trenches there were reports of frostbite, and even death from exposure. The weather also caused serious problems with railway construction and maintenance.

Railways after the Battle of Cambrai

On 5 January 1918, RCC III, which had been in charge of standard gauge railways for Third Army North, were moved to the Ypres sector, supporting the Fourth Army and later Second Army South. They never returned to the Somme sector. RCE V now took over the whole of the Third Army area. They only continued to look after the returning Fifth Army until 18 January, when RCC IV returned from the Ypres sector and took over (see Table 4.1, Chapter Four). Please refer to Figures 6.4 (page 108) and 6.5 (page 121) for the area north of Ham, and to 6.6 (page 127) for the rest of the 'new' area from Ham to Barisis. It was in early 1918 that many railway units were armed for the first time.

Standard gauge lines in the area of Third Army (south)

Aveluy yard and Pioneer Yard
The conversion of the line from Beaussart to Aveluy back to metre gauge continued (see metre gauge section), but in January 1918, RCE V agreed that Pioneer and Aveluy Yards should remain. On 8 March, RCE V moved their headquarters train to Pioneer Yard.

Authie Valley line (Doullens to Courcelles via Coigneux)
It seems that this line had been neglected since March 1917. No action was taken until 22 March, after the beginning of the German advance on 21 March, when labour was immediately diverted to make the line fit for traffic again.

Achiet-le-Grand to Bapaume and Marcoing
It was in December 1917 that the Hermies diversion was completed. It was extended east from near the northern portal of the Ruyaulcourt tunnel, using the north towpath of the dry canal for about 1 mile. Here it left the canal to rejoin the old formation at Havrincourt junction.

Miraumont to Le Transloy (The Miraumont - Rocquigny extension)
In December 1917, it was agreed to extend the Candas line from Achiet-le-Petit to the Maricourt to Rocquigny line at Le Transloy Yard. Among other considerations, it was noted that this would be useful if the enemy should advance on the Bullecourt front and make the Achiet to Bapaume line unusable. In this way it provided an additional west to east route from Candas, and from Doullens via the Authie Valley line. This also bypassed the restriction on British Army trains passing through Amiens. It was called the Miraumont to Le Transloy line.

The single track line left the Candas line at Achiet-le-Petit, and passed under the Amiens–Arras main line just south of Miraumont, with a chord connecting to the main line south towards Albert. The line then climbed east from the Ancre Valley onto the plateau, curving south east to join the Maricourt to Étricourt line at Le Transloy Yard. This was actually on the road from Le Transloy to Sailly-Saillisel, and nearer the latter. The line was about 10 miles (16km) long.

Plans were approved for construction to start on 5 February 1918. By 21 March, it is shown on maps as linked through and usable but reports of the reconstruction in September 1918 (Chapter Eight) indicate that long sections at the eastern end, and some stations, were incomplete.

Ancre junction to Épehy, via Plateau, Maricourt and Étricourt

Much work was done at 'Le Transloy', which became a very important yard, and a light railway transhipment. Major works began in December 1917, by 4th Bttn CRT. Construction included a rail head for four divisions, and ammunition sidings, the last completed by 15 February.

Standard gauge lines in the Fifth Army area

The Tortille Valley line (Étricourt to Quinconce)

This was designed to provide a new north to south link further from the front line than the Péronne to Épehy and Épehy to Étricourt lines, considered unsafe between Roisel and Fins.

Work was commenced at the end of December 1917. At the north end, the line started from a triangular junction at Étricourt, connected to the lines to Plateau and Miraumont, and to Vélu and Bapaume, and to Épehy. From there the line went south, following the dry bed of the incomplete Canal du Nord in the valley of the small Tortille river. At the south end the line went under the Maricourt to Péronne line, and then curved east to join that line between Quinconce and Flamicourt (Péronne). The line was 9 or 10 miles long (15-16km). Starting from the north end, stations were constructed at Manancourt, Moislains and Allaines. The line was constructed by 4th Bttn CRT, assisted by 11th US Engineers, and was open for traffic on 2 March 1918.

Froissy to Fay and Estrées-Deniécourt

Beginning on 17 February 1918, 4th CRT worked on reopening the old French branch from Froissy to Bois-Touffu (Fay). Track laying began on 1 March, and by March 20 it was usable to a rail head and ammunition dump at Estrées-Deniécourt.

Chaulnes to Péronne, Roisel, and Épehy

Additional work was done on yards and facilities, including a light railway transhipment at Flamicourt, opened on 28 February, on a short spur down the old metre gauge path towards Ham.

Roisel to Hargicourt

The German army are said to have taken up the track in March 1917. Maps of early 1918 show that a standard gauge line was under construction along the path of the former metre gauge line, probably completed by 20 March 1918.

Amiens to Chaulnes, Ham and Tergnier

This, and the other lines in the area south of this taken over by the Fifth Army, were established French *Compagnie du Nord* lines, under the control of French Engineers. Fifth Army took over facilities and stations as required, and supply railheads were established. Parts had been reconstructed in 1917 by French Engineers. The line was in use as far as Tergnier, very close to the front line.

Ham to Foreste

In 1917, the single track line of *Intérêt Local* from Ham to St. Quentin was reconstructed by French Engineers to beyond Foreste. On 5 January 1918, 3rd RC RMRE inspected the line, with instructions to take it over from the French, but the instructions were cancelled on 7 January. Fifth Army established two rail heads on the line, at Villers-St-Christophe and Foreste (Forest on some British maps). Here important light railway facilities were established.

Jussy to Montescourt and Essigny

This was the southern part of the line from Tergnier to St. Quentin, which before the First World War had left the Amiens to Tergnier main line east of Jussy, with a triangular junction. The line was restored by French Engineers in 1917 and opened on 30 June, rebuilt from a new junction west of Jussy, to join the old formation at Montescourt. The old bridge over the St. Quentin canal had been too visible from the German front line.

Noyon to Tergnier

The main line from Paris and Compiègne was restored in double track by French Engineers, for 34km (21 miles) from Ribécourt, south west of Noyon, to Tergnier, and reopened in April 1917. The Fifth Army took over stations from Pont l'Evêque to Chauny.

Appilly to Folembray

The French built this military line in 1917, from Appilly, on the main line from Noyon to Tergnier, to Coucy-le-Château, where it met the standard gauge line from Chauny to Anizy-Pinon. The line quickly left the Fifth Army area into the French Sixth Army area.

The Amiens avoiding line

This line was proposed to link the Amiens to Doullens line, from a junction just south of Poulainville, across the north east of Amiens to Vecquemont, on the Amiens to Albert and Arras main line, to allow through traffic without going through the centre of Amiens.

On 9 March 1918, RCC IV agreed that it should be built, but work was stopped on 26 March in view of the German advance.

Metre Gauge lines in the area of Third Army (south)
Beaussart to Aveluy and Albert, and Acheux to Beaussart

Dismantling the standard gauge track from Beaussart to Aveluy finally commenced on 5 February and was completed on 26th. Reconstruction in metre gauge was finished by 6 March, using French track. The first train ran over the completed line on 16 March, carrying a French inspection party, but no regular service was established before the German advance commencing 21 March.

Metre gauge lines in the Fifth Army area

In early 1918, parts of the formation of a number of these were taken over for the construction of light railways. This affected the Albert to Ham line between Péronne (Flamicourt) and Mons-en-Chaussée, the Ham to Ercheu line between Ham and Voyennes, and the line from Ham to Noyon between Ham and Guiscard. Civilian services may have continued as in 1917, but there is no definite information.

Light railways

In early 1918, light railways were refurbished and new facilities were installed in preparation for the expected German offensive. In particular, plans were made for the withdrawal of light railway rolling stock under its own power, and for this purpose tracks were extended west in places.

Rolling Stock

At the end of February 1918, the 15th (Aus.) LROC moved to Savy-Berlette from the Ypres area. On 1 March they were renamed the 1st Aus. LROC. Savy is on the line from Étaples to Arras, and it was by early 1918 a major light railway depot and transhipment, on the southern edge of the First Army area. Now Savy was designated as a supply depot for motive power for light railways, and over the next month considerable numbers of steam locomotives and tractors were delivered by standard gauge and distributed along the light railways.

Between 1 and 20 March, twenty steam locomotives were delivered, including nine 2-6-2T Alco-Cookes. Of these, eleven were dispatched south to the Fifth Army area. On 19 March, five were sent to Fins and five to Ham. Probably these reached their destinations. The locomotives going to Ham must have used the recently completed B line from Hancourt to Beauvois. A sixth locomotive was dispatched to Ham on 21 March.

This was Alco WD No. 1261, which only reached Quinconce (Péronne). This was the only locomotive we know of to escape from Quinconce during the German advance (see Chapter Seven). No petrol tractors were dispatched to the Somme sector.

The 5th Bttn CRT built an unloading ramp for light railway rolling stock at Euston Dump in January 1918, while building the X7 line extension. Two steam locomotives were delivered, one a Hudson 0-6-0WT, and some tractors and wagons, and a tractor shed was built.

Light Railways in the Third Army South area
The 1916 Somme battlefields (north of the Somme river)

Lines in this area from 5 December 1917 to 20 March 1918 are included in Figure 6.2 (page 103). The only new light railway extension west aiding the escape of rolling stock in this area was the X7 extension to Euston Dump (Colincamps)

Biez Wood to Puisieux (X7 line south extension) and Euston Dump to Puisieux

Between the end of December 1917 and the end of January 1918, A, B and D Companies of 5th Bttn CRT built an extension of the X7 line about 2½ miles (4km) long. The existing X7 line ran west from just north of Achiet-le-Grand, to a junction with the C12 line at Biez Wood, an important connection to the north west. The extension was built south to the standard gauge line at Puisieux, where there were ammunition sidings and probably a transhipment. From a junction just west of Puisieux the line was also built west nearly 3 miles (5km) to Euston Dump Engineer stores. parallel but not close to the standard gauge line.

Miraumont to Pozières and Fricourt

Because of a perceived lack of escape lines, a new north-south lateral line was proposed in January 1918. In February, it was decided to build a line about 8 miles (13km) long from Miraumont to Fricourt via Pozières, where there was still the terminus of the standard gauge branch from Méaulte. On 20 February, No 4 Company of 6th CRT moved to Pozières to start work. There was no attached labour, and in contrast to the normal performance of Canadian Railway Troops, progress was very slow. By 20 March, just over a mile of the formation had been graded, and although five miles of track material had been unloaded at the Pozières rail head on 22 February, no track had been laid. It is unclear why this project was not pursued with more speed.

Pozières to Aveluy

The line from Pozières to Aveluy is shown as still present on Third Army maps of 1 January 1918. However, by

21 March it had been dismantled. Without the line to Aveluy, there were no light railway connections south or west from the lines around Pozières to the Amiens to Arras standard gauge main line.

Maricourt to Cléry and Bouchavesnes
The light railway from Maricourt to just west of Cléry, with the branch north to Bouchavesnes remained or was restored. It was extended to Quinconce (Péronne) in February and March 1918.

The Y, BW and northern AX systems (Third Army South)

Lines in this area from 5 December 1917 to 20 March 1918 are included in Figure 6.4 (page 108).

The Y Lines
During December 1917, 5th Bttn CRT extended the main Y line east along the south bank of the dry cut for the Canal du Nord, and on to Havrincourt and Ribécourt. The latter section had to be constructed at night, because of the proximity of the final front line at the end of the Battle of Cambrai, but some German track was used. On 26 December, this line was linked up on the south bank of the canal with the BW line built north from near Neuville in May and June 1917 along the edge of Havrincourt Wood. This was the end of the Y line, and from this point the line east was part of the BW system.

Meanwhile, 5th CRT were also extending the Y4 line east from Vélu along the old standard gauge formation to Hermies, where there was a light railway yard, and further east. The work was frequently interupted by shell fire. In early 1918, one company of 6th Bttn CRT became responsible for construction and maintenance on the Y system.

Facilities were installed or improved along the line, notably at Frémicourt ration dump, with a supply rail head and transhipment. There were major transhipment yards at Bapaume and east and north of Bapaume, with rail heads for ammunition, supplies, and engineer stores, facilities for troop movements, and tank crossings.

The 6th LROC were operating from Bapaume from 9 November 1917. The 34th LROC moved to Bapaume on 7 March 1918 and took over the operation of this area.

Bapaume to Riencourt (Y5 line)
On 1 and 2 March 1918, 600 yards of track was put in at 'New Yard' on the Y5 line south from Bapaume to Riencourt-lès-Bapaume, adjacent to the main road from Bapaume to Le Transloy. The Y5 line, built in September 1917, was refurbished ready for the extension to Rocquigny.

Rocquigny–Riencourt (Y5 extension)
In February and March 1918, 6th Bttn CRT constructed this important link. Starting from a triangular junction with the Maricourt to Ytres line just south east of Rocquigny, the line curved north then west round Rocquigny, then north west between Beaulencourt and Villers-au-Flos to meet the Y5 line on the edge of Riencourt.

The straight line length of the line was 3 miles (5km), but with the bends it must have been 4 miles (6.5km). There is no definite statement that it was completed, but 5 miles (8km) of track was laid, more than enough to complete it with passing loops. On 14 March, the line was ballasted and surfaced, and on 16 and 17 March, reballasted and resurfaced. Probably it was ready for traffic by 21 March, forming an important escape link. There was no longer any link south west from Beaulencourt.

BW lines
The headquarters of 6th Bttn CRT remained at Lechelle, just south west of Ytres, until 23 March 1918. It continued to be responsible for the BW lines. Between 5 December 1917 and 20 March 1918, they built 16½ miles (26.5km) of line, despite the bitter winter and, in the eastern area, much hostile shelling. The greatest part was built in December (8¾ miles, 14km).

12th Bttn CRT, formed 'in the field' in November 1917, moved into the area. In November and December 1917, they worked on the BW lines around Flesquières and Havrincourt. From February 1918, they were based at Bussu just north east of Péronne but continued with general maintenance of the BW as well as the AX lines. Also, in December 1917, the 3rd Tramway Company (TWC) moved to Ytres and then on 15 December to a new camp near Neuville-Bourjonval. From there they worked on the BW lines and the northern AX lines and undertook some operating. They became the 3rd Foreways Company (FWC) on 1 March 1918.

By the end of January, the BW line was complete around the south of Havrincourt to Ribécourt. Another line north from near Metz-en-Couture, built through part of Havrincourt Wood by June 1917, was extended north to join the BW 'Y extension' near where the spur to Havrincourt Village left it. Further east the line from Metz to Trescault was extended north east to join the 'Y line extension' south east of Havrincourt. A branch from this line had been built in July 1917 into Havrincourt Wood, to the Place Mortemare, and in December 1917 this was connected to the Mortemare Tramway. The connection may have been a manifestation of the more liberal policy adopted by late 1917 on 'running through' between light railways and tramways.

Just east of the junction with the line from Metz, south east of Havrincourt, a branch began, from the BW103 control, north to Flesquières, which eventually connected with the Y4 line. On 25 November 1917, 2nd Company of 6th CRT moved to Havrincourt Wood to construct this, but building was halted during the Battle of Cambrai. The line was completed in December. Throughout December, there were frequent shell breaks on the more eastern lines, and particularly east of Havrincourt.

During December 1917 and January 1918, 6th CRT built a more southerly route from Metz to Trescault, a line south from Ribécourt to Beaucamps, and a line from the BW34 control point to Beaucamp to meet it. A branch south from this line joined up with the BW Gouzeaucourt Wood line of May 1917, but although it was slightly extended into the wood, it did not quite join up with the AX Gouzeaucourt Wood line. In February, nearly two miles of chalk ballast was camouflaged on the Beaucamps lines.

The direct line from Rocquigny to Étricourt and then north to Ytres station was built in January 1918. Whilst not labelled as a BW line, it linked with BW lines at both ends. There was never a direct line from Étricourt along the standard gauge line to Fins. There were many developments of yards and other facilities during this period. By March, tank crossings had been installed throughout the BW system.

The operating company based at Ytres from 20 May 1917 were the 9th LROC, who probably remained until at least February 1918. The 35th LROC were operating from Rocquigny from 1 to 22 March 1918 and may have been at Rocquigny before that. The 3rd TWC also undertook some operating.

AX lines (Northern part)

After the move of the Fifth Army back to the south in January 1918, the AX lines were divided between the Third Army South and the Fifth Army. The dividing line was the standard gauge line from Étricourt to Épehy.

In December 1917, No 3 Company of 6th CRT moved camp to Fins, but within a few days had to pull their camp west to Equancourt because of very heavy shell fire. In December and January B Company of 12th CRT, and 6th CRT, patrolled and maintained lines in the Fins area and 12th CRT handled light railway track at Fins yard.

Members of the Chinese Labour Corps unload duckboards at the transhipment at Ytres Yard on 2 February 1918. The light railway is nearest the camera. *(IWM Q8447)*

Gouzeaucourt and Villers-Plouich (AX system)
At the end of the Battle of Cambrai, the line built north from Gouzeaucourt through Villers-Plouich towards Marcoing, in parallel with the former standard gauge line from Épehy to Marcoing, had to be abandoned while the Germans occupied Gouzeaucourt village. They did not hold the village, but the front line settled closer to this line than before. The branch to Villers-Guislain was lost.

On 10 December 1917, 6th CRT salvaged a train from a tank crossing at the AX135 control point. On 29 December a small party from 12th CRT rescued six trucks and a hospital car during the night, from what was still regarded as 'No Mans Land' between Gouzeaucourt and Villers-Plouich. 12th CRT continued to maintain track around Gouzeaucourt.

On 15 February, an Officer from 3rd TWC, based at Neuville, and an Officer from 2nd Division of the Third Army reported on the work required on the 6km (3¾ miles) of track from the AX135 control point at Gouzeaucourt to 2.5km (1½ miles) north of Villers-Plouich. This was needed to support the front line towards Marcoing. The work was completed on 27 February.

The 3rd TWC were given the task of operating the line. Three men were sent to Bapaume to train on McEwan & Pratt 10hp tractors, and three of these tractors and drivers arrived from Bapaume. The AX127 control point was found totally unsuitable as a tractor base, and the tractors were sent to Metz-en-Couture on the BW system. These operations illustrate the difficulties and frustrations of Tramway and Foreways Companies at that time, even though in this case they were operating over 'proper' light railways.

The tractors were found to be in need of complete overhaul. Light push trucks arrived from Bapaume for use the same night, to convey material to Villers-Plouich and return with salvage. On unloading the trucks, it was found that due to defective construction only four could be coupled up. In addition, the trucks were found to be utterly unsuitable for the work required. New trucks were ordered with a report to Third Army Tramways.

By 4 March, one tractor was fit for operation but there were no trucks. On 5 March, nine Weston tipper trucks arrived. A train of two tractors and three trucks left Metz for Villers-Plouich at 6.15 pm, a distance 26km (16 miles) there and back, with RE stores for 2nd Division. It reported back at 2am with a load of trench mortar ammunition salvage. A similar train ran on 6 March.

However, the McEwan & Pratt tractors were insufficiently powerful for the grades on the light railway between Metz and Gouzeaucourt, even with that ratio of tractors to trucks. From 7 March, it was arranged with ADLR III South for a petrol electric tractor to convey the train to the AX135 control point. The train left with stores at 5pm and returned at 1.30am with 2 tons of trench mortar salvage. However, one tractor had broken down beyond AX135. On 8 March another unit had left trucks on the single track about a mile past AX135, and the goods had to be unloaded there.

This pattern of operations continued. On 11 March, the train arrived at AX135 and found a Simplex 20 tractor of 4th CRT going in to salvage the broken McEwan & Pratt tractor. There was a delay because of heavy shelling with high explosive and gas, and a gas shell landed on the line between Gouzeaucourt and Villers-Plouich. When the shelling slackened, an attempt was made to rush through, but the Simplex and truck derailed because the line was broken by shell fire. After rerailing the tractor and truck, both parties withdrew.

During the night of 11 March, the valley was heavily shelled with gas, and the track was broken in four places. The Sergeant in charge of the maintenance party based at Villers-Plouich was severely gassed but, realising the importance of keeping the line open, he refused to report sick and with three men who were also gassed repaired all the breaks in the line on 12 March even though the valley was still full of gas. The Sergeant was evacuated to hospital on the train the next night. He was later awarded the Military Medal.

On 13 March, the track was again destroyed between between Gouzeaucourt and Villers-Plouich, and the tractor and one truck were badly derailed. It was found impossible to rerail the tractor without proper tools. There was again heavy shelling and the valley was full of gas. On 14 March, another train left at 6.30pm with an officer and 11 men, armed with breakdown tools. Within a few minutes, salvoes of high explosive and gas shells were directed at the party. The valley became full of mustard gas. It was found impossible to resume work, and the party withdrew at 1am, with the officer slightly wounded.

On 15 March, the Assistant Chief Engineer and the Controller of Foreways (Third Army) inspected the line with the CO of 3rd FWC and gave orders that no further attempt be made to salvage the tractor at present. However, it was re-railed and brought out on the night of 17 March. The maintenance party was withdrawn from Villers-Plouich. The next day, a Sergeant and 11 men met a light railway train at the BW3 control point, and proceeded to Villers-Plouich to repair the track to allow the train to salvage material. However, the line was now unusable for regular supplies, and in any case was lost on 21 March.

Light Railways in the Fifth Army area
We have divided the area taken over by the Fifth Army from January 1918 into three parts. The northern part,

around and north of the standard gauge line from Péronne to Épehy, included the CY system and the southern AX lines, and connecting lines around Péronne. This part was taken over from Third Army South. The middle part consisted in part of the rest of the area taken over from Third Army South, both east and west of the Somme, south to the Amiens to Brie and Vermand road, including the DZ system. The rest of the middle part south to Ham was taken over from the French Army. The third part, wholly taken over from the French Army, consisted of the area from Ham south to Barisis.

The CY and southern AX systems, and Péronne connections (Fifth Army)

Railways in this area from December 1917 to 20 March 1918 are included in Figure 6.4 (page 108).

The southern AX lines

The line north from Quinconce (Péronne) to Fins, and the branch east to near Liéramont, were maintained from December 1917 by 6th CRT, who had one company based north of Nurlu, and 12th CRT, with one company at Aizecourt (AX line), and one near Villers-Faucon (CY lines). By the end of January 1918, 12th CRT had three companies in the Fifth Army area, and by 1 February, they had moved their headquarters to Bussu, near Péronne.

In January 1918, 12th CRT rebuilt the yards at the AX5, AX6 and AX7 control points. The last was at the branch junction towards Liéramont, the other two south of that. In January 2nd CRT constructed a 'Y' for turning locomotives at Nurlu. In February 12th CRT were visited by Canadian War Correspondents and undertook a great deal of small arms training.

The 12th US Engineer Regiment moved their headquarters to Quinconce in November or December. Units remained at Montigny Farm, operating the DZ lines, and new lines to the south and west (see Péronne to Ham section). From Quinconce they continued to operate the AX and CY lines. By February 1918, they operated 85 track miles.

The CY lines

D Company of 12th CRT moved to between Villers-Faucon and Liéramont on 15 December, and 2nd CRT headquarters moved to Beaumetz, south east of Péronne, on 6 January. The 3rd RC RARE left the area at the end of January. They had been at Tincourt since June 1917, and since then had built more than 40 miles of line, and two bridges. They were thanked for their work by the ADLR III South.

On 2 January, B Company of 2nd CRT moved to Tincourt, working under the direction of ADLR V. They took over the yard they called Marquaix, just east of Tincourt, on a spur of the standard gauge line, with transhipment facilities. They found that this yard had received no attention for a long time, and that rails, sleepers, points and bits of wagons were mixed up under 'several train loads of cinder ballast'. By 10 January they report 'some semblance of order'. Clearing could not be completed until a thaw on 18 January. Later, ballast was transhipped there, and timber for lines further south.

On 11 January, 2nd CRT were requested to take over construction of a line from the CY13 control point north west of Villers-Faucon towards Épehy. The line was to be constructed from the Épehy end to meet them by 12th CRT. On 14 February, 2 officers and 80 men of B Company travelled from Tincourt to

6.7 A light railway locomotive depot near Tincourt, probably in 1917 or early 1918. Amongst the locomotives parked in front of the sheds are two Baldwin 4-6-0Ts, and further back an Alco 2-6-2T. *(AWM P03608.026)*

CY13 and began work. A point had been installed, and 500ft of formation graded through 9 inches of frost, when word came at 3pm that the line was abandoned.

On 4 February, A Company of 12th CRT moved to Tincourt and took over the yard there on 11 February. During February and March, a great deal of light railway and other material was moved through the yard, which was also an ammunition depot and standard gauge ambulance train facility. 12th CRT also worked on the Yard at Roisel station and loaded chalk ballast at Roisel pit for use by 2nd CRT further south.

Roisel to Templeux-le-Guérard
Maps of early 1918 show a branch to Templeux-le-Guérard of the CY line from Roisel towards Épehy. This appears to have been built parallel to, but south of, the former metre gauge line to Hargicourt, now being rebuilt as a standard gauge line, and to have used a different route through Templeux. One map shows an extension of the line to Villeret as a trench tramway, with a branch to Hargicourt.

Péronne connections
The connection through from Cléry to Quinconce, and the connection on from Quinconce to Tincourt, formed an important new link to the west from the southern AX and CY systems and from the DZ system south from Roisel. In addition, the link from the south through Flamicourt would be a major new route, if open. Note however that there was still no light railway route from east and north of the Somme to the light railway from Froissy at La Chapelette.

The 7th CRT, moved to Péronne on 13 February for 'urgent light railway work'. This meant Quinconce to Cléry, Quinconce to Haut-Allaines, and Quinconce to Tincourt. They were assisted by more than 1,000 men daily as attached labour. In all, 7th CRT laid 8 miles (13km) of track in February.

Quinconce to Cléry-sur-Somme
This important link ran from the yard at Quinconce, to the existing line from Maricourt at Cléry-sur-Somme. It could not use the formation of the disused metre gauge line from Albert, already taken by the standard gauge line from Plateau. The line was 3.4 miles (5.5km) long and linked with the Maricourt line at the west end of Cléry village, where the line to Bouchavesnes turned off north. Grading began on 13 February, and by 24 February, 95 per cent of the track was laid.

Orders were given to double the track, and work began on 25 February. The bridge over the Tortille Creek at Halle was widened for double tracking on 2 March. On 9 March, 7th CRT laid 1.81 miles of track, bolted, spiked and lined, in 6 hours and 22 minutes. Probably both tracks were complete by 20 March.

Quinconce (Péronne) to Haut-Allaines
Leaving the Maricourt line at a Y junction just west of Quinconce yard, this short line curved north and east round Mont-St-Quentin to Haut-Allaines. The line was 2 miles (3km) long. Construction began on 23 February and the line was ready for operation by 15 March.

Quinconce (Péronne) to Tincourt
This line was surveyed by 12th CRT in January 1918, but built by 7th CRT, beginning on 16 February. About 5 miles (8km) long, it started from a junction on the AX line to Fins about ¼ mile east of the Quinconce yards, then took a big curve east of Péronne before following the north side of the Cologne river for 4 miles to Tincourt. The track was complete by 28 February.

Bussu branch
This was a ½ mile branch from the above line and was built by 7th CRT, with a ¼ mile spur to a gravel pit. The branch was ready for operation on 15 March. This might have served the headquarters of 12th CRT, based at Bussu at the time.

Doingt to Flamicourt (Péronne)
This was another important link, this time between the Quinconce to Tincourt line, and the standard gauge station at Flamicourt. The line could not use the disused metre gauge line from Albert, and its bridges, already taken by the standard gauge line from Plateau. Instead it began from a junction north of Doingt. There must have been a new bridge across the river (see image 9.3, Chapter Nine). The other end joined the line from Flamicourt to Vraignes.

The line was constructed by 4th CRT, with attached labour including 100 Chinese. Building started on 14 February and track was laid by 11 March. Some work was still being undertaken on 20 March, but the line was usable.

The Fifth Army area, Péronne to Ham, December 1917 to 21 March 1918

South of Péronne, both sides of the Somme, the Fifth Army took over from January 1918 the former Third Army South area north of the Amiens to Vermand road. To the south of this to Ham was the northern part of the area taken over from the French Army.

West of the Somme
Railways in this area are shown on Figure 6.3 (page 106).

Lines around Caix-Vrély
British units operated the network of lines south of the standard gauge main line from Amiens to Chaulnes,

and west of the standard gauge line from Chaulnes to Roye, in spring 1917. It is not known whether the French continued to operate them, but they were a long way from the front line. When the British Fifth Army took over this area again in January 1918, they were shown on Fifth Army railway maps, but there is no evidence that they were operated.

Wiencourt to La Flaque, Froissy and La Chapelette
By contrast this network of lines, north of the standard gauge main line from Amiens to Chaulnes, and with connections north from Froissy to Loop and the 1916 Somme battlefields, continued to be maintained and operated. The 34th LROC remained at Froissy until 8 March 1918, when 6th LROC took over.

East of the Somme, and new connections west
Railways in this area in this period are shown in Figure 6.5. The new connections west are shown in Figure 6.3 (page 106).

The DZ lines
The DZ system, south from the CY line at Roisel, was maintained and operated but no major new work was done. Operation was undertaken by 12th US Engineers based at Montigny Farm, and maintenance by 2nd CRT from Marquaix Yard (CY system).

Lines from Péronne (Flamicourt) south
The new standard gauge to light railway transhipment yards at Flamicourt became the focal point, from January and March 1918, of efforts to develop new lines south from the Péronne area to link with new lines to the west, and with the new line to the south (the B line). This linked Péronne with the lines taken over from the French Army in January 1918.

The line from Flamicourt to Vraignes was requested by the Cavalry Corps (Fifth Army). It was decided by ADLRV, on 7 January 1918, also to build a line from that line west to Estrées-Deniécourt, which is on the main Amiens to Vermand road on the west side of the Somme. Note that there is also Estrées-en-Chaussée, on the same road east of the river. The route across the river needed careful selection and a crossing at Brie was chosen.

Lack of light railway track material, and lack of locomotives and wagons for construction, are a recurring theme in the story of building these lines. Construction was by Canadian units, with operating support from the 12th US Engineers from Quinconce or Montigny Farm, and some contribution from RE units later.

Flamicourt Yard
The light railway transhipment along the old metre gauge alignment towards Ham was completed by 2nd CRT by 27 February.

Flamicourt (Péronne) to Vraignes
The route chosen followed the disused formation of the metre gauge line from Péronne to Ham as far as Mons-en-Chaussée, from where it ran parallel to the Amiens to Vermand road to just south of Vraignes. The total length of the line was about 7.5 miles (12km). Surveying began on 16 January. Some metre gauge rails and sleepers were salvaged between Flamicourt and Mons.

At the Vraignes end, a triangular junction was constructed by 2nd CRT with the B line from Hancourt to Beauvois, completed by 23 January, with a short spur. The rest of the line was constructed west to Mons by A Company of 2nd CRT, beginning in early February. Materials were delivered via the DZ and B lines to the junction, from the Marquaix and Hancourt yards. Track laying was complete by 14 February, except for 100ft at the end, because of lack of fish-plates. On 15 February, A Company moved south to Chauny, east of Noyon.

The other part of the line was built from Flamicourt towards Mons, by B Company of 2nd CRT. They experienced difficulties with material and rolling stock support. Work began on 6 February, when 6,000 sleepers were delivered to Flamicourt. More sleepers arrived on 12 February, but on both occasions, they had to be hauled to the work site by mule team. 500 yards of track salvaged from dugouts could not be hauled to the work site because of of lack of rolling stock. On 14 February, 200 yards of track was laid, but the rails had to be pushed to the end of steel by hand on light bogie wagons. However, things did improve; from 14 February, 3½ miles of track was laid, to connect through on 19 February. Operating support had been from the 12th US Engineers until 16 February, when 2nd CRT regretted the withdrawal of the Americans. One RE Simplex tractor and crew replaced them. The line was finished by 28 February and turned over to 12th CRT.

Le Mesnil Yard was built north east of Le Mesnil-Bruntel village. On 11 March, work started on an ammunition dump on an old industrial metre gauge branch formation north from here. On 20 March, work began on a marshalling yard about 1,000 yards (1km) futher south, probably at or very close to the junction with the line to Brie. Some track was laid on 22 March, but it was not finished.

Mesnil to Brie
This line started from the Flamicourt to Vraignes line, at a triangular junction, and was built south west to Brie. At Brie it skirted the north side of the village to reach the Somme and the Canal du Nord. The line was about 3 miles (5km) long.

It was built by B Company of 2nd CRT, who began work in early February. On 15 February, an officer on

Figure 6.5

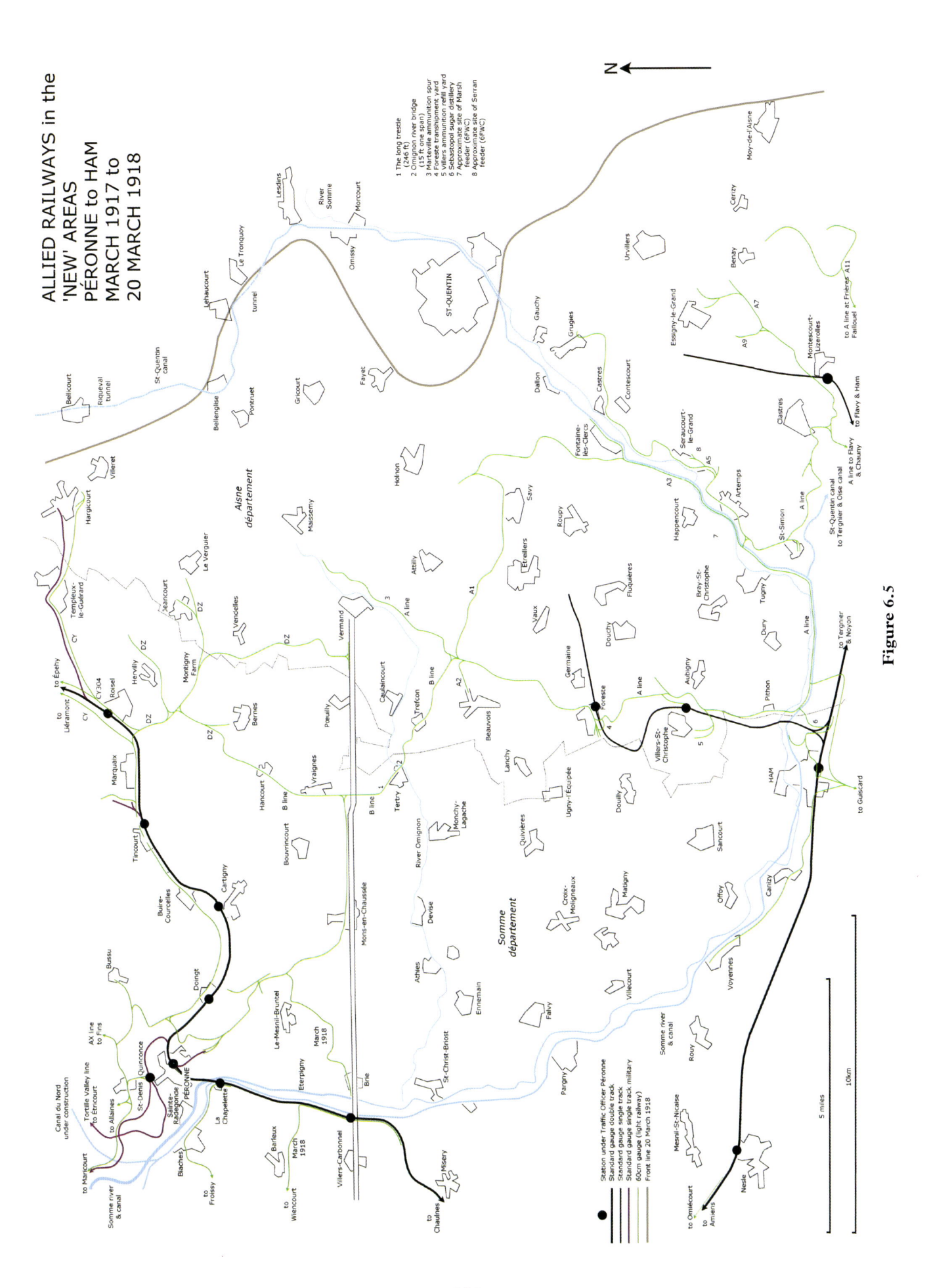

the staff of ADLR V asked for the line to be complete by 19 February. In fact, there were problems with supply of track material and with attached labour. Track was laid from both ends. At the Mesnil end this was brought from Flamicourt yard, and eventually two Simplex 20hp tractors and four flat wagons were available, but there was trouble with water in the petrol for the tractors. Time was saved by bringing the material up at night for laying next day. However, on 2 March, two loads of rails sent to Le Mesnil were 'taken by other units'. At the Brie end track material was brought from Flamicourt by standard gauge to the yard at Brie on the west side of the Canal du Nord, but because the light railway bridges were incomplete the material had to be hauled by road. The intense road traffic over this Somme crossing made this a very slow job. Later five flat wagons were secured behind a lorry and towed over the bridge on the road. The two ends were connected up on 6 March, but work continued ballasting and finishing.

The bridges at Brie
These bridges were to link the above line with the line being built to Estrées-Deniécourt on the west side. The canal is on the west side of the river, and the double track standard gauge line from Chaulnes to Péronne was immediately on the west side of the canal. The bridges were close to the bridges of the main road from Amiens to St-Quentin, on the north side, but the exact location is not known.

Materials for bridging were offloaded at the standard gauge yard from 19 February. However, as at 6 March, no work could be done because the pile driver had not arrived. After several days enquiry, it was located on 10 March at the railway junction at Mesnil, but it could not be moved because its PE tractor had returned to Montigny Farm. The pile driver was erected and working on 12 March. On the eastern approach to the bridges, huge piles of rubbish needed cutting through, several large tree stumps had to be removed, and Army Signals had to move some telegraph poles.

Three bridges were needed, two over branches of the Somme river and one west of them over the Canal du Nord. By 15 March, stringers and track were laid on the bents of the east river bridge, and 250 yards of track laid between the two river bridges. Probably the west river bridge was longer, and work was still in progress on 20 March. The canal bridge had probably not been started at the time of the German advance beginning on 21 March.

Estrées-Deniécourt to Brie
This line was constructed by 2nd CRT between 28 February and 22 March 1918. Starting from the existing line from Froissy via Chuignes to Estrées, it did not follow the obvious path straight east along the main road from Amiens to Brie. Instead it turned north almost to Assevillers, then east to pass near Barleux to reach the Somme river valley at Eterpigny. From here it followed the standard gauge railway from Chaulnes to Péronne south, with the Canal du Nord on the other side.

Construction began from both ends by B Company 2nd CRT towards the end of February, but track material seems to have been supplied exclusively from Péronne (Flamicourt), initally to the standard gauge yard at Brie, rather than using the line from Froissy. Supply to the west end therefore had to be by road, and this was helped by the loan of ten lorries from the Cavalry Corps. From the Brie end, tractors were lacking, and when two were available on 11 March, after overhaul, they were found to be without fan belts. On 12 March, one tractor failed at noon, and the other ran on only one cylinder. Word was sent to the 12th US Engineers at Montigny Farm, who quickly put both into good working order. On 17 March, work was held up by lack of petrol for the tractors, but some was eventually found at a mobile motor transport repair shop.

Track laying began on 6 March. The line was about 6½ miles (10.5km) long. A large mine crater was filled in at Barleux, and there were 13 road crossings. The crossing at Eterpigny, on the main road from Péronne to Amiens, was difficult because of the intensity of the traffic. On 16 March, in a competition against the other Companies of 2nd CRT, B Company laid 2,132 yards (1.21 miles) of track, in spite of a lack of tractors and spikes (another part of B Company, on the Ham to Guiscard line, did best). By 20 March, the track was complete and other work well on.

The good work of B Company on this and other lines was recognised in a letter on 2nd March from the Assistant Director General of Railways (Fifth Army) which he called a 'truly Imperial effort' (they were assisted by one British and one Indian labour company).

Brie to Marchelepot
On 8 March 1918, 7th CRT were ordered to build a light railway from the west side of the Canal du Nord at Brie to the standard gauge yard at Marchelepot, about 5 miles (8km) away. By 21 March only about one mile of track south from Brie had been constructed

Hancourt to Beauvois (the B line)
This important line was built in January and February 1918, to link the DZ system, and the new line from Flamicourt (Péronne) with the French lines in the new areas taken over to the south. Called the B line, there was little risk of confusion with the B lines around Arras.

The purpose of the line was stated to be 'to facilitate transfer of rolling stock from the English lines to the French system'. The line was started and finished before the connecting line to Flamicourt (Péronne).

Even in a time of many feats of railway construction, the building of this line was exceptional. The 2nd Bttn CRT headquarters was at Beaumetz, west of Hancourt. At least a part of all the companies of 2nd CRT participated in the work. The work was commisioned at a meeting of 2nd CRT with the ADLR and the LRCE (both Fifth Army) on 7 January. The same day the batallion took over the light railway yard just south of Hancourt at the end of the DZ system, and by 9 January more than 6 miles (10km) of rails and fastenings had been delivered there. Apart from track and some stringers for bridges, they promised the army to construct the whole line from salvaged materials. Some salvaged metre gauge rail was used, and every third wooden sleeper was metre gauge (ie longer).

Surveys started on 7 January in heavy fog and intermittent snow storms. The whole construction period was one of deep frost and snow, with short periods of thaw and rain, when road use was prohibited. At times the frost was so intense that in wooded areas dynamite had to be used to clear tree stumps. The line was divided into three parts, built at the same time. A Company was allocated the northern 45 per cent, across the chalk plateau south from Hancourt. C Company, helped by a detachment of B Company, were given the next 20 per cent, which involved the crossing of the valley of the Omignon river at Tertry. West of the river the line had to descend 100ft (30m) across a steep chalk hillside, and east of the river to climb again by 100ft through hilly country covered in bush. The last section (35 per cent), given to D Company, was again mostly across the plateau, skirting south of Trefcon to the junction with the former French line (now the Fifth Army A line) north east of Beauvois.

Work began on 10 January, with a big sick list, lots of men on leave, and a new draft 'in poor physical shape'. A Company reached the proposed junction with the Flamicourt line on 23 January. In the Omignon valley, the line was a series of cuttings and embankments, with much hillside work. At the beginning of the descent into the valley on the west side, it was decided to build a 264ft (80m) long and on average 10ft (3m) high trestle, to avoid an embankment across a re-entrant. This was claimed to be the longest trestle built for a light railway in France and was completed on 31 January. The bridge across the Omignon River at Tertry was a single span of 15ft, 11ft high, completed 1 February. Another trestle just east of Trefcon, also across a re-entrant, was 40ft long and 12ft high, completed 4 February.

On 20 January, the LRCE (Fifth Army) visited and wanted the line complete by 15 February. D Company were put in tents at Trefcon, and additonal labour was attached. C Company moved to Tertry on 23 January. On 25 January, 2nd CRT were visited by ARCE (Fifth Army). The Army now wanted the line finished by 5 February, so Sunday work was ordered. On 4 February, D Company laid 2,000 yards of track to complete the Beauvois end, and the track was linked through, a length of 5¾ miles. Work continued on ballasting and other finishing work, sidings and passing loops. Work was done to improve rapidly prepared grading, and to widen cuttings and embankments. On 8 February, the long trestle was strengthened by putting an extra upright in every bent (timber section). On 12 February ADLR V complimented the batallion on the line.

The line from Hancourt to the junction with the line to Mons and Flamicourt was handed over to 12th CRT on 4 February. On 9 February C Company left, and all work was complete by 16 February, but the tractors were still late because the radiators froze. As well as the line being used for traffic, probably mainly by the 12th US Engineers, 12th CRT used the chalk pit at Tertry for ballast for other lines.

A Journey
We have already noted the dispatch from Savy-Berlettes on 19 March to Ham of five steam locomotives. We presume that these reached their destination. They must have used the B line from Hancourt to Beauvois. We have only one other account of the use of this line. In summer 1917, 1st LROC were probably based at Montigny Farm, on the DZ system. On 15 September, 1st LROC moved to the area around and west of Rouen. Towards the end of October, a detachment of 1st LROC, probably a platoon, was sent to the Ypres area. If it was a platoon, the detachment would have comprised one or two officers and about sixty men.

Although the keeping of personal diaries was discouraged for security reasons, they were certainly kept and we have been fortunate to see one of these, kept by the family of Sergeant Leonard Atkins, who was a member of the 1st LROC. He was an experienced railway man, having worked before the war for the Great Western Railway. We have already referred to this diary, in relation to Plateau and Froissy in winter and spring 1917. There is no record in this diary relating to the period between 28 May 1917, before they left Froissy, and 2 March 1918.

The diary resumes on 2 March 1918, with Atkins' description of a long railway journey, and an account of such a journey during the First World War is a rarity. His journey was along the light railway 'main line' which ran north-south linking the British Army areas of the Western Front. It is not possible to compute the distance he travelled but 'as the crow flies' it is 130 km (80 miles). The probability is that the whole detachment travelled south in a convoy of trains; that there were two or more is indicated by Atkins, as a tractor driver, having at least two different brakemen on different days.

Atkins left 'International Corner', north of Poperinge in Belgium, at 3.30pm on 2nd March 1918, which he noted was a Saturday. He arrived at Romarin, which is south-east of Ballieul in France at 10.30 the same evening. He left there at 10.30 next morning and tells us that he was driving a British Westinghouse Petrol Electric tractor, No 2082, and pulling four empty wagons and a 'dead' 40hp Simplex tractor, No 2171, with its driver Tait. He also notes that his brakeman was W.H. Forsyth, and Guard T. Jones. Sadly, we do not have any other information about either of these locomotives.

They arrived at Barlin, headquarters of First Army Light Railways, at 7pm on 3rd March and left at 9am on the 4th. This time he pulled seven empty wagons and the brakeman was called Privett. He reached Bapaume at 9.30pm that evening. These must have been gruelling days, in still inclement winter weather, with the tractor driver only partially protected and the brakeman and the guard in the open. There would have been frequent stops on the busy and mostly single line, changing points, waiting at passing loops, and taking instructions from the frequent control points. Barlin to Bapaume is 30 miles (48km) in a straight line, and they were 12½ hours 'on the road'. The route took them up the long gradient south of Barlin to the top of the Artois Hills (580ft, 176m) at Verdrel junction, before descending through the hills to the handover from First to Third Army east of Artillery Corner at Arras.

They left Bapaume again at 10am the next morning. This time Atkins had eight empty wagons and the brakeman was Forsyth again. He arrived at 'Monteyny' (which must be Montigny) Farm which he describes as a British camp with some Americans (12th US Engineers were still there). He left the Farm on 6 March at 8am with six empty wagons and reached Foreste at 11am where the train was placed in a siding for the rest of the day. Rather sadly he records 'This depot took over our tractors etc.' The operating company at Foreste then was probably 2nd LROC. There are no diaries for 2nd LROC at the time, but Foreste was attacked just two weeks later on 21 March during the German advance, and 3 men of 2nd LROC were killed. Their graves are at Foreste. D Company of 2nd CRT was also there from 19 February. There were large yards and a transhipment here with the standard gauge line from Ham towards St. Quentin.

On the next page of Atkins diary there is only one entry. The party left Foreste the next day (7 March) for Ham, a distance he estimates as 4km, in fact 8km (5 miles), leaving the tractors behind. He was there for five days and then left on 12 March for 'Marlimouth' (which is identified later in the diary as Morlincort) east of Noyon, another 12½ miles (20km) south. Here they helped A Company of 2nd CRT extend the light railway along the Oise canal towards Noyon.

On the last day of this journey between the Ypres area and Foreste, the 1st LROC detachment must have travelled along the B line from Hancourt to Beauvois. Four weeks before, 2nd CRT were still finishing building this line. Two weeks later, the whole area was over-run by the German Army, with the loss of Atkins' route south from a point between Arras and Bapaume. And five weeks later the German advance in the north on the plain of the Lys cut the north-south main line for a long distance in the First and Second Army areas. It is a pity that we do not know how many other trains of light railway units supporting the Fifth Army made a similar journey in the short opportunity between 5 February and 20 March 1918.

The A lines from Ham north

The former French lines in the area taken over by Fifth Army were renamed the A lines. This was sufficiently far from Arras to avoid confusion with the A lines there. In this section we have described the lines north of the Somme at Ham, and around Ham as far east as the junction east of the bridge at Tugny. Beyond this, the lines are the subject of the next section. Lines around Ham include south to Guiscard and west to Voyennes. There was no link to the 'old' lines in the west. Branches of the A line were given even numbers if west of the main line, and odd numbers if east of it.

The Main A line

At the north end, this ran along the Omignon River to north east of Vermand. The junction with the new B line from Hancourt was near Beauvois. Just south of this, the A1 line went east, and the short A2 line went west to the edge of Beauvois village.

From here, the line south met the standard gauge line at Foreste (Forest station on British maps) and followed it on the east side past Villers-St. Christophe to meet the Somme canal east of Ham. At the canal the line turned east to Clastres, with a big loop north to cross the Somme Canal near Tugny.

From 31 January 1918, survey parties from 2nd Bttn CRT were at Ham advising ADLRV. On 1 February, a detachment of D Company 2nd CRT moved to Foreste. On 14 and 15 February they built an ammunition siding at Marteville, just south of Vermand, and did general light railway maintenance in the area. From 19 February, the whole of D Company was based at Foreste.

Also in February, C Company of 2nd CRT built an ammunition refill point at Villers-St. Chrisophe.

Surveys began on 15 February, and the work was complete on 3 March. More than 1¼ miles (2km) of track was laid. The work was slowed by the support labour being moved without warning on 19 February. Then on 22 February, they had only 20 fish plates for 2,000 yds of track, but an officer salvaged 350 'from places unknown'. Finally, on 25 February, track material was delivered at 3pm, 1½ miles from where it was needed, and it could not used until the next day.

On 28 February, ADLR V agreed to allocate five tractors, each with a bogie wagon and operating and breakdown crews, to 2nd CRT for maintenance of XVIII and III Corps areas. This was with a view to bringing the lines into good shape. D Company, north of Ham, placed one tractor and team north of Foreste, and the other at Pithon junction on the north side of the Somme canal.

French lines around Ham
The French had a network of light railways at Ham between the Somme Canal and the main line from Amiens. These linked with the main A line on the north bank of the Somme canal east of the standard gauge bridge for the line towards St. Quentin, with a bridge over the canal. There were probably transhipments in the east part of the main station yard, and from the Somme canal. The line ended near the main line passenger building. Some work was done on these lines in February 1918 by 2nd CRT, and in March the 22nd LR TCC were based near the Sebastopol sugar factory, on the eastern limb of these lines.

The Ham avoiding line (Ham–Pithon Wood avoiding loop)
From the main A line east of here, near woods south of Pithon village, 2nd CRT in March 1918 built another bridge and a line across the main railway, then west to join the path of the old Metre Gauge line from Ham to Noyon on the main road between Ham station and Muille-Villette. The line was about 2½ miles (4km) long. Track was laid from 4 March and mostly finished by 16 March, but the crossing of the Somme canal to join the main A line had not been completed by 21 March.

Ham to Guiscard
From 27 February, detachments of B Company of 2nd CRT started to clear the formation of the former metre gauge line from Ham to Noyon for 13.4 miles (21.5km), as far as Guiscard. The line was linked to the French lines in Ham station yard, with a 13yd crossing of the road south to Guiscard on 8 March.

Track laying began and on 16 March, as part of the 2nd CRT competition, B Company laid more than 2½ miles of line, 7½ft per man hour, and probably completed the line to alongside the main road at Guiscard. Also, on 16 March, the line was linked with the Ham avoiding line to Pithon Wood, on the main road ⅔ mile (1km) south of the level crossing at Ham station. On 19 March, rolling stock was moved onto the line, probably from the yard at Sebastopol (Ham).

Ham to Voyennes
This line, also built by B Company of 2nd CRT in March 1918, used the formation of the metre gauge to the junction at Offoy and then onto the loop line towards Nesle. Clearing and grading was completed as far as Voyennes by 14 March, and the track was probably laid by 18 March. This line was intended to be built on west over the Canal du Nord to link up with the line being built east from Omiécourt, near Chaulnes.

Omiécourt (Chaulnes) to Nesle
This line was built eastwards from Omiécourt, near Chaulnes (Figure 6.3). There was no connection with any other light railway at that end. However, the end of the line was close to the first British Army station on the line to Péronne, called Chaulnes Dump. From Omiécourt the line went south to meet the Amiens to Tergnier main line at Hyencourt-le-Petit, where there was a station called Fonchette by the British Army. The light railway then more or less followed the the main railway line south east.

The line was built by C Company of 2nd CRT, part of which moved on 25 February to begin work. A siding was built at Curchy, a station on the main Amiens to Tergnier line, and material was delivered there from 4 March, but later some track material was delivered to Omiécourt from Ham by lorry. Despite this there were shortages of material and on 8 March, no track could be laid. On 6 March, 2nd CRT moved two tractors and five flat wagons by lorry from the yard of the 22nd TCC (called now the 22nd Operating Company) at Sebastopol (Ham) to Curchy station. On 16 March, as part of the 2nd CRT competition, C Company laid almost 2½ miles (4km) of track.

By 20 March, the track had reached almost to the junction of the standard gauge line with the metre gauge line to Ham, just north west of Nesle. About 4½ miles (7.5km) was built. The missing link to Voyennes was 5 miles (8km) long, following the path of the disused metre gauge line, as was envisaged. It included the bridge over the Canal du Nord, whose status we do not know.

The A3, A5 and A7 lines
The A3 and A5 lines were former French lines. Both left the main A line at the bridge at Tugny. The A3 line to the west of the Somme and the St Quentin canal,

and the A5 line to the east, extended north east almost to the front line near St Quentin. The A1 line linked across from a branch of the A3 line to the main A line near Beauvois. The lines were probably being operated by 22nd TCC based at Sebastopol (Ham).

The 6th Foreways Company (FWC) RE was originally formed as 6th Forward Transportation Company RE at the Forward Transportation depot at Savy (Artois) between 8 and 21 February 1918, renamed 6th FWC on 25 February. Suitable personnel from the old 6th Army Tramway Company were transferred, and men picked from the Essex, Hampshire and Bedford Regiments were added. Some training on tractors and in other areas was given, but when the Company of five officers and 135 men left the Savy depot on 21 February, they had no transport or equipment, and only 12 rifles between them.

On 23 February, 6th FWC reported to the Chief Engineer of XVIII Corps, Fifth Army, at Ham. Headquarters was established at Ham and the Company camped at Happencourt, on the west side of the St Quentin Canal. Another camp was established at Seraucourt, on the other side of the canal, in early March.

Between 26 February and early March, 6th FWC constructed the Serran Feeder and the Marsh feeder. The Serran Feeder was 600 yds long, a branch off the A5 line at Seraucourt to feed two 12 inch Howitzer positions. The Marsh feeder was a branch off the A3 line south of Happencourt, about ¾ miles long, to feed a reserve battery position. Two other feeders were built but it is not known where.

On 3rd March, 6th FWC received two 20hp Simplex tractors, in need of repair, and by the middle of March they had four tractors and 35 wagons. A workshop had been established at Grand Seraucourt. W.J.K. Davies, in *Light Railways of the First World War* (1967), reports from an RE source the traffic for 6th FWC for the week ending 6am 15 March 1918. On tractor routes 122.5 tons of material were hauled, with average journey distances between 2.5 miles for 30 tons of ballast, to 9.15 miles for 3.5 tons of trench mortar bombs.

The Fifth Army area, Ham to Noyon, December 1917 to 20 March 1918

South of Ham, the Fifth Army took over from January 1918 the former area of the French Army, south to Barisis, due east of Noyon. Railways in this area up to 20 March 1918 are shown in Figure 6.6.

The A lines from Ham south
The former French lines were also renamed as A lines. In this section we describe the main A line and branches east of the junction which lay east of the bridge at Tugny. As with the areas immediately to the north, the story of light railways in this area in February and March 1918 is particularly linked with 2nd Bttn CRT, whose headquarters moved to Cugny on 14 February. This was just west of Flavy-le-Martel, a station on the main line from Amiens to Tergnier, where C Company moved on 10 and 11 February. On 15 February, A Company moved to Abbécourt, a station on the main line from Noyon to Tergnier, by the Oise and its lateral canal.

The main A line
From the junction with the A5 line at Tugny, the main A line went east to Clastres, then turned south to cross the St. Quentin canal at Jussy, and to cross the standard gauge line from Amiens just east of Flavy-le-Martel. From here the line followed a tortuous course south to the Oise canal and river at Abbécourt, passing through the Bois de Frières between Frières-Faillouël and Villequier-Aumont. At Abbécourt the line turned north east along the north bank of the Oise canal to Chauny, then south into the French area, probably just past the junction of the A15 branch to Barisis.

C Company were responsible for the line and branches from Tugny bridge to a point just east of the Château de Villette, near Caumont. A Company were responsible for the line and branches south from here to the end of the Fifth Army area.

The 2nd CRT C Company area
C Company divided their part of the main A line and branches into three maintenance sections, each with ten men under a corporal, the entire length of their responsibility being 40 miles (64km). It is probable that the A7 branch was worked, because one of the maintenance parties was based on part of it, at Montescourt-Lizerolles, but the other branches may not have been. The other two parties were based at Frieres-Faillouel and at Villequier-Aumont. Of the two tractors and bogie well wagons allocated to C Company, one set was based at Flavy RE siding, and the other in the Bois de Frières.

On 14 February, C Company were charged with building a new transhipment and ammunition refill point at Flavy-le-Martel, and work was completed on 23 February.

The main A line north of Flavy was said to be in good condition on 21 February. South from Flavy the line in the Bois de Frières was found to be in a poor state after heavy rain, and the light French fish plates were being sheared by the heavy British rolling stock. Parts of the line were reballasted using more than 100 tons of brick ballast, and some bent rails were replaced. Metre gauge sleepers were placed under some of the French joints. Trees were cleared from a branch line in

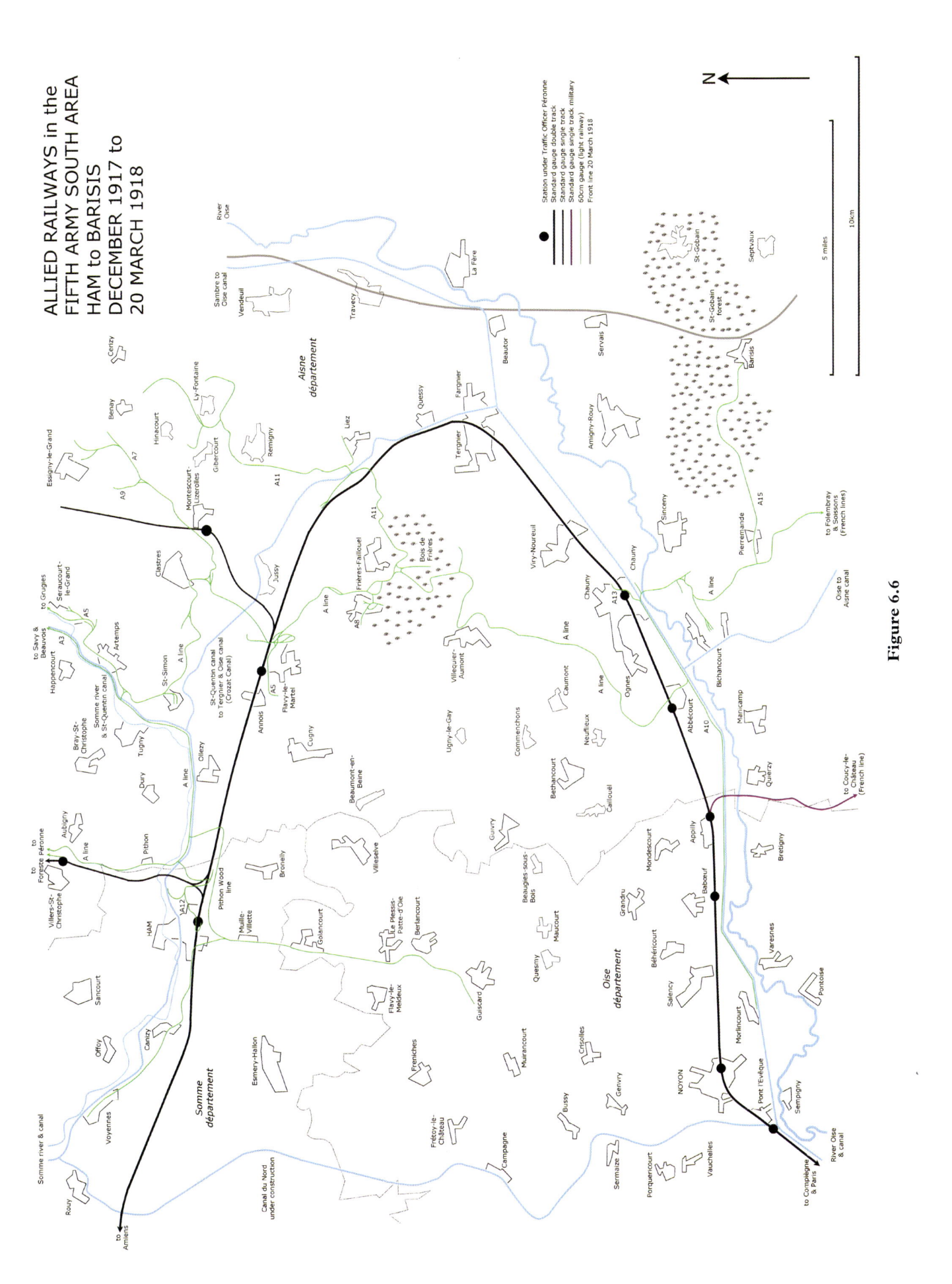

Light and metre gauge railways of the Somme sector 17 March 1917 to 20 March 1918

Figure 6.6

the wood being prepared as a diversion of the original route, but work was still in progress on 20 March.

The long A11 branch which began at a junction with the main line in the Bois de Frières was surveyed for more than a mile from the junction on 14 March, but it was probably not operational.

The 2nd CRT A Company area
A Company 2nd CRT moved to Abbécourt on 15 February and took over the A line and branches south to Barisis. On 18 February, four maintenance parties of four men, each under a corporal or lance-corporal, were placed on the main A line, one about one mile south of the boundary with C Company, one just north west of Abbécourt, one at Le Bosquet just south of Chauny, and one at Pierremande, near the junction with the A15 branch, where the line went south to the French Sixth Army. The operating companies were the 54th LROC and one of the South African LROCs, the 8th or the 9th.

The A10 branch already constructed by the French extended west along the north bank of the Oise Canal from Abbécourt to the bridge on the road from Dampcourt to Quierzy, marked on maps as the *Pont de Quierzy*, but usually known to the British army as Dampcourt Bridge. From 1 March, 2nd CRT started looking at an extension along the canal towards Noyon, and refurbished the existing A10 branch. On 9 March, they surveyed a route to Le Jonquoy, where the road from Noyon to Soissons crossed the canal, then up to the east end of Noyon standard gauge station along the formation of the existing metre gauge branch to the *ballastière* at Le Jonquoy. The whole was 6½ miles (10.5km) long. However the line was only laid out as far as the bridge on the Morlincourt to Varesnes road, which was 4 miles (6.5km).

Track material had already been unloaded from 59 wagons at Abbécourt yard, when construction started on 11 March. A Company were assisted by attached labour, and by the detachment of 1st LROC, who arrived at Morlincourt from Foreste on 12 March. There was difficulty getting material out of Abbécourt yard because of lack of a tractor, but the French lent a barge and two sailors to help move material along the canal. By 20 March, 3½ miles of track had been laid, so that the line was probably just short of the bridge on the Morlincourt to Varesnes road when the German advance started on 21 March. In the 2nd CRT competition on 16 March, just over 4,000 yds (2.3 miles) of track was laid, aided by the ability to move material along the canal.

The Expected German Offensive

The intensity of enemy shell fire increased steadily during the March 1918. On 17 March, at the St Patrick's Day services at 2nd CRT headquarters at Cugny, a 'general air of precaution' was noted. All around defence trenches with wire were being built. Rumours continued on 18 March. On 18 and 19 March, rolling stock was moved onto the Ham to Voyennes and the Ham to Guiscard lines from the 22nd 'Operating Company' (LRTCC) base at Sebastopol, near Ham.

At 5pm on 20 March, the troops in the area around 2nd CRT at Cugny were ordered to 'stand to'. An officer of 2nd CRT went to III Corps HQ at 9pm but was told that the order did not apply to them. They would receive orders if any move was necessary. Nevertheless, they did move their rolling stock onto the Ham to Guiscard line. Further north, in the Third Army area around Bapaume, ROD advised the CRCE (Third Army) that French workers, who were probably civilians, in the Achiet-le-Grand standard gauge yards had 'quit functioning', and British soldiers had replaced them. The ROD was standing by to move guns at 15 minutes notice.

Chapter Seven

Light and metre gauge railways of the Somme sector 21 March to 7 August 1918

The great German offensive on the Somme front in spring 1918 opened on 21 March. Codenamed Operation Michael but known to German commanders as the *Kaiserschlacht* (Kaiser's battle), the attack was mounted on the British Third and Fifth Army fronts, 50 miles (80km) long from Arras south to La Fère. It went almost as far south as the limit of Fifth Army responsibility at Barisis. The aims were to drive a wedge between the British and French Armies, and if possible to reach the sea and divide them completely. Another objective was to capture the railway yards and connections at Amiens, which would have crippled Allied communications. Troops were transferred from the Russian front, where an armistice had been agreed with the new government, and the German army wanted to attack before the arrival of large numbers of American infantry.

The attack opened at 9.40am on 21 March. An intense barrage began at 4.45am and changed to a creeping barrage at zero hour. Conditions were very foggy, and much gas was used. The German Second and Eighteenth Armies broke through on the British Fifth Army front, and the Second Army also broke through south of the Bapaume to Marcoing railway on the British Third Army (South) front.

As General Gough (Fifth Army) had warned GHQ, they were too thinly spread and there had been insufficient time to properly prepare. The British were outnumbered (26 divisions against 62) and outgunned (2,600 artillery pieces against 6,600) and they, especially the Fifth Army, retreated in considerable disarray, despite many individual and collective acts of bravery. By 23 March, the Fifth Army had retreated to the west side of the Somme from Péronne south, and by 24 March almost to Nesle. In the north Bapaume was lost on 24 March.

By 26 March, the attack in the Third Army area had almost reached Albert and the Ancre, and Albert was taken. However, the advance was stopped on the hills to the west of the Ancre. On 28th March, an attack at Arras and to the north, in an attempt to recapture Vimy ridge, pushed the front line back to the edge of Arras. North of that little progress was made.

The German army continued to advance rapidly in the south, taking Noyon on 25 March and Montdidier on 27 March. On 26 March, an emergency meeting of the Allied commanders was held in the town hall at Doullens. It was agreed that the French Marshal, Ferdinand Foch, should command the Allied forces. On behalf of the British Army, Field-Marshal Sir Douglas Haig agreed to this. Parts of the French Sixth Army were moved north to support the British Fifth Army, taking over the front line as far as Moreuil.

The German advance was finally stopped in front of Villers-Bretonneux, 10 miles (16km) short of the Amiens railway yards, and further south, just west of the Avre down to Montdidier. The German army had advanced up to 40 miles (64km) and taken more than 1,000 square miles (2,500 square km) of territory. On 5 April, General Ludendorff called a formal end to the offensive, but there were further actions around Villers-Bretonneux on 24 April. The German army had run out of steam and were short of supplies having advanced so far. They were also demoralised. Their best chance, although a devastating blow to the Allies, had proved indecisive.

The German offensive in the north

This meant that the Allied Armies were already very pressed when, on 9 April 1918 the German Army attacked between La Bassée and Armentières, on the plain of the Lys, with the intention of capturing the Channel Ports. On 10 April, they attacked north of the Lys, towards Ypres. When the advance was finally halted on 30 April, the west point of the 'Lys Pocket' was north of Béthune, only 5 km from the town centre. They did not get quite as near to Hazebrouck, and neither of these important railway centres were lost, but it was a close thing.

Railways during the Allied retreat
21 March - 5 April 1918

Railways in the Somme sector lost to the advancing German Army between 21 March and 5 April 1918 can be seen on Figure 7.1, with the initial and final front lines.

Standard gauge railways
Third Army

During the retreat, the British Third Army lost the French main line from Amiens from near Albert almost as far as Arras, with all standard gauge lines east of that. In May,

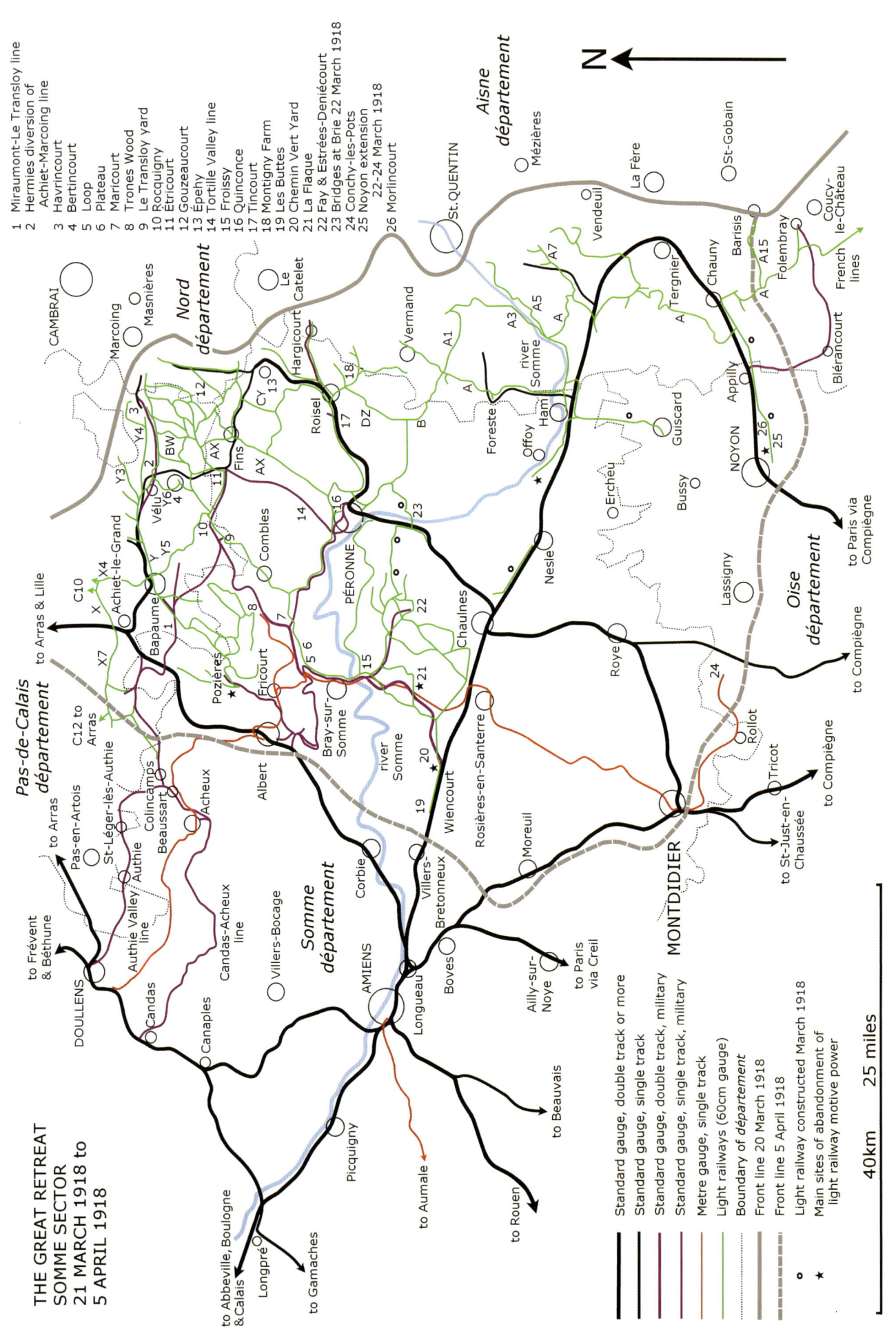

Figure 7.1

RCE V reported that 84½ miles (136km) of standard gauge track had been lost in the Third Army area.

On 21 March, the track was broken between Achiet and Bapaume, and the track on the Vélu to Ytres line cut in several places. Over the next few days, RCE V and associated Railway Companies withdrew. In general, standard gauge companies were able to travel by train, but it could be very slow.

RCE V had already moved on 8 March to Pioneer Yard (Aveluy). At 12.30pm on 23 March, their train left Pioneer Yard for Léalvillers. In 1917, they could have gone the short way via Acheux, before the standard gauge line had been changed back to metre gauge. Now they had to go by way of Amiens and Candas. They were delayed at Amiens from 7pm to 11pm because the station and city were being bombed. By 27 March, they were near Authieule, on the Authie Valley line, where they stayed until May. The HQ train was later parked at Dannes-Camier, on the coast on the Calais to Boulogne line, with several of the HQ trains of associated companies. From 29 March, the advanced HQ of the DGT Third Army was at Third Army HQ Bernaville, not far west of the Amiens to Doullens railway at Candas.

As they withdrew, bridges, track and infrastructure were destroyed. There were some problems. Railways were destroyed by blowing joints between rails, ideally every few joints, but in some cases shortage of explosives (usually Ammonal) meant that less joints could be blown. Most or all sets of points would be blown up. On 28 March, it was agreed that no water supplies at stations would be destroyed; the supply would be left for the troops. River bridges would not be destroyed until the infantry rear guard was across and the enemy in full possession of the opposite bank.

As one example of bridge problems, that of the Vélu to Ytres line over the Hermies diversion to Havrincourt was not destroyed. At 4.15pm on 22 March, the ADGT III ordered RCE V to destroy this bridge and the points and rails on the line when the line was clear of evacuating traffic. At 4.25pm, they were ordered not to do this. At midnight, the same office instructed that this bridge should be destroyed at once, but this was again countermanded. Finally, instructions were given to destroy this bridge at 1.30pm on 24 March, but it was already in the hands of the enemy.

Gradually the communication difficulties associated with the widespread destruction of telephone lines were overcome. Dispatch riders on motorcycles were widely used. When, near the end of March, it was realised that north of Albert the German army was likely not to advance far west of the Ancre, the situation settled somewhat. By 25 March all demolitions on the main Amiens to Arras line at and north from Albert, and all lines east of that, were complete.

On the Amiens to Albert section of the main line, demolitions were undertaken back to Corbie by 28 March. The congestion on this line is illustrated by the story of 3rd RC RMRE. When their train arrived at Buire-sur-Ancre from Ancre junction at 10.30am on 25 March, it was put into a siding. It had taken them two hours to move about 3 miles (5km). They found that all the French staff, and all the RTOs, had gone. ROD was trying to clear trains backed up buffer to buffer from Buire to Amiens, because enemy bombing had broken the line at Amiens. At 1am on 26 March, the 3rd RC RMRE train left Buire for Vecquemont, towards Amiens. ROD drew out the train without orders. Congestion was so great that no movement was more than 100 yards. They reached Heilly at 10am, where RCE V joined the train and they reached Vecquemont at 4.30pm. In 15½ hours, they had travelled about 9 miles (14km).

The Candas to Achiet line remained in Third Army hands as far east as Euston Dump. From Colincamps to Irles junction the line was destroyed during the night of 25 March. Probably the track was also destroyed from Colincamps towards Beaussart on 26 March, with the Authie Valley line demolitions. The line remained open to Beaussart but was in poor condition.

The whole of the Authie Valley line was held, but the eastern end was demolished from Courcelles junction, on the Candas to Achiet line, almost to St-Léger-lès-Authie, on 26 March. On 27 March, Authieule exchange yard, and the Authie Valley line as far as St-Léger, were found fit for traffic, and could be maintained. New rail heads at Orville and Authie village were constructed in early April 1918.

Fifth Army

During the retreat, there was considerable blurring of the boundary between Third Army (RCE V) and Fifth Army (RCC IV). Some Fifth Army units withdrew through the Third Army area from Fins-Sorel, Heudicourt and Épehy. In the area of Plateau, Fifth Army units did some of the rescue and salvage. The RCC IV HQ train withdrew from Doingt to La Flaque through Plateau, and then south through Bray and Froissy, on 22 March. This was probably because they, or ROD as the motive power agency, decided that this was a safer way than using the Péronne to Chaulnes line.

The RCC IV HQ train left La Flaque on 24 March at 8.15 pm and reached Chemin Vert (Wiencourt) at midnight. They moved on at 12.30 am on 25 March and reached the Longueau yards just east of Amiens at 6.30pm, reporting that the line in between was just one line of trains buffer to buffer. It had taken them 18 hours to cover about 12 miles (20km). The HQ train went to Romescamps, the regulating yards on the Rouen to Amiens main line, on 26 March. Finally, by 6 April the HQ and the train were at St-Léger-lès-Domart, on the line from Longpré to Canaples.

By 23 March, all demolitions east of Péronne were complete, and of the bridges at Péronne, accomplished under machine gun fire. The bridges over the River Somme at Bray were demolished on 26 March. Fifth Army lost all the British military lines in their area. On the main line from Amiens to Tergnier, all rolling stock was being evacuated from Chemin Vert as fast as possible on 25 March, and the process was completed by 26 March. The final front line was across the main line east of Villers-Bretonneux, towards Marcelcave.

Light Railways (60cm gauge)

This section describes the experiences of the light railway units during the retreat in the Somme Sector between 21 March and 5 April 1918. The light railways during the retreat are described mainly in relation to construction and operating units. There is little detailed information available about the demolitions on the light railways, although undoubtedly there were many. The units are described from north to south. Firstly, those in the Third Army area who stayed in the Third Army area, secondly those in the Third Army area who retreated into the Fifth Army area, and lastly those in the Fifth Army area. The final section looks at the attempts to salvage light railway rolling stock. Light railways are shown on Figure 7.1, which shows what was lost.

Light railway units evacuated by light railway, standard gauge railway, on road transport or on foot. Operating units were more likely to have rolling stock and motive power available than construction units, as long as there were lines open to use it. Moving the rolling stock west as far as possible was required anyway.

Third Army area

With the German attacks beginning on 21 March 1918, almost all of the light railways in the Third Army south area were lost. By 5 April, the front line had settled east of Gommecourt and Hébuterne, and west of Serre. South from Beaumont Hamel the front line lay along the crest of the hills just west of the Ancre. From Albert south the front was slightly further west down to the Somme river and canal. The boundary between Third Army and Fifth Army was just north of the Somme. Third Army retained some light railways south west of Arras.

Light railway escape routes can be seen in Figure 7.1. Of vital importance for the area south of the Achiet-le-Grand to Marcoing standard gauge railway was the C12 line south from Monchy-au-Bois. This joined the X7 line west of Bucquoy. These lines linked into the Bapaume area before this was lost in the advance.

The 13th (Canadian) LROC

The 13th (Canadian) had taken over from 6th LROC at Achiet-le-Grand in November 1917. Because they operated north and east from Achiet their story was told

7.1 On 23 March 1918, two days after the beginning of the German offensive and advance, men of the Royal Garrison Artillery unload shells from light railway wagons at a dump near Bapaume. *(IWM Q8610)*

in *Narrow Gauge in the Arras Sector* (2015). They are mentioned here because they returned to the Somme sector and are of importance later in this chapter, in connection with the A100 lines north east of Amiens.

6th Bttn CRT
On 21 March, the headquarters of 6th Bttn CRT, and No 1 Company, remained at Lechelle, just south west of Ytres. No 3 Company were forced to evacuate their HQ at Lebuquière, and their camp was destroyed by shell fire. All equipment was sent to Bapaume. In the afternoon, they learned that the enemy was nearby in Doignes, but they kept the track open to Beaumetz. No 2 Company, based at Neuville-Bourjonval, kept all available track open and worked all night to get out ammunition and guns.

Further enemy advance during the night drove No 3 Company back to Bapaume on 22 March, but No 2 Company continued to work on forward lines. HQ began moving stores back to Pozières at 2.30pm. On instructions from ADLR III, a permanent HQ was established at Pozières, where No 4 Company were already based. The enemy were in Fins at 8.30pm, and No 2 Company at Neuville were instructed to move by train. HQ, Battalion Transport and No 1 Company stood by to move. ADLR III, who was probably also based at Lechelle, was informed of the situation at 10pm, and advised that Army orders were to evacuate. No 1 Company moved off from Lechelle at 10.25pm, and HQ and Transport at 11.10pm.

Nos. 1 and 2 Companies reached Combles at 2.30am on 23 March, and HQ and Transport reached Pozières at 11.00am. We presume that Nos. 1 and 2 Companies travelled to Combles by light railway, probably using their own motive power. However, HQ could not have reached Pozières by light railway except from Rocquigny via Bapaume, and they almost certainly went by road using the accompanying battalion motor and horse transport. A salvage party went back to Lechelle later on 23 March. At 3.30pm, ADLR III staff said that the enemy were advancing on Bapaume. Nos. 1 and 2 Companies at Combles were ordered by ADLR to evacuate to Plateau. By the time No 1 Company left, enemy outposts were in Combles village. On arrival at Plateau they found it evacuated and marched to Pozières. Since there was no light railway link between Plateau and Pozières at that time, any remaining rolling stock Nos. 1 and 2 Companies had must have been abandoned, probably at Plateau.

On 24 March, at Pozières, 6th CRT were ordered to turn out all available men to work on changing the metre gauge line from Albert to Bray to 60cm gauge, but one hour later they were ordered to stop and move to Bouzincourt, west of Albert. This was not on the railway network. They spent the rest of the day moving.

At 3pm, ADLR III ordered them to be ready to reconstruct the line from Pozières to Aveluy. This was shown as still present on Third Army maps of 1 January 1918 but must have been taken up between then and 21 March. Nothing further came of this order. This must have meant that any 6th CRT rolling stock at Pozières, where No 4 Company had been based, was abandoned. This was ironic, because it was the failure to build the line from Fricourt to Miraumont via Pozières, the task of No 4 Company 6th CRT, which trapped light railway rolling stock there.

By the end of the afternoon of 24 March, an officer and 20 men were guarding stores and equipment at Pozières, everyone else was at Bouzincourt. At 7.30pm, an officer and 28 men of ADLR III staff arrived there with orders to evacuate in the direction of Amiens with 6th CRT. A few minutes later, another officer, LRCE III, arrived with other orders. After a conference it was decided to move all absolutely necessary stores, horses and motor transport to Louvencourt on the Doullens Road, and for an officer to go to HQ CRT for orders, because ADLR III had evacuated 'to where we didn't know, and had sent us word that he had ceased to function'. After all neccessary stores (rations, blankets, tents and equipment) had been loaded, motor transport moved off. At 11pm, the marching column moved off. They arrived at Louvencourt at 3.40 am and went into bivouac.

At 9am on 25 March, an officer arrived back from Doullens, having unloaded stores. All the men were sent in lorries to Doullens, as they were so tired they could not march. An officer returned to the stores at Bouzincourt but found that their guard had been 'rushed' by Imperial (ie British) soldiers, and their stores had been looted and destroyed. At 11am, they received orders from HQ CRT by dispatch rider that they were to go to Beauquesne to dig trenches. All personnel and stores were moved there, with the men going into billets at Raincheval. Gen Stewart (CO CRT) arrived about 5pm and gave orders to commence work on a defence line.

34th LROC
The 34th LROC had moved to Bapaume on 7 March 1918. On instructions from ADLR III South, the company evacuated Bapaume on 22 March, and moved to Pozières. They evacuated Pozières on 23 March, where they had to abandon all motive power units and rolling stock. Because of insufficiency of road transport, they also had to abandon most of the company equipment and records. They marched to Vecquemont during the night of 23 to 24 March, moving to Havernas on 27 March to dig trenches.

14th American Railway Engineers
On 21 March, part of the 14th American RW Engineers were based at Pozières. They also had to abandon their

rolling stock and evacuate west. On 24 March, two companies reported unexpectedly at the HQ of RCE V at Léalvillers. On 26 March, they were sent to assist 9th Bttn CRT at Thièvres, on the Authie Valley standard gauge line.

Third Army units going into the Fifth Army area
As can be seen on Figure 7.1, the layout of remaining light railways in March 1918 tended to force units to try to escape south west rather than north west. Pozières was a dead end. Units arriving at Rocquigny had to decide (or had orders) whether to take the newly completed Y5 extension to Bapaume, and then whether to take the X lines north and west or go south west to Pozières; or to take the line south west from Rocquigny to Maricourt. This led inevitably to Froissy and then to Wiencourt l'Équipée (Chemin Vert) on the main line from Amiens to Tergnier.

35th LROC
The 35th LROC was operating at Rocquigny on 20 March, with a detachment operating further north and east at Beaumetz-lès-Cambrai. The Beaumetz detachment was withdrawn on the night of 21 March with their rolling stock, to Rocquigny, but some may have gone to Bapaume. On the night of 23 to 24 March, rolling stock and personnel were moved to Sailly-Saillisel, and then on to Froissy via Combles and Maurepas. On 24 March, they moved on to Harbonnières, and then on 25 March to Wiencourt (Chemin Vert), travelling with their own motive power by 60cm gauge line all the way. At Wiencourt, as the War Diaries of the 35th LROC vividly describe:

'This was the end of LR (light railway) track, consequently any further evacuation of stock was not possible. BG (broad gauge, ie standard gauge) being unable to provide means of removing LR stock. Injectors were removed from Locos and magnetos and carburettors from tractors. ADLR V arranged to leave men for demolition of stock, all 35th Company men withdrawn to Chemin Vert BG railhead, loaded on BG trains.'

26 March found them on a standard gauge train en route to Candas, from where they moved to Vignacourt on 28 March to help dig trenches.

3rd FWC
The 3rd Foreways Company (FWC) were based near Neuville-Bourjonval and operated from their tractor base at Metz-en-Couture.

When on 21 March heavy shelling commenced at 4am with high explosive and gas, 40 attached infantry moved back to a new position at Rocquigny, and the balance of the company moved out of camp to high ground in the rear to escape the gas. The men in charge of the tractors at Metz were ordered to move them to Ytres.

On 22 March, the company and all stores moved to Rocquigny. On 23 March, they moved to Combles, leaving a captain and 18 men in charge of the stores at Rocquigny, which could not be moved because only one lorry was available. Four others promised by V Corps never arrived.

On 23 March, ADLR III South also moved to Combles, and 3rd TWC lent 60 men to assist with removing rolling stock and ammunition from Bus, Rocquigny and Le Transloy. Arrangements were made for a light railway train to bring back the balance of stores from Rocquigny, but the train could not reach them and men were sent to tell the Rocquigny party to make their own way to Combles. The 60 men returned late in the evening with the last of the light railway trains from Rocquigny.

Because Combles was being evacuated, the lorry and the company Ford car were sent to Maricourt, and the rest left Combles for Maurepas on foot at 8pm on 23 March amid heavy shelling. The majority of the men found it impossible to carry their kits and march the required distance. Later comments make clear that some of the Foreways Company men were older and less fit than the front-line infantry. Men unable to carry kits were ordered to leave them, keeping iron rations, water bottles and rifles.

Arriving at Maurepas at midnight, they were rejoined by the stores party from Rocquigny, and they found a number of LR trains there on their way to Maricourt. The 'majority of the Company especially old Pioneers and the attached infantry were much exhausted', and they were put on a light railway train for Maricourt. Two officers walked on ahead to Maricourt to get in touch with transport. Clearly the trains were not able to go fast, but there may have been more trains available at Maurepas because this was the junction with the line from Péronne. While the train was going up the heavy grades to Maricourt all ranks had to get out to help push. While doing so a lieutenant and a sapper were injured when a projection from a cutting threw them against the moving trucks in the dark.

From Maricourt, the company moved out on the last light railway trains to Froissy, which was reached at 10am on 24 March. At 11am, Froissy was also being evacuated and they moved on by train to La Flaque, while transport left for Amiens. Arrangements were made with the CO of the La Flaque dump to obtain tents for the unit, but because the evacuation of La Flaque was starting, and the only means of moving was on foot, it was thought advisable, owing to the condition of the men, to proceed slowly to Amiens and get in touch with HQ. The lorry had been sent for and was returned to Rivery Rest Camp near Amiens with the injured lieutenant, unable to walk with a crushed foot.

An officer went ahead and got in touch with the Fifth Army Controller of Foreways at Villers Bretonneux and made arrangements to billet the men there. However, he missed the company because they had obtained a lift on a motor lorry convoy. The road and villages were being bombed by the enemy, but he eventually got in touch with the company again east of Villers-Bretonneux, where the convoy had been stopped to remove POWs. The company therefore moved slowly on to Amiens arriving 5am on 25 March. They found accommodation at Rivery Rest Camp, on the edge of Amiens near the road to Albert.

On 26 March, orders were received by wire from the Third Army Controller of Foreways to proceed immediately to Contay and report to a Colonel at Albert. The men were sent to Contay by lorry 35 at a time, in four trips, which means that there were only 140 men, compared with the usual company strength of 250. As much rations and stores as possible were carried. Confidential documents and maps were burnt. Office dispatch boxes and survey instruments were taken in charge by a Road Construction Company at Rivery Camp, and 51 rifles handed to the CO at Rivery.

On arrival at Contay on 27 March, it was found that the enemy were in Albert, and it was impossible to get in touch with the colonel. Over the next few days, they were sent to various places on different orders. They went by road to Candas. Finding that Third Army Foreways had moved from Beauval, an officer went to Third Army HQ (Bernaville) and they were ordered to Bussy-lès-Daours. And so, on 29 March the men marched from Candas to Rubempré (9 miles, 15km), and the next day on to Querrieu (5½ miles, 9km), where they were stopped and given billets. Meanwhile, the big end had gone on their Ford car and it was towed back to Amiens by the lorry. The CO reported to the CRE as requested on 30 March, and finally on 31 March they were put to work; two officers and 31 men to Amiens for demolitions, and the rest wiring defences around Querrieu.

We have told the story of 3rd FWC at some length, because it illustrates the chaos and hardships, and the resourcefulness of the unit's officers in keeping the men safe and moving.

Fifth Army area

In the Fifth Army area, all light railways were lost. With the configuration of light railways already described (see Figure 7.1) it was almost inevitable that Fifth Army light railway units should evacuate west and stay in the Fifth Army area. The only possibility to do otherwise would have been north and a bit east up the AX line from Quinconce (Péronne) to Fins and from there to Bapaume via Rocquigny or Vélu. This would have been counter-intuitive with the German Army advancing rapidly from the east.

4th Bttn CRT
In March 1918, D Company of 4th Bttn CRT were working in the Péronne area, on construction of the Péronne to Quinconce light railway. On 22 March at 1am, they were called out to repair breaks in the track in forward areas. The next day, because of heavy shelling, they were forced to evacuate their camp leaving most of their equipment behind. They retreated to Plateau. A halt was made at Cléry and an attempt made to save some equipment, but it was found impossible. On 24 March, they made a forced march to Vecquemont to join the rest of the Battalion, working on the Amiens Avoiding line.

12th Bttn CRT
12th Bttn CRT were based at Bussu just north east of Péronne, working on general maintenance of the BW as well as the AX lines. On 21 March, A Company repaired shell breaks and maintained traffic, but in the evening had to withdraw detachments to Company HQ at Liéramont. An emergency gang repaired the line to a dump on the CY line to Heudicourt and dispatched three wagons of ammunition to Quinconce. Before noon on 22 March, the infantry had cut off the railway at the CY13 control, with a trench and wire line. The AX branch south of Liéramont was kept open, until evacuation orders were received at 2.30pm. One train left with all the company stores and equipment. The remainder left at 3.30pm for B Company HQ, probably on foot, and retreating parties of infantry reported that the enemy were approaching rapidly. During the first mile they were subjected to intense shell fire, and machine gun fire from both ground and air. Both parties met at B Company HQ near Aizecourt at 6pm. The train party proceeded with the train, and the rest marched, to a prelocated camp near Cléry. B Company continued to repair breaks until evacuation orders were issued, then they also retired on Cléry.

On 21 and 22 March, C Company repaired breaks breaks between Tincourt and Roisel. D Company continued to lay track on the Flamicourt to Quinconce line, Later, on 22 March, both C and D Companies retired to Cléry. The Battalion HQ evacuated from Bussu to Hem at about 2pm on 22 March, and all equipment and stores got back to the Hem yards west of Cléry, during the night. The rear party were forced to leave Bussu at 10am on 23 March, leaving some scrapers. The same day orders were received to retire to Cappy. This was on the other side of the Somme with no direct light railway connection. Battalion HQ left men to guard the stores at Hem to be picked up by the motor lorries. The military situation became such that the lorries could not return and at 4.30 pm the rear party had to leave for Cappy. The CO decided to retire to Corbie, and HQ moved out of Cappy at midnight.

Meanwhile, the companies also received orders on 23 March to retire to Cappy. A Company at Cléry loaded a train with stores and equipment, which reached Hem yards, but found it impossible to proceed further. We presume that this was caused by congestion or obstruction of the line ahead. The material was unloaded and left under guard. C Company managed to get two road wagons loaded and dispatched. D Company continued to build the Flamicourt to Quinconce line during the night of 22 to 23 March but then retired to Cléry with their equipment. Both A and B Companies had to leave for Cappy at 3am on 24 March after destroying the stores, and the others must have lost their equipment and stores too.

Battalion HQ bivouaced at Morlancourt in the early hours of the morning of 24 March. About 1pm, orders were received from GOC CRT (brigadier General Stewart) to proceed to Contay, and they arrived there in the early evening. All available motor lorries were dispatched to meet Company men and bring them in. By the end of 24 March, all four companies were at Contay. They were then ordered to Canaples. HQ arrived that evening and the companies marched through the night and arrived in the early hours of 26 March. At a muster parade in the afternoon, twelve men were missing but believed to be stragglers. Many of the men were without blankets or equipment.

6th LROC
The 6th LROC had moved to Froissy on 9 March 1918. They record that after the start of the German offensive on 21 March, the evacuation of Third Army South and Fifth Army areas caused the retirement of several light railway units to Froissy, with their rolling stock. 'In 48 hours upwards of 200 trains of construction troops, operating personnel, light railway rolling stock, repair trains, stores, machinery, ammunition etc' were handled in Froissy yard.

As the situation worsened, it was decided to work this stock to Wiencourt. This was successfuly accomplished, followed by the removal of the personnel and stock of 6th LROC, by 9pm on 24 March. Upon arrival at La Flaque, it was found impossible to proceed further because the line in advance to Wiencourt was too congested with the trains sent on previously. The position did not improve, and, next day, 6th LROC withdrew to Vecquemont, leaving one officer and 20 men in charge of the stock at La Flaque. They remained until the position became untenable and they were obliged to withdraw, after carrying out many demolitions, and rendering the stock useless.

7th Bttn CRT
The 7th Bttn CRT, whose HQ had been at Péronne, moved to Villers-Carbonnel, west of the Somme near Brie, on 20 March. This move had been in preparation since 5 March and was not a response to the threatened German offensive. On 22 March, when German activities threatened the area east of Somme, special efforts were made to put light railway rolling stock out of danger. Of the three bridges at Brie, the one over the east river was complete, that over the west river had been started, and the one over the Somme canal had not been started. The lines on either side of the bridge, from Le Mesnil to Brie on the east side, and from Brie to Estrées-Deniécourt on the west side, had completed track but were not fully ballasted and finished.

And so, on 22 March, the remaining two bridges at Brie, constructed of crib work and stringers, were built in ten hours. The Le Mesnil to Brie line was ballasted with earth and a 'large amount' of rolling stock reached Brie over this line by 6pm. By 9.30 pm, all rolling stock was over the bridges and cleared on its way to Estrées. Work had also been undertaken to ballast and finish the Brie to Estrées line. At midnight, word was received from XIX Corps that the battalion should move to a back area, so, on 23 March, all companies moved to Estrées. Work continued on the Brie to Estrées line and on the Le Mesnil and Flamicourt Yards. In the afternoon, 7th CRT moved to Chuignes. Work continued on the Estrées-Deniécourt line to remove rolling stock on 24 March.

From Estrées, the rolling stock could have gone straight to Wiencourt, or it could have gone first to La Flaque. In any event, the motive power units would have joined those disabled and abandoned at La Flaque or Wiencourt, and the wagons would have been burnt. On 25 March 7th CRT moved to Lamotte to help build the Amiens defences.

12th US Regiment of Railway Engineers
By March 1918, the six companies (A to F) of the 12th US Railway Engineers were operating from a main base at Quinconce (Péronne), and others including Montigny Farm on the DZ lines. South of Péronne they were probably the main operators on the Flamicourt to Hancourt and Le Mesnil to Brie lines, and on the Hancourt to Beauvois line (the B line).

After the German advance on 21 March, men based at Quinconce withdrew to Hem and then to Maricourt. It is probable that they moved by light railway with their own motive power, and that they moved on through Froissy yard. South of Péronne they moved back to Hancourt then Le Mesnil and were ordered to move their equipment to Fay by way of Estrées, so their rolling stock formed part, possibly the major part, of that dispatched across the Brie bridges by 7th CRT on 22 March.

Eventually, A Company assembled at Wiencourt and B to F Companies at La Flaque. By March 23, they were still repairing shelled lines but began destroying equipment. Then, lacking time to destroy equipment, they stripped the steam locomotives of injectors and side rods, and the tractors of magnetos and carburettors, which they buried since they could not carry them. They continued on foot, marching 14 miles (22km) the first day, and 22 miles (35km) the next. They reached safe billets at Vecquemont on 27 March, and from 29 March worked on the Amiens defences.

2nd Bttn CRT HQ and B Company
On 21 March, battalion HQ was at Cugny. At 4.30am, a most intense bombardment began, which did not decrease until after 11.30am, when the exceedingly thick morning mist had thinned a little. At about 2pm, artillery limbers started to pass through Cugny retiring. With their arrival, the attached Italian and Chinese labour was 'not slow' in also retiring. At 5pm, the CO gave orders to load heavy stores and pack up the rest ready to move.

On 21 March B Company were continuing to work on the Somme crossing on the Ham to Pithon Wood line. A party were also making the crossing of the main road in Ham to allow rolling stock to be moved onto the line to Voyennes. Considerable rolling stock was moved, but one locomotive ran out of water and in going forward for more ran off the track, stopping further work. High explosive shells were numerous. In the evening, the CO and an officer visited ADLRV South at Bussy. He had little information but wanted the work on the Voyennes line rushed, and the Ham to Pithon Wood loop completed to allow evacuation of rolling stock from the lines around Flavy. Heavy mist settled down again.

At 4.20am on 22 March, their dispatch rider returned from III Corps with orders to move. Battalion HQ moved to Guiscard, leaving a party of thirty. Five horse wagons returned at noon and took stores. The final party left at 6pm, by which time the farm west of Flavy was full of retreating guns. Great numbers of planes were shooting up roads and troops. Ham was evacuated by civilians at noon and 'the sight of refugees with their few treasured belongings in small carts was very pitiful'. The town was full of 'retiring' Italians and Chinese Labour. A small party of B Company continued work on the Somme crossing in order to clear rolling stock. By midnight, HQ and B Company were settled at Guiscard. The early hours of 23 March found Ham under machine gun fire and the enemy to the north of the town.

ADLRV South ordered HQ to move to Lassigny with B Company. The roads were full of French troops who were taking over part of the south of the British front. At Lassigny, everyone slept in the open in the centre of the old system of trenches which had been fought over by the French a year before. On 24 March, they moved to a French military hutment nearby. All day and night troops were retiring through Lassigny, and they stood ready to move if ordered. On 25 March, stores were loaded onto horse wagons and lorries, but a few unnecessary stores were left. The men went on foot to Ressons-sur-Matz, and then on by lorry to Tricot, south of Montdidier, where they met the transport and stores. The town was full of refugees, and French guns were moving up all evening. At Tricot on 26 March, 30 men of B Company reported in with D Company. They had been trying to make contact when rounded up by MPs as stragglers and some were sent up to the front line, but they had been allowed to leave when their battalion location became known. On 27 March, the battalion moved on to Ansauvillers. Later, on 27 March, Battalion HQ, and B, C and D Companies who had all assembled there, were ordered to Villers-Bretonneux.

2nd Bttn CRT C Company
On 21 March, C Company was based at Flavy-le-Martel. They received orders from Battalion HQ to withdraw the advanced maintenance parties to the battalion camp at Cugny. The light railway operating crews had already left. These may have been from 2nd LROC based at Foreste. The party at Montescourt-Lizerolles evacuated to Flavy, and then on 22 March on to Mesnil-St-Nicaise, where 3 platoons of C Company were based. The parties further south at Frieres Fallouel and Villequier Aumont retired to the rendezvous at Guiscard. Four horse wagons were loaded and moved to Cugny, leaving a small guard over the stores.

The platoons at Mesnil-St-Nicaise had been building the line from Omiécourt towards Voyennes. On 23 March, they laid 1,000 yards (1km) of track, with no labour available. Given the location, this must have been starting along the old metre gauge formation towards Ham, but they were still 3 miles (5km) from Voyennes, including the crossing of the Canal du Nord.

Civilians evacuated from Mesnil on 24 March on the orders of the French authorities, and the infantry were holding the road 1 mile away. C Company loaded their stores on horse drawn wagons, and marched with full kit via Nesle towards Guiscard, but were diverted to Lassigny. In billets near midnight, they were ordered to proceed directly to the Battalion rendezvous at Ansauvillers. They reached Popincourt at 5.30am, bivouaced until noon, and moved off again at 1.45pm to reach Montdidier at 4.40pm. There the 'English' area Commander refused to give them billets, but they finally obtained accommodation in huts from the French. They arrived at Ansauvillers on 26 March, where they were joined by HQ and B Company the next day.

2nd Bttn CRT D Company
On 21 March, Foreste was shelled from 4.30am, the track was blown up in four places but mended. Parties also repaired breaks at Pithon and Ham and they succeeded in delivering a train load of ammunition. By afternoon, front line troops were retiring through the village, so everything was packed ready to move. Most retired to Voyennes on 22 March. A small party was left at Foreste for maintenance, but they arrived an hour later, having been driven out by machine gun fire, leaving part of the equipment behind. The roads were blocked with traffic, chiefly civilians with their stock and carts. Several men from other units attached themselves and were brought along.

The Germans were advancing by night marches, so they left Voyennes at 2am on 23 March. By 2am on 26 March, they had marched to Conchy-les-Pots. The writer of the War Diary comments that the men behaved splendidly in trying circumstances, and that lots of farm stock to eat had been left behind in the villages, which they were 'happy to eat and deny it to the enemy'. Later that day, they moved to Tricot, partly by lorry, to join the rest of the Battalion.

2nd Bttn CRT A Company
On 21 March, A Company 2nd CRT were at Abbécourt, by the Oise canal. When the German offensive began, they had no definite information on the situation, but the company stood to, as all other units were doing. General maintenance was continued by the detached posts. The A line south from Chauny was under very heavy shell fire around Pierremande and broken for traffic. Chauny and Abbécourt yards were heavily shelled and bombed during the night but there were no casualties.

The company had already built the new line along the Oise canal to the bridge on the Morlincourt to Varesnes road. On 22 March, material was loaded at Abbécourt yard, and 600 yards of track was laid to extend this line towards Noyon. The A line south from Chauny was broken in 16 places. A Company had collected material for repair and were just starting work, when their attached labour party was ordered to go to Noyon. The operating company (probably 54th LROC) gave up operating, so there was no point in attempting further repair. At 6pm, all traffic beyond Abbécourt ceased, and later Chauny was evacuated. At 11pm, 54th LROC received orders from ADLR V South to move all rolling stock down the canal line towards Noyon, thereby blocking the line down which 2nd CRT hauled all the material to continue building.

The plan was still to extend the line along the canal in the hope that it could be built far enough for the stock to escape. Fortunately, they already had three wagons of rails at the end of line and ten wagons of standard gauge sleepers nearby.

All other units had evacuated by 23 March, so they moved camp to be nearer the work. One platoon was left in Abbécourt camp, where everything was loaded onto light railway wagons. In the evening, they were moved as far as track was clear, which was opposite Babœuf. Ahead, the line was blocked with 27 locomotives and 235 wagons, more than half of which were empty.

On 23 March, the track gang laid another 1,000 yards, which took the track end to just west of the bridge under the main road from Noyon to Soissons at Le Jonquoy. In the afternoon, a party took two tractors and seven wagons to Abbécourt yard and under shelling and direct enemy air observation loaded these, and three wagons found abandoned there, with 1½ miles of track, and other equipment. They hauled this to Babœuf. In the afternoon, the company had arranged with the French officer in charge of canal transport for a barge, as this was the only way of taking track material to the west of the blockage. When the barge had not reported at 9pm, an officer went to Pont L'Evêque where the 'English guard' (sic) had refused to allow it beyond Noyon bridge. With the officer on board and with some argument it was allowed to proceed to Babœuf bridge, reaching there at 1am.

On the next day at Babœuf, reveille was at 5am. Track material was transhipped from train to barge from daybreak, and another 1,100 yards of track was laid. This took the end of the track to south of Noyon, not quite half way between the bridge at Le Jonquoy and that at Pont L'Evêque. A party went to 'Quierzy' to collect sleepers. They found a complete travelling light railway workshop train of seven wagons, and a water tank wagon, in 'Quierzy siding' (that is, at Dampcourt bridge) on the point of being blown up by the Royal Engineers in charge. The Officers arranged to attach the workshop train to their tractors, which pulled the whole train back towards Noyon. The serial numbers (4183 to 4188, and 4209) show that this was not the workshop train in any of the known sets of photographs of these trains.

Also on that same day, 54th LROC abandoned a large part of their company stores and equipment and turned over the rolling stock to either the 7th or the 8th (South African) LROC, also operating in the Noyon area. They fired up the locomotives and moved the line of wagons about ¾ mile over newly constructed track so that the head of the line was at the bridge at Le Jonquoy under the main road to Soissons. A Company moved camp again to this bridge to bivouac in preparation for laying more track the next morning. However, at about 6pm, the South African LROC received orders to disable the locomotives, and to destroy all stores and withdraw, so laying further track was useless The workshop train, and the two tractors used by 2nd CRT, must also have been abandoned.

The civilian population had been leaving Noyon for three days. A Company, equipment and stores having been loaded on the barge during the day, they now moved down to Pont l'Evêque to bivouac. From this time, the moves of the company were governed by those of the barge, which was ordered back by the French authorities when needed. From 25 March to 4 April, they moved down the canal with the barge, sometimes on it and sometimes marching along the canal bank. On the way, they gave considerable help to the French officer in charge of canal transport, who was trying to salvage materials as they retreated, with little assistance. They helped load and unload steel rails, flour, navigation company records, and civilian property. Most notably, they made timber into booms for towing down the canal. The largest was composed of 55,000ft of large bridge timbers. On 28 March, they had orders from Battalion HQ to stand to, and move to Sains-en-Amiénois, but the buses did not arrive. On 30 March, they were visited, and told that the other Companies were in the line, and to work with the French Engineers until they could move. Finally, on 3 April, they were told to move by barge to Creil, where they would be picked up. On 4 April they unloaded four lorry loads of stores and some track material. The lorry convoy was delayed but it arrived piece-meal at Courcelles, south west of Amiens, the following morning, having been on the road 26 to 30 hours.

The rest of the barge was unloaded by 10.30am the next morning. The material was left in a barn and the track material on the river bank. The owner of the barn agreed to look after the supplies. Then they marched off but were forced to leave the main road because of traffic. We do not know where they were picked up by the lorries, but the transport and animals reached Wavignies on 6 April, and the men reached Courcelles on 7 April. By this time, the Battalion had gone to Villers-l'Hôpital, north west of Doullens. The animals were rested on 8 April, and the Battalion were reunited at Villers-l'Hôpital on 10 April, 70 miles (112km) in a straight line from Creil. A letter of thanks was received from the French officer on the canal for their work in the evacuation.

2nd Bttn CRT
When rejoined by A Company on 10 April, the rest of the Battalion had been resting and training at Courcelles, and then from 7 April at Villers-l'Hôpital, after their time in the front line (see **The Defence of Amiens** later in this chapter). From the middle of April, they were working in the north, in the Dunkirk area, but they reappeared in the Somme sector in September 1918 on standard gauge work.

1st LROC detachment
The detachment of the 1st LROC, including Sgt Leonard Atkins, had been at Morlincourt, just south east of Noyon, from 12 March. assisting A Company of 2nd CRT in building the light railway along the Oise Canal. They probably left Morlincourt on 24 March. They retreated towards Amiens, probably initially on foot. Eventually they arrived in the Frévent area, where they helped a Canadian unit convert part of the Lens to Frévent metre gauge line to dual gauge.

After a short period constructing a standard gauge siding north of Frévent, they travelled in small journies to Étaples, and from there they went to Calais. On 29 June 1918, the detachment boarded a train at Calais, arriving at Rouen just over 24 hours later, to be re-united with the rest of 1st LROC. They had been away 7 months and 2 days.

The evacuation of light railway rolling stock
The light railway escape routes can be seen in Figure 7.1 (page 130), with the places where significant amounts of motive power units and other rolling stock are known to have been abandoned. It is probable that much rolling stock reached the end of the available light railway track on the route they had taken. However, some had to be abandoned on the way. With the exception of the Maricourt to Quinconce (Péronne) line between Cléry and Quinconce, all lines were single track. It only required a breakdown, or a derailment or other accident, to block the line. Other causes of hold-ups were damage to the line from shell fire or aerial bombing. The light railway troops were expert at dealing with all of these quickly, but they were still a significant problem.

It would also have been impossible, or almost so, to travel against the main flow of traffic. To do so, against what was probably at times an almost continuous line of trains travelling west, would have required clearing successive sections between passing loops as the train going the other way progressed.

In the Third Army South area, all light railway lines were lost east of the Amiens to Arras main standard gauge line, almost as far north as Arras. We have already described the importance of the C12 line south from Monchy-au-Bois, to join the X7 line west of Bucquoy. These lines linked into the Bapaume area through the X and X4 lines via Mory. It is probable that all or almost all of the rolling stock which escaped from south of the Achiet to Marcoing standard gauge line used this route. Alternatively, stock could have been taken north from Mory on the C10 line to Boiry-Becquerelle, then north west to Mercatel and Wailly. With the German

7.2 A British Army dump near Cambrai, captured by the German Army in March 1918. The nearest wagon is German. May 1918. *(IWM Q61027)*

Army advancing rapidly this would probably have been considered unwise. Time was short. Bapaume was evacuated on 24 March. In the Fifth Army area all light railways were lost.

It was also assumed in planning that if light railway rolling stock reached a standard gauge rail head, stock could be transferred to standard gauge flat trucks and moved out. Colonel Henniker (*Transportation on the Western Front*, 1937) states that 'a small proportion' of stock from La Flaque was moved in this way, but in general other standard gauge traffic was too intense and time too short to allow much to be saved. Pozières was only served by a single track standard gauge line, demolished on 25 March. Other final positions of significant numbers of stock, at Voyennes and Noyon, were not in any case on a standard gauge line. With hindsight one can say that the situation was aggravated by decisions made in 1917 and early 1918, leading to a series of 'what ifs'.

With the demolition of the line from Aveluy to Pozières at some time between 1 January and 20 March 1918, Pozières became a dead end. If it had remained open, rolling stock could have reached the standard gauge yards at Aveluy. However, it is likely that there would still have been no opportunity to remove the stock on standard gauge wagons. But if the Ancre Valley line (see Chapter Five) had been completed, and if the line from Acheux to Beaucourt had remained in place, the two lines could quickly have been linked the 500 yards across the Ancre, using the existing road and bridge. But at the time, the priority had been to make track material available for construction further east.

The proposed lateral line from Fricourt to Pozières and Miraumont would not have helped much. It is possible that 6th CRT knew this, and that this is why they did not expend much manpower or material on it. There were no connections at Fricourt, and at Miraumont the problem of availability of standard gauge transport would have been the same as at Aveluy.

No doubt before the beginning of the offensive, Wiencourt (Chemin Vert), to where the lines had been built west by the French in 1916, seemed far enough. It was after all 29 miles (47km) from the front line at St-Quentin. But sadly, it was 5 miles (8km) short of the end of the advance at Villers-Bretonneux. A map of 1 February 1918 shows the light railway extended west from Wiencourt along the north side of the standard gauge line to just west of Marcelcave, but this also was not quite far enough.

Rolling stock escaping from the Ham area was dispatched along the line to Voyennes and became trapped there. What if the line had been linked the final 4 miles (6.5km) to the line being built east from Omiécourt? This would have allowed the stock to reach the standard gauge yard at Omiécourt but leading to the same problems with evacuation on standard gauge wagons. And in the south at Noyon, the best efforts of A Company of 2nd CRT and their assisting troops could not extend the track west fast enough to save the rolling stock there. The original proposal had been to extend the line to the main standard gauge yard at Noyon. But again, it is likely that there would have been no capacity to evacuate it on the standard gauge lines.

Might different decsions have saved more rolling stock? From what we know now, it never seemed a sensible decision to send any rolling stock to Pozières. The only way to Pozières was through Bapaume, and from Bapaume, stock could have been sent along the X lines to the C12 line and out north west. This would also have allowed the 14th US Engineers at Pozières to evacuate the other way to Bapaume, and then out as above, but the decision would have had to be made early, given the speed of the German advance.

It also seems that it was known from an early stage that the Fifth Army was giving way further and faster than the Third Army. Given that, any unit reaching Rocquigny with rolling stock should have been sent along the Y5 extension to Bapaume, rather than being forced south west through Froissy to Wiencourt. Also, the only locomotive known to have escaped under its own power from the Fifth Army area was Alco No. 1261. The crew from 1st Aus. LROC at Savy-Berlette were delivering the locomotive to Ham on 21 March, reaching Quinconce. They must have gone back the way they must have come, taking the AX line north from Quinconce to Fins, and from there to Bapaume via Rocquigny or Vélu. This would have been counter-intuitive with the German Army advancing rapidly from the east, and with the speed of the advance they must have been quick.

There might however have been so much congestion on the light railways in the Bapaume area that it was not practical to order more units to take that route. The crew of the single escaping locomotive may have made their own decision, sensibly going back the way that they knew.

From any point of view, the loss of light railways, and of light railway rolling stock, was a disaster wrapped up in the much bigger disaster of the retreat. An estimate in June 1918 was that the total loss of light railway equipment to the British Army in the German offensives of 1918 was 189 locomotives, 1,860 wagons, and 750 miles of track. This is far too low, although it may have been a good figure for morale. Colonel Henniker (*Transportation on the Western Front*, 1937) states that more than 300 locomotives were disabled at La Flaque and Wiencourt, and more than 2,000 wagons were burned. We think this is a reasonable assessment, by a man who was there at the time and had access to all the records afterwards. No comprehensive list of rolling stock lost exists now. We know that more than 200 trains were handled at Froissy during the retreat, all with at least one locomotive, and were dispatched on to La Flaque and Wiencourt. The 'large amount' of stock crossing the bridge at Brie on 22 March also went to Wiencourt or La Flaque.

In addition, we know that more than 27 locomotives and 235 wagons, as well as a whole workshop train, were abandoned at Noyon. Some locomotives were abandoned at Cléry and Hem-Monacu. A significant number must have been abandoned at Pozières, where they were left by two operating units (34th LROC and 14th US Engineers) and part of 6th CRT, who would have had a few tractors. Also, a considerable number must have been lost along the way, damaged or broken down. In all Fifth Army and Third Army South must have lost more than 400 locomotives. With the German attacks in the north, on the plain of the Lys and around Ypres, the British First and Second Armies lost almost no rolling stock.

In all, in excess of 1,500 light railway locomotives, half steam and half petrol tractors, had been delivered to the British Armies on the Western Front by March 1918. If they were equally distributed between the five armies, each would have had about 300. If Fifth Army lost all and Third Army some, more than 400 lost in total is about right. That would have been more than one quarter of all the British light railway motive power units in France. The loss of wagons would have been of the same order. This is certainly a more realistic figure than the 'official' 189 locomotives of June 1918.

The Defence of Amiens

During 26 March, successive defence lines on the approach to Amiens failed, but General Gough (Fifth Army) had put together an ad hoc defence force on 25 March. This consisted of various technical and Engineer units, infantry stragglers, and any other available men, but of most importance for this book, it included two companies (about 500 men) of the 6th US Regiment of Railway Engineers, and about 400 officers and men of 2nd CRT. The force was initially commanded by General Grant, Fifth Army Chief Engineer, but he was replaced by General Carey on 26 March, hence it is often called 'Carey's Force'. In all, between 2,000 and 3,000 men were placed on the old Amiens Defence Line, firstly to strengthen and repair it, and then to defend it. The line extended south from the Somme river near Vaux to the Amiens to Roye road at Mezières.

2nd CRT in the defence of Amiens

We do not have any details of the part played by the 6th US Regiment of Railway Engineers in the defence, but we know more about 2nd CRT.

By 27 March, C and D Companies, and part of B Company, 2nd Bttn CRT had moved to Ansauvillers, south east of Breteuil and 25 miles (40km) south of Amiens. A Company were still in the south retreating down the Oise canal. The main force was ordered by a Fifth Army Staff Captain to report to General Carey at Villers-Bretonneux. The men, who were told that they would be on unspecified construction work, were each hurriedly equipped with a rifle, 50 rounds, a box respirator, a steel helmet, and at least two days' rations. They embussed in 20 lorries at Wavignies, on the main Amiens to Creil road 1½ miles (2.5km) away.

Their arrival at Villers-Bretonneux was chaotic, but a detailed description of their time in the front line is beyond the scope of this book. From early on 28 March they held 1,000 yards (1km) of front line astride the main Amiens to Tergnier railway line between Villers-Bretonneux and Marcelcave, between the Bedford Yeomanry and a Battalion of the Gloucestershire Regiment. They were relieved early on 31 March, Easter Sunday, and they rejoined their transport and animals at Sains-en-Amiénois, around midday. Unshaven and very tired, they were given a hot meal and then allowed to sleep. They had been in the front line for 72 hours, with 29 casualties, including two killed. Later, 2nd CRT were awarded two Military Crosses (Officers) and ten Military Medals (other ranks) for their time in the front line. It may just be coincidence that 2nd CRT were formed in January 1917 from the 127th Canadian Infantry Battalion.

Reinforcing the defences - The Secondary Defence lines
General Byng moved the British Third Army Headquarters to Bernaville, west of Doullens, on 25th March. The Deputy Director General of Transportation (Construction) also opened a headquarters there, with orders to acquire all possible railway construction troops to construct a second defensive line. The main north to south light railway north of Arras, and the Lens to Frévent metre gauge line, was used to bring 18 companies from La Crèche, in the Nord *département*, to the Third Army area between 26 and 30 March 1918, and they and most of the locally retreating railway units were put to work on the defence lines.

Many were constructing the Pas-Condé defence line, a complete secondary defence line with trenches, wire entanglements, and machine gun emplacements. The line started in the north at Pas-en-Artois, just north of the Authie and the Authie Valley railway, and ended at Condé-Folie, on the south bank of the Somme next to Longpré.

Work began on 27 and 28 March and was probably complete by 13 April. This major effort was led Canadian railway troops. Another defence line was constructed in the rear defence zone, about 9 miles (15km) behind the front line established by 5 April, again mostly by railway troops. This probably began at the Pas-Condé line near Puchevillers and ran south to the Ancre near Vecquemont.

The aftermath of the great retreat
By the end of the retreat, the British Fifth Army was in severe disarray. Fifth Army HQ was suspended on 2 April. General Sir Hubert Gough was relieved of his command. Many have said that he was made the scapegoat for the failure. Whatever the reasons, it was a sad end for a General, and for an Army, which had fought with distinction in the later phases of the 1916 Battle of the Somme, and at Ypres in autumn 1917.

In May 1918, the Fifth Army was reconstituted under General William Birdwood, and put back into the front line on the plain of the Lys, between the Second Army (Ypres) and the First Army (north from Arras).

The Fourth Army under General Sir Henry Rawlinson had been moving back to the Somme sector from Ypres since the middle of March. In April they were put into the front line south of the Third Army, from Albert to Moreuil, south east of Amiens. RCC IV remained at St-Léger-lès-Domart as the standard gauge support for the Fourth Army. Units of the French Army had moved north to take responsibility for the front line from Moreuil south.

Further battles 6 April to 7 August 1918
There were a number of further battles on the Western Front between 6 April and 7 August. The German attacks against the British First and Second Armies on the plain of the Lys, and around Ypres, began on 9 April.

Most of the later battles, around the Marne and Aisne rivers and to the east, were fought by the French and American armies, and were south and east of the Somme Sector. The first was the German Noyon-Montdidier Offensive, from 9 to 13 June, known to the German Army by its code-name of 'Operation Gneisenau', but also known as the Battle of Matz. The German line after the advances of March and April towards Amiens was almost along the Montdider to Noyon metre gauge railway. Now they attacked south from Noyon, Roye-sur-Matz, and Montdidier, advancing at most 6 miles (10km) south from the first two, and hardly at all from Montdidier. The advance was halted by a French and American counter-attack.

Secondly, on 4 July 1918, Australian troops, supported by American infantry, tanks and by British and Australian aircraft, took the German salient at Le Hamel, in a quick and decisive attack. In some ways it was a dress rehearsal for the much larger attacks on 8 August.

From 27 May, the German Armies had attacked across the Chemin des Dames on the French front east of Noyon. They crossed the Aisne. In a further attack beginning on 15 July they crossed the Marne from east of Château-Thierry towards Épernay and made a large bulge in the French front line. The counter attack by the French, supported by four American and two British divisions, began on 18 July. By 2 August, they had forced the German Armies to withdraw, and were back to the line of the Aisne. With the failure of this, the last major German offensive of the war, the scene was set for the Allied attacks east of Amiens on 8 August.

Railways 6 April to 7 August 1918
This was initially a period of recovery and consolidation, merging into a period of preparation for the counter attack of 8 August. The overall situation, with the new developments, is shown in Figure 7.2.

Figure 7.2

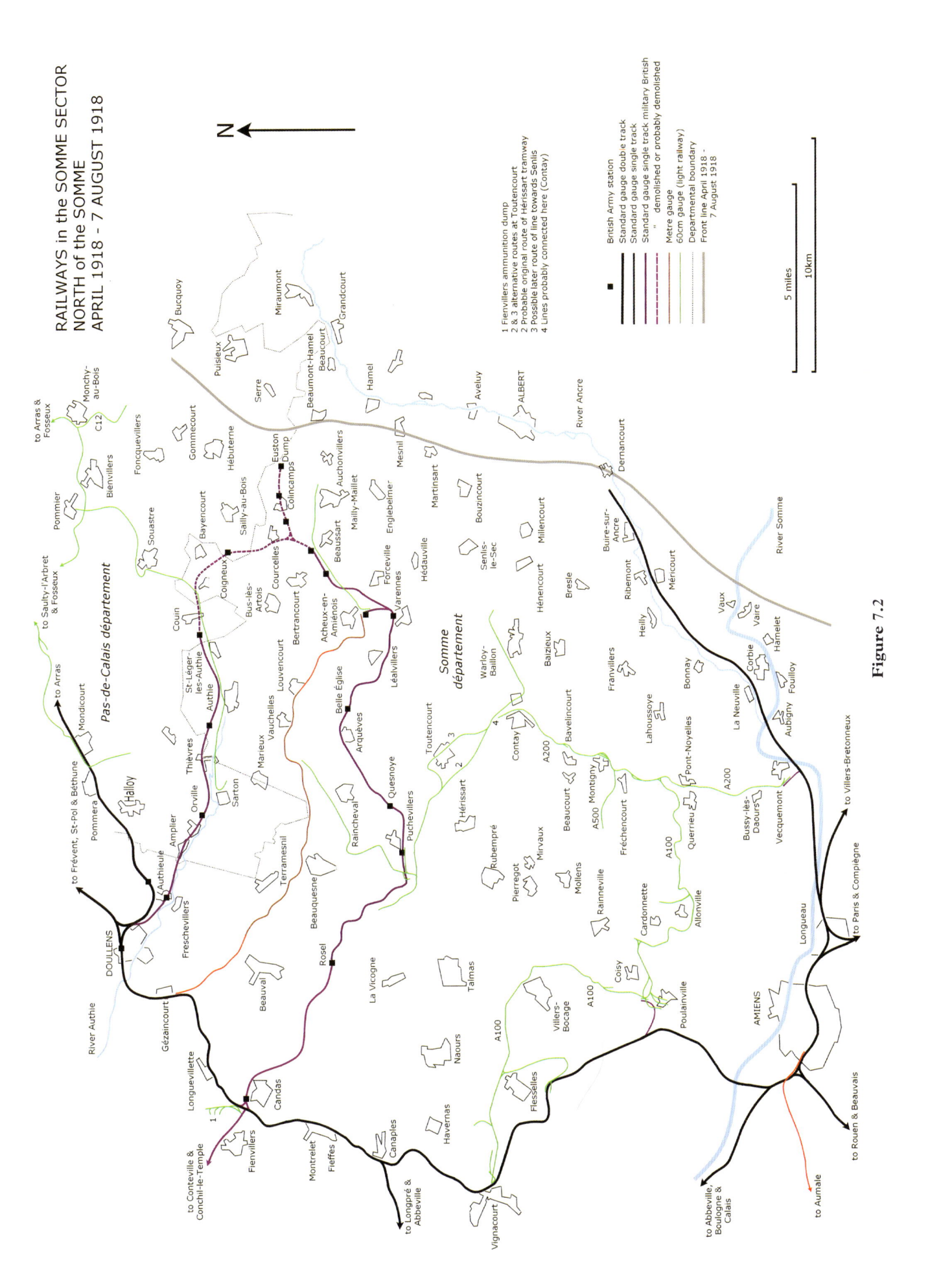

Standard gauge railways

The programme consisted of repairing and improving the existing lines near the front, while strengthening the lines further away, and adding new lines to replace those lost. With the British part of the front line in the Somme sector now east and north east of Amiens, this consisted of repairing the lines from Amiens east and north, that is the lines towards Albert, and to Doullens, and the military lines east from the latter towards the front. The French undertook similar work in their areas.

Doullens and the Authie Valley line

By the end of April 1918, the ROD limit of working was to St-Léger-lès-Authie. The destroyed line beyond St-Léger still required reconstruction in August 1918 (see Chapter Eight). The ROD was based at Freschevillers.

Candas to Acheux and Colincamps

By the end of April 1918, the ROD, based at Candas, was operating the line as far as Acheux, but was probably not from there to Colincamps. Improvements between Candas and Acheux were made in April and May 1918.

Amiens to Doullens and Longpré to Canaples

The line from Amiens to Doullens and the line from Longpré, which joined it at Canaples, had already been double tracked by early 1918. The operation and maintenance was taken over by the British during the German advance, and then taken back by the *Compagnie du Nord*. Following discussions about the inadequacy of personnel for this, at least bridge repairs were later handed back to RCE V.

A spur was built from a junction at Bertangles to Poulainville in April and May 1918, to a station alongside the main road to Doullens north of Poulainville village. Changes were also made at Vignacourt and Flesselles stations in June and July. All these were to link with the the light railway network being built from the end of May.

New lines from the coast

Between April and August 1918, new works were undertaken along the main line down the coast from Étaples to Abbeville, and from this line inland. The line inland from Conchil to Conteville, on the Abbeville to Frévent line, and the line on from Conteville to Candas, on the Amiens to Doullens line, provided a link through to the existing Candas to Acheux line. Later in 1918, with the reopening of that line to Irles junction, of the line from there to Le Transloy, and the opening of the line to Bellicourt, there was a continuous west to east British military line all the way from Conchil to Bellicourt (see Chapter Eight). This is a distance of 72 miles (116km) in a straight line. However, it is doubtful if, after the advances from August 1918, and the reopening of the Amiens to Arras main line, the more western parts were much used.

Quadrupling Étaples to Port-le-Grand - The coast line was part of the main line from Calais to Paris via Boulogne, Abbeville and Amiens, and had always been double track. Between May and August 1918, a double track military line was added. This started in the north at St. Josse, just south of Étaples and the beginning of the chord constructed by the British Army to the Étaples to Arras line. It ended in the south at Port-le-Grand, between Noyelles and Abbeville, where it linked with the existing line from Abbeville to Le Tréport. From Étaples to Quend station the work was done by British Engineers, and from Quend to Port-le-Grand by the French.

Conchil to Conteville - This single track line started at a triangular junction with the two new military lines down the coast, just south of Conchil-le-Temple. Called Authie station, a yard and ROD depot were built. From there the line climbed onto the plateau between the Authie and Somme rivers, and crossed it south east to Conteville, on the line from Abbeville to Frévent. Construction was commenced in April 1918, undertaken by 12th, 7th and 13th Bttns. CRT, and was completed during August.

Conteville to Candas - This single track line was built from Candas, on the existing line from Amiens to Doullens, and the beginning of the line to Acheux, to Conteville, on the line from Abbeville to Frévent, where it also linked with the above line from Conchil. Work commenced on 17 April, by 6th and later 11th Bttn CRT, assisted among others by 2nd LROC, diverted from light railway work. The line was about 11 miles (17km) long, and it was fully open for traffic by the end of June 1918.

Longpré to Longroy-Gamaches

This existing single track line was doubled by the British Army between April and August 1918. The work was undertaken by 4th Bttn CRT, assisted by 12th US Railway Engineers, and Labour Companies, including some from India. There was double line working to Martainneville on 15 July. The doubling was completed, and the line was handed over to the *Réseau du Nord*, on 15 September.

On 4 July Major-General Buckland, Chief Engineer, Fourth Army presented British decorations to Officers and other ranks of 12th US Railway Engineers, and on 25 July they left to join the US Army further east. They had served with British Army light railways around Péronne from August 1917 to the retreat after 21 March 1918, then on the Pas-Condé defence line,

7.3 The remains of three German standard gauge ammunition trains at Ham, attacked successfully by the French Air Force in July 1918. *(Authors' collection)*

until they joined the Longpré to Gamaches doubling on 23 April.

Amiens to Albert
This line was now cut by the front line near Dernancourt, south west of Albert. By the end of July 1918, one track of the main line had been restored to Corbie.

Amiens to Tergnier
With the front line across this railway immediately east of Villers-Bretonneux, no attempt was made to use this railway during this period.

Metre gauge railways

With the German advance between 21 March and 5 April 1918, almost all of the metre gauge railways in the Somme sector were lost.

Gézaincourt to Acheux and Mailly-Maillet
Only the section from Gézaincourt to Acheux, of the line from Doullens to Albert, remained workable and in Allied hands. The section from Acheux to Beaussart and on to Albert had just been converted back from standard to metre gauge when the German offensive began, and the front line was now just west of Albert, cutting the line at Martinsart. On 3 April, 1st FWC moved to Mailly-Maillet and were employed repairing the metre gauge line near there, as requested by a RE Special Company. This was night work because it was near the front line. On 4 April, most of the Company moved, but 12 men were left for maintenance. However, we have no evidence that the line was used beyond Acheux during this period, and the maintenance party rejoined the main company on 6 April, because the RE Special Company said that the line was no longer needed. Later the section from Acheux to Beaussart was taken over again for light railway use.

On the instructions of ADGT III on 18 April, the line from Gézaincourt to Acheux was prepared at once for demolition. Investigation showed there were on the line at this time, three locomotives, twelve passenger coaches, five brake vans, fifteen covered wagons, thirty-seven open wagons and two flat wagons. If the line were demolished, these would have to be destroyed, if they could not be evacuated on standard gauge flat wagons from Gézaincourt station. In July 1918, the standard to metre gauge transhipment facilities at Gézaincourt were enlarged and improved. A new metre gauge spur and passing loop was also constructed at Beauval, completed 18 July.

The civilian passenger service had ceased on 21 March, and was not resumed, but the line remained in military use by the British Army. On 21 May, RCE V were informed by ADGT III that light railways were to take over operation, and demolition duties, on the Gézaincourt to Acheux line. From 13 April to 15 June 6th LROC were based at Candas, and they probably operated the line from late May until 14 June. From 14 June, 34th LROC were based at Fienvillers ammunition sidings near Candas. A detachment took over operations on the line, based at Beauval, where the workshops had been established in 1915 or 1916. This is the only instance we know of British LROCs operating a metre gauge line.

Albert to Péronne and Albert to Montdidier
These lines were now entirely in German held territory. The bridge of the metre gauge lines from Albert to Péronne and to Montdidier over the main line north east of Albert station had been destroyed during the retreat on 25 March; two steel girders and the deck were destroyed, other girders cut, and the abutments damaged. Later maps show that the bridge over the Ancre east of this was also destroyed. The partial demolition of the metre gauge railway bridge over the Somme at Bray has already been described.

Noyon to Ham and Noyon to Montdidier
The line from Noyon to Ham was completely captured in the German advance between 21 March and 5 April, with much of the line from Noyon to Montidier. The rest was lost during the German Noyon-Montdidier Offensive, from 9 to 13 June.

The Reseau des Bains de Mer
The western Somme network, based on Noyelles, played little part in the war until 1917. After the German advance of March 1918, more material was imported through the port of St-Valéry, although it never matched the tonnage of larger ports such as Le Havre or Boulogne. The part played is well described in *Railways of the Baie de Somme* (Philip Pacey, Oakwood Press, 2000)

60cm (light) railways

After the German offensive and advance from 21 March to 5 April 1918, Third and Fourth armies undertook substantial work between 6 April and 7 August 1918, to consolidate, and to prepare for the planned major offensive.

Up to the German offensive of 21 March 1918, the central British Army light railway depot workshops were at La Lacque, near Aire-sur-la-Lys in the First Army area. After the German advance new workshops were built at Beaurainville in the Canche Valley between Montreuil and Hesdin, in the Arras sector. These workshops were a resource for all the British armies on the Western Front.

Third Army

Because the Third Army covered a large area, it divided itself for some purposes into Third Army North and Third Army South. The developments in the Somme Sector were in Third Army South, under the ADLR III South. Some developments were isolated bits of light railway, but there were also two more major areas of development, in the Authie Valley, and around Puchevillers. Light railways in this area from 5 April to 7 August 1918 are shown in Figure 7.2 (page 143).

Authie Valley and links north
Following the German advance, the X7 line connections to Achiet, Puisieux and Euston Dump (Colincamps) were cut near Bucquoy and north of Puisieux, close to the junction with the C12 back lateral line to Monchy-au-Bois.

In response Third Army built links south into the Authie Valley further west. A line from Saulty-l'Arbret, on the Doullens to Arras standard gauge line, was built south and then east to Bienvillers-au-Bois and then to the C12 line at Monchy-au-Bois, in June 1918. Also in June, from a junction west of Bienvillers, a line was built south west to Coigneux village, in the Authie Valley, on the destroyed part of the British military Authie Valley standard gauge railway. This was extended west along the valley, almost to Sarton, in July.

The line from Bienvillers to St-Léger and Thièvres was built by 9th Bttn CRT. D Company moved to Bienvillers on 17 June, and worked from that end, and B Company moved to Couin on 18 June, and worked from the St-Léger end. The whole route was about 9 miles (14.5 km) long. The two ends were connected up on 4 July, and D Company moved away on 9 July. B Company worked on finishing and maintenance until early August.

The 34th LROC had already been in the Authie Valley from 19 April 1918, at Couin, working on standard gauge spurs and stone for roads. From 14 June, when the Company base moved to Fienvillers, detachments were operating light railways in the Authie Valley, around Couin and Coigneux. In July, more of the Company were in the Authie Valley, maintaining light railway track for 9th CRT. On 1 August, the rest of the Company moved to St-Léger-lès-Authie, and and took over the operation of the new 60cm track in that area.

Saulty-l'Arbret to Mondicourt (and Thièvres)
Construction of this line was started by D Company of 9th Bttn CRT on 26 July. The line started from Saulty-l'Arbret and followed the standard gauge line from Doullens to Arras south west to near Mondicourt (5 miles, 8km). Here it turned due south. The intention was that it should end at Thièvres, joining the light railway already in the Authie Valley there.

Light and metre gauge railways of the Somme sector 21 March to 7 August 1918

In the event, it only got one third of the way south from the standard gauge line, which would have been a distance of 2½ miles (4 km). By the beginning of the Allied offensive on 8 August only some of the track had been laid, but work continued until 20 August. From 21 August D Company moved to maintenance of the C12 line, and the line never reached Thièvres.

Fienvillers ammunition dump
This was a good example of an isolated section of light railway serving one facility. During April 1918, 6th LROC laid track at Fienvillers ammunition dump. This was just west of Candas, on the line from Amiens to Doullens, and the junction with the British Army line to Acheux. Later, the new line from Conteville to Candas went through Fienvillers. The dump must have been close to the junction of these lines. Construction continued into May.

The line was operated from April by a detachment of 6th LROC. From 26 May, a detachment of 6th LROC moved to near Poulainville, in the Fourth Army area, to assist 11th Bttn CRT with the A100 line there. At least until 14 June, a detachment of 6th LROC was based at Fienvillers, with detachments elsewhere operating light railways, and probably the metre Gauge line from Gézaincourt to Acheux. On 15 June, the major part of the Company moved to Poulainville.

Lines around Puchevillers
From 2 April 1918, 6th LROC built, and then operated, a length of light railway track at Puchevillers Yard. We do not know the exact purpose of this, but it was associated with the standard gauge unloading sidings in the yard.

The Hérissart Tramway - On 18 April, 1st FWC, who had been undertaking mostly road work, moved to Hérissart, with instructions to build a light railway from Puchevillers to south east of Hérissart. Hérissart was the HQ of V Corps. This line became known as the Hérissart Tramway. The original end of the line was well west and slightly north of Contay. The line would have been about 4 miles (6.5km) long.

Work began on 19 April and by 27 April 2 miles (3.5km) had been graded, but there was no track to lay. Track was laid from 2 May, and by the end of June all of the track had been laid, and all ballasting and other work completed. The 1st FWC continued maintenance until early August, but from the middle of May, much of the company were engaged on other light railway work, and on Defence works. When they left the line later in August they handed over two Simplex tractors and seven 3 ton wagons to 9th Bttn CRT.

Other work by 1st FWC - In addition to the above work, 1st FWC undertook a lot of small light railway construction works between end April and July 1918. These illustrate the versatility of these companies. All of these lines were constructed with light track (9lb) and would only have been suitable for use with light petrol tractors. They were not connected to other parts of the light railway network.

These included, in the Somme sector, 1 mile of track near Beauquesne, 550 yards of track at 34th CCS at Fienvillers (in addition to that at the ammunition dump), and ½ mile of track at Hébuterne near the front line. This last was night work and one man was killed and three injured.

Later lines around Puchevillers
On 1 August, A and C Companies of 9th Bttn CRT moved to Puchevillers to construct light railway lines. Plans for a new light railway transhipment at Puchevillers were approved on 6 August. Later in August, a line to Rosel was also started. Work on the system was abandoned on 23 August 1918, no longer considered necessary.

Puchevillers yard – Considerable development work was undertaken in Puchevillers Yard, including more than 1 mile (1.6km) of new track.

Puchevillers to Beaussart and Sarton – The line to Beaussart was planned to run north almost to Beauquesne, until it met the metre gauge line Gézaincourt to Acheux just west of Vauchelles. From here a branch would have gone north the 2 miles (3km) to Sarton. The line to Beaussart would have followed the metre gauge line part of the way to Acheux, cut through the edge of Acheux, and met the metre gauge line again towards Beaussart. The line from Puchevillers to the junction would have been about 6 miles (10km) long, and on from there to Beaussart about 7 miles (11km) long.

Work began on the line to Beaussart on 2 August but was delayed by heavy rain. By the beginning of the offensive on 8 August only 1000 yards had been graded, and 600 yards of track laid. By 23 August, 6 miles (10km) of track had been laid, almost to the proposed junction, when work was abandoned.

Puchevillers to Senlis-le-Sec - The plans show that it was intended eventually to extend this line north from Senlis to Beaussart, to join the line to Beaussart coming more directly from Puchevillers. Later maps show a line starting from Puchevillers Yard on the Candas to Acheux standard gauge line, then going south east, passing Toutencourt village, then continuing to just east of Contay, a total distance of about 5 miles (8km). At Contay, the line turned east to end between Warloy-Ballon and Senlis-le-Sec, another 2½ miles (4km), making the total length of the line about 7½ miles (12km). The exact route of the earlier Hérissart Tramway is not known, but it probably passed south west of Toutencourt. The length of line laid by 9th CRT was 4¼ miles (7km), so it is probable that they used part of the Hérissart Tramway, branching off it in the area of Toutencourt. Matters are complicated by the fact that the two later maps showing the line towards Senlis, both from 1919, show different routes around Toutencourt, as shown on Figure 7.2. We think that the one south west of Toutencourt is more likely to be correct.

Work started on the line to Senlis on 2 August, and by the beginning of the offensive on 8 August 2½ miles had been graded, but no track laid. By 20 August 4¼ miles (7km) of track had been laid, when work was abandoned.

Puchevillers to Rosel – Between 20 and 22 August 1918, ¾ mile of track laid towards Rosel, before work was abandoned.

Acheux to Mailly-Maillet
On 1 July 1918 most of 2nd TWC moved to Léalvillers to work on light railways for V Corps, Third Army South. On 3 July, they began work on a light railway line from Acheux to Mailly-Mallet. Probably this followed, or used the formation of, the metre gauge line from Gézaincourt, and the route would have been via Beaussart, If this was the case, the section from Acheux to Beaussart would have been part of the proposed line from Puchevillers. From 7 July, they were unloading trucks of material from the standard gauge line in Acheux Wood. This and much, possibly all, of the other work was done at night because of the proximity to the front line. It is likely that the line was laid with 20lb rails, because it is called a light railway rather than a tramway, and because when an artillery spur was laid with 9lb rails this is mentioned, as if an exception. The Company received one 20hp Simplex tractor on 13 July, and two more on 3 August.

Work on the line continued until 24 August, and 2nd TWC moved on 25 August to Couin for work around Bucquoy (see Chapter Eight). We do not know how much of the line was built but given the length of time available it is probable that it was built all the way to Mailly-Maillet. The end of the work probably relates to the opening of the offensive on the Ancre front on 21 August.

Fourth Army
In consolidation of their position, and in preparation for the major offensive which began on 8 August 1918, Fourth Army light railways built an extensive system north east of Amiens between May and July 1918. This was linked to the standard gauge network at Vignacourt and Flesselles stations, and by way of the Poulainville spur, all on the line from Amiens to Doullens, converted to double track in 1917.

The process began with a meeting between RCE IV and ADGT Fourth Army on 24 May. Light railways in this area from April to August 1918 are shown in Figure 7.2 (page 143). The main system consisted of two lines. The A100 line ran mostly west to east from Vignacourt to Querrieu via Villers-Bocage and Poulainville. The A200 line ran north to south from Contay to Vecquemont, almost on the Somme. Presumably they were called A100 and A200 to avoid confusion with the A to A7 lines at Arras, but some units just referred to them as A1 and A2. Later, an A500 line was started from Fréchencourt to form a second east to west link between the other two lines, but was never finished.

The A100 line – Vignacourt to Querrieu
Construction of this line began from Poulainville on 26 May and from Vignacourt on 30 May.

Poulainville to Querrieu - On 26 May, C and D Companies of 11th Bttn CRT moved to Coisy, near Poulainville, and were joined by part of 6th LROC. The same day they commenced work, and by 12 June track laying was complete. Track material was unloaded at Poulainville standard gauge rail head.

Some work on a spur line at Allonville, north to the Amiens to Contay road east of Cardonette, was done by 11th CRT in June. The main work, to an ammunition dump by the road, was undertaken by No 4 Company of 6th CRT in July 1918. From 1 August, HQ 6th CRT moved to Bertangles, near Poulainville, and Nos. 2, 3 and 4 Companies were working on the A100 system.

Poulainville spur and station - Starting in April 1918, the British army built a branch about 1½ miles long from the standard gauge Amiens to Doullens line. It began at Bertangles junction, between Amiens and Bertangles, with the points facing towards Bertangles. Curving east and then north, it ended alongside the main road to Doullens north of Poulainville village.

The work was undertaken by 4th Bttn CRT, and completed by the end of April, when 263rd RC RE took over the maintenance. During May and June, a tank ramp, ammunition sidings, sidings for RE stores, a siding for light railway material, and an operating loop were added. A light railway station was constructed here, with transhipment facilities, which were ready for use on 14 June. The 4th CRT did some of the new work, including a tank crossing over the ammunition siding. ROD took over operation of the branch on 27 May.

The 11th CRT undertook light railway work at Poulainville station in June 1918, working on the general yard facilities and a locomotive yard, which included a

7.4 Baldwin 4-6-0T WD No. 652 with 5 wagons near Cardonnette, on the A100 line, on 28 July 1918. *(AWM E02768)*

round house. On 1 July, No 4 Company of 6th CRT moved to Poulainville and during the month added to the facilities at the station. They built about 300 yards of a second track into the locomotive round house and added sidings and a ration spur. Work at the Poulainville rail head continued into early August.

Vignacourt to Villers-Bocage - At about the same time, on 30 May, 13th (Can) LROC commenced construction of the light railway from Vignacourt towards Poulainville. They were already based at Vignacourt station, since returning to the Somme Sector on 16 April to work on roads.

On 6 June, they moved camp to an orchard on the road to Flesselles. Track material began to arrive on the standard gauge line at Vignacourt. By the end of June, 3.33 miles (5.36km) of track had been laid. On 29 June, most of the company, 146 men, moved to Poulainville by lorry, leaving the rest near Vignacourt for operation and maintenance. They returned on 7 July. The company constructed the line as far as Villers-Bocage, and remained responsible for maintenance and for operations on this section.

Vignacourt station - A station was constructed on the light railway, with transhipment facilities, which were ready for use on 31 July. Additional standard gauge works were undertaken by 260th RC RE and 263 RC RE. During June a shunting neck was sanctioned, and agreed by the engineer of the *Compagnie du Nord*, who were still responsible for the operation of the line from Amiens to Doullens. During July, it was agreed that 260th RC RE would maintain all sidings at Vignacourt built by the British Army, and dugouts were provided for the RTO and his staff, and for other rail head personnel. An additional stabling siding was agreed in August.

Villers-Bocage to Poulainville, and the Flesselles branch - On 5 July, C Company of 11th CRT moved to near Villers-Bocage. Between 6 July and the end of the month, they constructed the missing part of the A100 line between Villers-Bocage, the point reached by 13th (Can) LROC, and Poulainville station. From 10 July, they also constructed the branch from north east of Flesselles to Flesselles station. On 30 July, they were replaced by No 3 Company 6th CRT, based at Villers-Bocage.

Flesselles station - Another station with transhipment facilities was constructed at Flesselles. During June alterations and additions to the standard gauge track at Flesselles station were made by 263rd RC RE.

A200 line – Contay to Vecquemont
The A200 line ran north to south from Contay to Vecquemont, almost on the Somme, following the 1916 standard gauge British military line along the valley of the Hallue, and probably using its formation. The whole line was about 10 miles (16km) long.

At Vecquemont there was a yard alongside the British Army sidings, which branched off the Amiens to Albert main line there.

Construction was commenced by D Company and part of C Company 11th CRT in June and was probably completed during July. In June, C Company worked south to Vecquemont from the junction with the A100 line at Querrieu, and D Company worked north. C Company moved to Villers-Bocage on 5 July, and B Company remained at work on the A200 line until 30 July, when No 2 Company of 6th CRT moved to Fréchencourt. No 4 Company of 6th CRT undertook work on the A200 line in July. At some time, yards were installed at Contay. The 6th CRT were assisted in this and in their other work in the area by the 108th US Engineers.

A500 line
The A500 line began at Fréchencourt from a junction with the A200 line. It was planned as a second east to west link to the A100 line at Villers-Bocage, but only about 2 miles (3.2km) was built, by No 2 Company of 6th CRT, as far as the main Amiens to Contay road north of St-Gratien. Work started on 1 August and was abandoned on 9 August.

Operations on the A100 and A200 lines
The 13th (Can) LROC, based at Vignacourt, operated the line from there to Villers-Bocage, and probably the Flesselles line, which was a branch off this section.

A detachment of 6th LROC was based at Poulainville as the operating Company from 26th May, and they were joined by most of the rest of the Company on 15 June. They were also joined there on 16 June by 18th TCC. These two companies operated the rest of the system, a much larger area, but unlike 13th LROC they did not also do the construction and maintenance.

On 10 July, 13th LROC received two steam locomotives, one petrol tractor, two water tank wagons, and twenty-five other wagons, all delivered to Vignacourt on the standard gauge system. On 15 July, they received two ambulance wagons, and five more on 23 and 24 July, with one more steam locomotive. On 26 July, they started hauling general traffic, and by the end of July they had carried more than 3,000 tons of goods. We do not know what rolling stock 6th LROC and 18th TCC had available, but it must have been proportionately more, and it is almost certain that they were also able to offer a service for goods from some time during July 1918.

The North to South rear lateral
There was clearly a plan for a north to south rear lateral line linking the Third and Fourth Armies in early Summer 1918. At Contay two maps of 1919 show the end of the A200 line (Fourth Army), and the Puchevillers to Senlis line (Third Army), within a few hundred yards of each other but not joined. However, Col Henniker (*Transportation on the Western Front*, 1937) says that they did connect. Because this is the official history, and he was involved at the time, with access to all the papers, he was probably right.

However, the line from Puchevillers to Sarton was never completed. If it had been, it would have linked via Coigneux and Bienvillers with the Third Army system west of Arras. The link north from the Third Army to the First Army remained intact, but that further north between the First and Second Armies was broken by the German advance on the plain of the Lys and around Ypres, which had begun on 9 April. The latter was restored later in 1918.

Final preparations for the offensive
With the system in use for traffic, all was ready for these light railways to serve the northern part of the Fourth Army front when the offensive began on 8 August. On 7 August 6th LROC handed 9 wagons of wounded over to 13th (Can) LROC at Villers-Bocage.

Chapter Eight

Light and metre gauge railways of the Somme sector 8 August to 11 November 1918

The general situation

This chapter follows the development and use of railways by the Allied Armies, and especially that of the light and metre gauge lines, from the opening of the Battle of Amiens on 8 August 1918 until the Armistice on 11 November. 8 August, the 'Black Day of the German Army', began the retreat and final defeat of the German Army on the Western Front.

From the point of view of the British and Dominion Armies this period falls into three phases:

1. The Battles of Amiens and Montdidier, August 8 to 20
2. The Battle of the Ancre, and the advance to the Hindenburg Line, August 21 to September 28
3. From the assault on the Hindenburg Line (St Quentin Canal) to the Armistice, September 29 to November 11

These phases are shown in Figure 8.1, with the main standard gauge railways in the area involved. The railway developments are described in relation to each of these periods.

August 8 to 20 - The Battles of Amiens and Montdidier

The Battle of Amiens opened in fog on the morning of August 8, on a 14 mile (22km) front from Dernancourt in the north, on the Ancre just south of Albert, to the Avre north of Montdidier. From north to south were the British III Corps (which included one American Division), the Australian Corps, and the Canadian Corps (all Fourth Army). South of that stood the French First Army. The attack combined surprise, infantry advancing with tanks and armoured cars, and a carefully planned creeping barrage. By evening the allies had advanced 9 miles (14km), and 16,000 prisoners were taken in the first 2 hours.

On 10 August, the French Third Army attacked south of the Avre, retaking Montdidier, and also making good progress. By 20 August, the front line stretched south and somewhat east from Albert to the boundary with the French Army just west of Chaulnes, on the Amiens to Tergnier main railway line. From there the French front was straight south, then turning east near Lassigny and Noyon.

Railways 8 to 20 August 1918

In general, the railways, and other facilities, were less extensively destroyed than on the German retreat to the Hindenburg Line in 1917.

Standard gauge railways

On 16 August there was official notification that the War Office in London had approved a Directorate of Construction, to include standard gauge and light railway construction, and new construction in dock areas. Brig-Gen J.W. Stewart CMG, GOC Corps of Canadian Railway Troops, was appointed Director effective 12 August. The effects of this on the light railways are discussed later.

Third Army South

Although there was no advance in the Third Army South area between 8 and 20 August, considerable work was done to prepare for the next phase of the offensive, beginning on 21 August. Third Army standard gauge railways continued to be supported by RCE V. The Third Army workshop train was moved from Beaurainville to the Third Army HQ at Bernaville, on the Conteville to Candas line.

Candas to Acheux and Achiet
On 8 August 1918, this single track British military line was cut by the front line near Serre. It was operated by the ROD as far as Acheux. Although it had been said that it was usable as far as Colincamps, work was needed on this section. By 19 August, the line from Candas was ready for operation to Colincamps. On 12 August, the construction of standard gauge sidings at Puchevillers was authorised, for the light railway transhipment there, but construction ceased on 24 August.

Authie Valley line (Doullens to Courcelles junction)
On 8 August, the line was in use and operated by the ROD from Doullens to St-Léger-lès-Authie. From 16 August, the section from St-Léger, destroyed in March,

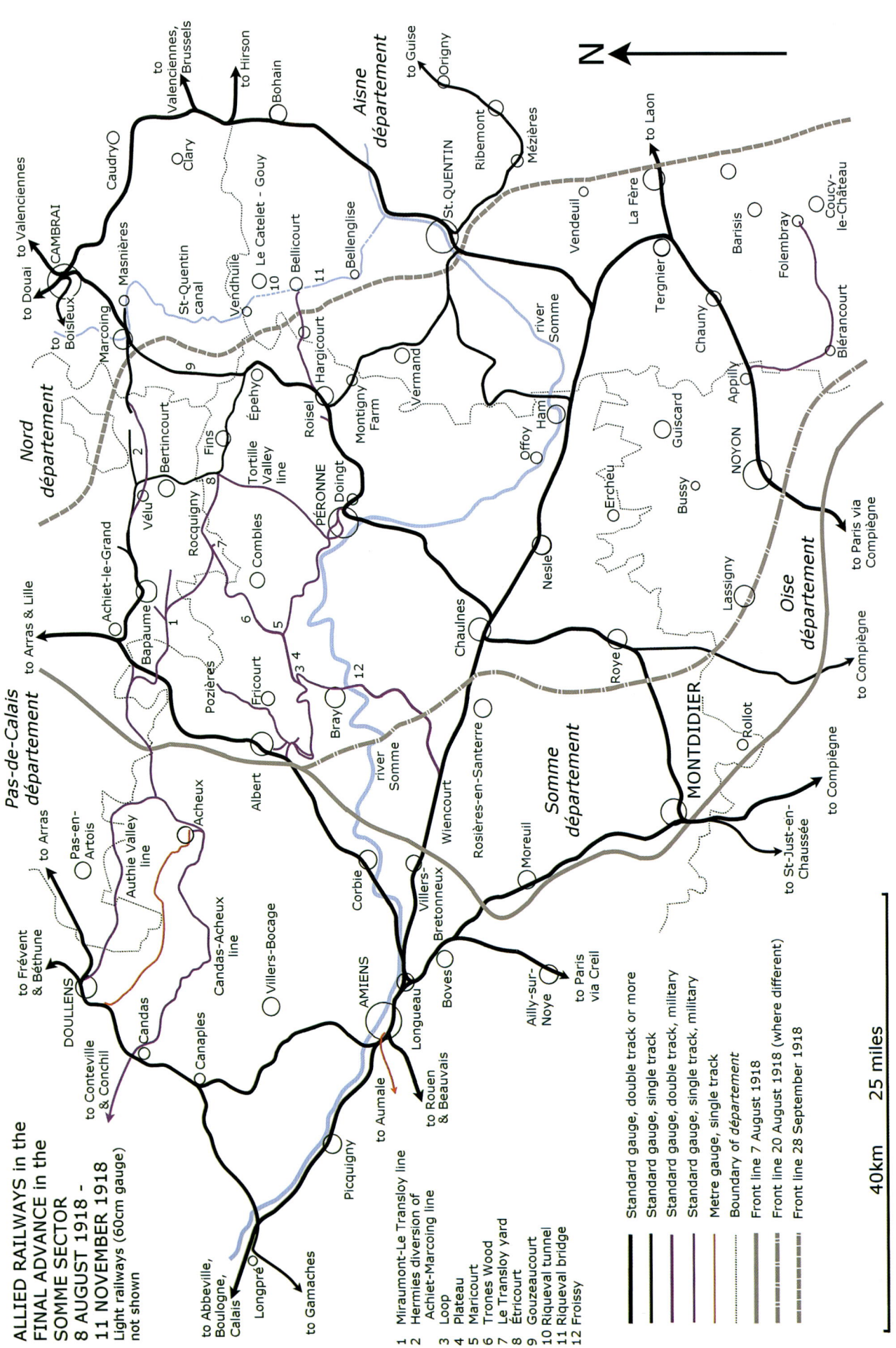

Figure 8.1

was reconstructed. By 20 August, the line was ready for operation to the Candas line connection at Courcelles.

Fourth Army
Fourth Army standard gauge railways continued to be supported by RCC IV. As soon as the German Army started to retreat eastwards, reconstruction of the occupied or otherwise unuseable standard gauge lines east of Amiens began.

Amiens to Albert and Arras
By 11 August, double track had been repaired from Amiens to the east end Corbie station. The ROD took over operation from Camon junction, junction with the line to Tergnier, on 17 August.

Amiens to Chaulnes and Tergnier
By 20 August, the front line was situated across this line between Rosières and Chaulnes. Reconstruction closely followed the advance east, and was conducted at times under shell fire and aerial bombardment.

On 8 August, 4th Bttn CRT moved to Longueau and began work at the Longueau yards just east of Amiens, and on the Amiens to Tergnier line, mostly between Amiens and Villers-Bretonneux. The work was under the command of the Commandant of Group A of French Railway Engineers, with assistance from 4th Bttn CRT, 1st Bttn CRT, 2nd Australian Tunnelling Company, and for a time E Company of the 108th US Railway Engineers, and 2nd and 5th APB. By 13 August, one track of the main line was open to east of Rosières, and by 20 August much of the second track was ready for traffic.

Chemin Vert to La Flaque, Bray and Loop
A reconnaissance of this former French and then British military line was made from Chemin Vert (Wiencourt) to La Flaque on 9 August. It was found generally in good order.

Metre Gauge lines
On 8 August, the only metre gauge line in the Somme Sector which remained workable and in allied hands, was the section from Gézaincourt to Acheux, of the line from Doullens to Albert. In the Third Army area, this continued to be operated as a British military line.

In the Fourth Army and French First Army areas, the Albert to Montdidier metre gauge line had been recaptured from near Proyart south to Montdidier. However, it is likely that the lines had been removed or in places converted to 60cm gauge, and the formation had been damaged. No attempt was made to bring this line back into operation until after the end of the war. North from Rosières to La Flaque, the formation had been taken over by a military standard gauge line. South from Rosières there was light railway (60cm gauge) track along the formation of the metre gauge line to south of the station at Arvillers-Hangest.

Light Railways
Third Army South
For these lines please refer to Figure 7.2 (page 143, Chapter Seven).

Lines in and around the Authie Valley
The 34th LROC based at St Léger-lès-Authie continued to operate the light railways in the area until 12 September.

Coigneux to Hébuterne
From 12 to 26 August B Company of 9th Bttn CRT built a light railway from Coignuex to Hébuterne. Starting from a junction with the line from Bienvillers to Thièvres between Coigneux and Couin, this line followed the standard gauge British military Authie Valley line south east to Coigneux station, and was then constructed east across country, passing north of Sailly-au-Bois to reach the edge of Hébuterne village. The whole line was about 5 miles (8km) long. Hébuterne was quite close to the front line until the attacks of 21 August, and this development was probably in support of that offensive.

The Puchevillers system
The development of the system around Puchevillers (see Chapter Seven) was abandoned on 23 August.

Acheux to Mailly-Maillet and Senlis-le-Sec to Beaussart
The 2nd FWC, who had constructed the line from Acheux to Mailly-Maillet, continued to work on it until 24 August, after which they moved to Bucquoy.

Fourth Army
The A100, A200 and A500 lines
These lines were operational before 8 August (see Figure 7.2, Chapter Seven). With the attacks of 8 August, 42 ambulance wagons were moved, and more on 9 August. A peak of 150 wagons was reached on 10 August, but mainly because the CCSs were being evacuated as the front moved further east.

The major part of the system was maintained by 6th Bttn CRT. On 8 August, some further track was laid on the A500 line from Fréchencourt towards Villers-Bocage, but after 9 August track laying was abandoned. Later, from 21 to 24 August, 13th Bttn CRT were based at Vecquemont and also worked on system maintenance. The main developments between 8 and 20 August were at Flesselles Dump, where more than 1¾ miles (2.8km) of track was added by 16 August.

On 13 August 13th (Can) LROC moved to Guillaucourt, and the 6th LROC, with 18th TCC, continued to operate the system.

Wiencourt to Marcelcave
On 10 August, No 1 Company of 6th CRT moved to Wiencourt to rebuild the light railway west to Les Buttes, on the standard gauge line between Marcelcave and Villers-Bretonneux. Between 14 and 22 August, the whole line was ballasted and ditched, and was open for tractor traffic as far as the yard and transhipment at Les Buttes, called Marcelcave Yard. Two miles (3.2km) of line had been laid, and 350 yards at the Yard. A tractor spur and brick and chalk ballast spurs were also installed. Meanwhile, between 18 and 20 August, 1st CRT laid more than 1½ miles (2.5km) of standard gauge track for the Marcelcave yard and transhipment.

South of the Amiens to Chaulnes standard gauge line
For the geography in this area see figure 6.3 (page 106, Chapter Six). Probably the main layout of the lines worked on had not changed much since then, and in any case, no other detailed information is available.

It was between the Amiens to Chaulnes main line railway, and the main Amiens to Roye road south of it, that the Canadian Corps had attacked on 8 August. As the front moved east, Canadian railway units began to arrive to support them with light railways. Between 11 and 13 August all four companies of 13th CRT, No 2 Company of 6th CRT, the 1st Tramway Company Canadian Engineers (TC CE), and the 13th (Can) LROC all moved into the area. The instructions to 6th CRT were to work on reclaiming 60cm gauge lines from Wiencourt east as far as possible into the area captured from the enemy.

The 1st TC CE moved from Liévin, in the First Army area near Lens, to Longueau (Amiens), on 11 August, and then moved east to Cayeux. The story of this unit at Liévin is told in our previous book, *Narrow Gauge in the Arras Sector*, 2015 (see area 4, Chapter Five), as is their story back with the First Army south east of Arras from 2 September (see area 7, Chapter Six). The two Canadian Tramway Companies were 'forward' units, constructing, maintaining and operating light railways close to the front line, using petrol tractors but with no steam traction. On 14 August, a construction sub-section moved up to Dougherty Junction, near Vrély, by the formation of the metre gauge line from Albert to Montdidier, and two operating subsections moved to a camp in the valley of the Luce, near to that of No 2 Company 6th CRT. The 13th (Can) LROC, a typical operating company, moved to Guillaucourt on 13 August.

From 11 August, No 2 Company of 6th CRT also camped in the valley of the Luce. 13th CRT entrained to Villers-Bretonneux on 11 August and on 12 August set up their HQ at Wiencourt. On 17 August, 1st TC CE moved their HQ from Cayeux up to Balloon Camp, in the valley just west of Vrély junction.

British units operated this network of lines from late April until 6 July 1917, mainly collecting salvage, before handing this area back to the French. We do not know whether the French continued to operate them, but they were a long way from the front line. When the British Fifth Army took over this area again in January 1918, they were again shown on railway maps, but we have no evidence of operation. Probably the German Army had used some or all of them from March to 8 August 1918. That they were quickly brought back into operation suggests that they were not too badly damaged.

Wiencourt to Caix and Vrély junction and Rosières – This line began at Wiencourt South yard. As the name shows this was south of the standard gauge line, and maps of February 1918 show no connection across the main line with North yard. From Wiencourt the line went south east to a junction in the Luce valley, which we have called Luce junction. From here, the line went south east past Caix village to the line of the Albert to Montdidier metre gauge line near Caix-Vrély station, and then followed the metre gauge formation to Rosières, on the standard gauge main line from Amiens to Chaulnes. It was regarded as the 'main line' in this area. Work on the line was done by No 2 Company of 6th CRT, and it was ready for tractor traffic to Rosières dump by 14 August. The line was operated by 1st TC CE until 18 August, then by 13th (Can) LROC.

From 17 August, 13th CRT were preparing material for salvage in Rosières yard. On 19 August, under heavy shell fire, a Lieutenant and eight men salvaged 44 pieces of French rolling stock from the yard, including locomotives, box cars, passenger wagons, and flat wagons. On 20 August, more rolling stock in Rosières yard was salvaged.

Luce junction to Beaucourt – From the junction the Beaucourt line went south west past Cayeux then south to Beaucourt. After replacement of 7 sections of track by 6th CRT, the line was ready and was taken over for operating by 13th (Can) LROC on 17 August. The first delivery of ammunition from Wiencourt rail head to Beaucourt was on 20 August.

Beaucourt to Le Quesnel – this was east from Beaucourt to Le Quesnel. The junction with other lines was east of Le Quesnel at Quesnel-Beaufort station on the path of the Albert to Montdidier metre gauge line.

Luce junction to Harbonnières – this line, also known as the Caix-Harbonnières cutoff, went north across the standard gauge line to meet the Wiencourt to Froissy line just north of Harbonnières. No 1 Company of 6th CRT worked on the line on 13 and 14 August and replaced 10 sections of track blown out by bombs.

Vrély junction to Le Quesnel – this line followed the metre gauge formation south to Quesnel-Beaufort station. It was operated by 1st TC CE until 19 August.

Le Quesnel to Rouvroy – this line east from Quesnel-Beaufort station was reconstructed towards Rouvroy by 13th CRT, and by 18 August it was being operated by 1st TC CE.

Vrély junction to Méharicourt – east from Vrély junction to Méharicourt, this line had originally in 1917 gone on to Chilly, and was known as the Chilly line. It is probable that now it was rebuilt from Dougherty junction slightly east on the line towards Rosières. On 14 August, 1st TC CE, with assistance from 10th CRT, commenced work on reconstruction and repair using track material from the dump at Rosières station. While getting the material two officers and an NCO were injured, and one sapper was killed by shrapnel. From 15 August, this line was the priority for 1st TC CE, and they were given six 20hp and two 40hp Simplex tractors for this, all but one from 13th LROC. By 18 August they were operating the line to Méharicourt village.

1st TC CE – On 19 August, the company was notified to be ready to move out at noon on 20 August. All operating was turned over to 13 (Can) LROC, and all construction to 13th CRT, at midnight. The construction sub-sections and the operating department moved down to Balloon Dump during the morning of 20 August, and the whole Company stood by there at noon. While the company was awaiting orders a long range high explosive shell landed among a group of men. Twelve were killed outright, one died before reaching hospital, and twenty-two were wounded, some very seriously. The dead were buried at Caix Cemetery in the evening. On 21 August, there was still no movement order, and the company moved down to the old camp at Cayeux, so that the men could bathe in the river. During the afternoon they marched to Boves, with lorries taking their packs. They remained in bivouac at Boves until 31 August, training and drilling, before moving back to First Army at Wancourt, east of Arras, on 3 September.

Wiencourt to Froissy, Bray and Plateau
On 8 August, the advance passed just to the east of Harbonnières. Just north of Harbonnières at 1.15pm a Baldwin 4-6-0T locomotive, WD No. 796, was found abandoned and derailed by No. 9 platoon of C Company of the 4th APB, who were not on railway work at the time. The photograph shows that the locomotive has derailed on points at a junction, almost certainly that just north of Harbonnières where the line to Proyart curves away to the left and another line, to Lihons, on the right. With the lifting jacks they were able to rerail it, and with 11 trucks and well wagons attached, took it back to a safe distance behind the line and notified the Canadian Railway Troops. This locomotive was later used on the Vis-en-Artois sugar beet network, south east of Arras.

8.1 Baldwin 4-6-0T WD No. 796 was captured by the German army in March or April 1918. It was found abandoned and derailed at Harbonnières on 8 August 1918. In this photograph it is being re-railed by No. 9 platoon of C Company of the 4th Australian Pioneer Battalion, who found it and then moved it to safety with eleven wagons. The locomotive was later used on the Vis-en-Artois sugar beet system. *(AWM E02787)*

No 1 Company of 6th CRT moved to Wiencourt on 12 August, to work on the line from Wiencourt to Proyart. They also maintained all lines north of the standard gauge line from Amiens to Chaulnes.

By 15 August, the line was open for tractor traffic to La Flaque. Next day all work was handed over to No 2 Company, assisted by 6th FWC for forward maintenance. By 18 August, the line was open to Proyart, close to the front line. Eighteen 16ft sections of track had been replaced at La Flaque dump, and 7 sections of track on the main line by 20 August. By that time 6th CRT had reconstructed more than 17 miles (27km) of track east of Wiencourt (including track south of the standard gauge line). The 35th LROC arrived at Marcelcave from the Ypres Sector on 15 August, and on 17 August started operating the lines from Marcelcave and Wiencourt towards Proyart.

August 21 to September 28 Battle of the Ancre and the advance to the Hindenburg Line

The attack of the British Third Army on 21 August on the German front line north from Albert towards Arras opened at 4.55am, again in fog. The Third Army consisted of eight Divisions, including the New Zealand Division. Fourth Army launched a new attack from the Somme north to Albert on 22 August. Albert was cleared by the morning of 23 August. On 24 August, Thiepval and Pozières were taken. Bapaume was captured on 29 August by the Third Army and the US II Corps.

By 31 August, the Third and Fourth Armies had recaptured the whole of the 1916 Somme battlefield, and the front line stood east of Bapaume and Flers. South of the Somme, the Australian Corps (Fourth Army) had, by 31 August, advanced almost to the line of the Somme canal south from Péronne to St-Christ. The French First Army took over from the Canadian Corps, south of the standard gauge railway from Amiens to Chaulnes, towards the end of August. By 31 August, they had advanced to Nesle and beyond.

On 31 August and 1 September, the Australian 2nd Division took Mont-St-Quentin, overlooking Péronne, in heavy fighting, and Péronne was recaptured on 1 September. From 4 September the German Army withdrew to the Hindenburg Line and its outpost positions, losing all the territory gained after 21 March 1918. On 18 September, the British Third and Fourth Armies, with units of the French First Army, attacked the Hindenburg outpost line on a 20 mile (32km) front. In the centre, the 1st and 4th Australian divisions advanced 3 miles (5km) to the main Hindenburg Line.

Railways 21 August to 28 September 1918
Standard gauge railways
Third Army

The RCE V HQ train moved to Acheux, on 4 September, and on to Boisleux-St-Marc, towards Arras, on 12 September. Between 17 August and 21 September, they opened 208 miles (335km) of track for traffic, of which 195 miles (314km) were reconstructed and 13 miles (21km) were new build. During this period operations were controlled by the Traffic Officer at Conteville.

Candas to Acheux and Achiet and the Authie Valley line (Doullens to Courcelles junction)
The line was reconstructed in single track from Colincamps. By the evening of 27 August, the Candas to Achiet line was ready for use to Achiet-le-Grand, and Achiet yard was sufficiently repaired to handle ammunition and supplies. On 7 September, ROD Candas took over operating to Achiet and Miraumont.

Beaucourt to Achiet-le-Grand and Arras (Third Army, Amiens to Arras line)
This part of the former main line from Amiens to Arras was opened by RCE V (Third Army), initially using the line from Candas. It was also being reconstructed south from Arras by RCE V, and from Albert north by RCC IV (Fourth Army). By 6 September, a single line through between Beaucourt and Miraumont was ready for use, linking Albert and Achiet-le-Grand.

Intructions were issued to lay the second track with French material as far as possible. The French were following behind making permanent bridges and replacing all track with French material. Double track was complete from Albert to Achiet on 16 September.

Achiet-le-Grand to Bapaume and Marcoing
An inspection of the part of this line near Achiet on 25 August found that it was not badly damaged. By 4 September, the double track to Bapaume was ready for use. The line east of Bapaume to Frémicourt was badly shelled and almost every joint had been demolished. Further east, there was less demolition. The German army had improved and enlarged Frémicourt yard, and the line had been doubled towards Vélu, using German rails. Summit and Vélu yards had been improved and enlarged.

One question was whether to use the Hermies diversion towards Marcoing along the Nord canal, built in 1917, or the 'old French' route through Hermies village. On this route it was found that the track via Hermies had been relaid by the Germans, with only occasional demolitions. Further east the German army had constructed a high level bridge over the Canal du Nord, now destroyed. The line was repaired to Hermies village, but the bridge was not rebuilt.

Instead, the decision was to repair and use the Hermies Diversion, now called the Lebucquière East Diversion. Reinstating the Nord canal bridge on the diversion line, at a lower level than that on the 'old French' line, would require three days. By 27 September, the line was complete to the west end of the bridge.

Vélu to Ytres and Étricourt
Inspections on 4 and 8 September showed that there were no formal demolitions, but there were some shell breaks. Much of the work on this line was done by 12th Bttn CRT. The whole line was in operation from 26 September.

Miraumont to Le Transloy (The Miraumont - Rocquigny extension)
An inspection by RCE V on 25 August showed that the German Army had been operating this line at the Miraumont end. Earthworks at the east end of the line were found to be far from finished, which must cast some doubt on the maps of March 1918 which show the line as complete. Work was delayed by lack of track material, labour, and motive power, but after a major effort by 2nd CRT the line was in operation from 26 September.

Fourth Army
The Amiens avoiding line
This link from Poulainville to Vecquemont was abandoned on 26 March 1918, in view of the German advance. Work restarted on 31 August. Some track must have been laid, because on 18 September RCC IV issued instructions to stop. Two companies of 12th CRT remained to complete the earthworks. Work continued into October.

Amiens to Albert and Beaucourt (Fourth Army, Amiens to Arras line)
RCC IV (Fourth Army) supervised the reconstruction of the Amiens to Arras line from the Amiens end.

By 6 September, three trains could be accepted nightly at Aveluy and two at Albert. The connection by 13th CRT with 2nd CRT (Third Army) south of Beaucourt was made on 2 September, and single line working to Miraumont and Achiet-le-Grand was possible from 6 September. Operation in double track to Beaucourt by ROD (Vecquemont), was established on 17 September. French Railway Engineers took over the line from Corbie to Albert on 23 September.

Dernancourt junction to Plateau
Work on the former British and French military lines, east from the junction with the main Amiens to Arras line, began on 18 September. The 275th RC RE based at Buire were charged with salvage and reconstruction on these lines from 28 September, but the line was not rebuilt to Plateau until October.

Amiens to Chaulnes and Tergnier
By 23 August, doubling was completed to Chaulnes, junction with the lines to Péronne and to Montdidier. During September, the line was extended east towards Ham by the French Engineers, assisted by D Company of 1st Bttn CRT, and later 262nd RC RE and part of 12th CRT.

Chemin Vert (Wiencourt) to La Flaque, Bray and Loop
Traffic was accepted to La Flaque from 26 August, operated by 260th RC RE. On 28 August, 264th RC RE took over operation, maintenance and reconstruction of the line. Operation to La Flaque was taken over by ROD Chemin Vert on 30 August.

On 24 August, a report on the Froissy-Bray peninsula was prepared by 3rd APB, who the previous day had helped 9th Australian Infantry Brigade capture the area. The peninsula lies between the Somme River at Bray and the Somme Canal, which cuts across the loop of the river through Froissy. The whole peninsula was isolated except for a footbridge at Froissy lock, and a temporary footbridge at the west end of the canal erected by 3rd APB. All other bridges had been efficiently demolished.

At Froissy, there appears to have been only one bridge over the Somme canal, carrying the road, and the standard gauge and 60cm gauge railways. Originally a bridge of brick with an elliptical arch had carried the metre gauge line, but that bridge was long gone. After a previous demolition, probably by the British Army in March 1918, six rolled steel joists had been placed over a clear span of 54ft (16.5m) using the brick arch as abutments.

The standard gauge bridge over the Somme at Bray was partly demolished. The 1st Bttn CRT commenced work on reconstruction on 25 August, and by 3 September both Froissy and Bray bridges were repaired, with at least standard gauge track laid. This allowed the line from Chemin Vert to be linked through to Plateau station the same day. 264th RC RE were to finish and operate the line from La Flaque to Plateau. A transhipment siding at Froissy and an ammunition siding at Merignolles were also ready for use. Operation all the way to Plateau was taken over by ROD Chemin Vert from 7 September. By 12 September, the bridge at Bray was sufficiently strengthened to take all types of locomotive.

Plateau to Quinconce and Péronne
On 30 August, two companies of 6th Bttn CRT arrived to reconstruct this line east from Plateau via Maricourt junction. As in 1917, part of the path of the former

metre gauge line from Albert to Péronne was used. Reconstruction was assisted by 2nd APB, who cleared the formation ready for track laying. From 13 September, the line was connected to Quinconce, but no trains could be accepted until the water supply was adequate at Plateau.

From 17 September, the line was connected through from Chaulnes to Péronne Flamicourt station. Therefore, from 18 September it was instructed that trains for Quinconce should travel via Chaulnes and Péronne. However, operating from Plateau to Quiconce was taken over by ROD from Chemin Vert on 19 September, and to Péronne from 21 September, so presumably the water supply problems at Plateau were solved.

Plateau to Trones Wood, Le Transloy and Étricourt
On 4 September, RCC IV diverted No 3 Company of 6th CRT to urgent work on the Trones Wood line. Traffic could be accepted at Trones Wood from 6 September. From 8 September, 263rd RC RE took charge of construction from Trones Wood to Étricourt. On 18 September, 12th CRT took over all work from Plateau to Étricourt, connecting through the same day. On 26 September, ROD Chemin Vert took over operation to Étricourt. The line from Miraumont was connected at Le Transloy on 19 September and in operation from 26 September, the same day as the line from Vélu to Étricourt.

Étricourt to Fins and Épehy
This line was taken over by RCC IV on 18 September. The 12th CRT moved to Étricourt on 10 September. They cleared up and laid new track in Étricourt yard. Elsewhere reconstruction was done by 2nd CRT, from whom 263rd RC RE took over on 20 September.

Quinconce (Péronne) to Étricourt - the Tortille Valley line
This British military line had been built in early 1918 and opened on 2 March. Repairs were started by 6th CRT on 14 September but taken over by D Company of 12th CRT on 20 September. They were instructed to complete the line to Moislains sufficiently to take trains by the night of 22 September, then continue the line to Étricourt with loops at Allaines and Moislain. On 28 September, the line was still being rebuilt towards Étricourt.

Chaulnes to Péronne
This French line, running as a commercial railway before the war, had been taken over as a British military line before the German advance of March 1918. Now it was reconstructed and reopened by the British army on the same basis. 1st CRT were instructed to commence reconstruction as soon as the line from Amiens had reached Chaulnes. The 1st CRT had been the main unit working on this line between April and June 1917. They were assisted by 260th RC RE and 1st APB. By 21 September, there was double line working by ROD to Péronne (Flamicourt). ROD moved from Chemin Vert to Chaulnes. A transhipment siding was built at Flamicourt.

Péronne to Roisel and Épehy
The main work on this section was undertaken by 1st Bttn CRT. The completion of the bridge over the Somme canal and river at Péronne on 12 September allowed trains to Doingt, and track material reached Doingt by train that night. The Fourth Army Commander wanted the line through to Roisel by 20 September. By 16 September, one train nightly could be accepted at Roisel, and there was double track working to Tincourt from 27 September, when operations to Tincourt were handed over to the ROD. The line was not extended to Épehy until October. On 22 September, RCC IV HQ train moved from Harbonnières to a new siding at Doingt.

Roisel to Hargicourt
The British Army CRCE advised on 22 September that the Roisel to Hargicourt metre gauge formation was again likely to be required, as in early 1918 (Chapter Six), for a standard gauge line. No 4 Company and later No 1 Company of 13th Bttn CRT was sent for the construction. Track laying began on 26 September, and work was continuing when the attack on the St-Quentin Canal began on 29 September.

Roisel to Vermand and St-Quentin
This French line of *Intérêt Local*, part of the longer line from Achiet-le-Grand via Bapaume and Vélu, was in the hands of the British Army in 1917, from Roisel as far as Vermand. Although there was a major light railway centre at Montigny Farm, on this line, in 1917 and early 1918, no attempt had been made to reopen it as a standard gauge line.

The 2nd Bttn CRT moved its HQ to the old British camp at Montigny Farm on 19 September. Men of B Company had been here in early 1918, working on the DZ light railway lines. They found that the German Army had reconstructed the standard gauge line from Roisel to Montigny Farm. From 28 September, it was agreed to accept one train per night to Montigny Farm, with 1st CRT to pilot the train to the Vermand line junction at Roisel.

Metre gauge railways
Gézaincourt to Acheux (Doullens to Albert)
This was still being operated as a British military line, although the facilities at Acheux station had been affected by the installation of artillery spurs, on which work had begun. On 23 August, work on these spurs was discontinued.

Representatives of the French metre gauge company, the *Société Générale des Chemins de Fer Économiques* (SE) called at RCE V on 27 August and were told that the spurs at Acheux had been abandoned, but that the British Army could not re-establish the line there at that time. SE offered to do the work with their own labour. Third Army Transporation agreed, and on 28 August, the French Inspector at Beauval was advised that there was no objection.

On 24 August, CRCE authorised the construction of standard to metre gauge transhipment facilities at Gézaincourt, but Third Army decided that this work was not needed. No attempt was made to restore the line back to Albert before the end of the war. It is not known what commercial operations if any were reinstated by SE.

Albert to Péronne and Ham
This line had been used from Albert to Trones Wood in 1917 and early 1918. The whole of the route of the line was recaptured during this period. However, the main stations along the line, at Albert, Péronne, and Ham were largely destroyed. The bridge across the main Amiens to Arras line north of Albert station, and the nearby bridge over the Ancre, had been demolished in March 1918, and not rebuilt. Between Maurepas and Péronne the formation had been taken over before March by the standard gauge line from Plateau, now rebuilt. South of Péronne, the line had been used by March 1918 for a light railway as far as Mons-en-Chaussée. No attempt was made to restore any of the line in metre gauge until after the war.

Albert to Montdider via Fricourt
There was no provision for the metre gauge line when the bridge at Froissy was rebuilt. The metre gauge bridge at Bray over the Somme river had been partially demolished during the British retreat in March 1918. No attempt was made to restore this bridge, or the line, until after the end of the war.

Noyon to Ham
This line had been disused and taken up during the German occupation. By March 1918, the formation from Ham to Guiscard had been used for a British Army light railway. Now Noyon station and facilities were extensively damaged. No attempt was made to restore the line until after the end of the war.

Noyon to Montdidier
This line had been entirely entirely in German hands since their Noyon-Montdidier offensive, from 9 to 13 June 1918. Lassigny became a major supply centre for German army. Lassigny was bombed by 120 French aircraft on 10 August and retaken by a division of the French Army on 21 August. No attempt was made to restore the line until after the end of the war.

8.2 Destruction at Ham station. Photograph by the French Army photographic section. *(Authors' collection)*

8.3 The ruined former German *Kantine der Eisenbahn* (railway canteen) at Ham station, in the building across the forecourt from the main passenger building, in 1918. A light railway is crossing the forecourt, probably the French line shown on British Army maps of early 1918 (see figure 6.6, Chapter Six). *(Authors' collection)*

8.4 Ville station, on the line from Noyon to Lassigny, as recaptured by the French in later 1918. *(Authors' collection)*

Light and metre gauge railways of the Somme sector 8 August to 11 November 1918

Roisel to Hargicourt
The use of the path of this metre gauge line for a standard gauge railway in early 1918 and again in September and October 1918 is discussed in the standard gauge section. The line was not reconstructed in metre gauge until after the war.

Light Railways

The formation by the War Office in London of a Directorate of Construction, to include light railway construction, has already been noted; and the appointment of Brig-Gen J.W. Stewart CMG, GOC Corps of Canadian Railway Troops, as Director, effective 12 August. In a circular of 26 August, the representatives of the Director of Construction for light railway construction in each British Army were named. In all cases these were the COs of a Battalion of Canadian Railway Troops, who were clearly taking the lead role in the construction of British Army Light Railways. For the Third Army Lt-Col W.H. Moodie, CO of 9th CRT was named, and for the Fourth Army Lt-Col A. Larchman of 6th CRT. From 26 August, responsibility for the construction and maintenance, but not operations, of light railways was transferred from the ADLRs to these officers.

Third Army

Third Army Light Railways began to move east to reconstruct and operate lines. For details of these lines please refer to Figure 6.2 (page 103) and 6.4 (page 108) (Chapter Six), which show the lines as at 20 March 1918. As reconstructed, they changed little. For the eastern parts refer to Figure 8.2 (page 166). Also refer to Figure 7.2 (page 143) for the more western lines in spring 1918.

The X7, X and X4 lines
The X7 line ran from Biez Wood, west of Bucquoy towards Gommecourt, to the north side of Achiet-le-Grand. At Biez Wood, it met the C12 line coming south from Monchy-au-Bois and had met the X7 extension to Puisieux and Euston Dump built by 5th CRT in early 1918.

From 22 August, C Company of 9th CRT, who had moved from Puchevillers, worked on this line under shellfire, salvaging and reconstructing, while D Company worked on the C12 line to Monchy. A Company joined them at Bucquoy on 24 August. On 25 August, 2nd FWC marched from Acheux to Couin and then travelled by light railway to Bucquoy, which must have been by way of Bienvillers and Monchy-au-Bois. From 27 August, 1st FWC also moved to Bucquoy. Both assisted with the X7 reconstruction.

From 31 August, 2nd FWC also reconstructed lines further north towards Arras, and between 1 and 7 September, worked on Bucquoy stone spur and tractor sidings. In September, 1st FWC continued reconstructing, and then maintained, the X7 line, and the yards at Achiet-le-Grand, as well as the X line and another line further north. They also had a detachment working on the line from Bienvillers into the Authie Valley at Coigneux.

Mory and the X4 line from there south to Bapaume are rather far north for the area of this book, but they did form the important link from Bapaume to the X7 and then the C12 lines to the west and north. From 7 September, 2nd FWC worked on the reconstruction of the X4 line. Later in September, D Company of 11th CRT continued the work on the X4 line between Favreuil and Bapaume, and the associated sidings and transhipments at Monument and Hun Dump. 2nd FWC maintained the X4 line, and the X7 line with 1st FWC at the end of September.

Lines south west from Bapaume
In September 1918, D Company of 11th CRT repaired and reconstructed the line south west of Bapaume along the main road to Albert as far as Le Sars, and the branch of this to Le Barque. This was where it probably met the branch to Thilloy of the standard gauge line from Miraumont to Le Transloy.

The Y5 line and extension to Rocquigny
On 9 September, 11th CRT moved to Villers-au-Flos and then the next day to Rocquigny, to reconstruct the Y5 line and extension from Bapaume to Rocquigny. They also extended the spur of this line to Beaulencourt, where it met the standard gauge branch to Beaulencourt from the Miraumont to Le Transloy line. From 23 September, 2nd FWC were also working on the reconstruction of this line and they continued to maintain it. The line was operated from 13 September by 1st Aus LROC.

The Y, Y3 and Y4 lines
Up to March 1918, the layout was as shown in figure 6.4 (page 108, Chapter Six). On 9 September, 1918 D Company of 11th CRT moved to Bapaume and commenced the reconstruction of these lines. By 13 September, the Y line had been relaid to east of Beugny, and Frémicourt Yard had been reconstructed. By 24 September, the Y3 line had been rebuilt to Boursies. They also worked on the reconstruction of the Y4 line.

On 25 September, 11th CRT were replaced by 9th CRT. By 27 September, the main Y line, being rebuilt by B Company, had joined the BW line coming north from Metz junction, and was open to Havrincourt. Also on 27 and 28 September, A Company built a bridge over the Canal du Nord, probably that for the Y line where it met the canal just north of Ruyaulcourt, linking the Y line back to Bapaume.

Meanwhile, D Company were continuing the reconstruction of the Y3 line, which by 27 September was open to Boursies, with a siding at Louverval. On 28 September, the line was complete to the Canal du Nord on the main Bapaume to Cambrai road.

Operations on the X and Y lines
The 54th LROC operated part of this area during September 1918, including the X line from Achiet-le-Grand to Mory, the X4 line from Mory to Bapaume, and some lines further north. On 12 September, 34th LROC moved to Bapaume. They set up controls along the Y line being reconstructed east, and probably on some other Y lines as well.

The 31st LROC, who had been operating light railways further north, transferred their HQ to Achiet-le-Grand on 25 September. They took over the X and X4 lines from 54th LROC, who moved their operations to the east. 31st LROC also took over operations on the X7 line and the branch to Achiet-le-Petit, and on the Y3 line to the Nord canal. For the Y3 line they placed their steam locomotives at Beaumetz Junction, and petrol tractors at Louverval. There must have been some sort of shared working with 34th LROC between Bapaume and Beaumetz Junction, where the Y3 line branched off, although 34th LROC managed the control points. The 54th LROC were probably operating the Y4 line with a base at Hermies, and the Y line east from Vélu towards Havrincourt.

From 13 September, 1st Aus LROC were based at Rocquigny, but had a control at Bapaume, and were operating the Y5 line and extension back to Bapaume, and the branch to Beaulencourt; also probably the BW/Y6 line from Bus Dump to Vélu. On 26 September, a detachment of 1st Aus LROC moved to Beaumetz junction. We do not know what they did there, given that 34th LROC were running the Y line from Bapaume, and 31st LROC were running the Y3 line, with 54th LROC east of there.

The BW and northern AX lines
It is not known if all of these lines were reconstructed and operated (see Figure 6.4 page 108, Chapter Six). The BW system had been very complex in 1917 and early 1918. Certainly, the main lines were brought back into use. These included the line from Le Transloy Yard to Rocquigny and Ruyaulcourt Yard (at Ytres village) and from there to Metz junction, north east to meet the Y line and on to Havrincourt. The line north from Bus to meet the Y6 line from Vélu, the line to Ytres Yard (towards Étricourt), the AX line from Metz junction towards Gouzeaucourt, and the AX line to Fins, were also brought back into use.

C Company of 11th CRT moved to the area of Ruyaulcourt standard gauge yard (Ytres village) on 16 September. They worked on the the reconstruction and maintenance of these lines until 27 September. Repairs to shell breaks were frequently needed. On 18 September work had to stop south of Havrincourt, and two days later near Dessart's Wood on the AX line to Gouzeaucourt. On 25 September, progress on both the Havrincourt (BW) and the Gouzeaucourt (AX) lines were stopped by enemy fire.

A detachment of 1st Aus LROC, who had been based at the Light Railway Workshops at Beaurainville since May 1918, moved to Achiet-le-Grand on 8 September, to operate light railways, and were followed by Company HQ on 11th September. By 13 September, the whole company were based near Rocquigny. They undertook repairs and proceeded to operate these sections which had not been worked since being retaken from the German army. This was the first time that this unit had operated a railway district on their own since arriving in France in May 1917.

1st Aus LROC established a district control at Rocquigny. In addition to controls at Bapaume and at Beaulencourt (Riencourt) on the Y5 line, there were controls at Bus Dump, Ruyaulcourt Yard (called Ytres control), Chalk Pit near Ytres standard gauge yard, Metz junction and Le Transloy.

In the week ending 27 September, 1st Aus LROC moved 5,399 tons of goods, of which 4740 tons was ammunition. Unusually, they record the WD numbers of motive power units, and of individual items of stock. At the end of September, they had six Alco 2-6-2T steam locomotives (one under repair), seven 40hp Simplex petrol tractors (one under repair), and one 20hp Simplex petrol tractor. Four more Simplex 40hp tractors were transferred to Beaumetz on 26 September, possibly for 31st LROC.

Fourth Army
The A100, A200 and A500 lines
No 2 and No 4 Company of 13th CRT moved to the Vecquemont district on 21 August to work on the light railway system. They were followed by Battalion HQ and No 1 Company on 23 August. They maintained the lines, did some grading and possibly did preliminary work on the link from Marcelcave (see next section). They were moved away on 25 August. No 4 Company of 6th CRT continued to maintain these lines until 5th September, when the Company moved to Plateau. Operations were probably continued by 6th LROC until they moved to Tincourt on 12 September, when the lines were abandoned until demolished in November.

Wiencourt to Marcelcave
Between 14 and 22 August, 6th CRT and 1st CRT had extended the light railway west from Wiencourt to Marcelcave Yard at Les Buttes. The whole line and yards were open to tractor traffic on 22 August.

Marcelcave to Villers-Bretonneux and Vecquemont
No 2 Company of 6th CRT moved to a site near Marcelcave on 22 August, to commence construction of a line from Marcelcave to Vecquemont via Villers-Bretonneux. The line would have linked up with the A100 system at Vecquemont, forming part of the planned south to north rear lateral line. Some work was done on the yard, but on 25 August construction was halted and was never restarted. The possible links north had already all been abandoned by 23 August.

South of the Amiens to Chaulnes standard gauge line
From 21 August, 6th CRT continued repairing the line to Beaucourt, and maintained the line to Caix. 13th CRT also continued maintenance, including from Dougherty Junction (near Vrély) to Méharicourt, where on 21 August seven shell breaks had to be repaired. 13th CRT moved to Daours on 23 August.

From 21 to 27 August, 13th (Can) LROC continued to operate the light railways from Wiencourt to Rosières dump, Le Quesnel, Chilly and Beaucourt. The French arrived on 28 August, when the French First Army took over from the Canadian Corps. They took over the operating from midnight on 31 August. On 2 September, 13th (Can) LROC moved to Marcelcave by Light Railway to relieve the 35th LROC.

Wiencourt and Marcelcave to Froissy, Bray and Plateau
By 21 August, this line was open to Proyart, close to the front line. No 2 Company of 6th CRT continued to work maintaining and repairing the line, with numerous shell breaks because much of the area was still under German observation. By 24 August, British troops had occupied the high ground east of Bray, and No 1 Company were ordered to put the line from Proyart to Bray in working order. The line was open for tractor traffic to Froissy on 29 August, after replacement of 82 sections of track, and No 2 Company moved to Froissy.

At Froissy there appears to have been only one bridge over the Somme canal, carrying the road, and the standard gauge and 60cm gauge railways. Maps suggest that there were two light railway lines on the bridge here. The road and standard gauge railway bridge was reconstructed by 3 September, by 1st Bttn CRT, and the standard gauge line from Chemin Vert (Wiencourt) to Plateau was opened the same day.

3rd APB suggested that a temporary bridge could be put over the lock slightly to the west. A photograph taken in 1919 does show a light railway across the lock. From 31 August to 2 September, No 2 Company of 2nd CRT worked on the 'Froissy-Bray diversion'. The light railway bridge at Bray, called 'No 2 Bridge', was reconstructed by 1 September, built from timber and steel, which was more than 30 yards long. Work was also undertaken on the line north from Bray to Plateau and Maricourt, requiring the filling of 50 shell holes and the replacement of 130 sections of track. The line was open for tractor traffic to Plateau and Maricourt on 2nd September, the day before the opening of the standard gauge line to Plateau. This all argues for a separate and new light railway route from Froissy to Bray, with a separate bridge at Froissy over the lock, and for a separate light railway bridge at Bray.

8.5 The Somme Canal at Froissy in 1919, showing a train crossing the light railway line which was built across the lock in September 1918. The Australian Corps Royal Engineers dump is on the right bank. *(AWM A00959)*

In early September, 6th CRT were also salvaging track in the back areas, including ripping up old sidings, and shipping the material forward from Marcelcave yard. They also constructed new sidings near Wiencourt (600 yards) and at La Flaque Dump (250 yards). Proyart Junction Ammunition Dump was reconstructed, extending and repairing spurs. The transhipment loop at Froissy yard was ready by 5 September, and an RE spur on 8 September. The transhipment and stone sidings at Plateau were ready for use on 6 September.

On 2 September, the 35th LROC, who were operating this line, were relieved by 13th (Can) LROC. They commented that the traffic from Marcelcave was by this time very light. Probably the main traffic was now by standard gauge line to Froissy and Plateau for transhipment there.

Harbonnières to Lihons and Foucaucourt
The line that branched off the line from Wiencourt to Froissy just north of Harbonnières, to Lihon, was reconstructed by No 1 Company of 6th CRT, with the branch towards Foucaucourt. It was open for tractor traffic to 1 mile south of Foucaucourt on 31 August.

Froissy to Fontaine-lès-Cappy
The line to Fay and Estrées was repaired via Chuignes as far as Fontaine by 5 September and maintained by No 2 Company of 6th CRT.

Froissy to Cappy and Herbécourt
The branch from Froissy along the south bank of the Somme canal to Cappy, and then across the Santerre Plateau to La Chapelette (Péronne), was repaired by No 2 Company of 6th CRT. It was open for tractor traffic to Herbécourt on 30 August, and to Biaches or just beyond on 31 August.

Plateau to Maricourt and Rocquigny
In early September, No 1 Company of 6th CRT started to repair the light railway from Plateau to Maricourt, Combles and Rocquigny. Presumably it was not in too bad condition, since only twenty sections of track needed replacement between Maricourt and Combles. It was ready for tractor traffic as far as Combles by 6 September, but we do not know when it was opened through to Rocquigny.

Maricourt to Péronne
No 3 Company of 6th CRT moved to Maricourt on 30 August and started work on the reconstruction of the line to Péronne on 3 September. By 4 September, 210 sections of track had been replaced, and the line was open to Cléry-sur-Somme, extended to Quinconce on 7 September, with a transhipment at Hem yard.

No 1 Company moved to near Quinconce on 8 September and reconstructed Quinconce light railway yard. Between 18 and 21 September, nearly ½ mile (1km) of track was laid in Quinconce Yard. Péronne transhipment siding was ready for use on 18 September, and the line probably reached Péronne well before that. They continued maintenance until they moved to Montbrehain on 12 October.

The CY and southern AX lines
The AX line from Quinconce north towards Fins was also reconstructed by No 1 Company of 6th CRT. Work commenced on 9 September and the line, which must have been in a good state of preservation, was open for tractor traffic to Nurlu by 11 September. It is not known when it reached Fins.

No 2 Company of 6th CRT moved to near Doingt to reconstruct the line from Quinconce to Roisel. The line was open to Roisel on 10 September, after the replacement of more than 100 rails. For the construction, they had three steam locomotives and eight petrol tractors. By 11 September, they had linked up with No 1 Company and the line was open from Roisel to Nurlu via Villers-Faucon. They comment on the heavy shelling between Roisel and Villers-Faucon, and the large number of mined wagons left on this line by the German Army. By 11 September, No 2 Company had also repaired the line from Quinconce to 'Péronne South', by which they must mean the link from Doingt to the line south from Péronne Flamicourt. By the middle of September, they had been joined by No 4 Company of 6th CRT, who worked on repairing and reopening all the sidings on these lines.

13th (Can) LROC moved from Marcelcave to Quinconce on 6 and 7 September, the first party by lorry and the second by light railway. From 8 September, they operated the lines towards Nurlu and Tincourt. They also salvaged rolling stock left on the lines. From 16 September there are details of goods carried; on that day they carried 793 tons of goods in 166 trips. As the month progressed total tonnage carried tended to increase, to reach 1816 tons on 27 September, during the preparations for the attack on the Hindenburg Line. Distances per ton varied between 6.2 and 9.0 miles (10 and 14.5km). Most of the loads were ammunition or rations, and most (96 per cent on 27 September) were carried on the 7½ miles (12km) of the AX line from Quinconce to Nurlu. They comment that constant supervision at the District Control and on the line, and prompt unloading of wagons, was necessary to ensure quick movement of traffic. On the night of 26 September, the standard gauge train due in the day before arrived late at night, and the ammunition due that day. The result was that the entire company, including the officer commanding, were obliged to work practically all night.

Two accidents occurred on 20 September, which illustrate the hazards of these operations. In the first, at 3.45am, at Aizecourt-le-Haut (AX line), sparks from a steam locomotive hauling a ration train set fire to cordite lying 18ft (5.5m) from the track. An officer and some men went to extinguish the fire and some shells close by exploded killing the officer and an NCO and wounding three men. In the second accident another locomotive also set fire to cordite alongside the track at Hem, on the line from Quinconce to Maricourt, a wagon of hay in the ration train caught fire, and salvage ammunition and the cordite exploded wounding an officer and some men. A sergeant took a 20hp tractor and brought the train out safely, then helped to extinguish the fire, at the same time carrying out boxes of explosives. The RTO also risked his life in carrying out the wounded and removing ammunition from the vicinity of the fire. Both men were recommended for an award.

South east of Péronne, DZ and B lines
During September, the light railway from Doingt to Vraignes via Mons-en-Chaussée was reconstructed. This met the line from Péronne Flamicourt, and then ran on to the junction with the B line south of Hancourt. The work was done by No 2 Company of 6th CRT, begun on 13 September 1918. The line must have been in quite good condition, because it was open on 14 September, and the B and DZ connection north to Roisel on 16 September.

The light railway work of 6th CRT was clearly considered important. At a time when other light railway units were being diverted to standard gauge work, No 4 Company was moved back to light railway work on 16 September and No 3 Company on 20 September. No 4 Company worked on Péronne South Yard (Flamicourt) where there had been a transhipment. On 15 September, a bridge building gang moved to Tertry to work on the bridge there (B line). The bridge was completed, and the line open to Villeveque, south of Vermand, on 18 September. It is not known if the trestle west of Tertry (February 1918) needed reconstruction, or if the line was rebuilt using different structures. Towards the end of September, the yard at Montigny Farm was repaired, and the line to Jeancourt. The principal lines were still being maintained by 6th CRT on 1 October, but we do not know for how long after that.

Roisel to Templeux-le-Guérard
From 16 September, No 2 Company of 6th CRT reconstructed the line from Roisel to Hargicourt as a light railway, that is to 60cm gauge, stating that they were using the 'old metre gauge line'. However, a light railway was built to Templeux-le-Guérard before 1 January 1918 and extended to Villeret and Hargicourt as a trench tramway. These appear to have been built parallel to but south of the former metre gauge line from Roisel to Hargicourt. It is probable that 6th CRT now reconstructed the line along the path of the old light railway, particularly since the old metre gauge path was to be used again for a standard gauge line. The line was open for traffic to Templeux-le-Guérard on 25 September, by which time 2¼ miles (3.65km) of track had been laid.

September 29 to November 11
The Hindenburg Line to the Armistice

South and east of the Somme Sector, the US Army with French support had retaken the St-Mihiel salient on 12 and 13 September. The main US army moved to the Argonne Forest. From 26 September, the French and Americans advanced to the line of the Meuse, and the Argonne Forest was cleared by the Americans by the end of October. North of the Somme Sector, the British First Army crossed the Canal du Nord towards Cambrai between 27 September and 1 October.

On 29 September the British Fourth Army, with Australian and two US divisions, and the French First Army to the south, attacked the St-Quentin canal. The section of the canal from St-Quentin north to Vendhuile had been incorporated into the Hindenburg Line defences. Except for the Riqueval tunnel 5.4km (3.4 miles) long around Bellicourt, much of the canal was in deep cuttings. The Americans had already unsuccessfuly attacked the defences at Bellicourt. On 29 September, the North Staffordshire Regiment (British 46th Division) captured the bridge at Riqueval, just south of the tunnel, intact. By 2 October 10½ miles (17km) of the Hindenburg Line had been breached. Between 3 and 10 October, the third defensive line around Beaurevoir was cleared and the Autralian 2nd Division captured Montbrehain, 5½ miles (9km) east of the canal.

Between 8 and 10 October, the British First, Third and Fourth Armies crossed three defensive lines and took Cambrai. The advances east and north continued until the Armistice on 11 November. By this time, the front line was more than 60 miles (100km) from the line near Villers-Bretonneux on 8 August, and the British were back in Mons in Belgium, where they had fought the first actions of the BEF in 1914.

Railways 29 September to
11 November 1918

Railways in the Third and Fourth Army areas from 29 September to 11 November are shown in Figure 8.2. As the Allied Armies advanced east, they tended to move to the north as well. We have regarded the front as moving east out of the Somme Sector when it was beyond the eastern limit of light railway development,

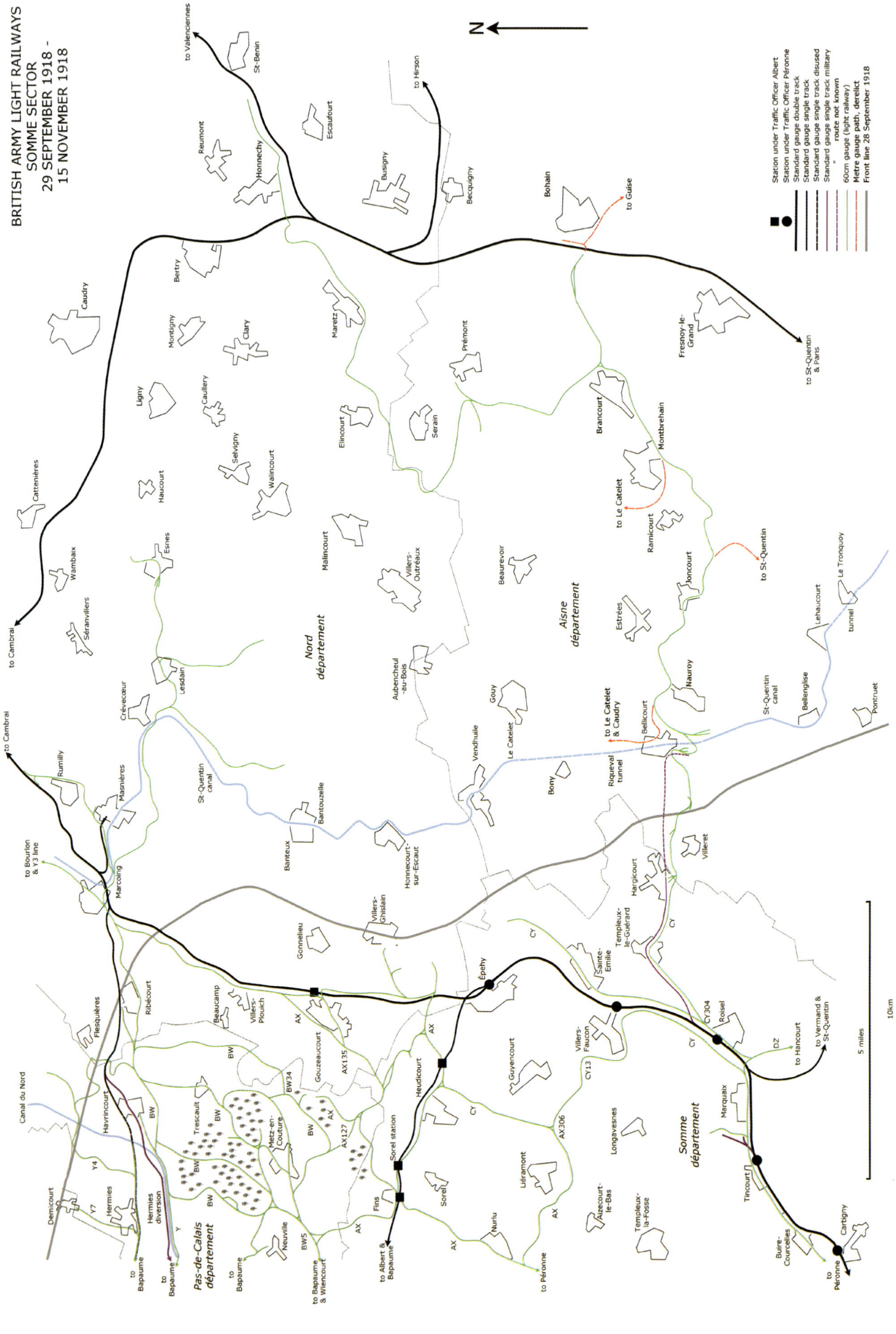

Narrow Gauge in the Somme Sector

Figure 8.2

which was to Bohain and just east of Honnechy. The standard gauge railway north and slightly east from St-Quentin to Le-Cateau-Cambrésis, which was the main line from Paris to Brussels, therefore forms the eastern edge of the area covered by this book.

Standard gauge railways
Third and Fourth Armies
On 31 October, RCE V moved from Boisleux to Somain and remained there until March 1919. Somain is in the Nord département between Douai and Valenciennes, in the British First Army area. RCE V had already handed over to RCC IV, on 11 October, all but two of their supporting labour companies. Since RCC I remained at Barlin, it seems that RCE V now became the forward (east) support group for the First Army and left the Third Army to RCC IV.

From 16 October, the train of the Third Army Commander was at Masnières, east of Marcoing and south of Cambrai. On 6 November, all lines west of the lines linking Chaulnes, Péronne, Épehy and Marcoing junction were handed over by RCC IV to RCE Comms (Railway Construction Engineers for the Lines of Communication), who were responsible for the back areas. RCE Comms were supported in this by 231st LRFC, one indication of the diversion of light railway units to standard gauge work towards the end of the War.

The Amiens avoiding line
After 9 October, only 1 platoon of A Company of 12th CRT remained at Vecquemont, until 1 November, when the project was finally abandoned.

Amiens to Achiet-le-Grand (Amiens to Arras main line)
This line was operating in double track by the end of September. By 28 October, French Railway Engineers had taken over the whole line.

Achiet-le-Grand to Bapaume and Marcoing
On 30 September, the Nord Canal bridge was open for railway traffic, and the Lebucquières east (Hermies) diversion was joined to the old French line east of Havrincourt on 1 October. There was one track back west into Havrincourt station.

Reconnaissance reports showed that the line on from Havrincourt to Marcoing junction, with the line from Épehy to Cambrai, was thoroughly demolished, and the St-Quentin Canal bridge at Marcoing, before the junction, had been destroyed. RCE V repaired the track and the bridge, and then worked on towards Cambrai until units under RCC IV came up from the south (Épehy) to take over. The ROD took over operation to Marcoing on 18 October. The line was maintained by 11th CRT until they moved east and it was taken over by RCE Comms on 5 November.

Miraumont to Le Transloy
On 6 October, 11th CRT took over maintenance from 13th CRT, and ROD, based at Candas, took over operating. Maintenance was taken over by RCE Comms on 5 November.

Dernancourt junction to Plateau
On 6 October, 275th RC RE were instructed to repair a single line track from Ancre junction to Loop, the junction with the line from Wiencourt and Bray, for the salvage of track materials, and two POW labour companies were moved from the Amiens avoiding line to Méaulte for this work.

Chemin Vert (Wiencourt) to La Flaque, Bray, Loop, Plateau, Quinconce, and Le Transloy
On orders from GHQ these lines were closed to traffic, to release operating staff and rolling stock, on 24 October. RE stores could be withdrawn by arrangement with ROD.

Le Transloy to Étricourt
After the closure of the line from Plateau on 24 October, this section remained open, leaving the through route from Miraumont. A detachment of A Company 12th CRT remained at Rocquigny at least until December 1918.

Étricourt to Fins and Épehy
On 20 September, 263rd RC RE had taken over reconstruction of the line. By 20 October, the line was ready for traffic to the junction with the line from Roisel at Épehy.

Quinconce (Péronne) to Étricourt - the Tortille Valley line
On 28 September, 12th CRT were still rebuilding the line towards Étricourt. The line was linked through on 1 October. D Company of 12th CRT was still maintaining the line in December 1918.

Chaulnes to Péronne, Roisel and Épehy
A siding at Eterpigny, south of Péronne, was ready for the Fourth Army Commander's train by 29th September. By the end of September, 1st Bttn CRT had completed the line from Péronne to Roisel in double track.

Before October, there had been no reconstruction from Roisel on towards Épehy. The 1st CRT began work on 4 October, with the German Army still close by. At 5pm on 24 October, a delayed action mine at Roisel destroyed all three main line tracks, leaving a crater 18ft (5.5m) deep. One line was reopened at 10.40pm and another at 11.16pm. From 7 November, there was double line working from Roisel to Épehy, taken over by ROD from 15 November.

Roisel to Hargicourt and Bellicourt
Work started at the end of September to use the metre gauge formation from Roisel to Hargicourt for a single track standard gauge line. Track laying to Hargicourt was complete on 1 October, and from 3 October Hargicourt could accept one train per night.

Instructions were received on 3 October from CRCE to extend the line from Hargicourt. Surveys were made north to Gouy (Le Catelet), possibly along the line of the disused metre gauge railway from St-Quentin to Caudry, but the railway was only constructed to Bellicourt. The remaining two companies of 13th CRT, No 2 and No 3, arrived in the area by 7 October.

From 14 October, ROD took over operation from Roisel to Templeux. On 24 October, 6th Bttn CRT took over the work from 13th CRT. The 6th CRT had been working on the light railway from Roisel to Bellicourt, and then on to Bohain (see light railways later in this chapter). Now they left No 3 Company and a detachment of No 1 Company on the light railway work and the rest moved to the standard gauge work.

The 13th CRT moved to Bouchain on 26 October to work for RCE V on railways around Valenciennes. This is an indication of how fast the war was moving east now. On taking over, 6th CRT reported that Roisel to Hargicourt was in reasonable shape. However, between Hargicourt and Bellicourt there were five severe curves, cuttings were too narrow, track laying was bad with poor drainage, and only about 5 per cent of the ballasting had been done. The section from Hargicourt to Bellicourt was closed to traffic from 29 October to 5 November to allow ballasting. On 7 November, No 4 Company moved to Montigny Farm, and on 16 and 21 November, No 1 and then No 2 Company moved to Aulnoye to work further east. Two platoons and one labour company remained for maintenance.

Épehy to Marcoing
The line was reconstructed by 1st CRT, assisted from 10 October by A and B Companies of 12th CRT. The double track bridge at Épehy, under the line to Étricourt, was completely destroyed. By 19 October, double track was complete to Marcoing junction, but the canal bridge to Marcoing station was still only single track. Traffic was exceptionally heavy. At 4.30pm that day, nine trains were standing between Gouzeaucourt and Marcoing because of congestion in Marcoing Yard.

ROD took over working from Épehy to Marcoing on 24 October. 1st CRT left by the end of October, replaced by 12th CRT, who were themselves replaced by 275th RC RE from 3 November. 12th CRT completed the doubling of the bridge at Marcoing just before they left.

Marcoing to Cambrai
From 10 October, the reconstruction of the line in double track through to Cambrai and then on to Caudry was of the utmost urgency to the Third Army. This was because of the increasing supply line problem with the rapid advance and the opportunities of the connections with other lines at Cambrai.

From 11 October, 9th Bttn CRT worked on doubling the line. 7th CRT moved to Marcoing on 15 October to continue this, and to construct a branch to Masnières. By 4 November, there was double line working to Cambrai.

Roisel to Vermand and St-Quentin
Vermand could accept one train daily from 5 October. By 7 October, there were four sidings on the main line at Montigny Farm, and operation from Roisel to Montigny was taken over by ROD.

During October, 2nd CRT continued work on the reconstruction of the line to St-Quentin. On 14 October, they began the reconstruction of the bridge over the Somme canal at St-Quentin, under German observation. St-Quentin Yard was reconstructed with the French, who were reconstructing the main line north from Tergnier. The link up by the French line was made on 12 October. The bridge over the Somme canal was finished on 15 October and the line opened for traffic at 4pm. ROD took over operations on 29 October.

St Quentin to Bohain, Busigny and Le-Cateau-Cambrésis, and Busigny to Cambrai
This is the line which we have regarded as the eastern edge of the area covered by this book. The standard gauge railway north and slightly east from St-Quentin to Le-Cateau-Cambrésis continued into Belgium and was part of the main line from Paris to Brussels. The line which branched off north west at Honnechy, just north of Busigny, went to Cambrai via Caudry, which was the centre of the Cambrésis metre gauge network.

These lines were reconstructed north from St-Quentin by the French, and east from Cambrai by British army units. However, the British Fourth Army wanted rail head facilities on the line from St-Quentin and assisted the French with the works. The track was complete to Busigny by the end of October. From the Cambrai end, construction was undertaken by 4th Bttn CRT and later 1st CRT. Later, 2nd CRT worked from Honnechy towards Cambrai to meet 4th CRT.

The station at Bohain was on the metre gauge line from Le Catelet and was reached by the light railway constructed from Bellicourt on 20 October. A survey in October, before reconstruction, showed that the metre gauge bridge over the main line was totally demolished, with the steel work lying across main line. A new large transhipment had been constructed 800

8.6 The British Fourth Army heaquarters train, under camouflage at Montigny Farm on 17 October 1918. A light railway is crossing the field to the right. *(AWM E03929)*

yards west of Bohain station. The whole yard had been demolished by blowing up the rails. Reconstruction was undertaken by 263rd RC RE, and 1st and 2nd CRT. The first standard gauge train reached Bohain station on 26 October.

Metre gauge railways
St-Quentin to le Catelet and Caudry
This line, owned by the CFC, ran north from St-Quentin to the centre of the network at Caudry (see Chapter Three). The line ran just behind the Hindeburg Line, especially near Bellicourt, and was destroyed by the Hindenburg Line on the western edge of St-Quentin.

When Allied forces reached Bellicourt on 29 September, the line was derelict, and the track had been taken up. The use made of it for light railway construction in October is described later in this chapter (see Roisel to Bohain, and Walk 4 in Chapter Twelve). Surveys of the standard gauge line from Roisel to St-Quentin in autumn 1918 confirmed that the metre gauge track had been demolished through the yard of Rocourt station, on the western edge of St-Quentin just east of the main Hindenburg defences (see Walk 5 in Chapter Twelve).

Le Catelet to Bohain and Guise
This line, belonging to the *Compagnie des Chemins de Fer d'intérêt local du Nord de la France* (NF), started from Le Catelet, where it met the above line from St-Quentin to Caudry. It ran east to Bohain and then on to Guise. When it came back into the possession of the Allied forces after 29 September 1918, it was also derelict, and the track had been taken up. It was also used for light railway construction in October, as far as Bohain, also described later in this chapter (see Roisel to Bohain).

Light Railways (60cm gauge)
During this period there were the last developments of military light railways. As the front moved east more rapidly it became difficult to maintain supplies even

with standard gauge lines. Increasing numbers of light railway units were diverted to standard gauge work. Light railways in the east of the Somme sector in this period are shown in Figure 8.2 (page 166).

This period also saw the introduction of the Light Railway Forward Companies (LRFC), formed from the Foreways Companies with the addition of tractor crews and other staff from some of the LROCs (see Chapter Four). On 1 October 1918, 1st FWC became the 231st Light Railway Forward Company (LRFC), and 2nd FWC became the 232nd LRFC, although for the latter the change of name was not officially confirmed until 21 October. They never filled the functions for which they were intended, becoming either operating companies with tractors rather than steam locomotives, or being diverted to standard gauge work.

The A100, A200 and A500 lines
These lines had not been operated or maintained since the middle of September and were now an isolated system entirely redundant to the Allied war effort. The lines had probably already been taken up when, on 4 November, an officer of 6th CRT was sent with 50 prisoners of war to load all the light railway material at Fréchencourt and Poulainville yards and send it to Vecquemont for shipment. Shipment to the Light Railway Workshops at Beaurainville was complete by 27 November.

The X7, X and X4 lines
On 1 October, C Company of 11th CRT completed the reconstruction of the light railway transhipment siding and RE spur at Achiet-le-Grand. From 1 to 5 October, 231st LRFC (formerly 1st FWC) continued to maintain the X7 line. They also maintained the X line from Achiet to Mory, the X4 line from Mory to Bapaume, and the Achiet yards. 232nd LRFC (formerly 2nd FWC), based at Mory, were also maintaining the X and X4 lines, and building the light railway yard at Achiet, until 10 October when they were moved to Marcoing.

The Y, Y3, Y4, Y5 and Y6 lines
The 9th CRT continued working on these lines. By 4 October, the Y3 line had reached the partly demolished light railway bridge over the Escaut river at Noyelles-sur-Escaut. By 10 October the line was connected over the bridge to the BW line, built north from Marcoing by C Company.

At the beginning of October, the Y and Y5 lines were partly being maintained by 232nd LRFC, based at Mory. On 6 October, 231st LRFC moved from Achiet to near Beaumetz Junction for maintenance work on the Y lines.

Operations on the X and Y lines
Meanwhile, between 5 and 11 October most of the control points on the X and X4 lines between Achiet and Bapaume were closed. On 12 October, HQ of 31st LROC moved to a yard just south west of Bapaume, on the line to Le Sars along the main road from Bapaume to Albert, where they set up a new district control. The same day, 34th LROC moved from Bapaume to Rocquigny.

31st LROC took over from 34th LROC the controls along the Y line as far as Vélu Junction, where the Y4 line branched off. Controls were also taken over from 54th LROC on 20 October, along the Y line east of Vélu, including two junctions with the BW system, at Canal Bottom by the Canal du Nord just north of Ruyaulcourt, and at Canal Junction, where the main BW line from Metz Junction came north to join the Y line. East from here this became a BW line, and 31st LROC also took over Knife Dump, on this line south of Havrincourt. Controls on the Y3 line reached Lock 3 on the St-Quentin Canal, near of Noyelles-sur-Escaut (north of Marcoing), on 29 October.

From 5 October, a Section of 232nd LRFC moved to Knife Dump near Havrincourt to operate ammunition trains forward for the attack on Cambrai. The goods carried by 31st LROC increased to a maximum of 1709 tons on 8 October, the day that Cambrai was retaken. This consisted of 1280 tons of ammunition, 98 tons of RE Stores, 82 tons of salvage, 83 tons of light railway materials, 5 tons of rations and 6 tons of water. 122 personnel were also carried that day. As the month passed and the front line moved away east, the total amount moved tended to decrease, the proportion of ammunition decreased, and the proportion of RE stores and later roadstone increased. On 31 October, 978 tons of goods were carried. Into early November some control posts were closed, and traffic further reduced. On 11 November only 376 tons were carried.

Before the take over by 31st LROC, 54th LROC had been based at Beaumetz-lès-Cambrai, for the Y line east, and at Knife Camp at Hermies, probably for the Y4 line. We do not know where 54th LROC went after 20 October 1918.

The BW and northern AX lines
The 9th Bttn CRT continued the maintenance of the Ytres Yards, the Ytres junction to Rocquigny line (BW), and the line from Neuville to Fins (AX). C Company of 9th CRT reconstructed the line from Metz Junction to Marcoing, which was open on 3 October. On 9 October, they met D Company, working on the Y3 line, at the bridge over the Escaut river at Noyelles-sur-Escaut. By 10 October, they were also maintaining lines from Ruyaulcourt (Ytres Village) to Metz Junction (BW) and from Vélu Junction to Rocquigny Junction (Y6 and BW).

In early October, 1st Aus LROC remained at Rocquigny. In addition to operating they repaired the line from Fins to Gouzeaucourt (AX) and brought it back into use by 6 October. From 3 October, they were assisted by a section of 232nd LRFC who moved to Rocquigny. 1st Aus LROC continued to keep a record of their rolling stock. In the week ended 11 October, they had six 2-6-2T Alco steam locomotives, one in repair, and four 4-6-0T Baldwins, two in repair. During that week, they received four more 4-6-0T Baldwins from 31st LROC. They also had fifteen 40hp Simplex petrol tractors, two in repair, and three 20hp Simplex tractor, one in repair. One of the 2-6-2T Alco locomotives was WD No. 1238, which worked on the Vis-en-Artois sugar beet system from 1926 to 1938.

During the week ending 11 October, 1st Aus LROC hauled 4694 tons of goods, including 2160 tons of ammunition and 1232 tons of stone, and carried 480 personnel.

On 12 October, 34th LROC moved from Bapaume to Rocquigny and took over operating the BW system from 1st Aus LROC, who moved to Lesdains. 34th LROC stayed until 9 November, when they were allocated to work with 58th (Canadian) Broad Gauge Operating Company based at Cambrai. During October, the 19th TCC were reformed as the 19th LROC at Rocquigny, and later moved to Marcoing.

Marcoing to Lesdains and Esnes, and branches
During October, a line was built east from Marcoing to Lesdains, then on along the valley east to Esnes. On 10 October, 232nd LRFC moved to Marcoing, and from 12 October and into November they were maintaining the lines from Havrincourt. From 28 October they were maintaining the line all the way from Bapaume to Esnes.

Meanwhile, on 12 October, the HQ of 1st Aus LROC moved from Rocquigny to Lesdains, and were working on the bridge over the St-Quentin Canal at Crévecœur-le-Grand. They remained working on these lines until 25 October, when they moved to Bergues, in the Nord *département*, to work for ROD on standard gauge operations.

In November, branches were built. One was along the north bank of the canal just east of Marcoing almost to Masnières, then north past Rumilly and back to the Marcoing to Cambrai standard gauge line. One was south from near Crévecœur-le-Grand, and the third south from Lesdains.

The CY and southern AX lines
From 29 September, 6th Bttn CRT continued to work on these lines. By 2 October, part of the former CY line north from the AX junction east of Liéramont towards Heudicourt, had been reconstructed, about 2 miles.

Also, on 2 October, No 1 Company moved back to their former camp near Mont-St-Quentin, to maintain the CY and southern AX systems.

In October, a new line was constructed from Éterpigny to La Chapelette and on round the north of Péronne to Porte de Bretagne. At Éterpigny the line connected with the existing line to Estrées-Deniécourt, and then followed the main road north to La Chapelette. From La Chapelette, it crossed the Somme canal and river and then followed the north edge of the town, probably along the line of the walls, to the existing line from Quinconce to Doingt and on to Roisel.

13th (Can) LROC continued to operate the lines until 11 October, when 6th LROC took over. On 29 September, the day of the attack on the St-Quentin canal, 13th (Can) LROC were thanked by ADLR IV for their service for the wounded, from a control on the AX line near Nurlu, to Doingt. In early October, loads carried gradually declined, to 684 tons on 10 October. They were operating from Hem to Quinconce, Quinconce to Nurlu, Nurlu to Roisel, and Quinconce to Tincourt. There was still a service from Tincourt to Roisel. The pattern of operations and other evidence indicates that the 'main line' from Quinconce was now to near Liéramont on the AX lines, and then on the CY line past Villers-Faucon to the junction with the line to Hargicourt, north of Roisel.

Roisel to Hargicourt, Bellicourt and Bohain
The light railways from Roisel to Bohain, and the branch from Brancourt almost to Honnechy, were the final great achievement of the 6th Bttn CRT, and indeed the final flourish of British light railway construction on the Western Front. The end result was a light railway all the way from Wiencourt, on the Amiens to Tergnier standard gauge line, to Bohain on the main line from Paris to Brussels via St-Quentin, a straight-line distance of 40 miles (64km).

The light railway from Roisel had been opened as far as Templeux-le-Guérard on 25 September. From 26 September, plans and preparations were made for the forthcoming attacks on the Hindenburg Line and the St-Quentin Canal. The plan called for the light railway to reach Joncourt at zero plus 96 hours, to deliver rations for eight divisions. The ration trains would be worked forward from Roisel for six divisions and from Tincourt for two divisions. Work continued on 28 September, with 1¾ miles (3km) of track laid and ballasted, assisted by twelve petrol tractors.

The plan for 29 September was that No 2 Company would leave Tincourt at 4am and move to the forward area. No 3 Company would leave Marquaix at 8am and relieve No 2 Company at 12 noon. Companies were to move by light railway and mules, with field kitchens and water carts by road. No 1 Company were ordered to leave their camp near Mont-St-Quentin at 5.30 am, and travel to the advanced Battalion HQ, just west of Hargicourt. Attached labour and one working party travelled by lorry, the rest by light railway. No 4 Company were to leave their camp south of Flamicourt at 7am by light railway and report to advanced HQ. Present camps were to be left standing with guards. Men were ordered to carry a ground sheet, great coat, rifle, steel helmet, box respirator, and 50 rounds of ammunition, with 24 hours rations per man coming on General Service (horse drawn, road) wagons.

No 1 Company was to work ahead, responsible for dismantling track, grading, bridging and so on, from Roisel to Joncourt. No 2 and No 3 Companies were to follow laying track in alternate 8-hour shifts. No 4 Company was to load material behind and keep the track in shape. Signallers were to be sent forward to string wires and to connect and man control boxes for operating construction traffic.

In practice, on 29 September the 'tactical situation' did not allow the work to proceed as expected, and 6th CRT were subjected to heavy shelling and gas attacks. Despite this, a siding was laid at Hargicourt, and 1,000 yards of track laid. On 1 October, work began to extend the line to Bellicourt. This was described as a 'reconstruction', confirming that a path already existed. This must have been a German light railway. Work was now unhampered, because of infantry advances.

Work to bridge a mine crater ½ mile (0.8km) west of Hargicourt was completed on 2 October, and the line to Hargicourt was fully open for traffic on 4 October. Track was completed to Bellicourt on 3 October and the next day, the track had joined the path of the previous metre gauge branch to the factory at Bellicourt. From here the branch and then the main metre gauge path from St-Quentin to Caudry were used to east of Joncourt, and because of this, extension was very fast. A loop and spur were put in at the former main line junction. (see also Walk 4, Chapter Twelve). The line was open for traffic to Joncourt station on 8 October. The line from Roisel to Joncourt suffered from heavy traffic on poorly ballasted track, and by 12 October, No 3 Company had to replace many bent rails.

Meanwhile, 500 yards of sidings and 2 sets of points had been put in at the St-Quentin Road near Bellicourt, and 800 yards of sidings and 5 sets of points at Bellicourt Yard. From 14 October, No 3 Company were constructing a link to the standard gauge yard being built at Bellicourt. Later, there was also a standard gauge rail head on the Bellicourt to Gouy road, but we

8.7 The light railway at Hargicourt on 1 October 1918. There are two Simplex 20hp tractors, and one Simplex 40hp tractor of open type, with a train of two wagons loaded with rails and other materials. *(AWM E03404)*

have few details of either of these yards, or of the light railway links.

A spur ½ mile (0.8km) long was built to the sugar factory west of Joncourt on 10 October and opened the same night. Because of the tactical situation the line was not extended beyond Joncourt until 12 October, when work by No 2 Company of 6th CRT commenced, with assistance from 350 men of the 102nd US Engineers. The line was extended east along the metre gauge path, then across country to join the formation of the metre gauge line from Le Catelet to Guise at Montbrehain. British Army maps show that there was already a rail link between the two metre gauge lines, which must have been of German construction, either 60cm or metre gauge. In the course of construction, some metre gauge line was dismantled and some converted to 60cm gauge.

The line was completed to Montbrehain by 5pm on 12 October and opened for traffic on the 13 October. From 14 October, No 1 Company took over the construction eastwards, assisted by 250 men from 105th US Engineers. From Montbrehain there was much metre gauge track remaining, but it was dismantled and replaced. Between Brancourt and Bohain there were problems with mines, especially at a bridge just by Haute-Cour Farm. Here there was a mine crater and blown up bridge, which was repaired from 15 October, with assistance from 105th US Engineers. Two more mines exploded here, the third on 17 October destroying the almost completed bridge. The bridge work was completed on 20 October, with help from 150 POWs. By this time the track was fit for traffic to Bohain, where the line ended just west of the former metre gauge bridge over the standard gauge line. By 22 October, a 400 yard ration spur and a 200 yard siding were completed. There was now little shelling even as far east as Bohain.

During October, many other facilities were completed along the line. Notable were the conversion to 60cm gauge of the metre gauge transhipment at Roisel (13 October), the construction of 'Y' lines for turning locomotives at Montbrehain (17 October) and near Joncourt (22 October), and sidings and other yard facilities along the line, particularly at Montbrehain and Brancourt. There were also frequent passing loops.

On 23 October, most of 6th CRT moved to standard gauge work, leaving No 3 Company and a detachment of No 1 Company on light railway work. No 3 Company maintained the line from Roisel to Joncourt, and by 31 October from Quinconce to Joncourt. No 1 Company detachment maintained Joncourt to Bohain, but were released on 31 October by the arrival of 33rd Labour Corps. By 10 November, No 3 Company were maintaining the line from Péronne to Bohain.

Operations Tincourt to Bohain - On 11 October, the 13th (Can) LROC moved from Quinconce to Tincourt, and the next day took over operating from Tincourt to Joncourt. On 15 October, the personnel of 6th LROC, 236th LRFC, and most of 18th TCC were placed at their disposal, and the next day they began operating to Montbrehain. By 20 October they operated to Bohain. This is a straight-line distance of 19 miles (30km) but would have been considerably more.

13th (Can) LROC were mostly carrying ammunition, rations and RE stores. Between 20 and 31 October, they carried an average of 1884 tons of goods per day, with a maximum of 2402 tons on 26 October, the day that the first standard gauge train reached Bohain. During this period, they had between 18 and 33 steam locomotives and 11 to 19 petrol tractors.

On 27 October 13th (Can) LROC suffered another accident, with sparks from a locomotive alighting on cordite and setting fire to an ammunition wagon. A 9.2 inch shell exploded wounding a Sapper of 18th TCC, who later died, and two other men. Five men were commended for saving the remaining four wagons of ammunition that were attached to the burning wagon.

From 1 November, 13th (Can) LROC were operating from Quinconce to Bohain, now also carrying some salvage. Loads were tending to decline. On 11 November, 4th APB were celebrating the Armistice resting and training at Ailly-sur-Somme, west of Amiens. On 14 November, they moved by standard gauge railway to Roisel. The next day they entrained on the light railway and detrained at Montbrehain. From the 21 November, they marched until on 26 November they crossed the border into Belgium, as part of the advance of the 4th Australian Division into the previously occupied territories. This was probably not the only use of this line for personnel movement, but it was a fitting use of the line in implementing the Armistice and marking the end of hostilities.

Brancourt to Sérain and Honnechy
On 6 November, 1918 6th CRT were contacted by ADLR IV to ask on behalf of Fourth Army about the condition of the metre gauge line from Brancourt to Honnechy. This was not a French line from before the war, but it is shown on British Army maps of Autumn 1918. It must have been a German military metre gauge line. From a triangular junction with the formation of the line from le-Catelet to Guise, now part of the light railway to Bohain, it followed a roundabout route north and east to the area of Honnechy.

6th CRT made a reconnaissance, and in the afternoon were ordered to convert the line to 60cm gauge as fast as possible, using No 3 Company and 102nd and 105th US Engineers. Work commenced on the conversion, which implies a regauging of existing track, on 10 November, with 93 men of 6th CRT, and 1,000 Americans. On 13 November, instructions were received in the evening from Fourth Army Transportation that conversion must stop at Honnechy. The line was ready for traffic to Honnechy on 15 November, when the US Engineers left.

A British army map after the war shows the light railway extending beyond Honnechy, to beside the main road and railway between there and Le-Cateau-Cambrésis, a total distance of about 11 miles (18km). We have no information about any use of the line.

The last month of the War

Light railways were best suited to a relatively static front line. With the German army in retreat east from August, the whole war had become more fluid. As we have seen, light railways were built to support the advance, and in some areas linked with captured German lines, but in the end the advance outran the railways. From October, the light railways entered a period of falling use, and were used to concentrate surplus supplies in the abandoned front line areas. By the Armistice on 11 November, the front line in the Somme Sector (for the British the Third and Fourth Army areas) was 30-35 miles east of the final eastward development of the light railways. There was also increasing difficulty supplying the troops by standard gauge railway in the face of the destruction of facilities by the retreating German army. By the end, most railway construction troops were working on standard gauge lines to the east.

Railway units doing light railway work were progressively transferred to standard gauge work. A summary of these for the Somme Sector is shown in Table 8.1. Some returned to light railway work later.

And so, at 11am on 11th November 1918 more than four years of hostilities on the Western Front came to an end. The story of the light railways in the Somme Sector after the First World War is told in the next chapter, and that of the metre gauge railways in Chapters Ten and Eleven.

Table 8.1 Somme Sector
Light railway units, and those doing light railway work, transferred to standard gauge work October and November 1918

Name of unit	Working at	Date of transfer	to	at	work	return to LR work?	details
6th LROC	Tincourt, Omiécourt	2 November	58th (Can) BGOC	Chaulnes	SG operating		
34th LROC	Rocquigny	9 November	58th (Can) BGOC Cambrai		SG operating	7 January 1919	Vox Vrie Farm, Poperinghe
231st LRFC	Lebucquière	28 October	RCE V	Achiet-le-Grand	SG maintenance	23 January 1919	Jenkes Sidings, Souchez took over from 1st TC CE
234th LRFC	(not Known)	3 November	RCC IV	(Cambrai)	SG maintenance	26 January 1919	First Army area (ADLR I)
1st Aus LROC	Lesdain	25 October	ROD	Bergues	SG operating	9 February 1919	Tincourt took over from 13th (Can) LROC
6th CRT (1,2 & 4 Companies)	Roisel	23 October	RCC IV	Roisel	SG construction and maintenance		
13th CRT	Daours	25 August	RCC IV	Henencourt	SG reconstruction and maintenance		
		23 October	RCE V	Somain	SG reconstruction and maintenance		

Chapter Nine

Light railways of the Somme sector 12 Nov 1918 to 1974

Following the Armistice on 11 November 1918 there was some celebration, but work had to continue. The Armies still had to be fed and otherwise supplied.

British Army Standard gauge railways

By the Armistice, the British forces had reached Mons in Belgium. Work was already well in hand to repair destroyed and damaged lines in north east France and in Belgium. Civilian railway staff in France and Belgium were anxious to restart work as soon as possible. Lines in France which had been civilian railways before the war, and in Belgium, were repaired and operated and handed over to the civilian authorities in due course. The process was largely complete by 1 February 1919, when RCE V handed over the line from Valenciennes to the Belgian border at Blanc-Misseron to the French.

British military standard gauge lines

The lines which had been built by the British Army were closed and then taken up. We have few details of this. Any new work in hand was cancelled soon after the Armistice.

In a very few cases, the French authorities considered taking over a line for civilian use. This is said to have been considered for the Authie Valley line and the line on from Courcelles junction to Achiet-le-Grand, to make a new route from Achiet to Doullens. In the end, none of the British military lines were saved. The French did not show any greater enthusiasm for saving their own military lines, which were also closed. Those lines which had been single track before the war but had been doubled either by the French or the British army, all reverted to single track working.

British Army standard gauge liquidation

In December 1918, the French government expressed a wish to buy British railway equipment in northern France, including about 3,000 miles of light railway. The British government was inclined to agree, since it would be cheapest to dispose of the lines *in situ*. However, it was not until May 1919 that the British government set up the British Transport Liquidation Commission (BTLC), based in Paris, with powers to work with an equivalent group in the French government. Another British group, the Disposal Board, based in Whitehall, were by this time negotiating deals with private companies, including the *Compagnie du Nord*, for some large standard gauge installations. The *Ministre des Travaux Publics* (Minister for Public Works, MTP) duly appointed the French Government Commission, but laid down that all disposals must be agreed by them on behalf of the government, even if the disposal was to private parties. By July, the BTLC had decided that they would not deal with 'Decauville track', by which they appeared to mean that they would not consider any 60cm track or related installations or material. The deal reached for light railways is discussed further in the light railway section.

A settlement for the standard gauge railways was not reached until November 1919, when the French agreed to pay 131 million francs (£3.64 million) for the fixed 'broad gauge' (standard and metre gauge) track and some dock installations.

Light railways (60cm gauge) under the British Army 12 November 1918 to Summer 1919

Even though the light railways had to a considerable extent ceased being involved with front line supplies by the end of the war, the light railway units continued to work after the Armistice. There were many army units in the back areas to be supplied, and an increasing amount of salvage work to be done. The light railway headquarters and the central light railway workshops at Beaurainville operated at least until March 1919, and the light railway forward training school at Savy-Berlette until April 1919 (both Arras sector). British Army and captured German steam locomotives were assembled for disposal at Beaurainville.

The light railway units were gradually demobilised. However, seven were still working in the Somme Sector into 1919, one of them at least until May 1919. These are shown in Table 9.1. After the Armistice, operations became concentrated into running from a few main centres. In the Somme Sector, these were around and east from Bapaume, and around and east from Péronne.

By 1 November, when it was clear which way the war was going, ADLR IV had said that light railway lines as far west as Quinconce would be required for salvage of ammunition, RE stores and other materials, and must be maintained under the existing arrangements. Lines west of Quinconce would if necessary be maintained by troops working directly for ADLR IV. Apart from 6th CRT completing the line from Brancourt to Honnechy

Table 9.1 Light Railway units still working in the Somme Sector after the Armistice

Unit	Based at	Sector	Area	date from	until
31st LROC	Bapaume	Somme	Bapaume	12 October 1918	21 December 1918
	Beaumetz Village	Somme	Bapaume	22 December 1918	February 1918
	Beaumetz-lès-Cambrai	Somme	Bapaume	1 March 1919	at least 31 May 1919
232nd LRFC	Marcoing	Somme	Bapaume	10 October 1918	at least 31 January 1919
19th LROC (TCC)	Marcoing	Somme	Bapaume	October 1918	at least January 1919
231st LRFC	Lebucqière, then Vélu	Somme	Bapaume	28 October 1918	21 January 1919 (1)
13th (Can) LROC	Tincourt	Somme	Péronne	11 October 1918	9 February 1919
1st Aus LROC	Tincourt	Somme	Péronne	9 February 1919	21 April 1919
18th LROC (TCC)	Tincourt	Somme	Péronne	21 April 1919	at least May 1919
236th LRFC	Tincourt	Somme	Péronne	15 October 1918	at least December 1918

'at least' = information ends without definite closure or demobilisation of unit
(1) moved to Souchez, First Army area, until June 1919

(Chapter Eight), there was no major new light railway construction by the British Army after the Armistice. ADLR III and ADLR IV continued to work into 1919, probably for as long as there were any light railway operations in their Army area.

Around and east of Bapaume
These lines remained in the Third Army area.

Maintenance
The 232nd LRFC, who had been based at Marcoing since 10 October, continued to maintain the line from Bapaume to Esnes. This was the Y line and the connecting BW line past Havrincourt to Marcoing, and the line beyond Marcoing east to Esnes. They also maintained other lines around these. In late December these had been reduced, but still included substantial lengths of line west and east of Marcoing, and part of the Y3 line north towards Fontaine-Notre-Dame.

Additional tractor drivers were trained at the light railway training school at Savy-Berlette, and by the middle of December, sixteen trained tractor drivers had returned from there. There was much interchange between units at this time. Some men were taken on the strength but remained attached to other light railway companies, but we do not know which ones. Ten men were detached to 31st LROC but returned on 30 November.

The 231st LRFC, who were based at Lebucquière and then Vélu, had been undertaking some standard gauge maintenance since 28 October, repaired the Y line light railway crossing of the Bapaume to Marcoing standard gauge line, which was in bad condition, on 2 December. Further maintenance was undertaken by 231st LRFC in January, on light railways at Bapaume and between Beugny and Frémicourt. On 21 January, they were moved to Souchez, in the First Army area, to take over from the 1st TC CE.

The 232nd LRFC remained at Marcoing. In January 1919, they constructed two spurs at Masnières, and on 23 and 24 January a dump was constructed at Ribécourt, on the BW line, probably for salvage. During January, a small number of men were demobilised, but when the War Diary ends on 31 January there were still 8 Officers and 277 Other Ranks.

Operations
The 31st LROC had been based at Bapaume since 12 October, operating a considerable area, as described in Chapter Eight. They continued to operate the area after the Armistice. Five further controls were closed on 12 November, on the Y and Y3 lines, probably reflecting the decrease in number of trains, which would allow longer distances between controls for single line operating. From 12 November to 30 November, they moved a total of 7744 tons, an average of 407 tons per day, no less than in the weeks before the Armistice. In December, it was 4293 tons, average 165 tons per day on operating days. They had Christmas and Boxing Day off, and from January did not operate on Sundays. They were carrying water, coal, rations, light railway material, RE stores and ammunition, and personnel.

On 22 December, the Company HQ moved from Bapaume to Beaumetz Village control, which was just north of the village, and by 1 March they had moved again a short distance to the Beaumetz-lèz-Cambrai control, just outside the village. There was little change in the pattern of operating. During January, ten men, and during February, fifteen men, were demobilised.

By March, business had increased, to 9557 tons, or 367 tons per day excluding Sundays. Of this, 9 per cent was ammunition, moved to standard gauge rail heads, and 12 per cent RE stores, moved to Bapaume, much of it from Ytres. They were now operating at least the Y5 line from Bapaume to Riencourt, the Y line from Bapaume to Lebuquières, and the Y6 and connecting BW lines from Lebuquières to Ytres. Since they were still based at Beaumetz, and had not closed any more controls, it is likely that they were still operating the Y and BW lines at least to Havrincourt and the Y3 line towards Marcoing.

There was no major change in April or May 1919, and in May they were still mainly moving salvage from collecting points to standard gauge rail heads. The War Diary of 31st LROC closes on 31 May without any further mentions of demobilisations, or of closing down the company. The 19th LROC, who had been reformed from the 19th TCC at Rocquigny in October, were operating from their base at Marcoing from October at least until January 1919.

Around and east of Péronne

These lines remained in the Fourth Army area. On 9 December, on the orders of the Director of Construction at GHQ all maintenance was handed over to ADLR III (Third Army).

Maintenance

On 17 November, No 3 Company of 6th CRT handed over maintenance of the lines from Roisel to Bohain and Honnechy, to various labour companies. A Lieutenant of 6th CRT remained with a small detachment of No 4 Company to supervise this.

By 1 December, the Lieutenant, based at Roisel, was in charge of all Fourth Army light railway maintenance, with attached labour only. On 9 December, orders came from the Director of Construction (GHQ) to hand over all light railway maintenance to ADLR III, with all stores and materials, ending the association of 6th CRT with these lines.

Operations

13th (Can) LROC, who had been at Tincourt since 11 October, continued to operate the lines from Quinconce. When 1st Aus LROC took over on 9 February, 13th (Can) LROC had been operating to Bohain, to Fins (CY and AX lines), to Montigny Farm (DZ), and to Villevecque (DZ, B and part A lines).

On 11 November, 13th (Can) LROC moved 1276 tons of goods, and, on 13 November, 1495 tons. However, later in November, traffic fell off and in the period 12 to 28 November, an average of 520 tons per day was carried. At the end of November, the unit records 'very little doing on light railways at present', but they did receive a letter of appreciation from ADLR IV.

There are no traffic figures for December 1918 and January 1919, but on 1 January they were carrying salvage, ammunition, RE stores, and personnel. On 9 February, 13th (Can) LROC handed over to 1st Aus LROC and on 15 February they moved to Étaples for demobilisation.

1st Aus LROC, who had been at Roulers (now Roeselare) in Belgium operating standard gauge railways, continued to operate the same territory, with two Officers and 174 Other Ranks. Table 9.2 shows the motive units available in February and March 1919, and their distribution within the network served.

Table 9.2 Motive power 1st Aus LROC February and March 1919

	Steam Locomotives				Petrol Tractors		
	Baldwin 4-6-0T	Alco 2-6-2T	Hudson 0-6-0WT	Total	Simplex 20hp	Simplex 40hp	Total
As at 28 February 1919							
Tincourt depot	29	4	4	37	8	1	9
Flamicourt sub-depot	1		4	5			
Bellicourt sub-depot					1	1	2
Montigny Farm sub-depot					3		3
Under overhaul at Beaurainville	1			1			
Awaiting removal to workshops					2		2
Totals	31	4	8	43	14	2	16
Total motive power units							59
As at 31 March 1919							
Tincourt depot	22	3	2	27	5	1	6
Flamicourt sub-depot	3		2	5			
Bellicourt sub-depot					1	1	2
Montigny Farm sub-depot					2		2
Awaiting removal to workshops					1		1
Totals	25	3	4	32	9	2	11
Total motive power units							43

Unfortunately, no numbers are given apart from the Baldwin (WD 501) which was sent to Beaurainville light railway workshops on 26 February. The workshops for petrol tractors were at Bancourt, just east of Bapaume. On 22 March, four Baldwin 4-6-0T locomotives were handed over to Fifth Army (north of Béthune) and on 31 March, thirty class F wagons were sent by standard gauge railway to Fifth Army. The distribution of locomotives also makes it clear, with the sub-depot at Flamicourt (Péronne), that 1st Aus LROC, and probably 13th (Can) LROC before them, were also operating the line from Doingt to Flamicourt, and probably the line from Flamicourt to Montigny Farm via Mons-en-Chaussée. The transhipment at Flamicourt is likely to have been a major collection point for salvage.

The categories of goods carried in February and March 1919 is also informative and is shown in Table 9.3. These figures illustrate that the work of the light railways was far from over at the end of March 1919.

On 21 April, 18th LROC (who had been 18th TCC) arrived and took over operations. On 23 April, 1st Aus LROC left for Roisel, and entrained for Le Havre, for demobilisation at the Australian Base Depot there.

Table 9.3 Goods carried by category, 1st Aus LROC February and March 1919

Category	9 – 28 February 1919	1 – 31 March 1919
(tons unless otherwise stated)		
Personnel (no)	1182	1357
Light railway material	1339	475
Light Railway stores		42
Water	88	661
Coal	589	646
Rations	349	349
RE material	105	184
Ballast		4257
Post		351
YMCA stores		28
Salvaged ammunition	1885	3566
Other salvage	780	4846
Dead steam locomotives (no)		60
Dead petrol tractors (no)		5
Total tons	5937	16827

9.1 Baldwin 4-6-0T WD No. 936 with wagon(s) at Péronne on 25 May 1919. The locomotive is still being operated by British or Dominion troops, probably the 18th LROC (formerly 18th TCC). *(AWM E05127)*

9.2 Baldwin 4-6-0T WD No. 853 crosses a trestle bridge with a central girder section at Péronne on 13 May 1919. There are two open bogie and at least two covered wagons, and a British soldier is sitting on top of one of the open wagons. The bridge is probably that over the Cologne river, and the operating unit probably the 18th LROC. *(AWM E05207)*

There is no further information about the activities of 18th LROC, but a series of photographs taken in Péronne in May 1919 shows the light railways there still being operated by British troops.

British Army Light Railway Liquidation

Following the decision of BTLC not to deal with light railways, they were dealt with separately. On 6 October 1919, the majority of the British light railways in France were sold to the French government for 85 million francs, about £2.4 million. The deal included all laid track east of the N16 (the road from north to south linking Dunkirk, Doullens, Amiens, Creil and Paris), with certain exceptions, and some of the stock at the Central Light Railway Workshops at Beaurainville.

The details were to be coordinated on the British side by the Army Director of Light Railways, who was still in post. Everything sold was to be completely taken over by the French by the end of October, with all liability for rents and land compensation. Some rolling stock, including locomotives and petrol tractors, was included in the deal. The French agreed to give priority, on the systems they had purchased, to the conveyance of British troops, labour companies, and prisoners of war, and their supplies and stores, subject to payment at agreed rates by the British Military Authorities. A further light railway contract was dated 6 November 1919, but we have no details.

Light railways (60cm gauge) under *the Ministère des Régions Libérées* (Ministry for the Liberated Regions, MRL) 1920 to 1923

As early as March 1919, the MRL expressed an interest in retaining as many as possible of the light railways, to help with reconstruction and general rehabilitation. The Minister asked the Chief Engineers of the Somme, Oise and Aisne, and the other involved *départements* to indicate which lines it would be useful to keep open. The Ministry's letter suggests, however, a wish to keep them all. By June, maps had been prepared in Paris showing which parts of the network were to be kept, but we have not seen these for the *départements* in the Somme Sector.

MRL were able to take quick control of lines where the transfer was from the French Army, as in the Oise

9.3 The Rue du Général-Foy at Ham. Reconstruction is being assisted with a 60cm gauge railway line. *(Authors' collection)*

and part of the Aisne *départements*. Some lines around Laon (Aisne) and Châlons-sur-Marne (Marne) were opened at the end of March 1919, and around Verdun (Meuse) in August 1919. However, the former British lines in Somme, northern Aisne and Pas-de-Calais had to wait for the contract described above.

Following the formal transfer of the former British lines in October 1919, MRL issued provisional instructions in November for the regulation of these lines. Despite subsequent disagreements about the contracts, MRL did take over and run these lines, in the Somme and Pas-de Calais *départements*, with operations beginning in January 1920, run on a departmental basis.

A good example of the use of these lines for reconstruction is provided by the application in September 1920 by an entrepreneur to occupy, for warehousing, 1018m2 of land belonging to the state adjacent to the N17 at La Chapelette, just south of Péronne. He had been awarded the contract, by Régions Libérées for the Péronne sector, for clearing rubble from seven villages, the construction of 1,000 semi-permanent houses, and the final reconstruction of the communes of Manancourt and Étricourt. A plan shows the warehouse area at La Chapelette, with the light railways, and the site of the 'Camp Anglais' and the 'Dépôt Anglais'. The line here connected around Péronne with the line north to Manancourt and Étricourt.

Description of the Network

It has been estimated that at the end of the First World War there were 300km (186 miles) of 60cm gauge light railways in the east of the Somme *département* alone. The number of kilometres operated by MRL in the Somme Sector *départements* as at 31 December from 1919 to 1923 was:

	HQ Office	1919	1921	1922	1923
Aisne	Soissons, St-Quentin	274	112	99	99
Oise	Compiègne (administrative) Noyon (Technical)	194	159	167	2
Somme	Péronne		123	132	83
Pas-de-Calais	Arras		479	484	268

There were no MRL lines in Somme or Pas-de-Calais in 1919 because the contracts with the British authorities were not concluded until late that year.

Light railways in the Somme Sector as they probably were in the period 1921 to 1922 are shown in Figure 9.1.

Light railways of the Somme sector 12 Nov 1918 to 1974

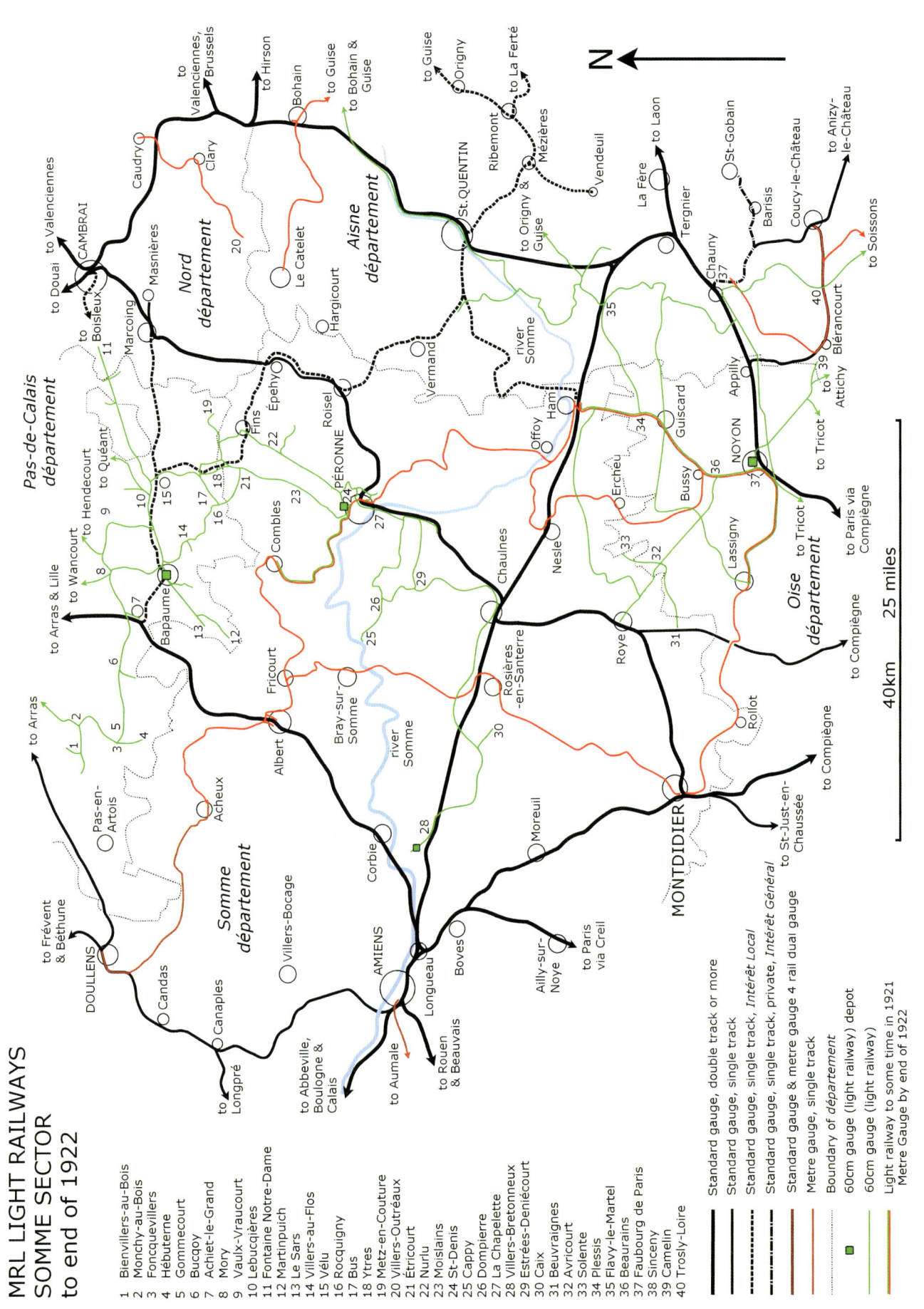

Figure 9.1

Pas-de-Calais network

Most of the extensive network in the Pas-de-Calais *département* is outside the area of this book, but we have included the lines in the southern Pas-de-Calais, based on the Bapaume depot, because they are in the Somme Sector as defined in this book. Some of these lines had closed by 1923, and all by the end of 1925. There were two connections south to the Somme network, one from the end of the former Y5 extension at Rocquigny to Étricourt, and then south to Péronne. This connection was probably closed in 1923, and certainly by the end of 1925. The second connection was from Ytres through Fins onto the former AX line to Péronne. This connection was closed by the end of 1923, probably with the section from Fins to Nurlu in the Somme network.

Somme network

Although it is known that British Light Railway units were operating the lines east and south east of Péronne until at least May 1919, by 1923 all lines east and south east of Péronne had gone. North of Péronne, the former AX line to Fins remained. There was also a spur east to Liéramont. Straight north from Péronne was a line to Étricourt. This followed the British Army line of early 1918 to Allaines, which had been extended, probably by the French, to Moislains, and then most likely along the alignment of the British Army standard gauge Tortille Valley line from Moislains to Étricourt. From Étricourt it followed former British light railways to Rocquigny, forming the second Pas-de-Calais connection, and on to Sailly-Saillisel, probably using the former British yard called Le Transloy, on the road north of Sailly. It also used former British lines north to Ytres Yard on the Vélu to St-Quentin standard gauge railway, and on from there to Ruyaulcourt on the Canal du Nord.

South and west from Péronne were lines to Cappy, and on to Froissy, and to Chaulnes via Estrées-Deniécourt. These all started from Péronne-Flamicourt standard gauge station, via La Chapelette. The two lines were linked from Herbécourt to Estrées-Deniécourt, and there were a number of branches south from them. Chaulnes was linked to Villers-Bretonneux by a line via Lihons, Harbonnières, Caix and Aubercourt, with a stub to Demuin. The Villers end of this, from Cayeux to Villers, had been added by the French at some time after summer 1918. The French had also completed the abandoned British plan of August 1918 and extended the light railway from Villers to Vecquemont on the Amiens to Arras main line. Most of the other lines were originally French lines, rebuilt by the British army in 1917 and 1918, and perhaps also by the German army in 1918.

During the First World War, much of the formation of the metre gauge line from Albert to Péronne and on to Ham had been used for light railway construction. At first, the light railway provided the whole service from Albert, which would have required some new track near Albert where the former British lines had been taken up. Later parts were used as the metre gauge reconstruction progressed. More information about this is given in Chapter Ten in relation to the reopening of the metre gauge line.

Oise network

The Oise network was based around Montdidier but had substantial parts in the Somme *département*. In the early involvement of MRL these may have had a connection with the Somme network north from Ham to the former B line near Beauvois, still being operated by British units at least until April 1919. However, any connection was soon lost, but the lines in southern Somme retained the Noyon connection so they were considered part of the Oise network. The principal line in this category was from Ham to Roye (Somme), and then on to Montdidier.

The path of the metre gauge line to Noyon, south from Ham, had been used for a light railway by the British Army in March 1918. By the end of the war in November, the French had used the rest of the formation to Noyon as a light railway track. More information about this is given in Chapter Eleven in relation to the reopening of the metre gauge line.

The line from Noyon to Roye (Somme) went to the Faubourg de Paris, and then probably followed the metre gauge path, to just north of the main road from Noyon to Roye. We do not know where it crossed the Canal du Nord, still under construction, but it followed very roughly the line of the main road to Roye. On the way, it was crossed by another north east to south west lateral line, definitely of French origin, and at Avricourt there were branches to Beuvraignes, on the Compiègne to Roye standard gauge line, and to Solentes. South and west of Noyon takes the Oise lines out of our area.

By 1923, only 2km of MRL light railway remained of the Oise network. This was the short section from Noyon main station to the metre gauge lines at Faubourg de Paris, on which the shuttle service had been replaced by road vehicles with the closure of the Noyon depot at the end of 1922. However, some of the linked lines between the Oise and the Somme *départements* must have remained open, becoming part of the Roye sugar beet network later in the 1920s. There were other sugar beet lines further south in the Oise *département*, outside the area of this book.

Aisne network

The line to Camelin went south east from the area of Noyon station. Camelin is near Blérancourt and was on the pre-war metre gauge line from Chauny to Soissons and to Coucy-le-Château, and on the wartime French military standard gauge line from Apilly to Coucy. The first part of the line probably followed the pre-war industrial metre gauge branch from Noyon station to the bridge at Le Jonquoy. After the branch to Camelin, the line continued to Cuts and Attichy.

East from the Oise canal at Le Jonquoy, the British line of March 1918 was used, then the former French lines to Chauny, in the Aisne *département*. From Chauny, a line went south to Trosly-Loire and Soissons, with connections to the rest of the southern Aisne network. From Abbécourt, on the Oise canal south west of Chauny, the former French and at one time British army A line wound its way north to Flavy-le-Martel, on the main standard gauge line from Amiens to Tergnier. From Flavy a line to Plessis, on the Noyon to Ham line, linked the northern Aisne network to Ham.

East of Flavy were connections east and north to St-Quentin and Bohain, and further east to Guise. However, even though British army units were still operating from Roisel to Bohain in April 1919, nothing remained of this line by 1921. Much of the path used was that of the metre gauge lines from Roisel to Hargicourt, from St-Quentin to Caudry, and from Le Catelet to Guise, which were now being reconstructed (see Chapter Eleven).

Rolling stock

Steam locomotives and petrol and diesel tractors were former military stock from the various armies. In the Pas-de-Calais and Somme *départements*, many of these were former British army locomotives. The British army had shipped some back to the UK but had then sold many in France. In other areas, more were of French origin, particularly the 0-6-0T Decauville type, but the French Army kept much rolling stock for future military use. Captured German locomotives were also used, mainly of the 0-8-0T *Feldbahn* type.

Wagons were also mainly former military stock. Later the American Pershing wagons were found particularly useful for sugar beet transportation. Passenger carriages were locally modified covered bogie wagons or built on the chassis of open bogie wagons. Probably some were fairly rough and ready.

Depots and Workshops

At the end of the war, the French authorities took over a major German army light railway depot and workshops at Haubourdin, on the south west edge of Lille, in the Nord *département*. This had been the German centre for light railway operations in the north-eastern Pas-de-Calais. When the need for regional light railway centres for major repairs and maintenance was recognised, it was quickly realised that the Lille area this was not central enough, so the centre was built at Les Hochettes, in the Baudimont district of Arras, at the junction of the lines into Arras. The other two regional centres were at Noyon in the Oise *département*, and at La Maltournée, near Châlons-sur-Marne, south east of Reims in the Marne *département*.

We do not know the location of the Noyon centre, but it may have been on or near the site of the metre gauge depot established after the First World War, west of Noyon station towards Faubourg-de-Paris. We know more about the Arras centre. The decision to build was made in September 1920, and the centre opened in June 1921. When it opened the Director was directly accountable to MRL in Paris. This enormous repair shop covered 4 hectares, and 13,000m^2 was roofed, with most of the repair lines raised above floor level for access.

There was also a workshop at Péronne, in the Somme *département*. The passenger services from Péronne generally started from Péronne (Flamicourt), the main standard gauge station. However, the services to Fins, and to Combles, came from St-Denis in the morning and went back there at night. St-Denis is on the north edge of Péronne, in the area where the British Army light railway yards at Le Quinconce had been, and it is likely that this was the site of the main depot and workshops. The locomotives for services going in other directions from Péronne may have travelled light to and from St-Denis. There was also an operating depot at Villers-Bretonneux.

La Maltournée was closed in January 1922, and the work and some of the equipment went to Arras. With the closure of the Noyon centre at the end of 1922, the Arras centre also took the work for the Oise and Aisne *départements*. They were now doing the work for seven *départements*, the whole of the MRL 60cm gauge network. With the leasing of the lines in each *département* from 1924, MRL decided on closure of the regional centre at Arras at the end of 1923. The equipment was liquidated, some going to other French state services.

Passenger Services

A considerable number of passenger services were run between 1920 and 1927, mainly between 1921 and 1923. Details of the times and routes were constantly varying according to reconstruction in the areas served. The lines served by passenger services are shown on Figure 9.2, which shows stops on these lines, and distances. Estimated distances are shown in brackets.

Stations and other stops

In the 1919 MRL regulations, there was an elaborate classification of stops, with the rules for use of them. In practice, matters were not so clear cut. On some published timetables all the stops were under the single

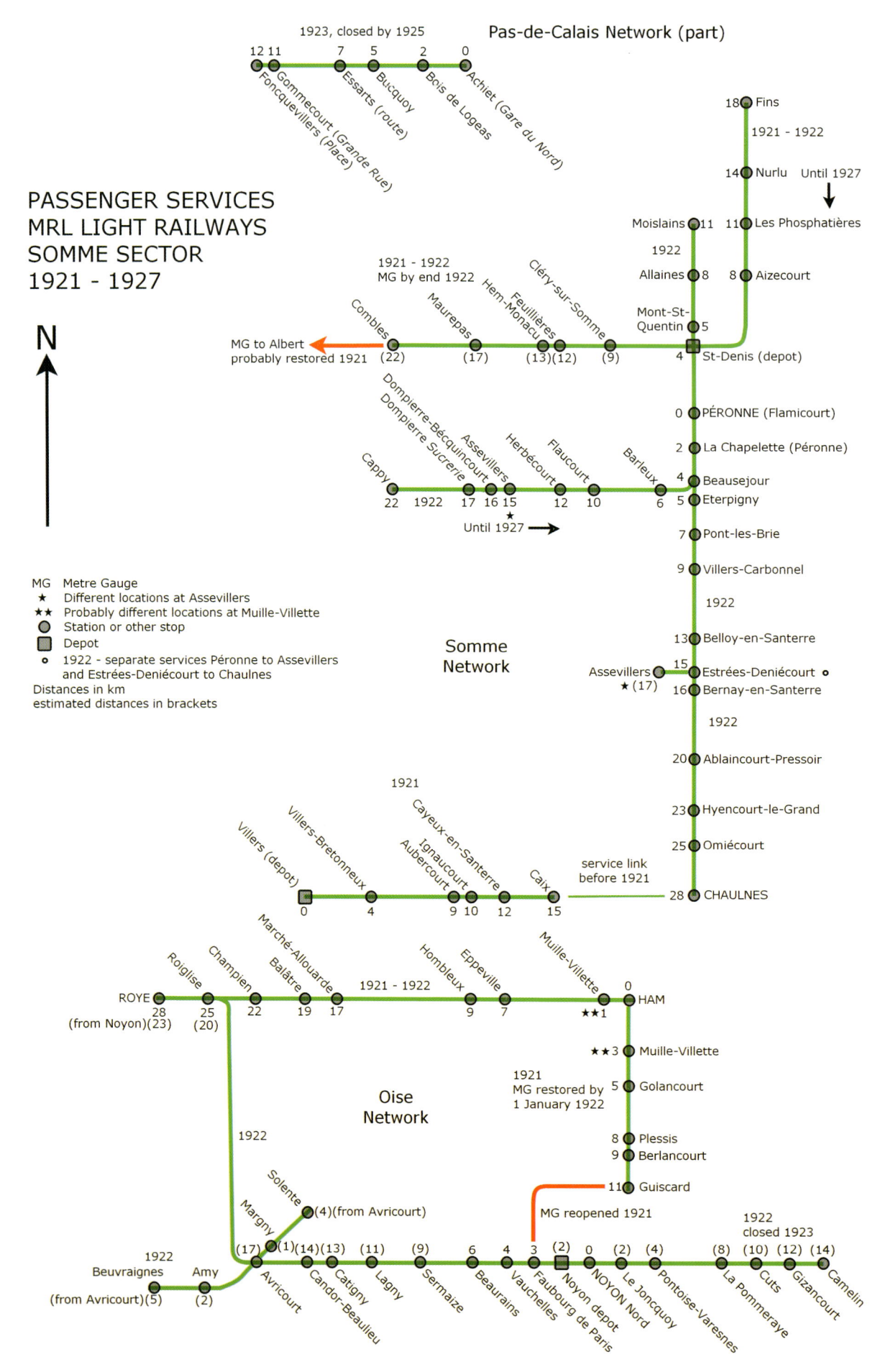

Figure 9.2

heading 'Stations', and on others were not classified at all. The location of some stops is difficult to identify precisely.

Passenger operations

Some passenger timetables of 1921, 1922 and 1927 are available. Many of these are marked that the connections with *Compagnie du Nord* trains is not guaranteed, and that the number of places on the train is limited. Many of the services start and end for the day at the location which is remote from the base depot. A train set may have been stabled at the remote location, but many of these services were less than daily. It is more likely that the set ran empty from the depot to the location. More details of the services on these lines are given in Table 9.4. The adult fare was 11 cents per kilometre.

Pas-de-Calais network – There was a considerable network of passenger services around Arras. The only one included here is the isolated service from Achiet-le-Grand to Foncquevillers, based on the Bapaume depot.

Somme network – The service between Villers-Bretonneux and Caix had at some time before June 1921 run on to and from Chaulnes. It also served Harbonnières, Vauvillers and Lihon. At Chaulnes there would have been a connection with the service there from Pèronne (Flamicourt), if the two services had been running at the same time.

The service from Péronne which had run to Fins in November 1922 only ran to Nurlu in June 1927. The service which in November 1922 ran between Péronne and Moislains had at some time previously run through to Étricourt. This suggests that the link

9.4 The *Route Nationale* at Nurlu, with the light railway station and shelter, after the First World War. Postcard postmarked 1922. *(Authors' collection)*

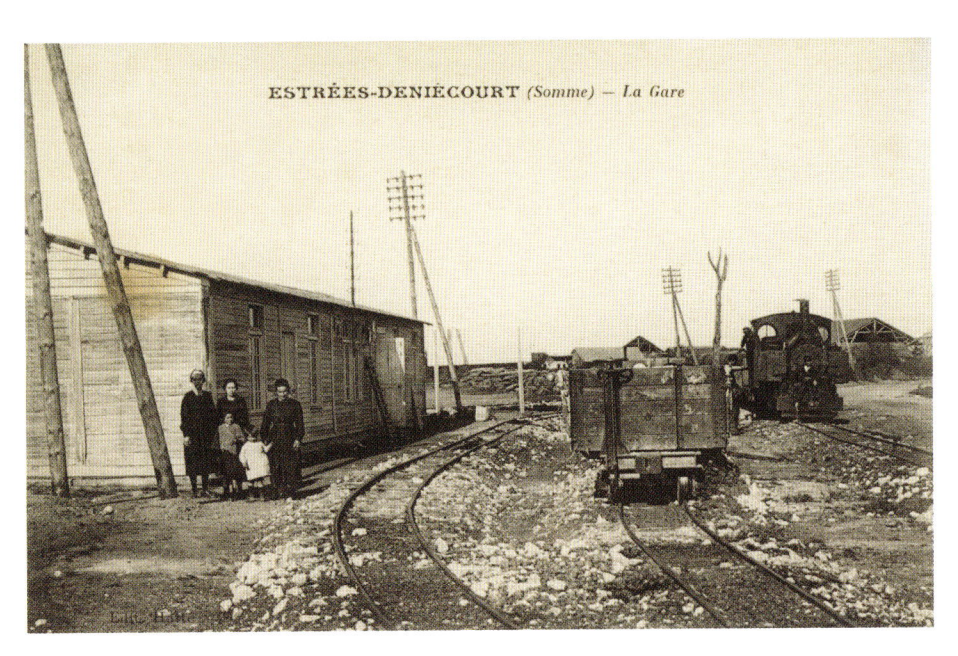

9.5 The station at Estrées-Deniécourt, on the line from Péronne to Chaulnes, when operated by the MRL. On the right are a former British Army bogie wagon, and a Baldwin tank locomotive, probably a former British Army 4-6-0T. *(Collection APPEVA)*

Table 9.4 Passenger services on the MRL Somme Oise and southern Pas-de-Calais lines 1921–1927

Département	Service from	to	Based on (depot)	Frequency	date	outward depart	arrive	return depart	arrive
Pas-de-Calais	Achiet (Gare du Nord)	Foncquevillers (Place)	Bapaume	Three times daily	1 Aug 1923 (closed 1925)	04.50 08.40 18.30	05.50 09.40 19.30	06.05 09.50 19.40	07.05 10.50 20.40
Somme	Villers-Bretonneux	Caix (Chaulnes)	Villers	Thursdays and Saturdays	Jun 1921 & 1 Jul 1921 (closed 1922)	04.35 08.25(1) 11.10(2) 17.05(1)	06.11 09.59 12.57 19.02	06.20 13.25 19.12(1)	08.21 15.45 21.05
Somme	Péronne (Flamicourt) (using metre gauge path to Albert - see chapter ten)	Combles	St-Denis (Péronne)	Wednesdays and Saturdays only	1921 & 1922	06.02(3) 15.05	07.50 17.20	08.20 17.40	10.40 19.25(3)
Somme	Péronne (Flamicourt)	Fins	St-Denis (Péronne)	Thursdays and Saturdays only	Jun 1921	15.15	16.50	08.04	09.30
				Thursdays and Saturdays only	1 Jul 1921	06.15(3) 15.15(4)	07.30 16.48	08.04 17.00	09.30(4) 18.15(3)
				Wednesdays and Saturdays only	Nov 1922	06.15(3) 15.15(4)	07.30 16.48	08.04 17.00	09.30(4) 18.15(3)
	Péronne (Flamicourt)	Nurlu	Péronne (St-Denis ?)	Saturdays only	Jun 1927 (closed later 1927)	15.15	16.30	08.27	09.30
Somme	Moislains	Péronne (Flamicourt)	Péronne (St-Denis ?)	Saturday only	Nov 1922	08.21	09.20	15.25	16.22
Somme	Cappy	Péronne (Flamicourt)	Péronne (St-Denis ?)	Saturdays only	Nov 1922	07.30	09.24	15.12	17.00
Somme	Dompierre-Sucrerie	Péronne (Flamicourt)	Péronne (St-Denis ?)	Saturdays only	Jun 1927 (closed later 1927)	07.50	09.34	15.12	16.38
Somme	(5)Asseviliers	Chaulnes	Péronne (St-Denis ?)	Saturdays only	Nov 1922 Estrées-Deniécourt	07.40 08.00	09.05	16.10	17.33 17.18
	(5)Estrées-Deniécourt	Péronne (Flamicourt)	Péronne (St-Denis ?)	Saturdays only	Nov 1922	08.10	08.40	15.02	16.30

Light railways of the Somme sector 12 Nov 1918 to 1974

Somme	Péronne (Flamicourt)	Estrées-Deniécourt/Belloy-en-Santerre(6)	Saturdays only	1922	06.21	07.55	08.15	09.40
		Péronne (St-Denis ?)			15.02	16.24	16.40	18.00
Oise	Ham	Roye (Somme)	Fridays only	1 Jul 1921	05.21	08.15	12.20	15.00
			Fridays only	1922	05.21	08.15	12.20	15.00
			Saturdays only	1922	11.35	14.27	06.03	08.54
Oise	Camelin	Noyon (Nord)	Twice daily	1 Jul 1921	06.55	08.05	09.00 (7)	10.07
			3rd on Saturdays		13.10	14.17	11.30 (7)(1)	12.37
					15.10 (1)	16.17	19.15 (7)	20.20
Oise	Camelin	Noyon (Nord)	Twice daily	Nov 1922 (closed 1923)	06.55	08.05	11.20	12.40
					15.19	16.20	19.15	20.25
Oise	Roye	Noyon	Once daily	Nov 1922 Avricourt	06.00	08.15	15.20	17.40
					06.42		16.50	
Oise	Solente	Beuvraignes	Once daily	Nov 1922 Avricourt	06.05	07.40	16.00	17.40
		Noyon			arr 06.35	dep 06.50	arr 16.50	dep 17.00

(1) Saturdays only (2) Thursdays only
(3) from or to St-Denis rather than Péronne (Flamicourt)
(4) does not stop at St-Denis
(5) on one table as Péronne-Flamicourt to Chaulnes
(6) to Estrées, comes back from Belloy
(7) From Noyon depot 30 minutes before

Note – Saturday market day in Péronne and Noyon, Friday market day in Roye (Somme)

to the Pas-de-Calais network through Étricourt had closed by November 1922.

Two services, from Péronne to Assevillers and from Estrées-Deniécourt to Chaulnes, are in one table headed 'Péronne-Flamicourt à Chaulnes'. In fact, the services connected at Estrées-Deniécourt, as shown in Figure 9.2 and Table 9.4. There were two stops called Assevillers, one in the village, and the other north on the road to Herbécourt where the line to Dompierre and Cappy turned west from the road. Both are shown in Figure 9.2. On one timetable for some time in 1922 the service from Péronne went to Estrées-Deniécourt, but returned from Belloy-en-Santerre, one stop back towards Péronne. This may just be a mistake on the timetable.

On the former metre gauge line from Albert to Péronne, a 60cm gauge service was started from Péronne to Albert via Combles in 1921, then progressively changed to metre gauge by 1922.

The last two light railway passenger services in the Somme Sector, from Péronne to Nurlu and to Dompierre *sucrerie*, were still open in June 1927, but closed later in 1927.

Oise network – The service from Ham to Roye was entirely in the Somme *département*, but was linked to the Oise network and not the Somme network. The service from Roye to Noyon was crossed at Avricourt by the service from Solentes to Beuvraignes, on the standard gauge line from Compiègne to Roye. The connecting times at Avricourt are shown in Table 9.4.

For the service from Noyon to Camelin, the train started from Noyon depot, where the train could be boarded in July 1921, but not in November 1922. This line was linked with the line from Noyon main line station to the Faubourg de Paris, with the location of the depot between, and on to Roye. We have not included the Oise services from Ressons-sur-Matz to Thourotte and to Tricot, which are outside the area of interest of this book.

From 1920, the 60cm line using the metre gauge formation provided the service from Noyon to Ham via Guiscard, and Noyon to Roye-sur-Matz via Lassigny, until the metre gauge service was restored in 1921. However, in 1921, these two lines met at Faubourg de Paris in Noyon, but the service from there to Noyon standard gauge station was provided by a 60cm gauge shuttle (see Chapter Eleven, Tables 11.1 and 11.2). This was linked to the Noyon to Camelin service. Both had closed by 1923, with the closure of the Noyon light railway depot. After that the connection was provided by road vehicles until the metre gauge lines returned to Noyon main line station area in 1925.

Aisne network – Because of a quicker approach to reconstruction, passenger services in Aisne disappeared in 1921 or 1922. We have not found any timetables for these services. Part of the southern Aisne network towards Laon consisted of lines constructed by the German Army to support the front along the *Chemin des Dames*. Part of the path of these was used after the war to establish a railway along the valley of the Ailette. This is only worthy of mention because the only photograph we know of showing a 60cm gauge passenger service was taken on this line in 1922.

Light railways (60cm gauge) under the *Société de la Voie de 60* 1924 to 1927

As early as 1922, MRL had wanted to cede some commercially viable lines to private concerns. By the

9.6 A Decauville 0-6-0T locomotive hauls a passenger train at Craindelain, on the line in the Valley of the Ailette, in 1922. *(Authors' collection)*

end of 1923, only 83km (52 miles) of light railway remained in the Somme *département*. From 1 January 1924, these lines were transferred to the *Société de la Voie de 60*, founded by a group of sugar manufacturers, and possibly other private companies. Many local industries, such as *sucreries* and *râperies*, quarries and brickworks, were connected with branch lines.

Also, on 1 January 1924 a private company took over the remaining lines in the Pas-de-Calais *département*. This company was the *Société des chemins de fer à voie de 0.60 du Pas-de-Calais*, a different but possibly related company.

The Sugar beet networks 1926 - 1974
Pas-de-Calais département

At the end of 1925, all light railway lines remaining in the Pas-de-Calais *département* were closed, except for those taken over by the *Société des chemins de fer à voie de 0.60*. This was, we think, yet another different company with a confusingly similar name. This company was mostly owned by the two principal sugar manufacturers in the eastern Pas-de-Calais, the *Société des sucreries et raffineries F. Béghin*, of Thumeries, and the *Société anonyme de la Sucrerie Centrale de Cambrai*. They took over the group of lines in the Vis-en-Artois area south east of Arras, fully described in *Narrow Gauge in the Arras Sector* (2015).

The Aisne département

When the metre gauge line from Coucy-le-Château was finally closed on 15 January 1948, part of the trackbed was used by the Ternynck *sucrerie*. They installed 60cm gauge track from their collection point at Montécouvé to their factory at Nogent-sous-Coucy. This operated until the beginning of the 1960s.

All but one of the twelve locomotives were of First World War military origin. There was one 4-6-0T Baldwin, formerly British Army, six 0-8-0T Orenstein & Koppel locomotives of *Deutsche Feldbahn* (DFB) type, and four later Franco-Belge 0-8-0 tender locomotives of similar type. The twelfth was an 0-6-2T from Decauville. For the present location of the survivors see Chapter Twelve.

Somme and Oise départements
The Roye network

The sugar factory (*sucrerie*) at Roye (Somme) has been active in various forms since 1831, and is still in production as part of the Saint Louis Sucre group, now owned by Südzucker of Germany.

As we have described in previous sections, Roye was on the lines from Ham to Montdidier and from Noyon to Roye, with passenger services until 1922. No doubt the Roye *sucrerie* used these lines to bring sugar beet into the factory. Maps of the 1930s show that a network remained around Roye, extending into the Oise *département*. We know very little about this network. It is likely that the sugar factory company took it over from 1 January 1927, when the Dompierre network was similarly transferred (see next section). We do not know when it closed.

The Dompierre network

The *sucrerie* at Dompierre-Bécquincourt, originally founded about 1881, was completely destroyed in the First World War. It was reconstructed and reopened in 1922 as the *Sucrerie Centrale de Santerre*.

There is no doubt that the Dompierre *sucrerie* was one of the users of the light railways in the area from 1922

9.7 The cross roads by the sugar factory at Dompierre in the 1930s. with four bogie wagons standing on the light railway. The nearest retains its British Army WD number. *(Collection APPEVA)*

Narrow Gauge in the Somme Sector

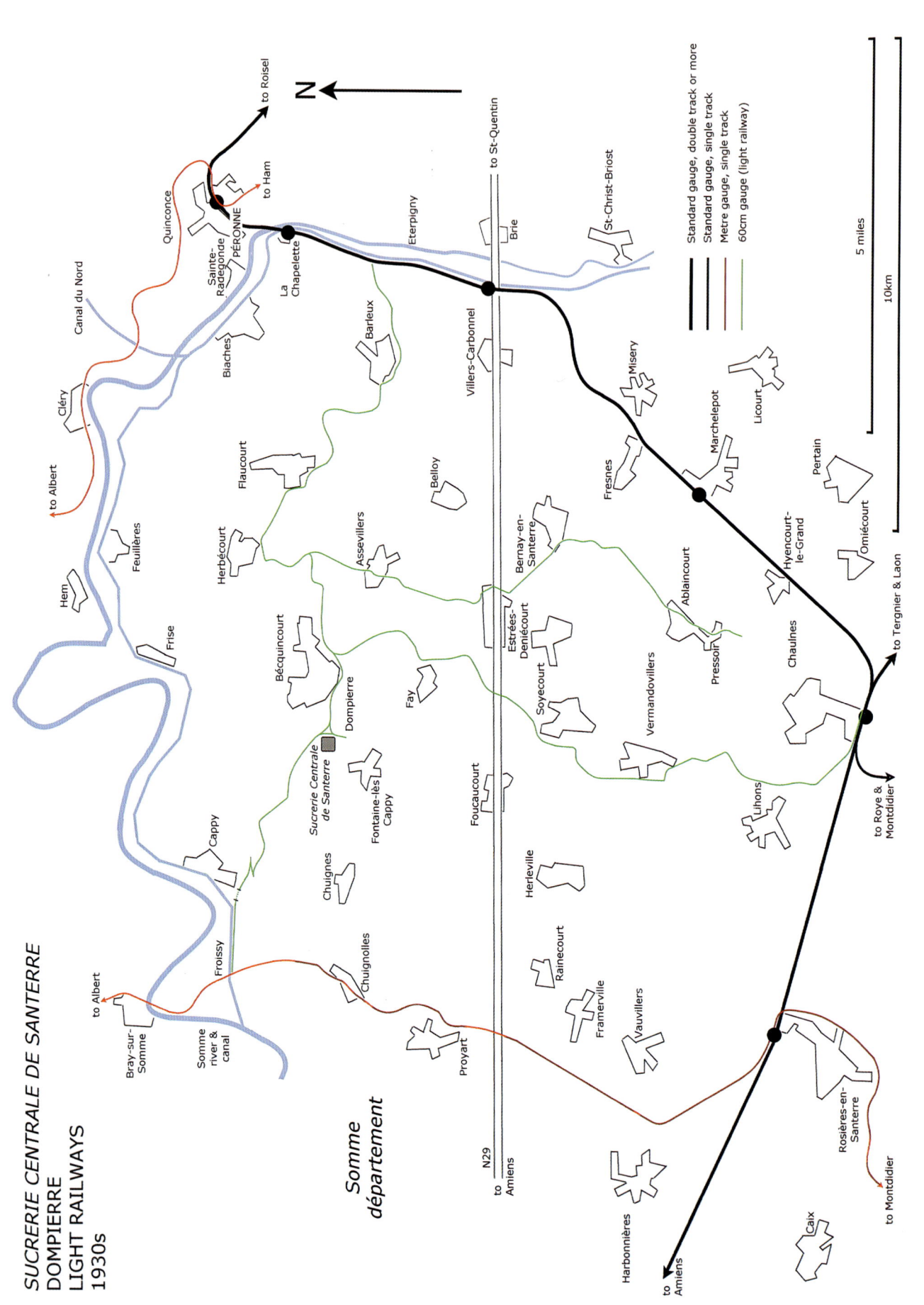

Figure 9.3

and was one of the companies who formed the *Société de la Voie de 60*, who took over the lines from 1 January 1924. In 1927 the network around Dompierre was bought by the *Sucrerie Centrale de Santerre*. The network is shown as in the 1930s in Figure 9.3. The two main lines from the factory were to Chaulnes and to Cappy Port.

The line to Chaulnes is said to have been constructed in 1930 using a different route from that of the network of 1921 and 1922 (Figure 9.1, page 181). Part of the other route to Chaulnes, as far as Pressoir, remained. In addition to collecting sugar beet, the line from Chaulnes was used to supply the *sucrerie* with coal and other requirements. The route of the line to Cappy and Cappy Port was altered in 1927 to avoid the village of Cappy. A tunnel 263m (288 yards) long was built, probably by the Cousot Company who owned the local stone quarry, and a double reverse line (zig-zag) was constructed to gain height onto the plateau. The line to Cappy Port was mainly used to take the produce of the factory to the Somme canal to load onto barges.

Steam was used initially for motive power. In 1942, the company introduced two locomotives built in 1941 by the *Société de Construction Ferroviaries et Navales* (Coferna), one with a 200hp Tatra air-cooled diesel engine, and the other with a 180hp water-cooled Iveco diesel engine. These were followed in 1946 by three Plymouth tractors, bringing the use of steam locomotives to an end. By the early 1950s road transport was becoming the predominant method of bringing sugar beet to the factory. In 1954 the network was dismantled, except for the line to Cappy Port, used for products for shipment until 1973, when it also gave way to road transport. The Dompierre *sucrerie* closed in 1988.

Chemin de Fer Froissy Cappy Dompierre - APPEVA 1970 to present

In 1970 a group of enthusiasts founded the *Association Picarde pour la Préservation et l'Entretien des Véhicules Anciens (APPEVA)*. In 1970 and 1971 they relaid the 1.5km (1 mile) of track from Froissy to Cappy port, which had been taken up, probably in the 1930s. This was rebuilt with First World War rails, but further away from the canal side than the original line. They also set about establishing a base and station near the Froissy end of the line. This is not the site of the First World War French and later British yard at Froissy, which was south west round the corner of the hill.

In 1974, APPEVA bought the line from Cappy Port to Dompierre, which they refurbished and then reopened. They also purchased some rolling stock. The *Chemin de Fer Froissy-Cappy-Dompierre* (CFCD), also known as the *P'tit Train de la Haute Somme*, is now the most important site in France for those interested in 60cm gauge railways, and especially those of the First World War (see Chapter Twelve).

9.8 The arrival of a train of wagons at Cappy Port on the Somme Canal in 1970. The wagons contain sugar from the Dompierre factory to be loaded onto the waiting barge. The train is hauled by a Coferna diesel locomotive, of which CFCD still has two in working order. *(Collection APPEVA)*

Chapter Ten

The metre gauge railways of the Somme département *12 November 1918 to 1955*

The eastern Somme network 1919 to 1929

After the First World War, much reconstruction was needed, especially on the lines around Albert. The eastern Somme network of metre gauge lines based on Albert continued to be run by the *Société Générale des Chemins de Fer Économiques* (SE). The lines mostly reopened between 1919 and 1921, except for Albert to Ham and the branch to Ercheu which were the most damaged. Albert to Péronne was not fully reopened until later 1922. The final war damages for the line from Ercheu to Bussy were not settled until 1931, and this was probably the timescale for the other lines too.

Doullens to Albert

This line remained operational from Gézaincourt to Acheux throughout the First World War. The dual gauge section from Gézaincourt to Doullens was probably converted to standard gauge only with the doubling of the line from Doullens to Amiens during the War. The section from Acheux to Aveluy had been converted back to metre gauge by March 1918 but was then again cut by the front line until late August 1918, with further damage.

A timetable, probably of 1922, indicates two locomotives and train sets based at Acheux, circulating between Gézaincourt and Albert. This provided two services each way per day along the whole line between these stations, with one additional service each way from Acheux to Albert and from Acheux to Gézaincourt. To get to Doullens it was necessary to change at Gézaincourt to the standard gauge line. The service to and from Doullens was subsequently restored, with the replacement or repair of the dual gauge section. This probably accompanied the conversion back to single track of the standard gauge line.

Albert to Péronne and Ham

The line from Albert had been used as far as Trones Wood, between Montauban and Guillemont, in late 1916 and in 1917, but was damaged and probably demolished during the German occupation from April to August 1918. Part of the path, from south of Maurepas to Péronne-Flamicourt station, had been used by the British Army for the standard gauge line from Maricourt. There was a parallel 60cm gauge line, which used the formation towards Albert as far as Combles. Operations on the standard gauge line from Maricourt to Péronne were abandoned on 24 October 1918, and the line was probably demolished soon after.

A timetable, probably of 1921 or 1922, shows a service from between Péronne-Flamicourt and Combles, on Wednesdays and Saturdays only. This ran in the morning from St-Denis to Combles, then back to Péronne, and in the evening from Péronne to Combles and back to St-Denis (see Chapter Nine, Table 9.5, and figure 9.2). St-Denis was the site of the main 60cm depot and workshops. The journey time from Péronne was 2 hours and 15 or 20 minutes, compared with the 1914 service which took 49 to 60 minutes. There can be no doubt that this was a 60cm gauge service. The stop at St-Denis, was not on the site of the metre gauge halt at Le Quinconce, but further north. The trains did not serve the halt at Porte-de-Bretagne.

In the other direction, the 1921 or 1922 timetable shows a service twice daily in each direction every day between Péronne-Flamicourt and the *arrêt* at Matigny, one stop short of Offoy. Even though it took longer than in 1914, by 25 to 44 minutes, this was almost certainly a metre gauge service, because there had never been a 60cm gauge line along the formation from Péronne further than Mons-en-Chaussée. The fact that the line stopped at Matigny meant that one or both of the Somme river and canal bridges between there and Offoy had not yet been repaired.

It is said that the metre gauge service had been restored along the whole length of the line by the end of 1922. Certainly, this was so by the timetable of February 1933.

Albert to Montdidier and Rollot

We have few details about the reopening of this line. We know that it was open from Montdidier to Rosières-en-Santerre by September 1921, and it was probably open over the whole length by 1922, with at least two services each way per day. The full story of the temporary takeover by SE of the service from Montdidier to Lassigny in 1921, and later more permanently from Montdidier to Rollot, is in Chapter Eleven.

The metre gauge railways of the Somme département 12 November 1918 to 1955

10.1 The Avenue de la Gare at Péronne in 1919, looking across the temporary bridge over the Cologne river to the wrecked station. The sign on the right is in English, and the part that can be read says 'Dead Slow All Traffic Tank Bridge'. *(Authors' collection)*

10.2 Not quite the same view in October 2016. *(Authors)*

Offoy to Ercheu and Ercheu to Bussy

In February 1919, SE proposed to the *Préfet* of Oise, that they should reconstruct the line from Ercheu to Bussy. By April, SE had signed an agreement with the *Préfet*. The line may have opened on 1 October 1920, and was certainly running by September 1921, and probably by that time between Offoy and Ercheu as well.

Bridges

See Table 2.5 in Chapter Two for the major bridges before 1914. All of these had been destroyed, often more than once, during the First World War, and many had been rebuilt, again often more than once, for military use. Now all needed definitive reconstruction for the reopening of these lines.

Albert

Before the First World War, the bridge over the standard gauge lines from Amiens to Arras, 0.75km (1/2 mile) north of Albert station, had carried the metre gauge line to Fricourt, Ham and Montdidier. With the changes at Albert station (see below), the bridge had to carry the line from Doullens into the new station east of the main station but continue to allow access to the metre gauge facilities on the west side. We do not know how the bridge was reconstructed to achieve this, but the old oblique bridge would not have allowed the necessary east side access.

Montdidier

At Montidier, a bridge was constructed to carry the metre gauge line over the standard gauge line from

193

Montdidier to Roye, where previously there had been a crossing on the level.

Offoy to Ercheu and Ercheu to Bussy
As noted in Chapter Two, construction of the Canal du Nord from Noyon to the Somme canal south of Péronne had started before the First World War, and had reached a stage when bridges were required for the lines from Offoy to Ercheu (at Rouy-le-Petit) and from Bussy to Ercheu (between Haudival and Béhancourt). They were reconstructed as before, similar to the Somme Canal bridge between Matigny and Offoy, of lattice girder type with brick abutments.

Stations and other stops
Most of the stations were rebuilt as they had been before 1914.

Albert
After the First World War, a new passenger station was built at Albert, on the east side of the main standard gauge station of the line from Amiens to Arras. Other facilities remained on the west side of the station.

10.3 Mailly-Maillet station, on the line from Doullens to Albert, under reconstruction in 1919. *(Authors' collection)*

10.4 The station at Proyart on the line from Albert to Montdidier. No date, but the new hut behind, the building materials on the goods platform, and the state of the tree behind left, all suggest rebuilding shortly after the First World War. *(Authors' collection)*

10.5 The ruins of the station at Albert shortly after the First World War, with temporary buildings. A metre gauge line and rolling stock can be seen on the right. *(Authors' collection)*

Ham

At Ham up to 1914, the terminus of the metre gauge line from Albert had been on the south side of the standard gauge lines (Figure 2.5, Chapter Two). After the First World War, both the line from Albert and the line from St-Quentin had termini on the north side of the main lines. The layout from about 1930 is shown in Figure 10.1. The metre gauge line from Noyon (see Chapter Eleven) came in to a short track south of the main line and west of the level crossing. West of this there was, by 1932 and probably from about 1930, a crossing on the level of the main lines, to give access to the goods and turning facilities on the north side.

Depots

The main depot and workshops remained at Albert, still in the yard area on the west side of the standard gauge lines. There were locomotive sheds at various sites, including Ham.

Rolling Stock

After the First World War, much rolling stock had been removed or destroyed, and supplementation was required in order to reconstruct and reopen the lines.

Steam locomotives

See table 2.7 for locomotives up to 1914. Locomotives added in 1919 and after are shown in table 10.1. These are for all the SE Somme lines, not just the network around Albert. The Baldwins were heavy locomotives constructed during the First World War for the 10ème Section of the *Chemins de Fer de Campagne* (French Army Railway Engineers), who were responsible for metre gauge military operations.

Table 10.1 Technical details of SE Somme locomotives from 1919
(see also table 2.7 up to 1914)

Manufacturer	Baldwin	HSP	SACM	BR
Year(s) of manufacture		1921	1893	1912
Wheel configuration	0-6-2T	2-6-0T	0-4-0+0-4-0T Mallet type	2-6-0T
Company No(s)	*	3.851-861	4.501-502**	3.614-615***
Year(s) put in service		pr 1921	pr 1922	pr 1939
Number put in service	14	11	2	2
Lines	SE	SE	SE	SE
Name				3.615 'Molinet'

BR – Buffaud & Robatel
HSP – Haine-St-Pierre (Belgium)
SACM – Société Alsacienne de Construction Mécanique
SE *Société générale des Chemins de fer Économiques* (SE)
*   Rented from the 10ème Section of the Chemins de Fer de Campagne (French Engineers)
**   transferred from the Allier network in 1922
***   transferred from the Allier network in 1939

Narrow Gauge in the Somme Sector

HAM
Compagnie du Nord station
shared with the MG lines to Albert & to Noyon
& the SG *Intérêt Local* line to St-Quentin
from about 1930

Lines (from top) -
SG to Eppeville sugar factory(2)
MG (SE) to Péronne & Albert
SG to Eppeville sugar factory
SG (CdN) lines from & to Amiens
MG (VFIL) to Guiscard & Noyon

Lines (from top, all SG) -
NE *Intérêt Local* line to St-Quentin
CdN lines to and from Tergnier

1   *Bâtiment des Voyageurs* (CdN Main station building)
2   *Cour des Voyageurs* (Forecourt)
3   *Buvette*
4   *Bâtiment des Voyageurs* (SE passenger building)
5   *Cour des Marchandises* (Goods yard) (CdN & SE)
6   *Halle à marchandises* (goods hall)
7   Turntables
8   Coal platforms
9   *Remise de machines* (Locomotive shed)(SE)
10 *Remise de machines* (Locomotive shed)(NE)
11 Terminus of VFIL line from Noyon

MG   Metre gauge
SG   Standard gauge
CdN   Compagnie du Nord
SE   Société Générale des Chemins de Fer Économiques
VFIL Compagnie Générale des Voie Ferrées d'Intérêt Local (also often abbreviated as CGL)
NE   Compagnie des Secondaires du Nord-Est
      (Ham-St-Quentin SG line)

— Standard gauge line
— Metre gauge line
▪ Building
▫ Platform

Figure 10.1

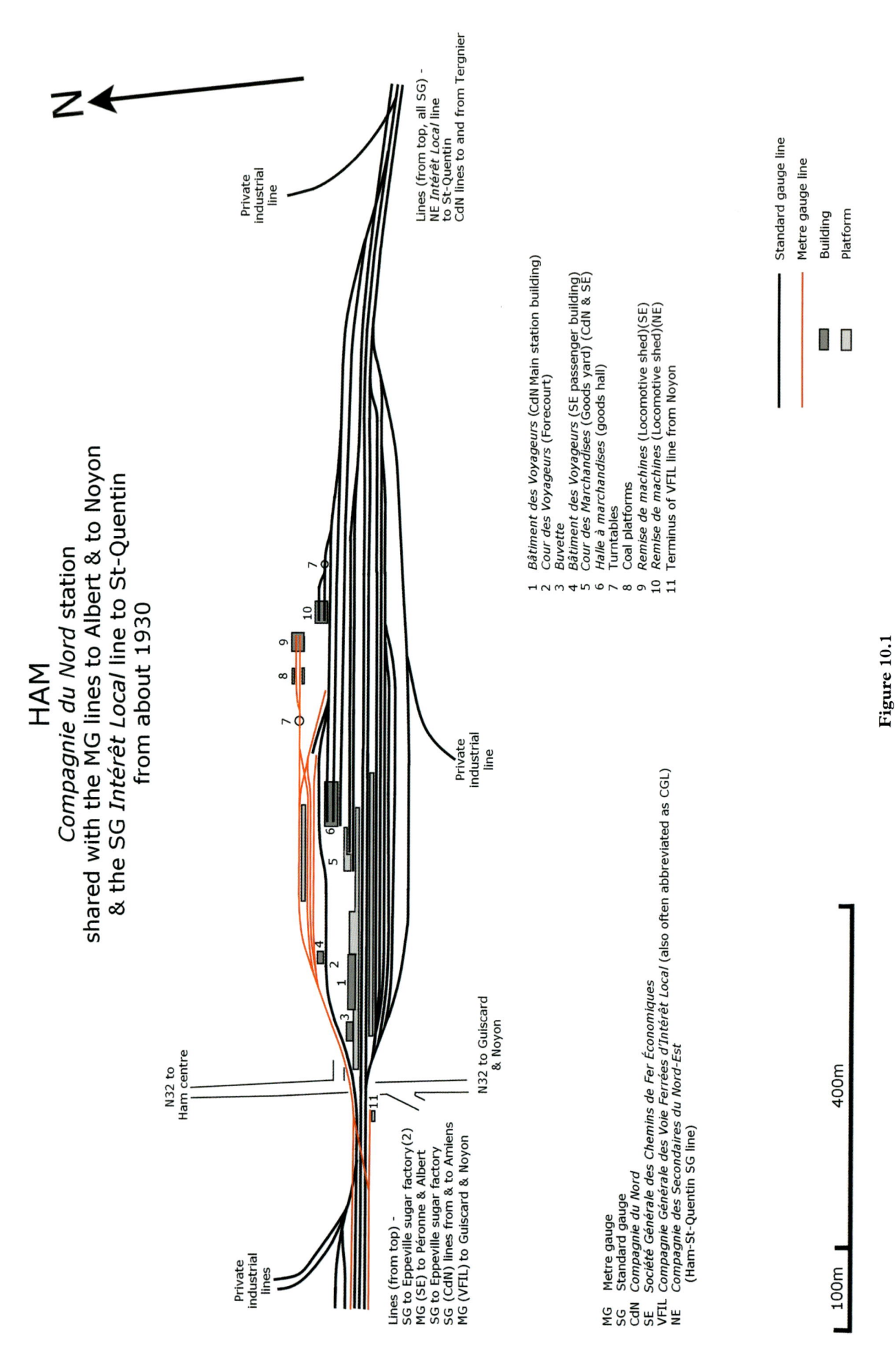

196

10.6 Ham station in April 2015, showing the passenger building as rebuilt after the First World War, on the main line from Amiens to Tergnier. *(Authors)*

10.7 The former SE shed for two locomotives in the goods area at Ham station. There is a disused standard gauge line in the foreground. April 2015. *(Authors)*

Some locomotives were recovered. An example is 3.572, reported missing on the Ercheu to Bussy line during the occupation in 1916, but subsequently recovered in 1922, repaired, and put back into service on this line. The other Ercheu–Bussy locomotive, 3.571, was never recovered.

In addition to the SE public line stock, there was one 0-6-0T Corpet-Louvet on the sugar factory branch from Guillemont to Longueval, and one similar at the sugar factory at Eppeville (Ham), both on the line from Albert to Ham.

Diesel railcars (Autorails)
The first diesel railcars were two manufactured by Renault and put into service on the line between Albert and Montididier in 1925. These are shown, with those purchased in 1936, in Table 10.2. They were numbered A-1 and A-2 and had 30hp diesel engines. They had two driving wheels at the 'front' end, and four trailing wheels, forming a bogie, at the rear. They could only be driven from one end, so had to be turned at the end of a route.

One of these railcars was third class only, and in 1933 was being used between Montdidier and Rollot. The other was second and third class, and in 1933 was providing at least some of the time a service all the way between Albert and Rollot.

Passenger carriages
These remained of the classical SE type, bogie carriages with a body finished with wooden planking,

Table 10.2 Technical details of SE Somme railcars from 1925

Manufacturer	Renault	De D-B	De D-B	De D-B trailers
Year(s) of manufacture				
Manufacturers type	KA	NJ	NJ	NO
Wheel configuration	2 driving	2 axle		
	4 (bogie) supp	(4 wheel)		
Manufacturer's No(s)				
Company No(s)	A-1, A-2	M-1 to M-10	M-11, M-12	R-1 to R-4
Year(s) delivered	1925	1936-7	1939	*
Number put in service	2	10	2	4
Line	SE	SE	SE	SE
Motor	Renault	Unic		
Power (hp)	30	85		
Driving position(s)	one end	one end		
	(unidirectional)	(unidirectional)		

De D-B – De Dion-Bouton
* From the *Réseau de la Nièvre*

and accessed from end platforms. Between the wars, this type was purchased from Manage & Vickers. Also, after the First World War, SE obtained unused carriages which had been intended for the *Chemins de fer Électrique de Champagne*. Later there were interchanges of passenger carriages with other SE lines, such as Allier and Valmondois–Marines.

Recovered passenger carriages were repaired where possible. As an example, one of the two mixed carriages of the line from Ercheu to Bussy was repaired in 1922 at a cost of 34,000 francs.

The eastern Somme network 1930 to 1939

During the 1930s, SE introduced the faster De Dion-Bouton railcars on the eastern Somme lines from Albert. However, during this period most rural metre gauge lines in France were struggling financially, with an increase of bus competition. Road transport had developed rapidly during the First World War. By the 1930s reliability had improved, prices had come down, and oil was cheap and increasingly available. Local railways, a wonderful innovation compared with walking or using horses, were now threatened by the flexibility of road transport. Railways were running at a loss, and bus services increased in an uncontrolled way.

The Coordination Committees and SNCF (also applies to Chapter Eleven)

In 1934, the National Economic Council (NEC), who had been asked to take evidence on the problems of local transport, presented their report. They recommended that each Region (in a railway sense) should have a 'coordination committee', to advise which transport mode or modes should provide local and long-distance passenger and goods services. The Coordination Committees represented local and national railway and road operators, but did not include users, as had been recommended. Closures of *Intérêt Local* lines, usually of metre gauge, were widespread in the 1930s and by 1937 France had lost nearly half of these. Many companies running *Intérêt Local* lines began to take an interest in owning and running bus services, often through a separate but related company.

In 1938, the major standard gauge railway companies were joined together to form the *Société Nationale des Chemins de Fer Français* (SNCF), which was, and still is, effectively a nationalised railway company. SNCF quickly started large scale closure of passenger services on less used rural lines.

Routes and industrial links

At Ercheu, the *râperie* acquired in 1933 an 0-6-0T manufactured by La Meuse. This came from the *Chemin de Fer de l'Artois*, from Béthune to Estaires in the Pas-de-Calais département, which had closed in 1932. This had been delivered in 1928 and given the number 12 by the Artois Company.

In 1939, a major change of the road layout around the halt at Porte-de-Bretagne, on the eastern edge of Péronne, was proposed. We are not sure that the work was carried out in 1939, but if not, it was done after the Second World War. Certainly, the proposals are identical with the road layout there now. This was to improve the flow of traffic, providing an eastern inner bypass for Péronne. The route of the railway line towards Albert was altered and new bridges were provided under the new roads. Adjacent to the halt was the sugar factory of the *Compagnie Nouvelle des Sucreries Réunies*. That the changes left the halt and the *sucrerie* surrounded by improved modern roads was symbolic of the times.

Rolling stock
Diesel railcars (Autorails)
The railcars put into service in 1936 or 1937 are shown, with those purchased in 1925, in Table 10.2. They were much more powerful, as reflected in faster journey times where they were deployed. These were De Dion-Bouton type NJ railcars, with 2 axles (4 wheels), and powered by 85hp Unic engines. They were driven from one end only, so had to turn round at the end of a route. Ten, numbered M - 1 to M -10, were put into service for the whole SE Somme network. In 1939 two more, identical or nearly so, were purchased, and numbered M - 11 and M - 12. Railcars purchased by SE after the closure of the lines around Albert are not included in Table 10.2.

SE also acquired four De Dion-Bouton trailers, from the *Réseau de la Nièvre*, but we are uncertain of the date these were put into service, or whether any were used on the Albert lines. They were numbered R-1 to R-4, the R for *remorque* (trailer).

Operations
In 1933, the service was predominantly steam, apart from a very limited railcar service on the Montdidier line. By 1936, there was considerable use of more modern railcars, and by 1938 these were providing most of the passenger services on these lines, except for the Offoy to Ercheu and Bussy loop. There was a considerable increase in speed. Between the First World War and 1933 there had been a tendency for *arrêts* (stops) to close. By 1938, most of these were again in use, with some new ones. No doubt the ease of stopping and then accelerating the light diesel railcars enabled this service improvement. The steam trains missed some of these *arrêts*. Some stops previously classified as stations and halts were downgraded to *arrêts*, probably to save staff. All *arrêts* were now *facultatif* (request), either by hailing the train as it approached, or by telling the *Chef de Train* that one wanted to alight. *Arrêts* were now only available to passengers, with their baggage and accompanied dogs, and tickets could be bought on the train.

The timetables of 1933 and 1938 refer to the existence of weekly season tickets, with use restricted to certain trains. The timetables of 1938 make clear that these are workers' tickets, as they probably were also in 1933.

Doullens to Albert
The timetable of February 1933 indicates much the same pattern as in 1922, apart from the extension of the service from Gézaincourt back into Doullens. The early afternoon service from Doullens ran 45 minutes later on Thursdays, market days in Doullens. Holders of weekly season tickets were restricted to early morning and later evening trains except on Saturdays.

However, by October 1936, railcars had been introduced, with one based at Acheux. There were four services each way per day along the whole line between Albert and Doullens, two steam and two railcar, with an additional railcar service from Acheux to Albert in the mornings and back at night. There was an additional Saturday evening service from Doullens to Beauquesne

10.8 A De Dion-Bouton M series railcar of 1937 or 1939 at Montauban station in 1949. *(Photo P. Laurent, collection Bernard Rozé)*

and back. The pattern indicates that the steam locomotive and train set was based at Doullens, and probably the steam services were mixed goods and passenger trains. This is consistent with the journey times of 1 hour and 7 or 8 minutes for the railcars, and 1 hour 48 minutes to 2 hours 5 minutes for the steam services. The steam times were almost unchanged from 1933 and indeed from the shorter length served in 1922.

By October 1938 (Table 10.3), there were three railcar services each way per day, which could be provided by one railcar based at Albert. Steam services were from Acheux to Albert in the morning, then the whole length of the line and back, then back from Albert to Acheux in the evening. This could be provided by one locomotive and train set based at Acheux, and these were probably mixed passenger and goods trains. There were new *arrêts* at Terramesnil, Forceville and Colincamps, but only the last was served by the steam trains.

Albert to Péronne and Ham

The metre gauge service was restored along the whole length of the line by the end of 1922. The timetable of February 1933 shows three services each way daily between Péronne-Flamicourt and Albert, and three between Péronne and Ham. The timetable is laid out to suggest two services all the way each way between Albert and Ham, but scrutiny shows long layovers at Péronne, from 1 hour to 3 hours and 56 minutes. Whether any were truly through trains, or one had to change at Péronne, is not clear. Either way, the service required two locomotives and train sets based at Péronne, and one at Albert. The most likely pattern is that there was one through train each way, based at Albert, and that the rest were partial, based at Péronne.

By October 1936, the whole passenger service was being provided by railcar. There were two through

Table 10.3 Doullens–Albert (SE)
Summary Timetable October 1938
Selected stops only

		(1)	*(1)	*(2)	(1)	*(1)
Doullens			07.23	13.29	15.05	19.09
Connection with CdN SG lines to Arras, St-Pol-sur-Ternoise, Amiens and Longpré
Gézaincourt (halt)			07.34	13.35	15.14	19.15
Connection with CdN SG lines to Amiens and Longpré
Beauval			07.39	13.40	15.32	19.20
Beauquesnes			07.46	13.47	15.49	19.27
Louvencourt			07.59	14.00	16.08	19.40
Acheux-Varennes	a		08.06	14.07	16.24	19.47
	d	06.12	08.06	14.08	16.24	19.48
Mailly-Maillet		06.30	08.17	14.18	16.42	19.58
Albert		06.53	08.34	14.35	17.05	20.15
Connection with CdN SG line Amiens–Arras.
Origin of MG SE lines to Ham, Montidier and Rollot

		*(1)		*(2)	*(1)	(1)
Albert		06.12	09.37	11.46	17.25	18.55
Connection with CdN SG line Amiens–Arras.
Origin of MG SE lines to Ham, Montidier and Rollot
Mailly-Maillet		06.29	10.03	12.03	17.42	19.21
Acheux-Varennes	a	06.40	10.18	12.14	17.53	<u>19.36</u>
	d	06.40	10.22	12.14	17.53	
Louvencourt		06.47	10.33	12.21	18.00	
Beauquesnes		07.00	10.54	12.34	18.13	
Beauval		07.07	11.13	12.41	18.20	
Gézaincourt (halt)		07.12	11.23	12.46	18.25	
Connection with CdN SG lines to Amiens and Longpré
Doullens		07.18	11.32	12.52	18.31	
Connection with CdN SG lines to Arras, St-Pol-sur-Ternoise, Amiens and Longpré

a   arrive   d   depart
Underlined – terminates, other than at end of line
SG   standard gauge   MG   metre gauge
CdN   *Compagnie du Nord*
SE   *Société Générale des Chemins de Fer Économiques*
*   railcar service
(1) Available to workers with weekly season tickets
(2) Available on Saturdays to workers with weekly season tickets

services each way between Albert and Ham, with a third service each way between Péronne and Albert and Péronne and Ham. There were additional services on Saturdays, market day in Péronne, to and from Albert, Combles, and Monchy-Lagache. The introduction of railcars reduced the journey time from Péronne to Albert from 1 hour 51 minutes–2 hours in 1933, to 1 hour and 5-9 minutes in 1936. For Péronne to Ham, the times reduced from 1 hour 16 - 32 minutes, to 53 minutes. Even allowing for the effect of mixed trains in 1933, this is a dramatic reduction.

In October 1938, the pattern was very similar (see Table 10.4), except for the reintroduction of a steam service from Albert to Péronne and back in the mornings, and an additional service from Albert to Combles and back in the mornings.

Table 10.4 Albert–Péronne–Ham (SE)
Summary Timetable October 1938
Selected stops only

	*(1)	(1)	*	*	*(2)	*(1)	*(1)
Albert		06.00	07.16		11.02	15.42	18.41
Connection with CdN SG line Amiens–Arras. Origin of MG SE line to Doullens
Fricourt		06.19	07.27		11.13	15.53	18.52
junction with SE MG line Albert–Montdidier–Rollot
Montauban		06.42	07.40		11.26	16.06	19.05
Guillemont		06.48	07.44		11.30	16.10	19.09
Combles		07.03	<u>07.51</u>		11.37	16.17	19.16
Hem-Feuillères		07.23			11.50	16.30	19.29
Péronne(-Flamicourt) a		<u>07.45</u>		12.07	16.47	<u>19.46</u>
Connection with CdN SG lines to Montdidier, Paris, Cambrai & Douai
d	06.03		08.24		12.13	17.47	
Mons-en-Chaussée	06.14		08.35		12.24	17.58	
Athies (Somme)	06.19		08.40		12.29	18.03	
Monchy-Lagache	06.27		08.48		12.37	18.11	
Matigny	06.39		09.00		12.49	18.23	
Offoy	06.45		09.06		12.55	18.29	
junction with SE MG line to Ercheu and Bussy
Ham	06.56		09.17		13.06	18.40	
connection with CdN SG lines to Amiens, Tergnier and Laon, and VFIL MG line to Noyon

	*(1)	*(1)	*		*(2)	*(1)	*(1)(3)
Ham		07.16			11.05	16.00	19.13
connection with CdN SG lines to Amiens, Tergnier and Laon, and VFIL MG line to Noyon
Offoy		07.27			11.16	16.11	19.24
junction with SE MG line to Ercheu and Bussy
Matigny		07.33			11.22	16.17	19.30
Monchy-Lagache		07.46			11.35	16.30	19.43
Athies (Somme)		07.53			11.42	16.37	19.50
Mons-en-Chaussée		07.58			11.47	16.42	19.55
Péronne(-Flamicourt) a		08.09			11.58	16.53	<u>20.06</u>
Connection with CdN SG lines to Montdidier, Paris, Cambrai & Douai
d	06.33		08.30		12.12	17.05	
Hem-Feuillères	06.59		08.58		12.29	17.22	
Combles	07.25		07.56	09.25	12.43	17.37	
Guillemont	07.38		08.03	09.39	12.50	17.44	
Montauban	07.45		08.07	09.46	12.54	17.48	
Fricourt	08.05		08.20	10.07	13.07	18.01	
junction with MG SE line Albert–Montdidier–Rollot
Albert	08.23		08.31	10.25	13.18	18.12	
Connection with CdN SG line Amiens–Arras. Origin of MG SE line to Doullens

a arrive d depart
underlined – terminates, not at end of line
SG standard gauge CdN *Compagnie du Nord*
MG metre gauge SE *Société Générale des Chemins de Fer Economiques*
  VFIL *Compagnie Générale des Voie Ferrées d'Intérêt Local*
* railcar service
(1) Available to workers with weekly season tickets
(2) Available on Saturdays to workers with weekly season tickets
(3) 10 minutes later Sundays and Feast Days 19 June to 18 September, except 14 August

By the time of the 1933 timetable there were other changes since the war. Hem-Monacu station had become Hem-Feiullières, probably on the site of the former Feuillières *arrêt*. Mametz had been downgraded to an *arrêt*, but the *arrêt* at Le Quinconce had become a halt. A new *arrêt* had opened at Eppeville, but those at Bécourt-Bécordel, Carnoy and Canizy had disappeared. By 1938, Maurrepas, Cléry, Mesnil-Bruntel, and Quivières-Guizancourt halts had become stations. The *arrêts* at Carnoy and Canizy had reappeared, and there were now new *arrêts* at Ginchy, Cléry-Église, and Matigny. There were also now separate *arrêts* at Bécourt and Bécordel, and at Croix and Moligneaux.

Albert to Montdidier and Rollot

In May 1929, VFIL, based at Noyon, were still running the service between Lassigny and Montidier, with trains in both directions once daily, and twice except on Wednesdays and Saturdays. The full timetable is shown in Table 11.3 (chapter eleven).

By 1933, SE had taken over most of the service from Montdidier to Rollot. Railcars were introduced on the Albert to Montdidier line by 1925. By February 1933, three trains each way were being run daily between Albert and Montdidier, with some being run through to Rollot. In addition, there were services between Montidier and Rollot, and some of the services were being run by railcar. The railcars were not particularly faster than the steam services.

By 1936, more services were being run by railcar, probably of a the more modern type introduced by 1936. However, these only ran between Albert and Rosières, with steam between there and Montdidier. The older railcars were being deployed between Montdidier and Rollot. There was only one through train daily, steam hauled and possibly mixed passenger and goods. Between Albert and Rosières, the new railcars were much faster, with a journey time 48-50 minutes, than the old railcars taking 1 hour 22-28 minutes.

Until 1937, VFIL, based in Noyon, were still operating some trains between Rollot and Montdidier. Some of these were withdrawn by agreement in spring 1937, when SE introduced one railcar service between Rosières and Rollot. VFIL continued one service through from Lassigny, but these were withdrawn on October 1937, leaving the whole service between Rollot and Montdidier to SE (see Chapter Eleven).

By October 1938, SE were operating four services each way per day all the way between Albert and Rollot, with no partial services. This timetable is shown in summary in Table 10.5. Three were by railcar and one steam, probably mixed passenger and goods. There were variable waits at Rosières and Montdidier for connections, the longest being just over 1 hour at Rosières. The actual railcar journey time was 1 hour 49 - 54 minutes. The steam time without waits was just under 3 hours, as in 1933.

Several *arrêts* had been closed by the time of the 1933 timetable, and were now reopened; Framerville, Rosières-Vrély, Bouchoir and Montdidier. All fifteen *arrêts* were now *facultatif* (request). This included two which had been stations (Caix-Vrély, and Assainvillers on the Montdidier to Rollot section), and three which had been halts (Froissy, Chuignolles, and Fignières). Caix-Vrély had been downgraded some time since 1921, and Assainvillers station since 1933, probably with the full takeover of this section by SE. There were two new *arrêts* since 1933, at Proyart and at La Neuville-lès-Bray. There were also now the two *arrêts* at Bécourt and Bécordel, on the common section between Albert and Fricourt.

Offoy to Ercheu and Ercheu to Bussy

Timetables for 1932 and 1933 show very little change from 1914 (Table 12.2, Chapter Two). Offoy to Ercheu and Ercheu to Bussy are still shown in separate tables, with extremely poor connections at Ercheu between the two services, even though both were operated by SE. By 1936, matters had improved. The timetables for October 1936 are shown in Table 10.6. This is now one table in the *Chaix*. There is one daily through service, not changing at Ercheu, and one more from Bussy towards Offoy on market days in Noyon. However, the only through service from Offoy to Bussy takes 3 hours 47 minutes, which is 1 hour 22 minutes travelling, 55 minutes waiting at Ercheu, and 1 hour 20 minutes waiting at Nesle, no doubt for main line connections. Some of the other connections at Ercheu are reasonable. This is still entirely a steam service, which could be provided by one locomotive and train set based at Ercheu and another at Offoy. There is also an evening bus service from Noyon to Ercheu and back.

The timetable of 2 October 1938 is similar to that of 1936, apart from some time changes between Ercheu and Bussy in the sugar beet season. The service remained entirely steam based. The evening bus service from and to Noyon remained, calling at most of the stops between Ercheu and Bussy, or somewhere nearby, but not at Bussy itself. The service is provided by a bus of the *Société des Transports Picardie-Citroën*, but it is not known if this was a company related to SE. Despite this timetable of 2 October, it is reported that SE closed the passenger service between Offoy and Ercheu on 7 November 1938, but the service from Ercheu to Bussy continued.

The eastern Somme network – Second World War to 1955

From 3 September 1939, France was once again on a war footing. The timetables of October 1939 show

The metre gauge railways of the Somme département 12 November 1918 to 1955

Table 10.5 Albert–Montdidier–Rollot (SE)
Summary Timetable October 1938
Selected stops only

		*(1)	*	(2)	*(1)
Albert		05.24	09.32	12.27	18.29
connection with CdN SG line Amiens-Arras. Origin of SE MG line to Doullens					
Fricourt		05.35	09.43	12.46	18.40
junction with SE MG line Albert–Péronne–Ham					
Bray		05.47	09.54	13.07	18.52
Froissy (*arrêt*)		05.50	09.57	13.12	18.55
Proyart		06.00	10.07	13.25	19.05
Harbonnières		06.07	10.14	13.38	19.12
Rosières	a	06.13	10.20	13.46	19.18
connection with CdN SG line to Amiens, Tergnier and Laon					
	d	07.16	10.26	14.12	19.34
Le Quesnel - Beaufort		07.30	10.40	14.36	19.48
Arvillers - Hangest		07.35	10.46	14.46	19.54
Davenescourt		07.44	10.55	14.59	20.03
Montdidier	a	07.59	11.10	15.23	20.18
connection with CdN SG lines Amiens to Compiègne and St-Just-en-Chaussée to Cambrai					
	d	08.05	11.30	15.28	20.25
Assainvillers		08.15	11.40	15.40	20.35
Rollot		08.22	11.47	15.48	20.42
origin of VFIL MG line to Lassigny and Noyon					
		*(1)	*	*(2)	(1)
Rollot		05.13	08.28	12.43	16.09
origin of VFIL MG line to Lassigny and Noyon					
Assainvillers		05.20	08.35	12.50	16.17
Montdidier	a	05.30	08.45	13.00	16.29
connection with CdN SG lines Amiens to Compiègne and St-Just-en-Chaussée to Cambrai					
	d	05.35	09.10	13.01	17.07
Davenescourt		05.52	09.27	13.18	17.31
Arvillers - Hangest		06.01	09.36	13.28	17.48
Le Quesnel - Beaufort		06.06	09.41	13.34	17.58
Rosières	a	06.19	09.54	13.47	18.18
connection with CdN SG line to Amiens, Tergnier and Laon					
	d	06.19	10.35	14.09	18.40
Harbonnières		06.25	10.41	14.15	18.48
Proyart		06.32	10.48	14.22	19.06
Froissy (*arrêt*)		06.42	10.58	14.32	19.18
Bray		06.45	11.01	14.35	19.27
Fricourt		06.56	11.14	14.46	19.50
junction with SE MG line Albert–Péronne–Ham					
Albert		07.07	11.25	14.57	20.07
connection with CdN SG line Amiens-Arras. Origin of SE MG line to Doullens					

a   arrive   d   depart
underlined – terminates, not at end of line
SG   standard gauge   CdN   *Compagnie du Nord*
MG   metre gauge   SE   *Société Générale des Chemins de Fer Economiques*
                              VFIL   *Compagnie Générale des Voie Ferrées d'Intérêt Local*

*   railcar service
(1) Available to workers with weekly season tickets
(2) Available on Saturdays to workers with weekly season tickets

some reduction of service, but still quite a good one. Between Doullens and Albert there are three railcar services each way all the way, plus one steam service from Acheux to Albert and back. From Albert to Ham and back there are two services all the way, but, with one exception, very long breaks at Péronne, so most are not really through services, as in 1933. There is one partial service based on Péronne along the whole line, and all passenger services are railcars.

On the line between Albert, Montdider, and Rollot, there were now three railcar services along the full route daily, but the fourth steam service had stopped.

Table 10.6 Offoy–Ercheu & Ercheu–Bussy (SE)
Summary Timetable October 1936
Main stops only

		(1)				(2)
Offoy		07.20		13.13	18.10	
connection with SE MG Ham–Péronne–Albert line						
Nesle	a	07.49		13.44	18.37	
connection with CdN SG Amiens to Tergnier and Laon line						
	d	08.05		14.39	18.51	
Ercheu	a	08.28		15.03	19.13	
	d	07.20	11.00	16.23		19.40
Bussy		07.54	11.37	17.00		
connection with VFIL MG line Noyon to Ham						
Noyon (bus service)						20.15

		(3)	(1)		(2)
Noyon (bus service)					18.25
Bussy		09.20	12.40	17.25	
connection with MG VFIL line Noyon to Ham					
Ercheu	a	10.01	13.17	18.02	19.05
	d	09.01	10.04	13.20	18.12	
Nesle	a	09.25	10.28	13.44	18.36	
connection with CdN SG Amiens to Tergnier and Laon line					
	d	09.54	10.43	14.38	18.52	
Offoy		10.22	11.06	15.01	19.15	
connection with SE MG Ham–Péronne–Albert line					

a arrive   d depart
Underlined - terminates, not at end of line
SG standard gauge   CdN *Compagnie du Nord*
MG metre gauge   SE *Société Générale des Chemins de Fer Economiques*
        VFIL *Compagnie Générale des Voie Ferrées d'Intérêt Local*
(1) Saturday, and the first Tuesday of each month, only (market days in Noyon)
(2) Bus service, probably not via Bussy
(3) Friday only (market day in Nesle)

The service between Offoy and Ercheu, which ceased in 1938, had been restored, but that between Ercheu and Bussy reduced. Overall, there was probably a shortage of crews with national call-up, and steam locomotives were being kept for essential goods work.

After the German occupation of northern France from June 1940, some steam services were reinstated, and others preserved, because coal became less scarce than petrol and diesel fuel. By May 1944, there was some further reduction of service, and on the line between Albert and Ham the services were completely separated at Péronne. Between Albert and Rollot there was one railcar service on Mondays, Thursdays and Saturdays, but otherwise all railcar services had ceased. Between Offoy and Bussy there was a very limited weekday service varying with the day of the week.

By 1947, the lines had largely recovered from the war. The timetables for October 1947 were very similar to those of 1938. The Offoy to Ercheu service had closed to passengers in November 1938 and was restarted during the Second World War with the service continuing well afterwards. In 1947, this, interestingly, had an additional train each way per day running through at Offoy to and from Ham. Overall these timetables give the impression of a well functioning railway.

Closures

At the end of the Second World War, the *Conseil Général* of the Somme *département* decided to close the central and eastern Somme networks. The feeling at the time was that roads and road transport were the future, and that metre gauge rural railways were failing.

The line from Fricourt to Montdidier and Rollot closed on 15 April 1948, except for the goods service between Fricourt and Froissy, which remained until 31 December 1948. The line from Offoy to Ercheu closed on 1 July 1949. Doullens to Albert closed on 1 July 1949 except for a goods service from Albert to Acheux, which remained until 31 December 1949. Albert to Péronne and Ham also closed on 31 December 1949.

The line from Ercheu to Bussy, now isolated in the Oise *département*, remained open for passengers until 1 February 1954. It remained open for goods, mainly sugar beet, until the closure of the VFIL Oise network based on Noyon in 1955 (see Chapter Eleven).

The metre gauge railways of the Somme département 12 November 1918 to 1955

10.9 At Albert station in December 1949, a few days before the closure of the lines, de Dion-Bouton railcar M-2 of 1937 is about to leave. *(Collection Bernard Rozé)*

Elsewhere in the Somme *département*, the SE line from Amiens to Aumale closed 1 June 1948, and the lines east from Noyelles in 1951, except for a goods service to Forest l'Abbaye until 1964. Of the Somme metre gauge lines, this left only the *Réseau des Bains de Mer* from Noyelles to St-Valéry, Cayeux and Le Crotoy. These are the lines which survive today as the *Chemin de Fer de la Baie de Somme* (CFBS) (see Chapter Twelve).

SE reformed itself into the the *Compagnie des Chemins de Fer et Transports Automobile* (CFTA). This better reflected their growing interests in road transport.

Disposal of assets

Very little is known about the disposal of assets for the eastern Somme SE lines. Some rolling stock went to the Noyelles lines. This included locomotive 3.856, Haine-St-Pierre (Belgium) 2-6-0T constructed in 1921 and put into service on the Somme lines in 1922. It was transferred to St-Valéry in 1951.

Chapter Eleven

The metre gauge railways of the Oise and Aisne départements *12 November 1918 to 1955*

Noyon to Guiscard and Ham, and Noyon to Lassigny and Montdidier (The Noyon Network)

After the First World War, very extensive reconstruction was needed. The line from Noyon to Ham had been taken up, then replaced by a 60cm gauge line. The line from Noyon to Lassigny and on to Rollot and Montdidier had been in operation to Conchy-les-Pots in 1917. However, all were destroyed with the German advance in 1918, which reached Montdidier, and the subsequent fighting to recover this territory.

Before the war these lines had been owned and operated by the Noyon–Guiscard–Lassigny Company, linked with the Milly–Formerie Company. This was a company associated with Alfred Lambert. After the war, the lines were not immediately taken back by the Lambert group. The *Société Générale des Chemins de Fer Économiques (SE)*, who operated the Somme networks, took over these lines until the end of 1921.

In the Pas-de-Calais *département*, the line owned by a Company associated with Alfred Lambert, Aire–Rimeux–Berck, had always been closely associated with lines associated with Émile Level, Anvin–Calais and the Tramway from Ardres to Pont d'Ardres. In 1919 these Companies joined together as the confusingly named *Compagnie Générale des Voie Ferrées d'Intérêt Local*, usually abbreviated to CGL by the French, but to VFIL in the British literature. In 1919 they also incorporated the *Chemin de Fer des Flandres* in the Nord *département*. It has been claimed that in 1920 they took over all the metre gauge lines in the Oise *département*, including those based on Noyon. However, they did not take over the Noyon lines from SE until 1 January 1922. By 1930 they had acquired a whole range of *Intérêt Local* lines in the north of France, including some of standard gauge. Among the last in 1930 were Boisleux to Marquion and Cambrai, Achiet-le-Grand to Bapaume and Marcoing, and Vélu-Bertincourt to St-Quentin, the last two of these in the area of interest of this book (see Chapter One).

Restoration of lines and services

In early 1919 the Minister of *Travaux Publiques* (Public Works) prescribed all necessary steps to re-establish as soon as possible the *Intérêt Local* lines destroyed by 'the enemy'. The Departmental Commission of Oise, at a meeting on 24 March 1919, requested the *Préfet*, with the shortest possible delay, to re-establish the lines from Noyon to Guiscard and Lassigny, Guiscard to Ham and Lassigny to Montdidier.

The path of the metre gauge line to Noyon, south from Ham, had been used for a light railway as far as Guiscard by the British Army in March 1918. By the end of the war in November 1918, the French had used the rest of the formation to Noyon as a light railway track. This was in use, from 1920 or earlier, until 2 May 1921, at least for goods services. We have seen claims that the passenger service was restarted using the 60cm gauge line, but we have seen no timetables for this except later in 1921 for the section nearer to Ham.

Similarly, at least from 1920, there was a 60cm gauge line using the metre gauge formation from Noyon to Roye-sur-Matz via Lassigny. These two lines would have met at the former junction of the metre gauge lines, west of Noyon standard gauge station. From the former halt at Faubourg de Paris (Route de Montdidier), a 60cm gauge line linked the two lines to Noyon standard gauge station, and also to the line to Camelin and on into the Aisne *département*.

In August 1920, the Chief Engineer announced the reopening of the line from Lassigny to the border of the Oise département (between Hainvillers and Rollot). This could be achieved from 1 October 1920. Because the section from Noyon to Lassigny was not ready to reopen, and SE were already operating between Montidier and Rollot, it was suggested that in the short term only SE should operate Lassigny to Montdidier. This they would agree in return for expenses plus 10 per cent. The Chief Engineer doubted that VFIL, who were at some time due to take over the Oise lines, could do it more cheaply than this anyway. In the event this service was opened by SE on 20 November 1920. There were two services each way per day, starting from and ending at Lassigny, with an extra service in the middle of the day between Lassigny and Roye-sur-Matz, weekdays only, for the connection with the line between Compiègne and Roye (Somme).

In August 1920, the Chief Engineer also announced the reopening of the line from Noyon (Faubourg de Paris) to Guiscard on 1 October 1920, but this was

206

11.1 Lassigny station shortly after the First World War, with soldiers on the platform, and a temporary building. Postcard postmarked 1923. *(Authors' collection)*

premature. There was a need for further discussions with the *Compagnie du Nord* about transhipment facilities at Pont l'Evêque. In the event these facilities were not provided until April 1921, allowing the reopening of the metre gauge line from Faubourg de Paris (Noyon) to both Guiscard and Lassigny on 2 May.

The Chief Engineer's report of 21 April 1921 said that the 60cm gauge line between Noyon and Ham would 'disappear' from 2 May. A van would provide for passengers beyond Guiscard to Ham, 'because the Somme *département* could not promise traffic on the 60cm'. It was hoped to open to Plessis-Patte-d'Oie (previously called Plessis-Flavel-Berlancourt) on 23 May, and to Golancourt on 13 June. However, the timetable for June 1921 shows the continuation of the 60cm gauge service, run by the *Ministère des Régions Libérées* (MRL), twice a day between Plessis and Ham until 13 June, and then from Golancourt to Ham. This timetable is shown in Table 11.1. As can be seen connections in the direction towards Noyon were good, those towards Ham less good especially in the morning. Carriage of passengers between Faubourg de Paris and Noyon main line station was provided by a 60cm gauge shuttle service (see Table 11.2).

The reopening of the lines from Noyon to Guiscard and Lassigy was undertaken by SE.

Noyon to Lassigny and Lassigny to Montdidier were clearly regarded as separate services, with separate timetables. Between Noyon and Lassigny there were two trains each way daily, with one more each way in the middle of the day on market days in Noyon. These were all mixed trains (passengers and goods). The service from Lassigny to Montdidier changed slightly, with two trains each way, but the morning service in the Montdidier direction went only to Boulogne-la-Grasse. It then turned back to Roye-sur-Matz, before turning again at Roye to go to Montdidier. The connections at Lassigny were very poor, with a 4 hour wait in one direction and 3 hours 15 minutes in the other.

The service to Guiscard was extended to Plessis on 23 May and to Golancourt on 13 June. There were two trains each way daily, and one in the morning from Bussy to Golancourt and back from Golancourt to Bussy in the evening. There was an additional train each way in the middle of the day on market days in Noyon. The service could have been provided by one locomotive and train set based at Bussy.

Between Noyon and Ham the line was opened from Golancourt to Ham at some time between 26 September 1921 and 1 January 1922, when the services were taken over by VFIL. Since the First World war, all

Table 11.1 Noyon to Guiscard and Golancourt (VFIL)
Plessis to Ham (MRL)
Timetable June 1921
All stops shown as in the *Chaix*

		**	**			
		(1)	(2)	(1)(3)	(1)	(2)
Noyon Faubourg de Paris	*arrêt*	09.35		12.45	18.55	
Origin of MG SE line to Lassigny and Montdidier						
60cm gauge connection to Noyon Nord						
Bussy		09.59		13.09	19.19	
junction with MG SE line to Ercheu, and Ercheu to Offoy						
Muirancourt	*arrêt*	10.09		13.19	19.29	
Guiscard		10.19		13.29	19.39	
Plessis-Flavy-Berlancourt		10.32	12.54	13.42	19.52	20.23
Golancourt		10.42	13.09	13.52	20.02	20.38
Ham (Nord)			13.36			21.05
Connection with CdN SG lines Amiens, Tergnier and Laon						
Origin of MG SE line to Albert						

		**			**	
		(2)	(1)	(1)(3)	(2)	(1)
Ham (Nord)		05.55			15.00	
Connection with CdN SG lines to Amiens, Tergnier and Laon						
Origin of MG SE line to Albert						
Golancourt		06.24	06.40	11.00	15.29	15.50
Plessis-Flavy		06.38	06.51	11.11	15.43	16.01
Guiscard			07.05	11.25		16.15
Muirancourt	*arrêt*		07.11	11.34		16.37
Bussy			07.27	11.47		16.13
junction with MG SE line to Ercheu, and Ercheu to Offoy						
Noyon Faubourg de Paris	*arrêt*		07.47	12.07		16.57
Origin of MG SE line to Lassigny and Montdidier						
60cm gauge connection to Noyon Nord						

** 60cm gauge (light railway) service (MRL)
SG standard gauge CdN *Compagnie du Nord*
MG metre gauge SE *Société Générale des Chemins de Fer Economiques*
  MRL *Ministère des Régions Libérées*
(1) Plessis–Golancourt only after 13 June
(2) Plessis–Golancourt not after 13 June
(3) Only on Saturdays and the first Thursday in the month (market days in Noyon)

stops on this line except Guiscard and Bussy had been downgraded to *arrêts*. The timetable from 1 January 1922 is shown in Table 11.2.

The lines from Noyon to Lassigny and from Lassigny to Montdidier were also taken over by VFIL on 1 January 1922, and the timetable is shown in Table 11.3. Noyon to Lassigny and Lassigny to Montdidier were still regarded as separate services, with separate timetables. The service was little changed from that at the reopening in May 1921. The connections at Lassigny were still very bad, with 4 Hours and 53 minutes to wait if travelling towards Montdidier, and 3 hours 15 minutes going towards Noyon. The only reasonable connection was of 52 minutes going towards Montdidier when the Noyon market day train ran. Since the war, all stops on this line except Thiescourt, Lassigny, Roye-sur-Matz, Boulogne-la-Grasse and Rollot had been downgraded to *arrêts*. In June 1924, an early evening train from Roye-sur Matz to Rollot and then back to Lassigny was added.

The timetables from 1 January 1922 in Tables 11.2 and 11.3 also show the connecting 60cm gauge services between Noyon main line station and Faubourg de Paris. These services were clearly designed to connect with the arrivals and departures at the latter. The 60cm gauge link had closed by 1923, with the closure of the Noyon light railway depot at the end of 1922. After that, the connection was provided by road vehicles until the station was restored and the metre gauge lines returned to the Noyon main line station area in 1925.

Reconnection to Noyon main line station
Even though it was claimed that the transhipment facilities at Pont l'Evêque opened in April 1921, before the services to Ham and Lassigny reopened in May 1921, VFIL wrote to the *Préfet* in August 1923, to say

Table 11.2 Noyon to Guiscard and Ham (VFIL)
Summary Timetable January 1922
Selected stops only

			(1)	
Ham		06.42	11.00	15.25
Connection with CdN SG lines to Amiens, Tergnier and Laon, Origin of MG SE line to Albert				
Golancourt	*arrêt*	06.54	11.12	15.40
Plessis-Flavy	*arrêt*	07.03	11.21	15.49
Guiscard		07.15	11.35	15.55
Muirancourt	*arrêt*	07.25	11.45	16.08
Bussy		07.37	11.57	16.13
junction with MG SE line to Ercheu, and Ercheu to Offoy				
Noyon Faubourg de Paris	*arrêt*	07.54	12.14	16.52
Origin of MG VFIL line to Lassigny and Montdidier				
Noyon Faubourg de Paris**		08.05		17.10
Noyon Nord (CdN station)**		08.17		17.22
Connection with CdN SG line Compiègne–St-Quentin (Paris–Brussels)				
			(1)	
Noyon Nord (CdN station)**		09.05	12.10	19.00
Connection with CdN SG line Compiègne–St-Quentin (Paris–Brussels)				
Noyon Faubourg de Paris**		09.17	12.22	19.12
			(1)	
Noyon Faubourg de Paris	*arrêt*	09.30	12.45	19.30
Origin of MG VFIL line to Lassigny and Montdidier				
Bussy		09.51	13.01	19.39
junction with MG SE line to Ercheu, and Ercheu to Offoy				
Muirancourt	*arrêt*	10.01	13.10	19.43
Guiscard		10.15	13.26	20.15
Plessis-Flavy-Berlancourt	*arrêt*	10.26	13.36	20.27
Golancourt	*arrêt*	10.34	13.44	20.35
Ham		10.45	13.55	20.45
Connection with CdN SG lines to Amiens, Tergnier and Laon. Origin of MG SE line to Albert				

**	60cm gauge (light railway) service		
SG	standard gauge	CdN	*Compagnie du Nord*
MG	metre gauge	SE	*Société Générale des Chemins de Fer Economiques*
		VFIL	*Compagnie Générale des Voie Ferrées d'Intérêt Local*

(1) Only on Saturdays and the first Thursday in the month (market days in Noyon)

that because they were still unable to get access to the main station at Noyon, a goods station had been constructed at the *arrêt* at Pont l'Evêque which would open on 5 September 1923. This had been achieved with state reconstruction money.

Plans for the reconnection to Noyon *Compagnie du Nord* station were made in 1922. The plan was to take the metre gauge lines into the north side of the station, avoiding the reconstruction of the bridge over the standard gauge lines to the old station on the south side. The plans required a bridge 4m wide, of *tablier métallique* type over the Grande Verse river, an arched bridge, probably of brick, 3.5m wide, over the Petite Verse river, and another bridge of *tablier métallique* type, 9m wide, over the road to Soissons, just west of the main station, where the road would also go under the standard gauge lines. There were to be two lines, one for Ham and one for Lassigny and Montdidier, all the way into the new metre gauge station.

In one report, the Chief Engineer said that the route had been established by the German Army during the war. In 1923, he reported that the project was held up at the Grande Verse river, but completion work would start in the spring of 1924. The new route and the new metre gauge station were opened in 1925, except that the bridge under the metre gauge and standard gauge lines for the Soissons road was replaced by a level crossing.

Stations
Noyon station

The new track layout at the standard gauge station was complete by 1925, with the new metre gauge station on the north side of the standard gauge tracks, at the west

Narrow Gauge in the Somme Sector

Table 11.3 Noyon to Lassigny and Montdidier (VFIL)
Summary Timetable January 1922
Selected stops only.

		(1)	(2)		
Montdidier				11.20	17.34
Connection with CdN SG lines Amiens to Compiègne and St-Just-en-Chaussée to Cambrai					
Origin of SE MG line to Albert					
Assainvillers	*arrêt*			11.39	17.51
Rollot		07.46		11.52	18.04
Hainvillers	*arrêt*	07.52		11.58	18.10
Boulogne-la-Grasse		07.59		12.09	18.21
Conchy-les-Pots	*arrêt*	08.04		12.15	18.27
Roye-sur-Matz Nord	a	<u>08.10</u>		12.22	18.34
Connection with CdN SG line Compiègne to Roye (Somme)					
	d			12.30	18.45
Canny-sur-Matz	*arrêt*			12.40	18.55
Lassigny	a			12.50	19.05
	d	06.55	11.15	15.55	
Dives	*arrêt*	07.06	11.26	16.05	
Thiescourt		07.19	11.37	16.19	
Cannectancourt	*arrêt*	07.23	11.43	15.23	
Ville	*arrêt*	07.32	11.51	16.37	
Noyon Faubourg de Paris		07.57	12.20	16.57	
Origin of MG VFIL line to Guiscard and Ham					
Noyon Faubourg de Paris**		08.05		17.10	
Noyon Nord (CdN station)**		08.17		17.22	
Connection with CdN SG line Compiègne–St-Quentin (Paris–Brussels)					
			(2)		
Noyon Nord (CdN station)**		09.05	12.10		19.00
Connection with CdN SG line Compiègne–St-Quentin (Paris–Brussels)					
Noyon Faubourg de Paris**		09.17	12.22		19.12
		(1)		(2)	
Noyon Faubourg de Paris			09.35	12.45	19.25
Origin of MG VFIL line to Guiscard and Ham					
Ville	*arrêt*		09.28	13.04	19.39
Cannectancourt	*arrêt*		09.35	13.14	19.46
Thiescourt			09.38	13.19	19.49
Dives	*arrêt*		09.45	13.30	19.57
Lassigny	a		09.52	13.43	20.05
	d	06.55		14.35	
Canny-sur-Matz	*arrêt*	07.04		14.46	
Roye-sur-Matz Nord	a	07.12		14.55	
Connection with CdN SG line Compiègne to Roye (Somme)					
	d	07.14	08.50		15.35
Conchy-les-Pots	*arrêt*	07.22	09.00		15.44
Boulogne-la-Grasse		07.28	09.08		15.51
Hainvillers	*arrêt*	07.37	09.17		16.00
Rollot		<u>07.42</u>	09.30		16.08
Assainvillers	*arrêt*		09.42		16.19
Montdidier			10.00		16.37
Connection with CdN SG lines Amiens to Compiègne and St-Just-en-Chaussée to Cambrai					
Origin of SE MG line to Albert					

a   arrive   d   depart
**   60cm gauge service (light railway)
Underlined – terminates, not at the end of the line (Lassigny is regarded as the end of a line)
SG   standard gauge   CdN   *Compagnie du Nord*
MG   metre gauge   SE   *Société Générale des Chemins de Fer Economiques*
                               VFIL *Compagnie Générale des Voie Ferrées d'Intérêt Local*
(1) between Boulogne-la-Grasse and Rollot as a trial only
(2) Saturdays and the first Thursday each month, market days in Noyon

11.2 Noyon station as reconstructed, which opened in 1932. The architecture is described on the plaque on the station as 'Art Déco', with the tall windows and the spire on the left giving it the appearance of a stylised church. November 2015. *(Authors)*

11.3 Billard A50D railcar 'Oise 1' at the terminus at Ham of the line from Noyon, in 1953. *(Photo & collection René Brugier)*

end. After the war there was a temporary passenger building, until the new station building was opened in 1932. This is in a gabled neo-classical style, which is still in use.

Between 1929 and 1931 a new bridge for the Soissons road was built over the standard gauge lines, and the dual gauge line through to the goods facilities east of the main station. This replaced the level crossing. There was probably some change to the metre gauge passenger terminus to accommodate this. Figure 11.1 shows Noyon station as it was from 1932.

Ham station and line

After the First World War, both the line from Albert and the line from St-Quentin had termini on the north side of the main lines. The layout from about 1930 is shown in Figure 10.1 (page 196) in Chapter Ten. The metre gauge line from Noyon came in to a short track

NOYON
Compagnie du Nord station
shared with the MG lines to Ham & to Montdidier
from 1932
details of SG goods yards and facilities not shown

Lines (from top) -
MG to Ham (VFIL)
MG to Montdidier (VFIL)
MG to VFIL depot
SG to yard areas (3) (CdN)
SG from and to Creil and Paris (CdN)

to St-Quentin, Valenciennes & Brussels
to Noyon centre
to Soissons

1 VFIL MG station (no buildings)
2 Hotel
3 New bridge 1929-1931
4 Bâtiment des Voyageurs (Main station building)
5 Cour des Voyageurs (Forecourt)
6 Cour des Marchandises (Goods yard)
7 Halle à marchandises (goods hall)

MG Metre gauge
SG Standard gauge
CdN *Compagnie du Nord*
VFIL *Compagnie Générale des Voie Ferrées d'Intérêt Local*
(also often abbreviated as CGL)

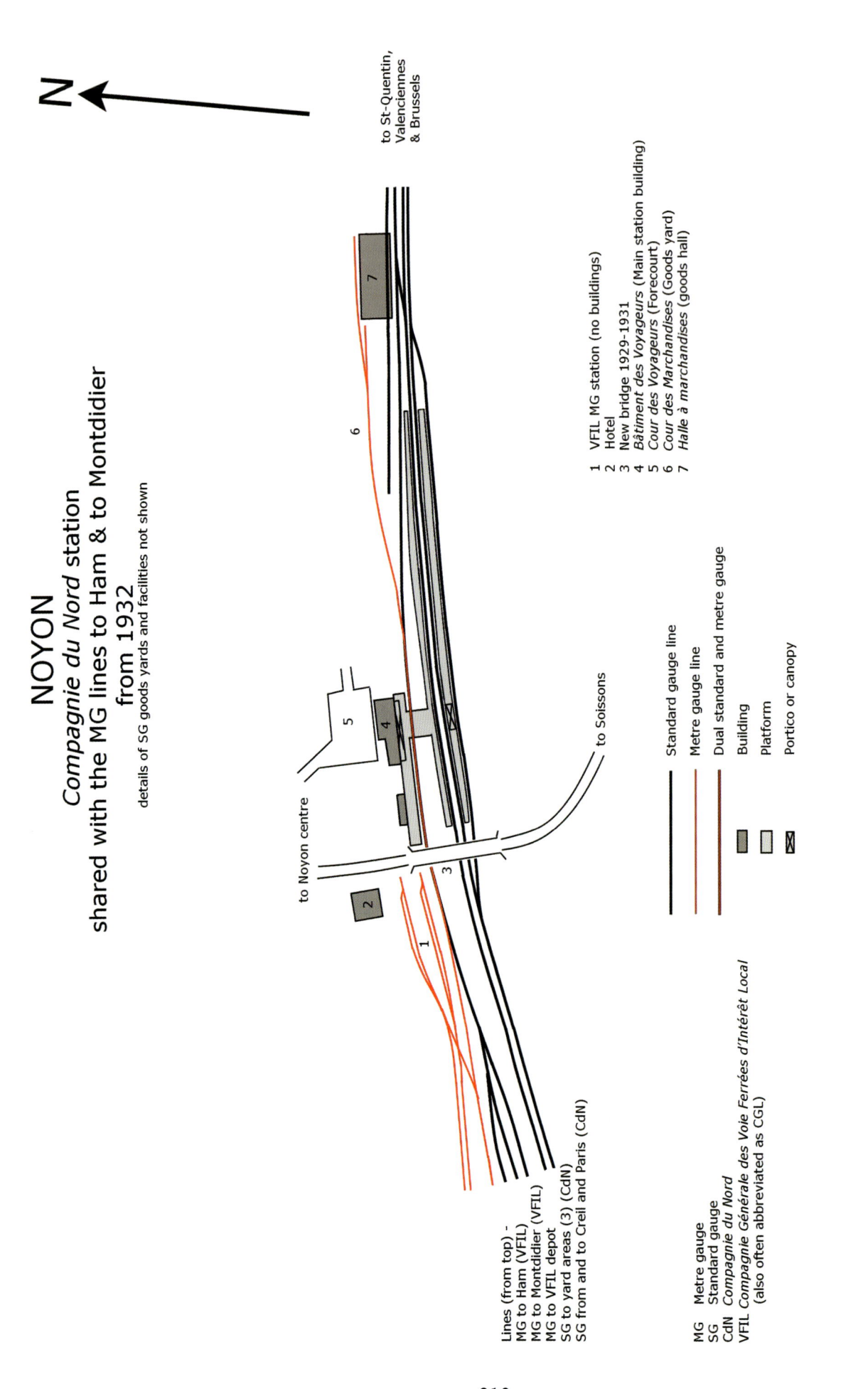

Standard gauge line
Metre gauge line
Dual standard and metre gauge
Building
Platform
Portico or canopy

Figure 11.1

south of the main line and west of the level crossing. There was no metre gauge link across before 1929.

In May 1929, the Chief Engineer of the Oise *département* wrote to *Préfet*, for him to pass on to his opposite number in the Somme *département*. The *Conseil Général* of Oise had voted for the re-establishment of facilities at Ham which had been present before the war, including a local service for goods, and a transhipment to standard gauge. They did not want a connection with SE, which would be costly especially for a tunnel under the Nord lines. Oise was not in control from the border for the last 3.70km to Ham. Oise had conceded operations to the Company Milly–Formerie–Noyon–Guiscard–Lassigny (NGL), Somme to SE. The Somme *département* had offered to hand the bit in Somme to Oise, but threatened that if no agreement was reached, they would declassify the part in Somme and cease operations. Oise objected that they could not unilaterally do this to a line declared of *Utilité Publique*. In the event, the Oise *département* accepted the offer and took over the line all the way to Ham, which they were in fact operating anyway.

No tunnel linking the VFIL line from Noyon with the SE line from Albert was built, but by 1932 and probably from about 1930, there was a crossing on the level of the main lines, to give access to the goods and turning facilities on the north side. By the early 1930s, a shelter had been built by the stub line which formed the terminus of the line from Noyon.

Montdidier station

Before the First World War, there had been a crossing on the level just south of Montdidier metre gauge platforms, allowing the line to Lassigny and Noyon to cross the standard gauge line from Montidier to Roye (Somme). After the war, this was replaced by a bridge. This facilitated operations, especially the through running of trains from Albert to Rollot.

Rolling Stock

During the war, many locomotives were removed, damaged or destroyed. Some items were recovered and repaired, replacements for others had to be purchased.

Steam locomotives

Locomotives up to 1914 for the Noyon network and the Roisel to Hargicourt line are shown in Table 3.4 (Chapter Three). In July 1923 the Chief Engineer of the Oise *département* was able to tell the *Conseil Général* that all the locomotives of the Noyon network had been repaired or replaced.

Locomotives added in 1919 and after are shown in table 11.4. These were an American military surplus Baldwin 0-6-2T, and two 2-6-0T Haine-St-Pierre 24.85 tonne locomotives, all of which were available

Table 11.4 Technical details of Noyonnais (VFIL) locomotives from 1919
(see also table 3.4 up to 1914)

Manufacturer	Baldwin	HSP	SACM
Year(s) of manufacture	1916	1920	1924
Wheel configuration	0-6-2T	2-6-0T	2-6-0T
Manufacturer's No(s)		?? & 1316	7381
Company No(s)	#	14 & 15	13##
Year(s) put in service	pr 1921	1921	1947
Number put in service	1	2	1
Lines	SE/VFIL	SE/VFIL###	VFIL###
Length (m)	7.89	8.61	7.89
Height (m)	3.10	3.30	3.40
Width (m)	2.20	2.45	2.31
Weight empty (tonnes)	20	24.85	22
Diam. of driving wheels (m)	0.87	1.025	0.90
Boiler pressure (kg/cm^2)		12.6	12
Heating surface (m^2)		54	56.50
Diam. of pistons (m)	0.33	0.36	0.32
Piston travel (m)	0.41	0.46	0.42

SE *Société générale des Chemins de fer Economiques* (SE) 1923-27,
VFIL *Compagnie Générale des Voie Ferrées d'Intérêt Local*
HSP Haine-St-Pierre (Belgium)
SACM *Société Alsacienne de Construction Mécanique*
\# 'American military surplus', possibly one of those shown as acquired by SE (see Table 10.1, Chapter Ten)
\#\# transferred from VFIL Pas-de-Calais network in 1947
\#\#\# on closure in 1955 Nos 13 & 15 transferred to VFIL St-Just-en-Chaussée network (Oise *département*); No 15 on CFBS since 30 July 1971

when the lines to Guiscard and to Lassigny were reopened by SE in May 1921. The latter were given the VFIL numbers 14 and 15. In 1947, number 13, which had been working on the VFIL Anvin-Calais and Aire-Berck lines in the Pas-de-Calais *département*, was transferred to Noyon. This SACM 2-6-0T of 22 tonnes had been built in 1922 for the Berck-Plage-Paris-Plage line in the Pas-de-Calais.

The Baldwin 0-6-2T was one of several based at Lassigny for reconstruction from 1919. They had been delivered between August and October 1916 to the 10° Génie of the French Army. These were used from 1920 by SE to provide the service between Lassigny and Montdidier. Only one remained with VFIL after they took over the Noyon lines in January 1922.

Passenger carriages and other rolling stock

We do not know how many passenger carriages or other rolling stock were available exclusively to the

11.4 Haine-Saint-Pierre 2-6-0T No 14 at the Noyon depot of VFIL in 1952. *(Photo M Rifault, collection J-L Rochaix)*

Noyon lines. However, by 1925 the Noyon lines and the Milly-Formerie line together had 18 passenger carriages, 9 *fourgons*, and 238 wagons.

Diesel railcars (Autorails)

In 1932 VFIL took delivery of, and put into service, three Billard A50D railcars for the lines from Noyon to Ham and from Noyon to Lassigny and Rollot. These were labelled Oise No. 1, Oise No. 2 and Oise No.3. Painted dark green, they had the appearance of a single decker bus on rails, with the engine under a bonnet sticking out at the front. With 2 axles (4 wheels), they had a CLM 50hp diesel engine, and could only be driven from one end (the 'front'), so that they required turning at the end of the route. There were 24 sitting and 5 standing places in two classes, officially first and second, but users considered these equivalent to second and third. They were 8.60m long and weighed 7.5 tonnes empty. They remained in service until the lines closed in 1955.

At Ham they had to cross the standard gauge lines to use the turning facilities of the SE yard on the north side. This may have been a major reason for re-establishing a crossing on the level between the two metre gauge lines.

Operations 1929 to 1937

This period saw the introduction of railcars, with improvements of passenger services and line speed, but also a period of wrangling with between VFIL and SE about the service between Rollot and Montdidier.

In 1929, the timetables show a better service than in 1924. Between Noyon and Ham and Noyon and Lassigny, the middle of the day train on market days in Noyon has become a daily service, making it three trains each way every day. One result is that there is one good connection at Lassigny every day each way, for passengers wanting to travel through. On the line from Noyon to Lassigny, an *arrêt* has been added at Le Guidon, where the lines diverged about 1km from Noyon main station. Between Lassigny and Montdidier there was little change, with two services daily, and a partial service in the morning. The evening service from Roye-sur-Matz to Rollot and then back to Lassigny, added between 1922 and 1924, remained.

The Billard railcars were introduced at the beginning of 1933. Timetables from the *Chaix* of February 1933 show that there were three services each way daily between Noyon and Ham, two railcar and one steam on Tuesdays, Thursdays and Saturdays, all railcar on other days. Times vary with market days in Noyon, Saturdays plus the first Tuesday in the month. Between Noyon and Rollot, there are three trains each way every day, two railcar and one steam, but with some adjustments of time for market days in Noyon. There is one additional train all the way each way on Saturdays, market day in Compiègne, for the connection with the Compiègne to Roye (Somme) line at Roye-sur-Matz. At least from 1933, and probably some time before, the service was no longer broken at Lassigny, with all trains through at least to Rollot. Most services were by railcar.

More detailed timetables of May 1935, produced locally for administrative purposes, show that almost

11.5 Billard A50D railcars 'Oise No. 1' and 'Oise No. 2' in the station at Noyon in 1953. Behind, on the northern approach to the bridge over the standard gauge lines, is the hotel, which is still there. *(Photo & collection René Brugier)*

all *arrêts* were now *facultatif* (request stops). The exceptions where stops were required were, on the line to Ham, at the level crossing at 1.31km in Noyon, where the lines diverged, and, on the line to Rollot, at Passel and Roye-sur-Matz *arrêt*. These had been the subject of *Arrêtés Prefectoraux* (Prefect's decrees) between 1931 and 1933.

The *Chaix* of 1936 shows all railcar services for passengers. Timetables for 1936 are shown in Table 11.5. Goods must by then have been going by steam on separate trains. Between Noyon and Ham, there were still three services each way daily, with time variations for market days in Noyon. Times with the railcars were faster, 41 to 51 minutes for the whole journey, compared with 1 hour and 5 to 10 minutes in 1929 with steam. This may not just be because steam is slower, but also some may have been mixed trains stopping to attach or drop of goods wagons.

Between Noyon and Rollot, there were three trains each way in 1936, all railcar. There was still one additional train all the way each way on Saturdays, market day in Compiègne. There was no service shown on to Montdidier, which was being provided by SE with some through services from Albert (see Chapter Ten, and Table 10.5). There were still problems between VFIL and SE about the section from Montdidier to Rollot, as is told in the next section. Between Noyon and Lassigny railcars had improved the journey time, from at best 36 minutes with steam to at best 25 minutes. The worst with steam was 1 hour, which must have been a mixed train, the worst with a railcar was 36 minutes.

Lassigny to Rollot and Montdidier

The line from Montdidier to Rollot had been reopened by the *Société Générale des Chemins de Fer Économiques* (SE) in 1920 and extended by them to Lassigny on 20 November 1920. From 1 January 1922 the service was operated by the *Compagnie Générale des Voie Ferrées d'Intérêt Local* (VFIL). Rollot was the last station in the Somme *département*, the next towards Noyon and Lassigny, Hainvillers, being in the Oise *département*.

Then, in 1930, the concession for the section from Montidier to Rollot was granted retrospectively to SE, who commenced operating the section. By May 1932, SE were providing the service three or four times daily, mostly running through from Albert, and in 1933 there were four trains daily, some provided by railcar. The pattern was the same in 1938 (Table 10.5, Chapter Ten).

In December 1932, the Local and Chief Engineers of Oise reported to the *Préfet*. The *Conseil Général* had voted in September, that the terminus of the line from Noyon to Lassigny and Rollot should be moved back to Montdidier. The Engineers comment that there was no doubt that the need to change at Rollot had wronged the Oise communes, Conchy-les-Pots, Boulogne-la-Grasse, and Hainvillers, for which Montdidier was the closest services centre. They thought that Somme found Rollot to Montdidier a heavy burden and were not interested in change. Costs would be reduced by railcars, about to be introduced. VFIL were going to try one service between Noyon and Montdidier by railcar in each direction, paying for the use of the Somme line. We assume that this recommendation was adopted.

Table 11.5 Noyon to Ham and Noyon to Rollot (VFIL)
Summary Timetable October 1936
Selected stops only

	★	★(1)	★(2)	★	
Noyon	09.01	12.18	15.10	18.40	
Connection with CdN SG line Compiègne–St-Quentin (Paris–Brussels)				
Origin of MG VFIL line to Lassigny and Montdidier				
Bussy	09.15	12.30	15.22	18.52	
junction with MG SE line to Ercheu, and Ercheu to Offoy				
Guiscard	09.28	12.39	15.31	19.01	
Ham	09.50	12.59	15.51	19.21	
Connection with CdN SG lines Amiens, Tergnier and Laon.				
Origin of MG SE line to Albert				
	★(1)	★(2)	★(1)	★(2)	★
Ham	07.23	07.30	11.08	12.22	16.44
Connection with CdN SG lines to Amiens, Tergnier and Laon,					
Origin of MG SE line to Albert					
Guiscard	07.45	07.51	11.32	12,46	17.05
Bussy	07.57	08.00	11.46	13.00	17.14
junction with MG SE line to Ercheu, and Ercheu to Offoy					
Noyon	08.12	08.12	11.59	13.13	17.26
Connection with CdN SG line Compiègne–St-Quentin (Paris–Brussels)					
Origin of MG VFIL line to Lassigny and Montdidier					

	★	★(3)	★(1)	★(2)	★	
Noyon	09.02	10.32	12.27	15.09	18.17	
Origin of MG VFIL line to Guiscard and Ham						
Connection with CdN SG line Compiègne–St-Quentin (Paris–Brussels)						
Ville	09.11	10.42	12.40	15.20	18.26	
Thiescourt	09.17	10.48	12.47	15,26	18.32	
Lassigny	09.27	10.58	12.58	15.37	18.42	
Roye-sur-Matz Nord	09.39	11.24	13.11	15.49	19.04	
Connection with CdN SG line Compiègne to Roye						
Boulogne-la-Grasse	09.46	11.31	13.21	15.58	19.11	
Rollot	09.53	11.38	13.30	16.07	19.18	
Origin of SE MG line to Albert						
	★(1)	★(2)	★(1)	★(2)	★(3)	★
Rollot	07.07	07.17	10.58	11.50	12.54	16.22
Origin of SE MG line to Albert						
Boulogne-la-Grasse	07.15	07.25	11.06	12.00	13.02	16.31
Roye-sur-Matz Nord	07.23	07.33	11.19	12.08	13.30	16.41
Connection with CdN SG line Compiègne to Roye						
Lassigny	07.34	07.44	11.30	12.19	13.41	16.53
Thiescourt	07.48	07.55	11.41	12.30	13.52	17.05
Ville	07.57	08.01	11.47	12.36	13.58	17.12
Noyon	08.10	08.10	11.56	12.45	14.07	17.25
Origin of MG VFIL line to Guiscard and Ham						
Connection with CdN SG line Compiègne–St-Quentin (Paris–Brussels)						

★   railcar service
SG   standard gauge   CdN   *Compagnie du Nord*
MG   metre gauge   SE   *Société Générale des Chemins de Fer Economiques*
                                     VFIL   *Compagnie Générale des Voie Ferrées d'Intérêt Local*
(1) Only on Saturdays and the first Thursday in the month (market days in Noyon)
(2) Except Saturdays and the first Thursday in the month
(3) Saturdays only, market day in Compiègne

In the *Chaix* of February 1933, there is no indication of any service beyond Rollot, but in May 1935 there was an evening train every day from Noyon to Montidier and back to Rollot. A morning train from and to Noyon was also extended to Montdidier, except on Saturdays and the first Tuesday of the month, market days in Noyon.

In the *Chaix* of October 1936, there are no VFIL services shown between Rollot and Montdidier (Table 11.5). However, letters of May and June 1937,

The metre gauge railways of the Oise and Aisne départements 12 November 1918 to 1955

11.6 Rollot station from the track side in May 2016. The original 'Lambert' type 2 station has been extended at the end opposite the goods hall. This was not there before the First World War, and it may have been added when the station became the permanent connection between the Albert and Noyon lines in 1930. *(Authors)*

11.7 The locomotive shed at Rollot was probably also built around 1930. May 2016. *(Authors)*

from VFIL to the Chief Engineer (Oise), state that the through services were continuing as in 1935. Now SE were introducing new services, one of which would effectively replace the morning service to and from Noyon, the one run when there was no market in Noyon. However, the evening service could not be replaced in a way which would continue to assure the connection with the standard gauge service at Montdidier, and SE had asked VFIL to continue this. The morning service was withdrawn, which VFIL said would save money as these services were largely loss-making.

The evening service was continued, but from 1 July to 10 October 1937 VFIL found that they only had 302 passengers, less than 3 per day. So the evening service was also withdrawn, leaving SE to provide the entire service between Rollot and Montdidier.

Operations 1938 and 1939

The services between Noyon and Ham, and Noyon and Rollot, continued much the same through 1938 and from May 1939, with minor adjustments of time, to allow for time changes of connections. By May 1939, the connection at Roye-sur-Matz, for the line

217

between Compiègne and Roye (Somme) was with a replacement bus service for the standard gauge line.

From the Second World War to closure (1955)

By February 1940, VFIL had moved their offices from Paris to Berck-Plage, at the end of the VFIL line from Aire-sur-la-Lys. From May 1940, the timetables show two trains daily each between Noyon and Ham, and between Noyon and Lassigny. There is a third train to and from Lassigny on market days in Noyon, still Saturdays and the first Thursday of each month. All the trains are now marked '*Trains Mixte Voyageurs*', suggesting a move back to steam and mixed passenger and goods trains. There is no indication of any service between Lassigny and Rollot, which must have been discontinued. This was just before the German occupation of northern France.

Timetables for May 1944 show that between Noyon and Ham and Noyon and Lassigny there was one service each way per day, plus a second on Saturdays and Thursdays on a trial basis. There is no service between Lassigny and Rollot. This is a steam service with slow times, but coal was less scarce than diesel fuel. It was based on one locomotive and train set based at Lassigny and one at Ham.

After the war, the service returned to two each way daily, at variable hours. The passenger service was provided by railcars but running more slowly than in 1936. In May 1955 Noyon–Ham took 1 hour 9-10 minutes, compared with 41-52 minutes in 1936. Noyon–Lassigny took 40-42 minutes in May 1955, but only 25-31 minutes in 1936.

In *The End of the Line* (Cleaver-Hume Press, 1955), 'a Book about Railways and Places Mainly Continental', Bryan Morgan describes (pp 46-48) a journey on dark green Oise railcars; No. 1 from Lassigny to Noyon and then No. 2 from Noyon to Ham. He had to wait 7 hours at Noyon, where 'the metric lines to Lassigny and to Ham meet but do not connect'. He then describes a journey to Ham through dark woods and wide landscapes, complete with poachers alighting at a thicket of their choice, abetted by the driver. We know of no finer epitaph for these lines.

Closures

The service between Lassigny and Rollot was closed in 1939 or early 1940 and was never restored after the war. SE closed the section from Montdidier to Rollot on 15 April 1948. VFIL closed the lines from Noyon to Ham and Noyon to Lassigny on 31 December 1955.

Disposal of assets

The old depot building at Noyon remains, the lines replaced with standard gauge, which are connected to the SNCF lines. It is used as a workshop to repair diesel locomotives.

On closure of the lines from Noyon in 1955, VFIL locomotives numbers 13 and 15 were transferred to the VFIL St-Just-en-Chaussée network, also in the Oise

11.8 Billard A50D railcar 'Oise No. 2' at Noyon in 1952. The bridge over the standard gauge lines can be seen behind. *(Photo M Rifault, collection J-L Rochaix)*

département. Both these locomotives survive. *Haine-St-Pierre* 2-6-0T number 15 now operates on the *Chemin de Fer de la Baie de Somme* (CFBS), and SACM 2-6-0T number 13 is on display at MTVS Valmondois (more details in Chapter Twelve).

St-Quentin - Le Catelet - Caudry (SQLeCC)

By the end of the First World War, the track had been completely removed, structures and buildings were damaged, and the rolling stock had been destroyed or removed. Part of the formation, from the industrial branch at Bellicourt to east of Joncourt, was used in October 1918 for part of the 60cm gauge line to Bohain (see Chapter Eight, and walk 4, Chapter Twelve). Around the western edge of St-Quentin, much of the path was badly damaged by the construction of the Hindenburg line (see walk 5, Chapter Twelve).

Reconstruction and reopening

The Nord and Aisne *départements* considered the advantages of reconstruction in standard gauge, but this was rejected. The *Société des Chemins de Fer du Cambrésis* (CFC) were put into administration in 1921, and the *Société Générale des Chemins de Fer Économiques* (SE) were charged with restoring operations in metre gauge.

From Villers-Outréaux to Caudry was reopened on 14 April 1921, and from Villers-Outréaux to St-Quentin-Cambrésis on 1 November 1923. From St-Quentin-Cambrésis to St-Quentin-St-Jean was reconstructed for goods traffic. From St-Quentin-St-Jean to St-Quentin-Nord was never rebuilt, and this section was formally declassified in 1933. St-Quentin-Cambrésis to St-Quentin-St-Jean was abandoned in 1936. The Cambrésis network, including St-Quentin to Caudry, was restored to CFC in 1924.

On reopening, there were at least three services daily in each direction, but it is likely that, as later, some of the services were broken at Le Catelet.

Stations

The stations were rebuilt as they had been before the First World War.

Rolling stock

Up to 1914, the rolling stock had been fitted with two buffers and central couplings, but during the war these were replaced with a central buffer with couplings below. Continuous vacuum braking was retained.

Steam locomotives

We do not know how many locomotives were recovered after the war. The steam motive power was reinforced by the purchase of second hand locomotives:

- 1 0-6-0T   Pinguely of 1921 acquired from a *sucrerie* (No. 21)
- 1 0-6-0T   Corpet-Louvet of 1907 coming from the Tramway from Versailles to Maule (No. 22)
- 3 2-6-0T   Pinguelys of 1903 bought from the *Chemins de fer Départementaux de la Côte d'Or* (Nos. 34 to 36)

11.9 St-Quentin-Cambrésis station, Postcard postmarked 1904. After the First World War this was the end of the passenger service from Caudry. *(Authors' collection)*

Railcars
During the late 1920s, the company put into service some railcars, because of a reduction in passenger traffic. Two small light railcars with a 30hp petrol engine and 18 places were put into service in 1927. These were followed by four Renault-Scemia type RS4 railcars, with a 32hp petrol engine and 24 places seated, delivered in 1928-1929.

Operations from 1930
The timetable for 1933 shows three trains each way per day between St-Quentin-Cambrésis and Le Catelet, and four per day between Le Catelet and Caudry. There were also two each way between Le Catelet and Villers-Outréaux, one of which appeared to run through from St-Quentin. There was one proper through service from St-Quentin to Caudry, but what appears on the timetable to be one through service the other way actually involved a 2-hour layover at Le Catelet. It was probably the same train set, because the timetable was marked when a change of train is required.

By 1934, many of the services were provided by bus. There were two bus services daily all the way between St-Quentin and Caudry, and one each way daily between St-Quentin and Le Catelet and between Le Catelet and Caudry. The only steam passenger services remaining were two services daily between St-Quentin and Le Catelet, so all services between Le Catelet and Caudry were by bus. At Caudry the buses arrived at and departed from the main square, and all but one each way daily cut out the standard gauge station. At St-Quentin they went on from the Cambrésis station to and from St-Quentin Nord.

CFC discontinued all passenger services on this line in 1936, and the whole service was being provided by bus. The bus services were two each way daily, and more on Sundays and Feast Days, and were genuine through services. The buses were also faster, taking about two hours, compared with more than three hours for the steam services, even without a layover or change at Le Catelet.

In 1936, CFC also abandoned the goods line between St-Quentin-Cambrésis and St-Quentin-St-Jean. The rest of the line was kept open for goods traffic. The Company took the opportunity to scrap or sell some locomotives. One of those sold was No.5 'Clary', an 0-6-0T Corpet-Louvet of 1888, which probably worked on the St-Quentin to Caudry line. It was bought by an English company and sold on to work at Loddington Ironstone Company in Northamptonshire. It is now on display at the Irchester Narrow Gauge Railway Museum at Wellingborough, with the name *Cambrai* (see Chapter Twelve).

The Second World War to closure (1960)
At some time during the Second World War, probably near the beginning, the passenger service between St-Quentin and Caudry was restarted. Coal was less scarce than petrol or diesel fuel, and on the Cambrésis system could come direct from mines near Denain in the Nord *département*. In the timetable of May 1944, there is one steam service all the way each way, based on Caudry, with one each way from St-Quentin-Cambrésis to Le Catelet and back, and one each way from Le Catelet to Caudry and back, based at Le Catelet. The service could be run with two locomotives and train sets, one based at Caudry and one at Le Catelet. The whole journey took just under three hours, much the same as in 1933.

In 1942 the network acquired three 2-8-2T Corpet-Louvet locomotives of 44.6 tonnes, built for a network in Guinée, which could not be delivered because Guinée was in the hands of the Free French. These were valued for pulling heavy goods trains, despite excessive axle weights for the track. When they returned to the manufacturer in 1947 to be delivered to Guinée, three lighter (36 tonnes unladen) but similar machines were ordered in 1947 and delivered by Corpet-Louvet in 1948, numbers 40 to 42. 41 was scrapped prematurely after a boiler explosion in January 1953, and the others worked until 1960. With the arrival of larger locomotives, some Corpet and Fives-Lille locomotives were sold to industrial users, in Sénégal, Algeria, Brazil and Great Britain. Probably the heavier locomotives were not used between St-Quentin and Caudry.

Closure
The passenger service between St-Quentin-Cambrésis and Caudry closed again at the end of the Second World War or soon after. St-Quentin-Cambrésis to Le Catelet was closed to the remaining goods traffic on 31 December 1954, and Le Catelet to Caudry on 1 September 1955. Of the Cambrésis network, only the line between Caudry and Denain remained, which closed for passengers on 16 October 1960, and for all traffic on 31 December 1960.

Tramways of St-Quentin
After the First World War, the service beween St-Quentin and Caudry stopped at St-Quentin-Cambrésis, and travel between St-Quentin-Cambrésis and the Gare Nord was by tram. Line 1 between the Gare Nord (*Compagnie du Nord*) and the Cimetière du Nord (adjacent to St-Quentin-Cambrésis metre gauge station), and the other lines, were closed in 1956, outlasting the passenger service on the Cambrésis line to Caudry.

The metre gauge railways of the Oise and Aisne départements 12 November 1918 to 1955

Guise to Bohain and Le Catelet (GBC)
After the war this line reopened in 1922 and closed in 1951.

Roisel - Hargicourt
In autumn 1918, the British Army used the track bed of the line for a standard gauge line and prolonged it to Bellicourt (see Chapter Eight). There was a nearby 60cm gauge line (light railway), also built on to Bellicourt. Since the original plan for the line had been to continue it to Bellicourt, to join with the metre gauge line from St-Quentin to Caudry, it is surprising that with the existence of a formation the opportunity was not taken to extend it with the reconstruction.

Standard gauge operation
After the war, the concessionaire, the *Compagnie des Chemins de fer d'intérêt local du Nord de la France* (NF), refused to take the line back at standard gauge, and it was placed in administration in 1919. A temporary standard gauge service was started from 1 April 1920 by the *Ministère des Régions Libérées* (MRL). For the standard gauge operations, the Aisne *département* made available two 0-8-0 locomotives, Nos. 4.652 & 4.656.

Metre gauge reopening
The line was restored to metre gauge and reopened in 1923, operated by the *Société Générale des Chemins de Fer Économiques* (SE), who also ran the Somme lines.

Buildings
The station at Roisel was reconstructed in 1921, for the standard gauge lines there.

Rolling Stock
Much of the metre gauge rolling stock was destroyed or removed by the German Army during the war.

Steam locomotives – One of the three pre-war locomotives (see Table 3.4, Chapter Three), which were all Corpet-Louvet 0-6-0Ts, was eventually retrieved. To this, SE, who operated the line from 1923 to 1927, added three more Corpet-Louvet 0-6-0T locomotives, unladen weight 17.5 tonnes, for the reopening in metre gauge in 1923. One more locomotive of unknown type was added in 1925.

Other rolling stock – Four new mixed class bogie carriages were ordered in 1920 for MG reopening 1923. Two *fourgons* and 43 wagons (thirteen covered, eighteen open and twelve flat) were also ordered.

Operations
Operations were allocated to SE from 1 November 1923 and restored to NF in 1927. From 1923 there were no more than two trains per day. The *Chaix* of July 1928 shows two passenger services each way per day (journey time 27 to 37 minutes), first and second class. This could be provided by one locomotive and passenger train set based at Hargicourt.

In the light of this, the passenger stock replaced seems excessive. However, the main purpose of the line had always been goods, and perhaps three locomotives and the wagons were all required.

Closure
The line closed on 31 December 1932 and was *déclassée* (declassified) by formal decree in 1933.

Tergnier - Anizy-Pinon
After the war, this metre gauge electric tramway did not reopen to St-Gobain until 1934, with a new branch to Charmes. St-Gobain to Anizy-Pinon never reopened. Operations were stopped by bombing in 1940, and the track and overhead wiring were later dismantled by the Germans. The line never reopened and was declassified in 1948.

Chauny to Coucy-le-Château and Soissons
During the war, the German army used this line from Chauny to Guny. After the German retreat to the Hindenburg Line in March 1917, the French army built a standard gauge line from Appilly to Blérancourt, and then used the metre gauge trackbed to Trosly-Loire and Coucy. After the war the French military line from Appilly to Blérancourt and Coucy reopened in standard gauge in 1919. In June 1921 there were two passenger trains each way on this line. After long discussions the metre gauge was laid as a four rail dual gauge system between Blérancourt and Coucy. The line was fully open from 1928, and the standard gauge military line from Appilly to Blérancourt was abandoned, but the dual gauge section from Blérancourt to Coucy remained.

In 1942, the German authorities closed the line from Chauny to Blérancourt and dismantled the track to recover the materials. After the Second World War, there were two weekly market day trains between Soissons-St Waast and Coucy, until closure in 1948. After 1948, Blérancourt to Coucy remained as a standard gauge line for goods traffic until 1963.

Chapter Twelve

Things to see and do now

In 1982, the *départements* of France were brought together again into 28 *régions* (regions). The Somme, Oise and Aisne *départements* became the modern *région* of Picardie, with the capital at Amiens. To the north, the Nord and Pas-de-Calais *départements* became the *région* Nord-Pas-de-Calais, with the capital at Lille, *Préfecture* of the Nord *département*. From 1 January 2016, 16 of the 22 *régions* of Metropolitan France were involved in mergers, so that now there are only 13. Picardie was joined with Nord-Pas-de-Calais to make one huge *région*, Hauts de France, for the north of France, with the capital at Lille.

The Track

In general, the original routes of railways can be identified using old maps; current large-scale maps showing remains; satellite images; and by walking the ground as far as is possible. Some of the original earthworks, and some bridges and other features, are shown on the IgN (Institut Géographique National) 1:25000 (1 cm = 250 m) maps. The older editions are in general more helpful in identifying earthworks and 'other linear features', which are often related to old railways, than the newer ones. However, there are far more of these clues for broader gauges than for the 60cm gauge lines. Satellite images of France can be seen on Google Earth or at www.geoportail.fr. In places, the lines of old railways are obvious on satellite images, but in some other places they can still be faintly detected by linear changes of colour in fields. Our suggested walks offer glimpses of some of what is left. Regrettably, most of the land was sold soon after the closure of the lines and much is now in private hands.

Stations and halts

A list of metre gauge stations and halts on the principle lines which have appeared in this book, with the location and current status of each, is available from the authors.

Type 1 stations were larger and in more important locations, type 2 stations smaller. The types on the lines built by SE, those from Albert and the line from Offoy to Ercheu, are described in Chapter Two. They were very different from those built by companies associated with Alfred Lambert, on the lines from Noyon to Ham, Noyon to Montdidier, and Bussy to Ercheu, which are described in Chapter Three. Sometimes stations built as type two later became more important, but retained the same buildings. This happened at Bussy (49° 37' 22" N 2° 59' 11" E), on the Noyon to Ham line, which later became the junction for the line to Ercheu and Offoy, and at Rollot (49° 35' 42" N 2° 39' 15" E), which after

12.1 The former line from Doullens looking towards Albert, and the halt at Vauchelles which is just round the corner. Now 'Rue de la Gare', with new posts and railings on the old bridge over a small stream, but the speed allowed has changed little. April 2015. *(Authors)*

the First World War became the interchange station between VFIL services from Lassigny and Noyon, and SE services from Montdidier and Albert. The original 'Lambert' type 2 station has been extended, and it is most likely that this dates from 1930, after which the services from Montdidier and from Noyon always ended here (see picture 11.6, Chapter Eleven).

After the closure, stations and the associated land were sold. Many of the stations and some of their associated buildings have survived. Most of the stations can be seen easily but a few are partly hidden up private drives. Most are now in use as private houses, after variable amounts of refurbishment and extension, but almost all are still easily recognisable. When looking at the stations please respect the privacy of the present occupants.

The Albert group of lines (SE)

The larger, type 1, stations at Acheux and Ercheu have been demolished. Of the rest, Offoy (49° 45' 37" N 2° 59' 57" E) is well preserved as a private house, and in the garden a sign, which must originally have been on the platform, points the way to the village. Bray-sur-Somme (49° 56' 23" N 2° 43' 15" E) has been much modified as a *Centre de Secours* (Fire and Rescue service station), but the name is still prominent (see picture 2.15, Chapter Two).

12.2 The SE type 1 station at Offoy, now a well preserved private house. April 2015. *(Authors)*

12.3 Some are less well preserved. The semi-derelict SE type 2 station at Louvencourt, now a store for farm equipment, in a field used for cattle. March 2016. *(Authors)*

There are many of the smaller, SE type 2, stations still to be seen. Some are smart private houses. A few are derelict, as is the one at Louvencourt (50° 05' 19" N 2° 29' 41" E) on the line from Doullens to Albert.

There are still many halt buildings to be seen, but many others have been demolished. The halt at Vauchelles (50° 05' 37" N 2° 28' 24" E) was at some time extended with a goods hall. The saddest of those that remain is the derelict halt building at Mametz (49° 59' 34" N 2° 43' 54" E). Some of the *arrêts* were at major level crossings, and at some there is still a crossing cottage, which was built for staff manning the crossing.

Of the shared stations at the ends of the lines, that at Doullens (50° 09' 37" N 2° 20' 27" E) was in one of those sad towns in northern France which has now lost all of its railways. The standard gauge lines from here

12.4 The derelict halt building at Mametz, on the line from Albert to Péronne. March 2016. *(Authors)*

12.5 The path after the First World War of the former metre gauge line from Albert and Péronne into Ham station. The site of the former metre gauge level crossing can be seen straight ahead. The terminus of the metre gauge line from Noyon was beyond the level crossing on the left, on the other side of the standard gauge tracks. April 2015. *(Authors)*

went to Amiens, to Longpré, to Béthune via Frévent and St-Pol-sur-Ternoise, and to Arras, as well as the metre gauge line to Albert. The track is still in place towards Amiens (through Gézaincourt halt), but the station area is now a retail park.

The stations at Albert and at Péronne are described in Walks Two and Three respectively. The standard gauge station building at Ham is as rebuilt after the First World War (picture 10.4, Chapter Ten). The SE metre gauge station building is almost opposite the main line station. The path of the metre gauge line into the station can still be seen.

Montdidier station (49° 38' 29" N 2° 33' 47" E) is still in use for the standard gauge line from Compiègne to Amiens. The remains of the station for the line from St-Just-en-Chaussée, going on to Roye (Somme) can be seen in the undergrowth. There are no remains of the metre gauge station, either that from Albert, or that of the line from Noyon and Rollot.

The Noyon lines (NGL, later VFIL)

There were only two 'Lambert' type 1 stations on the lines from Noyon to Ham and from Noyon to Montdidier. These were at Guiscard (49° 39' 32" N 3° 02' 50" E) on the line to Ham, and at Lassigny (49° 35' 07" N 2° 50' 29" E) on the Montidier line. There is a modern photograph of Lassigny station in Chapter Three (picture 3.2).

There are many examples of 'Lambert' type 2 stations on these lines. The station at Boulogne-la-Grasse (49°

12.6 The 'Lambert' type 2 station at Canny-sur-Matz, on the line from Noyon to Montdidier. November 2015. *(Authors)*

12.7 The name plate on the track side of the 'Lambert' type 2 station at Boulogne-le-Grasse, in red on white enamel. May 2016. *(Authors)*

36' 33" N 2° 42' 23" E) has a particularly good example of an enamelled station name. At Roye-sur-Matz (49° 35' 38" N 2° 45' 24" E), the standard gauge station building survives, with a French memorial of spring 1918 in the forecourt area. The *Maison d'Habitation* (living quarters) just up the road, is built in 'Lambert' style, like a station, but has been extended at the back. The whole area was probably rebuilt after the First World War, and the crossing cottage on the D27 at the end of the station approach has the date 1919 on it. Just across the field the A1 autoroute, and beyond it the TGV, both from Paris to Lille, thunder past.

Noyon station (49° 34' 38" N 3° 00' 23" E) was rebuilt after the First World War in Neo-Gothic style (see picture 11.2, Chapter Eleven). On the track side is a large gap between the passenger building and the modern tracks. This was where the dual gauge line came through to the goods area beyond (see Figure 11.1, Chapter Eleven). On the passenger building is a plaque with the history of the station, and a map showing the standard and metre gauge lines in the Noyon area after the First World War.

Depots and other remains

The VFIL depot at Noyon remains, in the Rue Marceau at 49° 34' 32" N 2° 59' 59" E. This was by the route of the dual metre gauge lines. The lines have been replaced with standard gauge, which are connected to the SNCF lines. It is used as a workshop to repair diesel locomotives.

At Ham, the former SE shed for two locomotives is at 49° 44' 24" N 3° 04' 33" E, in the large disused area beyond the passenger building still in use by SNCF (picture 10.5, Chapter Ten). There are a few standard gauge tracks left in this area, and the remains of a goods platform. This was the goods area for the main line, and the terminus of the Intérêt Local line from St-Quentin, as well as the metre gauge goods and terminus area. There is a modern picture of the locomotive shed at Bussy in Chapter Two (picture 2.9), and of that at Rollot in Chapter Eleven (picture 11.7).

Bridges

The site of the metre gauge bridge over the standard gauge lines at Albert is described in Walk Two at the end of this chapter. The bridges at Péronne, including the remains of the bridge of the metre gauge line over the standard gauge line from Péronne to Roisel, are described in Walk Three.

The abutments for the former oblique lattice girder bridge of the metre gauge line from Ercheu to Bussy over the Canal du Nord remain, at 49° 37' 27" N 2° 57' 22" E. This was between Semaize halt and Haudival *arrêt*. The eastern abutment is easier to reach, a short walk along the towpath on the east side. There is an access point 250m south where you can park, but you may prefer to park on the D91 and walk a bit further. On both sides the path of the former line continues along embankments.

The First World War and the French and British 60cm gauge railways

Many of the place names mentioned in the text on railways during the First World War, in Chapters Five to

12.8 The metre gauge depot at Noyon, built after the First World War, is now a standard gauge repair and maintenance facility for diesel locomotives. The fourth entrance, on the right, is obscured by a newer shed. November 2015. *(Authors)*

12.9 The eastern abutment for the former oblique lattice girder bridge of the metre gauge line from Ercheu to Bussy, over the Canal du Nord. There is an equivalent abutment on the west side. To the right the path of the former line continues along an embankment. May 2016. *(Authors)*

Eight, were local British forces names at the time. Most are not identifiable on modern maps. Examples are particularly numerous on the 1916 Somme battlefield, especially on the east side of the Ancre. Tara and Usna hills, and Nab (or Blighty), Usna, Tara, Mash, Sausage, Avoca and Caterpillar valleys are not marked on modern maps. However, they should be identifiable on the modern *Institut Géographique National* (IGN) 1:25,000 maps from the information on the First World War railway maps in this book. Villages have not changed name, or only slightly, and most of the farms are the same. Bronfay Ferme, Ferme Rouge, and Ferme du Mouquet are all marked.

War has been part of the scene of this part of France for centuries. The battlefields of Crécy (1346) and Agincourt (1415) are not far away. In 1940 the German Panzer divisions swept across this part of France. The British Guards Armoured Division under Lieutenant-General Sir Brian Horrocks crossed the Somme on 31 August 1944, and reached Douai by nightfall, having advanced 50 miles (80km). Both these forces crossed the junction of the D938 from Albert to Doullens with the D919 from Amiens to Bapaume at the south end of Hédauville village (50° 02' 33" N 2° 34' 14" E). In 1415 Henry V of England also came through here on his way to Agincourt, so it has been dubbed the 'Crossroads of the Three Armies'.

It has been estimated that more than 200,000 British soldiers died on the Somme, nearly 30 per cent of total British deaths on the Western Front. This compares with 250,000 at Ypres. The French probably lost 90,000 men here, but of course suffered higher casualties elsewhere, especially at Verdun. German deaths were probably nearly 120,000. Being in a railway company was less hazardous than service in the infantry, but despite this, many members of railway companies were killed during the First World War.

Of the First World War light railways themselves there is little to see. The abutments of one light railway bridge, probably from that conflict, can be seen in Albert (see Walk Two).

It is worth visiting the area around Aveluy. In the valley just north west of Aveluy village there is a water tank on a concrete frame in a field, at 50° 01' 38" N 2° 38' 40" E, close to the D129 to Martinsart. There are no identifiers on the water tank, but it just happens that it is precisely by the path of one of the tracks in Pioneer Yard, which was in this valley in 1916 and 1917 (see Figure 5.4, Chapter Five). This was where the standard gauge line from Acheux, which in 1916 took the path of the metre gauge line from Doullens to Albert, left the metre gauge line to join the main line north from Albert. Near to the tank is a cage full of old bits of concrete and a piece of corrugated iron, and a few items of old machinery. None is definitely identifiable to the First World War.

A little further north on the east of the D50 from Albert to Miraumont is Aveluy Wood Cemetery (50° 02' 43" N 2° 39' 37" E). This is on the site of the 1916 Lancashire Dump, which was on one of the first 60cm gauge tramways in this area. Across the Ancre from here is Authuille. When we visited in March 2016, the *commune* had marked the roads and tracks with the 1916 British Army names, in memory of the 1916

12.10 The water tank on the site of the former standard gauge Pioneer Yard, of 1916 and 1917. The cage contains bits of concrete and other artefacts. The path of the former metre gauge line from Doullens to Albert is up the hill at the back. March 2016. *(Authors)*

battle, but these will have gone now. At the corner of Thiepval Wood (50° 03' 09" N 2° 40' 11" E) the sign said 'Speyside Road'. From the corner of the wood, the 1916 tramway went up the south east side towards the front line. From here you can see the top of the Thiepval Memorial on the hill.

South of Authuille village is the entrance to Blighty (or Nab) Valley. It is worth parking by the D151 road (50° 01' 59" N 2° 39' 53" E) and following the footpath to Blighty Valley cemetery (50° 02' 00" N 2° 40' 07" E). The 1916 standard gauge Nab Valley railway came up here, and the 60cm gauge railway from Aveluy to Donnet Post and Ovillers. The light railway turned back at the end of the field by the cemetery and ascended the hillside opposite to reach the plateau (see Chapter Six). As you walk up to the cemetery you can clearly see the ledge cut into the hillside for the light railway 100 years ago. You can also look at bits of it from a local road at the top (50° 01' 54" N 2° 40' 05" E), but at the top the formation disappears into fields.

At the junction of the D1515 with the D20 from Aveluy to La Boiselle is Crucifix Corner (50° 01' 36" N 2° 39' 57" E). beginning of the first trench tramway up the hill to Ovillers. There is a modern commemorative sculpture here now.

Rolling stock

Surviving motive power units relevant to this book are shown in Table 12.1. Further details of all the locations and organisations where they are now can be found on their websites.

12.11 The Cross of Sacrifice at Blighty Valley Cemetery (CWGC). Behind on the hillside the ledge for the 1916 light railway from Aveluy to Donnet Post and Ovillers can be seen. March 2016. *(Authors)*

Things to see and do now

Table 12.1 Present location of some relevant narrow gauge rolling stock

Item of rolling stock	Organisation	Country	Type	Status
Metre gauge locomotives				
Haine Saint Pierre 2-6-0T No. 15 (1)	CFBS	France	steam	in regular use
SACM 2-6-0T No. 13 (2)	MTVS	France	steam	in static display
Corpet-Louvet No. 5 (3)	INGRM	England	steam	in static display
60cm gauge locomotives and tractors				
Hunslet 4-6-0T WD No. 303	WOLT	England	steam	in steam
Baldwin 4-6-0T WD No. 778	LBNGRS	England	steam	in use
Baldwin 4-6-0T WD No. 794	WHHR	Wales	steam	in restoration
Alco-Cooke 2-6-2T WD No. 1240	AMTP	France	steam	in static display
Alco-Cooke 2-6-2T WD No. 1257	Tacot des Lacs	France	steam	formerly CFCD
Alco-Cooke 2-6-2T WD No. 1265 (4)	FR	Wales	steam	being overhauled
Hudswell Clarke 0-6-0WT Works No. 1238	MRT	England	steam	in use
Decauville 0-6-0T Works No. 1652	CFCD	France	steam	in use
Kerr-Stuart 0-6-0T Works No. 2405 (6)	WLLR	England	steam	in use
Kerr-Stuart 0-6-0T Works No. 2451 (5)	L&BR	England	steam	in use
Kerr-Stuart 0-6-0T Works No. 3014	MRT	England	steam	in use
Henschel 0-8-0T	AMTP	France	steam	in use
Hartmann DFB 0-8-0T	AMTP	France	steam	in static display
Borsig DFB 0-8-0 tender	CFCD	France	steam	in use
Krauss DFB 0-8-0T	CFCD	France	steam	in static display
Orenstein & Koppel DFB 0-8-0T	CFCD	France	steam	in static display
Orenstein & Koppel DFB 0-6-0T	CFCD	France	steam	in static display
Orenstein & Koppel DFB 0-10-0T	CFCD	France	steam	in static display
DFB type 0-8-0T	Tacot des Lacs	France	steam	in static display
Decauville 0-6-2T (7)	AMTP	France	steam	in steam
Franco-Belge KDL 0-8-0T	CFCD	France	steam	in steam
Baldwin 2-6-2T (8)	Tacot des Lacs	France	steam	in working order
Dick Kerr PE	Tacot des Lacs	France	petrol electric	
Simplex 20hp WD No. LR 264	WHHR	Wales	petrol	in working order
Simplex 20hp WD No. LR 2832	MRT	England	petrol	in working order
Simplex 20hp Works No. MR 2197	MRT	England	now diesel	in working order
Simplex 20hp WD No. LR 2593	AMHC	England	petrol	in static display
Simplex 40hp 'open' LR 2228 (9)	FR	Wales	petrol	in working order
Simplex 40hp 'protected' WD No. LR 3090	MRT	England	petrol	in working order
Simplex 40hp 'protected' WD No. LR 3098	LBNGRS	England	petrol	in working order
Simplex 40hp 'protected' WD No. LR 3101 (10)	AMHC	England	petrol	in working order
Simplex 40hp 'armoured' WD No. LR 2182	LBNGRS	England	petrol	awaiting restoration
Simplex 40hp WD No. LR 3041	MRT	England	now diesel	in working order
McEwan-Pratt (Baguley) Works No. 736	WHHR	Wales	now diesel	in working order
Baldwin (US Army)	Tacot des Lacs	France	diesel	in working order

(1) Noyon–Guiscard–Lassigny (2) Valmondois (3) Cambrai, formerly Clary (4) Mountaineer
(5) Axe (6) Joffre (7) La Martroy (8) Felin Hen (9) Mary Ann (10) restored as 'open' type

DFB	*Deutsche Feldbahnen* (German field railways)
AMHC	Amberley Museum and Heritage Centre, West Sussex
AMTP	Association du Musée des Transports de Pithiviers
CFCD	Chemin de Fer Cappy Dompierre (P'tit train de la Haute Somme)
FR	Ffestiniog Railway, Portmadog, North Wales
INGRM	Irchester Narrow Gauge Railway Museum.
LBNGRS	Leighton Buzzard Narrow Gauge Railway Society Ltd
L&BR	Lynton and Barnstaple Railway, North Devon
MRT	Moseley Railway Trust, Apedale, Staffs
WHHR	Welsh Highland Heritage Railway
WLLR	West Lancashire Light Railway
WOLT	War Office Locomotive Trust

Metre Gauge locomotives

We have only included metre gauge steam locomotives known to have worked on the lines described in this book. Three such metre gauge steam locomotives have survived.

Haine Saint Pierre No. 15

VFIL locomotive No. 15, Haine Saint Pierre (Belgium) 2-6-0T, was constructed in 1921 as part of the programme of replacements after the First World War. It was put into service at Noyon in 1922. On closure of the Noyonnais lines in 1955 No 15 was transferred to the VFIL St-Just-en-Chaussée network (also in the Oise *département*). When that line also closed in 1961, No. 15 went to the proposed museum site at Verneuil, then in 1971 to the *Chemin de Fer de la Baie de Somme* (CFBS). Now restored, it is regularly in steam for passenger services.

Société Alsacienne de Construction Mécanique (SACM) No. 13

This locomotive was one of two 22 tonne 2-6-0T locomotives built by SACM in 1924 for the Berck-Plage-Paris-Plage (BPPP) line. This one was given the number 3, but was not really needed when it arrived as a replacement for a locomotive destroyed in the First World War. After a number of industrial moves, it was sold to VFIL in 1941 or 1942 for use on the Anvin-Calais-Aire-Berck lines. They gave it the number 13. In 1947 VFIL transferred it to Noyon. On closure of the Noyonnais lines in 1955 No 13 went with Haine Saint Pierre No. 15 to the VFIL St-Just-en-Chaussée network, also in the Oise *département*, for goods work until 1961. After various moves with a view to preservation, lastly at CFBS, it was moved in 1990 to the *Musée de Tramways à Vapeurs et des chemins de fer Secondaires français* (MTVS) at Valmondois. It has been in steam but is now only in static display in the museum, still with the number 13, but now called *Valmondois*.

Corpet-Louvet No. 5

In 1936, when the *Société des Chemins de Fer du Cambrésis* (CFC) abandoned the passenger service between St-Quentin and Caudry, the Company took the opportunity to scrap or sell some locomotives. One of those sold was No.5 *Clary*, an 0-6-0T Corpet-Louvet of 1888, which probably worked on the St-Quentin to Caudry line. It may have been fitted with the tanks of the original No. 1 *Cambrai*, sold for scrap in 1936. It was bought by an English company and sold on to work at Loddington Ironstone Company in Northamptonshire. In 1969 it was at the Towyn Museum (Talyllyn Railway). It is now in static display at the Irchester Narrow Gauge Railway Museum at Wellingborough, with the name *Cambrai*.

60cm gauge locomotives

There are numerous surviving locomotives from the British Army light railways (WDLR) of the First World War. A comprehensive list is provided in *Narrow Gauge at War* (Plateway Press, revised 2008) up to the time of that publication. There are also surviving examples of wagons (see pictures 4.12 and 4.13, Chapter Four). In respect

12.12 2-6-0T Haine-St-Pierre No. 15, built in 1921, in steam on 17 April 2016 at Lanchères, during the CFBS *Fête de la Vapeur*. (*Authors*)

of Motor Rail Simplex petrol tractors, the situation is complicated by the fact that the Simplex 20hp continued to be produced until 1932, and the Simplex 40hp until 1930, in identical or similar form to those used in the First World War. Very similar copies of the Simplex 20hp were produced by other firms until 1951.

There are no surviving examples of steam locomotives or petrol tractors known to have been used in the Somme Sector during the First World War. For British army petrol tractors and steam locomotives, it is usually the case that it is known that they were shipped to the western front and used, but not where and how. After the war, British, French and German 60cm gauge locomotives were used in the Somme sector, for reconstruction and then on industrial lines, especially for sugar factories. From the Dompierre sugar beet system, no steam locomotives survive, but some later diesel tractors are preserved at the *Chemin de Fer Cappy Dompierre (Le P'tit Train de la Haute Somme)* (CFCD). Four steam locomotives used on the Ternynck *sucrerie* lines at Nogent-sous-Coucy (Coucy-le-Château) have survived. We have indicated in table 12.1 where examples of the main locomotives types can now be seen in northern France and Great Britain.

Chemin de Fer Cappy Dompierre (CFCD) – Le P'tit Train de la Haute Somme
We have not given details of the other locations where rolling stock is now, but CFCD is undoubtedly the most important contemporary site for 60cm gauge railways in northern France, and especially for those of the First World War. As far as we know this is the only preserved 60cm gauge line on the site of one built for military use in that war.

The history of this area during the First World War has been told in Chapters Five to Eight, and that after that war in Chapter Nine, which ends with the early years of the *Association Picarde pour la Préservation et l'Entretien des Véhicules Anciens* (APPEVA), who own and run CFCD. Now there is a 60cm gauge line 7km long, and an extensive museum. These can be found on the D329 road at Froissy, 2km south of Bray-sur-Somme in the Somme *département*. APPEVA also publishes the journal *Voie Étroite* (Narrow Gauge).

Steam Locomotives
Hunslet 4-6-0T – Hunslet 4-6-0T of 1916, works number 1215, WD No. 303, was used in France, and there is a photograph at Boisleux-au-Mont, south of Arras, in September 1917. Repatriated from Australia, it is now in an advanced stage of restoration by the War Office Locomotive Trust (WOLT) and will be in steam in 2018.

Baldwin 4-6-0T – Both the Baldwin 4-6-0Ts in the UK served on the Western Front. That at Leighton Buzzard Narrow Gauge Railway (LBNGRS) and the associated Greensand Railway Museum, works number 44656 of

12.13 Baldwin 4-6-0T WD No 778, owned and restored by LBNGRS, in steam at Froissy on the CFCD on 7 May 2016. *(Authors)*

1917, WD No. 778, is regularly in steam. That at the Welsh Highland Heritage Railway (WHHR), works number 44699 of 1917, WD No. 794, is in restoration. Repatriated from India in 1985, it is now owned by the Imperial War Museum.

Alco 2-6-2T – The Tramway from Pithiviers to Toury (TPT) had at one time three Alco-Cooke 2-6-2Ts from British Army Light Railways of the First World War. TPT/AMTP No. 3-22, works No. 57131 of 1917, WD No. 1240, is preserved in static display at the *Association du Musée des Transports de Pithiviers* (AMPT) at Pithiviers (see picture 4.8, Chapter Four).

TPT No. 3-20, works No. 57148 of 1917, WD No. 1257, went to CFCD, where it was restored and was regularly in steam. This locomotive is now at *Tacot des Lacs*. It may be in working order, but was not in steam when we visited on 11 November, 2015.

TPT No. 3-23, works number 57156 of 1917, WD No. 1265, served with the 13th (Can) LROC at Coxyde on the Belgian coast in August 1917. After the First World War, it was used by the *Ministère des Régions Libérées* (MRL), probably on the Soissons-Laon network in the *département* of Aisne. It was acquired by the Vis-en-Artois sugar beet system in the Pas-de-Calais *département* in 1926. In 1935 it was sold to TPT. After the closure of TPT in 1964 the locomotive was given to the Ffestiniog Railway (FR) on indefinite loan and given the name *Mountaineer*, after an FR original of that name. The locomotive was modified to fit the FR loading gauge and was converted to oil burning during 1971. At the time of writing, *Mountaineer* is undergoing a major overhaul. Until this is completed it can only be seen by special arrangement.

Hudswell-Clarke 0-6-0WT (well tank) – Moseley Railway Trust (MRT) (Apedale Valley Light Railway) have a Hudswell Clarke 0-6-0WT, works number 1238, manufactured in 1916. This did not see war service but is identical with those which did. It has been fully operational since Autumn 2014.

Decauville 0-6-0T – Large numbers of these were produced for Franch Army Light Railways before and during the First World War. CFCD operate one (No. 5, Nord-Est), works number 1652 of 1916, which after the war operated at the *sucrerie* at Toury, restored to working order in 2006.

Kerr Stuart "Joffre" class 0-6-0T – Seventy of these were produced by Kerr Stuart of Stoke-on-Trent for French Army Light Railways in 1915 and 1916, based on the Decauville design. In 1956 five of the class were found derelict in a quarry at Rinxent, in the Pas-de-Calais *département*. Three of these are now in working order in England. Works No. 2405 of 1915 was acquired by the West Lancashire Light Railway (WLLR) in 1974. This locomotive, now named *Joffre*, has been fully restored (see picture 4.10, Chapter Four). Works No. 2451 of 1915 was acquired by the Lynton and Barnstaple Railway in

12.14 American Locomotive Company (Alco) 2-6-2T, built for the British Army in 1917, works number 57148, WD number 1257, formerly at CFCD, at Tacot des Lacs on 11 November 2015. *(Authors)*

1983. Restored and named *Axe*, it is regular use based at Woody Bay station. Works No. 3014 of 1916 was probably used by the French Army around Verdun. This locomotive is now operational at Mosely Railway Trust (Apedale Valley Light Railway).

Deutsche Feldbahn (DFB) locomotives – The most common locomotives of *Deutsche Feldbahn* (German Field Railways) were the 0-8-0T type. About 2,500 such locomotives were constructed between 1904 and 1919, by 14 different manufacturers

AMTP operate a Henschel of this type, built in 1917 (No. 4), and have a Hartmann of 1918 in static display. CFCD operate a Borsig 0-8-0 of 1918 of this type (No. 7), later modified in Poland with the addition of a tender. They also possess a Krauss and an Orenstein & Koppel (see picture 4.4, Chapter Four), the latter coming from the Ternynck sugar beet network at Coucy-le-Château. At *Tacot des Lacs* there is another ex-Coucy 0-8-0T, painted violet and without a manufacturer's plate.

US Army – From US First World War light railways Tacot des Lacs have a 2-6-2T Baldwin number 5104, works number 46828, now named *Felin Hen*. This is in working order.

Other former sugar beet locomotives – Of the former sugar beet system steam locomotives which were not from the First World War, two have survived, both in working order, and both from the Ternynck sugar beet network at Coucy-le-Château. Decauville 0-6-2T of 1902 *La Martroy* (No.10) is in steam at AMTP. Franco-Belge 0-8-0 tender locomotive of 1945, used at Coucy from then until 1963, operates at CFCD (No. 10).

Petrol and diesel locomotives (tractors)
Dick Kerr and British Westinghouse petrol electric (PE) tractors – The only examples we know of which are accessible to the public are at Tacot des Lacs, where there is a Dick Kerr PE tractor built for the British Army in 1917, which presumably saw service in France. It is in poor condition, with no number. Another Dick Kerr and a British Westinghouse PE tractor have been converted to standard gauge with new cabins, but there are no numbers. They are in very poor condition and part covered in vegetation.

Motor Rail Simplex 20hp tractor – We have listed four of these in the UK related to the First World War. Simplex 20 WD No. 264 is in private ownership, but is kept and displayed, in working order, at WHHR. At Moseley Railway Trust (Apedale) there are two Simplex 20 petrol tractors. Works No. 1111, WD No. LR 2832, built in 1918 but too late for service in the First World War, was used at Naburn Sewage Works near York, before arriving at MRT in 1992. It is in fully operational condition. Works No. 2197, was rebuilt in 1923 from a WDLR tractor, WD number unknown. Now powered by a diesel engine, it is also fully operational. Simplex 20 works No. 872, WD No. 2593, is on loan to Amberley Museum and Heritage Centre (AMHC). Built in 1918, this probably served in France. It was rebuilt by Motor Rail in 1925 and is on static display in the exhibition hall.

Motor Rail Simplex 40hp tractor – We have listed six of these in the UK related to the First World War. Three of these were of the 'protected' type and were delivered in 1918 too late to be sent to France. Works No. 1377, WD No. LR3098, is operated at LBNGRS, on long term loan from the National Railway Museum. Works No. 1369, WD No. LR 3090. has been rebuilt and is in working order at Moseley Railway Trust (Apedale) (see picture 4.11, Chapter Four). Works No. 1381, WD No. LR 3101, was donated to AMHC. It was of 'protected' type but has now been restored as an 'open' example. It is in operational condition.

The National Army Museum has given LBNGRS 'armoured' Simplex 40 WD No. LR2182, probably works No. 461, manufactured in 1917. This is thought to be the only 'armoured' Simplex in original mechanical condition, and it is in store awaiting restoration. In 1923 the Ffestiniog Railway (FR) purchased a reconstructed Simplex 40, probably WD No. LR 2228 of 'open' type, for work as a shunter. It was the first locomotive on the reopened railway in 1955, and in 1960 was fitted with a diesel engine. Called 'Mary Ann', she has now been put back in original condition with a rebuilt petrol engine. The second Simplex 40 at MRT (Apedale) is works No. 1320, WD No. LR3041. This locomotive was heavily rebuilt when in use at a quarry in the UK and is now fitted with a diesel engine.

McEwan-Pratt (Baguley) 10hp tractor – The only example of this type which probably saw service in the First World is at WHHR, restored with a diesel engine. Works number 736 was probably WD No. 273, the locomotive seen on a photograph at Teneur tank depot in the Pas-de-Calais *département* in 1917 or 1918.

US Baldwin diesel tractor – Tacot des Lacs has US Army Baldwin 0-4-0 diesel works number 48606, army number 2.053, which is in working order.

Standard gauge rolling stock
Association du Chemin de Fer Touristique du Vermandois (CFTV)
The only part of the *Intérêt Local* standard gauge line from St-Quentin to Guise which remains is the section

from St-Quentin to Origny-Ste-Benoîte, used for the cement factory and the *sucrerie* of Origny. Since 1979 it has also been used by the CFTV, which runs trains in the tourist season. They operate a North British 2-8-0 tender locomotive of 1917, which served in the ROD in the First World War, probably as ROD number 21651.

Walks

Walks have been more difficult to choose in the Somme sector than in the Arras sector further north. For the First World War period, there are many guides to the battlefields, particularly the 1916 Somme battlefield.

We have not included a walk in what was then 'Death Valley' and is now the Vallée Wagnon, by Mametz Wood. Walks around here are included in all the standard battlefield guides. But if you have not been before you should visit the 38th (Welsh) Division memorial (the Welsh Dragon), and Flatiron Copse Cemetery further up the valley. Caterpiller Valley, now the Vallée du Bois, on the right as you go up the valley, is not accessible. As you visit, imagine not only the epic struggle for Mametz Wood in July 1916, but also the valley full of railways, supply dumps and camps later in the year. By later 1917, the railways were all gone, save one light railway to Contalmaison. There is no trace here of the railway history now.

For the walks it is recommended to use these notes and sketch maps with the IgN (Institut Géographique National) 1:25,000 maps (1 cm = 250 m). The map number is given at the beginning of each walk. Latitude and longitude of starts and ends are also given to help those with GPS. All these walks are public rights of way.

Walk 1 - Railways and cemeteries behind the line at Beaumont Hamel

Map 2408 O. Distance about 4.5km (3 miles) there and back, allow 1½ hours, more if you want to linger and look at things. This walk follows part of the metre gauge line from Doullens to Albert, converted into standard gauge by the British Army in 1916. When this was not needed after the German retreat to the Hindenburg Line in March 1917, it was converted back to metre gauge by March 1918. Then the German army advanced and took Albert in March 1918, so the railway was not used again until reopened in 1920 or 1921. The line closed in 1949.

The walk follows the path of the line, now a track, from Mesnil-Martinsart to the D174 road from there to Auchonvillers. It is best to park at the Martinsart end (50° 03' 14" N 2° 38' 43" E). Before you start on the main walk it is worth walking down the small road south, the Rue des Veaux. After 120-140m, it is possible to discern Mesnil-Martinsart station building, now a private house, in the trees and shrubs. This is easier in winter when there are no leaves.

The main walk follows the track north, the Chemin Blanc, from the road where you have parked. The railway crossed the road 150m to the left, but after 500m the track joins the old formation of the railway. The going can be muddy especially in winter. The track gradually ascends, from 115m (377ft) at the start to 138m (452ft) at the end of the walk, giving an idea of the gradients with which the locomotives had to contend at several points along this line. As you walk up, the ridge on the right is where the German Army reached in March 1918. The front line was established here until the Allied advance in this area, which began on 21 August 1918.

The track curves to the left and in the folds of the hills here are two CWGC cemeteries, Knightsbridge and Mesnil Ridge. As you approach you can see on the skyline ahead the car park for the Newfoundland Memorial Park at Auchonvillers. The front line on 1 July 1916 was in the trees a short way beyond this, and the village of Beaumont-Hamel is in the valley below. The cemeteries mainly contain graves from the 1916 Battle of the Somme in this area, and there were almost certainly advanced dressing stations or casualty clearing stations in this area, using the railway, then standard gauge, to evacute the wounded.

Mesnil Ridge Cemetery is by the walk, with 95 graves, largely made by Infantry and Field Ambulances from August 1915 to August 1916. The other larger one 120m away across the field is Knightsbridge Cemetery, named after a communication trench. There are 548 burials, 141 unidentified. It was mostly used from 1 July 1916 to March 1917, and again March to July 1918. There are some Royal Engineers buried in these cemeteries, but none from railway units.

Continue the walk to the D174 road at the top. 400m and 500m along to the right on the other side are the remains of First World War fortifications, a strong point in concrete (50° 04' 19" N 2° 37' 58" E), and another further along which is half buried near the road. This is quite a busy road, hence the difficulty of parking with no laybys. Either retrace your steps down the hill or get someone to pick you up.

While in the area, it is worth visiting the Newfoundland Memorial Park at Auchonvillers, where there are preserved trenches, and a museum. You are also not far from the sites at Aveluy, Authuille and Blighty Valley described earlier in this chapter.

Walk 2 - Albert
Map 2408 O

This walk starts at Albert Station where SNCF still runs trains to Amiens, Arras, Douai and Lille. The station has a large car park (50° 00' 20" N 2° 38' 43" E). After

Things to see and do now

to Auchonvillers

to Auchonvillers

Newfoundland Memorial Park

D73

P

to Thiepval

WW1 concrete bunkers

to Doullens

Knightsbridge cemetery

Mesnil Ridge cemetery

WALK 1
Railways & cemeteries behind the line at Beaumont Hamel

D174 Rue d'Auchonvillers

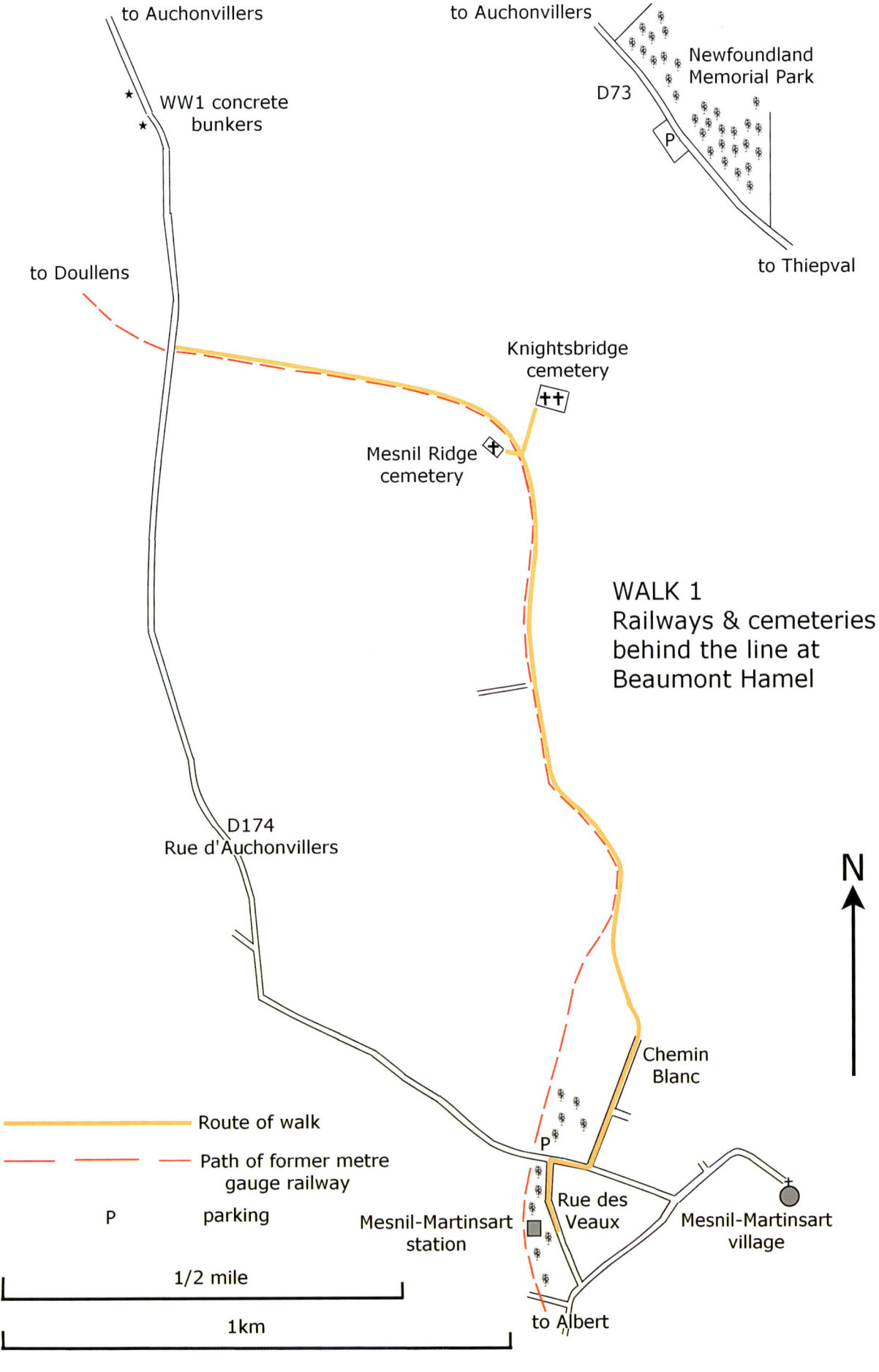

N

Chemin Blanc

P

Route of walk
Path of former metre gauge railway
P parking

Mesnil-Martinsart station

Rue des Veaux

Mesnil-Martinsart village

1/2 mile
1km

to Albert

Figure 12.1

12.15 *Walk 1.* View ahead where the path of the former metre gauge line curves left. Knightsbridge Cemetery is ahead, and behind to the right in front of the trees is the car park for the Newfoundland Memorial Park at Auchonvillers. The front line on 1 July 1916 was in the trees behind. April 2015. *(Authors)*

12.16 *Walk 1.* The concrete strongpoint on the road near the end of the walk. January 2017. *(Authors)*

parking, walk towards the station buildings. The one immediately facing you is the metre gauge station built in the 1920s, now apartments or offices. To the right of this building is set the old *buvette* which still carries that name. Walk into the main station and from the platform look across the tracks at the largely disused standard gauge yard and site of the metre gauge station in use until 1914. In the yard is an old gantry crane (see picture 2.7 in Chapter Two).

Return to the carpark and take the tarmac path between the carpark and the railway. This track is clearly marked as a jogging/walking track. Follow it as it runs parallel to the railway, where it becomes the path of the metre gauge line from the 1920s. After about 500 metres it goes under a road, and then climbs up to a road, Avenue de Parc. The old metre gauge goes straight on into new housing, and there is now no trace of the routes the old metre gauge line took to cross the standard gauge. Now take the Avenue du Parc to the left and continue as it becomes a track. It has a playing field down to the right. The track you see straight ahead has all the marks of an old metre gauge

Things to see and do now

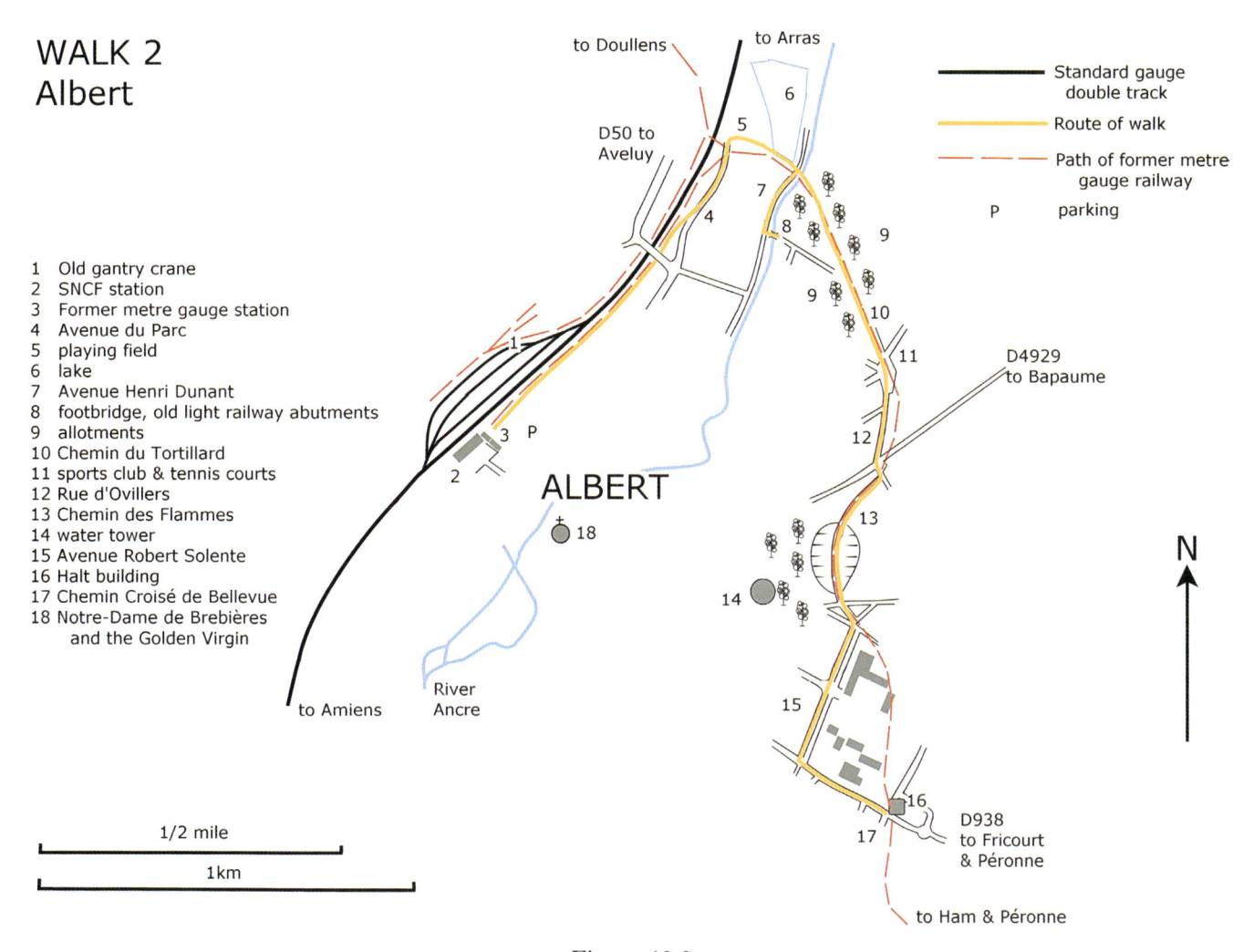

**WALK 2
Albert**

1. Old gantry crane
2. SNCF station
3. Former metre gauge station
4. Avenue du Parc
5. playing field
6. lake
7. Avenue Henri Dunant
8. footbridge, old light railway abutments
9. allotments
10. Chemin du Tortillard
11. sports club & tennis courts
12. Rue d'Ovillers
13. Chemin des Flammes
14. water tower
15. Avenue Robert Solente
16. Halt building
17. Chemin Croisé de Bellevue
18. Notre-Dame de Brebières and the Golden Virgin

— Standard gauge double track
— Route of walk
— — Path of former metre gauge railway
P parking

Figure 12.2

12.17 *Walk 2.* The former metre gauge station building at Albert, at the new station built after the First World War. October 2016. *(Authors)*

237

line but do not be fooled, our line turns sharply to the right on an embankment running along the side of the playing field. Climb down in the corner of the playing field and follow its edge to the far side, and you will come out onto a road. There is a wash-room-WC on the right. On your left is a lake with parking and picnic tables. The river Ancre is in front of you. On your right the embankment has disappeared at the entrance to a camp site.

There is a small detour you can take here by walking a short way along the road, the Avenue Henry Dunant. On the left between two bungalows is a path leading almost at once to a foot bridge (50° 00' 37" N 2° 39' 19" E). There was a First World War light railway bridge here. The remains of the abutments can be seen on both banks. The line is shown on trench maps, with a footbridge here, but the road and bungalows were built later.

Back to the line. The railway crossed the Ancre opposite the camp site entrance but there are no traces of the bridge. Cross the Ancre on the footbridge here and on your right, you will see a flight of steps. Take

2.18 *Walk 2.* The abutments for the First World War light railway bridge over the Ancre. There was a footbridge here too, but this one is not the original. October 2016. *(Authors)*

2.19 *Walk 2.* After crossing the Ancre the metre gauge line descended gradually along the embankment now marked by these pleasant lines of trees. October 2016. *(Authors)*

these and you will be able to walk along the old railway. Shaded by mature trees it makes a pleasant stroll. The track alongside is called the Chemin du Tortillard.

After 250 metres the light railway, whose bridge we saw above on the deviation, crossed the metre gauge on its way north-east up the Usna valley and on to the Aveluy to Ovillers line near Donnet Post.

You come out into a residential area with a school. The line has now disappeared behind housing on the left of the road half right which you need to follow, the Rue d'Ovillers. In a short way you reach the main Bapaume road. Cross this road and diagonally to the right opposite is a small road, the Chemin des Flammes, where you can pick up the line again. Follow the road until it turns into a track and you will see traces of a cutting. At the top, the track joins a major road across which the line disappears into a modern college development. You must now retrace your steps or alternatively, you can turn right and walk less than a kilometre into the town to visit the First World War museum, close to the church.

You can if you wish continue along the wide Avenue Robert Solente and then left into the D938 to the extended halt building that has survived. This is adjacent to the D938, Rue du 11 Novembre, opposite the junction with the Chemin Croisé de Bellevue (49° 59' 49" N 2° 39' 35" E).

Walk 3 - Péronne - Flamicourt
Map 2508 O

Péronne is another of those sad towns in northern France which used to have a main line as well as a metre gauge railway. Now there is nothing. This walk explores the area around the former main station. At the end are some other things to see in Peronne which can be seen more easily by car.

This walk starts at what used to be Peronne Station (49° 55' 40" N 2° 56' 27" E). You approach the old station from the centre of Peronne, crossing the Cologne River a few hundred yards from the station, which now houses a butchers' business. You should be able to park on the forecourt. Go round to the right of the building to examine the old track-side. The ground floor is covered by an ugly modern extension but above this you can see two station names. The lower one can just be seen above the new addition. It has Peronne-Flamicourt carved on a stone block. Above this is a simpler name plate in red, possibly a later addition. At the apex is a date carved in stone - 1921. Now head to the right of the station. In a south-west direction is the large area which used to be the station yards. Walk through this area and you will come to a parking area where a tarmac road ends. Cross the bridge over a small canal leading to a lake on your left. Ahead of you there is a path through the woods. Follow this path for a few hundred yards and you will come to the old standard gauge bridge over the river Somme. It is possible to climb up the bank and look along to see that the bridge was dual track but only one set of rails is left.

Return to the station to follow the track of the metre gauge line towards Ham. This can be walked but it may be easier to take the car. The line curves left out of the large former yard area, then joins a minor road. The road you are following was the metre gauge line, witnessed by the narrowing at bridges over culverts. These are edged by railings. Eventually you come to the end of the tarmac and housing and the line disappears into a field.

Return to the station. Cross the forecourt and take the road until you come to a crossing cottage on the Avenue de la Gare. At the cottage turn left. This is the track of the standard gauge line leaving the station to the north-east, and the path of the metre gauge line to Albert was immediately to the right. Follow this road until it leaves the houses and enters a wood. This track may be muddy. As you walk along, you will have glimpses on your right of the embankment that the metre gauge line needed to gain the height it needed to cross the line to Roisel and the Cologne River. You will soon reach the point where the metre gauge had climbed enough to cross the standard gauge you are standing on. At this point are the remains of the bridge. By the remains to the right is now a builder's yard but the railway remains are impressive. On the left hand side undergrowth masks the remains but they can still be seen. It was beyond this point that the metre gauge line crossed the river but unfortunately you cannot get anywhere near the river through the vegetation. You must now retrace your steps.

Although the next bridge is very close to the standard gauge bridge over the Somme it is necessary to drive round to find it. This is the standard gauge bridge over the Canal du Nord. Having parked the car in the Rue de la Digue du Canal (49° 55' 05" N 2° 56' 07" E), follow the tow path for a few hundred yards to the bridge.

Elsewhere in Peronne, it is also better to drive. Picking up the metre gauge line north of the Cologne river, the old crossing cottage at the D5937 can be seen (49° 56' 00" N 2° 56' 59" E), but on the other side of the road the site of the Halt for the Porte de Bretagne cannot be accessed. The crossing cottage at Le Quinconce (49° 56' 13" N 2° 55' 52" E), at the site of the metre gauge *arrêt*, is now surrounded by retail parks.

Whilst in Péronne you may visit the First World War Museum (*Historial de la Grande Guerre*) which is in the old castle. This is larger and with a wider scope than the Museum in Albert.

Narrow Gauge in the Somme Sector

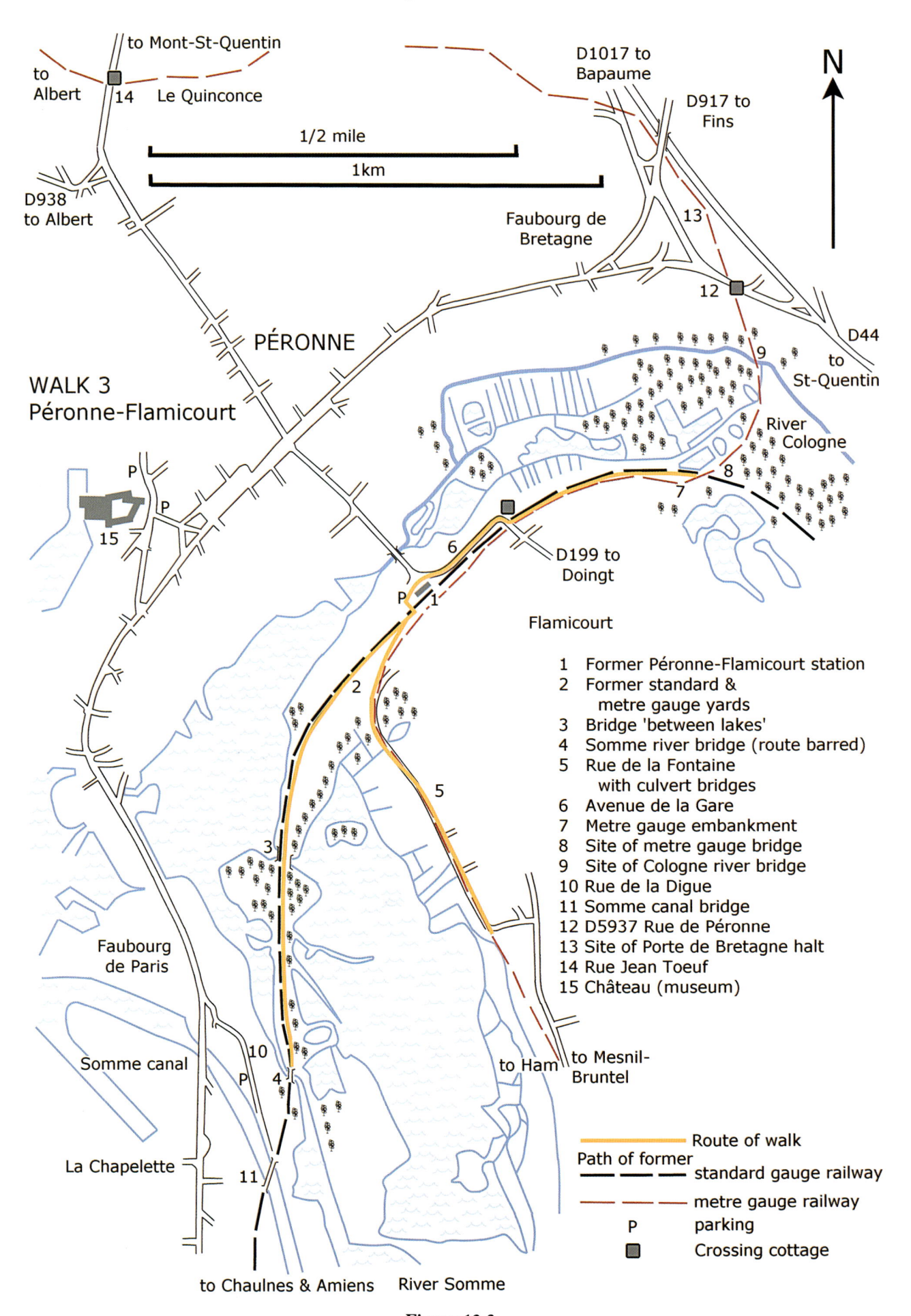

WALK 3 Péronne–Flamicourt

1. Former Péronne-Flamicourt station
2. Former standard & metre gauge yards
3. Bridge 'between lakes'
4. Somme river bridge (route barred)
5. Rue de la Fontaine with culvert bridges
6. Avenue de la Gare
7. Metre gauge embankment
8. Site of metre gauge bridge
9. Site of Cologne river bridge
10. Rue de la Digue
11. Somme canal bridge
12. D5937 Rue de Péronne
13. Site of Porte de Bretagne halt
14. Rue Jean Toeuf
15. Château (museum)

— Route of walk
Path of former
— standard gauge railway
— metre gauge railway
P parking
◼ Crossing cottage

Figure 12.3

240

Things to see and do now

12.20 *Walk 3.* The track side of the former station at Péronne, October 2016. *(Authors)*

12.21 *Walk 3.* The standard gauge bridge over the Somme river. October 2016, viewed from the route of the walk. *(Authors)*

12.22 *Walk 3.* The remains of the metre gauge bridge over the standard gauge line to Roisel. October 2016 (see also picture 6.1, Chapter Six). *(Authors)*

12.23 *Walk 3*. The standard gauge bridge over the Somme Canal. October 2016. *(Authors)*

Walk 4 - Bellicourt to Nauroy, metre gauge and First World War light railways

This walk is mostly on map 2608 O (Villers-Outréaux), but the west edge of it is on the edge of map 2508 E (Roisel). Distance about 4km there and back, allow 1½ hours, more if you want to linger and look at things. This walk follows part of the former metre gauge line from St-Quentin to Caudry, which was operated by the Chemin de Fer de Cambrésis. The basic walk is from Bellicourt station to Nauroy station. The walk can be extended in both directions, as described later. This is a pleasant countryside walk through low rolling hills, but it could be bleak and exposed in winter.

Before the First World War there was a branch line just east of Bellicourt village, curving round south of the village to a brickworks and a sugar factory. During the war, Bellicourt village was just on the German side of the main fortifications of the Hindenburg Line, and was held by the German Army from 1914 until late September 1918. The Germans had light railways here but took up the metre gauge track. The Hindenburg line here was taken and the village liberated by the US Infantry 30th Division, supported by the 5th Autralian Division, fighting as part of the British IXth Corps of the Third Army, on 29 September 1918.

The 6th Bttn CRT built the light railway from Hargicourt to Bellicourt by 3 October 1918 and linked it to the path of the industrial branch of the metre gauge line. Joining the main metre gauge formation east of Bellicourt, the line was open to Joncourt station by 8 October. From 12 October, the line was extended from this line east of Joncourt to the path of the Guise to Le Catelet metre gauge line at Montbrehain, and then on to Bohain. The line was operated by 13th (Can) LROC assisted by 18th TCC. Operations continued at least until May 1919, by 1st Aus LROC and then 18th LROC (formerly 18th TCC) (see Chapters Eight and Nine). The line here was reopened in metre gauge in 1923, and finally closed to all traffic in 1954 (see Chapter Eleven).

Park in the open area near Bellicourt station (49° 57' 48" N 3° 14' 07" E). You can also park at the other end near Nauroy station (49° 57' 32" N 3° 15' 41" E). Both are now private houses. Both are typical of *Cambrésis* stations, consisting of a two-storey building with ridge side on to track, a small round feature at the end at the top, and two windows each story at the side and one each at end. A single-storey extension has a roof with ridge parallel to the track, one window and one door on track side. These features are easier to see at Bellicourt, which has some modern extensions, and there is a sign *Attention au Train* on the end corner near the gate.

Starting at Bellicourt to the south, the obvious path of the line curves east through a cutting and then north east along a low embankment. The industrial branch to the factories at the south end of Bellicourt village, used for the light railway construction by the Canadians (and the Germans before that), was in the valley to your right, losing height down to the factories on the main road to St-Quentin. There is no trace of the branch now. Curving right again onto a straight section, you arrive at the point where the branch joined

Things to see and do now

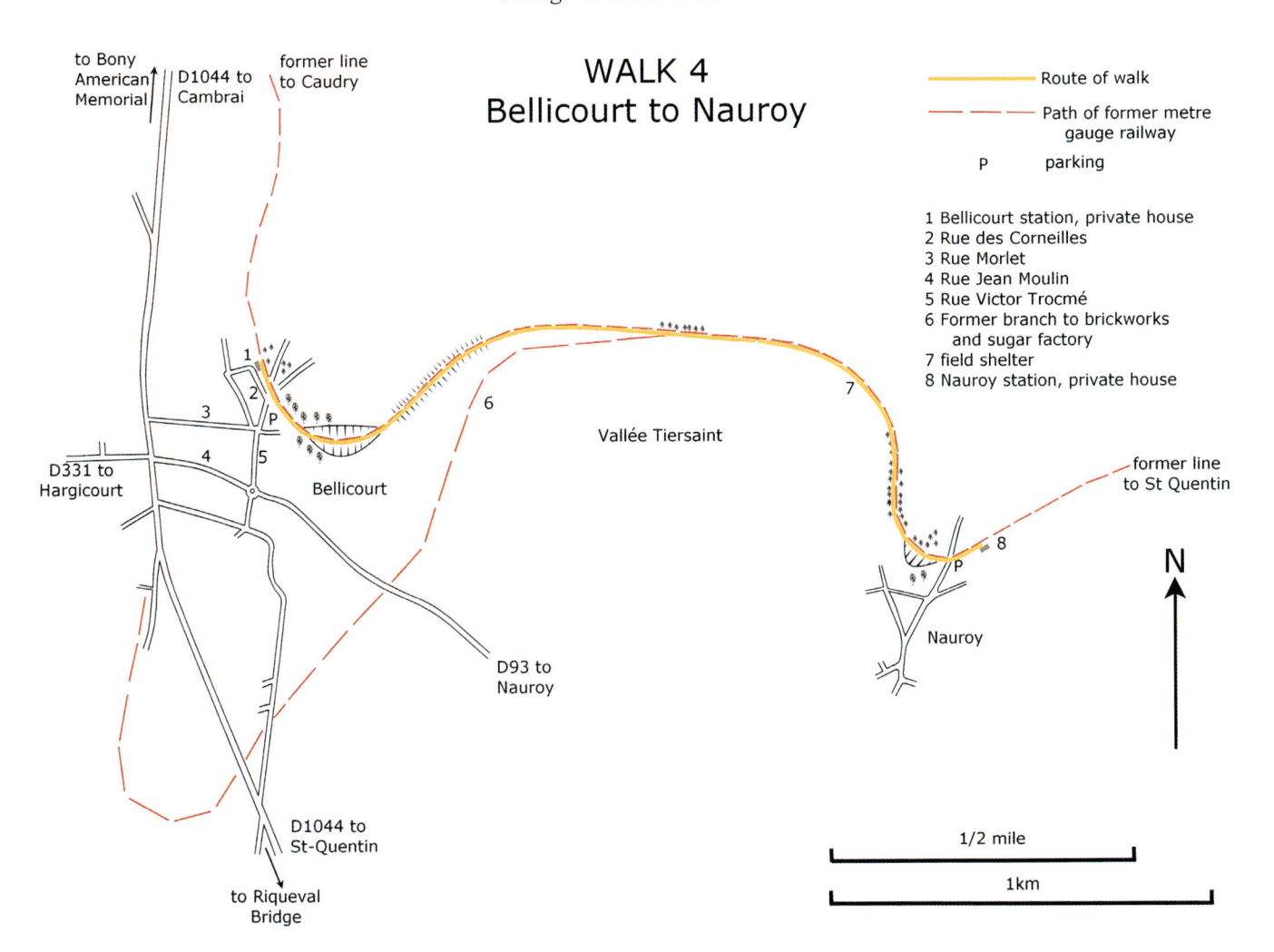

WALK 4
Bellicourt to Nauroy

— Route of walk
--- Path of former metre gauge railway
P parking

1 Bellicourt station, private house
2 Rue des Corneilles
3 Rue Morlet
4 Rue Jean Moulin
5 Rue Victor Trocmé
6 Former branch to brickworks and sugar factory
7 field shelter
8 Nauroy station, private house

Figure 12.4

12.24 *Walk 4* The track side of the former metre gauge station at Bellicourt. April 2016. *(Authors)*

243

the main line. Continue on through a more shrubby section and cross a farm track. The path bends right. From a distance you can see a wooden structure, which looks a bit like the shelter for an *arrêt*, but it is in the wrong place, and it turns out to be a modern field shelter. A sharper curve left through a more wooded area brings you to a road, in the north end of Nauroy village. The station is 100m ahead on the right of the path. If you wish to walk further the path along the old formation continues to Estrées halt and then Joncourt station.

From Bellicourt station you can extend the walk the other way along the former metre gauge line, or drive, to the Bony American Memorial (49° 58' 30" N 3° 13' 53" E). This is on the ridge over the Riqueval canal tunnel, and commorates the American units who fought as part of British Armies in 1918: and particularly to the 27th and 30th Divisions who fought here between 24 and 30 September 1918. There is a map showing their campaign on the back of the memorial.

Whilst in this area you may also wish to take the opportunity to visit Riqueval Bridge, which is just off the D1044 from St-Quentin to Cambrai, at 49° 56' 24" N 3° 14' 32" E. This important bridge over the St-Quentin canal near the south end of the Riqueval *touage* (tow tunnel) was captured intact by men of the North Staffordshire Regiment (British 46th Division) on 29 September 1918. At the east end of the bridge are some massive lumps of concrete, which were part of the Hindenburg line.

Walk 5 - St-Quentin, the metre gauge railway and the Hindenburg line

Map 2609 O (St-Quentin), but a very small part of the beginning of the walk is on the lower edge of 2608 O (Villers-Outréaux). Distance about 6km in one direction, allow two hours, more if you want to linger and look at things. This walk follows the former metre gauge line from Caudry, beginning at the site of the St-Quentin-Cambrésis station, around the western edge of St-Quentin as far as the bridge over the Somme canal. The story of this line has been told in Chapter Three up to the First World War, and in Chapter Eleven after that. St-Quentin-Cambrésis was named because it was the main station in St-Quentin for this line, which was part of the Cambrésis network based on Caudry in the Nord *département*. During the First World War the German Army occupied St-Quentin from 1914 until September 1918. They built a massive defensive line, the Hindenburg Line, to which they retreated in March 1917, and from then until March 1918 this was the front line, with Allied trenches only 1000yds (c. 1km) further out from the city. The main line of fortifications at St-Quentin followed the western edge of the city as it was then, although it is now more extensive. The fortifications followed on or close to the metre gauge line for quite a lot of this walk. It is no surprise therefore that the metre gauge line was destroyed by 1918.

Park in the area of the big road junction just by the *Cimetère du Nord* (north cemetery) on the D8 Lesdins Road (49° 51' 32" N 3° 17' 23" E). Alternatively, you can park at the other end, across the water from the *Port de Plaisance* on the Quai du Vieux Port (49° 50' 14" N 3° 16' 58" E) and do the walk in reverse; but in the recommended direction the net gradient is downhill, from 106m to 71m.

The site of the former St-Quentin-Cambrésis station was by the *Cimetière du Nord*, in the angle between the right-angled walls of the cemetery, about where the car park for the long block of flats is now. Nothing remains. This was the terminus of the line from Caudry via Le Catelet from 1892 until 1904 when the extension to St-Quentin Nord station was opened. After the First World War the line from Caudry was reopened to here in 1923. The passenger service closed in 1934, and the goods service in 1954. From 1923 to 1934 passengers going to St-Quentin Nord were advised to take the electric tram, which terminated outside the Cambrésis station (see picture 11.9, Chapter Eleven).

The walk begins across the main road, down the track between the pharmacy and a wall. From here to Faubourg St-Jean is gradually downhill, curving around the head of a small valley to the right, then slowly 180° left, then a bit right again. This is a quiet valley, full of trees and scrub and some allotments, and in Spring is full of blossom and birds singing. There are some back yards, noisome dogs, and fly-tipping but it is still remarkable for a place so close to the city centre. Near the end of the section is a very handsome house with large grounds on the right. At about 1.5km, you come out into the main road to Cambrai, the D1044 (formerly N2044), and the last part is named the Chemin du Cambrésis.

Across the main road the route of the railway is now a link between the Cambrai road and the modern D1029 (E44) to Amiens. However, there is a comfortable route to walk. On the right of the first part is a grassy area where the line ran, and just before the D732 to Gricourt (Rue Henriette Cabot) is the site of the former station of Saint-Jean. Although called a *gare* on the only picture of it which we have seen, it had a single-storey halt type building, now long gone. The line was restored to here in 1923, but only for goods traffic, and it only lasted until 1936. The rest of the line to St-Quentin Nord was never restored and was formally declassified in 1933.

Things to see and do now

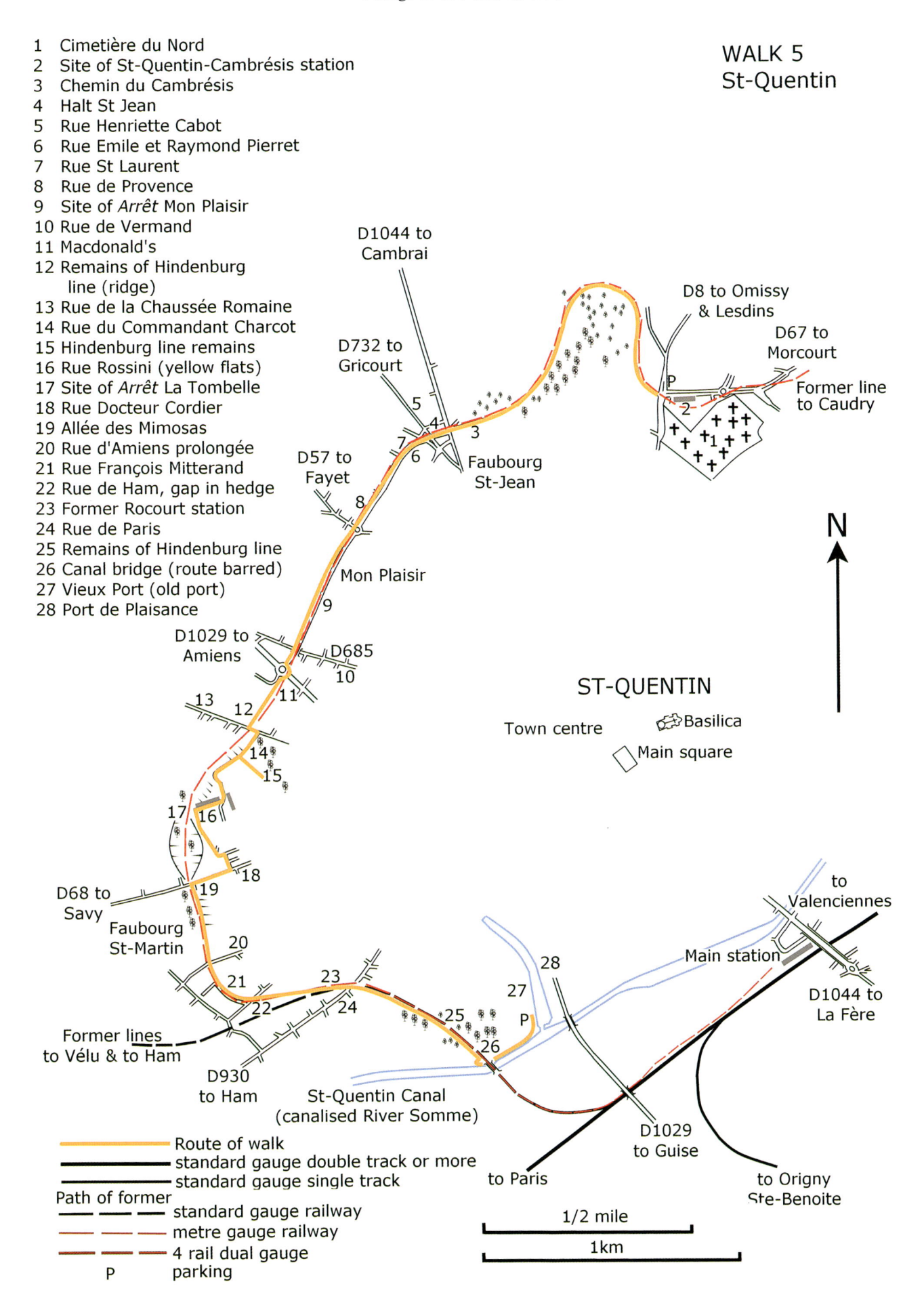

**WALK 5
St-Quentin**

1. Cimetière du Nord
2. Site of St-Quentin-Cambrésis station
3. Chemin du Cambrésis
4. Halt St Jean
5. Rue Henriette Cabot
6. Rue Emile et Raymond Pierret
7. Rue St Laurent
8. Rue de Provence
9. Site of *Arrêt* Mon Plaisir
10. Rue de Vermand
11. Macdonald's
12. Remains of Hindenburg line (ridge)
13. Rue de la Chaussée Romaine
14. Rue du Commandant Charcot
15. Hindenburg line remains
16. Rue Rossini (yellow flats)
17. Site of *Arrêt* La Tombelle
18. Rue Docteur Cordier
19. Allée des Mimosas
20. Rue d'Amiens prolongée
21. Rue François Mitterand
22. Rue de Ham, gap in hedge
23. Former Rocourt station
24. Rue de Paris
25. Remains of Hindenburg line
26. Canal bridge (route barred)
27. Vieux Port (old port)
28. Port de Plaisance

Route of walk
standard gauge double track or more
standard gauge single track
Path of former standard gauge railway
metre gauge railway
4 rail dual gauge
P parking

Figure 12.5

245

12.25 *Walk 5.* Near the start of the walk the path of the former line curves left, and there are sleepers forming a fence on the left. May 2016. *(Authors)*

At the lights, cross the Rue Henriette Cabot; on the other side the dual carriageway (Rue Emile and Raymond Pierret) curves gently to the left. Follow the service road (Rue Saint Laurent) on the right of the dual carriageway in front of the modern flats and shops, which was probably the actual line of the railway. It is from here that the main Hindenburg line was immediately on the right (north west). Just before the next roundabout, crossing the D57 to Fayet, there is row of older houses and the service road becomes the Rue de Provence. On the other side here, the road rises slightly; follow the cycleway on the right. Along here to the left are good views of the basilica in the city centre. After about 0.5km a bridge on the dual carriageway crosses the old road to Vermand (D685, formerly N2029). There was probably a railway bridge here. Beyond, the road drops to a roundabout on the much newer south west inner ring road, the D1029 (E44). You have now completed about half of the walk.

A McDonald's faces you across the roundabout. The railway went through the car park, but we must follow the grassy ridge straight on just to the right, with a soul-less white building wall to the right. This ridge is probably raised up by remains of the Hindenburg line. From the next road, the Rue de la Chaussée Romaine (ie a Roman Road), you cannot follow the railway. There is quite a hill, and the railway went round just to the right. You can follow the shallow ledge as it climbed, but then there is fence from where a long deep cutting runs through private ground, and it is a small scramble up to the block of yellow flats on the hilltop on the left.

Alternatively, turn left at the end of the 'grassy ridge' and quickly right up the hill along the Rue du Commandant Charcot (who was a polar explorer, not a military leader). There is a sharp left bend by the school (Ecole Jean Macé), then at the top turn right along the yellow flats (Rue Rossini) to join the end of the 'scramble'. Either way follow the Rue Richard Wagner and do a left and quickly right into the Rue Mozart to reach the D68, the Rue Docteur Cordier. Turn right up the hill, and after passing a day hospital for children and adolescents on the right you will find the railway again, at the beginning of the Allée des Mimosas on the left. At this point, the railway has climbed through the cutting from 80m at the bottom of the Rue du Cammandant Charcot to 101m. Straight down the road is a fine view of the west front of the basilica in the city centre (picture 1.1, Chapter One).

There is a worthwhile diversion on the way up the Rue du Commandant Charcot. Just before the school car park turn left across a flat piece of waste ground, follow the path over a small hump, and cross the asphalt area used by the school. On the other side is an opening into a grassy area with trees. Immediately inside is a large lump of concrete, turned half on its side (see picture 1.2, Chapter One). There is another on the right further in. These are remains of the Hindenburg line, probably a secondary line, as the main front line here was just the other side of the railway.

Pick up the railway footpath again at the beginning of the Allée des Mimosas. There is quite a high embankment (look left). There are steps down to the houses on the left, and then the path climbs gradually to a road (Rue d'Amiens Prolongée). This is a modern extension of the Rue d'Amiens, as the name implies. There used to be a cutting through here which has been filled in. Across this road a path drops down again to the Rue François Mitterand, with modern houses on the right and open grass to the left. The point where you join this road was the end of the cutting. The road curves left to the Rue de Ham, where across the road slightly left a gap in the hedge between two houses is held open in an arch by rusting rails. Through this the path, on the line of the railway, descends into a very pleasant open area, with further along a high bank on the left. This was Rocourt station. The former standard gauge lines of *Intérêt Local* from Vélu and from Ham (this part finally abandoned by SNCF for goods in 1992, see Chapter One) come in along the other side of the open area. This is now a footpath. At the end of the station area towards the road all the station buildings have gone, and there is modern accommodation.

Cross the D930 Rue de Paris, where there was a level crossing. There is a bar across the road, if you have resisted McDonalds further back. An old photograph (picture 3.4, Chapter Three) shows that the metre and standard gauge lines did not join into 4 rail dual gauge until the other side of the road, then running together to the main station (St-Quentin Nord). Follow the path along the old track on the other side of the road. Soon there is a wall on the left, then on old sign facing the other way, indicating the approach to PN (*Passage à Niveau*, level crossing) 22. The track continues through woodland to the old bridge over the Somme canal. On the left in places are piles of concrete lumps, part of the former rear defences of the Hindenburg Line. The bridge itself is shut off, but you can see that the sleepers are still there, although the rails have been taken up.

It is a long way to anywhere to cross the Somme canal, and is not worth it. Descend the steps to the canal side on the right just before the bridge and turn left under it. Follow the canal bank to the side arm of water with the Port de Plaisance on the other side. Looking back, you can see that a short way across the bridge there is catenary, where a standard gauge spur soon joins the main line into St-Quentin main station, still in use by SNCF. This is the old main line from Paris to Valenciennes and Brussels, now replaced for Brussels by the LGV.

There were two further halts or *arrêts* between Saint-Jean and the shared station at Rocourt. The best information that we have is that St-Quentin Monplaisir was just north of the bridge over the D685, the old road to Vermand: and that St-Quentin-La Tombelle was at the north end of the inaccessable cutting. We have found no trace of the stops, and there may have been no buildings. In any case all buildings in this area were destroyed in the First World War.

This is an ideal walk to have a party with two cars and to have left one at each end. Alternatively retrace the route or walk up the edge of the water and then through the semi-industrial area to the large junction of the D68, the D930 and the D1029 (E44) (49° 50' 36" N 3° 16' 42" E). From here you can take a direct route (about 2km) across the city to the *Cimetière du*

12.26 *Walk 5.* The walk through the woods down to the canal bridge. This is looking back towards the level crossing at Rocourt station, with the faded sign warning drivers of the approaching PN 22 in the foliage on the left. May 2016. (*Authors*)

12.27 *Walk 5.* The old railway bridge across the Somme canal, shared by the metre gauge line to Caudry and the standard gauge lines of *Intérêt Local* to Vélu and to Ham. May 2016. *(Authors)*

Nord. However, it is only a small dog-leg to take in the pedestrianised square in front of the fine Hôtel de Ville, where there are many refreshment places, and to visit the eleventh century basilica, now a cathedral.

And finally.....

As we found with our previous book, *Narrow Gauge in the Arras Sector*, in researching this book we have found a large amount of information on the railways we have described.

However, even though this is a sector on which there is already a vast literature, we found very little information on the sites of these railways. This contrasts with the abundance of information, including books and tours, on the battlefields which these railways supported. There are increasing signs that the enormous efforts behind the lines to support the troops at the front are being recognised. As before, we have found the identification of sites now, and matching them to known events and structures in the past, the most enjoyable and rewarding part of our research.

Much of the history of military railways on the allied side in the First World War in this area concerns the British and Dominion (now Commonwealth) armies. The French Army were also heavily involved, and the American Army to some extent, as described in the text. The British Armies held much this front from early 1916 until the end of the War, the period of most light railway development and use. The French, Belgian, American, and other allied armies made similar efforts in other parts of the Western Front. However, we believe that this makes this area, as the Arras Sector in our previous book, of especial interest to British and Commonwealth readers.

Bibliography

General
DAVIES, W.J.K. *Minor Railways of France*. East Harling, Norfolk: Plateway Press, 2000
DELATTRE, Daniel. *Les chemins de fer de la Somme au début du XX°*. Éditions Delattre, Granvilliers, 2011
DELATTRE, Daniel. *Les chemins de fer de l'Oise au début du XX°*. Éditions Delattre, Granvilliers, 2010
DELATTRE, Daniel. *Les chemins de fer de l'Aisne au début du XX°*. Éditions Delattre, Granvilliers, 2011
DOMENGIE, H. and **BANAUDO, J.** *Les petits train de jadis. Nord de la France*. Les Éditions du Cabri, Breil-sur-Roya, France, 1995.
FAREBROTHER, **Martin & Joan**. *Tortillards of Artois. The Metre Gauge Railways and Tramways of the Western Pas-de-Calais*. Oakwood Press, Usk, Mon., 2008
FAREBROTHER, Martin J B & Joan S. *Narrow Gauge in the Arras Sector. Before, during and after the First World War*. Pen & Sword Transport, Barnsley, South Yorkshire, 2015
MIDDLEBROOK, Martin & Mary. *The Somme Battlefields. A Comprehensive Guide from Crécy to the Two World Wars*. Viking, 1991: London, Penguin Books, 1994
PACEY, Philip, **ARZUL, Roland**, and **LEENE, Guy**. *Railways of the Baie de Somme. A Landscape with Trains*. Oakwood Press, Usk, Mon., 2000.

Chapter One
Northern France and the Paris Region. Michelin Green Guide, 2014 (in English)
Nord Pas-de-Calais, Picardie. Paris: Le Guide Vert Michelin, 2008 (in French, but more detailed than the English equivalent above)

Chapters Three and Eleven
BENNETT, Patrick. *Chemins de Fer Departementaux de l'Aisne*. SNCF Society 2013, Vol. 149, pp 30-38.
LEMMEY, Peter. *Chemins de Fer Departementaux de l'Aisne*. SNCF Society 2014, Vol. 153, pp 50-51 & 53.
WAGNER, Claude. *Voie métriques en Picardie. Histoire des voies ferrées d'intérêt local dans l'Oise*. LR Presse, Auray, 2013.

Chapters Four to Eight
Association du Musée des Transports Pithiviers (AMTP). *La voie de 60 et les chemins de fer militaires. Dés locomotives Péchot-Bourdon à la ligne Maginot*. Éditions AMTP, 1991.
AVES, William A. T. *R-O-D The Railway Operating Division on the Western Front. The Royal Engineers in France and Belgium 1915-1919*. Shaun Tyas Publishing, Donington, Lincs, 2009.
DAVIES, W.J.K. *Light Railways of the First World War. A History of Tactical Rail Communications on the British Fronts 1914 – 18*. David & Charles, Newton Abbott, 1967.
GITTINS, Sandra. *Between the Coast and the Western Front*. The History Press, 2014.
HENNIKER, A.M. *Transportation on the Western Front 1914-1918*. London, 1937. reprinted by the Imperial War Museum, London and the Battery Press, Nashville, USA, 1992.
HERITAGE, T.R. *The Light Track From Arras*. First published 1931. 2nd edition Plateway Press, East Harling, Norfolk, 1999.
Le HENAFF and **BORNECQUE, H.** *Les Chemins de Fer Français et la Guerre*. Paris: Librairie Chapelot, 1922.
LINK, Roy C. *WDLR Album*. RCL Publications, 2014.
PRÉVOT, Aurélien. *Les chemins de fer français dans la Première Guerre Mondiale*. LR Presse, 2014.
The Railway Gazette and Railway News. *Special War Transportation Number*, 1920. Reprinted by the Moseley Railway Trust and Railway Gazette International, 2013.
TAYLOR, A.J.P. *The First World War. An illustrated history*. New York: Perigee Books, The Berkley Publishing Group, 1963 (original publishers Hamish Hamilton).
TAYLORSON, Keith. *Narrow Gauge at War*. Plateway Press, East Harling, Norfolk, 2nd edition, 2008 (first published 1987).
TAYLORSON, Keith. *Narrow Gauge at War 2*. Plateway Press, East Harling, Norfolk, 1996

Chapters Six, Seven & Eight
BROWN, Malcolm. *The Imperial War Museum Book of 1918 Year of Victory*. First published 1998, this edition Pan Books, London, 1999.
DUNN, Richard. *Narrow Gauge to No Man's Land. US Army 60cm Gauge Railways of the First World War in France*. Benchmark Publications, California, 1990.

JOHNSON, J H. *1918 The Unexpected Victory.* Arms and Armour Press, 1997.

Chapter Nine
BLONDIN, Alain and **BLONDIN, David**. *Le P'tit train de la Haute Somme. Le Guide.* APPEVA, 2015 (in French and English).

CHAPUIS, J. L'Exploitation Commerciales De Certaines Voies De 60 Militaires Après La Guerre 1914-18. *Chemins de Fer Régionaux et Urbains* 1984, Vol 184, pp 27-48.

FRESNÉ, Eric. *70 Ans De Chemins De Fer Betteraviers En France* LR Presse, Auray, France, 2007.

VIERNE, Jacques. Principaux chemins de fer industriels et agricoles exploités en 1956. *Chemins de Fer régionaux et Tramways* 2008, Vol. 325, pp 6-11.

Chapter Ten
THOMAS, David. Coordination (parts 1 & 2). *The SNCF Society Journal* March 2006, No. 121, & June 2006, No. 122.

Chapter Eleven
MORGAN, Bryan. *The End of the Line. A Book about Railways and Places, mainly Continental.* Cleaver-Hume Press, 1955.

Chapter Twelve
BENNETT, Patrick. *Chemins de Fer Departementaux de l'Aisne.* SNCF Society 2013, Vol. 149, pp 30-38.

BLONDIN, Alain and **BLONDIN, David**. *Le P'tit train de la Haute Somme. Le Guide.* APPEVA, 2015 (in French and English).

CORK, Gerry and **SMITH, James.** *The Amberley Museum Narrow Gauge and Industrial Railway Collection.* Amberley Museum, Amberley, West Sussex, 2nd edition, 2001.

DUPUIS, Henri. Le Musée des Tramways à Vapeur et des chemins de fer Secondaires Français (MTVS). *SNCF Society* 2009, Vol. 133, pp 23-25.

HUGHES, I.G. *Hunslet 1215. A War Veteran's Story.* Oakwood Press, Usk, Mon., 2010

JONES, Mervyn. *The Essential Guide to French Heritage and Tourist Railways.* Oakwood Press, Usk, Mon., 2006.

LEMMEY, Peter. *Chemins de Fer Departementaux de l'Aisne.* SNCF Society 2014, Vol. 153, pp 50-51 & 53.

Index

Accidents, British Army light railways (WDLR), 102, 165
Acheux, 11, 19, 29, 73, 75, 77, 88, 89, 96, 99, 102, 114, 131, 140, 144, 147, 148, 151, 153, 158, 159, 161, 192, 199, 203, 204, 223
Achiet(-le-Grand), 96, 102, 107, 114, 128, 131, 132, 156, 157, 161, 162, 170, 175, 185
Achiet-le-Petit, 96, 102, 112, 146, 162
Aisne *département*, 1, 35, 179, 180, 183, 189, 206, 219, 222, 232
Albert, 4, 11, 14, 20, 29, 30, 56, 71, 74, 84, 96, 99, 104, 105, 113, 114, 129, 131, 132, 135, 142, 144, 146, 151, 156, 157, 159, 182, 188, 192-5, 197, 199-204, 213, 215, 222, 223, 225, 226, 234, 236, 238, 239
Amberley Museum and Heritage Centre (AMHC), 233
Ambulance trains (on LRs), 89, 90, 150, 153, 171
American Army, *see* United States Army
Amiens, 6, 56, 71, 99, 112, 113, 129, 131, 133-5, 137, 139, 141, 142, 144, 148, 153, 157, 158, 192, 225
Amiens, battle of, 151
Ammunition (on LRs), 89, 102, 111, 114, 115, 117, 119, 124, 125, 136, 138, 147, 148, 154, 164, 170, 171, 173, 175, 176-8
Ancre, battle of the, 151, 156
Ancre river & valley, 11, 75, 77, 80, 88-90, 102, 112, 129, 131, 140, 142, 146, 148, 151, 159, 227, 238
Armistice, 11th November, 1918, 151, 165, 173, 174, 175
Arras, xii, 56, 96, 102, 107, 113, 114, 129, 131, 132, 139, 183, 189, 225
Arras sector, xii, xiv, 10, 59, 61, 62, 102, 107, 146, 175, 234, 248
Association du Musée des Transports de Pithiviers (AMTP), 232, 233
Association Picarde pour la Préservation et l'Entretien des Véhicules Anciens (APPEVA), 191, 231
Atkins, Sgt. Leonard (1st LROC), 105, 123, 124, 139
Auchonvillers, 75, 89, 102, 234
Australian Army, 84, 142, 151, 156, 157, 165, 173, 178, 242
    railway companies: *see* railway & related transport companies
Authie river & valley, 11, 88, 142, 144, 146, 161

Authuille, 90, 227, 228
Autorails, *see* railcars
Aveluy, 71, 73, 77, 80, 88, 90, 96, 99, 104, 107, 112, 114, 133, 140, 157, 227, 228, 239
Aveluy Wood, 74, 80, 227

Ballast, 62, 87, 116, 118, 119, 123, 126
Bapaume, xii, 70, 74, 96, 102, 104, 107, 112, 113, 115, 117, 124, 129, 131-5, 139, 140, 141, 156, 161, 162, 170, 171, 176, 178, 185
Barisis, xiv, 6, 96, 112, 118, 126, 128, 129
Bazentin, 81, 83, 91, 92
Beaucourt(-sur-l'Ancre), 74, 75, 89, 90, 102, 140, 156, 157
Beaulencourt, 104, 105, 115, 161, 162
Beaumetz(-lès-Cambrai), 133, 134, 162, 170, 176
Beaumont-Hamel, 74, 75, 89, 234
Beaussart, 77, 88, 89, 96, 99, 114, 131, 145, 147
Beaurainville, 151, 162, 175, 178, 179
Beauval, 11, 77, 88, 145, 146, 159
Beauvois, 114, 120, 123, 124, 126, 136, 182
Bécourt, Bécourdel, 83, 84, 87, 91, 98, 202
Belgian Army, xii, 56, 58, 248
Belgium, xii, xiv, 2, 60, 61, 107, 124, 165, 168, 173, 175, 177, 232
Bellicourt, 51, 53, 144, 168, 169, 171, 172, 219, 242
Birdwood, William (General, Fifth Army), 142
Bohain, 53, 167, 168, 169, 171, 173, 177, 183, 221, 242
Boisleux, 61, 104, 156, 167, 231
Bony American Memorial, 244
Bordon Camp (RE) (England), 57, 60, 61
Bray(-sur-Somme), 14, 19, 30, 31, 83, 85, 91, 93, 99, 131, 132, 146, 153, 159, 163, 167, 223, 231
Brie, 120, 122, 136, 137, 141
Bridges, 16, 18, 38, 49, 122, 123, 131, 132, 136, 137, 141, 146, 157-9, 163, 165, 168, 170, 171, 193, 198, 209, 211, 213, 226, 227, 238, 239, 244, 246, 247
British & Dominion armies, xii, 56, 70, 96, 227, 234, 242, 244, 248
    First Army, xii, 70, 114, 124, 141, 142, 150, 155, 165
    Second Army, xii, 70, 112, 141, 142, 150
    Third Army, xii, xiv, 56, 59, 70, 71, 74, 102, 104, 107, 110, 112, 116, 118, 124, 128, 129, 131, 132, 136,

141, 142, 146, 148, 150, 151, 153, 156, 161, 165, 174, 242
    Fourth Army, xii, 56, 59, 71, 74, 90, 91, 102, 107, 110, 112, 142, 144, 146, 148, 150, 151, 153, 156, 161, 165, 168, 173, 174
    Fifth Army, xii, xiv, 56, 71, 74, 87, 88, 96, 102, 107, 110, 112, 113, 114, 116, 117, 118, 119, 120, 124, 126, 129, 131, 132, 135, 136, 140, 141, 142
    railway companies: *see* railway & related transport companies
British War Cemeteries (CWGC), 80, 227, 234
Bucquoy, 102, 132, 139, 146, 148, 153, 161
Bullecourt, xiv, 104, 112
Bus competition & replacement, 134, 162, 198, 202, 218, 220
Bussy, 11, 16, 17, 31, 32, 35, 38, 137, 192, 193, 194, 202, 204, 207, 208, 222
Byng (General, Third Army), 70, 142

Caix & Caix-Vrély, 73, 107, 119, 154, 155, 163, 182, 185, 202
Cambrai, 48, 165, 168, 171
    battle of, xiv, 96, 110-2, 115, 116
Canadian Army, 151, 154, 156, 163
    railway companies: *see* railway & related transport companies
Canal du Nord, 1, 18, 38, 98, 107, 109, 112, 113, 115, 122, 125, 137, 156, 157, 161, 162, 165, 167, 170, 182, 194, 226, 239
Candas, 73, 77, 88, 96, 112, 131, 134, 135, 144, 145, 146, 147, 151, 156, 167
Cappy & Cappy Port, 94, 95, 105, 135, 136, 164, 182, 191
Carey (General), 141
Casualties (railway troops), 112, 117, 124, 134, 142, 147, 155, 165, 173
Caterpiller Wood & Valley, 83, 84, 91, 92, 227, 234
Caudry, 48, 49, 51, 168, 169, 219, 220, 244
Chaix (French timetables), xv, 19, 202, 214-216, 221
Châlon-sur-Marne (Marne *département*) (now Châlons-en-Champagne), 180, 183
Chaulnes, 56, 71, 74, 85, 98, 99, 113, 119, 120, 125, 151, 157, 158, 167, 182, 185, 188, 191
Chauny, 55, 113, 128, 138, 183, 221

251

Chemin de Fer Cappy Dompierre (CFCD), 191, 231-233
Chemin de Fer de la Baie de Somme (CFBS), 205, 219, 230
Chemin de Fer Touristique du Vermandois (CFTV), 10, 233
Cléry-sur-Somme, 14, 85, 94, 105, 115, 119, 135, 136, 139, 164, 202
Closures, 202, 204, 205, 218, 220, 221
Colincamps, 77, 88, 96, 102, 114, 131, 144, 146, 151, 200
Combles, 19, 85, 93, 94, 133, 134, 164, 188, 201
Compagnie des Chemins de fer d'intérêt local du Nord de la France (NF), 53, 221
Compagnie du Nord, 8, 11, 16, 17, 113, 144, 149, 175, 185, 207, 209, 220
Compagnie Générale des Voie Ferrées d'Intérêt Local (CGL-VFIL), 10, 202, 204, 206, 207, 208, 213-218, 223, 225, 226, 230
Contalmaison, 81, 91, 104, 234
Contay, 73, 75, 77, 87, 135, 136, 147-50
Coucy-le-Château, 55, 113, 183, 189, 221, 231, 233
Crucifix Corner, 80, 228
CWGC (Commonwealth War Graves Commission): *see* British War Cemeteries

Decauville, 58, 59, 62, 84, 93, 175
Demolitions, 131, 132, 135, 136, 145, 146
Depots & workshops:
  British Army WDLR:
    Beaurainville, 61, 69, 146, 162, 170, 175, 178, 179
    La Lacque, 61, 62, 69, 146
    Light railway repair trains, 69, 138, 139
    metre gauge, 20, 24, 26, 40, 49, 53, 77, 146, 195, 218, 226
  MRL light railways, 183
Dernancourt, 73, 81, 91, 145, 151, 157
Director of Construction (British Army), 151, 161, 177
Director-General of Transportation (DGT, British Army), & Assistants, 59, 60, 70, 75, 80, 87, 88, 90, 142, 145, 146, 148
Doingt, 119, 131, 158, 171, 178
Dompierre(-Bécquincourt), 188
Donnet Post, 80, 81, 90, 102, 104, 239
Doullens, 6, 16, 29, 88, 112, 113, 129, 131, 133, 139, 144, 148, 175, 192, 199, 200, 203, 204, 224, 234
Dual gauge, 16, 49, 73, 74, 192, 221, 226
Dumps (British & other Armies, WW1), *see* Yards & Supply dumps

Épehy, 98, 109, 110, 113, 117, 118, 131, 158, 167, 168
Ercheu, 11, 16, 17, 19, 31, 32, 35, 38, 114, 192-4, 202, 204, 222, 223
Estrées-Deniécourt (Estrées-en-Santerre), 107, 113, 120, 122, 136, 171, 182, 188

Étaples, 114, 139, 144, 177
Étricourt, 98, 107, 109, 112, 113, 116, 157, 158, 162, 167, 180, 182, 185, 188
Euston Dump, 77, 88, 114, 131, 146, 161

Factory corner, 92, 104
Fares, 32, 48, 51
Faubourg de Paris (Noyon), 182, 183, 188, 206, 207, 208
Fay, 99, 105, 113
Ferme Rouge, 94, 98, 227
Ffestiniog railway (Porthmadog, North Wales), 59, 232, 233
Fins, 109, 110, 111-4, 116, 118, 119, 131, 135, 141, 162, 164, 167, 171, 182, 185
Flamicourt, *see* Péronne
Flavy-le-Martel, 99, 126, 137, 183
Flers, 83, 84, 93, 104, 105
Flesquières, 110, 115, 116
Flesselles, 144, 148, 149, 153
Foch, *Maréchal* Ferdinand (formerly General), 6, 74, 129
Foreste, 113, 124, 125, 128, 137, 138
Frémicourt, 96, 107, 115, 156, 161, 176
French Army xii, 56, 71, 74, 112, 118, 119, 129, 137, 142, 151, 159, 179, 183, 227, 232, 248
  First Army, 153, 156, 163, 165
  Sixth Army, 56, 71, 74, 85, 91, 113, 128, 129, 151
Fricourt, 11, 14, 19, 30, 31, 60, 74, 77, 81, 83, 91, 99, 114, 133, 140, 202, 204
Froissy 14, 30, 85, 87, 94, 99, 105, 107, 113, 119, 120, 122, 123, 131, 134, 136, 141, 155, 157, 159, 163, 164, 182, 202, 204, 231

Gares régulatrice – *see* Yards & Supply dumps
Gas shelling, 117, 134
Geddes, Sir Eric xiv, 56, 59, 60, 75, 80, 87, 88
General Headquarters (GHQ), 70, 87, 112, 129
German Army, 70, 71, 110, 128, 129, 156, 227, 233, 234, 242
  advance, Somme front (from 21 March 1918), 70, 114, 124, 128, 129, 131
  advance, Lys front (from 9 April 1918), 70, 124, 129, 141, 142, 150
  Black Day of (8 August 1918), 151
  Noyon-Montdidier offensive (Battle of Matz), 142, 159, 206
  retreat to Hindenburg Line, (March 1917), xiv, 95, 96, 102, 151, 221
Gézaincourt, 11, 16, 73, 77, 99, 145, 146, 148, 153, 158, 192, 199, 225
Ginchy, 84, 104, 105, 202
Gommecourt, 71, 74, 102, 132, 161
Goods wagons, *see* Wagons
Gough, Sir Hubert (General, Fifth Army), 74, 75, 112, 129, 142
Gouzeaucourt (& Wood), 109, 110, 111, 112, 116, 117, 162, 171

Grant (General), 141
Gueudecourt, 81, 84, 93, 104
Guillaucourt, 74, 85, 107, 154
Guillemont, 84, 197
Guiscard, 11, 35, 38, 40, 114, 124, 125, 137, 159, 188, 206-208
Guise, 53, 169, 173, 183, 221

Haig, Field-Marshal Sir Douglas (later Earl) 56, 129
Ham, 5, 11, 14, 16, 22, 29, 30, 35, 39, 40, 45, 48, 99, 112-4, 118, 120, 123-6, 128, 137, 138, 141, 157, 159, 182, 183, 188, 189, 192, 195, 200-204, 206, 207, 209, 211, 213-215, 217, 218, 222, 225, 226, 239
Hancourt, 110, 114, 120, 123, 124, 136
Harbonnières, 134, 154, 155, 158, 164, 182, 185
Hargicourt, 53, 54, 113, 119, 158, 168, 171, 172, 221, 242
Havrincourt, 98, 107, 109, 110, 111, 112, 115, 116, 161, 162, 167, 171, 176, 177
Havrincourt Wood, 109, 115
Hébuterne, xii, 71, 107, 132, 147, 153
Hédauville, 227
Hem, 85, 94, 105, 135, 136, 164, 165, 202
Hermies, 96, 107, 115, 156, 157, 162, 167, 170
Heudicourt, 109, 110, 111, 131, 135, 171
High Wood, 92, 104
Hindenburg line, xiv, 3, 71, 87, 89, 95, 96, 102, 107, 110, 151, 156, 164, 165, 169, 171, 219, 221, 234, 242, 244, 246
Honnechy, 167, 168, 173, 174, 175, 177

Irchester Narrow Gauge Railway Museum (Wellingborough), 220, 230
Irles junction, 96, 131, 144

Joncourt, 171, 172, 173, 219, 242, 244

La Boisselle, 77, 228
La Chapelette, 98, 105, 119, 120, 164, 171, 180
La Flaque, 85, 105, 120, 131, 134, 136, 137, 141, 153, 156, 157, 164
Lambert, Alfred (Lambert Group), 11, 19, 35, 38, 44, 48, 51, 53, 206, 222, 225
Lancashire Dump, 80, 227
Lassigny, 35, 38, 40, 45, 46, 48, 99, 102, 137, 151, 159, 188, 192, 202, 206-209, 213-215, 218, 225
Le Catelet, 48, 51, 53, 96, 168, 169, 172, 173, 220, 221
Le Transloy, 112, 113, 115, 134, 144, 157, 158, 162, 182
Le Sars, 74, 81, 92, 161, 170
Lebucquière, 107, 133, 157, 167, 176
Lechelle, 107, 112, 115, 133
Leighton Buzzard Narrow Gauge Railway Society Ltd. (LBNGRS), 231, 233
L'Équipée, *see* Wiencourt
Les Buttes, 71, 99, 154

Index

Level, Émile M. 10, 206
Liéramont, 110, 118, 135, 171, 182
Light railways xii, xiv, 56, 58, 60, 71, 75, 77, 80, 84, 87, 88, 90-2, 102
   Acheux area, 77, 88, 89, 102, 140, 145, 148, 153
   Anzac light railways, 60, 84, 107
   Aveluy lines, 80, 90, 114, 133, 140, 228, 239
   A lines, 123, 124-6, 128, 138, 140, 177, 183
   A100-500 lines, 147, 148, 149, 150, 153, 162, 163, 170
   AX lines, 107, 109, 110-2, 115-8, 135, 141, 162, 164, 165, 170, 171, 182
   British & Dominion Armies (WDLR), 59, 70, 75, 179, 180, 182, 226-228, 230
      1st Army light railways 124
      3rd Army light railways 161, 176
      4th Army light railways, 109, 148, 162, 177
      5th Army light railways 109, 178
      control posts 105, 109, 111, 116, 117, 176
      north-south 'main lines', 60, 70, 123, 124, 142, 150, 163, 182
   B line (Hancourt – Beauvois), 114, 120, 122-4, 136, 165, 177, 182
   BW lines, 102, 105, 107, 109-11, 115-7, 135, 162, 170, 171, 175, 176, 177
   C10 & 12 lines, 102, 107, 132, 139, 141, 146, 147, 161
   Coigneux & Hébuterne, 147, 153
   CY lines, 107, 109, 110, 118, 119, 135, 164, 171, 177
   Dompierre sugar beet system, 189, 191
   DZ lines, 110, 118, 120, 122, 123, 136, 165, 177, 178
   Flamicourt (Péronne) – Vraignes & Brie, 119, 120, 122, 123, 136, 165, 178
   French Army, 59, 71, 105, 123, 124, 126, 179, 182, 183
   Froissy to Cappy, Frise, Hem & La Chapelette, 94, 105, 119, 120, 164
   German Army, 59, 89, 91, 102, 104, 109-11, 115, 182, 188, 242
   Ham area lines, 125, 128, 137, 140, 206
   Longueval area lines, 84, 92, 93, 104, 105
   Marcoing – Lesdains & Esnes, & branches, 171, 175
   Maricourt – Trones Wood, & Péronne, & branches, 94, 105, 115, 119, 164, 165
   Martinpuich – Le Sars & Bapaume, 92, 161, 170
   Ministère des Régions Libérées (MRL), 179, 180, 183, 188, 232
      MRL sectors & depots, 180, 182, 185, 188
      Pas-de-Calais network, 180, 182, 185
      Somme, Oise & Aisne networks, 179, 180, 182, 183, 185, 188, 206, 232
   Nogent-sous-Coucy sugar beet system, 189
   Omiécourt – Nesle, 125, 137, 140
   operations, 70, 88, 90, 93, 94, 104, 105, 110-2, 117, 126, 134, 150, 162, 164, 170, 171, 173, 176-8
   Péronne & Quinconce area lines, 110, 118, 119, 136, 164, 165, 171, 177-9, 180, 182
   Plateau – Rocquigny, Étricourt & Ytres, 93, 94, 105, 116, 134, 164
   Pozières area lines, 84, 90-2, 104, 114, 133, 140
   Puchevillers area lines, 146, 147, 148, 150, 153
   Roisel – Bohain & Honnechy (via Templeux, Hargicourt & Bellicourt), 119, 165, 168, 169, 171-5, 177, 183, 219, 242
   Roye sugar beet network, 182, 189
   Saulty-l'Arbret – Bienvillers, Thièvres & Mondicourt, 146, 147, 153, 161
   trench tramways, 74, 80, 115, 119, 126, 227, 228
   Vis-en-Artois sugar beet system, 155, 171, 189
   Wiencourt area lines, 105, 107, 119, 120, 154-6, 162-4
   Wiencourt – Froissy, Loop & Plateau, 105, 120, 155, 156, 163, 164
   X lines 102, 107, 114, 132, 134, 139, 141, 146, 161, 162, 170
   Y lines 107, 109, 115, 116, 134, 141, 161, 162, 170, 175-7, 182
Lihons, 105, 155, 164, 182, 185
Longueval, 81, 83, 84, 91-3, 98, 104, 105, 197
Longueau, 6, 71, 131, 153
Longmoor Camp (RE) (Hampshire, England), 56, 60, 61, 93
Loop station, 73, 74, 81, 93, 99, 120, 167
Ludendorff, General, 129
Luisenhof Farm, 92, 104
Lynton & Barnstaple Railway, 232

Mailly-Maillet, 11, 89, 145, 148, 153
Mametz, 81, 224
Mametz Wood, 73, 81, 83, 84, 91, 234
Marcelcave, 74, 132, 140, 142, 154, 156, 162-4
Marcoing, 96, 107, 110, 111, 117, 156, 167, 168, 170, 171, 176, 177
Maricourt, xiv, 56, 71, 74, 81, 85, 93, 94, 98, 105, 112, 113, 115, 134, 136, 139, 157, 163, 164, 165, 192
Marquaix, 110, 118, 120, 172
Martinpuich, & junction, 74, 91, 92
Martinsart, 74, 145, 227, 234
Mash valley, 227
Masnières, 167, 168, 171, 176
Maurepas, 93, 94, 98, 134, 159, 192, 202
Méaulte, 73, 81, 83, 98, 111, 167
Metre gauge railways, xiv, 6, 10, 73, 198

Aisne *département*:
   Chauny – Coucy-le-Château & Soissons, 35, 55, 182, 189, 221
   Le Catelet – Guise (via Bohain), 35, 48, 53, 168, 169, 173, 183, 221, 242
   Roisel – Hargicourt, 35, 44, 53, 54, 110, 113, 119, 158, 161, 165, 168, 183, 221
   St-Quentin – Caudry, 35, 48, 51, 53, 168, 169, 172, 173, 183, 219, 220, 230, 242, 244, 246, 247
   Tergnier – Anizy-Pinon, 35, 55, 221
   Tramways of St-Quentin, 53, 220
Noyonnias (Oise) network:
   Milly – Formerie, 35, 38, 44, 214
   Noyon – Ham, 14, 16, 35, 38, 45, 114, 125, 146, 159, 182, 188, 195, 206-209, 211-5, 217-219, 222, 225, 226, 230
   Noyon – Montdidier, 16, 35, 38, 45, 46, 99, 102, 142, 146, 159, 188, 206-209, 211, 213, 222, 223, 225, 226, 230
   Noyon – Rollot, 192, 214, 215, 217-219, 223
   St-Just-en-Chaussée, 218, 230
Pas-de-Calais *département*, 39, 44, 70, 139, 143, 198, 206, 213, 230
Somme *département*, 11
   Albert – Ham, 14, 29, 35, 73, 83, 91, 93, 94, 99, 105, 113, 114, 119, 120, 146, 158, 159, 182, 188, 192, 193, 195, 198, 200-203, 213, 225, 226, 236, 238, 239,
   Albert – Montdidier, 14, 30, 73, 83, 91, 99, 133, 146, 153, 154, 159, 193, 199, 224, 225, 236, 238, 239
   Albert – Montdidier & Rollot, 192, 197, 202, 203, 213, 215-217, 223
   Doullens – Albert, 11, 29, 73, 77, 88, 96, 99, 145, 146, 148, 153, 158, 159, 192, 193, 199, 203, 224, 227, 234
   Ercheu – Bussy, 16, 19, 31, 35, 38, 40, 192, 193, 194, 197-9, 202, 204, 222, 224, 226
   Offoy – Ercheu, 16, 19, 31, 114, 125, 192, 193, 194, 199, 202, 204, 222, 224
   Réseau des Bains de Mer, 146, 205
metre gauge railways, First World War, 58, 73, 83, 91, 93, 94, 99, 102, 105
   Gézaincourt – Acheux, Beaussart & Aveluy, 73, 77, 88, 96, 99, 114, 131, 145, 146, 148, 158, 159, 234
   German Army, 73, 173
   Trones Wood link line, 91, 99
Metz-en-Couture, 109, 115, 116, 117, 134, 161, 170
Ministry for the Liberated Regions (*Ministère des Régions Libérées*, MRL), 179, 183, 207, 221, 232
Miraumont, 89, 102, 112, 114, 133, 140, 156, 157, 158, 167

Mons-en-Chaussée, 114, 120, 159, 178, 192
Montauban, 14, 83, 91
Montdidier, 11, 14, 22, 30, 35, 39, 40, 45, 46, 99, 129, 137, 142, 153, 182, 188, 189, 192, 193, 197, 202-204, 206, 208, 209, 213-217, 223
Montdidier, battle of, 151
Montigny Farm, 110, 118, 120, 122-4, 136, 158, 165, 168, 177, 178
Montreuil (-sur-Mer), 69, 71, 87
Mont-St-Quentin, 119, 156, 171, 172
Moreuil, 73, 99, 129, 142
Morlincourt, 124, 128, 138, 139
Mory, 107, 139, 162, 170
Moseley Railway Trust (MRT), 232, 233
Mouquet Farm, 77, 80, 90, 104, 227
Mule haulage, 74, 80, 93, 104, 105, 120
Musée des tramways à vapeur et des chemins de fer secondaires français (MTVS), 219, 230

Nab (Blighty) Valley, 80, 81, 90, 227, 228
Nesle, 16, 17, 24, 32, 99, 125, 137, 156, 202
New Zealand Army, 156
Newfoundland Memorial Park (Auchonvillers), 234
Nogent-sous-Coucy, 189, 231
Noyon, xiv, 4, 16, 22, 32, 35, 38, 40, 45, 46, 48, 99, 112-4, 124, 126, 128, 129, 138-42, 151, 159, 183, 188, 189, 194, 202, 204, 206-209, 211, 213-8, 222, 223, 225, 226, 230
Noyon Guiscard Lassigny Company (NGL), 11, 16, 19, 22, 35, 38, 206, 213, 225
Nurlu, 109, 118, 164, 182, 185

Offoy, 11, 14, 16, 17, 19, 32, 35, 125, 192, 193, 194, 202, 204, 222, 223
Oise *département*, 1, 35, 99, 179, 182, 183, 188, 189, 204, 206, 213, 215, 222, 230
Oise river & canal, 1, 124, 126, 128, 138, 139, 141, 183
Ovillers, 77, 81, 90, 104, 228, 239

Pas-Condé defence line, 142, 144
Pas-de-Calais *département* xii, xiv, 180, 183, 189, 206, 213, 222, 232, 233
Passenger carriages, 27, 45, 51, 54, 145, 183, 197, 198, 213, 214, 221
Péronne (& Flamicourt), 4, 11, 14, 29, 30, 74, 85, 98, 105, 107, 109, 110, 113-5, 118, 119, 120, 122, 123, 129, 132, 134-6, 144, 156-9, 164, 165, 167, 171-3, 175, 177-9, 180, 182, 183, 185, 188, 192, 198, 200, 201, 203, 204, 225, 226, 239
Petrol locomotives, *see* tractors
Picardie (Picardy), xiv, 71, 222
Plateau station, 81, 93, 94, 98, 105, 109, 111, 113, 131, 133, 135, 157, 158, 159, 162, 163, 164, 167
Pont l'Evêque, 38, 113, 138, 139, 207-209
Poulainville, 144, 147-9, 170
Proyart, 94, 153, 155, 156, 163, 164, 202

Pozières, 61, 77, 80, 81, 83, 84, 87, 90, 91, 98, 102, 104, 107, 114, 133, 134, 140, 141
Puchevillers, 73, 142, 146, 147, 148, 151, 153
Puisieux, 102, 114, 146, 161

Quarry sidings, 83, 84, 91, 92, 93, 98
Quinconce (Péronne), 105, 109, 110, 113-5, 118, 119, 120, 135, 136, 139, 141, 157, 158, 164, 165, 167, 171, 173, 175, 177, 183, 192, 239

Railcars (diesel), 197-9, 200-203, 214, 215, 218, 220
Railway & related transport companies, 56
  Anzac Light Railways & 1st Anzac LROC, 60, 91, 92, 104, 107
  Australian, 61
  Australian Light Railway Operating Companies (LROC), 60
    1st (formerly 15th), 60, 114, 141, 161, 162, 171, 177, 178, 242
    3rd (formerly 17th, later 3rd Aus. LRFC) 60, 70, 91
  Australian Pioneer Battalions (Aus. PBs)
    1st, 80, 91, 92, 104, 107, 158
    2nd, 80, 84, 91, 92, 153, 158
    3rd, 157, 163
    4th, 84, 91, 92, 93, 155, 173
    5th, 83, 91, 93, 104, 153
  British, *see* Royal Engineers (below)
  Canadian railway units, 57, 80
    13th (Canadian) LROC, 57, 60, 61, 132, 133, 149, 154, 155, 163, 164, 171, 173, 177, 178, 232, 242
    58th (Canadian) Broad Gauge ROC, 57, 171
  Canadian Overseas Railway Construction Companies (CORCC), 57, 99
  Canadian Railway Troops (Battalions, CRT), 57, 133, 142
    Brigadier-General J Stewart (CO, CRT), 90, 109, 133, 136, 151, 161
    1st, 75, 91, 93, 94, 98, 99, 105, 109, 153, 157, 158, 162, 163, 167-9
    2nd, 57, 88-91, 96, 98, 102, 107, 118-20, 122-6, 128, 137, 138, 139, 140-2, 157, 158, 163, 168, 169
    4th, 90, 91, 102, 107, 113, 117, 119, 135, 144, 148, 153, 168
    5th, 90, 114, 115, 161
    6th, 102, 105, 107, 109, 110, 111, 114-8, 133, 140, 141, 144, 148, 149, 150, 153-8, 161-5, 168, 170-5, 177, 242
    7th, 119, 122, 136, 137, 144, 168
    9th, 107, 134, 146-8, 153, 161, 162, 168, 170
    11th, 144, 147-50, 161, 162, 167, 170
    12th, 107, 115-9, 135, 136, 144, 157, 158, 167, 168
    13th 144, 153, 157, 158, 162, 167, 168
  Tramway Companies, Canadian Engineers (TC CE) 57, 61, 70
    1st, 57, 61, 154, 155, 176
  French companies, 58, 85, 87, 90, 94, 113, 144, 153, 156, 167, 168, 195, 213
  Labour forces and companies, 56, 98, 111, 119, 137, 144, 167
  Royal Engineers (RE):
    17th Battalion Northumberland Fusiliers, 57, 77, 80, 81, 88
    Chief Railway Contruction Engineer (CRCE), 88, 99, 159, 168
    Foreways Companies (FWC), 62, 115
      1st, 145, 147, 161, 170
      2nd, 148, 153, 161, 170
      3rd, 115-7, 134, 135
      6th, 126, 156
    Group Railway Construction Companies or Engineeers (RCC/E), 57, 167
      RCC III, 57, 112
      RCC IV 57, 98, 112, 114, 131, 142, 148, 153, 156-8, 167
      RCE V, 57, 75, 77, 80, 87, 88, 90, 93, 96, 98, 112, 131, 134, 144, 146, 151, 156, 157, 159, 167, 168, 175
    Light Railway Companies, 56, 57, 70
    Director(ate) of Light Railways, 57, 58, 59, 70
      Assistant Directors of Light Railways (ADLR), 58, 59, 161
      ADLR III, 59, 133, 176, 177
      ADLR III North, 59, 146
      ADLR III South, 59, 117, 118, 134, 146
      ADLR IV, 93, 110, 173, 175, 176, 177
      ADLR V, 59, 88, 102, 118, 120, 122-5, 134
      ADLR V South, 59, 137, 138
    Light Railway Forward Companies (LRFC), 60, 61, 70, 170
      231st, 70, 167, 170, 176
      232nd, 70, 170, 171, 176
      236th, 173, 176
    Forward Depot & Training School (Savy-Berlette), 70, 126, 175, 176
    Light Railway Operating Companies (LROCs), 60, 61
      1st, 60, 93, 94, 105, 107, 110, 123, 124, 128, 139
      2nd 107, 124, 137, 144
      4th, 61, 107
      6th, 61, 88, 89, 102, 115, 120, 132, 136, 146, 147, 148, 150, 154, 162, 171, 173

254

Index

9th, 61, 107, 109, 116
10th, 107, 109
15th, 16th & 17th (Aus), *see* 1st, 2nd & 3rd Australian LROCs
29th, 60, 102, 104
31st, 60, 162, 170, 171, 176, 177
34th, 60, 93, 105, 107, 115, 120, 133, 141, 146, 153, 162, 170, 171
35th, 60, 61, 91, 116, 134, 156, 163, 164
54th, 61, 138, 162, 170
Light Railway Train Crews Companies (TCC), 61
18th (later 18th LROC), 61, 94, 150, 154, 173, 178, 179, 242
19th (later 19th LROC), 61, 104, 107, 171, 177
22nd (later 22nd LROC), 61, 125, 126, 128
Light Railway Workshop & Miscellaneous Trades Companies, 61
Railway Companies, 56, 98, 157
3rd 'Royal Monmouth', 56, 73-5, 77, 87, 91, 98, 113, 131
3rd 'Royal Anglesey' 56, 109, 111, 118
119th, 77, 80, 88
260th, 99, 149, 157, 158
263rd, 148, 149, 158, 167, 169
275th, 157, 167, 168
277th, 77, 80, 81, 88
Railway Operating Division (ROD) 56, 58, 88-90, 96, 98, 128, 131, 144, 151, 153, 156-8, 167, 168, 171, 234
XIVth Corps LR Company, 60, 91
XVth Corps LR Troops, 60, 93, 105
New Zealand Light Railway Operating Companies (LROC), 60,
South African Light Railway Operating Companies (LROC), 60, 128, 138, 139
United States Railway Engineers, 61, 98, 113, 141, 150, 153, 173, 174
12th, 61, 110, 111, 112, 118, 120, 122, 124, 136, 137, 144
14th, 61, 104, 133, 134, 141
Rawlinson (General), 74
Ribécourt (Somme), 110, 111, 115, 116, 176
Riqueval bridge & tunnel, 165, 244
Roads:
Albert – Bapaume, 74, 75, 77, 81, 90, 92, 104, 161, 170
Amiens – St-Quentin (via Brie & Vermand), 110, 118-20, 122
Amiens – Roye, 87, 105, 107, 141, 154
Rocourt, 48, 49, 169, 247
Rocquigny, 98, 105, 109, 112, 115, 116, 133-5, 141, 161, 162, 164, 170, 171, 177, 182
Roisel, 53, 98, 107, 110, 113, 119, 135, 158, 164, 165, 167-9, 171-3, 177, 178, 183, 221

Rolling stock, *see* steam locomotives, tractors (petrol & diesel locomotives), diesel railcars, passenger carriages, & wagons
abandoned, 1918, 133, 134, 135, 136, 137, 139, 140, 141
Rollot, 22, 35, 38, 192, 197, 202-204, 206, 208, 213-218, 222, 223, 225
Rosières, 11, 24, 71, 73, 99, 153, 154, 155, 163, 192, 202
Royal Engineers (RE), *see* Railway and related transport companies
Roye (Somme), 87, 96, 102, 182, 188
Roye-sur-Matz, 38, 40, 46, 102, 142, 188, 206-208, 214, 215, 217, 226
Ruyaulcourt, 107, 109, 111, 112, 161, 162, 170, 182

St-Léger-lès-Authie, 131, 144, 146, 151, 153
St-Quentin, 2, 35, 48, 49, 51, 96, 112, 126, 140, 168, 169, 183, 219, 220, 233, 244, 246-8
St-Quentin canal, 1, 110, 113, 125, 126, 151, 158, 165, 167, 171, 244
Sausage Valley, 83, 84, 91, 227
Savy(-Berlette), 114, 123, 126, 141, 175, 176
Serre, 71, 74, 77, 88, 132, 151
SNCF, *see* Société Nationale des Chemins de Fer Français
Société de la voie de 60, 189, 191
Société des Chemins de Fer Départementaux de l'Aisne (CDA) 14, 35
Société des Chemins de Fer du Cambrésis (CFC), 48, 219, 230, 242
Société Générale des Chemins de Fer Economique (SE), 11, 16, 19, 22, 26, 27, 29, 35, 38, 99, 159, 192, 193, 195, 197-9, 202, 206, 207, 213-215, 217-219, 221-226
Société Nationale des Chemins de Fer Français (SNCF), 198, 218, 226, 234, 247
Somme, battle of (1916), xiv, 56, 59, 71, 74, 77, 81, 85, 87, 234
Somme, 1916 battlefield, 102, 120, 227
Somme *département*, 1, 11, 35, 38, 179, 180, 183, 188, 189, 204, 205, 213, 215, 222, 231
Somme river, canal & valley, xii, 1, 14, 75, 85, 94, 105, 119, 122, 124, 125, 129, 132, 135, 136, 141, 142, 144, 148, 157-9, 163, 164, 168, 171, 191, 192, 194, 239, 244, 247
Standard gauge railways, 6
British Army lines & facilities, 71, 175
Amiens avoiding line, 113, 135, 157, 167
Authie valley line, Doullens to Courcelles, 88, 112, 131, 134, 142, 144, 146, 151, 153, 156, 175
Aveluy – Mouquet Farm, 80, 90
Beaussart – Aveluy, 77, 96, 99, 112, 227, 234
Candas to Acheux, Varennes and Achiet, 73, 75, 77, 88, 96, 102, 112, 131, 144, 147, 151, 156, 175

Conchil – Conteville & Conteville – Candas, 144, 147
Hermes diversion (Achiet to Marcoing line), 96, 98, 107, 112, 131, 156, 157
Méaulte – Longueval & Pozières 81, 83, 84, 87, 91, 93, 98, 114, 140
Miraumont – Le Transloy, 112, 113, 144, 157, 161, 167
Plateau – Maricourt – Péronne, 98, 119, 131, 157, 158, 192
Roisel – Hargicourt & Bellicourt, 113, 119, 144, 158, 168
Tortille Valley line, 107, 113, 158, 167, 182
Vecquemont – Contay, 73, 75, 77, 87, 149
British & French lines:
Dernancourt – Étricourt (Plateau Line via Maricourt & Rocqigny), 73, 81, 85, 91, 98, 109, 111, 112, 113, 157, 158, 167
Froissy – Fay & Estrées-Deniécourt, 99, 113
Wiencourt – Loop, 85, 87, 99, 131, 153, 155, 167
French Army lines & facilities, 71, 175
Appilly – Folembray, 113, 182, 221
Les Buttes – Gailly, 73, 99
Moreuil – Loop via Wiencourt l'Equipée, 73, 74, 85, 87, 99
German Army lines, 92, 104
Lines of *Intérêt Général*, 6
Amiens – Tergnier (via Chaulnes, Nesle, & Ham), 14, 16, 17, 31, 32, 35, 56, 71, 73, 74, 85, 99, 107, 113, 119, 120, 125, 126, 132, 134, 141, 142, 145, 151, 153, 154, 156-8, 171, 183, 211, 213, 214
Amiens – St-Pol via Doullens, 11, 71, 73, 131, 144, 147, 148, 192, 225
Compiègne – Amiens, 16, 22, 73, 225
Compiègne – Roye, 38, 40, 46, 102, 182, 188, 206, 214, 218
Longpré – Canaples, 71, 132, 144
Paris – Brussels (via Noyon, Tergnier, St-Quentin & Bohain), 48, 53, 113, 126, 167, 168, 169, 171, 174, 211, 226, 247
Paris – Lille via Amiens, Albert, Achiet & Arras 14, 56, 71, 73, 75, 77, 89, 90, 96, 112, 115, 129, 131, 139, 145, 150, 153, 156, 157, 167, 182, 193, 194, 234
St-Just-en-Chaussée – Cambrai (via Montdidier, Roye, Chaulnes, Péronne, Roisel, Épehy, Marcoing), 14, 16, 22, 53, 98, 107, 110, 113, 118, 122, 131, 158, 167, 168, 171, 193, 194, 213, 225, 226, 239
Lines of *Intérêt Local* 6, 198
Achiet-le-Grand – Marcoing (via Bapaume), 53, 96, 107, 112, 115, 129, 131, 132, 139, 156, 167, 176, 206

255

St-Quentin – Guise, 10, 48, 233
St-Quentin – Ham (via Foreste), 14, 35, 48, 113, 125, 195, 211, 226, 247
Vélu – St-Quentin, via Étricourt, Épehy, Roisel & Vermand, 48, 53, 96, 98, 107, 109, 111, 116, 131, 157, 158, 167, 168, 182, 206, 247
Stations, 18, 19, 22, 24, 38, 53, 183, 185, 194, 195, 199, 209, 211, 213, 219, 221-226, 234, 236, 238, 239, 242, 244, 246, 247
Steam Locomotives:
  light railways (60 cm, and near Imperial gauges), 62, 69, 191, 231-233
    British War Department, 62, 69, 88, 89, 102, 114, 123, 128, 134, 137, 138, 139, 141, 150, 162, 164, 165, 171, 173, 175, 177, 179, 183, 189, 231, 232
      Alco-Cooke (Alco) 64, 114, 141, 162, 171, 177, 232
      Baldwin, 64, 88, 155, 171, 177, 178, 189, 231, 232
      Hudson (Hudswell-Clarke), 74, 104, 114, 177, 232
      Hunslet, 64, 94, 231
    Decauville 0-6-2T, 189, 233
    Franco-Belge 0-8-0 (tender), 189, 233
    French Army, 62, 183, 232, 233
      Péchot-Bourdon, 62, 64, 104
      Decauville, 62, 64, 65, 183, 232
      Kerr Stuart (Joffre class), 65, 232, 233
    German Army, 62, 175, 183, 189, 233
    US Army, Baldwin, 233
  metre gauge, 26, 44, 58, 145, 195, 197, 198-200, 202-205, 213, 218, 219, 230
    British War Department, 58
    French Army, 195, 213
    manufacturers 26, 51, 54, 195, 198, 213, 219, 220
      Corpet(-Louvet) 44, 51, 54, 197, 219, 220, 221, 230
      Haine-St-Pierre, 205, 213, 218, 219, 230
      Société Alsacienne de Constructions Mecaniques (SACM), 213, 218, 219, 230
  standard gauge, 234
Sugar beet, 1, 24, 45, 182, 183
Sugar factories (*sucrerie, râperie* or *distillerie*), 45, 51, 109, 110, 125, 173, 189, 197, 198, 231-4, 242
  Dompierre-Bécquincourt (*Sucrerie Centrale de Santerre*) 188, 189, 191, 231
Tacots des Lacs (Seine-et-Marne *département*), 232, 233

Tanks & tank facilities, 70, 74, 80, 110, 111, 116, 142, 151
Templeux-le-Guérard, 53, 119, 165, 168, 171
Tergnier, 55, 56, 99, 113, 168, 221
Thiepval, and Thiepval Wood, 77, 80, 90, 228
Timetables:
  light railways (MRL), 183, 185, 207, 208
  Noyonnais network, 45, 46, 48, 99, 206, 207, 208, 214-218
  Somme metre gauge network, 29, 30, 31, 32, 99, 192, 199, 200-202
  Roisel – Hargicourt, 54, 221
  St-Quentin – Caudry, 51, 220
Tincourt, 109, 110, 118, 119, 135, 158, 162, 164, 171, 173, 177
Track:
  light railway (60cm gauge), 62, 81, 88-90, 93, 102, 109, 111, 114, 116, 119, 120, 122, 123, 125, 126, 128, 138, 155, 156
  metre gauge, 16, 17, 18, 38, 49, 99, 114, 120, 123, 126
Tractors (petrol & diesel locomotives), 61, 65, 69, 77, 191
  British Army light railways, 61, 65, 69, 88, 89, 90, 102, 114, 117, 120, 122, 123, 125, 126, 128, 134, 137-9, 141, 150, 154, 162, 164, 170, 171, 173, 176-9, 231, 233
    Petrol Mechanical (PM), 61, 65
      McEwen & Pratt, 61, 65, 117, 233
      Simplex, 120, 147
      Simplex 20hp, 65, 66, 70, 74, 117, 122, 126, 148, 155, 162, 165, 171, 177, 231, 233
      Simplex 40hp, 65, 66, 124, 155, 162, 171, 177, 231, 233
    Petrol Electric (PE), 61, 65, 122, 233
      Dick Kerr, 65, 233
      British Westinghouse, 65, 124, 233
  British Army standard gauge, 77, 90
  diesel, light railway 191, 233
Transhipments, *see also* Yards & supply dumps, WW1:
  standard gauge to light railway,
    British, 77, 80, 83, 88, 91-93, 102, 107, 109, 113-115, 118, 119, 124-6, 147-9, 151, 153, 154, 161, 162, 164, 169, 170, 173, 180
    Flamicourt (Péronne), 113, 120, 136, 164, 165, 178
    Froissy, 87, 94, 105, 157, 164, 191
    La Flaque, 156, 164
    Le Transloy, 112, 162, 182
    Trones Wood, 84, 91
    French, 74, 87, 191
    German, 102
  standard gauge to metre gauge, 83, 145, 159, 207, 208, 213
Trench tramways, *see* light railways
Trescault, 109, 111, 115, 116

Trones Wood, 60, 73, 81, 83, 84, 91, 93, 94, 98, 99, 158, 159, 192

United States Army, xiv, 129, 142, 144, 156, 165, 233, 242, 244, 248

Vecquemont, 73, 75, 77, 87, 113, 131, 133, 135-7, 142, 148, 153, 157, 162, 163, 167, 170, 182
Vélu, 48, 96, 98, 107, 109, 113, 115, 131, 135, 141, 157, 158, 162, 170, 176
VFIL, *see Compagnie Générale des Voie Ferrées d'Intérêt Local*
Vignacourt, 73, 134, 144, 148-50
Villers-Bocage, 148, 149, 150, 153
Villers-Bretonneux, 74, 129, 132, 135, 137, 140-2, 145, 153, 154, 163, 165, 182, 183, 185
Villers-Plouich, 110, 111, 112, 117
Voyennes, 114, 124, 125, 128, 137, 138, 140
Vrély & Vrély junction, 154, 155, 163, 202

Wagons:
  light railway (60cm gauge), 61, 68-70, 88, 91, 102, 104, 114, 117, 122, 124-6, 136, 138, 141, 147, 150, 154, 178, 183, 230
  metre gauge, 28, 45, 51, 213, 214, 221
War Office Locomotive Trust (WOLT), 231
Weather, 60, 102, 104, 112, 119, 123, 124, 126
Welsh Highland Heritage Railway (WHHR) (Porthmadog, North Wales), 231, 233
West Lancashire Light Railway (WLLR) (nr. Preston, Lancashire), 232
Wiencourt (inc. Chemin Vert) 71, 73, 74, 85, 94, 99, 120, 131, 132, 134, 136, 137, 140, 141, 153, 154, 157, 162-4, 167

Yards & supply dumps, WW1: *see also* Transhipments
  British, standard gauge, 71, 73, 83, 88, 90, 93, 109, 112-116, 125, 128, 131, 144, 156, 162, 168, 172, 182
    Aveluy, 73, 77, 80, 90, 112, 140
    Pioneer, 77, 96, 99, 112, 131, 227
  British, light railways, 80, 81, 89, 90, 91, 93, 94, 102, 104, 105, 109, 111, 113-6, 119, 120, 124-6, 135, 136, 147, 150, 155, 162-5, 170, 172, 173, 176, 227
    Quinconce (Péronne), 110, 136, 164, 183
  French, standard gauge, 71, 129, 131
Ypres sector, xii, xiv, 58, 60, 99, 102, 104, 107, 110, 112, 114, 123, 124, 129, 139, 141, 142, 156, 227
Ytres, 98, 105, 107, 109, 110, 115, 116, 131, 134, 157, 162, 170, 176, 182